Letters of H. P. Lovecraft

LETTERS TO FAMILY AND FAMILY FRIENDS
VOLUME 2

Lilian Delora Phillips and Franklin Chase Clark,
on their wedding day, 10 April 1902

H. P. LOVECRAFT

LETTERS TO FAMILY AND FAMILY FRIENDS
VOLUME 2: 1926-1936

EDITED BY S. T. JOSHI AND DAVID E. SCHULTZ

Hippocampus Press

New York

Published by Hippocampus Press
P.O. Box 641, New York, NY 10156.
www.hippocampuspress.com

Hippocampus Press logo designed by Anastasia Damianakos.
Cover art © 2020 by David C. Verba.
Cover design by Daniel V. Sauer, dansauerdesign.com

First Edition
1 3 5 7 9 8 6 4 2

ISBN 978-1-61498-247-0 vol. 1
ISBN 978-1-61498-301-9 vol. 2
ISBN 978-1-61498-302-6 set

Contents

Letters to Lillian D. Clark and Annie E. P. Gamwell

1926

[152]   [ANS postcard][1] [HPL to LDC]

[Postmarked Brooklyn, N.Y.,
6 January 1926]
Wednesday Noon

Your card received & fully appreciated. These days I've been up to my neck in reading old weird material & writing that history of the spectral tale which Cook wants. It's good preparation for composing a new series of weird tales of my own. Yesterday & today I've had to wrestle with correspondence; but when I get one final line off to good old Moe I'll be ready again to start with the weird stuff. This afternoon I may go shopping & try to get another diary like the one we got in Elizabethtown last year. I think I'll omit the meeting this evening, since it's in Paterson where the fare is costly.

¶ Sorry you've had a cold, & hope it won't develop into a bad one. I'm astonished that my winter cold hasn't begun yet—but when it does come, I suppose it'll be the very hades.

¶ Will enjoy seeing the park guide if it's available, & shall be infinitely grateful for the Jeffrey book. Will await with pleasant anticipations the epistle you promise.

> Yr aff Nephew & obt Servt
> H P L

Notes

1. *Front:* Blank.

[153]   [ALS] [HPL to LDC]

Monday Night
Jany. 11, 1926

My dear daughter Lillian:—

Your much appreciated epistle & enclosures arrived this morning, & I am glad to hear that the worst of your cold is over. Pray be careful, however, to avoid such relapses as that of Friday; & let your kid sister do your shopping for you till every vestige of the disturbance disappears.

I'm glad you like "The Cats of Ulthar", & hope the public may do the same. In this issue of Weird Tales is also an announcement of my coming tale, "The Horror at Red Hook", with a sentence quoted from it. In the next issue—which will have no story of mine—will be an amusingly flattering announcement of my story "The Outsider", which will appear in the issue after that. No doubt a reading of "Ulthar" promotes one's sense of weirdness as one listens to a feline conflict—possibly suggesting that the object attacked is not one of the cat tribe, but rather some powerful enemy of the species! I've always had another cat story in mind, which I may write some day—about a mother-kittie whose offspring are ruthlessly drowned, & who in turn effects the drowning of an infant child of the one who drowned her children.[1] So you still have the poor little Manx kittie! I rejoice in his little brother, still intact, which you so kindly sent, & in the others of the same family which cluster around. Really, you ought to see the cat section of my museum! Enclosed is a kittie-cutting which Belknap gave me recently. I wish I could see the two whose manoeuvres you watch from your window!

As to the definition of a "moron"—this means a high-grade mental defective; definitely below the normal level of intelligence, yet in no sense a drivelling idiot, & sometimes capable of useful effort in a given direction. Taking as the normal the average type which can adapt itself to the community with ease & succeed moderately in a modest way, it is found that the number of morons in the United States has so increased that they now form almost a majority of the population. Most frankly peasant stocks are moronic en masse, & injudicious immigration privileges have brought about the deplorable condition here noted; a condition chiefly manifest in the increase of violent crime & reign of underworld gangs in the larger cities. There is no remedy for what has already occurred, but much can in future be done by applying rigid intelligence tests to candidates for admission & naturalisation.

As to Algernon Blackwood—no, he has nothing to do with the old Blackwood's Magazine; though as coincidence would have it, Blackwood's used to print an abundance of weird yarns. Algernon Blackwood is a living author still in his prime, whose handling of the unreal world has elements of power & convincingness unapproached by any other writer. Unfortunately his work is uneven, sometimes descending to a provoking sort of namby-pamby; so that in order to appreciate him one must be sure to begin with the right books. "Incredible Adventures" is a good one to start with, whilst "The Listener, & Other Stories" contains that magnificent masterpiece "The Willows", which Sonny & I agree is—so far as we know—the greatest weird story ever written. Some other good material is in "The Lost Valley, & Other Stories"—whilst great things are said of "John Silence—Physician Extraordinary", & "The Wave"— two novels which I've vainly been trying to get hold of. Thanks for inquiring about the park book—but don't go to the State House till you feel perfectly able. There's no haste in the matter. Glad Gregory's hasn't greatly changed, & hope you'll get the Marquand book at the library. Yes—A E P G said you'd read the Herford book, & I can imagine from the author's reputation as a humourist how strong the provocation to laughter must have been.[2] Thanks most prodigiously, by the way, for the stamps which make my new diary a present from you! I wish I'd seen the cloth-bound ones you saw in the ten-cent store—but fancy mine will do me. It's the same size & shape as the one you got me last year in Elizabethtown, but is a Standard instead of an ideal [*sic*],[3] & has a grey cardboard cover. Its number is 792, & if you chance to see one in any stationery shop you'll know exactly what I have. As to the tale Sonny is trying on the Atlantic—it is a phantasy entitled "They Call Me Shelley",[4] & tells of how the ghost of the poet came down to sail paper boats in a quiet English stream far from the bustle of the modern world. He talks at length with a little boy, & is joined by the ghosts of other great poets of his time. Then the honk of a distant motor horn is heard, & the shades all flee in panic to the celestial regions they have quitted; fearful lest the sight of gross mechanical modernism shall unfit them for the exalted sphere they inhabit. The sketch is a delicate & finely executed piece of work, yet I fear the Atlantic may balk at a still unknown name, & complain that the phantasy lacks substance. But the practice will do Belknap good, & before long he'll have less trouble with the editorial fraternity. I certainly believe the Child is a genuine poet, & can trace the faculty even in the sentences of his prose. For example—in the present story he speaks of the night coming on "with a wild rush of stars". It is in such colourful & graphic images that he does all his thinking—& that's what a poet is.

I wish I might have seen our municipal Christmas tree, & can well imagine its splendours. Its setting was especially felicitous, & I'll wager it surpassed both the N.Y. one in Times Square & the Brooklyn one in front of Borough Hall. As to the memorial—I still say that something of classic design & in a better location is what is needed. It is all very well to paint the Whitney design idealistically—as reproduced in yesterday's Sunday Journal—but in actual reality the clash of this exotic structure with a Georgian town would be highly disconcerting. I now await with keen expectancy the design to be submitted by the Rhode Island architects. I had a great dream about the city last night, in which I saw vast marble temples, palaces, amphitheatres, & a forum—yet placed in such a way that they did not conflict a bit with the colonial structures. One was on the site of the new Post Office, whose nondescript Renaissance bulk had been mercifully removed. City Hall, Butler Exchange, & Union Station had also given way to gleaming Graeco-Romanism. As to writing to the Journal about the Arcade—I may do it yet, though I hate officious obtrusiveness. I haven't pestered the editor with civic suggestions since 1913.[5] And say—that's *some* idea about framing the R.I. map with glass on *both* sides! No hurry—for the sheet is safe in its tube—but the notion certainly is worth keeping in mind! Yes—most of Mussolini's plan for Rome is excellent, tho' I don't like his idea (perhaps abandoned by this time, however) of erecting the world's tallest skyscraper in the Eternal City. That contravenes the classic Roman tradition. What I wish he'd do is to *restore completely* all the ancient structures—colosseum, forum, Circus Maximus, baths of Titus, arch & columns of Trajan, temple of Jupiter Capitolinus, &c. &c.—till the very image of Roman grandeur rose to mock the modern world. The Greeks are seriously thinking of doing that selfsame thing to Athens, & certainly the one-time Mistress of the World ought not to be far behind. Too bad the Pen & Pencil Club failed, but let us trust that the American Legion may add new laurels to the colonial dignity of the Clark–Taylor homestead in Thomas St. I wish some club would buy that house over Adams' market & let it down to the street level again. The elevation was, it must be admitted, tastefully & harmoniously done; but there's nothing like the real thing. Good specimens of Georgian architecture are too rare to be trifled with, & that hill by the 1st Baptist church is one of the loveliest colonial panoramas in America. Another desirable thing would be to get rid of that insufferably affected & out-of-place artists' building with its quasi-renaissance stucco gewgaws.[6]

All the cuttings you sent are delightfully pertinent & appropriate. Really, you ought to be an "exchange editor" of some prominent paper—selecting those items from contemporaries most worthy of reproduction. I saw that item about the Hawthorne statue, & enclose an editorial based upon it. What Salem ought to do now is to purchase Hawthorne's birthplace & outfit it as a museum, & also to acquire & restore the house in Herbert St. where the best years of his youth were spent. A tablet on the Mall St. house where the "Scarlet Letter" was written wouldn't be a bad idea, & if the old "Grimshawe" house abutting on the Charter St. burying-ground could be obtained & fitted with the Colonial doorway now removed & in the Essex Institute, the work of recognising Hawthorne might be said to be fairly under way.[7] When I establish my heirship to the Phœnecian gentleman who left the six copper coins, I'll see what I can do in the matter. Yes—I glanced at that Gardner speech & thought it fairly good, & also saw the headlines of the dreary rabbinical bickering about Jesus. Dry bones, for the most part, & without much significance in the biological, social & political questions of the day. All the issues that were alive in Bible times are dead now—as are the races. The so-called Jews of today are either Carthaginians or squat yellow Mongoloids from Central Asia, & the so-called Christians are healthy Aryan pagans who have adopted the external forms of a faith whose original flabbiness would disgust them. The day of belief as a significant factor is past—now we heed only the biological & cultural heritage of a stock as an index of its place. The mass of contemporary Jews are hopeless so far as America is concerned. They are the product of alien blood, & inherit alien ideals, impulses, & emotions which forever preclude the possibility of wholesale assimilation. It is not a matter of being orderly citizens & caring for their poor—the question is more profound than can be dealt with in superficial formulae, & vast harm is done by those idealists who encourage belief in a coalescence which never can be. The fact is, that an Asiatic stock broken & dragged through the dirt for untold centuries cannot possibly meet a proud, play-loving, warlike Nordic race on an emotional parity. They may want to meet, but they can't—their inmost feelings & perspectives are antipodal. Neither stock can feel at ease when confronted by the other, & Joseph Pennell the artist only speaks the unvarnished truth when he alludes in his recent memoirs to "the vague, un-formulated dislike of a Jew felt instinctively by every properly constituted person of my generation".[8] East versus West—they can talk for aeons without either's knowing what the other really means. On our side there is a shudder-ing physical repugnance to most Semitic types, & when we try to be tolerant we are merely blind or hypocritical. Two elements so discordant can never build up one society—no feeling of real linkage can exist where so vast a dis-parity of ancestral memories is concerned—so that wherever the Wandering Jew wanders, he will have to content himself with his own society till he dis-appears or is killed off in some sudden outburst of mad physical loathing on our part. I've easily felt able to slaughter a score or two when jammed in a N.Y. subway train. Superior Semites—especially those of rural heritage or of the Portugese stock typified by the Newport Touros & Mendezes of colonial times—can be assimilated *one by one* by the dominant Aryan when they sever all ties of association & memory with the mass of organised Jewry. But this process is necessarily slow & restricted, & has no bearing at all on the prob-lem of the alien mass. That mass must evolve its own aristocracy & live its own separate life, for the Asiatic & European cultures can never meet in common social intercourse. No member of the one, in good standing, can have any social dealings with the opposite body. The line is clearly drawn, & in New York may yet evolve into a new colour-line, for there the problem assumes its most hideous form as loathsome Asiatic hordes trail their dirty carcasses over streets where white men once moved, & air their odious pres-ence & twisted visages & stunted forms till we shall be driven either to mur-der them or emigrate ourselves, or be carried shrieking to the madhouse. Indeed, the real problem may be said to exist nowhere but in New York, for only there is the displacement of regular people so hellishly marked. It is not good for a proud, light-skinned Nordic to be cast away alone amongst squat, squint-eyed jabberers with coarse ways & alien emotions whom his deepest cell-tissue hates & loathes as the mammal hates & loathes the reptile, with an instinct as old as history—& the decline of New York as an American city will be the inevitable result. Meanwhile all one can do is to avoid personal contact with the intruding fabric—ugh! they make one feel ill-at-ease, as though one's shoes pinched, or as though one had on prickly woollen under-wear. Experience has taught the remnants of the American people what they never thought of when the first idealists opened the gates to scum—that there is no such thing as the assimilation of a stock whose relation to our own history is so slight, whose basic emotions are so antithetical to ours, & whose physical aspect is so loathsome to normal members of our species. Such is New York's blight. Our own New England problem, though less violently repellent on the surface, is yet of discouraging magnitude; for where New

York is swamped with Asiatics, our own streets are flooded with scarcely less undesirable Latins—low-grade Southern Italians & Portugese, & the clamorous plague of French-Canadians. These elements will form a separate Roman Catholic culture hostile to our own, joining with the Irish—who in a highly unassimilated state, are the pest of Boston. Many of these stocks could be assimilated—such as the Nordic Irish of Eastern Ireland & such of the French-Canadians as are of Norman extraction—but the process will be very slow. Meanwhile separation & mutual hostility must continue, though there is much less of that shuddering, maddening physical aversion which makes New York a hell to a sensitive Nordic. New England is by far the best place for a white man to live, & some of the northern parts are still astonishingly American. One could dwell very comfortably in Portsmouth N.H. Outside the N.Y. & N.E. belt other racial & cultural problems occur. The hideous peasant Poles of New Jersey & Pennsylvania are absolutely unassimilable save by the thinnest trickling stream, whilst the Mexicans—half to three-quarters Indian—form a tough morsel in the Southwest. The Indians themselves are very self-effacing & unobtrusive where they still remain—& the nigger is of course an altogether different matter involving altogether different principles & methods. In general, America has made a fine mess of its population, & will pay for it in tears amidst a premature rottenness unless something is done extremely soon. A better judgment, less idealism, & clearer scientific perspective at the outset would have saved a heap of disaster—for with a frank recognition of the unalterably Nordic character of this young, warlike western nation, we could have opened the general gates to Britain & northern Europe alone—admitting of alien races only such exceptional & superior specimens as could comfortably be assimilated by our Nordic population. In excluding the swarms of Mediterranean & Asiatic vermin that now ooze & creep over all the landscape, we could have avoided most of that very sense of intolerable repulsion which a foreign name now creates in us, & which reacts to a great extent even on superior foreign types who would otherwise have commanded our tolerance & respect. A sad & shortsighted mistake—thank God that Australia is avoiding it & admitting only an all-British population. In nations, as in society, *congeniality* is the all-important principle. As for me, I'm sick of Bohemians, odds & ends, freaks, & plebeians—C. M. Eddys & satellites & miscellany &c. They amuse me for a while, but begin after a time to get frightfully on one's nerves. People get on one's nerves when they harbour different kinds of memories & live by different kinds of standards & cherish different kinds of goals & ideals. The only company for a regular conservative American is that formed by regular conservative Americans—well-born, & comfortably nurtured in the old tradition. That's why Belknap is about the only one of the gang who doesn't irritate me at times. He is *regular*—he connects up with innate memories & Providence experiences to such an extent as to seem a real person instead of a two-dimensional shadow in a dream, as more Bohemian personalities do. But my recent campaign of emancipation is now a success, & I shall henceforward have around me none save such as are pledged to an undivided following of the conservative Anglo-Saxon tradition. It is well, for in chaotic heterogeneity there would never have been peace for me. All effort on my part would have been paralysed, since no effort would have seemed worth my exerting, if it could not earn me a place among those of my own mental type, free from common or alien social contacts & influences. And even if one cannot find a niche in congenial society, one can at least be *alone*, & that is enough for me. To be clear of irritant & hostile social fabrics is the thing— for otherwise, faced by a life of exile in hateful chaos, a bullet through the brain is the only solution. I was really meant for books & seclusion—& here I am, with the gang nicely tamed & yet unoffended. I still consider my escape rather a diplomatic triumph; for whilst the weekly meetings yet remain as an interesting punctuation to retirement, I am now liberated from the obligation of loafing about slum cafeterias & chattering endlessly for politeness' sake about things that don't concern or interest me in the least. My next step toward creative literary poise must be the abridgment of my correspondence. Here the task is of a different sort, for most of my letters are either to really congenial correspondents like Hoag or Moe or Alfredus, or connected with United business. My policy, as I now foresee it, will be one of shorter letters to the congenial, & total elimination of the official as soon as I can decorously manage it.

This course of reading & writing I am going through for the Cook article is excellent mental discipline, & a fine gesture of demarcation betwixt my aimless, lost existence of the past year or two & the resumed Providence-like hermitage amidst which I hope to grind out some tales worth writing. In the first place, it furnishes an admirable excuse for my absenting myself from engagements—breaking the social ties, as it were, that chained me too closely to the gang. In the second place, it exercises my literary inventiveness & prose style. And in the third place, it restores my mind to its natural field of bookish seclusion & accelerates my speed & retentiveness in reading to something like their old Providence standard. This article done—as it will be in two or three weeks—I shall devote myself to the composition of more stories to submit to Weird Tales—that magazine now having but four of mine awaiting publication.

Yes—nice old Tryout Smithy certainly did foil the real estate bandits most gloriously! He is now all out of the woods, & much nearer owning his house than he was before. The bank at Exeter complimented him warmly on his acumen, & the robbers now realise that they caught a Tartar in the outwardly guileless rustic whose naive questions they thought so simple at the outset. The rascals had been coining easy money through selling the same houses over & over again—trapping their purchasers on technicalities & foreclosing. So we now have a waffle shop in Providence? N.Y. is full of them, but I've never patronised any—tho' perhaps I shall now, on your recommendation. So that oil shampoo business is new? I rather thought King[9] had nothing of the kind, yet am sure he would have, had it then been in existence. It has certainly done wonders with my head—no itching or dandruff—& I advise you to try it. Your scalp problem seems to be about the same as mine, & I am sure the effect would be similar. I knew A E P G's sort of shampoo was different when she described it. Yes—I've heard of that cocoanut oil, too. I may indulge in future oil shampoos, with the intermediate washing you suggest. The latter won't be so much of a task now as it was (or would have been had I tried it) five years ago. The big thinning of my hair—a worse thinning than any which has come since—occurred during the first two months of 1922. I can still recall the bewildered way I felt of my hair at first, wondering what had happened! Instead of resistance, I met only flatness! But now all my brushing methods are accomodated to the new technique, so that I don't realise the loss any more. And in a decade, if I be still alive, I suppose I will be polishing with equal complacency a perfectly egg-bald crown!

As to S H's overcoat gift—I've already brought the strongest possible arguments to bear, & don't believe there's any further danger of this extravagance being perpetrated. Indeed, in a letter today I'm adding negatives & pointing out the thoroughly durable state of my present heavy protection. I suppose her idea was that she will now, while connected with a general department store, be able to secure it at reduced rates; whereas in another season she may be in a wholly millinery establishment where overcoats linger not. I expressed my appreciation whilst registering my conservative disapproval. As a matter of fact, my present coat is good not only for one more but for ten or twenty more years. Last month it celebrated its tenth birthday—it having been bought at Browning & King's in December, 1915, just a few months after the older of the two suits which were stolen last May. The same day I bought the heavy dark-blue felt hat which was never very becoming & which I discarded a couple of years ago despite the fact that it was not worn out. As to my alcove light—it is still out of order, & so is the tall lamp. So, I may pessimistically add, they seem likely to be till I pay myself for their repair! Believe me, I've exhausted all the potentialities of urbane rhetoric on rent days—but have so far received only equally urbane promises. Lately I've given up in sheer despair—what the deuce is the use of anything? But my emphatic lecture of last October has borne some fruit. I *do* get clean linen promptly each week, & I don't hear any more harangues about my electric light. Hot water is fine, also, but for this I believe I must thank the expostulant & bagpiping Arab next door, who brought the management up very sharply when the shutting-off experiment was tried. Said Arab often has company of kindred origin—& it's comical to hear them try to sing "Suanee River", "Old Kentucky Home", &c.[10] Eastern music is all in a humdrum minor key, & these Syrians don't know what it is to take the major intervals of European & American tunes. They whine & guess & drone & then wonder what's the matter! As to my radiator—it's all right when there's any steam in it! Once or twice a day, when there is any real fire worth noticing, the room heats up like a charm & my oil stove goes economically out. But the best of valves won't create caloric when there isn't any coal behind it—so most of the time I depend on my own Little Vulcan. Your new electric lamp must be piquant & delightful. Of course a dim hanging lamp in the middle of the room is no sort of thing to read or write by. My own reading-lamp is amply powerful. I buy my own bulbs, (50¢ each, & I've had two since I've been here, one bought last March & the other in November or December) since Mrs. Burns furnishes nothing but feeble apologies.

Glad A E P G had tea with you, & trust the call was mutually enjoyable. Tonight I must hunt up an all-night restaurant; since I find I haven't enough provisions here for a meal, & John's is closed—the hour being half past midnight. The Automats in Manhattan would also be closed before I could get there, so I guess I'll have to endure a cafeteria—maybe the Tiffany—despite my growing distaste for these depressing gang-rendezvouses. (poor French plural—I'll have to brush up before Alfredus descends on me with his new Parisian whiskers!) Upon my return—my letters being all done—I shall read Bulwer-Lytton till I am sleepy & then retire. Tomorrow let's hope I won't be snowed under again with such a stack of correspondence as came today. One item today was a poem by Mr. Hoag for revision—which reminds me that I must shortly evolve my annual tribute, this time for his 95th anniversary.[11] Good old boy! Two years intrinsically older than Gramp—yes, almost *three* years (Nov. to Feb.). Would that W V P had been dowered with equal longevity, so that his vigorous presence might still adorn Angell St! Well—such is which. Now I'll seal this & mail the whole stack of today's letters; then find a tolerable eating-place—at which latter I'll order cocoa on the strength of your recommendation. You'll find most of my diary in a contemporary letter to A E P G. I may add that I entertain a McNeil meeting here Wednesday night, & that next week S H may be here for a vacation, despite my cautions against extravagance. Not having attended the last meeting, I don't know where the Leeds meeting of Jany. 20 will be. ¶ And so it goes. More news later as news develops. ¶ Yr aff: Nephew & obt Servt

H P L

Notes

1. This plot idea bears a strong resemblance to the plot of Bram Stoker's "The Squaw," which is perhaps why HPL never wrote it up.

2. Possibly a book by Oliver Herford (1863–1935), an American writer and illustrator sometimes referred to as the "American Oscar Wilde" because of his various *bon mots* (e.g., "Only the young die good"). He had recently published a book called *What'll You Have?* (with Karl Schmidt; New York: Holt, 1925).

3. HPL probably meant to write "Ideal," the brand name of a diary, similar to Standard.

4. Apparently nonextant.

5. HPL published a letter in the *Providence Sunday Journal* (3 August 1913) titled "Seats for Park Concerts," suggesting the installation of seats on a grassy bank of Roger Williams Park for attendees of band concerts there. The *Journal* also published a letter dated 5 October 1926, after HPL's return to Providence, about the preservation of historic buildings in Providence. See "Asks Preservation of Old Buildings," *Providence Sunday Journal* 42, No. 15 (10 October 1926): Sec. A, p. 5.

6. HPL refers to the Fleur-de-Lys Studios (1885), a historic art studio at 7 Thomas Street in Providence. He mentions it in "The Call of Cthulhu."

7. Nathaniel Hawthorne's birthplace, built in 1750 at 27 Union Street in Salem, was moved in 1958 near the House of the Seven Gables (115 Derby Street) and is now open as a museum. The house at 10 Herbert Street, where Hawthorne intermittently lived from 1808 to 1845, the house at 14 Mall Street where *The Scarlet Letter* was written, and the house at 53 Charter Street that is the setting of *Dr. Grimshawe's Secret* are privately owned.

8. Joseph Pennell, *The Adventures of an Illustrator* (Boston: Little, Brown, 1925), 222.

9. Fernando King (1858–1937), HPL's barber at 171 Westminster Street in Providence.

10. "Old Folks at Home" (1851; sometimes referred to as "Swanee River") and "My Old Kentucky Home" (1852), songs by Stephen Foster.

11. "To Jonathan Hoag: (Upon His 95th Birthday)."

[154]   [ANS postcard][1] [HPL to LDC]

[Postmarked Brooklyn, N.Y.,
20 January 1926]
Wednesday Evening

Thanks enormously for hose! Precisely the right size! Hope you'll safely receive the candy S H is sending you. ¶ By this time you may have read my yesterday's epistle to A E P G.[2] Diary from that point on as follows: S H & I went out for an evening walk to Montague St. parapet, & returned to read till midnight & retire. Up 8 a.m. Bkfst. Spent day writing letters & gasping at portfolio of hideous drawings lent me by Clark Ashton Smith. At noon Kirk & Leeds telephoned, saying tonight's meeting will be at Chelsea Book Shop & urging me violently—yea, frantically—to come. However, if I go it will probably be late. I "tipped off" Orton, but it was too late for him to go, he having made other plans. Now—if I have time—I'm going out shopping. Then down town to meet S H for a restaurant dinner. Don't know how we'll spend the evening. ¶ Just heard from young Talman, who asks my help in deciphering the moon dial of an antique Dutch clock. His diagram is vague, but I'm doing what I can! ¶ Well—thanks again for the socks! More diary matter later, when there's more to record. // Yr aff Nephew & obt Servt
H P L

Notes

1. *Front:* Blank.

2. Nonextant.

[155]   [ALS] [HPL to LDC]

Tuesday Evening—
Jany. 26, 1926.

My dear daughter Lillian:—

I was delighted to receive yours of the 24th, with its piquant & interesting enclosures. The Wayside Inn rhymes are very clever—& I certainly envy honest old Henry with all my heart.[1] As I've just written A E P G, I should certainly be exactly like this worthy eccentrick if I had the cash—that is, like him as far as his Colonial tendencies go. Peace-ships & motors I would leave to more idealistick & mechanical souls.

Yes—the socks are perfect—for unfortunately my feet, hands, nose, & chin have not shrunk as obligingly as my neck & waistline. I am very grateful for this addition to my stock—for now my battery of apparel is quite practical & complete—or will be as soon as S H takes in my various shirt-necks to 14. It now seems plain that my proper neckband is 14, & my proper sleeve 34. As you will learn from the A E P G letter, my alcoves underwent a thorough overhauling last Sunday; as a result of which many decrepit garments were eliminated. Before long I shall have S H snap me with the camera in my new hat, & when the film is all taken up I'll send you views of myself in all the splendour of regained leanness & replaced apparel. There will be five or six views if all come out well, shewing me in (a) my new grey summer suit, (b) my dark grey best winter suit, (c) my new every-day brown winter suit, (d) my new brown hat, & (e) holding a delightful little kitty-cat. You'll be amused to see once again the familiar thin figure you knew prior to 1915–16. As to my light—I know you advised me to see to it, but Mrs. B. said that an Edison Co. man would have to come, (which was wrong—S H sent a man from the nearest electric appliance shop!) & that he would charge fabulously for even inspecting & prescribing. Of course, I am not electrician enough to be able to locate the trouble myself—it might have been anywhere—fixtures, walls, plugs, & all that—for all I could tell. But anyhow, it's all right now; & it's a relief to be able to dress, brush my hair, & black my boots in the alcove meant for that purpose. Glad you have your new bulb—I buy all mine myself, since those furnished by Mrs. B. are never powerful enough. Mine last very well, despite frequent all-night burning. The desk lamp which I replaced last month had been in use continuously since early in the previous March. Still, I know they tend to be uneven, so that one's rate of purchase is largely a matter of luck. Glad you like the candies; but keep the box if you find it of any decorative value in your room. Return it only in case you would otherwise throw it away. I am very fond of the design, which seems to me much above the average found on similar commercial products. As for letters & poems enclosed in former epistles—don't bother to return them. I can't keep my files crowded with miscellany, & nowadays retain only letters from you & A E P G.[2] Yes—I thought from the general style that the Arnold picture was an old one. Did he get more civilised-looking—more urbane & better-groomed—in his later years? Or perhaps you haven't seen him recently enough to venture a verdict. I shall tell honest old McNeil that you found his book a good seller at Gregory's, & strongly hope it may continue to be such. We all hope to see it put the good old boy on his feet in a modest way, & get him out of his unspeakable slum rookery—tho' results in any case won't be quick enough to permit of any move till next autumn. It would be very fortunate if the popularity of his new book could promote the sale of his earlier books as well, so that he might receive good royalties from them all—but of that only time can tell. As for Sonny-Child's book—it ought to be out in a week or two, & I'll surely send you a copy the very moment I get one. I think I saw that Cobb book of N.Y. once—he is very clever as a humourist, & the odd thing is, that he can write *weird* tales with a power which very few living Americans can summon. One could hardly ask for anything more ghastly or bizarre than his "Fishhead".[3] As to my article on the weird tale—it goes on very slowly because of the reading & re-reading necessary for its intelligent preparation. I find much valuable material in that 10-volume red-bound "Lock & Key Library" of strange tales which I picked up during my 1922 N.Y. trip.[4] My latest discovery is of the pair of French writers (19th cent.) who collaborated under the hyphenated designation of Erckmann-Chatrian. Their "Man-Wolf" is a marvellously effective tale of a Gothick castle & a transmitted curse, whilst some of their short stories are of ineffable power. However—they must all bow before my new idol of idols, the erudite Montague Rhodes James, Litt. D., erudite antiquary, student of old cathedral lore & architecture, & Provost of Eton College. James' mastery of horror is almost unsurpassable; & if you care to receive some absolutely authentick shivers, just read any one of his books of short tales—"Ghost Stories of an Antiquary", "More Ghost Stories of an Antiquary", & "A Thin Ghost, and Other Stories". Belknap has seen his book of *children's* ghost stories, "The Five Jars", & says that it's amply weird enough for any average adult.[5] I am eager to get hold of that, as well as of his very recent (just reviewed) new volume for grown-ups—"A Warning to the Curious". I shall give James very prominent mention in my article. Blackwood can be a mighty creator when he chooses, but is marred by occasional touches of namby-pamby sentiment, ethical bias, & the cant jargon of charlatanic occultism. I must read his somewhat recent & widely known "John Silence—Physician Extraordinary", which Sonny has just finished. As a sample of B. at his best, I'd recommend "The Willows", in "The Listener & Other Stories"—although "The Wendigo" in "The Lost Valley, &c." is exceedingly powerful in many ways. I think you'd enjoy Bulwer-Lytton's "Strange Story" again, despite its occasionally Victorian cast & almost interminable length. It certainly has the quality of real interest—so that one can't merely give it a duty skimming, no matter how hard one tries. Its genuine merit forces one to give it a real reading.

Yes—I certainly do hope we can get a tasteful memorial in the classic style, & believe that the local architects will evolve something perfectly appropriate if given their way. Simplicity, careful proportion, Georgian purity of design, & a general avoidance of sculpture in favour of wholly decorative elements are the things I would recommend. These punctiliously adhered to, I care not whether the structure be a tower, a column, an arch, or a Pantheon-like auditorium. Beauty & dignity, not practicality or utility, should be the guiding principles. Yes—I wish my dream of a classic marble city might come true—& as a step toward it I note the proposed design for a state office building near the state house, which impresses me very favourably indeed. Hooray for the art club & the Sidney F. Adams house!!6 Didn't the art club, by the way, do something toward mitigating the tragedy of the original raising—supervising the Georgian architecture of the connecting upper story & archway? That gives quite a pleasant old-world effect—but I'd rather have the real thing. Now to get rid of that infernal mess called the artist's building, & to get some tasteful neo-colonial house for the N. Main corner, to supplant Calef's prosaic 19th century market. As to Herbert Clemence's picture—bless you! I not only saw it, but enclosed it in yesterday's A E P G letter, telling her to give it to you for insertion in Grandma's red scrap book if you did not have one there already. In that letter I also answered A E P G's anti-oil-shampoo arguments by suggesting that the professional method of application drives the fluid into the scalp in such a way that the subsequent washing does not remove it. In any case, it may possess a peculiarly solvent & cleansing effect which ordinary shampoos lack—else why did it stop my itching when others didn't? The proof of the pudding, says the antique saw, is in the eating. Yes—I think I recall your use of cocoanut oil on my head. S H has bought some, & used it on me a week ago. Glad you've commenced treatments again, & hope results will soon be visible—& thanks tremendously for the box of pomade which you mention sending. Will it make the hair stay, & supplant that oil or tonic which you prepared for me? Seems to me I recall trying some a few years ago which didn't give results. But anyway, we'll see. Possibly, as you say, it will require a night's sleep to start the thing working. I'll let you know later how it works. Grandpa's hair is pretty thin & grey, but it still covers the old head completely. About another year will see a bald spot on the crown, & then will come general baldness in about a decade if the old man lives that long.

Yes—S H will be glad to hear from you, & according to latest plans she will be here still another week, making three in all. Too bad she can't make it a clear vacation, but she thinks that it will be better to pick up a little odd cash for herself, & many new ideas to enhance the value of her work upon her return to Cleveland. From now on, however, she probably *will* make the visit a vacation. When next you write, don't fail to tell about the pretty kitty-cat you mention—for all news of my favourite species is welcome, & the cats of Providence & Ulthar are much superior to those of New York. I think you'll like young Talman when you see him—I enclose the problem in horology &

astronomy which he recently submitted to me, & which I had to answer very gropingly because of my ignorance of old clocks, & because of the meagreness of his description. I can't really get the hang of the thing because Talman didn't say what the connexion & rotation rate of the various discs was; but from general principles I assume the following: that the two graduated circles move as one, describing a complete circle once in 29½ days, (note extent of graduation of outer circle) which is the time of the moon's apparent revolution around the earth. The outer circle, therefore, would indicate the *moon's age* in days; & therefore, by easy inference, its phase: 2 indicating the thin "shoestring" crescent in the west after sunset, 7 or 8 the 1st quarter or evening half moon, 14 or 15 the full moon, 21 or 22 the last quarter or morning half moon, & 26 or 27 the thin crescent of the "old moon" seen in the east before sunrise. Now the inner circle probably indicates the approximate time of the moon's rising (figure at left hand horizon) & setting, (figure at right hand horizon) which averages 51 minutes later each day except at harvest or hunter's moon. As for the moon disc itself—my *guess* is that it performs its revolutions independently of the other disc, once in 24^h 51^m—therefore following the average motions of the real moon: being above the horizon when that is above, & below when the moon is below. I may be all wrong—but I'm at least glad to have my attention brought to the matter, for it's something which anyone even half-interested in antiques ought to know. I shall try to look it up on clocks in the local museums & colonial houses, & shall inform Talman of my conclusions when I reach any myself. Speaking of astronomical matters—I enclose an interesting cutting which honest old McNeil gave me, quoting Prof. Moulton on the future of the universe. Moulton, in collaboration with Prof. Chamberlain, is author of the new cosmogonical theory which may replace the settled nebular hypothesis of Laplace.[7] I have not thoroughly investigated it as yet, but must do so in time—since it is taken with increasing seriousness in authoritative circles. I find that recent advances in both astronomy & chemistry have quite left me out in the cold as a hopeless back number.

Speaking of scientific matters—I am amused at the fresh discussion of Dr. Cook's polar claims as a result of Amundsen's visit to the poor old faker in gaol.[8] It's rather too bad that Amundsen let his personal sympathy sway him so far as to make statements favourable to a charlatan—for he ought to know that even the random utterances of a celebrity as great as he, carry a prodigious amount of weight—whether or not weight was intended. I saw Dr. Cook when he gave his lecture as part of the vaudeville show at Fay's Theatre—& he seemed rather cheap to me, though he was undoubtedly a serious & effective scientist in his early days—1900 or thereabouts. Another thing which interested me recently was a letter on the misuse of language in last Sunday's Times. None of these enclosures need be returned. And whilst I'm enclosing, I might as well send along a sample of the Brooklyn Library Bulletin— which I'll wager is vastly inferior to our new library publication—the transformed quarterly bulletin—as described in the recent Sunday Journal. This also need not be returned. As soon as I can get an extra copy, I shall send the new & long-delayed *United Amateur*—though it is a sadly slender issue as compared with those of the past few years. The dilatory printer, Marlowe, has been dismissed despite his frantic & illogical pleas for retention; & high hopes are entertained for the second issue—about to be printed by C. O. Hoisington of Idaho.

Under separate cover is coming an item which I think you will really enjoy—a copy of that State St. Trust Co. publication, "The French in New England", about which I waxed so enthusiastic when I secured my own copy a couple of months ago.[9] This copy is due to S H—who, when she heard that my calendar from the trust company (shewing an 18th century Nantucket whaling fleet) had come in crushed form, asked them for another; & received—with their characteristic generosity—not only the article in question but two booklets besides—as now forwarded to you. The smaller one—about Boston shipmasters—is by no means uninteresting; & is uniform with our "Ships & Shipmasters of Old Providence".[10] But the real *piece de resistance* is The French in New England book, with its wealth of pictures & allusions touching on Providence & Newport. I shall be acutely on the alert for the issuance of part 2, & will try to get you one when I get mine. The only mistake I've so far discovered is on page 40, where a picture of the Langdon house is given in place of one of the old Warner house. A E P G, if she recalls her last summer's visit to Portsmouth, will recognise the error. Now I only wish I could get the first part of the book on Towns of Old & New England, of which I have part 2.[11] I asked the company, but their supply is exhausted.

Well—by this time my diary is reached; though it will only extend through one day, since I carried it through yesterday in my recent communication to A E P G. And by the way—please tell the latter that I received her two programmes, & quite envy her both performances—Sothern, & the stock company at the Modern. S H has secured tickets for the popular Michael Arlen novel dramatised—"The Green Hat"[12]—for Thursday matinee, & I'll send along one of the programmes; tho' N.Y. programmes are exceedingly common & undistinguished as compared with the Providence product. But now to the diary—I rose at 8 a.m., ate breakfast, & washed the dishes as S H went down town. Then I wrote letters—& at noon S H telephoned to say that she was sparing the afternoon for diversion; arranging to meet me at the Milan in 42nd St. (where we all dined that night a year ago—with C. M. Eddy & the gang) at 2 p.m. Arriving on time, I found S H already seated; & we proceeded to stuff with an excellent full Italian dinner. From there we went to the inexpensive cinema next door, where we saw a very fair production entitled "The Tower of Lies"—based on a novel by the Swedish authoress Selma Lagerlof, present holder of the Nobel Prize in Literature.[13] After this we proceeded to Brooklyn—purchasing groceries & getting my coat at the tailor's. The latter says that the small spot on the inside of the coat (almost invisible, & not on the right side at all) is a basic defect of the material itself, & must have been there unnoticed when I got the suit. This may explain why I obtained a $34.50 suit for $25.00! Well—I really don't mind, since the thing is not exteriorly visible at all, & scarcely visible even when the coat is inside out. The suit as a whole is of immense sumptuousness, & far beyond anything else which $25.00 would have bought. It is now all pressed up for best again, & I am wearing the brown for every day. Returning to 169, we are now settled down for the evening; S H reading in the Morris Chair, & I writing letters. If I can get my letters done before bedtime, I shall turn to reading myself—& tomorrow I hope to get to the writing of my article again. As for the future—tomorrow night the gang meets at Belknap's. Thursday afternoon S H & I attend a matinee. Saturday night we *may* attend the Blue Pencil meeting. And the next Wednesday I entertain a (Leeds) meeting here. Such, then, is which. Two new white shirts (14–34) came this noon from Halle's in Cleveland, replacing those sent Christmas & found too large. I now seem to be pretty finely outfitted so far as garments go, & hope I shan't grow fat & have everything to readjust again! Not much danger, I guess—I stay thin without any effort at all now, & have quite graduated from the process of conscious "reducing". // Yr most aff Nephew & obt Servt H P L

[On envelope:] JAN. 27 / Retired last night 1 a.m. up 9 a.m., breakfast of hard-boiled eggs.—read weird material—dinner—lamb stew—out shopping—start for meeting at Sonny's 8:30 p.m.

Notes

1. Perhaps an extract from Henry Wadsworth Longfellow's *Tales of a Wayside Inn* (1863). The "Henry" is Henry Ford, who purchased the Wayside Inn (Sudbury, MA) in 1923.

2. In fact, no letters to HPL from LDC and only one from AEPG (12 June 1935) are extant.

3. HPL refers to Irvin S. Cobb (1876–1944), American writer best known in his lifetime as a humorist but now better known for a small number of weird tales. When "Fishhead" was published in the *Cavalier* (11 January 1913), HPL wrote a letter praising it (published in the *All-Story Weekly*, 8 February 1913). The book HPL refers to is *New York* (New York: George H. Doran Co., 1924), a humorous travel guide and part of Cobb's "Guyed Books" to American states.

4. A ten-volume anthology of weird tales, many of them from continental Europe.

5. *The Five Jars* is a novel, not a collection of stories.

6. Now known as the Seril Dodge House, 10 Thomas Street. It was built in 1786.

7. HPL refers to the Chamberlin–Moulton planetesimal hypothesis, a replacement of Laplace's nebular hypothesis as pertaining to the formation of the solar system. It was first propounded in 1905 by American astronomers Thomas Chrowder Chamberlin (1843–1928) and Forest Ray Moulton (1872–1952).

8. Frederick Albert Cook (1865–1940), American explorer who claimed to have reached the North Pole on 21 April 1908, a year before Robert Peary (1856–1920)

had done so, but later investigations cast severe doubt on Cook's assertion. In 1923 Cook was found guilty of fraud pertaining to oil companies he had founded in Texas and served seven years in prison. Explorer Roald Amundsen, a longtime friend of Cook, visited him several times in prison.

9. By Allan Forbes. No previous discussion of this book is found in the letters to LDC.

10. The book on Boston shipmasters has not been located. For the other book, see Bibliography under the title.

11 See Bibliography under [State Street Trust Co.]

12 Michael Arlen, *The Green Hat* (Broadhurst Theatre, 15 September 1925–c. February 1926); based on his novel.

13. *The Tower of Lies* (MGM, 1925), directed by Victor Seastrom (i.e., Victor Sjöström [1879–1960], a pioneering Swedish film director); starring Norma Shearer, Lon Chaney, and Ian Keith. Based on the novel *The Emperor of Portugallia* by Selma Lagerlöf (1858–1940), who won the Nobel Prize in 1909. George Bernard Shaw was the most recent winner.

[156]   [ALS] [HPL to LDC]

Early Saturday Morning
Jany. 30, 1926.

My dear daughter Lillian:—

Well—the packages have come, & bless me if I expected such a precious freight in that returned box!! Upon my soul, but I shall have to adopt a Spartan system of rationing if I expect to preserve the fruits of my reducing! Needless to say, the Hersheian shipment was vastly appreciated & instantly attacked—& the pomade, no less appreciated, will be employed when the occasion dictates; a full report to follow the trial. Abundant thanks for all—& may you enjoy your Viennese dainties as keenly as I shall enjoy my Pennsylvanian chocolate products!

I suppose you saw the memorial designs in yesterday's bulletin, & no doubt you have been as perplexed as I concerning which plan to favour. I certainly approve of Market Square as a site if it can be handled without injury to the Colonial quality supplied by the Market house & old (1816) warehouses in Canal & South Water Sts., but am not sure how well I like the obelisk as a central decorative element. Whilst of course the obelisk has been an adopted feature of classick art ever since Augustus conquered Egypt & brought specimens to set up in the publick squares of Rome, it is still to my mind something of an alien design. Two thousand years of *association* have naturalised it to such a degree that we are *used* to seeing it in connexion with Graeco-Roman architecture; yet for all that I cannot consider it *quite* compatible from the standpoint of genuine beauty of line. It is, essentially, an *Egyptian* form; & belongs properly only with architecture of the Egyptian sort, *in which rising lines converge as they ascend*. In classic Graeco-Roman designs, where vertical lines are perpendicular & parallel except in pediments, this Egyptian element has no *absolute artistick* place—its sole claim to tolerance being the accidental fact that a Roman conqueror brought it

to our western world as part of the spoils of his victory—thus giving it a sentimental or associational position. Of course, it does not clash *violently* with classic
art, else it would never have secured the foothold it has in Europe & America.
Far be it from me to say that the Washington Monument is intrinsically ugly as
viewed in line with the Arlington amphitheatre, Lincoln Memorial, & Capitol
dome. But I do think that, *caeteris paribus*, a purely Graeco-Roman form is to
be preferred. Therefore the Peirce design of an Ionick temple appeals tremendously to me—so much so that I am forced to give it my vote so far as
the major memorial is concerned—tho' I do like the R.I. Architects' plan for
the covering up of the Providence River & the decorative development of
that locality with trees, reflecting pool, & colonnades. Either plan, I may say,
seems to me superior in fitness for Providence to the Whitney design—
notwithstanding the great individual artistic merit of the latter. Yes—all told, I
am for the Peirce Ionick temple. What do you & A E P G think?

As for my diary, last carried to Wednesday evening—I arrived at Sonny's
in fair time for the meeting, & found assembled only Morton, Orton, & honest old McNeil. All hands were ecstatic in their admiration of the Smith drawings, & Sonny has vowed he will buy two of the hellish landscapes if the artist
will sell them. Refreshments were served at 10:30, & at 11:00 Orton had to
rush for his train. McNeil left at midnight, & Mortonius & I lingered till 1:00
a.m. Sonny's *real* grandfather is worse again, & is not expected to live long—
entirely out of his mind, & with two male nurses in constant attendance. He
has a combination of arterio-sclerosis & uric acid poisoning. Our next (Leeds)
meeting will be here. The next (McN) after that will be at honest old McNeil's.
The next (Leeds) after that will be at Sonny's. Returning to 169, I disposed of
some correspondence & retired at 4 a.m., rising again at 11 a.m. Thursday for
breakfast. After some letter-writing I went downtown to meet S H for a matinee at the Broadhurst Theatre in 44th St. just west of Broadway—& was
overcome with admiration at the facade of another playhouse (The Little
Theatre) just across the street, which is positively one of the finest bits of
modern imitation Colonial architecture that I have ever seen. The play was
that popular dramatised novel by Michael Arlen—"The Green Hat"—&
proved to be very cleverly constructed, tho' inclining toward the melodra-
matick. I send the programme under separate cover. After the theatre we returned to Brooklyn, did some grocery shopping, & enjoy'd an excellent home
repast of pressed beef & tongue sandwiches, potato salad, cream cake, & tea.
After dinner I hammered out three stanzas of my 9th annual Hoag birthday
poem, & retired at 11 p.m. Friday I rose at 11 a.m., ate breakfast, & helped
overhaul my linen whilst S H perform'd some necessary mending & alterations. I am marvellously well outfitted—9 shirts, 15 pairs of hose, 7 complete
suits of underwear with 2 undervests besides, 1 dozen collars of the correct
size, (14½) 9 good neckties, (all others discarded) & the full quota of outer
garments & hats noted in previous epistles—together with innumerable

handkerchiefs. In the afternoon we went out shopping, accumulating sundry domestick necessities (salt & pepper shakers, tacks, small nails, &c) at the 10¢ store, & seeing about the changing of S H's bargain fountain pen—which didn't work. You'll recall that I obtained a pen apiece for S H & myself last October at a sale of $1.28 specimens near Borough Hall. Well—we found the sale still on, & the salesman still willing to make exchanges. Looking over the stock, S H became impressed with the fact that all the $1.28 specimens are uncertain & mediocre, (mine worked only fairly) & that to obtain real satisfaction one must invest in a genuine Waterman. Accordingly—since she said she does not really care for a pen—she proposed, with characteristic generosity, the exchange of both her pen & mine for one good Waterman—the difference to be paid in cash! There was no stopping this Quixotically philanthropick resolve, & I did not escape from the emporium till a *$6.25* Waterman reposed in my pocket—a modern self-filler corresponding to the ancient $6.00 type which I bought in 1906 & lost seventeen years later amidst the sands of Marblehead in the summer of 1923. I am writing with it now—& the feed is certainly a relief after sundry makeshifts—tho' I think I'll change this especial model tomorrow for one with a slightly coarser point—one less likely to scratch on rough paper. It is certainly good to be back among the Watermans again, & I shall probably increase my writing output just for the pleasure of using the new device! At the 10¢ store S H secured some exquisite black & gold material to cover the lamp shade just discarded. This will not supplant the new lavender shade which she made in Cleveland & brought hither, but will alternate with it. The fabrick took my eye most emphatically— something in the design as a whole suggesting vaguely to my mind the wall paper on our front hall at 454. I enclose a tiny sample of this goods, (too small to convey any really adequate notion) together with a bit of the border that is to encompass it. I leave to your imagination the future aspect of the lamp—adding the information that the base (now of white enamel) is shortly to be bronzed or gilded to harmonise with the new decorative scheme of the shade. Altogether the outfit is likely to look much more dignified & sumptuous than it did when you saw it—& than it has looked during the past year. The white & pink combination wasn't quite appropriate for my austere desk & sober room, & I have frequently thought of changing it.

Well—we secured a slight lunch (cheese sandwich—egg salad sandwich—coffee—chocolate sundae) in the basement of the 10¢ store, & returned to 169 for the evening. I then finished my Hoag piece, typed it with suitable carbon copies, & prepared it for simultaneous sending to the *Troy Times* & *Greenwich Journal*[1] for publication on the birthday itself—February 10th. By coincidence, the 10th falls this year on Wednesday, the (weekly) *Journal's* publication day, so that that periodical may present the message on exactly the correct day as well as the (daily) *Times*. I shall mail to these periodicals in the morning—but shall not post Mr. Hoag's own private copy till Tuesday morning—Feby. 9th—so that he may receive it on his actual birthday. I resolved to get this one off in good season—you'll remember how I forgot all about last year's till Sunday, Feby. 8th. I recalled it during an all-night trip with Kirk, in a subway train nearing 168th St., & at once turned around & hit the trail for my desk. We had left Kleiner sleeping in Kirk's room upstairs, so Kirk slept on my couch as I hastened to my pen & paper & turned out the requisite lines. I shewed them to you, of course, at the time. Now see what you think of this year's specimen, composed at greater leisure. I enclose a copy which you may keep permanently after shewing it to A E P G. It's hard work thinking up anything new to say after 8 other poems of the sort—but I've done my best. I'm saving up my supreme effort for Mr. Hoag's 100th birthday! Well—after the typing we had a sort of supper, using up left-overs, & after that I settled down to write letters whilst S H commenced to make a hat. These processes are still in operation at 3 a.m., tho' a bit of sleep may be snatched ere dawn. Tomorrow afternoon I shall probably shew S H some sights, & in the evening we may drop in on the Blue Pencil meeting at the home of old Dr. Swift[2] in the Bronx—2498 De Voe Terrace, wherever that is. Neither of us, however, has prepared any literary contribution for the occasion. S H will remain here through next week—returning, in all probability, on Saturday, Feby. 6th. Letters from Cleveland indicate that she is greatly valued & appreciated at the Halle establishment.

I heard from the Alfredus-child Thursday. He has shaved off the facial fuzz because it wouldn't blossom into a real beard—but he absolutely refuses to get rid of the long hair, proferring many subtle arguments in defence of his contention that custom is a fraud, & that no really individualised person ought to give his head a "prison cropping." Grandpa will have to lecture him when he strikes N.Y. next May or June! ¶ Well—such is which. I may or may not add more diary matter on the outside of the envelope. In any case consider Friday the 29th as disposed of. ¶ Yr aff Nephew & obt Servt H P L

P.S. I enclose the latest from the Davis-child. Please shew to A E P G & return. And tell A E P G that if she hasn't already destroyed the other Davis epistles, I'll reconsider my decision & ask her to send them back. I think I want to shew them to Galpinius.

[On envelope? In RHB's handwriting:] Diary Saturday Jany. 30. Arose noon—breakfast—wash dishes—dust room—start at 4 p.m. on shopping & pleasure trip.

Notes

1. The latter appearance (assuming the poem was actually published there) has not been located.

2. The amateur journalist Dr. Edwin B. Swift.

[157]   [ALS] [HPL to LDC]

Friday, Feby. 12, 1926

My dear daughter Lillian:—

Your card of the 9th was very welcome indeed, & I rejoiced to learn of your emancipation from the trammels of the second cold. Pray be careful & avoid another coryzal visitation—this weather affords diabolical opportunities for their insidious acquisition! My 1925–26 cold has not yet arrived, but I suppose it will be here before the winter is over. The worst cold I ever had came in late April & early May of 1903*, & was so bad that it prevented my going to the Ladd Observatory on May 4th, though you & Dr. Clark had made an appointment for me with Prof. Upton. As a general thing, I think my colds of twenty & thirty years ago were worse than they are now.

I'm glad to hear that all the packages came safely, & trust you will enjoy them all. The colonial book seems to me a rare treasure, whilst all who have seen Sonny's little volume become enthusiastick. Kirk is going to include the latter in his next catalogue, & hopes to help the Child sell a number of copies. In this epistle I am enclosing a number of things which may possibly be of interest to you. Young Sandy's letter, which I trust your ingenuity will manage to translate from Sanduskese into English, will provide you with many reminiscences of seminary days at Norton; & will perhaps impel you to revisit your old Alma Mater when next you are in Chartley or vicinity. Another item is a sample of Orton's work, as shortly to be issued in Cook's monster *Vagrant*.[1] To me this sketch seems very good, tho' Orton himself professes to regard it as a contemptible trifle. Cook expects to use a good deal of his work in future. Another set of cuttings consists of miscellaneous archaeological, architectural, & antiquarian matter of self-explanatory nature—& the new catalogue of Kirk's Chelsea Book Shop. Of all this nothing need be returned except Orton's story—which I want to shew to other members of the gang. Orton has given me two more stories of his—in manuscript form—to read & comment upon, but I have had no time to attend to them as yet. I have, however, found time to polish up such parts of Loveman's poetical MS. as have reached Cook. Cook wants the Loveman book, when he publishes it, to be technically *perfect;* but is afraid of offending the temperamental poet by suggestions for revision. Accordingly he quietly sends me each section of the

---

*Incidentally—it was this very day of 1903—Feby. 12th—(which fell, however, on *Thursday*) that I bought the very first *new* book on *astronomy* that I ever owned. It was Young's "Lessons in Astronomy", & I got it at the R.I. News Co. for $1.25. Previously I had had only Grandma's copy of Burritt's "Geography of the Heavens". As I returned in the evening darkness on the rear platform of an Elmgrove Ave. car—415, I think it was; one of the graceful J. M. Jones cars—I looked over the pictures & chapter headings with perhaps the most delightful sense of breathless anticipation I have ever known. Most literally, a strange cosmos of new worlds lay before me!

long MS. as soon as he receives it from Loveman, & I supply the necessary changes without mentioning it to the bard. When the time comes, I shall read a duplicate set of proofs in the same silent way.

Speaking of local news—something which to our circle seems little less than a thunderbolt has just fallen. Kleiner—the settled, complacent business fixture—has lost his position with the old reliable Fairbanks Scale Co., & is looking for a new berth as accountant or bookkeeper! The matter involves no fault or deficiency of Kleiner's, but is an incident of that latter-day decadence which is undermining so many venerable & historick business institutions. The Fairbanks Co., despite its long years of fame, has come close to utter financial collapse; & has placed its affairs unreservedly in the hands of those banks who form its principal creditors. The banks, on their part, have taken over all the details of the company's administration; & are discharging employees right & left in a desperate effort to economise. Men of twenty & thirty years' experience, & with wives & children to support, are receiving tactful dismissals from the new authorities in charge; & with this policy ruthlessly carried out, it was inevitable that Kleiner, despite his ten years' faithful service, would be eliminated ultimately. Meanwhile the victim does not feel alarmed, or in the least depressed by his sudden ousting. Instead, he is grateful for the vacation; for with his skill in an important commercial field, it is only a question of time before he can obtain a new position as good as the old one if not better. His eye—whose affliction (he had a cold in it) I described in a former diary—is now better; & he is cheerfully going about his duties as chief arranger of tomorrow night's Blue Pencil Banquet—which Loveman, Sonny, & I plan to attend.

And now it behoves me to continue my diary, which hath not been extended beyond a week ago last Wednesday, when I was about to entertain a meeting here. Orton, you will recall, came early, bringing me Machen's "The Canning Wonder" as a gift; & S H & I took him out to dinner at Peter's. (the nice restaurant in Joralemon-St., near the corner of Clinton) The meal was very good, & as we walkt to & from the refectory we observ'd the beginning of the first of the two great snowstorms which have recently ingulph'd these parts of the country. On the return trip we purchas'd provisions for the evening's refreshments, & when we reacht 169 we beheld the first (or counting Orton, the second) of our guests—Kleiner—already come; & seated in the Morris-chair with an eye-cup & bottle of lotion with which he frequently sought to alleviate the discomfort of his afflicted optick. He was marvellously pleas'd with Sonny-Child's book, as Orton had been; & that delight was soon shar'd by Leeds, who represented the Chelsea Book Shop single-handed. Loveman, deterred by the storm & being in indifferent health, telephoned his regrets; & I promised to bring him the book as well as the Clark Ashton Smith drawings at his shop next day. Mortonius arrived late, having attended a Phi Beta Kappa meeting at Columbia College; but was heartily welcom'd &

very much in evidence after he did arrive. This comprised the meeting's entire personnel—since (although we did not know it at the time) Sonny's real grandfather had that day died, so that the child could not have come even had the weather permitted. Kirk was detain'd at his shop breaking in a new hired boy—a fine young blond American named Albert Fisher, of good aspect & pleasing manners, who is trying as hard as Belknap (& with slightly better success) to raise a moustache. Discussion was pleasing & vary'd; & involv'd not only the rapturous contemplation of Clark Ashton Smith's new weird drawings, but the introduction of Orton to a poet altogether new to him— viz., Andrew Marvell, Esq., the close friend of Milton, & author of very easy & agreeable verses. I copy'd one poem on the spot for Orton, upon the typewriter, for which service he profest himself very grateful. At 10:30 S H serv'd some delectable refreshments—sandwiches (tongue & cheese, with dressing) & cake—upon the blue china & tip-table; whilst I waded out thro' the snow for a can of coffee. All present declar'd the feast an unqualify'd success, & it was with reluctance that Orton tore himself away at 11 o'clock, in order to catch the 11:40 for Yonkers at the Grand Central. Kleiner was next to go, departing about 1 a.m., but Leeds & Mortonius stay'd till two. Upon their departure I pickt up the room & washt the dishes, retiring at 3 a.m. The next day—Thursday the 4th—I was up at noon, eat breakfast, washed the dishes, & set out on a tour of necessary errands which included both groceries & the barber's. Heaven knows I needed the latter uncommon bad, & 'twas with vast relief that I saw my head again clipt down to the condition of a gentleman's! Upon returning & delivering the edibles into the hands of S H, I rebrusht my scanty but neat locks (barbers never can brush hair correctly— even Fernando King fails to reproduce one's own strokes precisely) & set out on a fresh course of errands—this time down town, where I attended to some things for S H, got her ticket for Cleveland at the Grand Central, & mailed Sonnykins' book to you & A E P G. I then located Loveman by telephone, & finding him at the older of his employers' two shops,—the one in 4th Ave, whereas the new & sumptuous one is in 5th—proceeded thither to give him Belknap's book & the portfolio of Smith drawings. Both items delighted him to the point of ecstasy, & he promised to bring the drawings to the notice of his eminent friend Benjamin De Casseres as Smith had especially requested. It remains to add that he lost no time in doing so, & that De Casseres became wildly enthusiastick over the sketches & paintings; declaring (oddly enough, since no one else holds this opinion) that Smith is an even greater artist than poet. As for my main errand, the placing of Belknap's book on sale—this was not exactly a success; since for some commercial reason the Dauber & Pine firm will be unable to handle more than five or six copies. Loveman, however, said that Kirk could handle an indefinite number, & that he would include it in the next Chelsea catalogue; it having arriv'd just too late for inclusion in this one. To all these details he promis'd faithfully to attend; having indeed previously convers'd with Belknap about the matter over the telephone. In that conversation he had learnt of old Mr. Doty's death; which news being communicated to me, I writ that very night an epistle of condolence to the Child. Returning to 169 at 7:00 p.m., I found a lamb chop dinner prepar'd for me; the which I eat with relish & gratitude. After the disposal of the dishes I writ my note to Sonny; continuing later with other letters & retiring at 12:30 midnight. The next day—Friday the 5th—I rose at 11:00 a.m., eat breakfast & washt dishes, & later set out with S H for a sightseeing glimpse of something absolutely new to both—the celebrated *Hall of Fame*, which is, as you know, a colonnade extending round the domed classick library of N.Y. University on its commanding heights near Fordham, in the Bronx. You have, of course, beheld this at a distance; (you'll recall my pointing it out when we visited the Van Cortlandt mansion at the end of the West Side Subway. It is the edifice on a distant eminence to which I call'd your attention when the train emerg'd from underground at the Dyckman St. station & proceeded on an elevated structure.) but have never been close to it. In order to reach it, one takes the East Side subway—the one going to the Poe cottage, which we also used on Jany. 30 to reach the B.P.C. meeting at Dr. Swift's—& alights at the Burnside Ave. station. (one stop this side of Dr. Swift's, & two this side of the Poe cottage) Upon alighting, the course lies to the west steeply uphill through a district which, tho' newly built up, is nevertheless pleasing because of the curving, hilly streets, predominantly American population, & intangibly collegiate atmosphere. Mounting above the business section, we found a delightful residential district with new colonial houses peeping out from the dazzling snow, & a magnificent panoramick view of castled heights & wooded valleys spread out on every hand. This view, by all odds, form'd the finest prospect I have beheld since my trip to Washington. At the highest point of all, reach'd by a steep footpath winding betwixt two residual country-seats of Victorian vintage, towers that plateau which will some day be the main campus of the University. Now somewhat unfinisht & only partly built up, since the bulk of the college is scatter'd all over downtown New York, these heights are at present grac'd by several notable buildings of brick with stone trimmings, all in good classick taste as regards outline, but unfortunately of a *yellow* brick which subtracts from the Georgianism of the atmosphere. The great domed library, perch'd on the western precipice of the plateau with its circling colonnade overhanging the valley depths below, is flankt on the north by a Hall of Philosophy & on the south by a Hall of Languages. Lesser buildings appear here & there; & some day the whole plateau will be enclos'd as a scholarly and sequester'd quadrangle. The Hall of Fame itself, being a portico open to the four winds, was much chok'd with snow; but we manag'd to pick our way throughout its length without being bury'd. The bronze busts line both sides of the pillar'd passageway, resting betwixt the columns on the broad top of the low parapet, & having descriptive bronze tablets fixt upon the masonry beneath them. There are still many vacant spaces, & now & then a tablet without its corresponding statue—this latter being the case when the artist is still at work upon the effigy of some celebrity newly voted in. I rais'd my hat with proper local pride when passing that eminent South County citizen, Gilbert Stuart, Esq., (Mr. Williams' bust hath not yet arriv'd) & repeated that ceremonial out of aesthetick respect upon encountering the sombre gentleman whose home is only two stations away—that excitable visitant to Benefit St. & the Athenaeum, the gifted but unfortunate Mr. Poe. It was now near sunset, & the aspect of these pleasing heights in the magick glow of a gold-&-crimson sun was lovely & glamorous beyond description. The colonial past seem'd once more restor'd, & I cou'd well conceive of Fordham as a snug prosperous village but little concern'd with the distant New-York so many miles to the south. Only the extream *cold* prov'd annoying—for at these wind-swept altitudes there existed a biting chill which I found very difficult to shake off. Returning to Brooklyn by subway, we eat an excellent dinner at Joe's & later visited a cinema show at a theatre in Duffield-St., just off Fulton. Upon reaching 169, I read some in the new Weird Tales I had just bought, & retir'd at 2 a.m. The next day—Saturday the 4th—I rose at 11:00 a.m. & help'd clean the room in expectation of a visit from Orton in the afternoon. He wish'd to shew the nocturnal skyline to a young lady of his acquaintance, & was desirous of bringing her to call before the correct hour for exhibition. About noon we eat breakfast, & later the expressman call'd for S H's trunk. During the afternoon we read, & at about 4 o'clock our guests arriv'd; Orton's companion being a young woman of apparent intelligence & cultivated conversation, tho' not notable for extream beauty of face, named Elizabeth Hamilton. General literary topicks being for some time discuss'd, all hands set out at six o'clock to view the lighted turrets of Manhattan from the Montague St. parapet. Orton had been deeply im017press'd when first I shew'd it him last December, & was wishful to astonish the young nymph with that burst of magick constellated splendour to whose influence he had prov'd so sensible. Here, however, he was fated to be disappointed; for a sort of misty cloudiness accompany'd by snowflakes had arisen, so that the fiery spectacle across the water was quite compleatly obliterated. Bearing this frustration with the good grace which becomes a cynick & philosopher, Orton bow'd gracious adieux & departed with his guest. S H & I then proceeded to dine at the Taormina—that Italian restaurant over the grocery store in Clinton St. near Joralemon, which you may recall. Neither she nor I had been there for a year, & upon entering we were much repell'd by the boisterous aspect of the clientele. The prices, too, had become intolerably high—so that we could not help concluding that the proprietor had quietly turned to "bootlegging", & that regular patronage was now discouraged in favour of a sportier & more vinously inclined clientele. Still—having seated ourselves, we could not well arise & beat an inglorious retreat; so instead we bore the piratical prices with as good grace as possible, & were rewarded by finding the quality of the food still excellent. We shall not, however, repeat our visit to this refectory. Dinner done, we proceeded to Flatbush by subway to pay Mrs. Moran a call at 259 Parkside Ave. Finding her out, we left a note & proceeded to explore the once familiar reaches of Flatbush Avenue— winding up with a cinema show at the Linden. After this we returned to Brooklyn Heights, obtained some groceries at the shop under the Taormina, (whose excellence is unimpair'd by the extortion overhead) & proceeded to 169; where, after a modicum of reading, we retir'd at 1 a.m. Rising on Sunday at noon, I was subjected first of all to a cocoanut oil shampoo & then—after miscellanies such as cleaning, clothes-washing, &c.—to an excellent meal. Packing finally done, & some amount of reading indulg'd in, we set out at 5:00 p.m. for the Grand Central, there disposing of S H's luggage to a red-capt Nubian slave. In the interval before train-time we view'd the architectural beauties of the station & examin'd the books on sale at the contiguous Hall & Lyon—I mean Liggett—drug store; at length proceeding thro' the gate & concluding our colloquies at the steps of S H's Pullman car. As the train pull'd out at 6:30 p.m. I bowed my adieux & expressed my wishes for a pleasant journey. If all prospers at the Halle establishment, S H will not be here again till June; if asperities develop, however, she may return at an earlier date & seek some commercial opportunity here. I now quitted the Grand Central & proceeded at once to the publick library, intent to resume my weird reading in preparation for the article I am writing for Cook. On this occasion—&, I may add, on subsequent occasions—I encounter'd better luck than I had a month ago. Securing the volumes I call'd for, I proceeded to amend my ignorance by perusing two weird classicks which I ought to have read years ago— "The Monkey's Paw", (short story) by W. W. Jacobs, & "The Turn of the Screw", (short novel) by Henry James. These digested, I return'd to 169, did some reading, & retir'd at 4:15 a.m. The next day—Monday the 8th—I arose at 2 p.m., breakfasted, washed dishes, & began to cope with my piled-up mail. Toward evening I went down town to change the point of my new Waterman pen; & from the Waterman offices in lower Broadway (Cortlandt St. station of B.M.T.) proceeded uptown to the library via the Interborough East Side Subway—alighting at the Grand Central, traversing the arcade to the Shuttle line, & emerging to the surface at the very westernmost entrance, only a few doors from the library itself. I shall always use this route hereafter—in bad weather it pays to be an authority on the New York underworld! This time my reading consisted of the first two tales in Algernon Blackwood's enormously long "John Silence—Physician Extraordinary", & they certainly repaid my efforts—the second being an account of a weird French town, with dark intimations of Witches' Sabbaths.[2] Returning to 169 when the library closed, I wrote letters, read the Sunday Journal, & stayed up writing. From 11 a.m. to 3 p.m. Tuesday I rested; thereafter continuing with the letter-writing.

More snow appeared; but having perfected my new underground route to the library, I did not let it prevent me from getting down to read the third tale in "John Silence"—a hideous thing about a primordial curse, entitled "The Nemesis of Fire". Returning when the library closed, I stayed up & again grappled with my correspondence; receiving telephone calls from Sonny & Loveman, & resting from noon to 6:30 p.m. At this hour I started out for the meeting at honest old McNeil's—stopping en route at the Brooklyn library & succeeding in drawing out Algernon Blackwood's long novel, "The Wave". From there I went to the Milan in 42nd St. & indulged in the luxury of a spaghetti dinner, (35¢) after which I proceeded to the McNeil rookery in Hell's Kitchen—49th St. near 11th Ave. This meeting proved to be the slenderest one in the history of our club—for I was the *only* guest! Good old Mac with his simple ways is not much of an attraction for the majority, so that the Leeds meetings are likely to be the briskest these days. I, however, find something wholesome & refreshingly native-American in the old boy; so that I can generally be counted upon to turn up at the McNeil meetings. On this occasion we discussed all sorts of simple things, & I borrowed a copy of his "Tonty" to read at my leisure. He was pleased to learn of the book's good sale at Gregory's, & wonders how his other books are faring there—if indeed Gregory has them at all. About midnight he brought forth his simple refreshments—cocoa & cookies—& at 4 a.m. I departed, proceeding at once to 169 & staying up; my time being divided betwixt desultory readings in "The Wave" & weary attacks upon my accumulated correspondence. Later Thursday morning I cleaned my oil stove—a discouragingly sooty task—& after a rest from 12:30 to 6:15 p.m. arose to write A E P G. About 9 p.m. I started downtown to give Loveman the stories he wanted to shew to De Casseres, stopping en route for a pair of shoestrings. I can't for the life of me find the abundant supply which I know I must have somewhere. Do you recall where we put them? I've ransacked the chiffonier in vain! Loveman was at the *new* Dauber & Pine shop in 5th Ave.—the vacated quarters of the Macmillan Co.—& a prepossessing place it is indeed! The ground floor, devoted to new books, is in impeccable taste; & has an artistic balcony running around rear & sides. The basement is very capacious, & is filled with choice old books—one end being sumptuously fitted up with rugs, pictures, & mahogany as a reading room. I found a very desirable item there—an anthology of American Colonial wit & humour[3]—which I could not resist buying; especially since the courteous proprietor let me have it for half a dollar. Wishing to discharge *all* my social obligations with as little encroachment as possible on my time & seclusion, I made this a Kirk night also; & accompanied Loveman to the Chelsea Book Shop. There I found Kirk, Leeds, Kleiner, & the new boy Fisher, & indulged in general discussion & desultory reading of certain antiquarian items in Kirk's new stock. At midnight Loveman & Fisher left. At 1 a.m. Kleiner went. At 4 a.m. Leeds retired. At 5 a.m. I departed, leaving Kirk with a busy day before him. Upon returning to 169 I again grappled with correspondence, & rested from 8:30 a.m. to 2:30 p.m. Arising today at that latter hour, I have since been writing; & am now—6:30 p.m.—about to get ready for a trip to the library in which I hope to finish "John Silence". On the way, though, I'll try to get it at the Brooklyn library; & if I do (as I doubt) I'll return & read it here instead of going to N.Y. ¶ As for the future—tomorrow I am due at Sonny's at 6:30 p.m., to take the Child to the B.P.C. banquet, which is held at the Rainbow Restaurant, 18 E. 33d. St., near 5th Ave. (near the Waldorf-Astoria.) Next Wednesday there is a (Leeds) meeting at Belknap's, & the week after that a McNeil meeting at Loveman's. Aside from these things, & the possible call on De Casseres which Loveman is urging me to make with him, I hope to keep my programme free for weird reading, the writing of the Cook article, & the resultant recovery of my creative literary faculty. Then for some new weird stories! ¶ Hoping to hear from you soon, I have yᵉ honour to remain

Yr moſt aff. Nephew & obt Servt:

H P L

Notes

1. Cook's *Vagrant* no. 15 [Spring 1927] had 312 pages. It contained the following by Orton: "Change," 235; "To One Left," 271–72; "To One Gone," 273–74; and "To One at Delhi," 275–78.

2. The first two stories are "A Psychical Invasion" and "Ancient Sorceries." The latter was probably an influence on "The Shadow over Innsmouth."

3. By Carl Holliday.

[158]   [ALS]

Tuesday–Wednesday Midnight
Feby. 16–17, 1926

My dear daughter Lillian:—

Hurrah! At last I've wiped out the pile of dull correspondence & am able to take my pen in hand for home conversation. Just mailed a mile-high stack of junk, & am now safe till the morning mail. Here's hoping the postmen go on strike till I get this epistle finished & a book or two read!

I am indeed glad that you escaped the grippe, for a kind of mild epidemic seems to be sweeping the country from coast to coast. Out in California Clark Ashton Smith & both his parents have been down with it, whilst in N.Y. the latest sufferer is the critic Benjamin De Casseres, to whom Loveman wanted to shew my stories. However—it's nothing as compared to the scourge of 1918. You were, I think, wise in letting a good physician take hold of the case; & I trust you will supplement this wisdom with a cautious avoidance of unnecessary outdoor exposure. Today the dampness has gone, & a hellish frigidity has arrived in its place. This may be healthier, but it's a good deal more uncomfortable for me! Keep your establishment well stocked with provisions, as I do—so that going out on any given day will never be absolutely necessary. Yes—I noted the cutting concerning the amount of weather contain'd in February, & believe that the present month has amply demonstrated its truth! And yet think of the adventurous Barrington robin! Sowams is a great place for pioneers![1]

The more I reflect on the Architects' Plan for a memorial, the more favourably am I disposed to regard it—tho' I do insist that the Peirce temple is intrinsically more beautiful than an obelisk. However, the Architects' design, as submitted as a whole, certainly shews a marvellous degree of taste & comprehension of the needs of our particular landscape; so that it must undoubtedly stand very high amongst the various competing ideas. I only hope, though, that a mistaken devotion to the idea of abstract elegance will not cause the developers to tear down the old buildings near Market Square which give to Providence so much of its distinctively colonial character. Those Canal & S. Water St. Warehouses might well be spruced up & cleared of unsightly signs, but they ought never to be torn down. I had a depressing nightmare about the Arcade a few days ago—I dreamt that the steps were removed, & that the Westminster St. side was defaced by a hideous false front. Something drastic & immediate ought to be done to save this honoured & remarkable landmark. But returning to the memorial—the Architects' Plan is estimated as the least costly of all—& is the only one coming within the limits of the present appropriation of $300,000. Contractors figure that it could be completed at an expense of from $250,000. to $268,000. The Peirce Ionic temple (not counting landscape development) would cost $400,000. if of limestone, $550,000. if of granite, & $650,000. if of white marble, as of course it ought to be. The Whitney design, of course, is very costly. The pictures you missed in the Bulletin were only maps & diagrams so far as the Architects' Plan was concerned, but I'll send the article anyway, since it has the only good picture of the Peirce temple that I've seen. Please return with extreme care. I've just been trying to find a picture of the *Montana* design, but my files are so mixed up that I can't. I know it's there, however, & will send it in a few days when I indulge in the drastic straightening-out which I have long been contemplating. I'm sorry to see such a mass of untrained & superficial sentiment in favour of the Whitney plan—doubtless on account of its spectacular magnitude. The obstinate preference for it shewn by the American Legion may influence the city councilmen with whom the decision rests. That Sunday Journal view of the Architects' Plan was certainly alluring, & did much to incline me toward the design. I wish we could have both that & the Peirce design—the latter as a memorial to something else—such as the exploits of the Rhode Island sloop-of-war *Tartar* in the capture of Louisburg in 1745 under Sir William Pepperrell, Bart., & Admiral Sir Peter Warren,

K.C.B. The best place for the Peirce design would be the filled-in Hope Reservoir eminence. By the way—I note that the government has expressed a desire that all local war memorials be finished by 1928, in time for the celebration of the 10th Anniversary of the armistice.

I note with amusement the opinions of Capt. Hall anent Dr. Cook, but fear that none of these sensational speculations can be taken seriously.[2] The acceptance or rejection of an account is determined by a thousand considerations—details of evidence, character of participants & witnesses, &c—& although of course all instrumental records are subject to minor errors, it is fairly safe to say that Peary got as close to the pole as anybody will ever be able to get & prove it, whilst Cook did not. The one man was a scientific & reliable officer of the U.S. Navy, the other a brilliant but erratic soldier of fortune. The one was a gentleman of known honour, never known to deviate in the least degree from the exact truth, whilst the other was a demonstrated liar in at least one instance, (ascent of Mt. McKinley)[3] & has since become an outright criminal—being now in gaol. These facts speak for themselves. Nevertheless I hope Amundsen will make his expedition, since there is great room for geographical discovery in the neighbourhood of the pole.[4] Vast areas of the Arctic have never been trodden by man, & we know next to nothing of the distribution of land & water. Vast unknown islands, almost continental in extent, may lurk unsuspected in the white mists under the aurora; & none may say what strange wonders may not be found on them. As to the *universe*—there is nothing new in the conception of our visible universe of stars as a separate globular cluster, one of an infinite number scattered throughout infinity. Indeed, any other conception becomes almost absurd when we reflect upon its arrangement, & upon the nature of infinite & eternal space. Sir William Herschel, in my own 18th century, was the first to conceive of our local universe as a globular cluster; (stars in pie-shaped equatorial disc constituting milky way, nebulae rounding out the spherical form) & by this time the idea has passed almost out of theory into accepted fact. What *is* new in the astrophysics & cosmogony of Chamberlain [*sic*] & Moulton, is their doctrine of how the solar system was formed—a doctrine widely differing from the hitherto dominant nebular hypothesis of Laplace. I have not yet found a good recent book in which I can get a true working idea of the new "planetesimal hypothesis", but as soon as I do, I will write you as full an account as possible of it. One salient point is its belief that the sun captured its planets from outside space, instead of throwing them off as nebulous rings during its plastick & contracting period.

Haven't gotten to the Borgia book yet, but expect it will be interesting. The book you remember—about the bed which they poisoned with radioactive material four centuries & a half before the action of the story—was "The Grey Room", by Eden Philpotts [*sic*], who also wrote that still cleverer narrative of mystery, "The Red Redmaynes." Yes—it was good of Leeds to present me with the book, & I trust that I may some time return the favour.

Algernon Blackwood is indeed a great weird artist; but as I said before, he writes too much, & doesn't seem to be able to keep from publishing his poorer material. His "Empty House" & "Day & Night Stories" are very mediocre; yet the same man can turn around & write masterpieces like "The Willows" & the second, third, & fourth stories in "John Silence". ("Ancient Sorceries", "The Nemesis of Fire", & "Secret Worship".) I have his long novel "The Wave" from the Brooklyn library now, & hope to finish it in the hours following the conclusion of this epistle. Then (unless fresh mail swamps me) I shall go down & read more of his stuff at the 42nd st. library before the meeting at Belknap's. Blackwood has methods & subtleties worthy of the closest study, & is the most voluminous of all weird writers. His work ought to be known intimately to every student of macabre fiction, & only the large number of his dull books prevented me from knowing him better before. I still have many to read. Our library possesses a very good assortment of Blackwood material—you'll find it in the main room among the B's—on the open shelves, in the corner near the door to the stack, at the right of the delivery desk. Speaking of libraries, I note your Peck clipping. It's a good story—but if I recall rightly, Miss P. is no longer of an age to be annoyed by "mashers"! She is, I believe, a sister of that Peck who was until very recently principal of the Classical High School.

As for domestick matters—my domain certainly did need cleaning, but the trouble is that with bituminous coal about, it begins to need it again altogether too soon! But the big accomplishment was the picking up of the alcove, & the elimination of needless material, so that I can get at things & find what I want when I want it—except shoe strings! As for carpet-sweepers—I always have the use of one; that article, together with a broom, a mop, & a dustpan being permanently in the upper hall at the disposal of the fastidious tenant. I had a new tooth brush some time ago—about a year, I think—& it is still in fair shape; but I would be grateful for a soft one to hold in reserve. The one I obtained in the Christmas grab-bag at Belknap's is much too stiff for my aged gums. I'll preserve your directions for washing my hair brush; tho' I hate to do it, since it is no good for brushing purposes until dry again. I'll try that pomade after the next shampoo. I couldn't the last time because I was in a hurry—getting ready to see S H off at the station—so I used the fluid you made me a year or so ago. I use these substances only after a shampoo, since my hair no longer lacks oil as it did two years ago. I don't use them as *tonics*, because Fernando King says that hair-restorers & tonics are of no use. If a poor devil is going to be bald, he *will* be, despite all the frantic measures he may take!

Yes—I read of Stephen Leacock's intention to devote his pen & fortune to medical channels, & trust he may see the results he is looking for—but it is rather foolish to cramp one's artistic style by devotion to propaganda.[5] I fancy he'll find time to write a few things for the writing's sake! As for Archbishop Plunket[6]—he is undoubtedly of the Dunsany blood, though probably very remotely so, since the different spelling of the name argues no close connexion. The Plunketts are the greatest house of County Meath, with representatives in the nobility, in politics, in the professions, & in places of high dignity in both Anglican & Catholick churches. There has been a Cardinal Plunkett of the Popish church—tho' I'm not certain whether he's still living—in fact, I feel quite sure he's dead. And as for the sable barristress L. Marian Poe[7]—well, so long as she doesn't meddle wiv de white folks, Ah reckin she won' do no harm. Perhaps her great-great grandpaw was owned by Poe's grandfather, old Gen. David Poe! Now I suppose Delilah will try to enter professional life—possibly medicine or theology or statesmanship. As for the Aurora—too bad I always miss it! I've never seen a decent display. That fossil fish view is interesting—I well recall ours, & appreciate your intention of donating it to my museum!

Glad the Sayer establishment provides you with an interesting calling-place, tho' sorry the elder generation has departed. Bless me, but I'd like to see that nice kitty-cat who sleeps there so much! Kirk's cat died a natural death a month ago, & he has not yet secured another. He may, however, if he can find a very tiny kitten of just the sort he wants. Meanwhile the playful & whimsical Oscar from upstairs visits him frequently. If Grandma's red book is getting full, I'd advise matching it as well as possible at Preston & Rounds' & starting Volume II. I was interested to hear of Stephen Place's destination in the Hoag region, & trust the house of Briggs still flourishes there. As for trained fleas—I thought everyone knew about them! I recall my mother's having spoken of them at a museum in 14th St. in New York, which she inspected during a visit many years ago. The midget you saw on the street must have been connected with some vaudeville act at Keith's, Fay's, or the Emery, & I fancy a close study of the theatrical advertisements would have told you at once who & what he was.

Yes—Sonny is surely a great little writer, & Grandpa could see the touch of original genius even in the crude "Dr. Whitlock's Price", back in the 1919–20 season. By this time you'll have seen from A E P G's letter how he's represented in the new Anthology of Magazine Verse.[8] He'll be delighted to receive your note of thanks. And isn't it odd how my slangier grandchild, Sandy the Tough Egg,[9] is getting to know your good old Alma Mater! In his latest colloquial concoction he tells of hearing a sermon by the successor of the late principal (or perhaps his title was President) Cole—a man named Smart, who is holding the office temporarily till a permanent incumbent can be appointed. Last Friday I sent you a letter of Hard-Boiled Al's which forms quite a guide to the Wheaton campus of today, & which seems to settle the matter of name quite conclusively in accordance with your own impression. It would be interesting to look up the old catalogue & later visit the spot after so considerable an interval—& I wish that Sandy might be aroun' ter han' ya out a wise steer. I wonder if the Attleboro, Norton & Taunton cars are still running?

There was talk some time ago of abandoning the line, but they one-mann'd the cars & tried to keep on a little. The other Attleboro–Taunton line—the one that passed Briggs' Corners & the sanitarium & had a branch to Pawtucket—was abandoned & torn up years ago. However—if these aren't cars there must be omnibuses, & you won't need to worry anyway if you get free motor transportation from Chartley.

As to food—of course I keep a good supply constantly on hand! I don't bother with canned vegetables because they're an extra care & expense, but I suppose I could stow away beets, corn, succotash, &c. now & then. I've slowly come to like *peas* if they are *small & young;* but cannot bear string beans or asparagus. Yes—if I used them I would conduct the heating as you do. There are no Nicholson–Thackray stores in Brooklyn, but the Clinton Delicatessen under the Taormina keeps "College Inn" canned products. However—they are too expensive for regular use, & if I ever indulge it will be very sparsely, as a luxury. I think I'll try to see how much the Welsh Rarebit is.

I wish I knew that song—"Haste thee, Winter, haste away; Far too long has been thy stay"[10]—for if I did, I'd sing it about as soon as the autumn weather sets in. Even now I'm shivering at the thought of next fall! Yes—this Waterman pen is splendid, & I'm still debating whether or not I'll have the feed choked up a bit. As for that rich & royal lampshade—its stately dignity of hue doesn't affect my work in the least, since I always *tip* it to through [*sic*] the direct & unshaded light on the book or paper before me.* The aspect of the improved lamp is captivating beyond description! Glad the Davis-child's epistle amused you—here's another one, which you might return sometime. He certainly is a great boy! Also glad you liked the State St. Trust material. As to my inflated correspondence—I certainly am going to try & cut down on non-essential letters, but they do mount up hideously, & it's hard to neglect them without being discourteous. After the present United crisis (I wish these crises were less infernally frequent!) I ought to be able to reduce my daily epistolary output quite substantially, & put the energy into writing of a more permanent & creative sort.

And so it goes. I'll seal this document now, adding any needed diary postscripts on the envelope. I hope to read—& perhaps rest a little—during the day, & in there [*sic*] evening there is a meeting at Belknap's at which a very full attendance is expected. ¶ Hoping your cold is now absolutely all gone, I remain

Yr aff: Nephew & obt Servt
HPL

P.S. Glad the Mestrovic reference interested you. Thanks for the picture of the old boy in the old house. He & I can remember things! I enclose a printed copy of my new Hoag verses, which you may retain permanently.

P.P.S. And here are the UNITED AMATEURS for you & A E P G.

[On envelope:]

Diary extended to 8 p.m [*sic*] Wednesday.
Read "The Wave" but didn't finish it.
Rested 10:30 a.m [*sic*] to 6:30 p.m.
Am now starting for meeting at Belknap's.

Notes

1. Sowams was a Native American village where the Rhode Island town of Warren was later built.

2. HPL refers to Captain Thomas F. Hall (1841–1933), who defended Frederick A. Cook's assertion that he had reached the North Pole ahead of Robert E. Peary. See Hall's *Has the North Pole Been Discovered?* (Boston: R. G. Badger, 1917).

3. Cook claimed to have reached the top of Mt. McKinley in Alaska in 1906, but the photograph he presented as proof of his ascent proved to be a fake.

4. Roald Amundsen led an expedition that was the first to cross the Arctic in the airship *Norge* in May 1926.

5. Upon the death of his wife, Beatrix, of cancer on 15 December 1925, Canadian humorist Stephen Leacock (1869–1944) devoted much time to speaking about cancer and fundraising for cancer research.

6. William Conyngham Plunket, 4th Baron Plunket (1828–1897), dean of Christ Church Cathedral in Dublin and Archbishop of Dublin. The relationship to Lord Dunsany's family (the Plunketts) is unclear.

7. L. Marian Poe (1890–1974), the first African American woman to be admitted to the bar in the Southern United States.

8 Franklyn Pierre Davis (1868-1932), ed., *Anthology of Newspaper Verse for 1925* (Enid, OK: Frank P. Davis, 1926). The book contains Long's "A Man from Genoa" (9–10), which appeared in the *Hollywood Florida News*.

9. I.e., Albert A. Sandusky.

10. From "Winter Song," a song for schoolchildren.

[159]   [ALS] [HPL to LDC]

Friday Afternoon
Feby. 26, 1926

My dear daughter Lillian:—

I take my pen in hand to thank you for the park booklet & other material which arriv'd yesterday, & to exprefs the pleasure I have deriv'd therefrom. Zounds! I had no idea we had so many parks, for of most of those describ'd in the book I had never heard. If I am ever home again I shall have to spend the rest of my days exploring—& meanwhile I shall assiduously cherish the brochure for whose procuring I am so greatly oblig'd. The new Brown dormitories are certainly utter triumphs of the colonial tradition, & I had already cut them out of my Bulletin. I am deeply grateful for the duplicates, so that I may send them about with scant worry over loss or damage. Brown is certainly fast becoming a centre of colonialism—& my only regret is that the construction of these buildings entail'd the demolition of some *real* colonial houses. The Providence Bank item I am also delighted to have in duplicate. As you may have noted, the back encroaches upon Mortonius' precious crossword puzzle, so that after I cut it out I had to paste the puzzle fragment on white paper & fill it out by hand for the eager recipient. As to the merger—I'm largely neutral, but I hope the building will always be sedulously preserved. It is one of the finest colonial houses in the city built by the architect Joseph Brown (of the famous brothers) for himself in 1774, & alter'd during the 1790's. If ever abandon'd as a bank, I think it ought to be furnisht like the Pendleton House as a colonial museum—the facade being restor'd to its original residential state by the rebuilding of the double flight of stone steps with iron railing, & reopening of the colonial doorway on the 1st floor proper—now technically the second story. You will find a picture of the house in its pristine state in that yellow Isham[1] circular of colonial walks, publisht by the Chamber of Commerce. What Providence needs very much is a colonial museum in a *real* Georgian house, with the rooms fitted up in a more *intimately homelike* (& less selectively magnificent) way than in the Pendleton House. It ought to be designed to illustrate 18th century Providence life in all its phases—including kitchen & cellar. Then we ought also to have a *small* colonial house typically furnished.

And now for my diary, which last extended to Wednesday evening before the meeting. Well—I went out for the refreshments, & found Kleiner arrived when I returned. Orton soon added himself, & McNeil was on hand promptly at eight. Discussion had interestingly warmed up when Loveman arrived at 9:30, & at 10:15 the genial bulk of Mortonius made our festivities complete. I now went out for coffee, which I proceeded to serve as usual in the blue china. At 11:00 the departure of Orton for his train occasion'd universal regret, & sighs were repeated when Loveman evaporated at 11:30. Kleiner & honest old McNeil decamped on the stroke of midnight, but Mortonius lingered on till 1:15. On the whole, the meeting may be call'd highly successful. One of the topicks of discussion was the sale of ancient art objects now commenced by the Metropolitan Museum—terra cotta heads, Cyprus glassware, Greek & Roman lamps, &c. Mortonius asked me to pick him up something for a dollar when I went, but as it turn'd out, there was nothing any good as cheap as that. The worst & smallest sculptured head was 4 fish. After the meeting I washed dishes, read in Weird Tales, & retired at 3 a.m. The next day—

Thursday the 25th—I was up at 8:30 a.m., wrestled with correspondence, & at 1 p.m. started out on an expedition in the rain. First looking up the new municipal museum in the old Gracie Mansion (1813) at East River Park—foot of 88th St.—I was greatly disappointed; for the collection of prints & relicks is very meagre & badly displayed. There is no effort to furnish the old house in a homelike way—all is cold & formal, & the walls are defaced by some abominable quasi-historical murals. All I really liked were the mantelpieces in the upstairs rooms—fine specimens in the Adam tradition. In the office I saw the curator—Henry Collins Brown, editor of Valentine's Manual & compiler of that little ten-cent book of old N.Y. views which I sent you a year ago last summer.[2] He was not the courtly, white-bearded gentleman of the Old School I had expected, but a stocky, moustached person not yet very grey. From there I went to the Metropolitan Museum, raved properly at my empty purse when confronted by the fascinating antiquities for sale, & proceeded to brood on the past in the American Wing. I tried to find data on Talman's Dutch clock, but failed. Then I took the subway down to the library, read Blackwood till closing time, & concluded the day by returning to 169, wrestling with correspondence, & retiring at 4 a.m. Today I was up at 11 a.m., wrestled with correspondence, & received a telephone message from Sonny—who greatly enjoyed his meeting with the poet Harold Vinal.[3] It is now 3 p.m., & I am going out on a dual tour—first to see what the Long Island Historical Society (right here at Clinton & Pierrepont Sts.) is like, & second to do some more library reading. It's odd I never investigated this L.I. place so near at hand. Tomorrow I expect a call from Sonny & possibly Orton—& we shall probably visit some museum before the day is over. Next Wednesday is a Leeds meeting at Kirks [*sic*]—& that is all I know of the future. Such, then, is which. With renew'd thanks for the booklet & cuttings, & the hope that you are steering clear of colds, I am ever

Yr most aff: Nephew & obt Servt

H P L

Notes

1. See LDC/AEPG 166n1.

2. Henry Collins Brown (1862–1961), editor of *Valentine's Manual of Old New York* (1916–28). The other book HPL alludes to may be *New York of Yesterday* (New York: Gracie Mansion, 1924); but Brown compiled several similar volumes.

3. Harold Vinal (1891–1965), American poet, editor of the poetry journal *Voices*, and secretary of the Poetry Society of America.

[160]   [ALS] [HPL to LDC]

Thursday
March 4, 1926

My dear daughter Lillian:—

This is a sort of farewell to the world for a period of perhaps several weeks—the result of a modest but feasible & welcome *money-making* scheme. It seems that Loveman's bookselling firm need the temporary services of an envelope-addresser to help in mailing their catalogues; & since I was able to do such rapid & effective work in connexion with Kirk's catalogues, I am resolved to try my hand at the present venture. It will be very confining, involving regular hours at the establishment each day beginning at 9 a.m., but it will *not* be *mentally* exacting—having a purely mechanical cast & leaving my faculties free for whatever creative work they can accomplish. There are about 10,000 catalogues to be sent out, so that the work may last several weeks at (Loveman thinks) $17.50 per week. I shall use this matter as an excuse to abandon much correspondence; for if I thus sacrifice the major portion of each day, I certainly intend to have the leisure residue *purely & simply for myself*—my own personal reading & literary composition. I shall, too, indulge in at least two & perhaps three wholly recreational extravagances which I shall deem justified in view of the inconvenience with which I purchase them—(a) a $3.00 Philadelphia excursion, (b) a $5.00 Washington excursion, & (c) possibly a Roman terra-cotta head from that marvellous sale at the Metropolitan Museum. The addressing would seem to begin Monday at 9 a.m., but I shall of course reap no financial returns till the following Saturday. I'll let you know later how it turns out—& whether anything arises at the last moment to nullify the entire design.

As for my diary—last carry'd to Monday evening—I arrived at Sonny's in good season & found Orton & honest old McNeil there—Loveman being unable to come. Discussion was interesting & refreshments (served by the Child himself in the absence of the maid) excellent, & all regretted it when Orton had to leave at 11:00 for his train. McNeil & I stayed on till 1 a.m., whereafter I return'd to 169 & wrote on my weird article till 8 a.m. I then retired, rising Tuesday at 5 p.m. & going at once to the library, where I began to peruse the works of the celebrated Ernst Theodor Wilhelm Hoffmann, (1776–1822) whose fantastick tales had so great an influence upon Poe. I found Hoffmann freakish, extravagant, & grotesque rather than convincingly weird; & must own that to me his net impression is one of seldom relieved dulness—but his importance in the history of spectral literature is so great that no specialist in that field can afford not to know him, as a matter of general cultural background. Leaving when the library closed, I repair'd to 169 & spent the subsequent hours either writing on the article or pursuing necessary subsidiary reading. I retired at 7:30 a.m., & rose again Wednesday at 12:30 noon. Disposing of some correspondence, I hastened down town to attend to another bond matter for S H, after which I read more in Hoffmann at the library. At 8 p.m. I proceeded to the meeting at Kirk's, but found only Leeds at home. Kleiner soon arrived, closely follow'd by Kirk & Loveman; & Mortonius somewhat later completed the evening's quota. Discussion was mediocre but not oppressively wearisome, & refreshments were fair. Loveman left at midnight, & Kleiner at 2 a.m. Mortonius & I left at 4 a.m., after which I return'd to 169 & wrestled with correspondence—retiring at 9 a.m. This afternoon I rose at 1:30 & have been wrestling with farewell correspondence since then. It is now 4:30 p.m., & I shall proceed to the library to continue with Hoffmann till closing time. I shall then return & work more on my weird tale article. Tomorrow night Kirk, Orton, & I will probably take an all-night exploring tour, & Sunday I shall wind up all my earthly affairs before attempting this remunerative episode with the bookshop. I'll send more bulletins as events develop. Wish I could get some permanent *part time* addressing to do, for I can manage that sort of work very rapidly & effectively. And so it goes. Talman has sent some more data about the moon-dial of his old Dutch clock, & I am again constructing theories. This time we think the inner circle of figures may mean *high tide* as calculated for Amsterdam or Rotterdam.

¶ Yr aff Nephew & obt Servt

H P L

P.S. Please tell A E P G that my Wanamaker booklet has just come, & that I'm now sending for one apiece for you & for her.

[On envelope? In RHB's handwriting:] [P.]P.S. The Netopian just came. What delightful views of Rhode Island colonial fireplaces & mantels!![1]

Notes

1. "The Fireplace: An Architectural Tradition in America," *Netopian* No. 11 (February 1926): 7–10.

[161]   [ALS] [HPL to LDC]

Friday Afternoon
March 5, 1926

My dear daughter Lillian:—

Your welcome letter having arriv'd this morning, I will follow my note of yesterday with another. It is now 2 p.m., & I am hoping to get to the barber's before evening—when the all-night-&-all-next-day trip with Kirk & Orton will probably begin. I shall get Orton on the telephone about 4. Before going into eclipse with this addressing business I shall have one good jaunt!

I'm glad you enjoyed the archaeological cuttings in my former epistle, &

assure you that none need be returned. Neither need any of the letters—Sandy's, &c.—which I enclosed. One can't keep everything! Yes—I noticed the treadmill cartoon about the memorial in Monday's paper, & thought it rather clever—though spoofing aside, it is no light matter to decide on something which will be linked to the city's aesthetic scheme for better or for worse throughout an indefinite futurity! Here's hoping that something suitable is evolved in the end. The R.I. Architects' plan can still be consider'd, since the estimates given came well within the $300,000 appropriation. No—the Parthenon article need not be returned—but you might send back Orton's story, since I want to shew it to others. I thought this tale excellent, tho' its author professes to be ashamed of it. As to Miss Guiney's poetry—I read a volume or two many years ago, but found most of the moods rather remote at the time.[1] I have since been thinking of giving it a fuller critical survey when the opportunity presents itself. That Bullen article is a bit flattering—he isn't as important as I imply—but he is so amiable & eager that I thought it wouldn't do any harm to let him have his glory before a none too discriminating audience. Yes—I hope the United can survive, & think young Bacon is very praiseworthy & energetic in his efforts to keep it going despite every conceivable adversity. Yes—I have made the proper adjustments of credit on the park booklet business. You will, I think, enjoy the period furniture booklets when I send them, & if you'd like copies for permanent preservation I'm sure a postal would bring them. As I said yesterday, I've asked Wanamaker's to send you that tercentenary booklet which A E P G saw—& I fancy you'll derive some measure of entertainment from it. Collecting free booklets is quite a pastime—it grows on one!

Glad that Gregory's have another of honest old McNeil's books, & will tell him so next Wednesday when we meet at his rookery. I haven't read "Tonty" yet—& now only Pegāna knows when I will, since this commercial task is looming up. I am interested to hear of the peregrinations of the Empire Book Shop, whose disappearance from Empire St. I noted some 2½ years ago. I thought it had failed. The book—or rather books—which were lost in the transportation of my effects were Beers' large Atlas of Rhode Island, (1870) & the star atlas to Burritt's Geography of the Heavens, which lay flat for preservation within the covers of the stiffer book. No more desolating loss could be imagined—for the star atlas belonged to Grandma, whilst the R.I. Atlas gave in detail every inch of R.I. soil, & had Gramp's name as owner of half the land around Greene. So you recognise the names of the new Norton halls! It is interesting to be able to trace things so definitely. I note the cutting anent the Providence student honoured at Wheaton. But I never knew that the poetess Lucy Larcom was a graduate![2]

How unfortunate that another cold has beset you! It must be a misdelivery of the cold I ought to have had by this time. Stay in as much as possible, & let us hope that vernal weather will soon be an actuality. Glad you liked "Cool Air", & hope I can turn out some more material when this addressing siege is over. I'd like to concoct something which would bring in a fortune at one bound, so that we might settle down in that apartment you mention. As a location I choose that reclaimed Colonial section around Thayer St. which Theodore Francis Green is developing![3] Glad you approve of my 40¢ gorge—I think it's the best restaurant value available, & my ironclad "innards" will apparently cope with anything. I note your canned suggestions, but have to veto the *string beans*. I've come to tolerate peas remarkably, but string beans are a little too too much! My next innovation will be canned Welsh rarebit as per A E P G's suggestion. Glad you have such a good view of a Colonial college dormitory. Those pictures you sent fascinate me immensely, & I can imagine what a marvellously Georgian place the university is fast becoming. Now if only Sayles Hall & other intrusive Victorian features could be torn down! Even the clock tower with its Italian Renaissance implications is nothing to get enthusiastick over.

Yes—I noticed with much pleasure the honours extended to Dr. Chapin, & believe that few tributes have ever been better deserved! I wish Providence could produce a still larger number of international figures, & trust that the younger Chapin may adorn antiquarianism to as much advantage as his illustrious parent has adorn'd the art of Galen—if the younger generation of criticks will permit me to employ this latter flower of rhetorick! I think you will like young Talman when you meet him. Just now he's probably glad the Sunday Journal *didn't* publish his notes on his celebrated ancestress, the Goodvrouw Annetje Jans, since further research has caused an alteration in his point of view. And I hope the latest solution of the moon-dial of the old Dutch clock is the right one! So the Western Union has moved! I'll be glad to hear about the shiftings of the Tribune office when you find out—tho' of course there's no hurry. No—I'll be gentle & tactful in my tonsorial preachments to the Alfredus-child, & hope that his native good sense may step in at the last moment to cause a general shearing before he lands on American—or rather, New York—soil. As for *shoestrings*—I still look, off & on, but find nothing! And yet I know there's a large box of them somewhere hereabouts! So far my lapse of recollection has cost me nothing in cash, since a genial clerk at a shoestore (no doubt with an eye to future patronage) made me a present of the new pair I now have. Don't hurry about the toothbrush—my present one really shews no signs of decay.

So it was you & not A E P G who perused "Bat Wing"![4] I remember now, but usually think of her as the best-seller fiend! The same author's history of sorcery is quite entertaining, though a bit episodic & lacking in continuous development & detail. The best source of magical lore, I am convinced, is that odd Frenchman Constant who used the pseudonym "Eliphas Levi". I shall some time read through his large "Histoire de Magie" in Waite's excellent translation. Just now Hoffmann occupies me; tho' as I said yesterday, he is not intrinsically interesting. I hope to finish one series of his tales, "The Serapion Brethren", either tonight or tomorrow. My article is now dealing with Poe, & in preparing it I am re-reading whatever I describe in detail, in order to achieve perfect accuracy. What a marvellous yarn "Arthur Gordon Pym" is!

All the cuttings you sent were of keenest interest to me, & I shall carefully file the Scituate one in my collection of choice Rhodinsularia. What has become of the good old Lapham Institute these days? Is it frankly abandoned, or still in the hands of those Pentecostal fanatics? The last I heard of it, there was a fire there; but I believe it was said not to be extensive.[5] As one of the finest existing specimens of the early American academy, this place ought to be sedulously preserved. Its location is ideal, & it deserves a course of thorough repair & development as a high-grade boarding-school. The Philadelphia affair must have been interesting. I am going to take a Philadelphia trip if this addressing job really brings as much as Loveman says it will. Of course, the copy-books say that one ought to lay everything aside for the future—but meanwhile life slips by & one finds oneself old & incapable of enjoyment before one has really enjoyed anything! I want to see several parts of Philadelphia more thoroughly than I did before—especially the southeasterly colonial section around Old Swedes' Church, (1702) which I have never explored *by daylight.* I'll give that Saltus cutting to Loveman, who will undoubtedly be keenly interested & highly grateful. Not long ago he received an absurdly silly & gushing letter from Mrs. S. What she says about the reception of her biography is merely piffle—the thing is absurd, as you may have noted from Galpin's comment in the last letter I sent you. The book is a mess of trivial inanity; written without appreciation of Saltus' real merit, & gloating cheaply over every possible failing & eccentricity on his part—a most wretched way of repaying the man without whom she herself would never have been noticed by the publick. She uses her husband as a lever to promote her own literary pretensions—& then drags him through the mud in return. Mrs. S's influence on Saltus' work was unrelievedly bad. She curbed his natural style & point of view, & in his old age converted him to a mess of theosophical nonsense which ruined him as an artist & made him almost an object of ridicule.

Well—such is which. As for my diary since yesterday—I went to the library, read Hoffmann, returned & worked on my article, retired at 5 a.m., rose at noon, & have since been wrestling with correspondence. I shall now go to the barber's (3:30 p.m.) & telephone Orton about tonight. Then, the gods willing, I shall read at the library till the time comes for an assemblage of pedestrians. It's a bit cold for walking; but if Kirk & Orton can stand it, it would be unbecoming in me to back out! More later.

Yr aff: Nephew & obt Servt

H P L

[On envelope? In RHB's handwriting:] P.S. Just telephoned Orton—all-night hike called off on account of cold. Instead, I shall meet him at the library about 6 or 7 p.m. for dinner, & later we'll possibly see a cinema & return to 169 for literary discussion.

6:30 p.m. have been to barber's & am now starting down to meet Orton at the publick library.

Notes

1. Louise Imogen Guiney (1861–1920), American poet and essayist. She was a friend of Oliver Wendell Holmes, and it was apparently at her house in Auburndale, MA (where HPL and his family had, by his testimony, stayed in the winter of 1892–93), that HPL met Holmes (see LDC/AEPG 146n1). HPL had written of her poetry: "He [Holmes] was a devotee of Pope, and has been called 'the Modern Pope'. But Miss Guiney followed vaguer literary deities, of whom the Miltonic spirit *Chaos* seems to be the leader" (*SL* 1.20).

2. Lucy Larcom (1824–1893), American poet and author of a well-known memoir, *A New England Girlhood* (1889). She taught at Wheaton Female Seminary from 1854 to 1862.

3. Theodore Francis Green (1867–1966), who later became governor of Rhode Island (1933–37) and U.S. senator from Rhode Island (1937–61), was at this time president of the Morris Plan Bankers' Association.

4. By Sax Rohmer.

5. Smithfield Seminary in Scituate, RI, was a Freewill Baptist institution founded in 1839. In 1863 it was renamed the Lapham Institute. It was closed in 1876, and the site was later used as the campus of the Pentecostal Collegiate Institute (1902–18). In 1920, the site was used for the Watchman Industrial School, a school for African American youths. There were fires at the site in 1924 and 1926, purportedly set by the Ku Klux Klan.

[162]   [ALS] [HPL to LDC]

Saturday Evening
March 6, 1926

My dear daughter Lillian:—

Moriturus te saluto![1] Before the final plunge into the abyss I am squaring all my indebtednesses to mankind, & will reply briefly to your appreciated note—incidentally bringing my diary up to date. I'm glad these chronicles are of interest to you, & hope that their sameness does not tend to become a bore. During the coming orgy of remunerativeness they will no doubt dwindle largely to a record of reading & writing in the evening.

Yes—I trust the addressing matter may develop favourably, & fancy the novelty of it will get me there on time the first day or two. I probably shall stop in somewhere for coffee en route as you suggest. That old alarm clock is still here, but has no means of winding. However, I may be able to wind it with a pair of pliers till the stub of the former key is wholly worn down. I've already made a wicked nick in the blade of my favourite ivory paper-cutter trying to tinker with the beastly thing—which also lacks a crystal. But I shan't have the Burns outfit awaken me. The way to treat landpeople & proprietors is to keep them at a distance from one's own affairs, & never approach them except on the most insistent & necessary business connected with the house. As to spending the money—well, one doesn't undertake a hades of a bore unless one expects to get some fun out of it! I presume that the anecdote of the "huckleberry girl" which you cite is analogous to that of the barber's brother Alnaschar in the Arabian Nights.

Glad you saw that Netopian with the colonial matter. Yes—this Washington Memorial idea is excellent, & in conjunction with the proposed Roosevelt memorial will do wonders toward giving the capital that classick aspect which it has always sought, but which—as I noted a year ago—it can hardly be said to have fully realised. I hope to see Washington in a month or two! I like the temple design exceedingly, but on sober reflection am inclined to think that Market Square might not be exactly the place for such an object. More & more I favour the Hope Reservoir site—& more & more I wonder what—if anything—actually will be built! The spelling bee article is very apposite, & will interest such amiable non-spellers as honest old McNeil. Correct spelling seems to be due to two causes—care & practice on the one hand, & a vivid visual imagination—which quickly & strongly grasps arrangements of form—on the other. Added to which, I suppose, is the quality of rote memory.

As for my diary—last night I left off as I was starting for the library to meet Orton. Well—I found him there, & he insisted on treating me to an excellent Italian dinner at Bernardini's restaurant in 46th St. He doesn't like Italian food himself, but this place also has his favourite French cooking—which he patronised as liberally as a gathering cold of great severity would let him. After dinner he prolonged the treating streak by leading the expedition to the Capitol Theatre—a very elaborate cinema house of which I've probably spoken before—to see a film of Ibañez' novel "The Torrent", which deals with the Spanish scenes & characters he loves so well.[2] This is, by the way, coming to the Majestic next week. It turned out to be very artistically conceived, without the inane happy ending usually imposed on novels when distorted into moving pictures. The incidental orchestral musick was especially good, & one recurrent motif was so captivating that Orton means to write the management & find out its identity. I enclose the programme, which will give you some notion of the subsidiary features—all of which were smoothly & pleasantly presented. The performance being over, we proceeded at once to 169 for literary discussion; stopping en route at a chemist's shop for medicine for Orton's cold. Arriv'd hither, we talked on all imaginable themes—including the aesthetics of attire, in connexion with which Orton shew'd me the enclosed sample of Scotch tweed which he has ordered abroad for one of his new suits. It would be a bit informal for me, but for a younger man with a real wardrobe is in excellent taste for sport or careless business wear. At 2:30 a.m. Orton rested on the couch whilst I worked on my weird article—finishing with Poe & beginning on Hawthorne. At 10 a.m. my guest awaked & departed, & at 10:30 I rested, rising this afternoon at 4 p.m. & since then wrestling desperately to wind up my correspondence before renouncing liberty. It is now 6:30 p.m., & I am going down to the library to read more in Hoffmann & to find if possible a gruesome Hawthorne item I have never been able to get in Providence—"Dr. Grimshawe's Secret", whose scene is the old Salem house abutting on the Charter St. burying ground; a place I have often visited with appropriate sentiments. The house itself is the old Peabody place, where Hawthorne's wife dwelt—& the colonial doorway has now been detached & placed in the Essex Institute whilst the building has sunk to a cheap Polish boarding-house. Well—such is which. When I get back I'll either work on the article or read some Hawthorne items I have here. Meanwhile Orton plans to go to bed as soon as his work is over, & stay there all Sunday in an effort to break up his debilitating cold. ¶ More later—& meanwhile I have the honour to subscribe myself, with customary exprefsions of esteem,

Yr aff Nephew & obt Servt
H P L

Notes

1. "I, who am about to die, salute you!" In imitation of what gladiators said to the emperor.
2. *The Torrent* (Cosmopolitan/MGM, 1926), directed by Monta Bell (uncredited); starring Ricardo Cortez, Greta Garbo, and Gertrude Olmstead. Based on the novel by Vicente Blasco Ibáñez (1867–1928).

[163]   [ALS] [HPL to LDC]

Saturday Night
March 27, 1926

My dear daughter Lillian:—

Well!!! All your epistles arrived & received a grateful welcome, but the third one was the climax that relegates everything else to the distance!! Whoop! Bang! I had to go on a celebration forthwith, (vide subseq. diary) & have now returned to gloat & reply. A E P G's letter came, too—riotous symposium!! One thing, though, you will notice—& that is that I am *not* ill. That grippe was evidently only a mild imitation, & ever since Thursday I have been perfectly well—nothing but the ordinary blowing & coughing of a slowly yielding cold. So you needn't fancy that any case of convalescence is involved. Physically I am all right & ready for anything.

And now about your invitation. Hooray!! Long live the State of Rhode-Ifland & Providence-Plantations!!! But I'm past the *visiting*-point. Even if my physique is flourishing, my nerves are a mess—& I *could never board a train away from Providence toward New York again.* If I went to East Greenwich or Wickford I'd have to use trolleys—or busses in the case of Wickford, since the poor old Sea View has failed. I'm not eager for ignominious returns via the smaller orifice of the trumpet; but if you & A E P G think it's perfectly dignified for me to slip unobtrusively back toward civilisation & Waterman St., I'm sure I couldn't think of anything else logical for one who is an integral part of Rhode Island earth. Only last night I dreamed of Foster. If I ever use my brain, I guess it'll have to be in R.I.—though I might stand the Boston area if any imperative business fixed me there. But as to details—I'm all in favour of letting you & A E P G do *all* the planning, if you don't mind, & of sending my things ahead of me. When *I* land in person, I want my address to be *115 Waterman St.* Your plan for the little apartment is so ideal that I can't do anything save blister my palms applauding—& once I'm in it, I'll certainly hustle like the devil with writing to see if I can make enough to assure it permanence. I'll trust you to do all the arranging—you know how big the room at 169 is, & exactly what's in it; & can easily see that the new quarters come up to space requirements. There's no hurry—just wait till all is well, then hire your space & *let me know!* Packing will be a deuce of a job—but with a new lease of life at stake I shall have the energy of a daemon! I'll hire Kirk & his boy to pack my books, & will consult with the Excelsior Warehouses about other delicate things. Had I better wait till some Providence moving man has his van in N.Y. before arranging for any large shipments? All this can extend over weeks if necessary—I shall be perfectly content to camp out here amidst diminishing possessions. Only one thing must I have *new,* & that is a *couch.* I *will not* have a *bed* in my room, for it must be primarily a pleasant study as now. I am now used to sleeping on a narrow couch, (I never *open* the one here when alone) & wish a cheap specimen of the same (it needn't be an unfolding one—just a slim single steel-frame device) to precede me to the new place. Then I will dress it with green blanket, afghans, & pillows as I do this one here. If there are no alcoves to conceal dressing apparatus, I must have a cheap Japanese screen. Otherwise I am all right. I hate to think of the expense—but I'll cut out the Philadelphia & Washington trips I had planned, & will postpone any Salem, Marblehead, & Portsmouth jubilations till my purse may have had a chance to recuperate. Quinsnicket shall be my longest excursion for a time, & walks to Blackstone Park will cost even less. My library card expires on the 17th of next month, but I'll get it renewed, & with the address changed from 598. My stack permit has already expired—but good old William E. Foster has been tolerant of lapses before.[1] When the last load goes, I'll send change-of-address cards to Providence & Brooklyn post-offices, & to the Journal & Bulletin—also to the editor of the United & National Amateurs. Then—being tolerably well disposed of so far as my effects are concerned, I shall amble around myself—the least important part of the business. When I hit town the fact that I've been away will be only a sort of vague nightmare. I'll stock up on U E R tokens, (how much are they now—9¢?) take a tunnel car, (any one will do now) & show up ready for business. Three hectic days of arrangement, & the old man is back on the job. Slightly soured by exile, perhaps, but the same tough nut at heart, & ready for writing. I think, though, that I'll hustle up on the weird-tale history & get it done & mailed before migration.

As for nourishment—I *do* get enough; & if you & A E P G expect to fatten me up, you have a picturesque fight coming! I *will not* be fat again—& when I think of the discomfort & suffering I have escaped, I can only thank Pegāna I discovered how to do it. Two years ago I couldn't tie my shoes without puffing, or run upstairs without gasping. Even a brisk walk actually *hurt* my chest & abdomen by setting the great rolls of pendant fat in vibration. Now, thank Heaven, I have recovered something like the semblance of the human figure—& I certainly mean to *keep it!!* If I live as near down town as Brook St. I shall generally walk both ways—& I don't intend to get stalled half way up the hill on the return trip by any apoplectic adiposity! My thin hair is bad enough—I wonder what Fernando King will think of it! Well—he knew it was on the wane, & I won't be the first to go bald under his eyes!

As to Morton's museum—the parsimony of the trustees is such that the days of assistant-hiring now look very remote. And what is more, if there were any way of living at all in New England, anyone would be an ass to doom himself to that miserable huddle called Paterson—squalid enough in itself, & half inside the radius of New York's vaster squalor! For sheer depressing influence, that burg is excelled only by New York—& possibly Fall River. Even Pawtucket would be an elysium in comparison, & Woonsocket need feel no rivalry from it. It's very doubtful whether I'd ever have the nervous strength to consider tackling it after once getting home. I don't think I shall ever be west of the Connecticut River valley again.

Working backward to yours of the 25ᵗʰ—I beg of you not to overrate the slight indisposition I have been through. It may or may not have been a true form of grippe—certainly it was *not* the elaborate Spanish Influenza whose effects are so far-reaching—but at most it was an incident of three or four days in the midst of a long cold. All its signs are gone now as completely as if they had never existed—no nausea or headache, & not even a trace of physical weakness. All that lingers is the original cold—jogging along toward its end after the manner of my usual colds. But I am sorry that your own health has been so interfered with, & hope that a fine spring may serve to brush away all the traces of malady. Another thing—you needn't fear that I haven't been *eating*. My very fastidiousness during the shaky period had the effect of boring me with my simple home fare, so that I indulged quite frequently in good restaurant meals costing all the way up to 75¢—a thing my influx of wages permitted me to do. Accordingly I am lavishly well-fed—you ought to see the Italian course dinner I got in celebration of your invitation! That meal was a classic. It opened with "antipasto"—relish material, called by the French *hors d'oeuvres* & consisting of sliced salami, (spiced bologna) pimento, olives, &c—& next proceeded to an enormous tureen (2 plates) of "minestrone"—heavy soup full of vegetables & sprinkled with powdered cheese. Then an order of "ravioli"—meat encased in flat squares of pastry & smothered in tomato sauce & cheese. After that roast chicken & french fried potatoes—& then a course of assorted cheeses with bread. Next was fruit—a banana & an orange, both delectably small & fresh—& coffee, & finally I topped off with a plate of "spumoni"—or variegated Italian ice cream. I ate it all—some 75¢ worth! And when you come to read my diary you'll see an account of some marvellously regular sleeping, too. I'll get some lemons & other fruit as per your suggestion—lemonade is always practicable as long as the cold water of the faucet is really icy. Which reminds me—I suppose the kitchenette of the arrangement you mention would need a *refrigerator*. Have we still one tucked away in anybody's barn? My couch is comfortable enough—& I am *not* too thin! My shoulder-blades lost long ago the soreness they acquired that recumbent Saturday & Sunday. I don't need any tonic, so you needn't bother about having the prescription copied. I'm glad for your own sake, though, that it's palatable!

All your cuttings proved of interest, & I have noted them with care. "The Inferno of New York" is good—& if it has any fault, that fault is on the side of mildness! Incidentally—don't fancy that my nervous reaction against alien N.Y. types takes the form of conversation likely to offend any individual. One knows when & where to discuss questions with a social or ethnic cast, & our group is not noted for *faux pas*'s or inconsiderate repetitions of opinion. I don't think I fail to appreciate the genius & good qualities of the entire assemblage, for every member of which I entertain unaffected respect. As for that "Panchatantra"—I'll wager it can't equal the Arabian Nights.[2] I've read Hindoo tales & fables, but find them quite devoid of the peculiar atmospheric charm of the Saracenic masterpiece. I had heard before about those Dickens fireplaces, & am glad they will be preserved. It's really too bad, anyway, that the Parker House was torn down. I'm sure that more than half of this indiscriminate destruction could be avoided by the exercise of a little judgment & sense of proportion. So Cranston also has its Annetje Jans heirs! I'll have to send that cutting to young Talman, who is an enthusiast in the field of Jans research. The item on the creation of synthetic life is of the highest importance, & if sustained by further observations will prove the complete confounding & annihilation of all fundamentalists & believers in divine creation. The absence, so far, of authentic cases of laboratory abiogenesis, has been one of their crowing points—tho' I have always said it would be only a question of time before scientists would be able to metamorphose nitrogenous carbon compounds into elementary living protoplasm. I shall be interested to see how the Mazur experiments are treated by other commentators, & to what extent they will be developed within my lifetime.

Long life to the Congdon St elm—& may I soon pay it a pilgrimage of respect! One of the things I want to do is to visit *every* Laswell "Corner & Character" in the city, & eventually in the state. I was, though, disillusioned about Laswell in last Sunday's Journal; when in illustrating an account of the Capt. Pierce massacre in Central Falls during King Philip's War, he garbed the settlers in *18th* century costume! And so the Wheeler School has broken through to Angell St.! Before long I shall have to take a good long stare at that Banigan house out of Dr. Kalloch's office window—for I still have his cotton sealed into one of my molars. It was, of course, put there for an indefinite time—but was temporary none the less. I had myself cut out that item about the old lady who knew Hawthorne. Too bad she can no longer remember the old days! And I shall be glad to see a good memorial to Reeves go up. It is a shame that technical squabbles have caused his band to lose his name & sink to obscurity—& I wish that all hands might collaborate to straighten the matter out. It is obvious that *Fairman's Band* is the organisation which now bears to the community the relation which Reeves' once did. It is also obvious that the legally chartered "American Band" has become the merest shadow. Now what ought to be accomplished is the acquisition of the name & charter of the American Band by the Fairman organisation, with the adoption of the permanent title, "Reeves' American Band". That band certainly represents what is best in our military musical tradition—the band of Reeves, & of the Bowen R. Church of pre-delirium-tremens times. I'd like to see the day when one could glimpse on a *red* Elmwood car a dasher-sign announcing a Sunday concert at the park by Reeves' American Band. Any other name really seems outlandishly out of place, tho' I suppose it is about 20 years since Reeves' band ceased to play there. When it first left, they had the Banda Napoli—around '08 or '09—& then came Fairman's. And about the new Old Colony Coöperative Bldg.—I really must become semi-lyrical! Hurrah for Colonial Design! That & the Gas Co. will quite Georgianise good old Weybosset! Another *absolute gem* will be the new Providence Plantations Club in Abbot Park Place near the Round Top Church. Did you see the picture in the Sunday Journal? It is certainly a coincidence of the most delightful sort that my town should develop architectural leanings so perfectly in coincidence with my own personal tastes. I hope my window can command a colonial dormitory or something! As to food— I'm afraid I'm no Edison to acquiesce in a tame vegetable diet![3] I note the "Zed" circular, & remember that I liked the product a year ago when you sent a sample; but at present I don't seem to need a laxative at all.

I don't believe you'll find much sound science in Freud's "Dream Psychology", since his theory of dreams is perhaps the weakest link in his whole chain. Many of his hypotheses can be punctured quite readily by careful evidence, & it is one of Mortonius' many ambitions to refute Freud in a ponderous treatise on dreams. He is constantly collecting material for his enterprise, & is always ready to listen to a dream, or to hear a general account of anyone's dreaming tendencies. And so you've seen Montague Rhodes James' "A Warning to the Curious"! That is the volume I've just *bought*—so you'll soon have an opportunity to finish it at leisure! You've already read the best tale—"A View from A Hill"—tho' the title story is pretty good. On the whole, it's not equal to the same author's "Ghost Stories of an Antiquary", & "A Thin Ghost & Other Stories". That first-named volume contains the real cream of the James horror faculty. I must now get hold of "Cold Harbour", by Francis Brett Young, which Belknap has just finished. He says its quality of horror is very notable, & that it must certainly be included in my present survey of the weird tale. It is a full-length novel with a highly sinister background. By the way—I *do* want that story of Orton's again—to shew the gang. Enclosed are advance sheets of my "Moon-Bog", which need not be returned. I think the heading is pretty good—the artist[4] being a new one. It will be on the stands on the 1st. of May—a month & a little more—about which time I shall also receive a moderate cheque for "The Outsider". I've sent "Cool Air" to Wright, but have had no verdict as yet. A new magazine—"Amazing Stories"—has just been launched, & seems to favour the reprinting of pseudoscientific tales like Jules Verne's. This may possibly develop a later demand for original weird material—in which case I shall have a second market for my produce. I'll tell S H of the honours befalling the Boston Symphony conductor—his name is Sergei Koussevitzky.[5] Glad to hear of the curtains you & your slave are hanging, & hope to see them in person soon. I shall bring my brown portieres, & hope I can arrange for the segregation of dressing paraphernalia as here. Glad you have begun to take walks, & hope I may act as colonial guide before long! A E P G has certainly been a model child in helping you keep the establishment going without outside excursions! Your diet of Quaker Oats, vegetables, bread, & fruit sounds very sensible, tho' I am afraid I might get impatient with it. I shall probably do lots of prescribing for the menu when I blow in—& I hope those *canned dinners* (beef stew &c) are on sale readily. By the way—tell A E P G that I received her breezily delightful letter of invitation, as well as her Boston cards, & that I'll answer at the earliest opportunity. So far as the invitation goes, indeed, this present communication may be regarded as a reply to her as well as to you!

Sunday Noon

I had to leave off before getting to my diary, but will now add that "valuable" document plus the extra day which the delay has added to it. When I get home I shan't keep a diary, since you will be on hand to observe my motions directly—although I guess I'll finish out the book I bought this January. I paid 15¢ for it, & *must* get my money's worth![6] Now let me see—my last entry extended to Tuesday noon, when I was starting out for Sonny's. Well—I was so delayed in assembling my monstrous laundry (it came to $2.63) that I had to omit visiting the library & buying handkerchiefs; but by making these decisions I was able to be up at Belknap's on time. The lunch was an excellent one—lamb, dumplings, vegetables, & so on—& I resolved to make it the occasion for my return to solid food. Accordingly I ate very liberally, & was rewarded by a considerable influx of strength. Late in the afternoon orange cake & coffee were served, & I made this the occasion of shedding my new anti-coffee bias. Discussion, of course, was highly interesting; & at 6 o'clock I accompanied the Child forth to library & P.O. Having sub-lent him "Elsie Venner", I myself took out Dr. Holmes' "Guardian Angel", which I mean to read soon. By the way—it was during this afternoon, after a little spell of feverishness, that one of the major sudden improvements in my grippe occurred. I had rather tottered *in*, but when I walked forth it was briskly & easily! After bidding Sonny adieu I went down to the 42nd St. library & read Poe material till closing time. Then, returning to 169, I retired at midnight. Rising Wednesday at 9:30 a.m., I read the Sunday Journal & miscellany, & received a telephonic invitation from Orton to meet him at the library at 6:30 & dine before the meeting. At 5:30 I started out shopping, & bought a dozen 5¢ handkerchiefs at the Brooklyn Woolworth's. On the subway car down town a tragedy occurred—*I lost my new gloves!* This is the first time in 20 years that I have done such a thing, & I'm sure it won't happen again soon. (Tho' Sonny has lost 2 pair this winter alone!) Meeting Orton, I accompanied him to a glove shop in 6th Ave., where he helped me pick out a good $3.25 pair of Dent make—of the undressed finish called "Mocha". We then set out for a restaurant; & since he wanted a *French* one, I steered him to Budry's in 50th St., which A E P G will remember. This, however, was crowded; so we chose "Le Hibou" next door, where we enjoyed an excellent meal for which Orton insisted on paying. Proceeding thence to Sonny's for the meeting, we found attendance rather slim. The only others there, besides our little host, were honest old McNeil & Loveman—whose "Hermaphrodite" Cook has now fully set up for book publication, proofs being due at any time. On the whole the meeting was a good one. Discussion was brisk, & the refreshments consisted of one of Mrs. Long's inimitable Welsh rarebits. (I regretted that I couldn't accomodate a second helping after the titan dinner to which Orton had treated me.) Loveman brought me the second week's salary owed by his firm, as well as the book—"A Warning to the Curious"—which I had ordered. At 11:30 we dispersed, & Orton was so tired that instead of going home to Yonkers he accompanied me to 169 & spent the night on the couch whilst I slumbered blissfully in the Morris chair. At 8:30 he rose & departed, & I read "A Warning to the Curious" through. From noon to 7:30 p.m. I rested on the couch, & at night fared forth for a sumptuous beef dinner at Joe's which totalled *70¢!* I then returned, wrote letters, & retired at midnight. Friday I rose at 7 a.m. & desperately wrestled with accumulated correspondence all day, retiring at midnight. Saturday I rose at 9:30 a.m. wrestled with correspondence, & in the 11:30 mail received your letter. Whoopee!! Celebrations!! At 2:00 A E P G's letter came, & I could do nothing else but troop down to the Milan & absorb the hilarious dinner previously described. 75¢ & worth it! I then went to a cinema (25¢) & saw a revival of the famous transcontinental railway film of two years ago, "The Iron Horse".[7] Then I got a plate of *ice cream* at the Automat & returned to 169 to rhapsodise & write on the present epistle. At midnight I retired, rising again today—Sunday the 28th—at 8:30 a.m. & resuming my epistolary pursuits. It is now 1:30 p.m., & the mood of celebration is still upon me. I think I'll go out to John's or Joe's or some place where I can stuff indecently, & then take a spring walk in Prospect Park—imagining it is Roger Williams or Quinsnicket. The day is fair—if it isn't too cold & if the wind isn't raw. Next Wednesday I entertain the Leeds meeting here. The next M[c]Neil meeting is still unsettled. ¶ And now I await with interest & eagerness your opinion of my plans. Remember that I'm in good health, & that there's no hurry—but that the ideal thing would be a complete household slide back to God's Country.

> Yr aff Nephew & obt Servt
> H P L

Notes

1. William E[aton] Foster (1851–1930), a graduate of Brown University who assisted in the opening of the Providence Public Library in 1877 and served as its director until his retirement in 1930.

2. The Panchatantra is a series of Indian animal fables written in Sanskrit dating to around the 3rd century C.E. A new translation by Franklin Egerton appeared in 1924.

3. In his later years, the inventor Thomas Alva Edison (1847–1931) was a vegetarian.

4. Ed Whitham.

5. Serge Koussevitzky (1874–1951), Russian-born conductor and composer, conducted the Boston Symphony Orchestra from 1924 to 1949. On 13 March, Koussevitzky and the Boston Symphony Orchestra performed at Carnegie Hall.

6. HPL's diary for 1925 (the basis of his letters to LDC and AEPG) covers the calendar year 1925 and the first six days of 1926 (see *CE* 5.149–75). The diary that HPL purchased for 1926 is apparently nonextant.

7. *The Iron Horse* (Fox Film Corp., 1924), directed by John Ford; starring George O'Brien, Madge Bellamy, and Charles Edward Bull.

[164]   [ALS] [HPL to LDC]

> Monday Afternoon
> March 29, 1926

My dear daughter Lillian:—

Well—I have your note of yesterday, & by this time you have my communication of similar date. This letter will have disabused you, I trust, of the notion that I am ill; & will have shewn you how favourably I regard the migration idea if thoroughly & deliberately carried out. I am sorry that you gained the idea that I am ill, & fancy the reason is that Providence had the grippe epidemic in severer form than N.Y. What I had was not true influenza in any sense—merely a few shaky days in the midst of a cold—& by this time it's hard to remember that I ever felt weak at all. So I don't fancy I'll have to look up any hospitals for a while!

Yesterday I decided on Joe's for dinner, & took baked country sausage & mashed potato. For dessert—throwing financial discretion to the winds—I celebrated by taking strawberry shortcake with whipped cream (30¢), but this is a final fling & I won't do it again. I am all back to normal physically, & there's no further excuse for de luxe dietetic indulgence. Hereafter economical considerations will have to rule again—though not, of course, to the extent of depriving me of ample & wholesome material. Today I'll plan a dinner approximating about half a dollar. Well—yesterday afternoon I read Holmes' "Guardian Angel", kept it up through the evening, & retired at 2 a.m. Today I was up at noon & have been writing ever since. I shall probably continue writing till late afternoon. Then I shall dine & read the Sunday Journal—after which I shall begin honest old McNeil's "Tonty of the Iron Hand", which I promised the old boy long ago I would peruse. Oh, yes—& Sonny called up last evening, saying that he would like the Leeds meeting next Wednesday instead of having it at my place. I consented, & he will issue cards countermanding my invitations. He's going to get Young's "Cold Harbour" out of the Womrath Library[1] & have it ready for Grandpa Wednesday.

Now about migrations—there is no question of disillusion involved. I don't expect to live in a seventh heaven of happiness anywhere, & only want to drag out my last few days in some quiet backwater where the general environment isn't too obtrusively offensive. There is no question of illusion or disillusion about Providence—I know what it is, & have never mentally dwelt anywhere else. When I look up from my work it is Angell St. I see outside the windows, & when I think of going out to buy anything it is Westminster St. that comes to my eyes until objective realism painstakingly corrects the image. I have no emotional as apart from intellectual conviction that I am not in Providence this moment—indeed, psychologically speaking, I *am* & always will be there. Whenever I hear a whistle in the night I always think it is some boat on the bay, or some train down at the Bristol Depot.

But as I have said before; if all hands think Boston or Cambridge a more appropriate haven, I am not disposed to pit against their judgments an opinion from a mind whose ghastly rashness & idiocy of 1924 brought about this New York move. I could certainly work well in Cambridge, & the general atmosphere there is—apart from the single detail of early personal associations—of course even closer to my particular cast of mind than is Providence. Naturally, since Providence is a commercial port whilst Cambridge is a cultural centre, the latter would be expected to fit a literarily inclined person much better—& the only reason it would not, is that I am essentially a recluse who will have very little to do with people wherever he may be. I think that most people only make me nervous—that only by accident, & in extremely small quantities, would I ever be likely to come across people who wouldn't. It makes no difference how well they mean or how cordial they are—they simply get on my nerves unless they chance to represent a peculiarly similar combination of tastes, experiences, & heritages; as, for instance, Belknap chances to do. To all intents & purposes I am more naturally isolated from mankind than Nathaniel Hawthorne himself, who dwelt alone in the midst of crowds, & whom Salem knew only after he died. Therefore, it may be taken as axiomatic that the people of a place matter absolutely nothing to me except as components of the general landscape & scenery. Let me have normal American faces in the streets to give the aspect of home & a white man's country, & I ask no more of featherless bipeds. My life lies not among *people* but among *scenes*—my local affections are not personal, but topographical & architectural. No one in Providence—family aside—has any especial bond of interest with me, but for that matter no one in Cambridge or anywhere else has, either. The question is that of which roofs & chimneys & doorways & trees & street vistas I love the best; which hills & woods, which roads & meadows, which farmhouses & views of distant white steeples in green valleys. I am always an outsider—to all scenes & all people—but outsiders have their sentimental preferences in visual environment. I will be dogmatic only to the extent of saying that it is *New England* I *must* have—in some form or other. Providence is part of me—I *am* Providence—but as I review the *new* impressions which have impinged upon me since birth, I think the greatest single emotion—& the most permanent one as concerns consequences to my inner life & imagination—I have ever experienced was my first sight of *Marblehead* in the golden glamour of late afternoon under the snow on December 17, 1922. That thrill has lasted as nothing else has—a visible climax & symbol of the lifelong mysterious tie which binds my soul to ancient things & ancient places. But I was not born in Marblehead, & I did not live all the best days of my life there—although the place (in common with Salem, Portsmouth, & all old New England scenes) gives me at times an intensely poignant illusory sensation of having done so in the period around 1750–1760. Providence is my home, & there I shall end my days if I can do so with any semblance of peace, dignity, or appropriateness. Industrially I suppose Cambridge has more openings—in fact, Orton has promised to speak a good word for me with Boston publishers, whilst only last week I asked Mrs. Miniter for exact particulars of the occasional proofreading she used to do for Ginn & Co. at their plant in Cambridgeport. But Providence would always be at the back of my head as a goal to be worked toward—an ultimate Paradise to be regain'd at last.

Whether it would be advisable for me to see Providence if I am not to live there, yet remains debatable in my mind. If Cambridge is decided upon, it might be best (tho' I know it is a frightful imposition upon you, & am duly ashamed to make the suggestion) for you & A E P G to pick my quarters there & have me make the move directly—taking the train that goes thro' Springfield & Worcester. Then, once settled in New England, you could be my guests now & then—& I could see how advisable a trip to Providence might be, if I were only 44 miles away. The point is that I am perfectly well, & that there is no haste. I can vegetate indefinitely if let alone, & at this moment—glory be praised—I haven't seen a soul to speak to since last Wednesday. As to the packing at this end—I think I had better attend to that myself, ordeal tho' it will be whilst it lasts. S H's plans are so unsettled that her next move is always uncertain, & she might just as likely be in Cleveland or Chicago as in New York when the moment for moving arrived. It would hardly be fair to depend on her as packing agent, & I think—as I said yesterday—that it would be best to let me wind up here myself as soon as a New England address is assured me. Take all possible time to think things over. I must finish my article on the weird tale anyhow before embarking on any radical move which would disrupt systematic writing (for which my bookshelves are absolutely necessary) a month or more. Then, when everyone has done with revolving contingencies in their minds, I will abide by the result of a clear majority vote. As to weight—I'll wager Dr. Chapin would tell you that different physical types call for widely different dimensions, & that any one chart of figures is at best approximate & empirical. "Oughts" are limited & relative in a case of the kind—for clearly a man with the physiology of Andrew Jackson or Abraham Lincoln can't be expected, in normal health, to take on the proportions of a man with the physiology of William H. Taft or Samuel Johnson. Some are natural fat-builders, whilst others are not—& I trust in divine Pegāna that I'm *not!*

More later ¶ Yr aff Nephew & obt Servt

HPL

Notes

1. Arthur L. Womrath ran both a circulating library and used bookstore at 21 West 45th Street in Manhattan.

[165]   [ALS] [HPL to LDC]

> 10 Barnes St.,
> Providence, R.I.,
> April 1, 1926.

My dear daughter Lillian:—

Whoopee!! Bang!! 'Rah!! For God's sake jump at that room without a second's delay!! I can't believe it—too good to be true! Bet it'll evaporate like that one we picked out in Garden Place a year ago.

Somebody wake me up before the dream becomes so poignant I can't bear to be waked up!!!

Take it? Well, I should say so!! I can't write coherently, but I shall proceed at once to do what I can about packing. Barnes near Brown! What deep breaths I can take after this infernal squalor here!! I'll wait & finish my article at home! I can't write connectedly now—too excited—but merely dash off an ecstatic affirmative & appreciation! Hope you can get a room yourself in the same place—hurrah for the Corners & Characters of Providence!!

I'll manage the packing somehow, even if I have to be wildly extravagant & let the warehouse man do most of it. Let me know about *moving methods*—whether to wait for a Providence mover making a N Y trip. The Exc. Warehouse will probably *trust* me for fees, because they have so much of my stuff. I must have my hanging bookcase from there again, & really ought to have *another* case for new books. Would it be asking too much to suggest that you or A E P G get me some cheap standing bookcase at an auction room—charging it to me & placing it in the room? I would greatly like those books which I have in storage—I've missed many—& believe I could even have gotten them into this room had I known how large it is. I note all you say of rugs. Will talk the whole matter over with Mr. Perry, the chief man at the Excelsior Warehouses.

S H endorses the move most thoroughly—had a marvellously magnanimous letter from her yesterday. She may be in Cleveland 2 wks. or more to come, so there's no need of bothering her with the packing. Excitement will keep me as capable as necessary, I fancy, tho' of course if A E P G could *conveniently* take the trip at the last it would be an enormous help. I haven't given Mrs. Burns notice yet—I can't really believe it's happening, & have a most haunting sensation of dream!

Well—as for diary since my last—I dined at John's Monday night, returned & wrote letters, read honest old McNeil's "Tonty", (interesting but naive) & retired at 3:45 a.m. Tuesday I rose at nine, entertained a window-cleaner, wrote letters, & went out to get a new wick for my oil stove. (Shall I bring it, or get my gas Vulcan out of storage?) The day was so good that after a 60¢ dinner at Peter's I took an all-afternoon vernal stroll in Prospect Park, (pretending it was Roger Williams—I *must* see that Benedict Memorial!) reading *Weird Tales* on a bench. Great day—fine sunset. Then I went down to the publick library & read Constant's History of Magick. Back to 169 at ten—finish Weird Tales & retire at 3:45 a.m. Wednesday up at 10:30 a.m. & write letters all day. In evening up to Sonny's for meeting—all present but Loveman, who was calling on the poet Harold Vinal. (Vinal wants to go home to New England, too!) Child had new honours to shew—poem spontaneously copied from L'Alouette in N.Y. Tribune, fine review of his book in *London Times*, & new letters from celebrities, including *Arthur Machen*. Good meeting—live discussion, dainty refreshments. Dispersed at 2 a.m. Orton was so tired that he repeated his last week's visit to me, resting on the couch whilst I wrote letters & leaving 8:30 a.m. today. I kept on writing, & rested from noon to five. *Then came the letters from you & A E P G.* Wow!! This note is my next move, & after I've dropped A E P G a line I shall go down town to celebrate with a dinner at the Milan—returning 2 library books & calling on honest old McNeil to return Tonty. I think he'll have the next meeting. The next Leeds one will be at Kirk's, *& I hope to write it a letter from #10 Barnes!!!!* Heigho! More later, & I'll be all alert for future advices. ¶ Yr aff Nephew & obt Servt

H P L

[P.S.] And thanks tremendously for the generous *chocolate* shipment!
[P.]P.S. Has the room electricity? If so, I'll bring bulbs. If not, I must have a Welsbach.

[On envelope? In RHB's handwriting:] P.S. I'll need a haircut just about in time to patronise Fernando King.

[166]   [ALS] [HPL to LDC]

Tuesday Noon
April 6, 1926

My dear daughter Lillian:—

Before starting up to Sonny's I'll drop a line in reply to yours of yesterday. I enclose a note & pictorial cutting from the Child to shew you where we're going during the afternoon. This new Roman wing must be exquisite—I shall visit it again before migrating in order to fix it inextricably in my mind. Thank Heaven it opened when it did—I wish you could get here to see both it & the American Wing, which is worth a second inspection.

Hurrah for your coming move to 10 Barnes! Cohesiveness is the word for what's left of the House of Phillips! From your descriptions I judge that the whole thing is so well suited to my idea of a room & neighbourhood that I'll have difficulty in persuading myself it isn't a dream. Yes—my environment certainly won't keep me from doing good work, though of course that's no guarantee that I will do it. I don't amount to much, after all, & it isn't well to hope for too much from a tired old head.

As to details of packing—I'll try to follow your advice as closely as possible, & will label & identify all keys. S H may possibly be here to help; &, as I said yesterday to A E P G, I hope she won't consider the move in too melancholy a light, or as anything to be criticised from the standpoint of loyalty & good taste. I will begin intensive packing as soon as the Wednesday meeting is over, & may find a use for the *tags* I have carefully saved—though the warehouse will doubtless provide more. I think I won't have the books in boxes at all, but use what boxes I have for fragile ornaments. Yes—my rug will need cleaning. Shall I have it sent to the cleaner's directly? If so, tell me the address & I will tag it separately—unless it is best for everything to be delivered together. Electric lights? Good! Then I shan't feel extravagant about the two bulbs I just bought. Yes—S H will send my linen—tho' there is more than I can use. All renters of rooms are supposed to supply fresh linen as well as light & heat. Shall I bring my gas Vulcan as well as the oil stove?

Glad to hear of the bookcase cupboard—that may obviate the need of a new bookcase. Had I better bring *all* my books—storage ones & all? I'd like them very much. I hope your room in the same place will be equally attractive.

As to the rent business—it really doesn't matter so long as what I pay covers the exact period agreed upon. Rent is usually in advance—it is here— & I shall pay Mrs. Burns up to the end of the last week I shall be here. I gave her a sort of tentative notice when paying last night. The rent here, as you know, has changed from a monthly to a weekly basis. At the outset we gave Mrs. B half a month's rent, & I gave the other half as soon as I moved in. That was for January—the basis was always fully in advance & still is. I'll see to the packing shortly. Kirk can pack books finely *without boxes*—in neat, tight, newspaper bundles—& I'll ask the Excelsior man what he can do in that line. Meanwhile I'll await full word of all particulars. I'll arrange a valise camping outfit for the last couple of days—probably choosing the brown suit to wear. I really don't know which overcoat to keep out—being colder-blooded than in my youth. Glad the couch will be ready at the Providence end.

Well—as for my diary since yesterday—I got two new light bulbs, took them back to 169, & then started out to John's for dinner. After that I went down to the bookshop to pick up Loveman, & from there to his place— stopping en route at his behest for coffee & ice cream. At his establishment we carefully went over the Herm proofs, & put them into what is probably the most definitive conceivable form. Then, after some discussion, I returned to 169, read the Sunday Journal, & retired at 4 a.m. Today I was up at noon, & am hustling this epistle off before calling on Sonny. Then museum—& dinner in the evening with Orton & Harold Vinal present. I shall dress up in my best suit, with fresh linen. I enclose some timely cuttings, which please save for me. This widening of Angell St. at the cost of noble elms is atrocious. As a native I protest! Who wants vulgar wide streets anyway? And the news that the Stephen Hopkins house is really coming down desolates me immeasurably![1] Well—I shall be all on edge for messages!

Yr aff Nephew & obt Servt

H P L

P.S. I note your inventory of goods. A E P G will shew you mine, which I made yesterday. Shall I bring storage material? I have only 2 of the 454 dining room chairs, & 2 of mother's paintings—duck & roses—are in storage.

Notes

1. The Stephen Hopkins House (1743; original cottage built 1707 by John Field), 15 Hopkins Street, Providence. In the late 1920s the house was carefully restored by Norman M. Isham. It formerly stood at the foot of Hopkins Street on South Main Street and was moved halfway up the hill in 1804.

[167]   [ALS] [HPL to LDC]

Thursday Evening—
April 8, 1926

My dear daughter Lillian:—

Yours of yesterday duly arrived, & I note with minute attention everything therein. I *shall* want the blacking box, for since reacting against New York's squalor I have adopted a somewhat higher standard of neatness—not only as concerns shoes, but as concerns hair cutting & clothes pressing as well. As to the needed storage stuff—I can tell better when I see it at the warehouse. S H won't want my phonograph records, for they are not of the classic type she likes; but I want them kept safely in case I ever have a machine again. I'll leave the sewing machine. No—we didn't sell the two shaky dining room chairs, for as you'll recall, that second-hand man refused to pay anything whatever for them. I can't bear to let them go, for they are 454 relics & could be mended if given to an expert. Couldn't Mrs. Glazen or somebody find stable space for them? I won't bring them *now*, but hope they can be kept available somehow. I have their mates in use, & if we ever kept house again it would be a pity not to have the fuller set of four. I'll bring the round table & mattress—but where shall we keep them? I really won't need to bother about the mattress, for I'm not at all particular about sleeping arrangements at all. Half the time I don't go to bed at all, but sleep in my clothes on top of the couch. As to paintings—I really must bring both duck & roses. The duck, of course, is not appropriate except in a dining-room, but it is my mother's work, & ought to be in Providence. If I had any hope of having a dining-room I'd keep it sedulously—but in any case it would be better at Butler Hospital than out of Rhode Island. Maybe we can find a corner to tuck it—though it is not suited to the walls of my room. The *roses,* also in storage, we may be able to hang. Is the new room larger than the present one at 169? If so, I think there will be no trouble as to wall space. S H is of the opinion that the stag ought to be with his fellow-paintings despite her ownership—& she also insists that I take her little mahogany book stand, (on which I had my typewriter at 259, & which now stands betwixt my desk & my typewriter table under the left hand front window, with a Japanese box on top of it) which I have always valued highly. By the way—what shall we do with material not wanted immediately at 10 Barnes—like the mattress & round table? Will the

Cady man stop later at Mrs. Glazen's stable & deliver them, or must we make a separate item of the secondary transportation? Yes—I'll bring old Vulcan for future eventualities. About the large trunk—do you mean to tell me that I have my *fourth yellow blanket* in it? Glory to Pete in the highest!! If that is so, *then none of my blankets was stolen last year, & I still have my full set of four!!!!* It seems too good to be true—& probably is. I think that trunk contains my stuff only, but it can just as well come later. As for *pillows*—great scott! Have I been using *mine?* I thought these were Mrs. Burns's!! They're all right, though, whoever they belong to. And as for *linen*—I get *3* towels a week here—two ordinary & one turkish. I hope the Excelsior man will be able to do boxless book packing. The Magnalia had better stay in the lower drawer of the library table, stuffed with protective papers.[1] As to details—I'll have the packing man begin with the books as soon as possible, & tell him to deliver the storage material just before the day the Providence man calls—so that the place will be as little cluttered up as possible whilst the packing is going on. I shall take all of my books—for I have missed many. After all, that first Providence elimination of 1924 really pared my library down to an absolute minimum. You can bet I'll bring my heavy alcove curtains—those are delightfully rich, & ought to be kept whether or not we need them at the moment.

S H will arrive here Tuesday morning to help with final details—I enclose her letter. You can see what she says regarding her possible Boston settlement. If she wishes me to accompany her to Boston before proceeding to Providence I think that I ought to do so—for I suppose the day of my arrival will be immaterial so long as you are on hand to receive the moving men & their load. I will supply you with all possible particulars, & will guarantee to arrive at a respectable daylight hour. I shall come first to 115 Waterman, & you can—if convenient—accompany & introduce me at 10 Barnes. If I do go by way of Boston, (which seems by no means certain, tho' S H appears to favour it) I shall proceed to that city by way of Springfield & Worcester, or perhaps the Boston & Albany—for when I first see Providence I want to be able to debark & settle. No fleeting glimpses from car-windows for me!

Yes—as my letter to A E P G[2] will shew, I saw the Mencken items & was considerably amused.[3] Orton was quite excited, being in the American Mercury office & hearing everything from the inside. He means to see me in Providence shortly, since in May he will go "on the road" for the Mercury. In July I shall see Mortonius, who is resolved not only to conquer Durfee Hill at last, [let me see—I suppose the Chepachet cars have stopped, tho' there is presumably a 'bus service in replacement] but to explore Newport under my guidance. Tho' a born New-Englander, he has never seen this ancient & historick port. I, for my part, simply must see *Plymouth* & its neighbours Hingham & Duxbury—a region hitherto absolutely untapped by me. I hope the trolleys still run thither from Brockton. I must likewise explore *New Bedford* intelligently. I saw much of it in 1912, but didn't know how to perform Colonial exploration then. Another summer, when I feel I can better afford it, I must see *Cape Cod* & *Nantucket*. And I can never really die in peace till I have seen the Connecticut Valley towns—*Deerfield* &c. Orton says he will take me to these, & to Athol some time, in his father's motor—which he has the privilege of using when at home in Athol on vacations. The drive to Providence is not excessive. Later in the summer, if he can get a vacation, Kleiner says he may take the boat trip to Providence & renew 1918, 1919, & 1920 memories. You doubtless recall his poem "At Providence in 1918". The Galpinius-child will pass through N Y in May, & I shall expect Belknap to tell me how his long hair looks. He says he is now brushing it straight back from his forehead, which makes it a bit less obtrusive. He comes on the Leviathan, due to land May 17, & will precede his sailing with a bicycle tour of Brittany. No—I don't think I shall miss such social activities as I have had here—the Longs excepted. And I can discuss things as well by post as by word of mouth with Sonny. What I want are rest & oblivion—or at least, a seclusion amidst ancient scenes wherein I may cast off the actual modern world in a quiet round of reading, writing, & pilgrimages to quaint & historick places. I want to dream in the atmosphere of my childhood—to sit on Prospect Terrace with an old book or a pad & pencil in my hands . . . . Grandpa is a pretty old gentleman!

As for current news notes—Orton is moving into Greenwich Village, taking a ground-floor apartment with a cousin of his in quaint Grove Court—that colonial byway whose arched gate opens southward at the bend of Grove St., some two blocks west of Sheridan Square. (where we got the veal cutlet which you didn't like at Hubert's Cafeteria) The neighbourhood is very colonial, though like all New York neighbourhoods somewhat verging on squalor. Roaring Italian slums are just around the corner. And Loveman has secured bookshop positions for both Leeds & Kleiner—Leeds with the place where Dauber & Pine used to be, & Kleiner with the Breslow shop where I got my copy of Trumbull's poems. Oddly, it was through Kleiner, in one of his delicious illustrated epistles of a decade ago, that I first heard of Breslow's! The job came just in time to save our urbane poet, for he was beginning to have to sell his books. Leeds still rooms with Kirk, though he is anxious to get quarters of his own. Kleiner, by the way, is soon to call on honest old McNeil & make his peace. He didn't mean to offend or neglect, but the old boy is touchy, & stayed away from my meeting last night. At least, I think it must have been on this account that he was absent.

And this brings me to my diary. After writing A E P G yesterday I cleaned the room & welcomed Orton as an early arrival. He was so tired that he had to sink speechless into the morris-chair whilst I went out for provisions. Shortly after my return from the Scotch Bakery (I tried to get Kirk on the telephone but failed) Kleiner arrived, & soon afterward Loveman. Thus far the meeting was very dull, & Orton finally succumbed to his exhaustion & sank sound asleep on the couch. Then Mortonius arrived, & things brightened up. At 11 p.m. Loveman had to go—sacrificing refreshments. Kleiner went out with him & returned with the coffee. All this time Orton had slept like the dead, & we had not the heart to wake him. From this time till 1 a.m. the triangular meeting of Morton, Kleiner, & me progressed finely & briskly. Then my two conscious guests departed, leaving their regards for the unconscious one. Shortly afterward Orton waked at last, & was astonished to learn that Morton had been there. He took some belated coffee & cake & returned to the couch to sleep till morning, whilst I successively wrote on my article & slept in the morris chair. At 8:30 a.m. Orton left; & I wrote some letters & worked on my article. (which is now down to modern times.) In the afternoon I rested a bit, & am now finishing this to get off this evening—it's about 10 p.m. Tomorrow I'll begin breaking up—starting with a trip to Flatbush to interview the warehouse outfit. In my exact procedure, I'll be very largely guided by their advice; & on Tuesday S H will be here to assist with counsel & dexterity. Next week there'll be a Leeds meeting at Kirk's—my final personal appearance with the gang. ¶ Well, I'll keep you fully informed about everything, & we'll all hope for the best. Now I'm going out to the post office, & afterward will do a bit more on the article & rest preparatory to the manoeuvres of the morrow. And so it goes—hope to see you soon!

Yr aff: Nephew & obt Servt
H P L

P.S. I wish the Bulletin would go back to its old size—this new broad format is inconceivably awkward!! Will they deliver it wrapped & addressed by carrier—on the same day—at 10 Barnes? Where there are many boarders, wrapping & addressing would seem to be necessary.

Notes

1. HPL refers to the first edition of Cotton Mather's *Magnalia Christi Americana* (1702), which had long been among his family's most prized possessions.

2. Nonextant.

3. HPL refers to the controversy inspired by the publication in the April 1926 issue of the *American Mercury* of a story, "Hatrack," by Herbert Asbury, about a prostitute who solicits among the parishioners of a Methodist church. On 30 March, J. Franklin Chase, secretary of the New England Watch and Ward Society, demanded that Boston newsdealers return their copies of the issue to the publisher. On 5 April, Mencken went to Boston and publicly sold a copy of the issue to Chase, who had him arrested. Mencken hoped for a jury trial to create greater publicity, but on 7 April a judge declared that "No offense had been committed" and released Mencken.

[168]   [ALS] [HPL to LDC]

Friday Noon
[9 April 1926]

My dear daughter Lillian:—

Well—I hope to get to the warehouse & make ar-
rangements today, & you may be sure that I won't wear myself out in social affairs. My only engagement is the meeting next Wednesday at Kirk's, & I doubt
if many unexpected things turn up. I shall try to plan things simply; having the
packer first fix all the books & stack them up in front of the empty shelves on
the door side of the room, & then attend to the ornaments & the Fra Angeli-
co—& anything else which needs expert care. Meanwhile I'll have my trunk up
from the cellar, & begin filling it with clothing & other material. I'll send the
chiffonier just as it is—drawers filled—merely adding stuffing to prevent shifting cargo. Ditto the library table, my desk, & my cabinet. Then when all this is
done, I'll have them deliver the storage stuff for transportation. If it won't all go
into the room, Mrs. B. might possibly let one or two items stay in the basement
storeroom a day or two. As soon as it becomes necessary to disorganise desk &
chiffonier, I'll begin to pack my valise for the camping period at both ends. I
may buy some cheap suitcase or fibre bag for extra space—since as you know,
the Philadelphia trip was the last of my smaller valise. Yes—I'll sleep & eat!

As for edibles in the room—there's no hurry, but my staples are the National Biscuit products *Cheese Tidbits* & *Zu-Zu,* canned beans, canned spaghetti, cakes of Hershey's milk chocolate *without* almonds, & what are called
"canned dinners"—things like beef stew all complete. These are the things
which can be bought ahead. When I arrive, I'll add such perishable things as
bread & cheese. I never lay in large supplies, since groceries are so near; but
at Barnes St. I presume one has farther to go. What is the nearest "neighbourhood" group of shops—the Thayer–Angell aggregation? As to crackers
& milk—*nothing doing!* I honestly believe that it was this lacteal diet which
caused my original wave of fatness, & I certainly intend *never* to be fat again!
I'll take *nutritious* food, but nothing *fattening.* Great Heavens! the way I used to
pile up the flabby poundage by that ocean of milk, first with crackers &
cheese, & then with ginger cookies for dessert! Never again! I'm in the 150-lb.
class to *stay* this time! Oh—as for *fruit,* of canned stuff I suppose peaches or
pineapples are as good as anything. Of fresh fruit I like peaches best, but
think the *banana* is an excellent staple, since it requires so little bother.

Yes—I'll bring the jar—& I'd like to have my bowl & pitcher in Providence, anyway, tho' I had hoped the sink in the lesser room would serve as a
bowl. I don't want any bedroom stuff visible in the main room, for that is
first of all a *study.* You know how sedulously I exclude all such stuff at 169. If
any bedroom stuff has to be present, I must have a Japanese screen to conceal it. I'll consult with S H about the desk lamp, but I think she means me to

have it. You'll hardly know it in its novel golden splendour—you recall the sample I sent a couple of months ago.

Well—as to a diary, there isn't much this time. Since posting your letter I've done nothing but write on my article & rest around—& begin a letter to the Galpinius-child. Now, after dropping a line to A E P G & taking another snatch of rest, I'm going to give Mrs. B. definite notice & interview the Excelsior Warehouses. I'll have to get some more postage stamps, too.

Such, then, is which. I'll bring the storage trunk, &c., & hope that a good place can be found for all such material as will not go toward the furnishing of my room—or of yours. More later, & at the very last I'll tell you when I arrive. I'll guarantee to shew up at a decent hour, & not incommode anybody—in fact, I'll come to 115 & go over with you if you like.

But Hades! I've just overslept! Had to snatch a second's rest, & here it is 4:30! May be too late for warehouse—but I'll see. Anyway I'll notify Mrs. B & attend to some other necessary errands in Brooklyn & Manhattan. Will write A E P G tonight, & *surely* attend to the warehouse matter early in the morning. More later.

In haste, but ever yr obt Servt & aff Nephew,
H P L

[On envelope:]
Just recd. a $14.00 cheque for "Nemesis" in Weird Tales 2 years ago! The firm is paying up Henneberger's old debts. Will send to A E P G to be cashed in my next note to Providence.

[169]   [ANS postcard][1] [HPL to LDC]

[Postmarked New York, N.Y.,
9 April 1926]
Friday 8 p m.

Well, I *did* get in time for the warehouse, & Mr. Perry is coming to look over the place tomorrow at 10 a.m. He will tell me when I can see my things in storage. Packing will begin Monday—& the warehouse says it will have to furnish *paper cartons* for the books. ¶ After that, the day being warm & fine, I walked in Prospect Park in the golden sunset & read E. F. Benson's "Visible & Invisible" on a bench. Then I came down to the N.Y. Post Office to get a British money order cashed (United business) but found I must be there before 5 p.m. Being at 33d St. & 8th Ave., I'll now proceed to the Milan for dinner; after which I'll return to 169 & write A E P G &c. More later.

Yr aff Nephew & obt Servt
H P L

Notes

1. *Front:* Blank.

[170]   [ALS] [HPL to LDC]

Monday–Tuesday Midnight
April 12–13, 1926

My dear daughter Lillian:—

Your epistle duly arrived, & likewise A E P G's epistle with financial service. I'll answer her shortly. Since I must leave *some* things in storage, I suppose I might as well leave as much as possible; hence in selecting material will bring only what I need for immediate use. I'll leave records & dining-room chairs—also duck painting. If I *ever* had a dining room I'd want the latter. The roses, & all paintings now in my room, will come.

S H has abandoned the immediate Boston plan, but will in all probability accompany me to Providence, so that you may expect two callers at #115 instead of merely one. I'll let you know the exact *day*—Saturday or Sunday or Monday—in a subsequent bulletin, but you may depend upon it that we'll arrive in time to accomplish the introduction at 10 Barnes at an eminently decorous hour. Probably we'll choose the train which I employed in that other April homecoming of mine four years ago—after the brief visit—a train leaving New York at about 8 a.m. & reaching the Union Station about 1 p.m. We ought to be at 115 somewhere around 1:30—but of all this you'll hear more in subsequent communications.

Yes—I'll bring the mattress & the round oak table. I think I'll bring typewriter table & book stand too—the table is more convenient, & I like the top of the stand bare except for the Japanese box—it adds an aesthetic touch. Glad to learn of the convenience of Thayer St. shops. Now that I think of it, they do run considerably north of Angell. Isn't the new East Side P.O. Station on the corner of Cushing? I have never seen it. As to packing—drawers, library table, &c.—all due precautions will be taken, & S H will remember anything I forget. I shall bring the desk lamp with black-&-gold shade—you'll agree it's a work of art! S H doesn't recall whether the pillows here are ours or not, but I'll ask Mrs. B. tomorrow. Pillow-ticking is such a non-committal thing. Your description of Mifs Reynolds[1] sounds promising, & I certainly think she won't find me a noisy or undesirable tenant. Mrs. B. will testify that I have been the most inconspicuous & unobtrusive of mortals, even if I do burn the electric current at night! Oh, yes—& I'll write you full particulars about the arrival of the Cady truck— or as much as I can glean from the men when there [*sic*] are here. Why not let me have your *telephone number* to give to the men, so that they can call you up as soon as they get within the radius of our exchanges, & let you know when they expect to arrive at 10 Barnes? If you answer this immediately, I'll receive the number in time to give it to them. Or if there's no telephone service at 115, you could give me A E P G's number—for surely the Ripley household wouldn't be unprovided. I'll ask the men to avoid an early morning arrival if they can— surely they wouldn't mind loafing a bit in some Auburn or Elmwood cafeteria when they stop off for breakfast. No—I suppose our restaurants aren't as varied as those of N Y, but I hardly fancy I'll starve. I shall patronise the Belvedere very often—the Italian place at the S.E. corner of Washington & Aborn—for minestrone & spaghetti are my favourite comestibles. S H received your letter in the same mail with mine, & is answering in this mail.

Now as for my diary—I left off as I went down to the station Sunday morning to meet S H. Finding her without difficulty, I adjourned with her to the Automat, where we had a breakfast of bacon & eggs, (for S H) sausages & fried potatoes, (for H P L) coffee, & fruit. We then proceeded to 169, where S H read Sunday papers whilst I wrote on my article. At 5 p.m. we adjourned to Peter's for dinner, having a repast in several courses which no epicure could afford to despise. Mine was grapefruit, soup, spaghetti, beef with potato pancake, sweet potato, & onions, coffee, & spumoni. (Italian ice cream) After this we bought a Brooklyn Standard-Union & looked up the cinema shows, deciding on a picture in a theatre out toward Kleiner's neighbourhood. Taking a Gates Ave. car, we had not gone far before we saw that the locality was depressingly undesirable; wherefore we changed our plans & kept on till we reached an elevated line—which we took as the beginning of a circuitous journey (with 2 changes) to good old Flatbush, the only undecayed spot in the whole decomposing fabric of Brooklyn & New York. Arriving there whilst the evening was still young, we had ice cream at Reid & Snyders (or rather, *I* had ice-cream whilst S H had two coca-colas) & attended the familiar Parkside Theatre, only a few steps from 259. The film was Locke's "Stella Maris" in re-issued form, & aroused in my mind an interesting reminiscence. I attended the *old* issue of this film in January 1918 at the Strand, but was forced to leave before it was half over because of a digestive attack— my stomach was not then as reliable as it is now. In that old film Mary Pickford was the star, but the new version has a wholly new cast of younger actors whose names & faces were utterly unfamiliar to an old-timer like me. This time I saw the picture through, & learned for the first time what the ending was![2] Well—after that we returned to 169, where I wrote more on my article (I'm half through Arthur Machen now) & retired at 12:30 midnight. Monday I arose at 10:30 a.m., read papers, & at 2 p.m. accompanied S H to the Milan, where we ate the regular 65¢ lunch. After this we attended a French cinema of Rostand's "Cyrano de Bergerac"[3] (which S H has wanted to see for years) at the Cameo in 42nd St., after which we took the air by means of a walk up 5th Ave. & along 57th St. Subsequently, because of S H's wish to remove to some extent my extreme disgust with N Y, & to substitute in my mind some more favourable parting impressions, we took dinner at a really nice restaurant in East 56th St.—the Elysée, where an atmosphere of genuine taste & repose attracts a fastidious clientele of regular people—not the beastly scum which one sees on the streets & in cheaper places. Here she insisted on treating me to a dinner for which *exquisite* is the only appropriate adjective—fruit cocktail, soup, lamb chop, french fried potato & peas, coffee, & an utterly superlative cherry tart of which we could not resist taking two helpings apiece. I suppose I overate, but I always feel more like eating nowadays in decent surroundings—& this place was of the sort to brighten one up & make one feel comfortably at home. After this we walked toward downtown along 5th Ave.; ending at the 34th St. subway station, where we took a train for 169. Reaching that rookery in due season, we both began to write letters; a pastime in which I am still engaged, whilst S H has turned to the perusal of Bulfinch's "Age of Fable". Tomorrow (as per telephone message of today) we shall call at the Excelsior Warehouses between 9 & 10 a.m., picking out what we wish transported & returning at once to receive the packers between 11 a m & noon. From then on feverish dismantling & packing will ensue, & the storage material will arrive in safe season for trans-shipment on Thursday. Tomorrow night (Tuesday) S H wants to take me to another really decent eating-place— the restaurant of the Hotel Gotham at 5th Ave. & fifty-somethingth street, which she pointed out to me this evening—still further to remove my drab impression of N.Y. & encourage a kindly feeling toward the poor dead city. Wednesday night there is a Leeds meeting at Kirk's, & some other day Sonny wants me to have dinner up at his house. Well—more soon. Will let you know when to expect the delegation; & if you'll send me your telephone number at once, I'll tell the Cady man to call you up as soon as he hits town. Tell A E P G I'll answer her appreciated epistle shortly. Now I shall retire, so new diary will begin with rising Tuesday. ¶ Yr aff Nephew & obt Servt

H P L

P.S. Here's a cutting about that new museum wing which Sonny, Orton, & I saw last Tuesday. I'm going to take S H to see it if I get a chance.
P.P.S. I'll pass that Wheaton news on to Sandy

Notes

1. Florence Reynolds, HPL's landlady at 10 Barnes Street.
2. *Stella Maris* (Universal, 1925), directed by Charles J. Brabin; starring Mary Philbin, Elliott Dexter, and Gladys Brockwell. Based on the novel by William J. Locke. HPL also refers to *Stella Maris* (Pickford Film, 1918), directed by Marshall A. Neilan; starring Mary Pickford, Ida Waterman, and Herbert Standing. The film is a melodrama about a love triangle.
3. There does not appear to be a French production of *Cyrano de Bergerac* at this time. HPL may have seen an Italian production, *Cireno di Bergerac* (Unione Cinematografia Italiana, 1923), directed by Augusto Genina; starring Pierre Magnier, Linda Moglia, and Angelo Ferrari.

[171]   [ALS] [HPL to LDC and AEPG]

Thursday Night
April 15[, 1926]

Dear Children:—

Everything packed & gone. Have recd. all letters from both of you, & will try to answer all in note form in extreme haste. Sorry L D C has been indisposed, & hope recovery will be soon & complete. Will have sent telegram by time letter is mailed. [9:30 p.m.—have just sent it & am resuming this chronicle.] All A E P G remittances recd.—regular hebdomadal banking & both instalments of Weird Tales cheque. No further cash will be needed—I have enough for all fares, tho' of course the Excelsior storage & Cady movers are still unpaid. The Excelsior merely added their charge ($30.00 *complete,* for all packing & bringing goods from storage) to the regular bill, as I thought they would. Packing was all done Tuesday, & today the Cady men took everything but the details saved out for my valises. We are now using a table & 2 chairs lent from the next room by Mrs. B.—she also lent us an oil heater & let us keep the storage stuff in the next room (now vacant) from Tuesday to Thursday. We are not bringing the trunk in storage, nor the linen there, nor the shaky dining room chairs, &c.—but we *are* bringing the duck painting because it is packed securely with the roses. The amount of stuff is appalling—& I hope it can all be judiciously distributed at the Prov. end. Have we good storage facilities at Mrs. Glazen's? The yellow blanket was *not* in the storage trunk; proving that it *was* stolen last year after all.

Cady men—as night letter says—will be at 10 Barnes about 1 p.m. Saturday. There were two brunet gentlemen of Delilah's shade—undoubtedly Zulu princes in disguise—& they will have the office try both Angell 0476-W & Angell 4462-J if necessary when they reach the city. The call ought to come at about noon, & will certainly precede the arrival of the van by a safe margin. I've written them full instructions. It is not likely that S H & I can get around till the middle of the afternoon, so have Delilah by all means. L D C mustn't tackle any arduous job when her health is in the least below par. We shall telegraph upon starting from the Grand Central for Providence—at such an hour that the message will reach L D C at 115 Waterman before noon. Then, upon alighting at the Union Station, we shall telephone 10 Barnes—Ang. 4462-J—before setting out for that point. If Miss Reynolds reports that L D C is already there, we shall proceed thither at once. If she does not, we shall call 115 Waterman—Ang. 0476-W—& seek further instructions. My departure from my original intention to proceed to 115 in any case is due to the fact that we shall apparently arrive just as the ebon Cadyites are discharging their burthens at the Barnes St. haven. But with the telephones working in spite of the absorption of the Prov. Tel. Co. by the N.E. Tel. & Tel. Co., (which Mayor Gainer valiantly opposed) I fancy there'll be no ultimate slip-up. I've had my hair cut for the occasion—couldn't wait to let King do it this time! Yes—packing was a deuce of a job, & S H helped valiantly. We shall—as implied above—cut out Boston & the North Shore & come directly to Providence. S H has to attend some interview about a possible position in N Y tomorrow at 3 p.m.; but whatever the result, the chances are 8 to 2 that she will accompany me to Prov. to see me settled. She has sent her trunk by our van. It would be a good idea to have a couch that folds down into a double bed—exactly like Mrs. Burns' which we have now, unless one could be had which sits higher from the floor when down—for use when S H is here, so that double rent might be obviated. If Miss Reynolds has none, there is no more useful piece of furniture which we might *buy*, since it will save vast amounts in rent, & since a regular double bed is **absolutely impossible** for a room like mine, which **must** be a **study or library** with the atmosphere of such. I cannot for a moment consider any visibly bed-like furniture in my room—whose whole purpose is to furnish a nerve-soothing atmosphere—yet a bed which can *at times* be made double would constitute a very great economy. Mrs. Burns' specimen—which I have now—is really quite ideal so far as I am concerned; & is of such liberal size that I can sleep as well when S H is there as when I am alone. If no such device can be obtained by Saturday, we'll adopt such provisional accomodations as may be available—& of course it may be that the utter congestion of the van-packed room will make necessary a night or two's stop at the Crown or Narragansett in any case. As to the high cost of packing—as before stated, Perry finally included the moving of storage goods in his 30-fish holdup. Of course it's exorbitant—but I doubt if any other company could do better. The Excelsior Co. has a very high standing—being really the leading thing of its kind in Flatbush. It's a regular old Yankee concern—L D C will recall the corpulent giant James A. Perry, who forms its head & nucleus. By the way—the pillows here are Mrs. Burns's, as I thought. Comically enough, *I'm not sure* whether or not we've packed the two pillows in storage! If not, I'm sure it would be quite customary for the landlady at #10 to furnish these commodities as Mrs. Burns did. It is odd what oversights & ambiguities tend to occur in the exciting bustle of moving!

Well—so much for this! This is probably the last *letter* I'll have time to pen before seeing you children, tho' L D C will hear from me both by telegraph & by telephone before meeting the Theobald delegation. Now for my diary—which, coming down to Thursday night, will leave but two days for oral narration before that reunion which will render diaries unnecessary.

Tuesday the 13th I rose at 9 a.m. & wrote postcards. At 9:45 I started for the warehouse with S H, inspected the goods, (which were brought down by elevator to a vast barnlike space on the ground floor) & selected what seemed necessary for transportation. The packers agreed to be at 169 with the extra material at 1 p.m. We then took a walk through Flatbush, dined at a new spaghetti place there, (S. side Flat. Ave. just this side of Church Ave.) & returned to 169 in time to meet the men. Then ensued a feverish round of industry, terminating about 4 a.m. [*sic*] Just after the men left, we found we had forgotten to send one carton of goods to storage—so took it ourselves in the subway; afterward enjoying a long sunset walk down Flatbush Ave. Dining at a place near Bedford Plaza, we afterward attended the Farragut Theatre, where we saw a tremendously impressive cinema spectacle of the Johnstown Flood of 1889—with late Victorian costume reproduced with minute & amusing accuracy.[1] Returning to 169 by Interborough subway, we retired at midnight—rising on the following morning about ten. On this occasion we read & wrote letters, & at 2 p.m. started down for lunch at the Milan. This done, we proceeded by 'bus to the Metropolitan Museum; where I shew'd S H the new wing which Sonny, Orton, & I had seen the preceding week. At closing time we left, strolling southward through Central Park to the 59th St. Plaza, & thence along 5th & Madison Aves. to the Grand Central, where we took the subway for Brooklyn. The district just traversed was that of the Elysée, where we dined Monday night; & is perhaps the last surviving fragment of the old American New York of taste & opulence. Arriving at Borough Hall, we had a bite & sip at the Scotch Bakery, & afterward went to the barber's at State & Court Sts., where S H sat reading whilst the tonsorial artist reduced my scant locks to something like civilised proportions. I then returned to 169 to give the new-cropt hair a *real* brushing, & later set out for the farewell meeting at Little Sonny's—where I found only Mortonius ahead of me. Loveman straggled in later, & Kirk & Kleiner were next to shew their tardy faces. Orton presently ensued, & Leeds (who had had to wait for a telephone call at the Chelsea Book Shop) came just in time to bid Mortonius adieu—the latter having to hustle back to Paterson to be on hand early the next day. Following discussion, an exquisite supper (grapefruit, soup, meat pie with mushroom sauce, coffee, & jelly-whipt-cream dessert) was served by 18th century candlelight—with Grandpa Theobald at the head of the table as guest of honour, & Little Sonny at the foot as host. Afterward some spirited literary conversation was indulg'd in, & Sonny produc'd a new horror book from the library—a short-story collection by John Metcalfe entitled "The Smoking Leg"—in which I had time to read three stories. One of the tales—"The Bad Lands"—is full of such genuine cosmic horror that I am almost resolved to mention it in my article. Leeds also had a book—"Uncanny Stories", by May Sinclair,—which he forced on me as a loan, & which I shall have to return by mail from Providence. I've read one of the tales so far, & am not at all impressed.[2] This book I shall probably read on the train, unless I read the philosopher Hobhouse,[3] (which Mortonius has urged me to read for the last 4 years) my Morton-lent copy of which I have saved out for my valise. Well—Orton had to follow the Patersonian Curator in about ten minutes, since he was forced to get the last Yonkers train in order to superintend his moving to Greenwich Village on the following day. Loveman, exhausted by a devastating day's work, was next to depart; leaving Kirk, Leeds, Kleiner, & me to join with our little host in promoting wisdom & merriment. At 1:30 a.m. the gathering dispersed, & Kirk & I prepared for a final & typical all-night walk downtown. Kleiner stuck with us as far as 86th St., & Leeds as far as 72nd.; but after that the two "champeen hikers" had it all to themselves. We threaded our nocturnal way through Greenwich Village, stopping to stroke many a friendly kitty-cat, & afterward descended the dominantly Colonial tho' hideously decay'd Hudson St., where we found two ancient houses we had never seen before—fine Georgian specimens with stone-faced, arched & fanlighted doorways with pillars—doorways having suggestions of New-England & Philadelphia as well as New-York influences. I say these specimens were *fine,* but I speak only architecturally. In conditions they sank to the depths of squalor & decrepitude. Finally we reach'd Greenwich St. & the Planters' Hotel, (where Poe stopt when it had sunk to a dingy boarding-house) & explored Carlisle St., one block south, where a guide-book (our little brown Biltmore one) had told us to expect a fine old Colonial house in recognisable condition. We found it, & it resembled the pretentious Kennedy house (1 Broadway) where Genl. Washington once stopt; though its decay is pitiful to behold. We now, after petting a great white (and *clean*) kittie with a red collar, who mewed a wistful "hello" to us & who purred like a Rolls-Royce motor when scratched under the chin, proceeded to the Battery; where we viewed the sea, had coffee, & bade effusive & courtly adieux in the grey dawn that was swiftly turning pink. I returned to 169, retired at 6 a.m., & was up the next day (today—Thursday) at 10 p.m., [*sic*] reading & writing till lunch time, when S H went out for some excellent sandwiches & I went out for coffee—one having constantly to be on hand for the Cady men. In the early afternoon I read aloud to S H., when finally the movers arrived; & we were at once neck-deep in sordid & prosaic toil. Oh, what a time! But by seven p.m. we were fairly well cleaned out, and the movers went their way—the golden way that leads to the 1st Baptist steeple. I then began to write, but just at this juncture Loveman telephoned; saying that the author Benjamin de Casseres (who does not know a word of Latin) was badly in need of some one who could give him the sentence *"I am the Shadow-Eater"* in good & idiomatic Latin to serve as a fake classical motto for the title-page of the 3d. edition of his volume of philosophical prose-poems entitled "The Shadow-Eater".[4] He asked Loveman; but the latter having no Latin, the epistle was referr'd to me. I suggested the words *"Esor umbrarum sum"* eater of shadows I am;[5] but not being sure of anything in my old age, went out to the Bklyn. Library in Montague St. to look the matter up & see if my phraseology was as purely idiomatick as possible. It *was* all right, & I at once telephoned Loveman to that effect. De Casseres may give me a copy of his book when it appears. I now met S H at Peter's, had a fine course dinner, & proceeded to the Western Un-

Fig. I.

ion office in Fulton St. to send your night-letter. From there I return'd to 169 & the borrow'd table & chair; writing steadily till the present hour of 12:00 midnight. I shall now retire at once, so that my next—& doubtless oral—diary will begin with the morning of the 16th. As to the future—telegraph & telephone messages will apprise you. It will be great to see a real town again, & my pleasure in hailing you children can scarcely be described. I won't stop to correct this text now, but will hustle it into the box. See you (since 'tis Friday already) *tomorrow*—Saturday—& will have on my best grey suit. Also will have my winter overcoat, which the rawness of the lingering winter hath forc'd me to chuse as the one to save out from the packing. And so it goes. Homeward bound, & sing hey for the devil's own job of straightening out a Titan load of domestick sundries.

⁋ In all expectation—

Yr aff Nephew & obt Servt

H P L

Notes

1. *The Johnstown Flood* (Fox Film Corp., 1926), directed by Irving Cummings; starring George O'Brien, Florence Gilbert, and Janet Gaynor.
2. HPL mentioned both Metcalfe's "The Bad Lands" and Sinclair's *Uncanny Tales* in "Supernatural Horror in Literature."
3. Leonard Hobhouse (1864–1929), British political philosopher best known for his book *Liberalism* (1911).
4. No such edition appeared.
5. The words "eater of shadows I am" are written above *"Esor umbrarum sum."*

[172]   [ALS] [HPL to LDC]

Wednesday
[15 September 1926]

My dear daughter Lillian:—

Well—here's another instalment of my diary! The cinema show Monday—John Barrymore in "Don Juan"—was excellent, & was accompanied by a remarkable device for the synchronisation of music with the film, called the "Vitaphone".[1] It is a new invention, & its results are so marvellously excellent that I fancy it will have an important effect on the history of the amusement industry. After the performance we returned to the Astor, reading for a time & finally retiring. The following morning S H had to attend early to business, & was to be rushed so crowdedly that she could not have a moment of the leisure she had planned. Accordingly she bade farewell immediately after a waffle-&-syrup breakfast at the St. Regis in Broadway & 43d St.—where we used to dine—& departed for a round of business which was to last until the very moment of her train-time. She sent to you & A E P G her best & sincerest regards.

I then telephoned Sonny, & after closing negotiations at the Astor, (where we had an excellent 3d floor room & bath—$7.00) took a 5th Ave. 'bus for the headquarters in West End Ave. The entire house of Long displayed a gratifying cordiality, & insisted that I take every meal there during my sojourn in the vicinity. Lunch occurred at 12:30, & about that time I telephoned to Loveman & Orton. Kirk, as coincidence would have it, was coming that very day to have a tooth filled, so I saw him at 2 p.m. Sonny was as interesting an arguer as ever, & time did not hang heavily. In the afternoon Kirk, Belknap, & I visited the Hispanic & Indian Museums & the Spanish Church in 156th St—none of which Kirk had ever seen before. We then bade Kirk adieu & returned to Belknap's, where more discussion & an excellent dinner followed. After that I went down to Kirk's—picking up my checked valise at the Astor en route—& found my host sound asleep! Kleiner soon arrived—& has promised to send you a fine copy of "Roll On, Silver Moon" in his own incomparable monastic uncials![2] Loveman quickly followed, & after a time awaked our host. From then on conversation was general & interesting, & after a cup of coffee at the Chatham all disbanded; Kirk & I returning to the Chelsea Book Shop, reading some, & finally retiring. Kirk is the living symbol of all cordiality, & insists on my staying with him as long as I possibly can! And he has just given me a fine guidebook to Germantown, Pa.![3] He has a fine new cat—who sleeps on the foot of his bed—& a second cat who is a constant visitor but whom he does not technically own. This same feline is now on the table beside this sheet of paper, & has tracked some dust on it! We rose today at 9 a.m. & are now about to go out for coffee. At 11 a.m. I shall call on Orton (whose feud with Loveman has healed) at his colonial quarters in Grove Court, & at 12:30 I shall be at Belknap's for lunch. In the afternoon I am going with the Longs to a cinema of the old novel "Ben Hur".[4] The meeting is in the evening, & we hope for a good one. Both Belknap & Loveman will be present—this occasion possibly marking the beginning of the end of their feud.

Tomorrow *I may be in Philadelphia,* since S H insisted on treating me to the trip despite my most sincere & vigorous protests. I'll send particulars later in the day, or early tomorrow, when I find out about excursion rates & timetables. Needless to say, this will be an expedition of the utmost delight—including the sesquicentennial with its reproduction of Colonial High Street. Philadelphia is, second to Providence, my favourite town. In returning home I shall use 'buses all I can. Direct service betwixt Providence & N.Y. is temporarily suspended on account of bad roads betwixt Hartford & Prov., but I shall take a local 'bus from N.Y. to Hartford or New Haven, & there connect for home. I *know* these Hartford & N. Hav. 'buses are running, for I've seen them recently at the terminals around Eddy & Fountain Sts. I'll keep you informed by card of my movements. Probably you'll see me before the end of the week, although my violently cordial hosts are waxing almost rhetorical in their efforts to prolong my stay. The Longs even offered to have Sonny sleep on a couch in their room & let me take his couch in the parlour if I found Kirk's quarters too messy & dusty for comfort—but I'm all right at Kirk's for the very few nights of my stay.

Well—now to call on Orton & get up to Belknap's for lunch. More soon. Hope you're flourishing, & that Delilah hasn't torn my room all to pieces!

Yr aff Nephew & obt Servt

H P L

P.S. Had a great time at Orton's—fine Colonial place, but he's leaving on the 15th on account of insufficient heat for winter. Met two interesting chaps there—one being editor of a Brooklyn magazine. Now I'm up at Sonny's & about to start for Ben Hur.

[P.]P.S. 6 p.m.—"Ben-Hur" was *great!* Now dinner & meeting at Kirk's.

Notes

1. *Don Juan* (Warner Bros., 1926), directed by Alan Crosland; starring John Barrymore, Warner Oland, and Estelle Taylor. This was the first film to use Vitaphone, a sound film system devised by Warner Brothers and used from 1926 to 1931.

2. "Roll On, Silver Moon," a traditional Ozark folk song set to music by many composers. HPL may have been thinking of the version set to music in 1902 by Charles N. Ernest. See further LDC/AEPG 336.

3. Probably Charles Francis Jenkins (1865–1951), *The Guide Book to Historic Germantown* (Philadelphia, PA: Site and Relic Society of Germantown, 1902).

4. *Ben-Hur: A Tale of the Christ* (MGM, 1925), directed by Fred Niblo; starring Ramon Navarro, Francis X. Bushman, and May McAvoy. Based on the novel by Lew Wallace.

[173]   [ALS] [HPL to LDC]

Sunday–Monday Midnight
[19–20 September 1926]

My dear daughter Lillian:—

Oh, what a day! I've just seen the most marvellously beautiful scenery which has ever met my eye, & am still whirling in the ecstasy it inspired! You'll recall my brief dip into the Wissahickon Valley in 1924, as recorded in my diary at that time. Well—I've done the whole thing now, & I can truthfully say that every bend of the ravine brought out new glories. It's superb beyond words—& I fancy one would have to go to Northern New England to find even a faint parallel. I got lost twice by following tributary creeks by mistake, but was *glad* each time, since I merely stumbled upon fresh beauty. On my first "losing" I hit on the ancient mill

(1707) where the celebrated astronomer & public official David Rittenhouse was born—a thing I tried in vain to find two years ago.[1] The whole region is lovely in the highest degree. Enclosed (for identification) are its characteristic flowers, & I will later shew you a typical mineral, whose omnipresence gives the soil an appearance of being powdered with star dust. The accompanying map (torn from my old trolley guide upon the purchase of a new one) illustrates my route of the day. As you see, I returned via ancient Germantown; & appreciatively reabsorbed the sights I saw in 1924. Our own R.I. Gilbert Stuart resided in this place for a time, & did one of his most famous Washingtons in a studio upstairs in the stable. He had followed the General—who, having been driven by yellow fever from Philad^a., (then the capital) was staying at a mansion (still standing) in the neighbouring village. Night overtook me in Germantown, & I returned to Phila. about 9 o'clock. Dinner was at the Automat, & I am now in my Y M C A room reading guidebooks & writing letters. Tomorrow shall be devoted to scenic odds & ends—probably including Fairmount Park. Phila. is a great town, & probably the largest of all really American cities, as it was in colonial times. One can't count N.Y. in America any more—& I fancy Chicago is too parvenu to be anything in particular.

Monday night I shall have to return to N.Y., & I shall probably stay for the Wednesday gang meeting. It's at Loveman's, & I can see that he will be offended if I'm not there. Then—Thu. or Fri.—I shall come home via New Haven by stage coach; though Kirk & the Longs have been urging me most desperately—with offers of free lodging & meals, respectively—to extend my stay longer. I trust you're saving all the Bulletins & today's Sunday Journal in consecutive order. I haven't seen a newspaper since leaving, since only the Journal & Bulletin appeal to me. I'm using "car checks" just as you are, althhough those in Phila. are much smaller than ours. I guess I'll bring home a sample to shew you. They are 8¢ each—2 for 15¢.

But now I must desist & retire. (1 a.m.) Will note time of rising on envelope. I'll leave the Y M C A in the morning & check my valise at the Broad St. station—tho' I wish to Pete I dared spend 2 bucks more on another day!! I have your 10 safely stowed away, & a good 8 for coach fare home. I hope New Haven will be some good, & that I shan't regret following the advice of Orton & Morton, & choosing it instead of Hartford.

And so it goes. Trust you're flourishing, & that my cheese in the bread box hasn't spoiled.

> Yr aff Nephew & obt Servt
> H P L

P.S. Hope Miſs R. isn't impatient about her rent cheque—which doubtless reposes in an unopened epistle from A E P G.

[On envelope:] up 11 a.m. & off for Fairmount Park. Glorious weather—warm & sunny—makes my whole sojourn absolute perfection.

Notes

1. David Rittenhouse (1732–1796), astronomer, inventor, treasurer of Pennsylvania (1777–89), and first director of the U.S. Mint (1792–95).

[174]   [ALS] [HPL to LDC]

Wednesday–Thursday
[22–23 September 1926]

My dear daughter Lillian:—

Well—this is the last or next the last epistle I'll be writing before I hit the homeward trail. Oddly enough, I've decided *not* to stop extensively in New Haven, & for this reason: if I do, I'll have to do the New Haven–Providence stretch *after dark*, whereas I want the benefit of the whole ride by daylight, in order to see & enjoy the colourful New England roads of the Connecticut back country. Therefore I shall probably be home late Friday instead of early Saturday—Friday being spent wholly in coaches in the road. Old times—stage & wayside inns—coach leaves the Queen's Head Tavern, in New-York over against Broad-Street, & arrives in Providence at the Golden Ball, in Back-Street near Gaol-Lane, over-against the Colony-House. But don't stay up on my account, for there's no telling how late the stage may be. And what a pile of Evening Bulletins & correspondence I'll have to wade through!

As for my diary—I couldn't drag Sonny to the meeting after all! I got him as far as Loveman's door, but at that point his determination gave out, & he refused to face the ordeal of a publick reconciliation. So he went home, the little imp! The meeting was especially good, a visitor being present in the person of one William Forman *of Philadelphia,* a college student, Dunsany-admirer, & son of a U. of P. professor. As long as he stayed we discussed Philadelphia with affection & detail—& he hates New York as much as I do. The other participants were Kirk, Loveman, Kleiner, Mortonius, & honest old McNeil. At 10 o'clock "The Mikado" was broadcast by radio, & Loveman got it on his splendid new set. Everybody but honest old Mac was delighted, but this good soul retreated to the corridor when the rendering was about half through, & did not return till the last echo had vanished. Then he reappeared with many a childish diatribe against the music, & many a naive censure of the singers for not enunciating distinctly. Simple old boy! He finds the world a strange place! We later adjourned to a cafeteria for refreshments, & finally dispersed—Kirk & I repairing to Chelsea & doing some reading & writing before courting slumber. Tomorrow—my final day in Manhattan—I shall lunch with Sonny & try to get in touch with Orton again, lest the latter be offended.

By the way—guess what waked me up this morning? It was a soft & mysterious tread upon my silent form—which jarred open my sleepy eyes to gaze upon the most exquisite little grey & white kitty-cat imaginable! A visitor—& the son of the late lamented Oscar, whose elegy I wrote this summer after his untimely demise beneath the wheels of a speeding motor.[1] This littlest Oscar is a frequent caller at the Chelsea Book Shop, since Kirk leaves the French windows open in order to admit as many of the neighbourhood cats as care to share his hospitality.

And so it goes. I'll see you Saturday morning, & hope you've been flourishing during my days of active peregrination. I'm looking forward to a glorious New England coach ride Friday, & only hope the day will be fair. I must have a "pull" with the weather bureau, since all of my sightseeing period has been marked by ideal skies.

Hoping my room is not greatly upset,

I am

Very truly yr aff Nephew & obt Servt
H P L

P.S. Gang assembles at Belknap's tonight for a farewell. We shall hear Dempsey–Tunney fight returns by radio.[2]

Notes

1. "In Memoriam: Oscar Incoul Verelst of Manhattan."
2. Jack Dempsey (1895–1983) and James Joseph "Gene" Tunney (1897–1978) fought for the heavyweight championship on 23 September 1926 in Philadelphia. Dempsey had held the title since 1919, but Tunney won the fight; he defeated Dempsey again on 22 September 1927 (the celebrated "long count" fight).

[175]   [ALS] [HPL to LDC]

Friday
[24 September 1926]

My dear daughter Lillian:—

This epistle ought to begin with some violent profanity—for behold what happened! I found a 'bus at the proper terminal with a Rhode Island license plate, & bearing the name "Miss Providence". Boarding it, I complacently awaited the beginning of a delightful journey; when lo! I found too late that it was for Boston only, & that I had indeed *missed* Providence for that day! Tableau! Well—at first I thought I'd come by train; but finally decided I didn't want to sacrifice the New England rural scenery, so changed the ticket for one good tomorrow. Therefore I am hereby sending a special notification that I shall *not* be home tonight—but that I may be expected at a corresponding hour tomorrow—Saturday—night. And this time, believe me, I'll be mightily careful about the stage coach I board!

As for my diary—yesterday afternoon I read through Dunsany's new book of plays[1] at Belknap's, & afterward went for a walk to see the yacht which had burned & capsized in the river off 96th St. Then came dinner, & finally a gathering of the clan at Belknap's to hear the Dempsey–Tunney fight returns over the radio. Loveman actually came, thus marking the beginning of the end of his feud; & Kirk brought two visitors from Akron—newspaper men of considerable talent.[2] The results were a surprise to all, but involved no betting losses for anyone present. At 1 a.m. the assemblage broke up, Loveman leaving at the subway & the rest walking downtown. Then reading & retiring— & a hasty rising at 8 a.m., only to encounter the disappointment above chronicled. I have now returned to Kirk's, & am uncertain what I shall do during the day. Probably I shall look up at the library certain items which are not in ours—but it is an infernal anticlimax to be stranded here when I had expected to be coming home. Possibly I'll take a book to Prospect Park—that is, if it doesn't rain. I'll let you know tomorrow what I did or didn't do.

And now I must desist & accompany Kirk to the Chatham for lunch. Expect me tomorrow unless some fresh & unexpected blunder knocks my programme awry.

Hoping that all is flourishing at #10, & that the accumulation of unanswered mail is not too formidable, I have the honour to remain

Yr aff Nephew & obt Servt

H P L

["Special Delivery" written at top of letter in RHB's handwriting.]

Notes

1. Presumably *Alexander and Three Small Plays,* published in October 1925. Dunsany's next volume of plays, *Seven Modern Comedies,* did not appear until 1928.
2. One of these was Howard Wolf. See further LDC/AEPG 193.

1927

[176]   [ALS] [HPL to LDC]

Y.M.C.A.—Boston
Sunday Morning
[17 July 1927]

My dear Daughter Lillian:—

Well, we had a great meal at Jake's, (I took peach short-cake—delicious!) caught the stage-coach, & alighted at the museum at 2 p.m. Wandrei was delighted with everything, especially the Greek vases & Japanese prints, & we saw the entire establishment before leaving at 4 p.m.

A thunderstorm was now brewing, so we established ourselves in a restaurant opposite the Y.M.C.A. & awaited the final returns from Jove's armoury. It was long rather than sharp, so we produced books & writing materials, answered all our correspondence, & took dinner at 8 p.m. The rain had by that time ceased, so we crossed the street, took rooms at the Y.M.C.A., (I'm on the 5th floor & Wandrei's on the 7th) & departed on a nocturnal tour of archaic sights.

Late as was the hour, I think I managed to shew Wandrei quite a bit of the surface of archaic Boston. We threaded the colonial lanes of Beacon Hill, saw the State House, Brimstone Corner, the Granary Burying Ground, King's chapel, Old Corner, Old South Church, old State House, Faneuil Hall, Paul Revere's house, (built 1676) birthplace of Mortonius' grandfather, old North Church, hellish colonial byways of the North End, (the scene of "Pickman's Model"—I was heartbroken to find the actual alley & house of the tale utterly demolished; a whole crooked line of buildings having been torn down) & the relatively commonplace Chinatown along Beach St. The oddest thing we saw was an immense throng of persons of every aspect—the largest concourse of people either had ever seen, filling endless blocks like a frenzied mob in a siege—who formed the purchasing personnel of Boston's Saturday-night public market. We had no idea that any such ancient institution survived in any city today, hence were interested & delighted beyond words. Wandrei insisted on identifying himself with the scene to the extent of purchasing an immense lot of pressed figs for a quarter, & a pound of cherries for 20 cents.

Having returned to the Y M C A we retired about midnight, & I am now writing this at about 8:30 a.m., after a fine sleep & a shower-bath in the lavatory. BUT—confound the luck, it's RAINING—& this was the day we picked for Salem & Marblehead! I haven't seen Wandrei yet, so can't tell what he'll decide; but will add final details on the envelope after I meet him (our rendezvous is the lobby at 9 o'clock) & learn what he thinks. I wish we could hire umbrellas in this place—they seem to have about every other known facility! Well—I can't tell when we'll be home, but of course it will be before Tuesday night, when Mortonius is due. You'll receive postcards from us later, unless we get utterly disgusted with the drizzle & come back ourselves on an early coach—which I don't fancy we'll do. Hades, what luck! It was the blinding of Polyphemus—his son—which set Neptune against Ulysses, but I wonder what the deuce set Jupiter Pluvius against Wandrei & me the very moment we struck Massachusetts!

Yr aff Nephew & obt Servt
H P L

[On envelope:] Well—it's stopped raining, & we're going to risk the Salem–Marblehead trip!

And here's news! See what faithful walking does! I'm down to *138*—exactly Wandrei's weight!

———

Well, here we are! Old Salem at last, & it looks as if it were clearing up!

[177]   [ANS (envelope only)] [HPL to LDC]

[Postmarked Athol, Mass.,
21 August 1927]

Well—back from Deerfield to Athol again! Here's a pictorial idea of the celebrated capital of amateur journalism—which is truly a delightful place of the sleepy Central-Massachusetts type—like Leominster, Fitchburg, & Gardner. Cook has a cottage on a side street, & I have a fine room upstairs—the room which Wandrei occupied before me. Food is excellent—we had *Friends' Yellow-Eye Beans* tonight! Weather superb so far—here's hoping it will keep good for tomorrow's trip to Lake Sunapee, N.H.

¶ The scenery hereabouts is *absolutely superb!* Great domed hills & breathlessly majestic valleys; impressive river gorges & exquisite stretches of great-elmed, stone-walled farmlands. The villages are delectable—though many of them (such as Enfield, Greenwich, & Dana) are doomed by the coming reservoir. The scenic views in this envelope are perfectly typical of what I am seeing.

Have seen Cook's business place, where *Recluse* & *Vagrant* are printed, & have read proofs on Bullen book.[1] ¶ More later. Just now two splendid kitty-cats (one a little black boy!) are crawling all over me! ¶ Yr aff Nephew & obt Servt H P L

[P.S.] It has certainly been *some* birthday! Cook made me a present of an enormous set of Deerfield postcards.
[P.P.S.] *SUNDAY* Day's all right. Starting for Lake Sunapee.

Notes

1. John Ravenor Bullen, *White Fire* (1927), which HPL edited (he also supplied a preface—a reworking of his article "The Poetry of John Ravenor Bullen").

[178]   [ANS (envelope only)] [HPL to LDC]

Friday Morning
[26 August 1927]

Had a glorious ride to Portland yesterday—unbroken fine weather, & today promises to be the same. Arrived 2 p.m., & registered at the gorgeous new Y M C A—Georgian architecture, & only finished last month. Portland is not really so colonial as Providence, but has a fascination all its own as a once mighty seaport & as the metropolis of a remote northern realm. It is really very metropolitan, & looks as large as Prov. although it is actually ⅓ smaller. It is built on a peninsula with hills at eastern & western ends, these being made into exquisite parklike drives & promenades. The old colonial town grew up along the water, Fore St. (see guide within) being the original main street. This is now a slum, but has many remnants of the old days. On Munjoy Hill is an old ship signalling tower (vide picture within) built in 1807 & now open to the public. By ascending this I had the finest view of my life— including the White Mountains. Trees overshadow the houses throughout the residence sections, giving rise to the nickname "Forest City." H W L was right when he called it "The beautiful town that is seated by the sea."[1] I've explored it pretty thoroughly, I shall finish it today. Made a side trip to the colonial village of Stroudwater, & am going to the ancient seaport of Yarmouth today. That will be my farthest north. I shall also visit Portland Head lighthouse (1791) & both Longfellow houses—birthplace & later residence) [*sic*] besides walking in Colonial sections. From here, Portsmouth, Newburyport, & Haverhill. Probably shan't be home till Monday. I'm tempted to take a one-day White Mt. excursion if it's very cheap—I'm going marvellously economically, & the chance would be too good to miss! H P L

Notes

1. From Longfellow's poem "My Lost Youth" (1855), ll. 1–2.

[179]   [ALS] [HPL to LDC]

Friday Evening
[26 August 1927]

My dear Daughter Lillian:—

Hurrah! I shan't have to miss Mt. Washington after all! Went to the station to make inquiries, & found that on account of heavy demand a special excursion runs *Saturday*—tomorrow—which will permit of the full stop-over! So before 24 hours are through I shall be 6290 feet above sea-level! This Saturday excursion is doubly fortunate, since it will save a day of my trip—the Portland sightseeing being absolutely completed. Thus Sunday will be devoted to Portsmouth & Newburyport. If I like the White Mountains—& I am sure I shall—I shall regret having let the Old

Corner bookstore buy my mother's large book on that region. I saw it in the store the other day—wonder how much is charged for it now?

Today's sightseeing has been very important. Yarmouth was delightful, & the later trip to the old Portland Head light equally so. But the main items were the two Longfellow houses. The birthplace is in great lack of funds, & in a rather shabby state. Few people ever visit it, & the attendants are two seedy old men who move with deliberation & circumspection. It is intelligently managed, however, & not long ago the ugly Victorian doorway (shewn in the card I sent) was removed to make way for a reproduction of the original colonial portal. There are no postcards of this; but the old men gave me a dozen blotters shewing the restored doorway, so that you will see the present aspect of the place when I bring them home. The popular neglect of this place is probably due to the fact that Longfellow never actually lived there for any period of time. The more famous brick house in Congress (formerly Main) St. is the one which he always considered his home.

This afternoon I explored the Congress St. house (of which I send cards) & was delighted with its architecture & contents. It is a complete museum not only of the Wadsworth & Longfellow families, but of the whole Georgian period as well. I'll shew you the historical booklet upon my return. Many features are directly connected with some of the allusions in the early poems—as is also Deering Park, known in Longfellow's time as Deering's Woods.

Have finished all the correspondence I brought along, & may tackle the one revision job I have with me—an article which came on the morning of my departure & which I first surveyed in the Worcester 'bus. Hope a new lot hasn't piled up during my absence—I'll assume it hasn't, or else I shan't enjoy the White Mountains!! I am writing these lines on a bench along the Western Promenade, in plain sight of those mountains. They are now just at the limit of visibility in the sunset. I hope most fervently that tomorrow will be clear— if it isn't, I'll sacrifice Mt. Washington & try Sunday after all. This is going to be quite a sunset—it reminds me of a pencil scrawl on the window sill of the boys' room at the Longfellow house. The room then overlooked the back cove & the distant White Mountains, & some member of the family recorded his pleasure at a gorgeous sunset which he witnessed in July 1830. The view is now entirely hemmed in by buildings, for the house is in the very heart of the present business section.

Well—more later. Some good weird effects in this sunset, but my pen will need refilling before I can tell about them.

Yr aff Nephew & obt Servt
H P L

[P.S.] Back at the Y M C A & filled up again. The N.W. view from my window—all across Portland's back cove,—is as magnificent as the view from Longfellow's window in 1830. Here's a weight card shewing how I'm endeavouring to train down after stuffing at Cook's. Slow work—142½ at last report! Had a great beef dinner at a one-arm joint today, & am having supper (cheese sandwich & chocolate) in my room.

[180]   [ANS postcard]¹ [HPL to LDC]

[Postmarked Newburyport, Mass.,
30 August 1927]

Hopping off for Haverhill at last! Took a walk to Old Newbury, 4 miles south of Newburyport, & had a magnificent view from a high hill which I climbed—sea, river, meadows, farms, & the spires of Newburyport in the distance.

¶ Am mailing back all my soiled linen in various parcels. Got a complete new outfit here at *incredibly* low prices—wish I could lay in a large stock at these pre-war rates. It pays to buy in small towns. The extra shirt I took was too shrunken to button—neckband burst when I tried to put it on—so I've mailed it back clean. You can mend it later on. Yr obt H P L

Notes

1. *Front:* Spire of Unitarian Church, Newburyport, Massachusetts.

[181]   [ANS postcard]¹ [HPL to LDC]

[Postmarked Haverhill, Mass.,
31 August 1927]

Well, I reached Haverhill safely, after passing through quiet & attractive Amesbury, home of Whittier's later years. Am at the Y M C A—which is the oddest one I've struck yet. It hasn't the money to build a suitable structure, so spread out over a lot of former private houses in a once residential neighbourhood. I'm in a place about the size & style of 10 Barnes St.—& for 75¢ have secured an enormous front parlour like the one Miss Reynolds has rented to my various guests. Have called on good old Smithy, & he hasn't aged a jot in the five years since I saw him last. 75 this coming October, but lean & spry & hardy as a boy. Talked with him till midnight, & caught the last car back to Haverhill—he lives in a suburb. Instead of shouting—for he is stone deaf—I used a pencil this time; which is a much better method. Well—see you later.
Yr aff Nephew & obt Serv H P L

P.S. Am coming home through Ipswich, Gloucester, Salem & Marblehead if I can arrange it. Ought to be home abt Fri.
[P.P.S.] Haverhill is an extremely live & busy city—somewhat like Prov.

[On front:]—here is where I got most of my data on antique Newburyport. I've sent you a Newburyport booklet—hope it arrives.

Notes

1. *Front:* Historical Society, Newburyport, Mass.

[182]   [ANS postcard]¹ [HPL to LDC]

[Postmarked Haverhill, Mass.,
31 August 1927]

Haverhill is an enormous city! The business section really looks as widespread as ours, though the population is only 60,000. Am seeing whether there is good transportation to Ipswich & Gloucester.

Yr aff Nephew & obt Servt
H P L

Notes

1. *Front:* Merrimack Street, Looking East, Haverhill, Mass.

[183]   [ANS postcard]¹ [HPL to LDC]

[Postmarked Ipswich, Mass.,
31 August 1927]

Have just been over this original *Whipple* homestead.² Great! En route for Gloucester. Ipswich is a fine old town.

Yr aff Nephew & obt Servt
H P L

Notes

1. *Front:* Historical House, Ipswich, Mass.
2. HPL presumably refers to the John Whipple house at 53 South Main Street in Ipswich, originally built c. 1638 and then sold to John Whipple (1596–1669), who expanded it. His son, Capt. John Whipple, is not identical to John Whipple (1641–1700), an ancestor of HPL.

[184]   [ANS postcard]¹ [HPL to LDC]

[Postmarked Gloucester, Mass.,
1 September 1927]

In Gloucester at last! Didn't half appreciate it the first time. Was given a fine guide book at Y M C A, & have discovered marvellous things by its aid. Later had a splendid view of city & harbour from top of Y M C A. Am doing the town very thoroughly, & will probably include Rockport. Pre-Revolutionary houses are more numerous than I expected, & there is a ghoulish hidden graveyard just off a side street. An 1805 belfry dominates the skyline. I climbed a high hill & had a stupendous view. Gloucester has an *active* maritime atmosphere not possessed by any other town I have seen. Its whole community life is unique & local, & the main street retains most of its Georgian brick buildings. More anon.

Saved a lot of fare today by walking.

Yr aff Nephew

H P L

Notes

1. *Front:* The Cape Ann Scientific and Literary Association Building, Gloucester, Mass.

[185]   [ANS postcard][1] [HPL to LDC]

[Postmarked Gloucester, Mass.,
2 September 1927]

Cliffs at Magnolia as glorious as ever.[2] Drawing homeward—shall see Salem & Marblehead before night.

Yr aff Nephew & obt Servt

H P L

Notes

1. *Front:* Along the shore, Magnolia, Mass.
2. HPL had visited the region in 1922 with Sonia Greene.

[186]   [ANS postcard][1] [HPL to LDC]

[Postmarked Manchester, Mass.,
2 September 1927]

Manchester is a delightful old town! En route to Salem & Marblehead. You'll see me pretty soon—possibly before this card.

Yr aff Nephew & obt Servt

H P L

Notes

1. *Front:* Congregational Church and Town Hall, Manchester-by-the-Sea, Mass.

[187]   [ANS postcard][1] [HPL to LDC]

[Postmarked Marblehead, Mass.,
3 September 1927]

You can't beat Old Marblehead! Next to Providence, it's the home of my spirit! It certainly eclipses all other towns in pure colonialism. Pretty near home now—you may see me before this card. Salem was great—as usual. Beverly is too modern to be interesting.

Yr aff Nephew & obt Servt

H P L

Notes

1. *Front:* A quaint old street in Marblehead, Mass..

[188]   [ALS] [HPL to AEPG]

Providence-Plantations,
Septr. 17, 1927

My dear Grandchild:—

I was yesterday much pleas'd to receive your note, & to learn that you are finding agreeable diversion in the archaick & elegantly cultivated town of Newport. I am sensible how great a difficulty attends the purchase of suitable pictorial cards, & wou'd suggest that the only shop having a decent variety is *Rugen's,* 295–297 Thames St. You can there obtain a very fair number of photographick designs such as the one enclos'd, for the not unreasonable sum of tuppence ha'penny each. I extend my profoundest gratitude for the picture of His Majesty's headquarters at Mr. Bannister's house—a view which I have, but of which a duplicate is exceeding welcome. I trust you are not missing any opportunity to bask in the vivid atmosphere of antiquity, & hope that it forms a pleasing prolongation of influences dominant during your Truman Beckwith sojourn.[1] It is indeed unfortunate that so many of the ancient places are in a state of decay, but one may only be thankful that they are there at all. At least, they are better than the colourless abodes of unimaginative luxury, in whose mechanical perfections there is little or nothing to stimulate & satisfy the aesthetic consciousness. The decadent state of the old city hall or market is indeed exasperating to consider, & many plans for its restoration have been proposed—so far in vain. It is especially irritating to realise that its final downfall—the destruction of the arches & creation of shops in Thames St.—did not come till *1891.* The Ionick purity of Mr. Harrison's art in this building (circa 1763)[2] is especially notable, & it will indeed be a crime if the structure is not eventually rehabilitated & well maintained. There has been talk of this in connexion with the removal it will have to undergo if (hideous thought) Thames St. is ever widened for the benefit of the vulgar trading element. I am glad you have had a chance to discuss the antiquities of Philadelphia—a city as colonial as Newport in many places, tho' those places are generally slums of one grade or another.

I shall now endeavour to append a table of those historick places which you ought to see, & which I shall describe in that order which wou'd be encounter'd by the explorer desirous of seeing them all in the course of the briefest possible walk. Let us assume that the trip is started at the Long Wharf. (Obtain a good map at any bookshop)

Long Wharf—observe ancient buildings, contour of harbour, & skyline of town, all suggesting the scene existing in the time of Prescott & Rochambeau.[3]

Thames St. & Parade—Observe City Hall—Peter Harrison, 1763—glance up at panorama of colony house (1739) & occasional old buildings on all sides. Note house on right-hand side (South) of Parade (Washington Sq.) now occupied by Salvation Army. Oliver Hazard Perry once resided here. This same house, & the old gambrel-roofer on the other side of the square now occupied by the Newport National Bank, are rivals in the claim of having housed Quartermaster-General de Béville of Rochambeau's troops.[4]

Now walk south along Thames St., glancing at all the ancient roofs, & at the colourful courts, alleys, & streets leading up the hill or out to the water-front. Note the exquisite views of Trinity steeple obtained by looking up Church or Frank or Mill St.—also view of corner of Vernon house (Rochambeau's headquarters) up Mary St.

After going about as far as the Post Office, return to the Parade & start north along Thames. Note heavy cornices, with corbels, on some of the ancient houses; a particular characteristic of Newport colonial architecture. Study doorways carefully, noting greater simplicity than in Providence. The typical colonial architecture of Newport is of about a generation earlier than that of Providence, & belongs to an entirely different tradition. Gambrel roofs are abundant, whereas Providence discarded them relatively early. The average date of an old Newport house is about 1730; that of an old Providence house (of the plain, slant-roof type) about 1770. Note, somewhere on the seaward side of Thames St., a **very** old house with stack or clustered chimney in centre. This is almost undoubtedly a survival from the 1600's. Glance up & down all the side streets—quaint vistas are certain to reward you on every hand.

At *Bridge St.* turn seaward, to the left, traversing the slums & crossing the railway tracks till *Washington St.* is reached. Several interesting old houses lie along the route, & on the right-hand near corner as you turn into Washington is a pair of hellishly sinister abandoned houses, crumbling & boarded up, (date circa 1730) whose picturesquely ghastly aspect impresses all beholders.

Washington St.—Water St. in colonial times—was the great residential thoroughfare of the ancient town, & has fortunately kept much of its pleasing character, together with most of the old gambrel-roofed mansions. On the water side, at the foot of Elm St., will be seen the Nicholls-Wanton-Hunter house; now occupied by a Popish convent, & probably the place visited by your converted friend. This has the gambrel roof & heavy cornice overhang typical of Newport colonial architecture. It was the headquarters of Admiral de Ternay,[5] who lies buried in Trinity Churchyard, & formed the scene of his death—the death room on the second floor being still pointed out by antiquarians. On the same side of Washington St., at the foot of Poplar, will be found the great old Robinson house, with its railed gambrel roof, Quakerishly plain doorway, & facade set flush with the street without intervening grounds. This was the town house of "Quaker Tom" Robinson of the celebrated South County family;[6] for it must be remembered that Newport, & not Providence, was "town" or "the city" to the opulent & squirearchical planters of the Narragansett Country across the bay. With the Robinson family in this house was quartered Vicomte de Noailles (Lafayette's brother-in-law, their wives being sisters) of Rochambeau's staff, whose wife (later guillotined by the rabble in the French Revolution) presented Mrs. Robinson with a set of china as a recognition of the courteous hospitality extended her husband. The present owner & summer occupant, whose residence is in Philadelphia, (Miss Esther Morton Smith) is a descendant of the Robinsons & still an adherent of their Quaker faith. In her possession is not only the historick set of Sévres ware, but also a bronze teakettle from the French camp equipment which the Vicomte gave to his hostess upon his departure. The interior of this house, which I have never seen, is said to be very fine; several lantern-slides of it being shewn by Norman M. Isham in his lecture of last winter.[7] Farther on, at the foot of Walnut St. & also on the water side, is the white gambrel-roofed house occupied in revolutionary times by Solomon Southwick, publisher of the Newport Mercury. Its rear abuts directly upon the water, & it was at one time associated with vague but baseless rumours of hidden pirate gold. In Walnut St.—somewhere—the home of Matthew Colbraith Perry, younger brother of Oliver H., & opener-up of Japan to the western world, is said to be; though I have never been able to find any building conclusively identifiable with it. All of Washington St. is worth close study. At the end of the broad part is old Fort Greene, a bit of 1776 masonry & embankment now used as a publick park. From here continue along the newer part of the street to *Van Zandt Avenue*. Turn to the right—inland—there, walking back across the railway to *Farewell St.* & the great cemetery where ancient & modern slabs both have place. Here decide whether or not you wish to secure a splendid skyline view of Newport from the pleasing rural slopes of Miantonomi Hill, about a mile to the north. If you decide affirmatively, keep on along Van Zandt Ave. to *Malbone Road,* then turning to the left & curving around past the site of picturesque old Godfrey Malbone's burned-down country-seat to *Miantonomi Place,* which leads up the hill into the memorial park now covering the summit. There roam about & pick your vistas at will—the best being from the westerly slope, as the vegetation is now grown up. Having beheld all you desire, retrace the same route back to the cemetery & the corner of Van Zandt Ave. & Farewell St. You are now prepared to resume the urban part of the tour.

Proceed south—toward the town—along Farewell St., noting the more ancient parts of the cemetery on the left as you draw near the southern end &

the junction forming the head of Thames St. From here continue along Farewell, noting on the right the small, shady, & picturesque old burying ground where several colonial governors—Coddingtons, Eastons, & so on—lie. At the corner of *Marlborough St.* (left hand, nearer) note one of those bleak, spectral-looking gambrel-roofers [gable-end, with pedimented door, toward Farewell St.] which give certain parts of Newport such a characteristic ghostliness. This was a favourite doctors' location in colonial times, the house having been successively occupied by Dr. Norbert Vigneron (circa 1730—a French Huguenot) & Dr. Benjamin Waterhouse, (circa 1800) who introduced the practice of vaccination to America. At this corner turn to the left into Marlborough, keeping a lookout on the left for the old Quaker Meeting House, (1699) still in good condition at the back of its extensive grounds—now used as a publick playground. All the side streets around this section have finely quaint colonial vistas to offer the discriminating urban landscapist. Keep on along Marlborough to *Broadway,* (Broad St. in colonial times) there turning sharply in to the right, back toward the Parade & the Colony House. On the left-hand side of Broadway, at the corner of Stone, will be found a queer old house (17th cent., with 18th cent. additions) with stack or cluster chimney, which has lately been taken over by the Newport Historical Society for preservation. This is the Wanton-Lyman-Hazard house, which in 1765 was the scene of a stirring riot. It was then inhabited by Martin Howard, Esq., His Majesty's collector of revenue under the Stamp Act; & on account of the unpopularity of the tax was stoned & besieged by a lawless mob of provincials. The ruffians broke into the building, drank up all the liquor in the cellar, & under the influence of this patriotic inspiration proceeded to demonstrate their virtuous love of liberty by breaking up the furniture, slashing the family portraits, tearing out door & window frames, & even attempting to pull down the great chimney with ropes. Mr. Howard, though born & bred in Newport, departed for England on His Majesty's sloop *Cygnet;* & did not return to the colonies. He spoke well of the general temper of the better sort of provincials, however, in subsequent reports & addresses to Parliament.

Now returning to the old Colony-House, put up in 1739 from the designs of Rich^d. Munday, Esq., (a Boston man come to Newport) it is incumbent upon us to inspect the interior of that antient & celebrated edifice. Here will be found some carving & panelling of the very first order, & in the attick there are many traces of the old-time school kept there—with initials & mural scrawls of scholars extending back as far as 1776. In emerging, do not fail to note the Union Jack arrangement of panels on the soffit (or under side) of the small balcony from which all official matters & governmental accessions (including the coronation of His Majesty, George the Third) were proclaim'd in the palmy days. This, together with the crown on Trinity, form'd the sole vestige of our lawful government's heraldry to remain in the town during the treasonable outbreak of 1775–83; & it is by some surmis'd, that the stupid destructive mob refrain'd from harming it merely because they were too dull to perceive what it signify'd. At this point it is well to look long & appreciatively about the Parade; imbibing the quaint beauties of every vista, & observing the excellent Georgian architecture of that new court-house whose dedication occurr'd less than a month ago.

Proceed now thro' *Clarke St.*, noting all the old houses, & in particular the fine square Vernon house at the corner of Mary. This edifice, which serv'd as Rochambeau's headquarters in 1780–81, is of an especially fine & classically mature design far beyond the average conceptions of local architects of its period (1758); so that although nothing is positively known of its designer, Norman M. Isham feels virtually certain that it is attributable to the erudite & English-trained Peter Harrison. "I can say with confidence", piped & whispered Mr. Isham during his lecture last January, "that either Peter or the devil planned that house!" This applies only to the *exterior,* the interior being of ordinary provincial design. It was built as the town house of Metcalf Bowler, from whose country-seat in Middletown was taken the panelling used in the Rhode Island room (top floor) of the American Wing of the Metropolitan Museum in N.Y. When the French took it over, it was owned by William Vernon, Esq., who became rather dissatisfied with the way Gen. Rochambeau took care of it. Vernon was in Boston during the Revolution, serving on the eastern navy board, but he wrote his son Samuel to keep a sharp eye on the property. Samuel wrote back—"I believe the General takes as much care of the house as the Frenchmen generally do, but it will sustain more damage than a family living in it seven years. The floors will be entirely spoiled!" Rochambeau built a recreation hall for his officers in the rear garden, a thing of which Mr. Vernon said, "I can't think it polite of him." Afterward Mr. Vernon sent Rochambeau a bill for £135—covering repairs only, since he charged no rent as a matter of patriotism. This was promptly paid in good French livres. A second son of Vernon—William H.—lived much at the court of France before the French Revolution, so that upon his return to Newport he was widely noted for his polish'd manners, & locally nicknam'd "Count" Vernon.

From the Vernon house proceed up *Mary St.* past Spring to *School St.,* noting on the corner the birthplace of William Ellery Channing,[8] now hideously defaced by a French roof. All the streets in this region are deliciously quaint & narrow, & deserve careful inspection for scenic & antiquarian vistas. At this point one may well detour to the left through School, visiting the Newport Historical Society where this street terminates in Touro St. Everything in this building—all three floors—deserves minute inspection; & one must not miss the woodwork from the old 7th day Baptist church at the rear of the ground floor. The pulpit & stairs leading thereto have been praised by Norman M. Isham as the finest examples of their kind in this region, & a fair sample of Trinity's probable arrangement before its enlargement. Just below the Hist. Soc. is the old Jew's Synagogue in its walled grounds—erected in 1763 by Peter Harrison for the rich Jews who had become such a dominant element in Newport commercial life. These Jews hailed from Holland, Portugal, & the West Indies, & were utterly unlike the Mongoloid rats from Central Europe that clutter up our slums today. They established the whaling industry in R.I., formed a monopoly of the spermaceti & candle trades, & donated largely to the publick life of the town—especially the *Touro* family, which has left its name on everything. They could not subsist, however, except by trade; so left Newport in a body when the revolution—plus the rival supremacy of rising Providence—put an end to Newport's commercial prosperity. The exterior of this building is very unprepossessing—a fault due not to Mr. Harrison, but to the Jews who employed him & who insisted on certain proportions. The interior, however, is an absolute marvel of classic beauty; representing Harrison's unhampered work & being classed with the interior of King's Chapel in Boston (also by Harrison) as one of the two finest public interiors in American colonial architecture. I have never found it open, but last July Wandrei & I climbed around & peered in the windows—finding it fully up to the expectations aroused by Isham's lecture. Return now through School St.; keeping on to *Church St.,* turning down that to the right, & pausing at *Spring St.* Here we behold old Trinity (1726) & its churchyard in all their archaick glory—exquisite steeple topping the city skyline as its dominant & typical feature, & over all the Golden Crown symbolick of His Majesty's rightful authority in these dominions, unharm'd & refulgent thro' all these years of sedition & alienage! God Save the King! With Trinity (design'd by *Rich.* *Munday,* built 1726 & once enlarged in colonial times by an extension of the apse end) you are yourself too familiar to require any description; but I wou'd urge you to immerse your fancy once more in its peerless antiquity & quaintness. Church St. being exceptionally narrow & colonial, 'tis worth surveying all the way betwixt Spring & Thames. This is true of all other streets in this neighbourhood, & no true antiquary wou'd rest content till he had threaded them all. At the corner of Church & Thames stood Mrs. Cowley's celebrated Assembly Room where most publick functions were held, & where Genl. Washington danc'd on the evening of March 6, 1781, upon the occasion of his visit to Comte de Rochambeau.

We will now proceed southward from the rear of Trinity along Spring St., noting in detail all the colonial houses we find. Sharp eyes will detect in at least one place detect [*sic*] a specimen of that rare combination of hipped & gambrel roof found only in Newport, & forming (according to Norman M. Isham) the result of a French influence brought by Ayrault & the early Huguenots. At the corner of Pelham we behold the antient Bannister house— whose picture you so kindly enclos'd—where His Majesty's forces had their headquarters from 1776 to 1779. At *Golden Hill St.* we see ahead & on our left the pleasing expanse of *Aquidneck Park,* within whose bosky umbrage reposes the People's Library. It is best here to turn up Golden Hill St., all of whose houses (built on one side only) are colonial. At the top, where the street bends into *Thomas St.* & becomes a slum of increasing Africanism, we behold through a gate on our right the closely-hedged colonial burying-ground in which the Wanton family & other ancient worthies repose. We now keep along Thomas to where it ends in John, there turning down to the left until the first cross street (Martin, I think) is encountered, & then edging to the right through this aperture to *Prospect Hill St.* Then down to the left again, & through the first street to the right (name forgotten) to Pelham St. All this serpentine edging has given us an excellent taste of the general atmosphere of colonial Newport. We now continue to the right up the hill—along Pelham to Touro Park; noting the excellent later Colonial house along the way. This was the very edge of the town in the old days, & the places hereabouts were virtually country-seats. At Touro Park the Old Stone Mill[9] deserves a kindly recognition even from those too wise to credit its Norse mediaevalism; whilst the student of history will not overlook the ancient "Governor Gibbs" house at 142 Mill St. opposite the park, where Gen. Nathanael Greene for some time had his headquarters, being there visited by the Marquis de Lafayette & other notable officers of the French & rebel armies. Advancing now to Bellevue Ave., (antiently call'd Jew St.) & turning a little to the left, we cannot fail to recognise on the right hand side the spacious grounds & noble Dorick facade (marr'd tho' it is by trivial & impertinent wings* erected against the architect's advice) of Peter Harrison's supreme triumph of 1750—the Redwood Library. Like Trinity, this building is too well-known to you to need any description; but I wou'd call your admiration again to its classick excellence of design & elegant maturity of workmanship. For the colonies in 1750 it was a marvel of architectural assurance & urbane polish; & Mr. Isham does not hesitate to assert that at the time of its building it surpassed in artistic merit any other edifice on American soil. There are usually historical exhibits of great interest in the cases in the main room of this institution, & the collection of oil-paintings of early Newport gentry is ever deserving of the traveller's attention. We now proceed northward along Bellevue Avenue till we come to the open space made prominent by the graceful neo-colonial bulk of the modern Hotel Viking. On the right, where Kay St. branches off, will be found the old Jews' burying ground, established in 1677 & the subject of a poem by Longfellow. The granite gate, put up in the period just before the Revolution, is a copy of the gate of the old Granary burying ground in Boston.

We are now at the head of Touro St., ready to return to the Parade & Long Wharf past the Historical Society & old Synagogue, which were visited at an earlier stage of our trip—although they can just as well be postponed

---

*whilst the asymmetrical bulk *behind* the original structure represents later additions, the two small *lateral* wings are of the original fabrick.

for this stage, except that the Hist. Soc. closes at 5 o'clock. This really completes a layman's survey of the old town proper, so that any subsequent time can be spent on outlying sights. If one have an horse & chaise, one may drive out Broadway to Two-Mile Corner, take either of the forking roads, & behold on the high ground betwixt them (on the left if one be on the East road; right if on West Road) the last of the region's ancient windmills. Farther out along the west road is the (much alter'd) Overing house, at which the young rebel colonel W^m. Barton so audaciously captured Genl. Prescott in a night expedition by rowboat. "Sir," conceded the eminent prisoner to his captor, "You have made a damn'd bold push tonight!" He was rowed across the bay to Warwick & taken thence to Providence, where the learned barber John Howland (later to gain fame in educational matters) shav'd, curl'd, & powder'd him. Later he sent to Newport under a flag of truce for his powder, perfume, wardrobe, & body-servant; all of which were at the Bannister house in Pelham St., whose likeness you so kindly sent.

Another outland pilgrimage is to the Bishop Berkeley country, some four miles beyond Newport beach on the road to Middletown. For this also a carriage is needful to such as are not hardy & accomplisht pedestrians. Proceed by any route—Bath Road is the main one—to the beach, continuing up the hill beyond to where the neo-colonial belfry & Gothick church tower of St. George's School peep picturesquely out from the hill-crowning verdure. At the crest of the hill, where the road sweeps down to the left to Second Beach, turn in along the sand road that goes to the right, & cut across to the edge of the great rock cliffs on foot. Here will be found the celebrated chasm or tidewashed rift known as "Purgatory"—a majestick formation which compares very favourably with its analogues at Magnolia (Rafe's Chasm) & Marblehead. (The Churn on M'head Neck) Proceeding onward—down to Second Beach—we see silhouetted above the shore to the north the bold crags known both as "Paradise" & as the "Hanging Rocks". On the flat ledge three-quarters of the way up, with the topmost section overhanging as a canopy, was the favourite afternoon seat of the good Bishop (then Dean of Derry) who adorned this region with the cultivating influence of his presence from 1729 to 1732. It was on this ledge that he composed the greater part of "Alciphron; or, the Minute Philosopher", the fifth book of which opens with a very pretty description of the Newport countryside, & of the fox-hunting of the local 'squires. The whole scene here is exquisitely delightful—blue of sea & sky, white of gleaming beach & fleecy cloud, grey of noble crag & ledge, & deep, restful green of kine-dotted pasture & hillock. Over all, on the inland side, towers the grey Gothick church of St. George's school; giving in that setting a perfect & poignantly lovely fac-simile of a gentle English landscape, with hedge, croft, & distant abbey. One cannot resist the inclination to burst into numbers at such a sight:

Note: Another sight—don't miss the old frigate *Constellation* (1797—sister-ship of *Constitution*) in the harbour. I saw & went over it when it was at Phila. Sesquentennial last year.

Where the bright Blue aſſaults the chaulk-white Strand,
The beetling, ledge-lin'd Cliffs titanick ſtand;
Here verdant Fields in ſunny Calm extend,
Whilſt the low waves agreeable Echoes lend.
On yonder Knoll an Abbey Tow'r is ſpy'd,
And paſtur'd Kine ſurvey the riſing Tide;
O'er all the Huſh of ruſtick Virtue glows,
And antient Mem'ry grants the Soul repoſe.

Where now the Idler ſcales the craggy Ground,
Philoſophy in Triumph once was found;
For each grey Rock above the Blue upthrown
A *Berkeley's* Feet and *Berkeley's* Thoughts hath known!
Beneath yon hanging Peak's petrifick Shade
An *Alciphron* in all its Parts was made,
And ev'ry Path ſome ling'ring Trace contains
Of the great Clerick's wife melodious Strains:
Wou'd that my ſterile Muse might here ignite
With ſome reſidual Spark of that vaſt Light!

Those desirous of scaling The Hanging Rocks & sitting in the Bishop's Seat can do so by taking the right-hand road at the junction now at hand. Otherwise one keeps on to the left—& later takes the middle road where three branch. A sign on the left hand by a grove of pines tells the location of "Whitehall", Dean Berkeley's country-seat, & by threading the grove one comes upon the house—on the right, set well back from the path. This edifice, built by the Dean in 1729, is an excellent specimen of its period; the wide front door bespeaking an overseas influence not common in the colonies. The property is well maintain'd by the colonial dames, & accessible for the sum of 15 cents—theological students free. The interior is plain but very fine—& postcards are on sale. One may return [*obliterated*] if desired, by another route—going inland as directed by signboards & striking Broadway in its remoter reaches.

And so it goes. Don't miss anything if you can help it! No news here except that L D C's cold vanished before developing far, & that I'm as busy as the devil with revision. Am going downtown today—first time out in a week.

Hoping you'll fully appreciate Newport's antiquities—I remain
Yr aff Nephew & obt Servt H P L

P.S. Oh! I forgot to mention (a) that Wilfred B. Talman will probably be here next week-end, & (b) that L D C plans to get hold of Delilah & tackle the storage problem next Monday or Tuesday.

[AN enclosure, JHL][10]

Probably Gov. Arnold's windmill, built circa 1675.

[AN enclosure, JHL][11]
Here, amidst the primal thunders of the antient river Ocean, we salute thee.

Notes

1. AEPG had lived for a time in the Truman Beckwith House (42 College St.), built by the celebrated architect John Holden Greene in 1826–28.

2. Peter Harrison (1716–1775) designed the Brick Market Building (1762–72) at 127 Thames St. in Newport. It is now a museum.

3. William Prescott (1726–1795), American colonel during the American Revolution. Jean-Baptiste Donatien de Vimeur, Comte de Rochambeau (1725–1807), French general who commanded 7000 troops in assistance of the Continental Army during the American Revolution. He landed in Newport on 10 July 1780.

4. Oliver Hazard Perry (1785–1819), American naval commander. Pierre François de Béville, quartermaster-general for the Comte de Rochambeau.

5. Charles-Henri-Louis d'Arsac de Ternay (1723–1780), French naval officer whose forces carried Rochambeau's troops to Newport.

6. Thomas "Quaker Tom" Robinson (1731–1817), Newport merchant and advocate for the abolition of slavery.

7. Norman Morrison Isham (1864–1943), prominent professor at Brown University and RISD, architectural historian, and author. He was a pioneer in the study of early American architecture. HPL attended a lecture titled "Early Rhode Island Houses."

8. William Ellery Channing (1780–1842), a leading Unitarian preacher.

9. HPL refers to the Old Stone Mill in Touro Park, Newport, the remains of a windmill probably built by Benedict Arnold (colonial governor of Rhode Island, 1663–66, 1669–72). Longfellow's poem, "The Skeleton in Armor" (1842), hints of Norse origin.

10. *Front:* Ancient Viking Tower / The Old Stone Mill, Newport, R. I. Uncertain that the postcard was enclosed with this letter.

11. *Front:* Purgatory, Newport, R. I. Uncertain that the postcard was enclosed with this letter.

1928

[189]   [ALS to LDC]

395 East 16th St.,

Brooklyn, N.Y.,

Begun—April 29, 1928.

Continued on Roodmas—April 30—

Just before the Witches' Sabbath,

Finished—May Day

My dear daughter Lillian:—

At last I am reserving a day free from engage-
ments & am about to clear up some of my correspondence. The weather has
been wretched, so that thus far sightseeing & antiquarian exploration have been
impossible except for Friday's trip in the Longs' closed car. None the less, every
minute has been closely crowded with this & that; including the preparation of
a critical synopsis of old de Castro's Bierce book, about which we may or may
not be able to arrive at an arrangement. I have been breaking in my small
grandchild Belknap on the process of revision, & we are now forming a part-
nership for the joint handling of manuscripts—each to take the phase of
work most naturally suited to him. If our guesses are correct, this system will
enable us to cover more ground than either could possibly cover alone, & will
increase the net profit of each member substantially. Sonny has given up his
attempts to write cheap fiction altogether, & is about to put all his non-artistic
energies into revision. We are going to insert an advertisement in *Weird Tales,*
where our names are likely to prove drawing cards, & perhaps in other magazines later. The form which we have adopted—& which I prepared—is this:[1]

FRANK BELKNAP LONG, JR.——H. P. LOVECRAFT
Critical and advisory service for writers of prose and
verse; literary revision in all degrees of extensiveness.
    Address
Frank B. Long, Jr., 230 West 97th St., New York, N.Y.

I am making the Child attend to the negotiatory part because young heads are
better than old in matters of business & detail. He will handle MSS. involving
reconstruction in modern technique, whilst his aged Grandpa will tackle more
conservative cases & deal with niceties of final form—spelling, punctuation,
& so on. Sonny is quick to catch on to the necessary steps, & is handling one
of the Reed MSS.—which I found impossible to do on time—as a preliminary exercise.[2] I shall do some of the typing now that my machine is in decent

shape—which reminds me that Belknap will need a new machine soon. His portable Corona is beyond further repair, & the next time it gives out he will have to invest in one of the current small-sized models. I am advising him to choose a Remington instead of another Corona, for the ancient make has fairly maintained its supremacy over all competitors. The new portable Remingtons are scarcely larger than Coronas—I'll probably get one four or five years hence, when the need will have arisen.

S H's new business venture develops more visibly than my own, & the modestly tasteful establishment just around two corners in East 17ᵗʰ St. has acquired an exquisite decorative elegance at surprisingly little expense owing to her own designing of details & her personal work in preparing & fitting the hangings & other accessories. It is in a brick row of tasteful neighbourhood shops like the new row on the west side of Thayer St. opposite Bunn's & the Mayflower; & though small in area, has been arranged & furnished in such a manner as to make the most of every inch & convey an impression of ample room. Inexpensive pine tables mahoganised, panels for window-background shaped & stained with economical ingenuity, mirrors bought unframed & appropriately provided with inconspicuous frames, linoleum flooring whose clever imitation of tiling deceived even me—all these things combine to give the shop a far greater air of selectness & distinction than the same financial outlay could possibly have given it under any less effective management. S H made the portieres, window draperies, & table-covers entirely herself—on our old Angell St. sewing machine—& the carpentry was done by a highly dexterous semi-amateur who charged comparatively little; a slender, wistful-looking young ex-seaman—the son of a retired sea-captain—who has lately tried to find some landsman's business because his wife does not wish him to go to sea. The shop has a working space partitioned off in the rear by portieres, & is freshly painted in a quiet & tasteful way. New & classical-looking sconces from the electric company unite with three overhead lamps to provide the illumination, & the six chairs are small colonial *Windsors*, made in *Gardner, Mass.*—near Athol, & in the Westminster district where mother & I spent the summer of 1899. These Windsors are exactly like one which Belknap has just bought. S H has six larger & finer ones for the apartment. You & A E P G have doubtless received the announcements of the new venture. The text is revised & amplified by me, from originals prepared by the alert young advertising man who called last Monday. On account of an accident to the press, his firm could not handle the job on time; so I took the chance to waft back some bread cast upon the waters in the dim past, & had S H give the job to those kindly printers in Flatbush Ave. who let me use their typewriter so freely—refusing all pay—when I was here six years ago & had an imperative Bush order to fill. They remembered me, & were quite pleased to see how faithfully I recalled their favour. As you will see from your specimens, the quality of the work performed did not constitute any anticlimax to the agreeable episode. They are clearly high-grade workmen, & S H will patronise them in future whenever she needs printing done. Another distinctive feature of the new establishment is the striking hat-box for deliveries which S H has designed. It is round in contour & black in colour, with a green-bordered cover & green name-&-address inscription in small, tasteful letters at the centre of the cover. There is a good supply of these, & more can be obtained when they are gone. Signs for the shop-front & window have been ordered & will soon be delivered, while a goodly supply of hat material will be obtained tomorrow. Metal hat-trees for the display of goods in the show-window is another feature. S H will engage one assistant, & is arranging with a bright nigger-boy with a bicycle (who will have a motorcycle in a short time) to take charge of deliveries. The formal opening was yesterday*, but of course the enterprise will not be really finished & running for a week or so. About a thousand dollars will have been invested after everything is obtained, & I surely hope the venture will prove a success. I advised against such enterprises by letter when the plan was outlined,

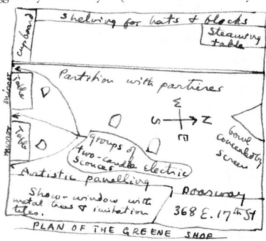

but upon viewing the location I cannot help feeling that it may survive & prosper after all. The neighbourhood is good, there is no other establishment of the kind near by, the adjacent shop-owners are friendly & disposed to help, & the diminutive elegance of the place itself invites congenial patronage. With cautious & intelligent management, it ought to make itself a permanent standby of the most select local business centre in Old Flatbush; & S H is working furiously & diligently under the influence of the highest hopes. I append a plan of the place to assist in conveying an idea of its aspect.

As for the apartment in East 16th St.—it has four rooms, & looks very much like 259 Parkside before I altered the original decorative scheme by the importation of my things. The apartment-house, called the "Hilda Arms", is the only thing of its kind in a region of Providence-like single houses, well-kept lawns, back-yards, & tree-shaded streets. I am not sure whether you saw much of this especial part of Flatbush, but I think A E P G did. It is beyond & westward of the ancient church & churchyard which I love so well. Societies &

---

*Two customers appeared, & carried away a very favourable impression even though the place was not ready to accomodate their needs.

agreements among property-owners preserve the quality of the section. The flat is on the third floor, & is known as Apartment 9. The general contour of its four rooms may be seen from the foregoing diagram, though a chart can scarcely do justice to its pleasant & aesthetic appearance. The dining or sitting room is panelled in squares of dark oak, whilst the woodwork elsewhere is white or oak of varying degrees of richness. Papers on the walls & rugs on the floors are uniformly in good taste. The dining-sitting room has a great central indirect-lighting fixture, whilst the library has a group of chain-hung lamps precisely like those in my room. I am now using the secretary as a desk & centre of activities—illuminated at night by a wrought-iron adjustable bridge-lamp with a *hundred-watt* bulb. Belknap agrees with me in pronouncing the whole apartment an extremely tasteful little haven. The household cuisine is of the same sumptuousness which characterised Parkside fare, & I am duly on guard to protect my 146 lbs. against further increase. I cannot make 140 by Roodmas, but I must do so by St. John's Eve

or Lammas![3] The effect of this luxury on my digestion is excellent—so that I need not regret having omitted the Phenolax wafers from my valise. Spaghetti with S H's inimitable sauce, meat prepared in magical ways beyond the divining of the layman, waffles with maple syrup, popovers with honey—such are among the challenges to leanness wherewith my pathway is beset! And in case I wish a touch of home, there is a Downyflake Doughnut Shop not far off in Flatbush Avenue. On account of the uncertain weather I have not yet had my suit pressed, though it now resembles a tramp's disguise. As soon as the present series of endless rains looks fairly over, I shall patronise the establishment of Signor Narcisi around the corner. I am now on my second set of linen, & S H has insisted on washing the non-ironed pieces of the week's quota. I may send back the collar & shirt, or I may let a local laundry attend to them. I now have on the shirt from Bossy Gillis's town,[4] & have decided not to complain to His Honour about the quality of his local merchandise.

Shrinkage is very slight indeed, & the garment forms a genuinely worthy addition to my not unlimited wardrobe. I will close this description of immediate surroundings with a concise chart of the neighbourhood about the Cortelyou Rd. subway station; shewing the relative locations of 395 East 16th, & the shop at 368 East 17th. The whole district is quite a long walk south & west (the equivalent of three subway stops) from the Parkside neighbourhood, & is infinitely more pleasant & small-village-like. Clearly, Flatbush is the one habitable spot in all the depressing welter bearing the name of New York.

Another new flat of great interest is that of the Longs at 230 West 97th St., Manhattan. This is a vast improvement over 823 in that it has more rooms. Otherwise it resembles 823 closely, both in date of building & general architectural cast. The general

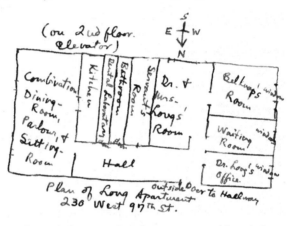

layout will be seen in the accompanying diagram. Belknap has a room of his own at last, & the parlour need no longer be invaded by patients. Old Felisboy stalks about as of yore in a serenity occasionally tempered by mild spittings & clawings; but the faithful Ottie left a fortnight ago to embark on the seas of matrimony, so that the servant problem is in a state of transient acuteness. Just at the moment, after several unsuccessful trials, there is a new German domestic of rather high quality; who accepts a very low salary in exchange for lodgment offered to her husband as well as herself. Thus, in a way, the House of Long may be said to be taking a boarder! The name of the apartment-house is The Wilmington. It is in the same general location as 823—being on the S.E. corner of 97th St. & Broadway. I do not think the building looks *quite* so spic-&-span as 823—on whose site, by the way, a tall & gleaming new apartment-house has arisen. The accompanying chart will illustrate the relative positions of good old 823 & 230 W. 97. Belknap's uncle, whose sudden illness I mentioned on my card, is slowly holding his own; so that there is now no acute worry about him. That book of travel impressions by the aunt, for which I wrote an introduction, will shortly be published by W. Paul Cook. [Cook is also setting up my "Shunned House" & having Belknap write a preface for it.][5] In closing this account of Long matters I must not forget to mention with becoming regret the sad & gaudy repainting of the family Essex, whose sober dark outlines drew up in front of #10 last July. Alas! Some daemon of sporty taste impelled the good doctor to have the faithful roadster tricked out in a glossy maroon, with upper body in a kind of olive-grey, & with a vivid light scarlet around the window-indentations. It is, in short, a decidedly snappy affair; & Sonny vows that everyone turns to look at it whether it be moving or stationary. Dr. Long is now a highly capable driver, with occasional bursts of genuine speed mania.

The scenic setting of the visit being now sufficiently outlined, let me turn to the various events & take up the diary which my postcards carried to Tuesday morning. Starting out before noon, I did some shopping with S H, (incidentally getting this paper at Kresge's—exactly the same sort which you got me last autumn) surveyed the new shop in East 17th St., took a walk through the vernal semi-rusticity of Prospect Park, & finally embarked on an Interborough subway train at the Plaza station. By 2:30 I was at Belknap's, & there then followed a highly entertaining afternoon of discussion. Returning to #395 for dinner, I set out in the evening to see Loveman at the new shop to which he has moved his business—uptown in the 59th St. book belt instead of in the Wall St. downtown section. It is a prepossessing place, & Loveman seemed delightfully genial & unchanged. He had with him one of his numberless prodigy-proteges, a quiet blond youth, whose accomplishments seem to be, so far, appreciative rather than creative. We soon adjourned to a coffee-house for quiet discussion, & later I accompanied Loveman home—to the familiar brownstone mansion in Columbia Heights which you & I discovered. Just now Loveman is alarmed over some financial disputes which are causing dissension among the gentle old sisters who own the place. He fears that they may sell it, & that he may in such a contingency be forced to seek a haven elsewhere—a prospect which he very naturally & sensibly does not welcome! However, it may not be so. Loveman has taken a large front room next his former small one, & has moved in his long-dormant bookcase. His walls are gradually acquiring the Hellenic pictures needed to make them expressive of himself, & his mantel is embellished by some queer-ish cylindrical sculptured heads made especially for him by a modernist artist of his acquaintance. The type of technique is original with the sculptor, & the mood symbolised by the work is one of infinite serenity & repose—a Nirvana-like ataraxy beyond anything which earth can afford. I will attempt to convey in a sketch some idea of the bizarre technique, though naturally I cannot hope to hit upon even a hint of the real expression or emotional background. There are two of them—one of which seems to me rather better than the other. At a guess I'd say that the sculptor has quite a future before him. But these are only minor features of the contemporary Lovemanic ensemble. Titanically overshadowing them, & forming one of the most distinctive art objects ever housed in a single room, is something which arrested my glance the moment I crossed the threshold, & from which it is impossible to keep one's eyes long averted. I have mentioned many times how intensely Loveman admires a certain Greek athlete's head shewn in the classical corridor of the Metropolitan Museum, & how many times he has wished he could obtain a good cast of it. Well—he has had his cast made at last—especially for him, by the museum authorities, & at a cost of something above $12.00. It is utterly magnificent—life-size, like the original, of course, & of a splendid ivory finish involving a darkening of the shadows calculated to bring out all the facial expression & convey the grace of the curling hair as chiselled in the original's tinted, delicate-veined marble. The head is on a great cube of the same ivory plaster, & the massed effect of the whole spectacle is ineffably poignant. I had not realised that one could have actual casts thus made from real Graeco-Roman statuary. In effect, almost anyone can have in his home the authentic essence of classical art, & at a merely nominal cost. I am strongly tempted to save up for a purchasing space some day—for as you know, it was my original design in youth to have a private museum of Greek & Roman casts. The thing I most desire in this line is a head at the Metropolitan which I admire nearly as much as Loveman admires his Greek athlete's head—I refer, of course, to that inimitable old Roman with the tight lips & corrugated brow (now on a pillar in Wing K, but in the corridor when you were there) of whom I have so often spoken to you. I can see him now on top of my bookcase beside Milton . . . . he is a great old boy, & as expressive of me as the languishing young Greek is of the author of "The Hermaphrodite". Well—to return to the diary—Loveman & I discussed art & literature & Bierce & George Sterling till well into the small hours; my host crowning his hospitality by making me a present of a forgotten old book of weird antarctic adventure entitled "Revi-Lona", which I have not yet had time to read.[6] I left at 3 a.m. after inviting Loveman over to 395 the next evening with a young friend of his, whose neo-Hellenic verse he had shewed me. Reaching 395 in due time, I retired early at the hour of four. The next day—Wednesday—I accompanied S H on some errands & did considerable reading at 395. At 2:30 p.m. Small Sonny came over; & after he had sufficiently observed & admired the flat & the neighbourhood, we both set out to call on honest old McNeil at his quarters in Fifth St., Brooklyn. I had never before seen this place; for as you know, Mac inhabited the roaring slums of Hell's Kitchen in Manhattan when I was last here. We went by surface car to save Sonny the ordeal of climbing subway stairs, & I finally beheld the new habitat of our quaint & simple friend—a dingy though not unclean unit of a seedy brownstone row in one of the streets which slope downward toward the west from Prospect Park to the Gowanus & Erie Basin regions. Mac answered the jangling bell in person, & was quite speechless at sight of his expected guest's unexpected companion. He led us upstairs to his three-room quarters, & I was pleased to see the familiar face & familiar furniture in a setting less squalid than the old joint in West 49th St. The place is of about the same degree of squalor as 169 Clinton St.*, though Mac does not seem to mind the unaesthetic frowsiness. It is exclusively a stag retreat, run by an old German bachelor named Muck, with whom Mac frequently holds converse in a not altogether unamiable manner. During the present session all sorts of topics were discussed, & I promised to call on my honest host again before my departure from metropolitan shores. Sonny overstayed his usual time, but finally departed; & after a while I likewise bade Mac adieu & proceeded 395-ward. Dinner being over, I got in touch with old de Castro by telephone; & found that he wished to see me very much the following day. The guests now came—Loveman & the young poet Alan Taylor Devoe[7]—& the evening passed quickly in general aesthetic discussion. Devoe is a fine, quiet youth of ancient & patrician New Jersey stock, though his verse still shews something of youthful immaturity. Blond & delicate, he affects rudimentary side-whiskers. He read Belknap's "Man from Genoa" & Wandrei's "Ecstasy", which happened to be lying about, & expressed a keen wish to meet Belknap in the near future. S H served cocoa & cookies, & the evening may very fairly be adjudged a success. Retiring at 12:30 midnight, I arose at 8 a.m. Thursday, & accompanied S H out on some errands. In the afternoon I went up to Belknap's to pick him up en route to old de Castro's, but he was considerably delayed by having to be on duty at his uncle's while his aunt went down town. Finally, however, he arrived; & together we set out for 55 West 88th St., where lodges the unctuous old hypocrite whose story ruined my winter. 88th St. was soon reached, & #55 turned out to be a decaying brownstone—or red sandstone—mansion between Columbus Ave. & Central Park West, whose ornate & carven facade bespoke the lavishness of the gay 'nineties, when architects like Stanford White made of the private dwelling a thing of pomp & ostentation. Old 'Dolph is on the second floor in a suite of which we saw only the main large room. He is not practicing dentistry, & Sonny & I can't guess what his daily occupation really is. His chief possession is a lively little fox-terrier which never keeps still for a moment, but jumps upon everyone in a perfect ecstasy of diffusive friendliness†. In the hall below I saw a fine coal-black kitty-cat, but he does not belong to de Castro. Old Dolph is a portly, sentimental, & gesticulating person given to egotistical rambling about old times & the great men he has intimately known. He has nearly a score of books lying

---

*Loveman tells me that 169 Clinton is now uninhabited, with broken windows & an air of ghoulish desertion. I think I shall take a look at it from sheer curiosity.
†De Castro had to brush my clothes for me twice. To make matters worse, the doglet is *white!*

about in MS.—mostly bound like the one you saw—& he is desperately anxious to have me rewrite the Bierce volume.[8] He also wants me to approach Cook about the publication of "The Monk & the Hangman's Daughter" in a new edition—to have additional passages from the German original, to include the illustrations used in the defunct 1892 edition, & to be retitled "Ambrosius & Benedicta".[9] I'm afraid the old duffer can't or won't pay a decent advance price, hence I doubt if I take the revision job after all; though I shall read the book fully & prepare a helpful synopsis & list of suggestions. My own interest impels me to do this—& I have promised him such a list by next Thursday. At the proper hour, Belknap having left, de Castro dutifully changed his suit & led me forth to a sumptuous repast in the dining room of the Peter Stuyvesant Hotel in Central Park West. Later we returned to his quarters, & I had a hard time breaking away at 10:30 p.m. Returning via elevated & B.M.T., I retired at just about midnight. The next day—Friday the 27th—I was up early & hastened northward to join the Longs on their projected motor trip through the wild hill country. En route I purchased a present in honour of The Child's birthday, (a Modern Library copy of Bierce's "In the Midst of Life") for the little rascal was just turning twenty-six.[10] Twenty-six! To think of that small boy as a middle-aged fat man! In due time the gaudy car started northward with its load—papa, mamma, Sonny, & grandpa—the child having lent me an old brown overcoat of his for the occasion. I recall once that I borrowed an old overcoat from Dr. Long for a ride on a 'bus top, [*sic*] for in those days I could not think of getting any garment of Belknap's on. How turned are the tables today! I was veritably lost in the young imp's apparel! The day was cold & showery, but a closed car made exploration not only possible but enjoyable. We swung into Riverside Drive & made for the north, noting as we did so the unfinished new viaduct which is to remove the inward curve of the Drive at 135th St, where the cliffs recede from the shore along the line of a former cove. Up near the Dyckman farmhouse (1783) we beheld the first great evidence of change since 1926. What were then rural or semi-rural roads have now become monotonous rows of light brick apartment houses, so that the old Dutch cottage is the sole surviving remnant of a brighter age of light & air & verdure & leisure. Van Cortlandt Park next engaged our vision, & I was glad to see the old stone mansion (1742) again. I shall later visit & enter both Dyckman & Van Cortlandt houses. You have seen the latter yourself, as you will recall; whilst A E P G has seen both. We now struck northward along the Bronx Parkway, observing en route some extremely pleasing suburban villages—mostly high-grade modern real-estate developments. The scenery is surprisingly fine for a region outside New England, bold wooded hills, deep sinuous valleys, & picturesque twists of roadway combining to form a panorama which unfolds continuously before the admiring spectator. The great dams of the Kensico reservoirs—for the region is, like Scituate in our state, a source of urban faucet-material—are here & there visible, like reliques of a vanished cyclopean race, whilst at one point the fountain jets of a purifying or aërating station suggest an assemblage of fantastic geysers. But the great moment of the journey was when the trammels of suburbanism were wholly shaken off, & we entered at last the real American countryside of rolling meadows, grazing kine, farmsteads with sloping apple-orchards, & stone walls winding in zigzag negligence up hill & down dale. The past! His Majesty's lost Province of New-York! God Save the King! From several lofty hilltops we obtained vistas of domed hill & furrowed plain, distant village & gleaming river, which rivalled in sweep & magnificence anything to be seen in Cook's Connecticut-Valley district . . . . . . I say *rivalled,* though I do not think these vistas could really be said to *equal* the best stretches of landscape along the Athol-Greenfield highway. But for New York they were astonishingly fine, & I surely enjoyed them to the full despite the showery greyness of the day. The region around Somers, highly colonial & full of splendid quasi-Novanglian landscape touches, was the scene of many of Dr. Long's boyhood years; when he was sent out of the city to have his then feeble health built up. At many turns of the road he indulged in bursts of reminiscent admiration unusual for one whose daily mood is so prosaic; recalling here & there a brook he had fished in, a pool he & the other boys had swum in, an apple-orchard he had sampled, & a slope on which he had lounged through the long summer afternoons of the bygone 'seventies. Once, when the car topped a rise beside a reservoir-sunken valley, he waxed almost lyrical about a day when he had first been driven there in a jolting carryall by his uncle—a day in spring, when the magic of scented fields & delicately-leaved trees blended with the song of robins & the charm of apple-blossoms. Good soul—he had to grope & fumble for words in order to stammer out the picture & sensations he wished to convey; yet behind the rough ineptitude there lurked a genuine & unmistakable aesthetic feeling which might, under other conditions, have made him an artist or poet. It took one generation more to crystallise the emotions into articulateness—so that Little Belknap instead of Big Belknap became the author of "The [*sic*] Man from Genoa." Some of the old-American villages of the region are delightful. Bedford Hills, built quaintly upon a congeries of slopes & curves, suggests some such place as Apponaug or Cumberland Village or Rehoboth Village; whilst Somers is a colonial cluster like Moosup Valley or Rice City. On the central green of Somers is the effigy of an elephant upon a tall pole, said to commemorate the first publick exhibition of that quaint animal in these colonies, which took place near the tavern (still standing) on this spot. I regretted that I had neither camera nor postcards to immortalise my impressions of the village. The apex of the trip was Lake Mahopac, a favourite summer-resort whose central feature is a picturesquely irregular & island-studded sheet of water whose shores are lined with shady drives & capacious hostelries. The beauty of this region is undeniable, but I was not sorry to turn back toward the wild hills & pastoral farmlands. Lunch—an enormous & elaborate affair of the typical Long sort—was eaten on a rambling back road of extreme picturesqueness, & the return voyage was fully as pleasing as the outward jaunt. At one point the road revealed an inimitable panorama of agrestic slopes & kine-dotted meadows to the westward—with the gleaming Hudson beyond, & in the far background the vapour-draped heights of the mystic domed hills. Not far off two rural swains were ploughing their ancestral acres in the old, ancestral way—each plough linked to two horses of a hardy breed. It was a picture to remember, & I cannot ever recall having seen a more impressive glimpse of age-old rural life. We were back in Manhattan by five o'clock, having traversed a middle stretch of Van Cortlandt Park which I had never before seen. Subsequently Belknap & I argued about philosophy, & after dinner (the family had fish, but they had provided 2 lamb chops for me) we planned our new revision service & exchanged ideas as to procedure. Leaving at 10:30 p.m., I arrived at 395 an hour later & found S H busy addressing announcements for the new millinery venture. I offered my help in the process, & we laboured jointly until 3:30 a.m., covering a list of important Flatbush families furnished by the local real estate company. We sent these announcements to you & A E P G, but yours has just come back for deficient postage—the stamp having fallen off the letter. It has now gone out again—this time, I hope, successfully. The next day—Saturday—I rose at 9:30 a.m. & helped S H with sundry errands. In the afternoon I called on Talman, with whom I had previously held telephonic communication; finding him in the small Willow St. room which I recalled so well from room-hunting days of old. Brooklyn Heights is not so much changed as one would think from that illustrated booklet Talman sent—indeed, the whole of N Y seems to me exactly the same, with nothing of novelty or unfamiliarity about it. At 3 o'clock Talman & I joined Little Belknap at the American Museum of Natural History, where we spent most of the time studying the Mexican–Central American section— interest having been aroused by the Spence book on Atlantis which I read so hurriedly just before departing on my trip. We saw some dinosaur bas-relief paperweights at the publication window, whose price (25¢) was so low as to tempt us sorely—but the window closed before any of us made a purchase. Talman looks much the same as ever. He is preparing a colossal genealogy of his family in book form, which will probably be published some day. The scholarship & labour which must have gone into such a work is truly prodigious—endless tables, charts, references, & lists of data, & all the various coats-of-arms drawn out with the highest artistic skill. After our museum session Talman had to go off on a newspaper assignment, (he is working for the Times now) but Belknap & I proceeded down by elevated to the 42nd St. library, where we unearthed some more Atlantis material. Sonny then left for home, whilst I took dinner at the Automat—having told S H not to bother with my dinner on the opening day of her enterprise. Upon my return to 395

I did some necessary writing; & at 10 o'clock S H arrived, bearing a prodigious load of groceries & insisting on preparing one of her matchless spaghetti suppers. I could not refuse a repast so carefully chosen to suit my palate, so that on this one occasion I was perforce thrown back to the conventional three meals per day. Retiring at 12:30 midnight, I was up again at 9 a.m.—daylight time—Sunday, & spent the morning in writing. In the afternoon S H & I went out for a delightfully circuitous walk; the first half of which included the choicest scenic bits of Prospect Park, whilst the latter half comprised a representative survey of the best parts of still-unspoiled Old-American Flatbush, with its separate houses & lawns, & its general Brown St.–Keene St.–Lloyd Avenue–Hope St.–Thayer St. atmosphere. The Parkside Ave. section is no longer representative of the ancient & exclusive Flatbush, but south of Church Ave. the pristine tone is not even threatened. Here the normal American life of the New York area is making its last stand, & I was encouraged to note how much more *extensive* the unspoiled territory is, than I had ever suspected. The total area of still-American Flatbush must be nearly a square mile—a rectangular strip roughly half a mile across from east to west (Flatbush Ave. to Coney Island Ave.) & two miles from north to south. (Church Ave. to Avenue H.) Apartments have invaded some sections of this area, but most of it is all untainted, & exceedingly suggestive of the East Side of Providence. Churches are numerous—all Protestant except one excellent Catholic specimen whose chimes make magic on the Sunday-morning air. The premier edifice, of course, is the old Dutch meeting-house which you saw. On this occasion we had an exquisite glimpse of it from the rear—transfigured by the elfin golden sunlight of late afternoon, & rising above its venerable churchyard behind the delicate tracery of a stately maple's still unbudded boughs. The steeple has been painted white, so that it now makes a prodigiously New-Englandish appearance—although of course its simple grace cannot compare with the elaborate majesty of our one & only First Baptist. Another magnificent Georgian church—brick, with an old-time white belfry—is just around the corner from 395 E. 16th St.,—in Dorchester Road, the next beyond Cortelyou. I had never seen this (it is the Flatbush Congregational Church) before, hence was quite overpowered with surprise & pleasure upon beholding it during this walk. I rather think it is a clever & faithful modern reproduction rather than a really old building, but the architecture is so correct that I really cannot be sure. All that makes me think it is not old is the fact that it is in the midst of 1900-period houses. I rejoice in having so pleasing a fane so close to the scene of the visit. After this walk we returned to 395, where S H prepared a magnificent lamb stew—which served also for the next day's dinner. Then followed a period of writing—with retiring at midnight. Monday, April 30, I rose at 8 a.m., & wrote letters all the morning. At noon I set out for Belknap's—stopping en route to see about my fountain pen at the Waterman Co. Repairs will cost 50¢, & the pen will be ready in a few days. When I reached Sonny's neighbourhood I did a little local shopping for a cheap stop-gap pen—& obtained the device with which I am finishing this epistle. It cost only a dollar, & is made by the same Eagle Pencil Co. which manufactures the commonest sort of penny lead pencil. The point is a bit scratchy, but the feed is good; & I fancy it will be a good reserve to have on hand for emergencies like the present one. It is a self-filler, & the pen is supposed to be gold. Arriving at Belknap's, I discussed revision with the Child for a while; & we then set out for the Bronx Zoölogical Park, (which you have not seen, although A E P G has) having been led by the warmth & fairness of the day to abandon a previous plan of visiting the Nat. Hist. Museum. As A E P G can tell you, Bronx Park is full of exceedingly beautiful, New-England-like scenery; & this we enjoyed to the utmost, though Belknap perhaps found more of interest in the various beasts caged here & there. We left at about 6 p.m., Belknap going home & I returning to 395 for dinner. S H spent the evening at her shop conferring about her business & advertising campaign with some local commercial authorities—especially the wife of the real-estate man who rented her the shop. This lady is a leader in the local D.A.R. chapter, & thinks she may be able to induce some of her fellow-members to patronise the new establishment. I spent the time writing letters, & retiring was at midnight. The next day—today, Tuesday, May 1st—I arose at 9 a.m. & have been writing continuously ever since. I am making no engagements, but shall spend all the time getting some of my neglected correspondence attended to, & reading up some of the material which has accumulated on my hands. I can't get my report on old de Castro's book done in the time I promised, but I'll drop him a card of explanation & further promise. Tomorrow night the gang (which has almost dissolved, but which Sonny thinks can be temporarily revived during the present visit) meets up at Belknap's, & I shall be there during the afternoon preceding, taking dinner with the Longs. Thursday is unplanned, but will doubtless be full enough. Friday I shall again accompany the Longs on a rural trip in their gaudified Essex, probably witnessing the impressive 5 o'clock drill at West Point. Saturday is unplanned, but Sunday S H & I will both have dinner with the Longs. I must find time to look up Kirk, who is keeping a bookshop in Greenwich Village, & has recently added a circulating library. Then, too, I must work in a trip to Paterson to see the one & only James Ferdinand. I shall, though, probably see both Kirk & Mortonius at the meeting tomorrow night. Too bad I haven't Monday's & Tuesday's crossword puzzles to give Mortonius! The spell of rainy weather seems to be broken now, so I think I'll let S H take my suit out to be pressed before I go up to Sonny's tomorrow. I'd hate to have the assembled gang behold me in my present hobo-like state! Fortunately my *face* has been behaving *marvellously* well, (the permanent extractions of the past winter have been of the highest value in coping with the handicap) so that I shall be spared one source of annoyance usually very acute.

11:30 a.m.

The mail has just come, & in it your very welcome letter. Your mention of having sent *four* Bulletins (whereas I received only Wednesday's & Thursday's) convinces me that two were lost in the mails; hence I hope you can get duplicates of Monday's & Tuesday's (April 23–24) at the Journal office. I hate to miss one, on account of the High Lights of History, &c., & of course it would be a grave blow to Mortonius to lose two of his puzzles. You might try sending these two if you can get them, since I have read Wednesday's & Thursday's, & want the record solid to that date. As for later issues—I noticed the exorbitant postage (7¢) on each of the two papers that came, & agree with you that remailing is highly impracticable. So just save the issues as they come, & I'll indulge only in the minor extravagance of buying one now & then at the out-of-town newspaper stand at 42nd St. & 6th Ave., back of the public library. But send last Monday's & Tuesday's, & let me see any cuttings of great interest; (needn't send whole papers) especially things concerning the new railway, colonial antiquities, & further instalments of the local reminiscent articles. I believe that one on Italian Federal Hill is due, & Olneyville, Elmwood, &c. are yet uncovered. By the way—you needn't fear the loss of *letter* mail at this end. This is a regular apartment-house like 259 Parkside, with individual letter-boxes in the lobby. It was all right not to forward poor Hennessy's letter, (though you might slip it in one of yours if you happen to be using an envelope larger than his) but I'd like to see Tryout when it appears. You can recognise Smithy's homely brown wrappers. What I am avidly waiting for, of course, is the 78-fish cheque from Weird Tales,[11] which will form the backbone of my southward peregrinations. How much, by the way, is my bill? I have forgotten how much the Bulletin amounts to each time. Is it $1.75? I know the Sunday Journal is $1.25. I may pick up a Sunday Journal here in order to get it read & disposed of, but save all until further notice. You need *not* save the N.Y. Times for the past two Sundays, since I have seen them here & extracted everything I wish to save. I am herewith returning the Chapin article, which afforded me much pleasure. The old Coventry house must be tremendously interesting—I shall keep the cutting for my files. In Sunday's Brooklyn Eagle—which S H takes—there is a highly interesting article on some old pewter in the Brooklyn Museum, which I shall send you after I have seen the exhibit in question. As for overcoat & umbrella, I have *not* really needed them; since the cold has not been excessive, whilst the rain has been more or less intermittent. What I wish I *did* have is my *summer suit**; since the weather around Washington will be radically warmer than here. It was almost too warm for my regular thick suit (that fuzzy grey one bought in 1921 & now stolen) on Easter Sunday, 1925, during my one memorable dip into the near-South. If I

---

*Belknap & Loveman have both just bought new summer suits of very light grey—almost exactly alike.

had needed an overcoat, either Belknap or Talman would have lent me one to keep during the whole of the visit. Both offered to, & with my present figure (I am still holding to 146, as the enclosed card proves) I can wear the garments of either of these children. As for food bills—S H has so far refused to accept anything toward their defrayment despite the most emphatic down-settings of my foot, though she says she may let me help later on if the new shop entails any great loss during its opening period. I must have all my bills paid up & all my dishes washed at all times . . . . I shall send you what I owe as soon as the W.T. cheque comes. I may try some Reed work soon—I must get a 5¢ pad of cheap paper—& my course with the de Castro book depends on the outcome of my next conversation with the old boy. Glad you have followed my example in adopting the Cavalier pad—it's the best dime I've seen since the war. You aren't as rusty at the art of letter-writing as you think—indeed, your present communication seems fully as graceful & informative as any epistle could be. S H sends you her warmest regards, & wishes you could get around here to participate in the visit. How about it? It would be *great* if you could. There are comfortable sleeping accomodations, (you could have the bedroom) & a Pullman journey is no ordeal at all. Nor would there be any expense except the railway fare. Thousands of sights await your seeing, yet the Flatbush neighbourhood is as restful as a slice of Providence. I wouldn't overwork you in sightseeing—just one thing per day. Honest Miss Reynolds could take care of our effects at #10 for a week or so. Let me know if you can make it, & I'll arrange a monster welcome & easy programme.

And so it goes. More later. Shew this epistle to A E P G when you see her.

Yr aff nephew & obt

H P L

P.S. I hope nobody is wreaking any havock among my *chists* in de *Cornders,* or disarranging any objects on my *ivory* table by de fireplace! I can't permit work around my quarters! ¶ Had a card from A E P G in Boston. Shall drop her a card today. ¶ If this afternoon is good, I think I'll take some of my work out in the open—Prospect Park or the Japanese Garden near the Brooklyn Museum—where we got lost in Dec. 1924.

Notes

1. The ad appeared in *WT* 12, No. 2 (August 1928): 281.

2. FBL was acting as agent for Zealia Brown Reed Bishop. HPL revised at least 3 stories for her.

3. St. John's Eve, 23 June, is the eve of the feast day of Saint John the Baptist. Lammas is 1 August (in the Northern Hemisphere).

4. I.e., Newburyport, MA. See further LDC/AEPG 258n1.

5. Cook's edition, printed in an edition of 300 copies, was never bound or distributed.

R. H. Barlow bound a very small number of copies in 1934, but the bulk of the edition was circulated only in 1959–61 by Arkham House.

6. By Frank Cowan.

7. Alan Taylor Devoe (1909–1955), wrote poems early in his career but then became a naturalist and devotee of birds. See such books as *Down to Earth: A Naturalist Looks About* (1940) and *Our Animal Neighbors* (1953).

8. HPL refers to *Portrait of Ambrose Bierce*. HPL eventually declined the revision job because de Castro would not pay him in advance. FBL revised it and wrote a preface.

9. *The Monk and the Hangman's Daughter* is a translation by de Castro (as Gustav Adolphe Danziger) of Richard Voss's *Der Mönch von Berchtesgaden* (1890–91); the translation was revised by Ambrose Bierce. The work was serialized in the *San Francisco Examiner* (13–27 September 1891) and published in book form in 1892. It was included in Volume 6 of Bierce's *Collected Works* (1909–12). A reissue of that volume did appear (New York: Boni & Liveright, 1926), but no edition as described by HPL was published.

10. In fact, FBL (b. 1901) turned twenty-seven on 27 April 1928. See Peter Cannon, "Frank Belknap Long: When Was He Born and Why Was Lovecraft Wrong?" *Studies in Weird Fiction* No. 17 (Summer 1995): 33–34.

11. For "The Lurking Fear."

[190]   [ALS] [HPL to LDC]

395 East 16th St.,
Brooklyn, N.Y.,
May 3, 1928.

My dear daughter Lillian:—

I take my pen in hand to continue my diary, whose principal topic today will naturally be the meeting of last night.

But first I must request a favour, much as I hate to put you to severe trouble. It is that you send me my *grey summer suit* by express or parcel post at the earliest convenient date. Yesterday's temperature is what impels me to make the request with such emphasis. It was an exquisite day, with the magic of summer in the air; but the weight of my winter suit almost stifled me with oppression & drowned me with perspiration. It would be *absolutely impossible* for me to make my southern circuit in such gear, so I surely hope that the packing of the aestival raiment will not prove a formidable or unfeasible task. I am sure A E P G would be glad to take it down town, & I will cheerfully submit to the addition of the express or postal fee to my bill. [I'm a poor man, but I've got a $78.00 cheque!] I will return the heavier suit by parcel post when I myself return. During the sojourn there will probably be many cool days (in N.Y., not in the south) when I shall still require the winter weight.

Incidentally, when you pack the suit you might include the following additional articles in the large bundle:

(1)   The nice belt that Sonny gave his Grandpa on Christmas—now in red tissue paper in the lowest small drawer of my chiffonier.

(2)   *All Evening Bulletins which have accumulated to date.* (& last Sunday's Journal if it doesn't affect the weight badly)

Regarding the latter—I have just solved the problem of avoiding an accumulation of reading on my return by being a sport & sending the Journal Co. 60¢ for a duplicate subscription for the shortest possible time (one month) at this address. I used the name of Greene in order to avoid confusion on the Journal books, for I don't want them to disturb my regular home subscription through any mistake. The paper will probably begin coming by Saturday or Monday, (May 5 or 7) so if you will send (with the suit) all issues up to that date, my record will be complete. You might also send the "Trader Horn" page from the Sunday Journal—saving the rest very carefully. Incidentally, I may remark with a blend of surprise & amusement *that Morton does not want any more puzzles from the Bulletin!* It is not that he has given up puzzling—bless my soul, no! It merely means that he finds the crossword in the N.Y. Tribune enough for him. But who can say that this is not the beginning of the end? It is hard to think of the old boy without his puzzles . . . . I am sure I shall continue to tear them instinctively out of the Bulletin each night, as I have done so steadily for the last four years!

But let me advert to the diary proper. I think my card of yesterday told of the arrival of the Monday & Tuesday (April 23–4) Bulletins [I have now recd. April 23–6 inclusive. Further shipments should begin with Friday, April 27] & of my intention to start for Sonny's. I had previously had my suit pressed & shoes blacked in honour of the gang, & had done some errands for S H— seeing locksmiths, sign-painters, &c. Well, I reached Belknap's on time, but found the household plunged in chaos through the dismissal of the new maid that very morning. She had proved intolerably impertinent, & there was nothing for Mrs. Long to do but emulate Mayor Gillis[1] & 'tell her where she got off'. Accordingly all plans were plunged into chaos, & the events for Friday & Sunday are still uncertain. On this occasion Belknap & I went out in Central Park to discuss aesthetic matters & improve the balmy summer weather, afterward dining at an excellent cafeteria at Broadway & 96th St.—a place, by the way, where Sonny, Morton, & I once ate six years ago. I had beef loaf, fried potatoes, peas, coffee, & ice cream in reasonable amounts not inconsistent with the reducing policy of a conservative old gentleman, but that small Sonny-rascal stuffed his little self with all the rich & fattening things he could find on the day's menu; including *a whole glass of thick cream!* The child is determined to be a Rabelaisian fat man, & is disconsolate at having dropped to *148*—two pounds more than his aged grandpa weighs!

At 7:30 p.m. we returned to 230 to await the gang—all of which finally filtered in except Loveman & Kleiner. Loveman was obliged to be at his bookshop that evening, whilst Kleiner has virtually dropped out of everybody's sight save for the Paterson Sunday hikes. Honest old Mac was the first to come, & Talman was the next. Then the one & only James Ferdinand rolled ruddily & globularly in & spread an expansive cheer & animation over all the scene. Orton, a little graver & quieter than the irresponsible Orton of yore, next appeared on the scene. He is now thoroughly sick of New York, & hopes to return permanently to Vermont in the late summer or autumn. A rather uncongenial marriage has given him a tinge of melancholy, though he is still the same fastidious dandy in dress that he was three years ago. Next & last was Kirk—good old Georgius—whose marriage has proved extremely congenial, & who is still the same happy-go-lucky, unsubdued old night-hawk of yore. It was the regular old gang—as loquacious & argumentative as ever for the nonce, though I am told it is harder & harder to get them rounded up for the meetings. Mrs. Long served her famous Welsh rarebit despite the absence of any maid—giving the Child a chicken sandwich instead, as is usual in such cases, since he has an aversion for cheese almost equivalent to my abhorrence for fish.

The meeting broke up at midnight, after designating Kirk's place in Greenwich Village as the scene of next week's conclave. He has a basement flat in West 11th St.—separate from his shop & circulating library in West 8th St., although he lived over the latter at first. Kirk, honest old Mac, & I walked down Broadway together, & when we came to the elevated at 66th St. Kirk insisted that Mac & I hop on & accompany him home for a further session. We did so, & found Mrs. Kirk half-expecting such a codiciliary assemblage. She is a pleasant, blonde person, not especially young or good-looking, but apparently a highly congenial partner for the carefree & irresponsible Georgius. The household served tea, crackers, & cheese, & I had to exercise a very Spartan austerity in order to fend off un-reducing amounts of this *third* collation of the evening. Discussion was brisk & not uninteresting, & it was 3 a.m. before I put the good old boy on his right train—the subway is always too complex a problem for the honest wight—& rode with him as far as De Kalb Ave. Then I changed to the Brighton Local & was at 395 by 4 a.m. Retiring at once, I arose at 10:15 today (Thursday) & found that S H had left an excellent breakfast on the kitchen table. Since then I have been writing letters, but very shortly (it is now 2 p.m.) I am going out. I shall stop at the emporium around the corner to see S H, shall go down to the Waterman Co. to get my fountain pen, [this cheap stop-gap device grows much *better* as I use it!] & shall probably call on Loveman at his bookshop, which I have not yet had a chance to look over. For the days ahead, there exists a social programme of amusing fulness in view of my recent hibernation; since all the gang were anxious to make engagements. Tomorrow I shall probably see Belknap. Saturday I am going to meet Orton at noon at the Saturday Review office where he is employed (he receives $100.00 per week!) & go out to his home on the northern rim of the city for dinner. Sunday S H & I may possibly dine at the Longs', & may possibly be taken by them for a ride in the gaudily repainted Essex. Monday I have promised to visit honest old Mac at 2 p.m. Wednesday the gang meets at Kirk's. Saturday, May 12, Orton is going to take me—& possibly Belknap as well—out in his automobile to Paterson to see good old James

Ferdinand & his museum. At odd moments I must get the de Castro book looked over, though I doubt exceedingly whether I can ever come to any real arrangement with the author. I shall also do other revision & reading—preferably in the open air. And many items of exploration are on the docket, especially a trip with Talman to find the ancient Schenck houses, neither of which has ever been seen by either of us. On a lone trip I intend to discover Forest Park in the borough of Queens near Kew Gardens, which I have never hitherto beheld. It would make an ideal scene for a day's reading or writing.

And I shall see my interesting correspondent Bernard Dwyer of West Shokan, N.Y. I had not had time to write him myself; but honest old Mac told him I was here, & he wrote that he means to come down before my visit is over. I shall be exceedingly glad to meet the handsome young giant, for he has one of the most genuinely fantastic & delicately Machen-like minds I have ever encountered. Probably I shall visit him myself, by Hudson River boat, before I return home; since I am anxious to see the wild & glamorous countryside he inhabits—a thing whose charm he has so colourfully described in his letters. None of our gang except Wandrei has ever met Dwyer in person, but Wandrei found him prodigiously congenial & prepossessing.

The June *Weird Tales* with my "Lurking Fear" is now out—Kirk had a copy last night—& I shall purchase it this afternoon. I perused the Bulletins, of course, with the keenest interest; & was infinitely glad to hear that Gov. Case has signed the new railway bill. Now it remains for the company to proceed with the construction & justify the faith the state has reposed in it. I certainly do hope that all the Grand Trunk work will not be wasted in the end!

And so it goes. More diary material as it develops. I hope it won't be inconvenient for you to send the light suit, for there can be no comfortable southerly tripping without it. Washington, Alexandria, & Annapolis must be glorious in the spring sunshine & blossoms—ancient & eternal with their centuried roofs & spires. I surely must see them before this cycle of peregrination is over! Give my regards to A E P G & let her see this diary instalment. And come along yourself if you can! ¶ Yr aff Nephew & obt Servt H P L

Notes

1. See further LDC/AEPG 258n1.

[191]   [ANS postcard][1] [HPL to LDC]

[Postmarked Brooklyn, N.Y.,
6 May 1928]
Saturday noon.

Diurnal Diary
EXTRA—The Bulletin has begun to come for its special month here—the

issue for Friday, May 4, being the first. Therefore, please send me by express or parcel post (that will avoid the high postage which you paid on individual copies) all the issues up to that time, as follows:

Friday, April 27
Saturday, April 28
(Sunday Journal if convenient)
Monday, April 30
Tuesday, May 1
Wednesday, May 2
Thursday, May 3   this will fix me up properly & continuously

---

My last diary extended to Thursday afternoon at Prospect Park. That evening I wrote letters & retired at midnight, & the following day I was up at Belknap's at 9 o'clock for the motor trip. The day was warm & ideal, & the excursion was one long pageant of unalloyed delight. We went up the Sawmill River Road through a hilly countryside of the most exquisite description, finally mounting the heights near the Bear Mountain Bridge & obtaining the finest possible view of the Hudson & its adjacent domed hills. At length we crossed the bridge & visited West Point, where under a sunny sky we witnessed the impressive evening dress parade—with pomp & music—at 4:35 p.m. We sat near Maj-Gen. Smith, commandant of the Academy.[2] Returning through marvellous scenery on the Hudson's west [*continued on front*] bank, we traversed the outskirts of Talman's home country & arrived in N.Y. at about 8 o'clock. Lunch—of the usual Long sort—was eaten en route. In the evening Belknap & I discussed things in general, & I returned to 395 at 10 p.m., retiring at midnight. The Longs have another new servant—Irish by persuasion & bearing the grotesque name of *Angel!* Today I am going to meet Orton at noon & go out to his place near Van Cortlandt Park.
Yr aff Nephew & obt Servt H P L

Notes

1. *Front:* Blank.
2. The commandant of cadets at West Point from 1926 to 1929 was Campbell B. Hodges. Morton F. Smith was commandant from 1914 to 1916.

[192]   [ALS] [HPL to LDC]

395 East 16th St.,
Brooklyn, N.Y.,
May 7, 1928.

My dear daughter Lillian:—

Yours of May 4th is at hand, & I am on the lookout for the parcel post package. (Your postal just recd.) Just as well to send only important parts of the paper—but I hope you included the "High Lights of History". I shall certainly need the suit. On account of the innumerable engagements incident to meeting so large a gang after so long a time I can't possibly get down on my real exploring trip till next week; & by that time it will probably be scorching in Washington—if not here as well. Hope you didn't forget to include the belt Sonny gave me—I want to shew the Child that his grandpa is an appreciative old gentleman! Incidentally—you need *not* save yesterday's N.Y. Times. I've gone through it thoroughly & have cut out all I want. I shall be glad to see the Bulletins which bridge the gap between April 26 & May 4. I do not read any N.Y. daily papers—the Bulletin is the only news medium I have ever found perfectly satisfactory, although the Times is of course the greatest Sunday paper & general compendium of current civilisation in existence.

I shall get weighed again soon, though I scarcely dare do it after all the spaghetti & kindred luxuries in which I've lately been wallowing. Like ex-Secretary Daniels, I must put my foot down![1] I shall make S H accept what I think the price of my food is—& I can assure you that I don't add any difficulty to the household work. I've even washed the dishes two or three times! But I must have my bill! Tell A E P G to square me up without telling me how much it is, so that I won't have to undergo the painful process of shelling out when I get home. I'm a poor man, & the ordeal of paying out good hard cash is a terrific strain upon a sensitive nervous system! Don't bother to send Weird Tales unless I ask for it. Open it & read it yourself. I haven't been able to pick up a copy yet, but believe I can when I get around to the larger news stands in Flatbush Ave. Send me the Netopian, but (if it's no trouble) get me *another* fresh, flat copy at the Hospital Trust to keep for my file. I want my permanent file copy spic-&-span & unmarred by the wear & tear incident to repeated transmission through the mails. Don't bother about the other items of non-letter mail—except, of course, Tryout.

S H's establishment seems to be taking hold very well for a new enterprise, & it looks as though it might succeed quite solidly. The location is good & free from competition, the shop is modest & tastefully attractive, & the merchandise is naturally of the best & most piquant possible order. She has the highest hopes for its future, & is certainly much more contented than when subjected to the uncertainties of outside employment.

As for Wednesday—ah, me! To think that as Belknap & I were basking in the warm sunlight of Central Park, a dark shadow of upheaval was flitting about de chists in de cornders of mah inner sanctum! And worse still—to think that my very windows are denuded of their dust-mellowed hangings in the interest of that vague illusion called household cleanliness! Eheu! Eheu! Why didn't I set my foot down & lock the door before I left!

Sorry you can't get around & participate in the present outing—& I still believe it would be easier than you think. You can't imagine how free from N.Y. bustle & restlessness this one quiet oasis is. I'll distribute your regards with appropriate cordiality—the Longs always send theirs most lavishly to you & A E P G. That was a great ride last Friday. In the morning we stopped at Van Cortlandt Park to let Dr. Long play a round of his beloved golf, & during this pause Belknap & I climbed a steep bank which afforded one of the finest views I have ever seen. Unlike my early Cable Cottage experience, I had no trouble at all in getting down! The West Point drill was exceedingly impressive. I had never been around the grounds before, & was highly interested to see the environment which gave the finishing touch to Manton Mitchell. Despite two or three classic buildings, the dominant motif is Gothic; many of the newer structures having been designed by the famous Ralph Adams Cram.[2] One mediaeval gate in particular is impressive beyond words.

I'll wager Miss Reynolds has stirred up the fire a bit today & yesterday, for the weather has taken a decided turn toward rawness. Heat is off here, but the kitchen gas range makes matters very comfortable in a few minutes. I've done some small odds & ends of Reed revision, but am still in doubt about old de Castro. I must make him his synopsis soon.

As for my diary—I believe my last postal took matters up to the time of my starting on the trip to see Orton. I met Orton at the Grand Central Station Saturday, 12:30 p.m., as per schedule; & we caught the 12:35 to Van Cortlandt Park. This place, as you know, is usually reached by the West Side Subway; but Orton knows the time-tables of the railway trains, & prefers to patronise their quicker service. We made the journey in about 20 minutes; & after a brief pause at the local shops began to wend our way toward Orton's apartment. Right then & there came a vast surprise; for I had always thought the Hudson shore line came rather near Broadway, so that no great area could exist in the vicinity unknown to me. For once in my life I was wrong, & a moment was enough to convince me of the real facts regarding the topographical layout. The truth is, that a whole separate & hidden world of semi-rusticity lies north of Spuyten Duyvil between Broadway (opposite the Van Cortlandt Mansion) & the river; almost unknown to the throng, & comprising sleepy colonial farmland & modern parklike estates in approximately equal parts. It is as striking & incredible an old-American oasis in the New York desert as is this southwestern region of Flatbush—in some ways even more striking, since the *rusticity* of the older stretches is vastly more profound & primitive. The curving road which gradually rises from Broadway & roughly parallels it for a while is the original Albany Post Road, & along its length are many fine specimens of colonial cottages virtually unchanged during the last 150 years. There are alluring ancient gardens with moss-grown bank walls, & farmyards whose quaintness has scarcely felt the touch of time. The incredible thing is that all this has existed hitherto without my knowledge. To think that I have been time & again within a stone's throw of the locality without even imagining its existence! I had thought that no more undiscovered worlds could remain in the New York region; but here, at last, was one more! A few apartments have invaded this cryptic countryside, but the invasion is not likely to be extensive. Of course, the absolute rusticity will go in time—the stone walls & straggling orchards & weedy banks by the roadside—but the change is less likely to be in the direction of apartment blocks, than toward a garden-street arrangement like our Freeman Parkway or upper Elmgrove Ave. or Blackstone Boulevard. Meanwhile much of the primal colonial atmosphere remains, & I was marvellously glad to see it before any urbanisation or ultra-civilisation comes to spoil it. The bulk of the territory (from about 225th to 262nd St) is exploited by a real estate firm under the name of Fieldstone Manor, & the restrictions both as to buildings & inhabitants are very strict. The whole terrain is marked by bold hills & curving roads, & many of the estates have picturesquely high, steep terraces. Along the river front are several impressive mansions with broad, sloping lawns, while at other points one encounters winding glens & deep, wooded ravines almost reminiscent of the "Sewer-Chimney Forest" or Butler Hospital Grotto.3

Orton lives in one of the few apartment houses of the district, quite near Broadway at the corner of the Albany Post Road. His flat has five rooms, & within that space he has managed to stow an almost record-breaking accumulation of family, consisting of one grandmother, one father, one mother, one wife, & one infant son—Geoffrey Dean Conrad Orton, aged 8 months. The furniture is all colonial, & many ancient family reliques are to be found on every hand. Orton's library is a magnificent accumulation, & the proportion of rare books explains why he finds $100.00 per week a somewhat small salary. The volumes are all housed on maple shelving which Orton made with his own hands, & form a collection considerably larger than my own. This library, moreover, is only a fraction of what Orton really owns—being merely what he has picked up since coming to N.Y. At home in Athol he has a family library just as large again! Orton's marriage seems to have been a characteristic bit of his precipitate, good-natured blundering; for his wife is a colourless, stupid, plaintive-voiced little Jew girl devoid of any visible sort of attractiveness or brilliancy. The baby, though, looks as though he would be a real Orton; & he will have the benefit of a colonial atmosphere & Vermont ancestral environment from the start. Orton's own family are delightful—real, old-time Yankee folks with unspoiled ways & a Massachusetts back-country twang. Mr. Orton senior has lost his left arm—whether in the Spanish War or through some peace-time accident I did not enquire. Orton's mother appears to be the real lady of the household, & was responsible for the excellent New England dinner with which I was regaled. The senior Ortons know Providence well, & have stopped many a time at the Narragansett. Mrs. Teachout—Orton's maternal grandmother—is in some respects the most delightful member of all the household; being a typical Yankee rustic gentlewoman of the fine old school. She is about 80 years old, & a connoisseur & creative artist in the domain of rag carpets, crazy quilts, & such-like products of the pristine New England family circle. If Orton is to be commiserated upon an uncongenial marriage, he is surely to be congratulated upon having so many of his own old family circle left to keep the ways of the past alive. With both of his parents & a grandmother as integral parts of his household, it cannot be long before his wife is at least moderately well assimilated culturally; whilst his little son can scarcely be less than a regular Yankee under the mass tutelage of a father, grandfather, grandmother, & great-grandmother of the ancient line. The Ortons come of a fine old line of English gentry with an ancient coat-of-arms. The original seat of the family in America is Farmington, near Hartford, Conn., though this particular branch has for generations been domiciled in Vermont. Orton senior owns the largest department store in Athol, but is evidently semi-retired, since he is able to spend so much time with his son. They all know Cook & Munn well—& like them both. Orton's uncle—the youngest brother of Orton senior—is in charge of a biological laboratory in Yonkers—you will recall my visit to his home when Orton lived there, in February 1926.

As I said, on this present occasion Orton's mother served a delightful dinner; & afterward Orton & I went out for a walk through the marvellous rural oasis in which he lives. Every turn was a fresh surprise to me, for I had no idea that any such hidden world existed within the corporate limits of Greater New York. At one point we struck a section as new to Orton as to me—where on a noble height stands a tall column (like our coming war memorial in P.O. Square) erected in honour of Henry Hudson, but at present strangely devoid of identifying tablets. Only through asking a stranger were we able to ascertain what the monument signifies. The whole scene was astonishingly beautiful, & was further favoured by delightful afternoon sunlight & warm weather. It left an impression which may best be summed up as Freeman Parkway indefinitely extended . . . . . certainly, there was absolutely nothing in the picture to suggest that New York was less than a thousand miles away. In the radiance of sunset we returned to Orton's apartment & were favoured with another excellent meal. (*How* in Pegana's name can I be 140 by St. John's Eve??!!) After this we discussed sundry literary & antiquarian topics, & rejoiced in Orton's coming return to New England. This summer he will send his family to Somers, N.Y. (by coincidence, the same quaint village with the elephant's effigy on a pole where Dr. Long spent much time in boyhood, & which he shewed me a week ago last Friday!) while he himself remains in N.Y. City. Then, if he can purchase a farm in the Vermont backwoods, he will retire thither for the rest of his life. He is thoroughly disgusted with N.Y. & wishes to break away from it for good. At length Orton took me to the subway in his automobile, & I returned to 395 E. 16th; reading en route an excellent work on architecture ("Sticks & Stones", by Lewis Mumford) which Orton had lent me. Arriving about 11, I retired at midnight, & was up at 9:30 a.m. Sunday. Sunday I did little save read the architectural book & the N.Y. Times, & write letters in the evening. Monday the 7th I rose at 8 a.m., wrote letters, went to see honest old McNeil at 2 p.m. The old boy was glad to have a visitor, & I helped correct the introductory chapter of the book he is writing.[4] Toward evening I walked Flatbushward across Prospect Park, Mac accompanying; leaving my host at the Ocean Ave. gate as I entered on the last lap of the journey. After a sumptuous dinner I accompanied S H to her shop (she keeps it open evenings & likes company there) & wrote letters in the secluded space behind the portieres; later returning with her to 395, & stopping en route at a drug store for ice cream. Since then I have been writing letters, & when this is concluded I shall retire—about 11 p.m. The next diary, then, will start with Tuesday morning.

Tomorrow I am reserving for my own work, & for some errands for S H. Wednesday I had intended to have Orton over here & accompany him to the meeting at Kirk's, but Sonny has just notified me of the presence in N.Y. of a man we would like to meet—Clifford Gessler, poet & editor of the Honolulu Star-Bulletin, with whom Belknap came into correspondence through sending his "Man from Genoa" for review[5]—so Orton & I may decide to go up to 230 & join the Child as he takes his distinguished friend to one or another of the museums. In the evening, of course, the gang will meet at Kirk's—& I fancy that Belknap may bring Gessler along. Thursday & Friday are open, but Saturday Orton is to take Sonny & me out to Paterson to see Mortonius. Sunday S H & I are to have dinner at Sonny's, & next Monday I may go to see honest old Mac again, since he was so pathetically eager to have me call soon & stay to supper with him. After that I shall be thinking of Washington trips & such like. Dwyer writes that his coming to N.Y. is less certain than he hoped a week ago, but I shall probably go to see him on his native heath anyway. The boat fare is very slight.

I must not close without mentioning the exquisite little grey kittycat with whom I played at a drug store near Orton's. He was the cutest little divvle I have seen in years; & the way he climbed up Grandpa's trousers & played with the Old Gentleman's watch-chain formed the extreme of captivating fascination. His mamma was recently killed by a motor, so his masters are taking extra precautions to safeguard his young life. More anon.

                  Yr aff Nephew & obt Servt

                      H P L

Notes

1. Josephus Daniels (1862–1948), Secretary of the Navy (1913–21). HPL refers to the fact that, on 2 May, Daniels stated that he would "put his foot down" against running on a third-party ticket in the upcoming presidential election.

2. Ralph Adams Cram (1863–1942), celebrated American architect who was a leader

of the Gothic revival movement. He was also the author of a slim book of weird tales, *Black Spirits and White* (1895), some stories of which HPL discussed in "Supernatural Horror in Literature."

3. For the "Sewer-Chimney Forest," see LDC/AEPG 254 and 256. "Butler Hospital Grotto" refers to an area on the grounds of Butler Hospital in Providence. HPL would customarily meet his mother there during the time of her confinement there (1919–21) rather than in the hospital itself.

4. Presumably *The Shores of Adventure; or, Exploring in the New World with Jacques Cartier* (New York: E. P. Dutton, 1929), McNeil's last published book.

5. Clifford Gessler (1893–1979), author of poetry volumes (*Kanaka Moon*, 1927; *Tropic Earth*, 1944), travel books (*Road My Body Goes*, 1937; *Hawaii: Isles of Enchantment*, 1937; *Tropic Landfall*, 1942), and other writings. His review of *A Man from Genoa* (*Honolulu Star-Bulletin*, 28 July 1928) is now reprinted in HPL and Clark Ashton Smith, *Dawnward Spire, Lonely Hill* 687.

[193]   [ALS] [HPL to LDC]

Thursday Afternoon
May 10, 1928

My dear daughter Lillian:—

I take my pen in hand to inform you of the safe arrival of the summer suit & accompanying matter, for the transmission of which I am abundantly grateful. I perceive that the postage came to 27¢—which must be relentlessly added to my bill! Needless to say, I was gratify'd by the Bulletin fragments enclosed; which fill up the gap to date, with the exception of last Sunday's Journal. I have perused them all with the keenest interest, including the separate cuttings & marked items. I reënclose the Whipple cutting for Grandma's red book & also send an item about a new restaurant opportunity—right in your daily line of march—of which you ought to avail yourself, at least to the extent of sampling its fare. I was interested to see that Pres. Edwards of the State College has such stalwart defenders.[1] Possibly the Bulletin was a little over-eager in its intensive crusading. The anecdote of the futuristic painting hung wrong side up caused considerable amusement at the meeting last night—whilst the reference to Providence's status among metropolitan centres will afford me material for many a boast when things as mundane as vulgar prosperity are under discussion. I also clipped a good deal from the Sunday Journal—including the admirable Gilbert Stuart portrait in the Rotogravure section.

I am enclosing—*to be saved carefully for my scrap book*—a cutting which Kirk has been carrying around in his pocket for a year, & which has some amusingly complimentary references to my fictional attempts. I met this young chap Wolf—a fat, genial person—on my last visit to N.Y., in Sept. 1926, but did not fancy he remembered me at all. He is wrong in saying that it was a tale of *mine* which caused an issue of *Weird Tales* to be barred from the stands in Indiana. The story in question was Eddy's "Loved Dead"—which, however, had much of my work in it.[2]

The belt duly came, & I shall wear it tomorrow if I go to ride with Sonny & his parents. Whether or not I do so, will depend on whether or not Belknap's uncle lives another day or two—his demise being hourly expected. Belknap's aunt is a Christian Scientist, but the patient's son by a former marriage sees to it that he has proper medical attention—even going so far as to call in an *osteopath* in addition to the regular physician.

As for my diary—I think I previously carried it through Monday, when I went to call on honest old Mac. Tuesday morning I was up early & wrote letters, & was pleased to receive a call from my small grandchild Belknap. On this occasion I shewed the child all around the Flatbush neighbourhood, & he was truly moved with admiration for an oasis so remote from the life & atmosphere of repellent New York. In the afternoon I decided to pay a couple of Manhattan calls which courtesy demanded, so visited the bookshops of both Loveman & Kirk. Loveman—in 59th St.—was very cordial, & sold me two books I had always wanted (Petronius' "Satyricon" & Apuleius' "Golden Ass") at an incredibly low rate—a dollar each for absolutely new, uncut copies—besides making me a present of an amateur book (Miss Hyde's poems) which has become a drug on the market. Whilst in this shop I was introduced to the son & the nephew of the head of the Anderson Galleries—Mitchell Kennerley, who was once a publisher & brought out the first American editions of Dunsany's work. The son—Mitchell Kennerley Jr.—was especially attractive & well-informed; though pathetically *fat* for a young man. He can't be over 25, yet makes Jeremiah Phillips look like a shadow by comparison. Safe to say, he'll never be 140 by St. John's Eve or even by Lammastide! The cousin was also very genial, & had read some of my weird stories. Equal cordiality held sway at Kirk's—this being my first visit to the attractive shop in W. 8th St. near Sixth Ave. After leaving there I proceeded to explore certain parts of Greenwich-Village to see how much of its colonial antiquity was impaired by modern decadence. Great was the devastation which I found. Varick St. as a Georgian relique is a thing of the past, whilst the tangle of the Minettas has been virtually ruined by the new subway & extension of Sixth Ave. Charlton St. has escaped the peril of this latter operation only to succumb in part to another—four of its best colonial houses being torn down to accomodate a wretched apartment-house whose use of Georgian motifs is only an insulting mockery. After this depressing spectacle I returned to 395, had dinner, & wrote all the evening in S H's shop. Retiring about midnight, I was up Wednesday at a moderate hour & did some errands for S H. I then went to the *barber's*—the local artist at 16th St & Cortelyou Road—& had an excellent haircut (tho' no better than Fernando King could give me) for the exorbitant sum of **75¢**. These select neighbourhood places charge more than the barber shops in downtown N.Y.—the standard metropolitan price being 60¢. I could have secured a haircut for only 40¢ had I been willing to patronise the Court St. joints which I frequented in Clinton St. days—but I thought I'd be festive this time.

For that afternoon I had an engagement with Orton—to shew him around the Flatbush oasis—& I kept it despite Belknap's wish to have me come up & meet a rather distinguished N.Y. visitor with whom he had come into touch—the poet Clifford Gessler of Hawaii, who is editor of the Honolulu Star-Bulletin & a lecturer of some note. Gessler had reviewed Sonny's "Man from Genoa" very favourably when it was sent to him, & had naturally looked up the child when he passed through the metropolis. He had wished to meet me also; & when Belknap relayed the wish to me, I asked Orton over the telephone whether he wouldn't like to change the scene of the colloquy to Belknap's. Orton, however, seemed very averse to any change of plan; so that—since my engagement with him was a prior one—I was compelled to forego the acquaintance of the celebrity. Gessler, by the way, says that Belknap is quite famous in San Francisco literary circles; "The [*sic*] Man from Genoa" being somewhat widely perused & discussed there. Well—Orton arrived at 3:30 p.m., & despite the weary greyness of the day we explored the entire Flatbush oasis. He was as strongly impressed as Belknap with its utter un-New-Yorkishness, though (as I have said in a previous diary) he himself lives in a delightfully rural oasis. At six o'clock—having stopped at the shop for instructions—we made the necessary purchases for a sumptuous repast, which S H served in due splendour a half-hour later. After that we took the subway for the gang meeting at Kirk's, arriving thither about 9 p.m. Orton is obliged to go to Vermont next Saturday, so that he cannot take Belknap & me to Paterson as planned. We shall probably go by 'bus.

The meeting was a good one, with Kirk, Orton, Belknap, Mac, myself, & Kleiner present. This was my first sight of good old Kleiner during the present visit, & he seems just the same as ever. The absent members were Morton, Loveman, & Talman. All sorts of things were discussed, & Kirk's wife served refreshments almost as lavish as Mrs. Long's typical ones. At 2 a.m. we dispersed—Orton & Belknap having left at 12:15 a.m.—& Kleiner, Mac, & I took to the B.M.T. subway for subsequent dispersal to our respective destinations. The next meeting will be at Kleiner's in the labyrinthine Bushwick section, & I have promised to act as guide for honest old Mac, who vows that he could never find his way about in such a tangle of involved streets which "don't lead nowheres"—as he expresses it. On this occasion I reached 395 & retired at 3:30 a.m.; rising this morning (Thu., May 10) at 9:30 a.m. & going through the pile of Bulletin back numbers. This noon—a *glorious* warm day— I set out for Prospect Park with enamel-cloth bag full of work & writing materials; resolved to do something with the de Castro book in order that I may make some kind of a report to the old geezer. It is now 3 p.m., & I hope I can have some progress to shew before I return to 395 for dinner at 6:30. Tomorrow I may or may not take a motor trip with the Longs, according to whether or not Belknap's uncle lives. Saturday I go to Paterson to see what that fat rascal Mortonius did with the rocks we sent him.[3] Sunday S H & I may or may not (according to the condition of Belknap's uncle) dine with the Longs. Then next Wednesday the Kleiner meeting will come. After that I shall be reflecting upon Washington–Annapolis–Alexandria–Richmond–Williamsburg matters. The spring suit looks very well, & I almost wish I had worn it today. I shall put on soft collars (which I have with me) when I go southward. By the way—Loveman tells me that C. A. Brandt, the Literary Editor of *Amazing Stories,* wants to get in touch with me before I go home. He has asked that I call him on the telephone some morning before 10 o'clock & arrange for a colloquy. This I shall probably do eventually—although I haven't forgotten that his skinflint magazine gave me only $25.00 (& that after long months & repeated requests!) for a story ("The Colour Out of Space") of the same length as one for which *Weird Tales* paid me *$165.00.*

The part of Prospect Park where I am now sitting is one of the most attractive rural spots I have ever beheld. I am seated upon a rock under delicately leaving trees, & before me winds a pebbly crystal brook in which a blithesome host of twittering birds are bathing. Passers-by are very few, & when I tire of this vantage-point I can seek another where diverse scenic effects prevail.

By the way—Belknap's friend Gessler is going to **Providence** tonight to deliver a lecture. I shall watch the Bulletin (which comes with admirable regularity) for particulars of the event. Possibly it will be at the Plantations Club—or if a free lecture, at Sayles or Alumnae Hall. I hope to see him as he returns through N.Y. Belknap has lent me a copy of his book—"Kanaka Moon"—& I find the poetry of a very high order.

This is a great afternoon! If it weren't that I've got to tackle de Castro's book, I'd hire a boat on the park lake & row around amongst the mystic wooded isles that dot the placid blue. I'll wager Roger Williams Park & Quinsnicket are flourishing in this weather! I must drop old de Castro a card & tell him I'll call on him soon. Belknap says he's getting impatient.

You might shew this to A E P G—& tell her I'll answer her note shortly. I forgot to bring it with me today.

Yr aff Nephew & obt Servt

H P L

Notes

1. Howard Edwards (1854–1930), president of Rhode Island College (1906–30). HPL refers to a dispute that arose at this time between Edwards and the director of the college's Agricultural Experiment Station, Burt L. Hartwell. Most of the faculty and alumni supported Edwards.

2. HPL refers to Howard Wolf, author of the column "Variety" for the *Akron Beacon Journal.* In his column of 12 December 1927 (p. 10), Wolf recounts how he met George Kirk

and HPL in New York. The column is reprinted in Cannon, *Lovecraft Remembered* 403–5.
3. Morton had visited HPL in early June 1927, and the two of them had gone to western Rhode Island to secure some mineral samples for Morton's museum.

[194]   [ALS] [HPL to LDC]

Monday Afternoon
May 14, 1928

My dear daughter Lillian:—

I take my pen in hand to say that I am well & hope you are the same. The particular pen in question is my regular Waterman, which I've just had fixed. It still scratches a bit, so that I think I'll take it down once more.

My diary, I believe, extended to Friday night—after my trip with the Longs to Stamford. Saturday I rose early & wrote all the morning, setting forth at noon for Paterson, to beard the one & only Mortonius in his den. I went by 'bus, but found the scenery so utterly rotten that I wished I'd gone by train. The 'bus line crosses to New Jersey by way of the new Electric Ferries at 23d St, landing at Weehawken, where the Burr–Hamilton duel took place in 1804. At this point the Palisades have been frightfully desecrated by oil tanks & factories, so that the landscape is truly pathetic. All the way to Paterson the road extends through ugly & depressing factory towns & monotonous flatlands. Paterson, however, has the bold ridges of the Watchung Range as a background; hence is scenically beautiful despite its infamous architectural ugliness & factory atmosphere.

I found the Museum a marvellously prepossessing place—nothing but the brick outer walls of the old stable having been allowed to remain. The whole lower floor is one vast exhibition hall containing miscellaneous objects—Indian & African relics, birds, insects, & butterflies, the old Submarine,[1] &c. &c. Upstairs the front half is all one large hall of minerals, whilst the rear half is subdivided into laboratory & offices. The mineral collection is not yet classified, so that the upper story is still closed to the public. One elderly attendant guards the lower floor whilst James Ferdinand lords it above in solitary majesty. I found the fat & genial Czar in his office, & his delight at having a visitor seemed to be unfeigned. Save for Kleiner, I am the first gang member to see the new Museum. Morton shewed me all the collection in detail, & afterward took me to dinner at his favourite restaurant—the same old place where we ate three years ago. He insisted on buying me a dollar course dinner despite my protests on behalf of my reducing campaign. How, oh, how, shall I be 140 by St. John's Eve!! Afterward we visited some of the wild & rugged scenery of the region—a rocky, daemoniack gorge which is a waterfall at high water, & the lofty eminence of Garrett's Mountain, whence we had an unparallelled view of all the neighbouring countryside. This precipitous crag—of which you'll find a picture in the folder we sent you—is really a magnificent thing; & quite outdoes our Neutaconkanut in intrinsic grandeur. I still prefer Neutaconkanut, though; since the spectacle of outspread Providence infinitely surpasses that of outspread Paterson. Atop Garrett's Mountain is a sinister & deserted stone tower, built years ago by an eccentric & now deceased millionaire. Lower on the slope is a spreading & ambitious Norman castle constructed by the same lavish person & now used as a sanitarium.

Having seen the sunset from this lofty point of vantage, we proceeded to James Ferdinand's rather seedy-looking apartment in Summer St. near the Museum. It is a five-room affair in a dingy old-time building called "The Franklin", & is maintained in the usual Morton way—slipshod, & without artistic neatness or decorative harmony. The principal contents are books & minerals, & I'll own that I've never yet seen so fine a private library. In books, Mortonius surely has the rest of the gang licked to a frazzle; his present collection comprising not only his own old library—which I saw years ago at his niggerville place in Harlem—but his mother's library as well. The massed result completely lines the walls of three rooms, & is grouped according to a very intelligent system of classification. Here we discussed things in general till nearly 11 p.m., at which time I took a train to N.Y. Arriving at 395 after midnight, I read the paper & retired about 2 a.m.

Sunday I arose about 10, read the N.Y. Times, & at noon set out with S H for a trip. First walking southward along Ocean Parkway, we later took the subway & proceeded toward Bryn Mawr Park, where S H wished to look over her piece of real estate. As she may have mentioned to you or A E P G, she has managed to sell the long, narrow lot & pay fully for the more artistic triangle by Tibbets' Brook—so that there are now no yearly expenses save taxes. She has let the Homeland Co. list the property for re-sale, though now & then half-tempted to try building a small Colonial house in case her present venture proves really remunerative. Going to the end of the West Side Subway—Van Cortlandt Park—we changed to a Yonkers car, & at Yonkers took the 'bus for Bryn Mawr Park. The scene was just as beautiful as ever, & the property is certainly improving without the least symptom of deterioration. After an interesting talk with the Homeland representative on the plot—a genial person named McGuire—we reëmbarked for Yonkers & returned to N.Y. by the railway along the shore—now operated with electric trains. Then subway to 395, a reprehensibly elaborate repast, a perusal of the Brooklyn Sunday Eagle, & retiring at 12 midnight.

Today—Monday—I rose at 10 a.m., did some writing, went to Manhattan for some errands, returned to Flatbush at 3 o'clock & got S H some lunch from a neighbouring cafeteria, & have now gone to the rural ravine in Prospect Park for letter-writing & de Castro work. I shall have to hurry like the deuce with this latter, but hope to be able to shew the old boy something by tomorrow or Wednesday. It is now 5:30 p.m. At 6:30 I shall be back at 395 for dinner, & shall later do more de Castro work at S H's shop. That will finish Monday, so that the next diary will begin with Tuesday. Wednesday night the gang meets at Kleiner's, & (as I have previously said) I shall call at honest old Mac's at 7 to guide him thither.

Enclosed is some antiquarian material which may possibly prove of interest. I also enclose my small grandchild's latest portrait—taken on one of those quarter-in-the-slot self-photographing machines—which shews a very serious, reflective, moon-faced, & almost-moustached little cynic indeed! Save this for my collection. And by the way—you might send back that extravagant praise of me by Kirk's friend, since some of the gang have expressed a wish to see it soon. Netopian safely arrived & gratefully perused. Shall be glad to see High Lights of History (Apr 26–May 3) whenever convenient to you. And I wouldn't mind a look at the Sunday Journals of May 6 & 13 if some cheap & easy way of sending them happened to present itself. Nothing like being up to date!

More diary later. This is a great afternoon, & the birds & squirrels are delectably lively.

Yr aff Nephew & obt Servt
H P L

Notes

1. The Paterson Museum had acquired the *Fenian Ram* (launched in 1881), the first practical submarine, built by John Philip Holland (1840–1914), an Irish engineer who had emigrated to the U.S. The vessel had been commissioned by the Irish Fenian Brotherhood.

[195]   [ALS] [HPL to LDC]

Thursday Night
May 17, 1928.

My dear daughter Lillian:—

Yrs. of yesterday duly arrived, & again I take my still unfixed pen in hand. It will not cost any more to have it further rectified, & I certainly mean to attend to it shortly.

Yes—of course those figures atop Garrett Rock are Mortonius & me! It was a great old climb, & the resultant panorama surpassed anything I had expected. At that distance, & in the golden magic of sunset, all the ugliness of Paterson fell away; & we beheld only an enchanted city of spires & domes which might have been Sarnath or Carcassonne or Samarcand for all we could tell. James Ferdinand certainly knows how to manage a museum, & he has made marvellous use of the limited space at his disposal. What I envy him most, though, is his *library*. I thought that Cook had the best library of anybody in the gang, but now realise that the actual championship belongs to Mortonius.

I haven't calculated my exact time schedule ahead, but fancy I shall do my southern adventuring around the turn of the month & be home about the first week or so in June. The weather has been too cool for really satisfactory exploration, & I've been so busy that so far I haven't even seen the places in N.Y. that I want to look up—save the Jumel Mansion, which Sonny & I visited Tuesday. Too bad we couldn't get in when you were there—I enclose a couple of postals illustrating interior treasures, just to tantalise you! I'd like to meet the genial curator again some time—he wasn't in on this occasion. He is now 88, & as active as any young fellow. I haven't worn the summer suit yet, but shall need it on the southerly trip. Sonny has bought his new straw hat—a black-banded, conservative affair of which his Grandpa Theobald thoroughly approves—& the Old Gentleman may shortly follow suit. The Child got his at Truly Warner's, & I fancy I shall try the same joint. I shall wear my new purchase south—& probably home as well, shipping my brown felt veteran home by parcel post. Very shortly I shall have to attend to my other end also—obtaining my new Regals whilst I get the present pair tapped. After the repairs, I shall resume the old shoes & send the new ones home by parcel post. I have some soft collars along, & think I shall adopt them on the southern trip. I may & may not get to Kenmore. It will depend mainly on my finances, & the question of how economically I can do Washington, Annapolis, & Alexandria. If Sechrist is at home, I may stop with him in Washington; thus saving Y M C A rent.

I shall be glad to see the parcel post package of Sunday Journals &c. Keep for me the Vermont picture on the cover of the N.Y. Times magazine for last Sunday. That is the only Times item which I want kept. The one I have here I have folded to lend to correspondents, but I want an unfolded copy for my permanent files. Yes—I saw by the Bulletin that the Sunday Journal meant to print its feature & book section in magazine form. I shall be exceedingly interested to see it. The reminiscence of cycling days will indeed fill me with envy—I knew that bicycles were still used in Europe, & wish they were not obsolete here. If I can ever get hold of any real cash, I shall certainly obtain a modest Ford—which may be regarded as the bicycle's lineal descendant. I am surprised to hear that the Guernsey has undergone such a metamorphosis & absorption—bless my soul! While I am absent in the enemy's country, the enemy steals around to Providence & captures strategic points! But if they keep up the St. Regis food standard you will have no reason to complain. You doubtless recall the excellent food & liberal portions served at the Times Square St. Regis at Broadway & 43d St. I wonder whether the Guernsey Plaza will still be a jazz-orchestra dancing place when it is reopened? If it fails, it will serve people right for tearing down the stately old Butler Mansion!

Old de Castro still hems & haws about that Bierce revision job, & I don't yet know just how able he is to pay. It is clear that he wants it badly—he calls up now & then on the telephone, & came over to 395 in person yesterday morning, as you'll see by the official diary postal sent to A E P G. Last night I took him to the gang meeting at Kleiner's, where he entertained everybody with his loquacious egotism & pompous reminiscences of intimacies with the great. Old 'Dolph obviously wants the book in a hurry—& without an advance fee. I am endeavouring to convince him that he won't get it thus! His latest scheme is to have me do the book & submit it to some literary magazine for first publication—dividing the profits equally. All this *sounds* well— but I think I'd like to see some cold cash first.

As a matter of coincidence—guess who has just called me up on the telephone, while I have been writing this letter? *Henneberger*—the glib Weird Tales promoter of other years!! His voice sounds as suave as ever—he got my telephone number from Little Belknap, & hastened to exchange remarks with the Old Gentleman to whom he still owes forty dollars. He is in N.Y. for some time—staying up near 181st St.—& he invites both S H & me to take dinner with him some time soon. Apparently his wife & family are with him on this excursion. I spoke civilly to the young reprobate, but took care not to broach the subject of business. I don't think he is really *dishonest,* but he is so blithely *irresponsible* that I wouldn't trust him across the street with a plugged nickel. I hope he forgets his invitation & doesn't set any date!

Stamford is quite a place—makes one think of Pawtucket or Woonsocket or Brockton or Taunton or Fitchburg. I didn't know that the Wayland Square Jacksons now reside there. It would have been amusing indeed to step back into a Providence past antedating my own birth!

On account of the expected death of Belknap's uncle, the Friday trip has been cancelled tomorrow. In the evening I may have a call from Loveman, who telephoned his intention of coming. The next gang meeting will be at Belknap's unless developments in the case of his uncle forestall it. My diary for Tuesday, Wednesday, & Thursday will be found on postcards to A E P G, which she will doubtless bring over Sunday. Apparently she is having quite an exciting time attending to the asinine Ripley upheaval.

Cook has sent me proofs of "The Shunned House", & Belknap is now writing a preface for it. I don't know when the book will be issued, but it will be interesting to step into the ranks of book authors like Sonny & Loveman & Clark Ashton Smith & Wandrei!

Yr aff nephew & obt Servt

H P L

[196]   [ALS] [HPL to LDC]

Saturday Night
May 19, 1928.

My dear daughter Lillian:—

I take my pen in hand to continue my diary, which

stopped with Thursday night. Friday I arose at 9 a.m., read & wrote letters, & went out for various errands; writing again for the major part of the afternoon. In the evening Loveman came over, & about 10 p.m. we started on a nocturnal walk toward downtown Brooklyn in the manner of bygone years. After passing through the Georgian byway of Albemarle Terrace & beholding the ancient Dutch church & churchyard we stopped to observe 259 Parkside Avenue & to note the slow deterioration now overtaking its neighbourhood. After that we walked through Prospect Park, which was very glamorous in the mist & lamplight, emerging finally on the impressively Roman-arched expanse of the Plaza. Thence our path led along seedy Flatbush Ave. & dingy State St., till at last we stood on that most hateful of corners—*169 Clinton St.!* We had expected to find the marks of decay & vacancy which Loveman had noted some months ago, but instead beheld a fresh coat of paint, & all the concomitant marks of rehabilitation. The landscape was very little changed—same old dismal oppressiveness & incipient squalor. After muttering an appropriate curse we turned along once-familiar paths toward Loveman's house— observing as we did so the new tall buildings of the Borough Hall section, whose mist-lost pinnacles lent a novel background of mysticism & wonder to the dreary scene. I stayed at Loveman's until 1 a.m., conversing & appreciating the various objets d'art distributed about his room. It is a pity that he will soon have to leave that congenial haven which we found for him, but the mounting financial difficulties between the elderly Laverty sisters will presently make the sale of the property necessary. At 1 o'clock we adjourned to a cafeteria near the Clark St. subway station, & at 2 I returned to 395, retiring at 3 a.m.

Saturday the 19th I rose at 10 a.m. & did some reading & writing. At 2 p.m. I set forth on a lone trip of exploration, in quest of two historic houses & one historic site which I had never seen before, but which I had long been anxious to visit.

First on the list was the famous Dutch farmhouse of Capt. Jan Martense Schenck Van Nydeck, built from the timbers of a privateer in 1656, & still preserved in excellent condition without alterations. This is the oldest house within the corporate limits of New York City, & probably the oldest in New York State as well. It is one of only two surviving houses in Greater N.Y. built during the actual sovereignty of the Holland States-General—the other being the Nicholas Schenck homestead, which stood next on my visiting list. This notable object stands near the so-called Mill Basin in Flatlands, or southeastern Flatbush, a considerable distance beyond the Cortelyou Rd. neighbourhood. The district is given over to factories & cheap houses, & the terrain is one of flat salt marshland & beach sand. Reaching the place by surface car, I found it fully up to expectations; & I shall certainly recommend it as a major sight to be seen by all metropolitan visitors. It is amusing to reflect that I

Jan Schenck ho. 1656

myself never found it before—but as I once told you, I had temporarily lost my set of directions during my former N.Y. sojourn. Capt. Schenck, the builder, was a privateer of note, & suspected of being a pirate. During the Revolution the house was owned & occupied by Joris Martense of Flatbush, & it was there that Maj. Moncrief of His Majesty's forces was captured by the rebel captain William Mariner. Having seen the Jan Schenck house, I now proceeded by a long & circuitous surface & elevated journey to the dingy seaside suburb of Canarsie, to view the other of the two Schenck homesteads—the Nicholas Schenck house, built in 1659 & now in a painful state of decrepitude. This is a Dutch gambrel-roofer now standing in one corner of Canarsie Beach Park, & surrounded by a palisade to guard against the danger of its possible collapse. The city may some day restore it to strength & splendour, but action in this direction is exasperatingly slow. During the Revolution this house was used as headquarters for a division of His Majesty's forces, though its owners were permitted to continue their occupancy. Its appearance today is very depressing—& I greatly fear the upper story will cave in before many weeks have passed. This being seen, I turned via elevated to my third & last destination—the site of the old stone Cortelyou house (1699) at 3d St & 5th Ave in the Gowanus district of Brooklyn, not far from honest old Mac's. The lower story still exists in a *buried* state in the backyard of a deserted building, & there are rumours that the city may excavate it & make a public park of the place. It was at this farmhouse that the Battle of Long Island was most hotly waged, a fact commemorated by a bronze tablet that broods squalidly in the shadow of the elevated. Having viewed this site, I proceeded to 395 by subway, had dinner, & have since been writing letters. My next diary will begin with Sunday the 20th. More soon.

Yr aff Nephew & obt Servt
H P L

[197]   [ALS] [HPL to LDC]

Wednesday Night
May 23, 1928

My dear daughter Lillian:—

As I take my pen in hand to reply to your esteemed communication of the 22nd, I must lose no time in imparting to you the *genealogical* research which Talman & I this afternoon accomplish'd at the publick library, with the aid of John C. Cooley's book on the Rathbone family, & other authorities. Pray get out your charts & prepare to set down the most important addition to our family stock of ancestral information which we have had since Dr. Clark's tracing of the Whipple line! In a word, *we have traced the Rathbone line clearly, & without a break, back to the original Richard Rathbone of England,* who came to the colonies in the 17th century, & who had married, prior to his advent, one *Marion Whipple,* sister of the Capt. John Whipple who subsequently emigrated to *Ipswich, Mass.,* & whose Ipswich homestead I last year visited. This discovery brings us a wholly distinct Whipple line, only distantly related to our R.I. Whipples. Here is the complete line from Rhoby & Sarah Rathbone (your grand-mothers & my great-grandmothers) up:

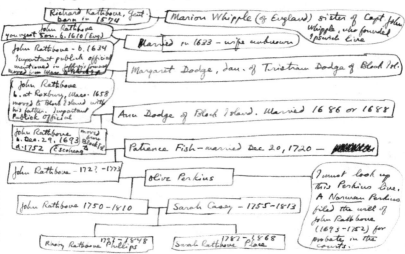

We are now, for the first time, *completely placed* as regards the whole Rathbone family in America; i.e., we can now figure out our exact relationship to any other Rathbone in the country, since they all come from Richard Rathbone & his wife Marion Whipple. It is interesting to note that we have a double share of the blood of the Block Island *Dodges,* now so famous as dar-ing pilots. I shall investigate this line further. Talman has looked up the *Fish* line, (mother of the John Rathbone who married Olive Perkins) & finds that they have an excellent coat-of-arms. I shall gather more data, if possible, before my return. Throughout the seventeenth century the Rathbones seem to have been of extreme importance in Rhode Island. We also gave the Whipple line some attention, & appear to have found that the Revolutionary captain Benijah Whipple was half-brother of our ancestor Benedict W.—i.e., a son of Benjamin W. & his *first* wife Sarah Bernon. But unless new data has been uncovered since 1873, (the date of the Whipple book we consulted) we shall *never* know our exact relationship to Capt. Abraham Whipple the privateer & naval of-ficer—for odd as it may seem, no one can place the father of this celebrated personage, although he undoubtedly came from the North Providence Whip-ples.[1] But the big feat of the season is completing our Rathbone lineage. This really gives us—in connexion with all the other lines pushed through to the first American member (i.e., Casey, Place, Hazard, Whipple, Mathewson, Field, Clemence, Brownell, &c)—a far from contemptible array of genealogical information. I hope to do some research on the *Phillips* line soon.

———

Needless to say, your epistle was of great interest; as were likewise the two Sunday Journals which safely arrived by parcel post. I like the new magazine section exceedingly, & hope this convenient feature will be retained. I am saving the bicycle article & other things—bless my soul, but I'll have a pasting siege when I get back! I must get some more of those cardboard files at Woolworth's.

Glad to hear the news—& to learn that our local niggerville is disappearing. As I said long ago, the picturesque Providence custom of tolerating negro settlements amidst good neighbourhoods is bound to perish. This is the *third* to vanish within my recollection—Grotto Village & Cole's Village being the other two. I fancy the Wayland Ave. one will be next, with the large Meeting St. settlement after that. The two permanent local niggervilles will undoubtedly be Winter St. & Constitution Hill.

Glad the new Sharpe estate promises picturesque developments. There's no place like the ancient hill, & I fancy the advance of the slums is definitely checked. Now the logical thing to do is to *push back* the slums if possible, & save such places as northern Benefit St., Jenckes St., &c. Mrs. Pettis's home must be in a sort of semi-slum.

End so Meesder Frenk, who iss ah poor men, shood get it de maw-nee to feegs ubb de house-a'ready by No. 10!! Oy, oy! Vot a cost! Vot a cost! De piezza, de belcony posd, de paindt . . . . . . oy, he shell get ruint, he shell get ruint! I hope he won't try to do any interior decorating in my study—the upheaval in de cornders must be bad enough as it is! Speaking of cornders—& cornder cupboards—I'm glad that the estimable Mr. Nutting has come out so well in his litigation. I have the Susanna Hopkins grave cutting.

I trust the renamed Guernsey is keeping up to its former standards—I noticed its St Regis advertisement in the Sunday Journal. As for *straw hats*—I am considering your advice with mature deliberation, & am almost inclined to follow it. In fact, I had thought of the same thing myself; recalling how my 1927 straw was ruined by rain in Portsmouth & Gloucester last August. I may yet wait & make my purchase in Providence. The same goes for *Regals*, too. Last Monday S H took my old shoes out to a local cobbler & brought them back in an hour's time—completely renovated, & with new thick soles & rubber heels. It only cost $1.35, & I fancy the things will wear for months if not years.

Sonny's uncle still hovers betwixt life & death. A few nights ago all his children & grandchildren were summoned to his bedside about 2 a.m. for a last farewell, but he did not expire as then feared. The meeting for tonight at Belknap's was cancelled; but unless something happens, the Longs want me to accompany them on their motor trip next Friday. Belknap's aunt is going ahead with the travel-book plan—the MS. being sent this evening to Cook. Loveman may not lose his boarding-place till fall, since the Laverty sisters have patched up a sort of truce. The gentle old lady we saw is apparently the injured party in the dispute—Loveman sympathises strongly with her. He is going on a visit to Cleveland next week, & will later make a New England tour—on book business—including *Providence*. As for me—I guess I'm paying for all my food & incidental expenses. In about a week I shall probably get on the move, first visiting Bernard Dwyer up the Hudson, & then staging the long anticipated southerly odyssey. I shall prolong some of my social activity after my return; for Mortonius will attend the Harvard Commencement, & I may meet him for a day around Boston before his advent to Providence. Late in June we shall be sampling Mrs. Maxfield's 28 flavours of ice cream at Warren. *Wandrei* may come East again, too.[2]

As for my diary—I believe I last brought it up to Saturday night. Sunday the 20th I rose at 11 a.m., read the Times, & went out for an afternoon exploring trip whilst S H rested. My route covered colonial & Victorian Manhattan—the tip of the island, (Fraunces' Tavern &c) Bowery Village, Gramercy Park, & Murray Hill—ending up at 42nd St. It was all territory previously known to me, & I was pleased to see that less change had occurred than in Greenwich Village. Returning to 395, I had a sumptuous dinner & went out with S H to the cinema; (first I've seen since last August) retiring, after a season of reading, at 3 a.m. Monday the 21st I rose at 10:30 a.m. & wrote letters. In the afternoon I paid a visit to Theodore Roosevelt's birthplace at 28 E. 20th St., which I had never entered before, & was fascinated by the ugly but homelike Victorian atmosphere, & by the plentiful & magnificently arranged reliques of the greatest American of my generation. Under separate cover I am sending a set of postcards of this impressive shrine, & I am herewith enclosing some circulars which describe it much better than I could. I remained until closing-time, after which I returned to 395 for dinner. In the evening I went up to Sonny's & accompanied him in a call on that wily old braggart De Castro, who had expressed a very urgent wish to see us. As usual he boasted & haggled inconclusively, tried to persuade me to undertake work on a promissory basis, & regaled us with tedious anecdotes of how he secured the election of Roosevelt, Taft, & Harding as Presidents. According to himself, he is apparently America's foremost power behind the throne! But Belknap & his aged grandpa were not born yesterday, so that we finally made a highly ceremonious exit on the very rational basis of "no pay, no work"! Returning to 395, I retired at 1 a.m.

Tuesday the 22nd I rose at 12:00 noon & wrote letters. At 3 p.m. that old leech De Castro came around, & I could not get rid of him in any way. He was full of plans for making both our fortunes—to say nothing of Belknap's—& advised me to do all sorts of things from revising his immortal works to going to Portugal & writing a descriptive treatise on that country.

He says he is going to Europe next week on an important mission. I hope so. After a couple of hours of rhetoric, I told my voluble guest that I had an engagement to meet Loveman at his shop at 6 o'clock—& he obligingly trailed along with me. He says he is *reducing*, (Pegāna knows he needs it!) but nevertheless stopped at a restaurant near the subway station & consumed an enormous slice of strawberry shortcake to stay his gastric gnawings until he might reach home & absorb the sumptuous meal prepared by his solicitous spouse. We reached Loveman's bookstall (in East 59th St.) on time, & De Castro finally broke away after being introduced to everybody in the place. His last words to me were an urgent request to meet him the following noon for a call on a man who might probably . . . . er, that is, *possibly* . . . . be interested in a gigantic money-making publishing venture, &c. &c. &c. I told him I would telephone him if I could go . . . . . & I did not telephone. Heaven speed him to Europe unless he wants to fork over 150 fish in advance for the Bierce revision!

Well—what Loveman had planned for the evening was to have me meet three friends of his for dinner at a restaurant, & to spend the evening at the Greenwich Village home of one of them. The restaurant was an excellent French one in West 45th St., & all three fellows proved delightful. One was a quaint youngish professor named White. Another was a budding short story writer named Paul Allen. The third, a vivacious, intelligent youth whom they called "Ted" Blanchard, was from **East Greenwich, R.I.**; & discussed the widening of the post road & the 'busses to Apponaug with all the eclat & assurance of a regular guy from God's country. I ordered spaghetti, coffee, & ice cream, whilst the others gorged themselves sybaritically on a huge table d'hote course dinner whose central feature was roast chicken. At length the parting came—Blanchard going to the theatre to see a revival of "She Stoops to Conquer",[3] White going home to write, & Allen taking Loveman & me home with him. The Allen flat is at 88 Horatio St., in a semi-antique district, but not till we entered did I realise why Loveman had had me invited there. Then I saw the reason—& *what* a reason! Bless Grandpa's bones, *what* a 'ittle **kittie!!!** His name is "Boojum", & he is about two months old. His head is tigerish Maltese, his paws & tail are dark tiger, & the rest of him is white. His length is about 8 or ten inches . . . . yet within that brief compass what a cosmos of kinetic & fatigueless playfulness resides!! The precious little atom was not still a second, but rolled & chased & boxed & leaped & tumbled & cavorted all the evening without intermission. He climbed & chewed his way all over his Grandpa Theobald, & certainly kept the old gentleman well absorbed & entertained throughout the session. At odd moments my host's books, wife, old china, & furniture were pointed out to me. Tea, I believe, was served. But my one persistent impression is of small "Boojum". As adieux were exchanged, I was given the loan of a clothes-brush—at whose moving bristles Boojum leaped ecstatically even as I strove to remove his capillary vestiges. My wrists still bear the delicate tattooing of his delicate claws—& as I gaze reminiscently at the artless tracery I again give vent to the sententious reflection—*some* kitty-cat! As Loveman & I were returning to Brooklyn on the subway we ran accidentally into *Talman;* who, as coincidence would have it, had been trying to get me by telephone all the evening to arrange an all-day tour of his ancestral countryside on the other side of the Hudson. We repaired at once to a cafeteria near the Clark St. station, & after Loveman's departure went to Talman's room—where we talked art, genealogy, bookplates, heraldry, & exploration until 3 a.m. In the end we made two engagements instead of one—Wednesday to pursue genealogy at the library, & Thursday to make the great excursion. Returning to 395, I retired at 4 a.m. & was up today—Wednesday the 23d—at 11 a.m. Wednesday morning I did some errands for S H. Belknap telephoned, & I included him in the afternoon's genealogical engagement at 2 o'clock. I reached the library on time, finding Talman there & soon greeting Little Sonny. There then followed a period of intensive delving, during which Talman helped both Belknap & me unravel the mysteries of the ponderous tomes touching on our respective ancestries. The crowning achievement of the day was my completion of the Rathbone line straight back to Richard Rathbone, Gent., of England. I shall make similar researches on the Perkins, Phillips, Dyer, &c. lines before leaving the radius of the N.Y. library.

About 3 o'clock we adjourned to visit the Dyckman cottage far north on Manhattan Island—which you have not seen, but which I have pointed out to A E P G. This is the best preserved Dutch farmhouse & museum in America—& I will give you an idea of its nature by means of postcards mailed under separate cover with the Roosevelt cards. We took the west side subway to 207th St. & reached the cottage about 4, lingering appreciatively over its varied delights. Later we took a walk through the wild woodland of Inwood—a permanent reservation of the Quinsnicket type—seeing the great old tulip tree under which Henry Hudson treated with the Indians, & the rock caves in the hillsides where the Indians used to make their winter homes. We emerged to the world of decadent modernity near the Dyckman St. subway station—our trip parallelling almost exactly one taken by Morton, Belknap, & me in Septr. 1922—nearly six years ago. In that interval the Dyckman St. region has changed from virtual open country to a dreary apartment-house desert.

Returning to 395, I had an excellent dinner & have since been busy writing. I must soon cease, for my ambitious trip of the morrow with Talman will necessitate my rising at *4 a.m.*—since I am to meet him at the Clark St. subway station at 5:30 a.m. preparatory to catching the 6:15 for Spring Valley. We are going to his home, & he is then going to take me out in his automobile—shewing me the ancient Dutch region where he was born & bred, & where all his ancestors have dwelt for the last 300 years. It will be a great experience, & you can expect quite a travelogue based upon it. In the afternoon we may cross by ferry to Tarrytown on the east shore, & explore the Washington Irving country—including the 1690 Dutch church at Sleepy Hollow.

Pegāna grant us good weather—& grant me the power to be—& stay—awake at 4 a.m.!

As for incidentals—my revisory clients are doing very well. Wright of *Weird Tales* has accepted De Castro's novelette[4] (which spoiled my whole winter & for which I received only $16.00) for *$175.00*, & has also taken "The Curse of Yig", which I wrote for $20.00 from Mrs. Reed's notes, for $45.00. I hope that I can banish revision sufficiently this summer to write a few things of my own—it would really be financially profitable as well as aesthetically preferable. I am expecting a Reed cheque of $28.25 for back work, & have one more plot to write up at a dollar per page. Sonny is busying himself with revision like Grandpa's little man—our joint advertisement will soon appear in *Weird Tales.*

And so it goes. More soon. Give my regards—& S H's—to everybody, including any kitty-cats whom you may encounter. The size of this epistle necessitates its transmission in one of those long & rotten envelopes. Here's hoping it will hold together till it reaches you!

With sincerest compliments, believe me,

Yr moſt aff. Nephew & obt Servt

H P L

[On envelope? In RHB's handwriting:] Well, I made it! (Vide within) It is now 5 a.m., & I am on the station platform bound to meet Talman!

Notes

1. Commodore Abraham Whipple (1733–1819) and HPL's great-great-grandmother Esther Whipple (1767–1842) were both descended from the Providence settler John Whipple (1617–1685). Thus, HPL was a third cousin, four times removed, of Commodore Abraham Whipple.

2. Wandrei, who had visited HPL in 1927, did not return to Providence until 1932.

3. Oliver Goldsmith's *She Stoops to Conquer* (1771) was revived in May 1928 at Erlanger's Theatre (246 West 44th Street) in May 1928. It was staged by William Seymour and starred Fay Bainter, Lawrence D'Orsay, and Horace Braham.

4. "The Last Test."

[198]   [ANS postcard][1] [HPL to LDC]

[Postmarked Tarrytown, N.Y.,
24 May 1928]

Still on the move amidst colonial antiquities. This is the heart of the Washington Irving country—Sleepy Hollow. Talman left me at Nyack, on his own side of the Hudson, & I have come here by ferry. I've wanted to see this church for years. More later—watch for the travelogue!

Yr aff Nephew & obt Servt

H P L

Notes

1. *Front:* Old Dutch Church, "Erected 1685," Tarrytown, N.Y.

[199]   [ANS postcard]¹ [HPL and Wilfred B. Talman to LDC]
[Postmark obliterated;
25 May 1928]
Having a great time—wait for my travelogue! Surprisingly beautiful scenery &
fascinating antiquities. I owe my expert guidance to the undersigned member
of the landed gentry of the region.
Yr aff Nephew & obt Servt
H P L

Wilfred B. Talman

Notes

1. *Front:* '76 House, Major Andre's Prison, Tappan, N.Y.

[200]   [ANS postcard]¹ [HPL and FBL to LDC]
[Postmarked Spring Valley, N.Y.,
26 May 1928]
Taking today's hosts to see the scene of my yesterday's revels! Great trip!
Yr aff Nephew & obt Servt
H P L

Francis Lord Belknap.

Notes

1. *Front:* High School, Spring Valley, N.Y. Postmarked erroneously as 25 May.

[201]   [ALS] [HPL to LDC]
Saturday Night
[27 May 1928]
My dear daughter Lillian:—
            I take my pen in hand to continue the diary,
whose last entry was for Wednesday the 23d. As you may infer from enve-
lope-inscription & cards, I did manage to rise Thursday at 4 a.m. & meet
Talman at 5:30 at the subway station. Crossing to New Jersey in the Hudson
Tubes, we caught the 6:15 for Spring Valley; enjoying a long & leisurely journey of the typical Erie-accomodation kind. The scenery, at first flat & unin-

teresting, grew better & better as we fared north & west; till at length we reach'd a region comparing quite favourably with the typical New-England landscape. Shortly after 8 we reached the village of Spring Valley—a wretchedly ugly place of about 3000 inhabitants—& set out on foot for that adjacent rural region in which the Talman family have dwelt for the past 300 years. The route quickly became very pretty, & after something more than a mile we attained the broad acres of the Talman estate—which adjoins on the north the celebrated school for girls conducted by Edwin Gould, Esq., of the well-known family. "Knollwood", the Talman home, is a spacious square edifice of rubble stone & clapboards built in 1905 by the present owner & set on a gentle rise far back from the roadway, with which it is connected by a tree-lined driveway & stone pillar'd gate. Its situation has a very high landscape value, & was carefully planned in every detail by Mr. Talman. Northward & southward are great sweeps of exquisite country, whilst across the road are the graceful trees of an alluring wood. The lawns stretching toward the road are extensive & well-kept, & near the house take the form of double terraces. Stables & other farm buildings are in the rear, & behind them are the orchards & cultivated fields. Within, the house is furnished with excellent taste, many family antiques being included in the equipment. The hall clock is over three centuries old, & was brought from Amsterdam by the first Tallman to emigrate to the New-Netherland colony. Many Chinese objects—due to a son who is a missionary in China—add a note of the exotick to a decorative scheme predominantly early-American. The Talman family consists at present of Mr. & Mrs. Talman & an elderly maiden sister of Mr. Talman's—all well-bred & affable, & true representatives of the ancient Dutch aristocracy of the region. Mr. Talman has several sons, most of whom are clergymen; but Wilfred is the only one who has remained within a visiting distance of home. He is the youngest.

Arriving at Talman's home at 8:30 a.m., we were hospitably regaled with breakfast. Mr. Talman said grace before the meal, being of a simple devoutness in keeping with his position as a leading rural 'squire of the region. He is of wholesome & markedly rustic aspect, though no longer engaged in the business of agriculture. He is vice-president of the local bank. Talman having shew'd me the house & its family treasures, we set out upon our antiquarian pilgrimage around the region. The Talmans have two automobiles, & for our expedition the older one was chosen on account of the roughness & muddiness of the back roads we design'd to traverse. The day was ideal for sightseeing, & the winding ways beckoned invitingly through new-plough'd fields & along picturesque alternations of hill & dale, stone-wall'd meadow & brook-bubbling grove. Colonial farmsteads were of surprising numerousness, & Talman took pains to acquaint me with all the minutiae of the antient architecture. You can get a general idea of the type from having seen the Lefferts Cottage at the edge of Prospect Park—& from consulting those views of the

Dyckman house which I lately sent. In Talman's particular region, the houses are of a somewhat more primitive cast—only a story & a half in height, & with the upper story unplastered & unpartitioned. The lower half, & sometimes all the gable ends, is almost invariably constructed of the native brownstone of the region; roughly dressed in the earlier specimens, but quite artistically squared & smoothed in the more ambitious houses of the later 18th century. Most of the dwellings are augmented by additions—ells or lean-to's—built at various times during the colonial period. Some are spoilt by tawdry Victorian excrescences added by recent owners, & a few have been very happily preserved or restored in their original condition. The outer doors are double—in the Dutch fashion, with separate upper & lower halves—except where ugly modern doors have been substituted. In this particular region the dates of the buildings vary from 1690 to about 1800. The very earliest structures have plain peaked roofs, but the characteristic Dutch gambrel with short upper pitch & concavely curving lower pitch soon gained universal ascendancy. One house—the home of Major Smith, an ancestor of Talman's—we explored on the inside as well as outside, it being now inhabited by a worthy peasant family friendly to the 'squire's folk. In this edifice I was shewn the unprotected staircase down which Major Smith fell (without injury) whilst practicing a military drill in his attic in 1754.

Thus was spent the morning, amidst the pleasing scenery of an antient countryside, & in close communion with the Dutch life which hath there held unbroken sway since the earliest ages of the colony. Ruined mills beside lovely streams were common sights; & these, together with frequent ruined farmhouses, added a touch of melancholy to an idyl otherwise joyous. I secured a brownstone fragment from one of these archaick ruins as a souvenir. Picturesque in the extreme were the innumerable family burial plots & spreading churchyards, all filled with the mortal remains of Talman's ancestors from about 1650 to the present time. The Dutch colonial families of that district, like our early families in Rhode-Island, are all closely intermarried & related; so that virtually any person of Talman's generation is a descendant of the Harings, Van Ordens, Talmans, Blanchs, Blanvelts, Mabies, &c. &c. whose quaint red sandstone markers slant crumblingly above the sometimes neglected grass & matted weeds of the little railed-in plots. The stones (of the same material as the paperweight on my desk) are of every degree of crudeness & proficiency in workmanship; from roughly & illiterately scratched fragments [of a primitiveness never found in New-England] to Georgian carving of the highest workmanship, including the conventional fat & bewinged cherubface. It is a curious commentary on the cheerfulness of the Dutch disposition, that none of these old slabs have the gruesome skull-&-crossbone embellishment so common in New England & in all other colonial regions of English settlement. Never the skull—always the little fat cherub! I secured a fragment of a gravestone of one of Talman's ancestors—a small red sandstone chip bearing the single carven letter M. (The last letter of ABRAHAM) Some of the slabs had quaint epitaphs; but most were undecipherable, & I could not pause for recension & copying. In a few cases one would find the burial plot all overgrown with trees & saplings, like some of the neglected burying-grounds in our own Foster, Glocester, & Burrillville. At length we returned to Talman's house for dinner, after which we set forth once more in the car; this time bound for the colonial village of Tappan, so famous in history, which I had glimpsed three weeks previously as Dr. Long raced his car through on the way back from West Point. All the village is ancestrally connected with Talman, & he promised to shew me everything there is to be seen. Tappan is an ancient Dutch village, & in the autumn of 1780 became the headquarters of Genl. Washington, who was then investigating the celebrated Arnold plot for the delivery of West Point to His Majesty's forces. The whole region was a constant scene of sporadic guerilla [*sic*] warfare between unauthorised bands of robbers professing allegiance to one or another of the contending armies—the "cow-boys", allied to the rebels, & the "skinners", said to favour the lawful side of the king. Talman's own lineal ancestor, Douwe Talman, was murdered in his home by the band of Claudius Smith, a leader of the "skinners", whilst guarding his hoarded gold at the advanced age of 90. He was seated on the chest holding his treasure when run through with a bayonet—& it is interesting to note that Talman has just bought this chest from a distant relative at a cost of $50.00. When Gen. Washington took up his residence at Tappan, his prisoner Major Andre was transferred thither as well; & it was in the stone tavern of Mr. Mabie (a relative of Talman's) near the village green that the brilliant, brave, witty, & honourable young soldier was incarcerated pending the rebel court-martial. History knows the result of that court-martial, & laments the needless hanging of that admirable & virtuous youth whose only offence was to serve his sovereign & his country faithfully & unswervingly. In 1821 the remains of Maj. Andre were exhumed from the lone hilltop grave by the site of the gallows, & transferred with appropriate ceremonies to a tomb in Westminster Abbey. Still later—in 1880—the hilltop was marked by a suitable memorial to the intrepid officer. God Save the King!

We approached Tappan at about 2 p.m.; & surveyed its pleasing green, its ancient houses, & its brick Georgian church with a lively & fitting delight. Our first stop was at the tavern where poor Maj. Andre was confin'd—a brown stone edifice built in 1755 & still in good condition, now fitted up with reliques as a private museum & refreshment stand. I sent you a card of this building day before yesterday. Within are many memorials of the past, & I leaned reminiscently on the tavern bar which has felt the elbow of many a rebel officer & Dutch squire. The small room where Maj. Andre was confin'd is fitted up with table & chairs as it was during his occupancy; & the large front parlour, where the sentence of the court-martial was read, is likewise equipped in the manner of 1780. The place is now colloquially known as "The '76 House", & some agitation is in progress to secure its purchase by the state & its equipment as a really effective museum & historick shrine. Intrinsically it is scarcely a beautiful building. From the tavern we proceeded to that dwelling—now forming part of a larger building—where Genl. Washington himself resided & maintain'd his headquarters. It is an early Dutch house with great chimney & steep roof, set considerably back from the road in a grove of pines. We could not enter—or even closely approach—this place, since it is now in new hands & has an owner as hostile toward visitors as the present owner of the Hawthorne birthplace in Salem. It was formerly in the family of Talman's mother, & that gentlewoman herself was born within its walls. We thence bent our steps toward the ancient Dutch cottage called "The Manse", built about 1750 & forming the residence of the pastors of the Reformed Dutch Church. This is an excellent curving-roofed specimen, & we study'd its lines with an acute satisfaction. Last of the buildings to be examin'd was the splendid Georgian church shewn on the enclos'd postcard. This is a very late specimen—1835—but is nevertheless a phenomenally good example of the colonial tradition. We explored the galleried interior as well as the exterior, & found that each was worthy of the other. Our final Tappan pilgrimage was to the melancholy hill where Maj. Andre met his undeserv'd end, & where now stands the memorial to him erected by Cyrus W. Field of Atlantick cable fame.[1] Silently we ponder'd upon the moving inscription— compos'd by Dean Stanley of Westminster[2]—& thereafter drove away; young Dutch rebel & aged Rhode-Island Tory alike honouring the memory of a youth whose life & death were equally devoid of stain.

Paſsing thro' the decaying Colonial villages of Sparkill & Piermont—now inhabited wholly by Italians & negroes—we at length reach'd the shoar of the Hudson & were soon in the nondescript hillside town of Nyack. Here I bade my generous host adieu, & set out for the other side of the river on the ferry. The Hudson is here at its broadest, forming a hill-fringed basin known to the early Dutch as the "Tappan Zee"; & throughout the long ferry-voyage I surveyed the wide stream & its green banks & promontories with the keenest of gratification. At length I was deposited in Tarrytown, where at once my mind reverted to the life & tales of Washington Irving, who caught so well the spirit & colour of the region's wild beauty & rich legendry. Tarrytown is a precipitous hill village of large size & considerable dignity, which climbs above the water to a table-land of great scenick charm. Half-way up the hill I secured a stage-coach for North Tarrytown, & was soon in the wraith-haunted domain of Sleepy Hollow, whose ancient Dutch churchyard has grown to the proportions of a cemetery as large as Swan Point. The church itself—built in 1685—is still standing in fine condition & active use. Save for the Old Ship Church at Hingham, Mass., (1681) it is the oldest continuously used publick meeting-house in the United States. A card which I sent you shews the general aspect of the place. Note the *Gothick* cast of the windows—one of the few examples of *original* (as distinguish'd from *revived*) Gothick architecture in the country. The only other one I know of is a certain church in Virginia, which I have never seen. It is obvious that the Dutch held to the Gothick manner much later than we.

Having enjoy'd the old church & the neighbouring antient gravestones, I proceeded to digest the beauties of Sleepy Hollow itself—a Quinsnicket-like wooded ravine of considerable length, at whose bottom flows a crystal stream with many rocky waterfalls. Pursuing this to its head, I return'd to the road & walk'd back to Tarrytown; where at the top of the hill I secured a stage-coach for Sunnyside—Irving's manorial home—which lies southward toward New York. Alighting at Sunnyside Lane, I walkt down toward the Hudson, but soon found that the great Irving estate is in private hands & closed to the publick. I obtain'd several indifferent views of it by peering thro' the high slat fence, & at last return'd to the roadway to hail a coach for Hastings-on-Hudson—the next stage in my journey back to New York. Hastings is a river port of no great beauty, & I there secured a trolley car for Yonkers & the New York subway. Arriving at Van Cortlandt Park, I took a subway train for downtown, alighting at 50ᵗʰ St. & dining at the Times Square automat. (Broadway & 47ᵗʰ St.) Thereafter I took the B.M.T. for Cortelyou Road; reaching 395 about 10 p.m. & retiring in fairly respectable season, in pleasant retrospection of a day well spent, & agreeable anticipation of another bracing jaunt on the morrow with the Longs.

The next day—Friday—I was up at 6:30 a.m. & reached Sonny's promptly at 8:30. Belknap's uncle is slightly more comfortable, & much clearer mentally, though the physicians extend no hope for his recovery. He has been vastly cheered & soothed by a little fox-terrier which his wife had Sonny & his mamma select for him—& whose purchase was inspired by the mental improvement he shewed when a friend called with a small dog to see him. Mrs. Long & Belknap spent all Thursday afternoon selecting the dog—going from place to place in a taxicab at Mrs. Symmes' expense. On this Friday we started promptly for Van Cortlandt Park, where Dr. Long played his usual round of golf whilst Mrs. Long sat in the car & Belknap & I roamed the wild brookside behind the region of links & graded lawns. At 12:30 we had lunch in the pavilion by the golf-course, & thereafter set out across the Dyckman St. ferry for an indeterminate trip on the west bank of the Hudson. On this occasion we used a brand-new road north of the ferry—a ledge blasted out of the palisades since my former sojourn in New York. From this road—called the Alpine Boulevard—we obtained some of the most magnificent river vistas conceivable by the human mind; the finest being from a lofty parapet opposite Hastings, whence one might observe the lordly stream & its mountainous banks for uncounted miles in both directions. Continuing northward we pafs'd thro' Sparkill to Nyack—at which point, perhaps influenced by my description of the previous day's delightful trip, the party decided to turn directly west toward Spring Valley, which lies 7 miles inland. Of the beauty of this region I have already spoken—& it remains only to say that the Longs, who had never seen it before, fully endorsed my approval. At the village Sonny & I alighted to procure & mail some postcards, & later I took the expedition along the south road to see Talman's home & the broad Talman acres of rolling meadow-land. We then decided to continue west & north to Suffern & Tuxedo, where a spur of the wild Ramapos lends to the landscape a touch of mystery & expectant magnificence. The hills were soon upon us—& as we neared Suffern I felt these same sensations of breathless awe which I experienced last August as the train pafs'd through Crawford Notch in the White Mountains. Suffern is detestably ugly—there are no decent small towns outside New England—but the rugged natural scenery excuses all. Toward Tuxedo the landscape becomes even more impressive, & north of that fashionable centre still vaster ranges of hills stretch off to fill the soul with ineffable wonder. When we came to the Seven Lakes Drive, which runs eastward toward the Hudson through Harriman State Park, we decided to double back toward the river; hence embarked upon the silent roadway whose sinuous & hilly length affords unending vistas of peak & valley, lakelet & ravine, distant trail & far-off village steeple. It was a very poor road in a mechanical sense, & its frequent bumpings gave good Dr. Long's prosaick soul more than one occasion for verbal emphasis. But even he could not regret having selected this route, for its dizzying loveliness of panorama formed ample payment for almost any physical hardship. Toward the end we passed by the pathetic expanse of Letchworth Village, New York's spacious rural asylum for the harmlessly feeble-minded. Boys with close-cropped hair & vacant visages played about all the hills, & waved inanely at the passing traveller. One stolid youth of about 17 sat on the turf, busily plucking & eating large handfuls of meadow grass. He alone seemed oblivious to the traffick & novelties of the road! Finally we reached West Haverstraw & veered southward, repeating the return from West Point as made three weeks ago except that this time we took the Alpine Boulevard south of Sparkill instead of turning inland to Tappan, Dumont, Teaneck, &c. The vistas were just as glorious as on the northward trip, & we ultimately recrossed Dyckman St. ferry & returned to 230 by way of Riverside Drive. There we had a sumptuous chicken dinner, after which Sonny & I discussed Spain, fiction, whaling, science, philosophy, & a dozen other absorbing topicks till 11 p.m. Felis was in his glory—even if Belknap does think of obtaining a lively little dog to throw his whiskered nose out of joint! At 11 I set out for 395, reaching it an hour later & retiring in decent season. It had been a great two-day spree, & I thoroughly appreciated the imaginative stimulation it had afforded. Upon my return I found a note from that old fox de Castro, saying that he may not want any work done till after his return from Europe. Thank gawd—& good riddance! Today—Saturday—I have attended to writing & have not been out of the house at all. S H left breakfast, & came in at 7 p.m. to get dinner. Her shop has so prospered in the last few days that she has had to have a woman come in to assist with the repairing & manufacturing. Tomorrow S H & I are going to take dinner at the Longs' unless Belknap's uncle has another sinking spell. We shall probably, weather favouring, go for a motor ride in the afternoon—which reminds me that it did *not* rain in the N.Y. region yesterday. More later. Just recd. a card from A E P G.

Yr aff Nephew & obt Servt
H P L

P.S. Just recd. your note. Shall be glad to see Sunday Journal for May 20. I like the new magazine section. ¶ Have just got a fine new antiquarian N.Y. guidebook through Talman, which shews scores of fine colonial houses I have never seen. I shall put in most of the remaining N.Y. days searching out these places.

Notes

1. Cyrus West Field (1819–1892), American businessman who founded the Atlantic Telegraph Company and in 1858 laid the first telegraph cable across the Atlantic Ocean.
2. Arthur Penrhyn Stanley (1815–1881), Dean of Westminster (1864–81) and a leading British cleric of his time.

[202]   [ANS postcard][1] [HPL to LDC]

[Postmarked Brooklyn, N.Y.,
29 May 1928]

Better send me proofs of "Shunned House"—Cook seems to be in a hurry, & I can correct them here or on the road. He is also going to print the travel book by Sonny's aunt. ¶ As for diary—Sunday we rose at 10 & went up to Belknap's at 1 o'clock. After dinner all hands went for a delightful ride through the same scenic region as that covered by the first Long tour of the season—the wild hills of the Kensico & Katonah regions. Supper was eaten as a lunch en route. We returned in the evening & retired at 1 a.m. Today—Monday—I rose at noon & went up to Sonny's to meet our client Mrs. Reed, who was in town Sun. & Mon. She seems quite prepossessing & intelligent. After her departure Sonny & I went to the Nat. Hist. Museum, where we both bought 25¢ dinosaur paperweights. We then took a walk in Central Park, saw an exhibition of Spanish Inquisition paintings, & called at Kirk's shop. I returned to 395 at 7 p.m., had a spaghetti dinner, & later went to the library to look up genealogy. I found more Rathbone material, but did not have time to copy it all. Am now returning to 395, which ends today's diary. Will probably be on the road in less than a week. My duplicate Bulletin didn't come to-day. Better begin saving our regular copies. Regards to A E P G.

Yr aff Nephew & obt Servt H P L

Notes

1. *Front:* View from Top of R.I. Hospital Trust Building, East Side Along College St., Providence, R.I.

[203]   [ANS postcard][1] [HPL to LDC]

[Postmarked Brooklyn, N.Y.,
31 May 1928]

Here's a diary continuation from Monday night. ¶ Tuesday rose 10 a.m., & read Sunday Journal. Was greatly interested in Quinsnicket article, & am sorry that my beloved wildwood tract is to be spoilt by overcivilisation. They've ut-terly ruined the picturesqueness of Break Neck Hill road! In the afternoon I took a long exploring walk in Southern Brooklyn & discovered many colonial houses & an ancient milestone. Back for dinner, & in the evening went up to see that pestiferous old leech de Castro in response to an urgent telephone call. Inconclusive talk, as usual! I hope he goes down to Mexico & gets shot or imprisoned! Back at midnight to 395 & retire. ¶ Wednesday up 10 a.m. On account of holiday S H did not keep shop open, hence she accompanied me on my exploring tour. Went to Forest Park & Middle Village in Queens, but rain started before any colonial houses were sighted. Proceeding to Manhat-tan, we ate at the good old Milan; after which we returned to 395. Evening spent reading & writing—retiring at 11 p.m. Tomorrow I shall spend all day exploring—in fact, all the rest of the N.Y. stay will be spent in visiting the ob-scure colonial sights mentioned in the new guide book I got through Talman. ¶ Belknap's uncle died this morning at 7 o'clock, & all the family are busy see-ing to details—hence I shan't see Sonny for a couple of days.

Yr aff Nephew & obt Servt H P L

Notes

1. *Front:* Soldiers and Sailors Arch, Brooklyn, N.Y.

[204]   [ANS postcard][1] [HPL to LDC]

[Postmarked Flushing, N.Y.,
1 June 1928]

Well—here's another diary—covering a day & a half. As I told you, I am now spending all my time seeing the colonial sights described in the new Guide Book. Yesterday (Tuesday the 31st) & today I have been doing the borough

of Queens, (Long Island N. & E. of Brooklyn) & have uncovered an astonishing amount of colonial material both Dutch & English. My route yesterday
led up to the N.W. corner of Long Island—the Astoria & Bowery Bay districts—where I found a gratifying number of old Dutch farmhouses. Much of
Bowery Bay is still open country & farmland, just as when Petrus Stuyvesant
was Governor-General. Returning, I followed Northern Blvd. where the
modern real estate development of Jackson Heights is situate. At one point
there, I found—all amidst the new streets & tawdry rows of brick cottages, &
in full sight of the distant towers of Manhattan—a primitive 18th century farm
with house, barns, orchards, & ploughed acres complete. There was an old-
fashioned yard with tall flowers & kettle-&-tripod, & everything else suggesting the rural past; & the inhabitants seemed oblivious to all the ugly modernity pressing in upon them. It was the old *Hazard* homestead—perhaps
connected with our R.I. Hazards.

Yr aff Nephew H P L

[On front:] middle section built in *1661*

Notes

1. *Front:* Old Perry Estate showing Old Bucket Well, Elmhurst, L.I., N.Y.

[205]   [ANS postcard]¹ [HPL to LDC]

[Postmarked Flushing, N.Y.,
1 June 1928]

CARD #2—DIARY CONTINUED

After surveying the old Hazard homestead I looked up other archaick houses
in the ancient Bowery Bay Road, & thereafter returned to N.Y. because of the
approach of nightfall. Dining at the Automat, I later went to the Publick Library to copy Rathbone data & look up the Dodges of Block Island—whose
blood I have discovered that we possess in a double dose—but the volume
covering the Dodges was not available. I am going again tonight. After the
library closed I returned to 395, read a bit, & retired at 1 a.m. Today—Friday,
June 1st—I rose at 11 a.m., read some, & have again set out on a course of
colonial exploration in Queens. I began with New Lots in Bklyn—a dingy section—& worked northward to Middle Village & Maspeth, which were both
disappointing. Then I struck *Elmhurst*, (the ancient Newtown) & am repaid for
all my searching! This is a delightful old place—a colonial village with shady
streets, venerable steepled churches, & picturesque churchyards. The present
cards illustrate a trifle of the atmosphere. I am still here—6 p.m.—& in the remaining 2½ hrs. of daylight I mean to go on to ancient Flushing—a favourite
stamping-ground of mine in Clinton St. days. Then library, Automat, & 395.
Yrs H P L

Notes

1. *Front:* Queens Boulevard and Broadway, Elmhurst, L.I., N.Y.

[206]   [ANS postcard][1] [HPL to LDC]

[Postmarked Brooklyn, N.Y.,
2 June 1928]

CARD #3—DIARY FOR JUNE 1st, Continued:
After mailing cards I & II in Elmhurst, I took the elevated for Flushing, arriving there about 6:30 p.m. The village seemed much as of yore, save that (alas!) there are more apartment houses [due to the extension of the subway-elevated thither. There used to be no direct route, hence Flushing stayed unspoiled & rural]—& that the new colonial belfry of the Sloane furniture factory [in process of construction in 1925] now dominates the sky line. I visited the places I knew, & later searched out the old mansion of His Majesty's Governor of the Province in 1765—Cadwallader Colden, Esq.[2]—which is in good condition though engulfed by a cursed Jew cemetery. I also found the ancient Coe–Rapalye farmhouse on Flushing Creek, but night descended before I could find more. I then returned to N.Y.—too late for the library—& had dinner at the Automat. Then back to 395, write, & retire in reasonable season. ¶ S H's business is progressing beyond all expectations. She has one assistant now, & has just advertised for another! ¶ More anon.
Yr aff Nephew & obt Servt
H P L

Notes

1. *Front:* "Broadway." Tarrytown, N.Y.
2. Cadwallader Colden (1688–1776), governor of New York (1760–62, 1763–65).

[207]   [ANS postcard][1] [HPL to LDC]

[Postmarked Brooklyn, N.Y.,
2 June 1928]

UTILITARIAN POSTSCRIPT: *Saturday noon*
(a) Can you send me 2 pairs of socks? My pedestrian activities have destroyed that many beyond the hope of repair. Don't hurry unduly—I shan't need them till I go southward, & can pick them up as I pass through Bklyn again on my way back from West Shokan. I shall leave for W. Shokan Wednesday.

(b) I am herewith sending home, by parcel post, my winter suit—newly pressed, & carefully packed by Signor Narcisi. Better take it out of the box & hang it up on its shoulders as soon as it arrives, so that no wrinkles may be perpetuated. There are some grease spots on the trousers, where some salad capsized during a picnic lunch in Belknap's car, but Signor Narcisi says that a thorough dry-cleaning will remove them.

Today looks like a good day for exploring, so I'm starting out again, historical guide book in my hand. I shall possibly finish up the southern Brooklyn region & tackle the villages at the extreme Northern rim of New York City. Watch for the diary instalment covering the day's activities. Shall probably copy Rathbone data at the library tonight. Dwyer has just sent me explicit directions on how to reach him in West Shokan.

Yr aff Nephew & obt Servt

H P L

[On front:] P.S. The Shunned House proofs have not yet arrived.

Notes

1. *Front:* Entrance Midwood Manor Ave. J and Coney Island Ave., Flatbush, Brooklyn. N.Y.

[208]   [ANS postcard][1] [HPL to LDC]

[Postmarked New York, N.Y.,

5 June 1928]

The Shunned House proofs duly arrived! Thanks. As for stockings—if you haven't sent them already, better make it 3 pairs instead of 2—since another pair shew signs of succumbing to the stress of pedestrian exploration. ¶ As for my diary—after mailing my suit home Saturday, I proceeded to explore unknown corners of southern Bklyn—Gravesend & New Utrecht—& found a splendid array of colonial material. I then proceeded far uptown in New York—to the Bronx village of Westchester & the University Heights region—but found most of the ancient buildings torn down. Then I finished my Rathbone copying at the library, ate at the Automat, & returned to 395, retiring about 2 a.m. Sunday I was up at 11 a.m., glanced at the Times, & embarked with S H on a trip of Staten Island colonial exploration. The village of New Dorp was full of fine Dutch material, whilst the neighbouring town of Richmond (which we reached at twilight) was one of the finest & most unspoiled Georgian villages I ever beheld. Busses have replaced trolleys on the island, & the railway is now electrified. Back at 10 p.m., dinner, & retired 1 a.m.

Yr aff Nephew H P L

[On front:] P.S. Today I arose at 1 p.m. & am about to telephone Sonny about the day's plans. Will probably leave for West Shokan Wednesday or Thursday. ¶ Will you buy a **July** Weird Tales for me? I don't want to bother with it here. And *save all Bulletins from now on.*

3 p.m. On my way up to Belknap's. Afternoon's plans still unformulated.
10 p.m. Forgot to mail this on my way to Sonny's, so will complete the day's diary here. Had a fine afternoon & evening of discussion, & took dinner with the Longs. Now I'm returning to 395, & will retire in good season.

Notes

1. *Front:* Dutch Reformed Church, Port Richmond, S.I..

[209]   [ANS postcard][1] [HPL to LDC]

[Postmarked Brooklyn, N.Y.,
6 June 1928]

Postcard & socks just came—Wednesday morning. Glad the suit arrived in good order. As you'll see by my preceding card, the proofs did arrive after all. Too bad the Times came defectively—it's a wonder it comes at all in such loose form. I'll mail you the whole issue if I can still find it here. I've torn one article out of the magazine section. Save all Journals & Bulletins now. My duplicate Bulletin stopped yesterday. [Later—alas! 395's Times has been thrown away!] ¶ I suppose you saw the recent Bulletin editorial announcing that the old Spring St. school in East Greenwich is to become an historical museum. The news gratified me prodigiously, for I had feared the structure might be torn down despite its dignity as original home of the E. Greenwich Academy. Today looks like a good day, so I believe I'll devote it to antiquarian research—finishing up Brooklyn & possibly finding some rare nooks & corners in the Bronx. I may try Staten Island, though, instead of the latter. Orton left word, asking me to telephone him at 4 o'clock, but unless I happen to be near a telephone I'll be hanged if I spoil a rustic trip on that account! Tomorrow the Longs leave for Atlantic City for a trip of three days. They will take Belknap's aunt with them, since she needs recuperation after the siege of her husband's fatal illness. More soon—& thanks for the socks.
Yr aff Nephew H P L

[On front:] I've just received the letter which you forwarded from that comical Brooklyn eccentric David W. Cade. I shan't answer it while I'm here, for if he knows I am so near him he'll expect me to call, & I am quite sure the poor fellow would bore me to death. I guess I'll answer from West Shokan.
P.S. I must thank & congratulate you on the repairs which you gave that shrunken shirt—enlarging the neck & setting the buttons out. It works finely & hangs well—so that I shall ask you to give similar treatment to its counterpart—which is also with me, & which I am wearing in its shrunken state. As for that 3d pair of socks—you can use your own judgment about sending it. It may not be absolutely necessary.

Notes

1. *Front:* Queens Boulevard and Broadway, Elmhurst, L.I., N.Y.

[210]　[ANS postcard][1] [HPL to LDC]

[Postmarked Brooklyn, N.Y.,
6 June 1928]

Greetings! Notice the difference in penmanship! I've been to the Waterman Co. again at last, & instead of trying to fix the point a second time they've given me a brand new gold pen—with the privilege of exchanging it as many times as I wish without any cost beyond the 50¢ I paid for the original repairs 2 or 3 weeks ago! I'm trying a finer point this time, but am not yet quite sure whether I'll keep it. I must try it on different kinds of paper before I decide. ¶ If pleasant, I shall go to West Shokan on the 9 a.m. boat—which reaches Kingston at 2:25 p.m.—FRIDAY, JUNE 8. If violently rainy, the next day. Continue to forward all mail here, since I'll be able to pick it up on my way South. Also the stockings. And KEEP ALL EVENING BULLETINS FOR ME, IN ORDER, BEGINNING WITH TUESDAY, JUNE 5th. Earlier ones need not be kept, since the duplicate month expires only today. ¶ As for my diary—I rose today (Tues. June 5) at 11 a.m. & read Shunned House proofs. S H came & got a midday meal at 2 p.m., & after that I went out for errands—including this pen. Then I proceeded to Flatlands, S.E. of Flatbush, to find the ancient tide-mill on Gerritsen Creek; a venerable relique built in 1688. I came on it in the misty twilight, & it was not a disappointment. Then back to 395 & retire.
Yrs H P L

[On front:] P.S. Sonny is getting an astonishing number of replies from a revision advertisement he inserted in the *Writers' Digest.* Our joint advertisement in *Weird Tales* will appear July 1st, [proofs have just come, & look highly prepossessing] at which time I'll be home & ready to cope with any inquiries which may come my way. The Longs are going to take a motor trip as they did last summer, & I have agreed to forward all their mail to various weekly destinations (named by telegraph) as I did before. The trip is not likely to include Providence this time—I fear the good doctor remembers our tangled traffic & absence of golf links. Heaven speed the Whitten Plan!

[Vertically at left margin:] I hope my suit arrived in good shape.

Notes

1. *Front:* Queens Boulevard and Broadway, Elmhurst, L.I., N.Y.

[211]　[ANS postcard][1] [HPL to LDC]

[Postmarked Brooklyn, N.Y.,
6 June 1928]

The Diary—WEDNESDAY, JUNE 6—Continued

Well—I had a call from Sonny before noon, so planned to include him in the latter half of my afternoon's explorations. Prior to that I went alone on another visit to Flatlands, & found the ancient Bergen house (circa 1660) in a state of desertion & virtual collapse. Meeting Belknap at the 42nd St. Library at 2 p.m., I planned the residue of the course on Staten Island. We proceeded thither by ferry, & first explored very thoroughly the colonial village of Stapleton—of which I sent you cards 4 years ago. Then—to gratify the Child's love of the sea—we went down to South Beach & stayed for a time on the shore. On the return trip I left the car again at Stapleton, observing some old houses & taking the 'bus for archaick old Richmond, (here illustrated) the scene of last Sunday's trip. It looks as splendid in full daylight as in the twilight, & I shall now see whatever I missed Sunday. The chief point in Richmond is the late-Colonial court house on the hill—part of which is visible in the card I am sending A E P G. Later bulletins will describe the rest of the day's voyaging. On the whole, I am inclined to deem Richmond the most primitive & picturesque small village in the N Y area.

Yr aff Nephew & obt Servt H P L

[On front:] Just climbed an exquisite towering hillside in the sunset, & saw all the primal countryside outspread in a mystic golden glory—the village looking exactly as in this picture. Now back to N Y by 'bus—sorry anticlimax!

Notes

1. *Front:* Panorama of Richmond. Staten Island, N.Y.

[212]　[ALS] [HPL to LDC]

Thursday Afternoon
5 p.m.
[7 June 1928]

My dear daughter Lillian:—

Well, what do you know about this! Talk about sudden changes of plans—I'm as quick in my way as our amiable hostess Mifs Reynolds to take advantage of a sudden & unexpected invitation!

Listen to this! I said yesterday that my Friday trip was to be up the Hudson to West Shokan. Well—it isn't, after all—but is to be, instead, the beginning of a week in that enchanted region in my own New England—*Vermont!*

Orton is responsible for the change. He tried to get me on the telephone for two days, & only succeeded this morning. When he did, he sprang his Vermont invitation—& made it so insistent & so free of all expense that I couldn't civilly refuse it—if, indeed, I had wished to refuse it. I called at his office this afternoon, & he renewed his cordial pleading with double vigour; so that in the end I sent Dwyer a card postponing the West Shokan jaunt, & agreed to let Orton be my host. He has bought a farm near Goodenough's place in West Brattleboro, (although he has never met Goodenough in person) & simply can't start in rusticating until he has his old Grandpa Theobald's blessing on the enterprise! Naturally, I shall see Goodenough whilst I'm there—& shall introduce Orton to him. I shall also try to get to see good old *Cook*—since Athol is no prodigious 'bus ride away. From there I shall go to West Shokan at last, then down the river, & finally the long-contemplated Philadelphia-Southern antiquarian tour. Some dizzy social whirl for a confirmed hibernator!

This, then, is my immediate programme: to meet Orton at 4:45 p.m. tomorrow at the Grand Central, & accompany him to the mystic vistas & avenues of glamorous & half-fabulous Vermont. Archaick New-England! I shall help one of its sons to re-acclimate himself to its venerable hills! Orton also wants me to pay him another & longer visit in the fall, when I take that long motor trip with Cook to see Walter J. Coates.

Naturally I'll send full bulletins all along my route—& give you the Vermont address for forwarding purposes through next week. Orton advises me to wear rough clothes, but I guess my best clothes are rough enough for any region short of the Dakota bad-lands. I am promised a rich array of rural towns & colonial steeples—if you want to know more about the locale, read the Vermont article in the National Geographick on my table.

As for my diary since dropping you the sunset-hill card at Richmond—I returned to N.Y. last night by 'bus & ferry, dined at the Automat, & finally proceeded to 395 to write & retire at a moderate hour. I was up at 10 this morning, wrote letters, & later went to see Orton at the *Saturday Review* office, (which is also the office of *Time*) 25 West 45th St. I am now sitting on a bench in front of the Publick Library, watching the 5th Ave. 'busses go by & writing such letters & cards as are made necessary by my altered plans—to Dwyer, Goodenough, Cook, &c. Later I shall dine at the Automat & pay a final call either on Loveman or honest old Mac—after the thundershower which seems to be brewing, & which will shortly drive me into the library. My duplicate Bulletin subscription stopped June 4, but I have bought Bulletins for the 5th & 6th at the 6th Ave. I shall probably do likewise tomorrow, but in case I don't, it might be well for you to begin saving Bulletins with the issue of FRIDAY, JUNE 8th.

Have now adjourned within, because of the descending drops. The one good thing about N Y is the way one can defy a rainstorm through underground travel. I shall get from here to Loveman's book shop without leaving the subway except at the last end—by taking the Interborough for the Grand Central at the new 5th Ave. station, & then transferring to the East Side Subway for 59th St. & Lexington Ave. More soon.

Yrs for the hills of New England
—Grandpa Theobald

P.S. I'm still undecided about the new pen-point. On this Cavalier paper it is as smooth as silk! I guess I'll give it a trial till I pass back through N Y on my way South.

[213]   [ALS] [HPL to LDC]

Friday Afternoon
[8 June 1928]

My dear daughter Lillian:—

Your welcome epistle arriv'd this noon, just as I was packing for my Vermont excursion. I am also packing a large box of stuff to send home—which I trust you will shortly receive in good condition. This includes all my stiff collars (I have adopted soft ones for the residue of the summer) & the belt Sonny gave me. That belt is too good to wear for every day yet—I only wanted the Child to see it on me once & realise that Grandpa appreciated his gift. Among the miscellany included in this shipment is the 25¢ dinosaur plaque which I obtain'd at the museum. Here's hoping it reaches #10 unbroken. I have not purchas'd any straw hat so far—though the weather scarce befits my heavy felt. Possibly I shall get the benefit of late-season prices when I patronise Mr. Warner's Providence branch upon my return.

I shall buy a Bulletin (for yesterday) this afternoon, so would advise you to begin saving papers with FRIDAY, JUNE 8th. Yes indeed, I am on the alert for all trunk line developments, & have read with interest of the resumption of the Providence Line of New York boats. I surely did note the Benefit St. garden article; & as you know, paid especial attention to the East Greenwich school news. If I'd known of that when I met the young man from East Greenwich a couple of weeks ago, I surely would have had a golden topick of conversation! I wish that someone would buy the Smithville Seminary from the niggers & fit it up as a memorial to New England's old academy system.

Yes—weather has been rotten, but I've managed to see some sights in spite of it! Here's hoping it's decently sunny next week—for in the wild country one can't do anything when it's rainy. I could better stand a little rain during the southerly lap of the journey, since with an old felt hat & the price of a suit-pressing one can tramp about colonial towns in a drizzle without disastrous results. I wouldn't want a rubber coat & hat on a voyage like this. Too much bother.

I note the cuttings you enclosed—though I doubt if Federal Hill's Signor Santayana is any relative of Belknap's philosophical idol.[1] Deesa boy is-a Ee-taliano, while the eminent philosopher is a Spaniard. As for kitty-cats—I agree that they are essentially a masculine animal: a delight of unsentimental & disillusion'd aesthetes who appreciate abstract beauty of line & motion without reference to the petty quality of fawning affection for mankind. I saw the article you clipped in my Bulletin, & shewed it to regal old Felis—who spat in critical acknowledgment! I'd like to see the Maltese you mention.

I regret the leak which messed up my alcove, & am rather glad I was not on the spot. No doubt you recall the day that 598's kitchen plaster fell on my head. Speaking of 598—I find that *Dr. Farnell* is a patron of Loveman's book shop, & that he has mentioned seeing my name written in juvenile fashion about his cellar!

As for my diary—last night I went to Loveman's shop but found him gone, so called on honest old Mac instead. Mac was glad to see his fellow-ancient, & insisted on going out & purchasing some ice-cream & cake in honour of the occasion. At 11 I returned to 395 & retired in good season. Today I rose at 9:30 a.m., went out for errands, & have since been packing. Now I must mail my bundle home & do some more errands—& possibly go to the barber's. I want Dwyer to see me for the first time with decently cut hair—though I suppose I could get the job done in Brattleboro if there isn't time here. Finally—I shall meet Orton at 4:45 at the Grand Central & take the 5 o'clock train for Vermont. More soon—

Yr aff Nephew & obt Servt
H P L

P.S. In order to avoid crowding, I am taking S H's large suit case to Vermont & West Shokan, instead of my 99¢ valise. When I cross back through N.Y. I'll return it, take my own, & arrange a suitable condensation for the shorter southern sojourn.

Notes

1. HPL refers to George Santayana (1863–1952), Spanish-born American philosopher who influenced HPL's later thought.

[214]   [ANS postcard][1] [HPL to LDC]

[Postmarked West Brattleboro, Vt.,
12 June 1928]

Hurrah for New England again! Have meant to write a diary letter, but have had no time. Reached our destination safely—& *what* a destination! Orton has hired a real colonial farmhouse of the most traditional type, & conducts everything as primitively as possible—oil lamps & candles, wood fireplace fires, no plumbing save cold water piped from a neighbouring spring, &c. I have learned how to build a wood fire, & have helped the neighbours' boys round up a straying cow. Foster blood tells! As for the *scenery*—it is utterly beyond description! Illimitable vistas of wild green hills, mysterious sloping forests, & remote glimpses of purple peaks where strange gods dwell. I shall make the most of it during the week I expect to be here. I hope to call on Goodenough soon, & also wish to work in a trip to Athol to see good old Cook. I shall then go by motor coach to Albany over the famed Mohawk Trail, stop at the Y.M.C.A. there, & ultimately proceed down the Hudson toward West Shokan. There are lots of old books & Farmer's Almanacks in the attic here, & I may get some of them soon, since the owner has commissioned Orton to dispose of them. Vermont is a great place, & I look forward to my trip with Cook in the autumn. More soon.

Yr aff Nephew H P L

Notes

1. *Front:* Suspension Bridge, Connecticut River, Brattleboro, Vermont.

[215]   [4 A.Ms. postcards (in envelope?)]¹ [HPL to LDC]

[No Postmark;
12 June 1928]

TUESDAY, JUNE 12, 1928.

I'll herewith endeavour to catch up with my diary. Friday noon I got a haircut & shampoo at the Parkside Barber Shop, & caught the 5:02 train with Orton. It was glorious to reënter the ancient realms of New England, & when we struck real farming country toward Hartford I was ready to emit loud cheers! I caught the merest glimpse of Hartford from the train, & night came on before we changed cars at Springfield. Of this latter I could glimpse only the tall illuminated tower of the celebrated Campanile. At Greenfield the train stopped for 20 minutes, & I found time to scrawl some postcards with a Massachusetts postmark. At length the lights of Brattleboro appeared, & the rail trip was done. We were met with a Ford, owned by a neighbour, & hurried out of all earthly reality amongst the vivid hills & mystic winding roads of a land unchanged for a century. Back to ancient New England! After so long an absence I was actually—by virtue of the train's route—taken into no less than *four* New England states: Connecticut, Massachusetts, New Hampshire, & Vermont. Orton's home is a real story-&-a-half Colonial farmhouse, exquisitely situated beside a wooded, brook-bearing ravine on a shady mountain road. Towering green slopes loom on every hand, & no artist could paint a nobler bit of agrestick loveliness. There is an inimitable quality of fantasy & mystery in the beetling proximity of almost perpendicular cliffs of vivid greenery. From the higher peaks views of the utmost magnificence can be obtained—range on range of far-off violet pinnacles, [II.] including Mt. Monadnock & the hills that line the misty Connecticut. Certainly, Orton has selected the place of places to ensure the Novanglian atmosphere & background of his new family! He tries to duplicate the life of old-time Vermont in every possible way—including the playing & singing of psalm tunes by the ancient Estey organ (made in Brattleboro) in the best room. He wears overalls & cowhide boots around the farm, & surely looks the indigenous rustick to perfection. I have induced him to add a boot-jack & Farmer's Almanack to his array of antiques around the settin'-room fireplace. The interior of the house is very colourfully furnished in every detail—absolutely in the old farmhouse tradition—as you will see when I send the pictures Orton took Sunday. Only the ground floor is finished & plastered, the attic being devoted to picturesque accumulations of cobwebs & ancient household accessories. Among the latter are many books, which the owner of the place has commissioned Orton to sell—taking half the profits for his trouble. We are now cataloguing the items in question. My room is the regular guest room on the ground floor, adjoining the best room with the Estey organ. The windows look across the road directly into an ancient wood. [III.] I retired in good season Friday, & awaked Saturday to a rainy day. In the morning Orton & I catalogued the attic books, & in the afternoon we worked on the neighbouring woodland brook—building a dam in an effort to change its course & form a small pond. In the evening Orton sang psalm tunes & I wrote letters, retiring somewhat late. Sunday all rose in good season, & Orton & I joined the Lee boys (nearest neighbours)[2] in an ultimately successful quest for a lost cow. Our course led through some of the most magnificent countryside imaginable—a region famous for fox-hunting, so that we saw many a fox's den. You will see pictures later on of many phases of this expedition. The Lee boys are great fox-hunters—there are four of them, & they live in a brick colonial house which their ancestors have inhabited for 5 generations. They have sugar maples & sell syrup & sug-ar—& they shewed me the first sap-boiling or sugar house I ever saw. In their modest way they are local oracles, & I learned from them all the best mountains of the locality. Governor's Mountain is the highest, & I intend to climb it. Whilst Orton & I were with the Lees, honest old Goodenough called in person, but did not wait to see us. Cook, though expected, did not appear. [IV.] Some guests did come, though, in the person of Orton's friends (cousins) from Athol—a young fellow with his wife & small son, all very pleasant & prepossessing. The cousin helped fix the new dam after dinner. In the evening all hands went to Brattleboro for errands, & retiring was very late. Monday I rose late & spent the whole day exploring the mystic hollow & domed hills beside the house. Wrote in the evening & later retired. Tuesday—today—I rose early & explored the hills. In the afternoon I walked to Brattleboro for errands—finding scenic beauty at every turn of the winding hill road. On the return trip, I stopped in at Goodenough's & found the old boy as quaint & delightful as before. Next Sunday Cook will visit him, & we shall all assemble at the G. home for a sort of amateur convention. Cook may take me along to Athol in his car, so that my coach ride to Albany will have good old Athol as a base. Returning to the house from Goodenough's, I had dinner & have been writing letters ever since.

WEDNESDAY, JUNE 13.

Rose today at 9 a.m. & have planned some extensive rural hiking, perhaps including an ascent of Governor's Mountain, the highest elevation hereabouts. More soon.

Yr aff Nephew & obt Servt H P L

[On front of card 4:] P.S. Last Friday I was in too much of a hurry to get a Bulletin in N.Y., so *save all my Bulletins beginning with* THURSDAY, JUNE 7th. I haven't the slightest idea of what's happening in the world!

P.S. #2 I am getting some laundry done at a neighbour's, so that I won't have to bother with sending it by parcel post. Hope it'll be decently laundered & ironed!

Notes

1. *Front:* 1) Main Street, Brattleboro, Vermont. 2) Bird's Eye View, North from Mt. Wantastiquet, Brattleboro, Vt. 3) Bird's Eye View from Mt. Wantastiquet, Brattleboro, Vt. 4) Main Street, Brattleboro, Vermont.

2. In "The Whisperer in Darkness" (1930), set largely in Vermont, HPL cites a "Lee's Swamp" (*CF* 2.485).

[216]　[ANS postcard][1] [HPL to LDC]

[Postmarked West Brattleboro, Vt.,
14 June 1928]

Well—here's a brief continuation of my diary. Wednesday I was up in good season & started out to climb Governor's Mountain—1823 feet above sea level. The lower slopes were gently rising pasture land, but higher up it became very steep & thickly forested; so that my climb became a perilous & perpendicular adventure having some of the picturesque elements of fantastic nightmare. The summit proved to be covered with second-growth trees, so that I didn't get much of a view after all. I descended the other side & wandered all the afternoon thro' the unbelievably lovely & picturesque wooded valley & brook-bearing forest ravines of the region. I never saw such exquisite sylvan brooks in all my life—celestial music & crystalline loveliness! Some of the waterfalls are beyond description. If anything is more typical of Vt. than the green hills, it is the omnipresent multitude of marvellous limpid *brooks*. Toward sunset I traversed some old-time farmland, (for Vt. is *real* New-England still—what R.I. was 75 or 100 yrs ago) & paused at the white-steepled crossroad-village of Hinesburg. This is an idyl out of a story book! Then back to the house for dinner, & write all the evening.

Yr aff Nephew & obt Servt

　　H P L

[On front:] P.S. Today—Thursday—I am up & out in good season, visiting an especially fine brook which Goodenough recommended to me. I am now sitting on the bank, not far from G's house. I shall now go to Brattleboro & try to climb Mt. Wantastiquet on the N.H. side for the view. Then back to the house & catalogue books all the evening. This will complete Thursday's diary. I'll let you know how I come out with the mountain. Certainly having a great time!!!

Notes

1. *Front:* Bird's Eye View from Retreat Tower, Brattleboro, Vt.

[217]   [ANS postcard][1] [HPL to LDC]

[Postmarked Brattleboro, Vt.,
14 June 1928]

I am writing this in His Majefty's Province of *New-Hampfhire*, tho' it is only juft acrofs yᵉ River from Brattleborough, & this card will have to bear a Vermont poftmark. After dropping my other card I call'd on Goodenough & went to town, at once crofsing over to yᵉ N.H. fide & climbing up Mt. Wantastiquet by a narrow winding path. I am now on yᵉ Summit, where a monumental marker is fituate. The view is magnificent paft defcription—all of Brattleborough & half the world befides—hills, hills, hills, & the interminable windings of the Connecticut. A shower halted me a moment—but only a moment. Now to descend & return to Orton's, & catalogue books for the rest of the evening. That finishes Thursday's diary. This is a great country—old New England in its most typical & unspoil'd state. If *northern* Vermont is any better, as Orton claims, it must be *some* region!
Yr aff Nephew
H P L

Notes

1. *Front:* Covered Bridge, Vernon Road, Brattleboro, Vermont.

[218]   [ANS postcard][1] [HPL to AEPG]

[Postmarked West Brattleboro, Vt.,
15 June 1928]

Greetings! I thought you'd recognise the Greenfield card—the place is extremely pretty, as I recall from the time when I passed through it by daylight with Cook last year. Yes—I knew that Helen Gamwell is now there, & I'll at least ring the bell at 32 High St. if I am there in any other way than on a moving vehicle.[2] I may not have occasion to stop off there, for Cook will probably take me to Athol Sunday in his motor, & when I pass through on the 'bus en route to Albany & Dwyer's place, there will be no opportunity for a pause. ¶ This is, I really think, the finest countryside I have ever seen. It is *old* New England, absolutely unspoiled, & leading the same life that R.I. & Mass. led a century ago. Every house contains an old Yankee family which has dwelt there for generations, & the town of Brattleboro itself is entirely old-fashion'd & straight-American. *It is our own world of the past,* miraculously preserved for the present & tolerably well guaranteed for the future! Let there be no mistake—*the early New England is still alive & vigorous.* The real change is merely a sad *restriction of its area.* The Brattleboro & Guilford of 1928 are the Providence & Foster of 1800. Today I am simply roaming the lovely hills & dreaming. In the afternoon I (OVER) [on front] (CONTINUED) shall return to the Orton place & finish the cataloguing of some old books & almanacks which the owner has commissioned Orton to sell & keep half the profit. I shall take my pay for this service in books—for some of the items are old New England things which I would give my eye teeth for. There are also a lot of old readers—at which we are going to give good old James Ferdinand Morton the first chance. In the evening I'm going to Brattleboro in a neighbour's car to meet Orton, who had to go back to N.Y. for a while to attend to his business. Sunday *Cook* is coming up, & all hands will meet at Arthur Goodenough's place. Then all aboard for Athol! Yesterday I climbed Mt. Wantastiquet, across the river from Brattleboro, in New Hampshire. The view was utterly magnificent! Certainly, for real scenic beauty & pristine New England rusticity, this region excels all others which I have ever seen. More soon. Yr aff Nephew & obt Servt H P L

[Marginal note:] I am now sitting in a sunny meadow beside a brook.
[Marginal note:] This is a diary letter—shew it to L. D. C.

Notes

1. *Front:* Suspension Bridge, Connecticut River, Brattleboro, Vermont.
2. Helen Sears Gamwell (1874–1938), a nurse, was the sister of HPL's uncle Edward F. Gamwell. She and her brother are buried with their parents in Arms Cemetery, Shelburne, MA.

[219]   [ANS postcard][1] [HPL to LDC]

[Postmarked Deerfield, Mass.,
18 June 1928]

Deerfield again! Your letter recd.—will answer presently. Wait till I send you the writeup Orton gave me in the local paper![2] Athol next week, & then Cook is going with me in his car to see Dwyer at West Shokan. It's clouding up at this moment—9 a.m.—but I hope the day won't be spoilt. This place is entrancing beyond description—here we have the *vast & massive* colonial houses

that Vermont lacks. Massachusetts is a great old state after all—second only to R.I. More soon—
Yr aff Nephew & obt Servt
H P L

P.S. Sky is clearing! Good!

Notes

1. *Front:* Mohawk Trail, Deerfield Valley from Whitcomb Summit, Observation Tower.
2. HPL refers to Orton's article "A Weird Writer Is in Our Midst," *Brattleboro Daily Reformer* (16 June 1928): 2; rpt. in Joshi, *A Weird Writer in Our Midst* 51–54.

[220]   [ANS postcard][1] [HPL to LDC]
[Postmarked Newport and Springfield, Mass.,
18 June 1928]
Waiting for a Brattleboro 'bus already overdue. The day has turned out fine & sunny, & I may go to Newfane, an old town N.W. of Brattleboro which everyone tells me is exceedingly quaint.

Read page-proofs of "The Shunned House" yesterday. Cook is going to make a 60-page book of it by using liberal spacing & wide margins. He's just dropped a line to Little Belknap asking him to hustle up the preface. I'm dedicating the volume to Cook. You'll see the first copy.
Yr aff Nephew & obt Servt
H P L
(I'll answer your letter shortly)

Notes

1. *Front:* East Main Street, Greenfield, Mass.

[221]   [ALS] [HPL to LDC]
Tuesday Night
June 19, 1928
My dear daughter Lillian:—
Yours of the 14th (financially momentous date!) duly arrived—& meanwhile you have doubtless received my postals from archaick Deerfield & picturesque Greenfield. I have likewise received the additional socks, for which I am duly grateful. Holes have begun to appear in one of the new pairs—an illustration of how hard Vermont rusticity is on one's clothing! I am certainly glad I did not get a straw hat!

The weather has, all told, been astonishingly favourable. Today is damp

& unpleasant, & I am writing indoors by a wood fire of my own building; (for I have become astonishingly expert in xylo-pyrology) but this is the exception, as my diary amply demonstrates. The trip has been a marvellous pleasure & mental stimulation, for it has brought me magically close to those basic & surviving well-springs of early-American life which we in cities, & in southern New England generally, are accustomed to regard as extinct. Here life has gone on in the same way since before the Revolution—the same landscape, buildings, families, occupations, & modes of thought & speech. The eternal cycle of sowing & reaping, feeding & milking, planting & haying, here constitutes the very backbone of existence; & old traditions of New England simplicity govern all things from dairying to fox-hunting. That Arcadian world which we see faintly reflected in the Farmer's Almanack is here a vital & vivid actuality—in all truth, the people of Vermont are our contemporary ancestors! Hills & brooks & ancient elms—farmhouse gables peeping over bends of the road at the crest of hills—white steeples in distant valleys at twilight—all these lovely reliques of the old days flourish in undiminished strength, & bid fair to transmit themselves for many generations into the future. To dwell amidst this concentrated old-fashionedness for two weeks, seeing about one every day the low-ceiled, antique-furnished rooms of a venerable farmhouse, & the limitless green reaches of planted fields, steep, stone-walled meadows, & mystical hanging woods & brook-murmurous valleys, is to acquire such a hold on the very fundamentals of authentic Novanglianism that no amount of urban existence can counteract or dilute it. Whether you believe it or not, the rustics hereabouts *actually* say "caow", "daown", "araound", &c.—& employ in daily speech a thousand colourful country-idioms which we know only in literature. The books & almanacks in the attic—all old New England things, & in many cases having Vermont & New Hampshire imprints—contribute greatly to the general effect. I have selected several—as you will realise when they arrive by parcel post. Old readers & geographies with the long ſ, naive books of travel, histories with curious old New England woodcuts—these are the things which fascinate me; bringing back as they do a chapter of civilisation distinctive in the extreme, & fresh in the memory of all but the youngest natives of these colonies.

I enclose a few snap-shots illustrative of my agrestick idyll. Please save these for my arrival, for Orton has lost the negatives & thus cannot get duplicates for me. Later I will send some more pictures, including some splendid views of the colonial living-room & fireplace where I am now seated. I will also try to get a copy of my write-up in the Brattleboro Reformer—though the office has no more left. The view of Orton & myself in costume represents us as we were when we worked on the dam in his brook. What I have on my shoulders is an ancient yoke employed in carrying milk-pails.

I am indeed sorry to hear of your lame back, & hope that you will be very careful of it. Did any unusual exertion bring it on? You must guard against strenuous efforts until the effects of former strains have had a long time to wear off.

As to my cash—it is certainly holding out miraculously because I have had so few chances to spend it! Food, board, & even transportation now & then, is costing me absolutely nothing—so that if I do go broke it will be on postcards! Really, it is almost incredible how events have conspired to give me a continuous travel spree at virtually no expense. And the joke is, that most of the rest of the trip is likely to be just as non-pecuniary! On Saturday the Ortons expect to visit cousins in Athol, & I shall get a free ride in the automobile which will come to fetch them. Then Cook insists on my being his guest for a few days. And then, if all goes well, I shall get a free ride all the way to West Shokan N.Y. in Cook's car—since Cook wishes to pay Bernard Dwyer a visit at the same time that I do! The southern part of the trip, of course, will demand a greater cash outlay; but it will be worth it. I shall certainly return home with a wholly new & gratifyingly ample fund of inspiring travel imprefsions!

As for Bulletins—*do not save any prior to Thursday, June 7th, for I have read all before that.* Do not save any N.Y. Times prior to *Sunday, June 10th.* Save, however, all Sunday Journals & parts of Sunday Journals which have not been sent me. By casting out Bulletins & Timess [*sic*] prior to the dates mentioned, you ought to be able to conserve much space. No—I won't buy any more Bulletins, because I can't up here. Outside of R.I. one can't get them except on the out-of-town-paper stands of very large cities.

I regret to hear of the mortality in Barnes St. lately—& am correspondingly glad to learn of the reposeful prosperity of Horatio Valentine. I recall reading of his activities in the G.A.R., & can imagine how he enjoyed himself Memorial Day. I hope you can pay him the visit he suggests—it would be a delightful change for you. Where does he live? I assume that it is in Rhode Island.

So honest Eddy has been inquiring about Grandpa! I'm dropping him a card from Vermont. I shall be interested to see the article by Marc Greene—there's a boy after my own heart! If I had his brains & energy I'd roam about the world exactly as he does, except that I'd probably stop off at Providence rather oftener than seems to be his custom.

I trust that all the ceilings & cornders at #10 will be fixed up before I return for another indefinite period of vegetation. Oy, vot a eggsbense for a poor man like Meesder Frenk! End by der top of diss, heh shood heff to baint der houze-a'ready! Vell, ef he baints der leedle elcove by my room, I only hope he does it vhile I'm avay!

I can imagine how busy A E P G is. Her trip to Maine will surely complete the scattering of our family over the expanse of New-England! When I get back I am going to make you go on some short afternoon trips—notably to Bristol & Newport.

Now as for my diary—I think it concluded last Friday night. Saturday morning I was up early & accompanied Orton on a fishing trip through one of the most delightful brook-bearing forest ravines that I have ever seen. He caught 12 small trout, but I believe I enjoyed the expedition more than he; since the scenery at every turn was enough to take one's breath away. In the afternoon there arrived a very welcome visitor—none other than Walter J. Coates of North Montpelier, editor of the Vermont periodical—Driftwind— which printed my article on Vermont last winter. He had heard of my presence at Orton's, & motored down with his wife a distance of some 75 or 100 miles to meet me—an honour which I surely appreciated. We discussed literature all the afternoon, & after dinner settled down to a fireside argument on philosophy which lasted till 3 a.m. At that hour everyone retired save Orton & me—& we proceeded to the top of one of the neighbouring hills to build a fire & watch the sun rise. The spectacle was glorious in the extreme, & after witnessing it we retired for a brief snatch of rest. We were awaked by the arrival of good old Cook from Athol—& we surely were glad to see him! He brought page-proofs of "The Shunned House"—which I read on the spot & let him take back—& galley proofs of the new edition of that Bullen book, which I shall read very shortly. In the afternoon all hands repaired to the Goodenough home for the literary conference—there being two others also present: a schoolmarm-poetess named Miss Miller, & a man from the Brattleboro Reformer named Paul Jones. Jones is a typical Vermont Yankee in speech & aspect—quaint & grotesque, but shrewd & kindly. Discussion was brisk & interesting, & at the close Goodenough served a repast of typical rustick lavishness—lavishness to the point of redundancy, with the usual groaning board so highly favoured by country folk. Dispersal soon followed— Coates going homeward, whilst Cook adhered to the Orton party. I enclose an item descriptive of the conference—which please return to me for ultimate return to Orton, it being his only copy.[1]

The conference being over, all hands repaired to the Orton house, & in the evening Cook took everybody for a scenic ride in his car. After that we sat around the ancient fireplace & discussed various things—finally retiring.

Monday morning we rose at 5 a.m., since Orton had to get to N.Y. on an early train. Cook took him to Greenfield to get his train, & I went along as a sightseeing passenger. After seeing both companions off toward their respective destinations I took the 'bus for archaick & historick Deerfield; & was thereafter lost in admiring contemplation of elm-shaded antiquity. Returning to Greenfield, I caught the 'bus for Brattleboro, which went by a different route from the one taken by Cook, Orton, & I [*sic*] on the downward trip. We had come all the way on the West side of the river, but the 'bus detoured Eastward to include Northfield, Mass., & Hinsdale, N.H. Arriving in Brattleboro, I had hoped to make a trip to Newfane—a quaint old town to the north—but found that there was no good round-trip service in the afternoon. Accordingly I returned to the Orton place, took my writing materials to a neighbouring hillside, & wrote letters throughout the later afternoon, continuing the practice after dinner during the evening. Retiring at a reasonable hour, I awaked the next day to find rainy weather, hence have done nothing but write letters indoors. That will complete Tuesday's diary; but I will leave this epistle unfinished for a partial Wednesday entry, since the rural mail does not leave till 4 p.m.

Wednesday

Rose today at 11 a.m. to find the weather still dismal but not rainy. I shall do a little writing, & then shall set forth in quest of a tall & splendid waterfall south of here which the Lee boys have described to me. Later I shall return & read proofs of the 2nd edition of that pestiferous Bullen book which Cook brought up Sunday. That, you will recall, is the burden which made last autumn a nightmare both in Providence & Athol. We thought we were rid of the thing—but an unexpected sale developed, & here we are tackling the same job all over again! Of course, the financial backer (Archibald Freer of Chicago) will see that we lose nothing by it.

And so it goes. I'll conclude now & put this in the R.F.D. Box. During the rest of this week my temporary addrefs will remain unchanged, but it will thereafter—barring sudden changes of plan—be ℅ *W. Paul Cook, Box 215, Athol, Mass.* Cook is anxious to leave Athol nowadays, & is talking of coöperating with Orton to buy adjacent farms in Northern Vermont. More soon.

Yr aff Nephew & obt Servt
H P L

Notes

1. [Unsigned], "Literary Persons Meet in Guilford," *Brattleboro Daily Reformer* (18 June 1928): 1.

[222]   [ALS] [HPL to LDC]

Thursday Afternoon
[21 June 1928]

My dear daughter Lillian:—

I add this postscript to my epistle of day before yesterday in order to enclose some material which has recently come to hand—more pictures, & some newspaper material which I could not get before. You may now see what publick Vermont characters my host & I are getting to be! You might return the cuttings to me while I am at Cook's, since I want to shew them to him & to Dwyer; but you can retain the snapshots if you find them interesting. If I can't get more, I'll annex these again when I get back. And by the way—you needn't hurry about returning the cuttings. Shew them to A E P G before sending them.

As for my diary—I think I ended up with Tuesday night. Wednesday was damp & dreary, but not so bad as the day before; so I went out in the afternoon to find the woodland waterfall about which everyone has been telling me. I failed once more to locate it, but came on another fall—an artificial dam in a meadow where a mill used to be—which amply repaid my expedition. On the way back I met the Lee boys with a motor truck, & they gave me a lift. After dinner I wrote letters & retired at a reasonable hour. Today—Thursday—I rose early & accompanied the Ortons into Brattleboro; they having been given a motor lift by the poetess-teacher, Miss Miller, who attended the Goodenough conference Sunday. I had hoped to make Newfane by 'bus, but learned that the schedule permitting return on the same day does not go into effect till July 1st. After this disappointing discovery I was taken to the Reformer office & introduced to Charles Crane of their staff—"The Pendrifter"[1]—& he secured for me a copy of the Saturday paper with Orton's writeup, which I had been unable to obtain through regular channels. Crane is a typical Vermont Yankee & proved highly congenial. He took me over to his private office (he is also in the advertising business) on another street, & gave me many advertising booklets containing bits of Vermont local colour. Miss Miller introduced the Ortons to him, & he was invited out here for dinner tonight—to which invitation I added one of my own for the evening; namely, to accompany me when I visit the eccentric artist & recluse Akeley,[2] whom Charley Lee has promised to take me to see tonight after his chores are done. I'll tell you about this visit in my next diary. Crane is the person in whose special column Orton's writeup of me appeared. After my morning call on Crane I returned to the Orton place, expecting to go out & search for the waterfall; but showers have so far kept me indoors writing. I am well caught up on my correspondence, but have yet to read the Bullen proofs. Probably I'll do a lot of work on that Bullen book in Athol—for which, of course, I shall receive pay from the same generous Archibald Freer who forced that $100.00 cheque on me last Christmas.

P.S. Just had word over the telephone that Crane can't come tonight after all. Too bad—but I shall see the hermit-artist just the same. I must finish this quickly for the postman, who calls at four each day. More later.

Yr aff Nephew & obt Servt
H P L

Notes

1. The column in the *Brattleboro Daily Reformer* was in fact called "Pen-Drift"; Charles Edward Crane (1884–1960) usually signed himself "The Pendrifter." A selection of his columns was published as *Pen-Drift: Amenities of Column Conducting* (Brattleboro, VT: Stephen Daye Press, 1931). The column is cited in "The Whisperer in Darkness" (*CF* 2.474, 476).

2. Bert Gilman Akley (1871–1946) painted as a hobby. He and his rustic dwelling served as the basis for Henry Akeley and his remote farmhouse in "The Whisperer in Darkness." Note that HPL has misspelled his name, just as the fungi from Yuggoth misspell the name (as "Akely" [*CF* 2.493]) in a telegram sent to Wilmarth.

[223]   [ANS postcard][1] [HPL to AEPG]

[Postmarked West Brattleboro, Vt.,
23 June 1928]

Greetings to my fellow-wanderer! We surely are spread out all over New England. On Saturday I move down to Athol, & after that will come West
Shokan. I'll tell L D C not to exert herself too much—although I shall try to
arrange easy trips for her—Bristol & Newport—when I get back. No need to
worry about my cash! Without bills for food & lodging, & with most of my
transportation free, I am spending virtually nothing—even my transit to West
Shokan will probably be free—with Cook. ¶ Better attend to all money matters with cheques. Needn't begin the *weekly* ones till I let you know, for I expect some more cash for work done while away—especially the proofreading
for the second edition of the Bullen book, on which Cook & I are now busy.
But of course the large July & August funds will be welcome. ¶ Be back by
Sept. 10, so that we can take that London trip—although about that time
Cook intends to take me on a motor ride up to northern Vermont to see Walter J. Coates. It's a gay round! If I get up to Boothbay Harbour I'll drop in on
you. ¶ And so it goes. You'll hear from me often—both from the road &
from archaick Providentium. When in Athol I may make a side-trip down to
North Wilbraham to see Mrs. Miniter—who said she felt slighted because I
didn't drop in last year when there. I may see Deerfield again, too. More
Soon—yr aff. Nephew & obt Servt
H P L

[On front:] Ancient Farmhouse Abode of the West Brattleboro Artist / Bert G.
Akley. Here is where I was last night—calling on a rustic artist who lives all
alone & has never taken a lesson in his life. He is one of the old stock hereabouts—of the very family who used to own this house that Orton is hiring. He
paints all kinds of pictures, & with a native skill arguing the greatest possibilities
if he had only had an artistic education. He is also a photographer of marked
attainments. He paints coats-of-arms for all the families hereabouts—& can
beat even our young heraldick friend Talman in that field. ¶ Rainy weather
has prevented my doing much this week—hope it'll be better in Athol. L D C
will send you all my diary epistles, including my writeup in the local paper.
ADDRESS ME FOR A WEEK—or until further notice—% W. PAUL COOK, BOX
215, ATHOL, MASS.

Notes

1. *Front:* [Printed line crossed out by HPL and replaced by his written note.]

[224]   [ANS postcard (in envelope?)]¹ [HPL to LDC]

[No postmark;
24 June 1928]

SUNDAY JUNE 24

Well—here's another diary instalment, written as we hop off for Athol. I last wrote Thursday, as I was about to go to the artist Akeley's. [*sic*] At the proper time Charley Lee called for me—on foot, since the Ford was broken down & would take some time to repair. We walked 'cross-lots, thereby seeing some exquisite scenery which I would otherwise have missed. Akley—who lives alone in the ancient farmhouse shewn on the other side of this card, turned out to be a highly remarkable rustic genius. His paintings—covering every field, but specialising in the local scenery, are of a remarkable degree of excellence; yet he has never taken a lesson in his life. He is Talman's equal or superior in heraldic painting, & is likewise a landscape & still-life photographer of the highest skill & taste. In other fields, too, he is a veritable jack-of-all-trades. Through it all he retains the primitiveness of the agrestic yeoman, & lives in unbelievable heaps & piles of disorder. About 10 o'clock Bill & Henry called for us in the Ford, & I returned to Orton's, retiring early. Friday was wretchedly rainy, so I spent the time reading proofs till late afternoon, when the downpour eased up. I then took a pedestrian tour, found the lovely waterfall I had been seeking so long, & explored the sleepy hillside village of Guilford Centre, whose ancient roofs & white church tower would make a delectable picture. I returned through Hinesburg, whose delicate steeple & breathless hillside vistas so deeply impressed me on a former occasion. After dinner I read weird material & retired in good season. Saturday I rose at noon & read weird material. In the afternoon W. Paul Cook & his wife arrived, to stay overnight & move the Orton party down to Athol the next morning. That morning has now arrived, & I am all packed up. We shall probably start about noon. The day—confound it—is abominably rainy.

More later—Cook may postpone his West Shokan trip, causing changes in my itinerary. You'll hear from me soon.

Yr aff Nephew & obt Servt H P L

[On front, vertically in left margin:] I suppose A E P G is in Maine now—I've just sent her a card, to the Boothbay Harbour address she gave.
[Vertically in right margin:] My addreſs for the next few days will be % W. Paul Cook.

Notes

1. *Front:*

Ancient farm home of the artist
[Best Christmas Wishes From

Bert G. Akley,]
Weſt-Brattleborough, Vermont.

[225]   [ALS] [HPL to LDC]

℅ W. Paul Cook,
Box 215,
Athol, Maſs.
Monday, June 25
Midnight

My dear daughter Lillian:—

I take my pen in hand to bring my diary to date & enclose a few items of timely interest. Today—after a literary discussion with Cook & Munn last night which lasted till 4 a.m.—I rose at noon, & spent most of the afternoon on a bench on the green or common of the "Upper Village." Athol, like Providence on a smaller scale, is composed of two distinct entities; the ancient hill, where the first colonial houses clustered, & the modern valley, where the factories & business streets are. The hill section, or "Upper Village", is still very rustic & colonial; with little white houses, a triangular green called Phillips Park, & a pair of attractive white-steepled New England churches. Cook neither works nor lives up there; but it is my favourite part of Athol, & I use it for sitting outdoors & writing when I do not feel disposed to visit the wilder open country & the neighbouring hillsides. Still higher up on this hill is the site of the original settlement of 1735; (then called *Pequoig*) but this does not fall within the compact area of the village proper, since the centre of activity shifted soon after the first colonisation. Cook shewed me the original site last night—bronze tablets marking the spot & pointing out its historical significance.

I like Athol very much, although it is by no means so good as Brattleboro. Here we do not find the pure, untainted America which we find in Vermont; for manufacturing industry has brought its curse in the form of a slum mongrel population. But much of the elder life still survives, of course; & it is infinitely more traditional & American than any average section of Southern New England. It is, too, within easy reach of the wild domed hills & hanging woods of the primal wildernefs.

The first thing I have had to do in Athol is to reclaim the wreckage which the Vermont wilds wrought upon my attire. My shoes, after a cleaning & blacking & new pair of strings, now have a tolerably respectable appearance; but my suit was a total loss which only a 2 or 3 day course of cleaning, mending, & pressing at the tailor's could make fit for wear in the publick highways of a civilised community. Accordingly, since I needed a new summer suit anyway, I have taken advantage of a removal sale & bought a cheap bargain which to me seems incredibly good. Mr. & Mrs. Cook agree in praising it as a remarkable piece of luck, & Cook may buy one at the same place for himself. It fits finely after two rounds of vest alterations—both of which were effected within a few hours after the purchase. The suit is a plain, dark-blue summer affair much like the old 1918 wreck now hanging in my wardrobe. It is, naturally, of a very conservative & elderly cut; & it cost me only *$17.50,* although it bore a price-tag of $29.50. As soon as I finally donned it, I delivered my old suit into the hands of a Semitic shentlemans vot hess a shop right near Cook's Transcript office—& he say heh shood heff it by me a'ready een a couble uff days—shoost like eed shood be new-a'ready, end ferry sheab! When I get it I shall decide which one to wear on the residue of my trip—sending home the other one by parcel post. It was a relief to get into decent looking clothes again—& to have on respectably blacked shoes—after my two weeks of roughing it.

Well—after dinner tonight Cook took me for a motor ride southeast to Petersham & Barre—an exquisite section full of fine old colonial estates, & containing the vast forest tracts owned by Harvard University for use in forestry courses. Petersham & Barre are both splendid steepled villages of the old New England tradition. I saw many *Templeton* guideposts, which made me think of you. We returned at dusk after some magnificent sunset vistas, & after that Cook & I discussed books in his library till 10:30. Since then I have been writing letters, & after that I shall do some necessary reading—weird work of A. Conan Doyle, unobtainable in Providence, which I must appraise for a possible 2nd edition of my weird fiction article. Cook is now printing my "Shunned House"—I stopped in at the office this afternoon & saw the press at work on it. Here is a sample sheet—which need not be returned. Tomorrow I shall read & write—if possible, in the open. In the evening Munn is coming over to take Cook & me to his home in Partridgeville to shew us his weird library. You'd hardly know Munn now—he's *reduced,* & looks as radiantly handsome as a young Northern god. Wednesday Cook & I may go down to North Wilbraham to see Mrs. Miniter. More bulletins soon.

Yr aff Nephew & obt Servt

H P L

P.S. Here is a review of the Bullen book which Cook has just received. It is from the Honolulu Star-Bulletin, & is by that Clifford Gessler—the poet whom I *almost* met in N.Y. last month when he called on Belknap.

[On envelope:] Safe in Athol after a rainy though not unpleasant ride. Am spending the residue of the day amidst the weird items of Cook's library.

11 p.m.
P.S. *H. Warner Munn* has been over, & has given me a copy of "The King in Yellow", which I've wanted for 2 years. And he may take me on a 2-day motor trip around *Cape Cod* later in the summer!

[226]   [ANS postcard]¹ [HPL to AEPG]

[Postmarked Athol, Mass.,
27 June 1928]

Well—here we are in good old Athol! Have just bought a new bargain suit to replace the one Vermont wrecked—the latter is at the tailor's. The new one is navy blue, summer weight—very conservative & elderly, & only *$17.50*. Have been out to Munn's & am going again. You wouldn't know the kid—he's *reduced*, & looks as handsome as a radiant young northern god—a boyish Thor or Freyr or Sigurd! His weird library is a wonder. Friday I leave for North Wilbraham to see Mrs. Miniter, & for 2 or 3 days mail will reach me ⁰⁄₀ *Miss E. O. BEEBE, N. Wilbraham, Mass.* Miss B. is Mrs. M's cousin—& incidentally the local superintendent of schools. Today I'm seated by a shady roadside reading proofs for Cook. Having a great time. ¶ Hope you're enjoying Maine—& that I've remembered the right address.
Yr aff Nephew & obt Servt—H P L

Notes

1. *Front:* New Arch Bridge, Main Street, Athol, Mass.

[227]   [ANS postcard]¹ [HPL to LDC]

[No postage, no postmark;
27 June 1928]

Well—here's another brief diary. Spent Tuesday in the open—on the hill toward the sentinel elm, reading & writing. In the evening Cook & I went to Munn's place—a fine old rambling farmhouse southwest of Athol—& saw his excellent weird library. Today—Wednesday—I shall spend all my time reading proof for Cook beside a shady road north of the village. Tomorrow I'm going over to Munn's again. Friday I leave for North Wilbraham to see Mrs. Miniter, & for 2 or 3 days mail will reach me ⁰⁄₀ *Miss E. O. BEEBE, North Wilbraham, Mass.* Miss B. is Mrs. Miniter's cousin—& incidentally the local Superintendent of Schools. Cook says that she is quite a local magnate—that what she doesn't *own* of North Wilbraham she has a mortgage on! More bulletins shortly. Having a great time. Yr aff Nephew & obt Servt
H P L

[P.S.] Am reading the proofs of Belknap's aunt's book²

[On front:] "The Shunned House" is now all printed, but not bound.

[On envelope:] P. S. I'll put this in an envelope after all, in order to enclose a picture of the Vermont conference at Goodenough's. Please keep this for me, since it is my only one. You might lend it to A E P G.

P. P. S. Just got my old suit from the tailor's finely fixed up. Since it is newly pressed, while the new suit is already getting out of press, I'll send it home & wear the new one on the rest of the trip. It will arrive shortly—please take it out of the box & put it on shoulders before it becomes creased. Thanks in advance!

Notes

1. *Front:* New Arch Bridge, Main Street, Athol, Mass.
2. See Bibliography under Mrs. William B. Symmes. HPL ghostwrote the preface for FBL.

[228]   [ANS postcard][1] [HPL to AEPG]

[Postmarked Athol, Mass.,
28 June 1928]

Thanks for the Boothbay Harbour collection! Looks like quite a place, though a trifle too summer-hotelish to suit my pastoral & antiquarian eye. Vermont is the place—though of course it'll be ruined as soon as tourists discover it. ¶ Shall be moving on to N. Wilbraham at 8 a.m. tomorrow. More bulletins from there. Dwyer is having a house full of company, so I may postpone my visit there till a month later, when Cook means to take me in his car. But I think I shall go down the Hudson just the same en route to the long-deferred Southern half of my trip. You ought to see my new blue suit—though it looks like all my other suits. More anon. Yr aff Nephew H P L

P.S. I'd like to see that Blockhouse, even if it is a relatively late specimen.

Notes

1. *Front:* Windings of the Trail and River, Mohawk Trail, Mass.

[229]   [ALS] [HPL to LDC]

Phillips Park, Athol.
Thursday, June 28. [1928]

My dear daughter Lillian:—

I was delighted to receive your epistle this morning, though sorry to hear that the results of your overexertion have been keeping you indoors. I hope that the warm summer sunshine of the past three days may continue with sufficient geniality to bring you out. It has been very good of Mrs. Hodgdon to attend to your muffin shopping—but in a couple of weeks I shall myself relieve her of that office unless you are yourself on the trail again by that time. I hope that you are getting a good array of food—a rather difficult matter, I fear, without the help of the Guernsey-St

Regis or Shepard's Cafeteria. The Cooks are literally stuffing me—but I am managing to keep my weight down to 144.

As for the rural artist Akley's house—it most emphatically has *not* any modern conveniences! He is a slovenly & eccentric character of the most pronounced type; going about unshaven & in a sweater, & keeping his farm in the wildest possible state of dust & disorder. But for all that he is a natural genius, & could have made his mark in the world had he cared to leave his native scenes & apply himself systematically to a career of development.

Glad the pictures & cuttings were of interest to you. I do not think you will find my suit permanently injured; for as you know, the trouser-bottoms were fraying & the lining wearing out anyway. I needed a new one, as I had indeed frequently remarked; & the one I have purchased in Athol is as fine a bargain as I could have obtained anywhere. The old blue is no longer fit to wear in public—or except on rough trips to Quinsnicket & so forth. I shall keep it—though perhaps not on shoulders as part of my wardrobe proper. The new blue looks just like it, except that it fits my present figure. I shall, after this trip, save it carefully for future years or to be buried in; wearing the old grey as the principal summer suit. I think the tailor made a very good job of that—almost as good as our "alterating" [*sic*] friend Meester Bernstein, late of the Golden Ball Inn, could have done.

No need of bothering about cash—I have hardly made a dent in my fund except for the suit! Without any expense for food, & with all the transportation expense still in the future for the solitary part of my wanderings, I have been existing absolutely free all these weeks; a most fortunate & extraordinary condition for which I am suitably grateful. I've told A E P G that she need not forward anything but my $40.00 on the 14th of July & August. I've actually been living *more* cheaply than as if I had been at home! As for my mail—you might send the Van Dusen book % *E. O. Beebe, North Wilbraham, Mass.* I may stop & see Van Dusen in Philadelphia, & I'd like to see what he has sent me in order to discuss it with him. Don't, though, if it's any trouble, or if it involves going out of the house when you wouldn't otherwise be going. As you may see, the matter is most decidedly not an important one.

Dwyer is having company, so I may omit stopping there on this trip, especially since Cook means to take me there in his car as a special trip from Providence next month. I shall, however, probably go to Albany & down the Hudson just the same; for I want to see the scenery, & that is a marvellously cheap way of getting toward Philadelphia & the South. I don't think I shall stop any length of time in New York City—S H is renting the apartment at 395 E. 16th St. to an elderly couple & taking a room elsewhere. I may merely look up two or three people during the course of a day or two, & move right on to Philadelphia. My Southern trip will be determined by my purse—& my final return will be by 'bus in easy stages through His Majesty's Province of Connecticut & over the Plainfield Pike through Rice City & Greene. I shall probably be home in about a couple of weeks—let us hope the plastering & plumbing at #10 may be in a condition to receive me!

Well—be careful of yourself! Thanks for the cuttings. I appreciate the kitty poem, & shall send a double flood of postcards after July 1st. Remember the lot I sent from Washington just before the rates went up? ¶ Yr aff Nephew H P L

[230]   [ALS] [HPL to LDC]

Sunday, July 1ˢᵗ· [1928]
℅ Mifs E. O. Beebe,
North Wilbraham, Mafs.

My dear daughter Lillian:—

I take my pen in hand to record the progrefs of my tour since last reports. On Thursday evening Munn came down to dinner in his Efsex Roadster & afterward took Cook & me on a trip to one of the finest scenic spots I have ever seen—Bear's Den, in the woods southwest of Athol.[1] There is a deep forest gorge there; approached dramatically from a rising path ending in a cleft boulder, & containing a magnificent terraced waterfall over the sheer bed-rock. Above the tumbling stream rise high rock precipices crusted with strange lichens & honeycombed with alluring caves. Of the latter several extend far into the hillside, though too narrowly to admit a human being beyond a few yards. I entered the largest specimen—it being the first time I was ever in a real cave, notwithstanding the vast amount I have written concerning such things. Munn says there is another & still larger cave near Athol, to which he will take me the next time I am there; & Cook promises to shew me the extensive caverns in Cavendish, Vermont, when we go there in the early autumn. Having seen Bear's Den with sufficient minuteness, we proceeded to Munn's house & looked over the old books in the barn. Munn made me a present of a Bible in the long ſ—something I have always wanted—printed at Edinburgh in 1795. That, & several other books I received or am borrowing, will be brought down by Cook the next time he visits Providence in his car. After this we returned to Cook's & chatted till quite late, when all dispersed & retired.

I arose Friday morning at *6:30,* & took the 8 o'clock train for North Wilbraham—on a line which is doomed to go out of existence when the beautiful Swift River Valley is flooded to make a reservoir for Boston. The scenery was very fine, though of course I did not get so good a sight of it as I did last year when Cook took me through the region by motor. At the station I was met by Mrs. Miniter in a neighbour's Ford, & taken at once up the beautiful shady road that winds around Wilbraham Mountain. (For a description of this country, see the Dowe Memorial booklet.)[2] The scenery is lovely in the extreme, with just the right balance of hill & plain. It is not so vivid as Vermont, but much richer & statelier; with larger trees & more luxuriant vegetation generally. The houses are old, but not notable. The population is quite sharply divided—the good families maintaining their old standards whilst the common folk are going downhill. A Polish invasion further detracts from the atmosphere in many localities—the house of the "Natupskis" being visible from the Beebe front porch.[3] The home of Mrs. Miniter's cousin is a large rambling late-colonial structure built as a tavern, & is stuffed utterly full of magnificent antiques, none of which are for sale. They occupy every inch of floor, wall, shelf, & table space, & 7 cats & 2 dogs perambulate & gambol through the lanes between. Miss Beebe, a woefully fat but highly intelligent & cultivated gentlewoman of 70 is the 'big man' of all the surrounding countryside; & decides the fortunes of the school committee, town council, & everything else from her seat beside the telephone. She is a mine of local history & tradition, & a fountain of weird anecdote—& of course a past master & connoisseur of antique collection. She means to leave her possessions to the Museum in Springfield upon her death. She drives about in a horse & buggy, though not scorning to accept a motor lift to town from neighbours in bad weather. The house is set high near a curve of a road lined with magnificent maples. Southward the graceful rise of Wilbraham Mountain can be seen—this mountain & all the land for miles around belonging to Miſs Beebe. A curious abandoned road connects the house with the mountain—it is picturesque to see the tall grass growing between stone walls where chaises & farmers' wains once ran. The whole region is full of odd rural lore, & ought to prove a mine of inspiration for any writer. I have already learned many things about old New England life previously unknown to me—such as the institution of *cat-ladders* inside the chimney of farmhouses, to enable the cats to climb from floor to floor when all the doors are shut. There is a fine system of cat ladders in this house—though only one ancient feline (Printer, aetat 17) knows how to use them. The place is very neat, though the only help is a boy named Chauncey, who sits at table with the family. He was taken from the poorhouse in *Attleboro*—but seems a delightfully gentlemanly person. My room is at the head of the stairs, & is furnished in the manner of about 1830. *Lard-burning* lamps are among the contents—these articles being formerly wholly unknown to me.

Mrs. Miniter does not appear to have aged at all in the 5 years since I last saw her, but is very active in literature & takes long rural walks. My diary so far is devoid of great events because of the showery weather. Friday I spent largely indoors inspecting antiques & watching cats—though in the evening I walked briefly down the road to imbibe a bit of the scenery. Saturday better weather enabled me to take a walk through some of the picturesque country to the north, Mrs. Miniter serving as guide whilst both dogs *& one of the cats* acted as a quadrupedal retinue. I never before saw a cat which followed persons over hill & dale like a dog. The country is very beautiful & traditional indeed, & undoubtedly represents the inland landscape of Western New England at its best. Upon returning I was shewn the extensive barn belonging to the place—Miſs

Beebe keeps 2 horses & several cows. The *cats* all have different & highly individualised personalities—2 are grey (including a patriarch 17 years old) & five (including a very little kitten) are yellow. Of the dogs one is a mature & very well-bred collie, whilst the other, an Airedale puppy, is a trifle uncouth & over-demonstrative. Sunday—today—we attempted a walk up Wilbraham Mountain, but were overtaken by a thunderstorm & forced to accept a lift back from motorists—who stopped at the house & proved to be delightful persons quite prominent in Springfield educational circles. Tomorrow better outdoor luck is hoped for. ¶ You'll receive further bulletins in the course of time. I am now reading "A Mirror for Witches", by Esther Forbes, which Munn has lent me.

Yr aff Nephew & obt Servt

H P L

P.S. Toward the end of July Sonny & his family will make a New England tour, & I may then meet them in Marblehead for purposes of guidance. Since that is about the time Munn expects to get there, I am going to see if I cannot make the two events coincide.

[On envelope:]

P.S. Sunday–Monday Midnight

I must add a reference to the absolutely marvellous *firefly* display which I have witnessed this evening! All agree that it was unprecedented, even for Wilbraham. Level fields & woodland aisles were alive with dancing lights, till all the night seemed one restless constellation of nervous witch-fire. They leaped in the meadows, & under the spectral old oaks at the bend of the road. They danced tumultuously in the swampy hollow, & held witches' sabbaths beneath the gnarled, ancient trees of the orchard. Never have I seen fireflies leap so *high!* The treetops were alive with them, & a few soared even higher; blazing like meteors against the violet dusk & rushing into the cosmic vault to join their brothers, the stars. As evening advanced, the spectacle diminished; & now I am retiring to dream about those spectral torches, & about the lean brown marsh-things (invisible to mortal eyes) who wave & brandish them in the gloaming when the unseen nether world awakes.

Notes

1. Cited in "The Dunwich Horror" (*CF* 2.444).

2. *In Memoriam: Jennie E. T. Dowe*, ed. Michael White (Dorchester, MA: [W Paul Cook,] 1921).

3. HPL refers to the name of the Polish immigrant family that is the focus of Miniter's professionally published novel *Our Natupski Neighbors* (1916).

[231]   [ALS] [HPL to LDC]

Thursday, July 5, 1928

My dear daughter Lillian:—

You were just in time to catch me in North-Wilbraham, for tomorrow or next day I move onward. Yes indeed—I appreciate the good luck which has provided me with this remarkable series of places to visit; for truly, the present outing has come to be one of the most remarkable vacations on record. Counting in the Munn & Cook events to come, the summer of 1928 is likely to prove unique & unparallelled as a whole; a bright sunset gleam to illuminate an old man's declining years.

That firefly display was undoubtedly a rare occurrence even for Wilbraham, as Miss Beebe & Mrs. Miniter both agreed. There have been plenty of fireflies since then, but no concerted display even comparable to the one described. Only by a piece of the rarest good fortune did I chance to catch it. Yes—the scene & house alike are well calculated to suit one of my archaic & feline tastes. A E P G may be enjoying Boothbay, but I am sure I had rather be in this primitive & un-touristed bit of ancient countryside.

I'll wager the accumulated Bulletins & Sunday Journals will keep me busy a fortnight after I get home! "Elektra" must have been quite a performance[1]—no doubt the Industrial Trust took advantage of its advertising value when they inaugurated their *electric* display! Sterling's poem[2] is very fine—he was certainly a bard of the first rank, & one of the finest in America during the past generation. The Cohan celebration will doubtless be somewhat distinctive & entertaining—are they placing a bronze tablet on his old Wickenden St. birthplace?[3] Not all of the Corky Hill & Fox Point gang turned out so well!

The temperature lately has just about suited me, though I certainly could use a little more sunshine! I shall shortly be parcel-posting home a parcel of used clothing for the laundry. The drawers & stockings are so riddled with holes that I will leave it to you whether to send them with Mr. Seagrave or throw them away. If perfectly convenient, you might send a clean outfit—white shirt, undervest, drawers, & socks—to me in care of S H's shop—*368 East 17th St., Brooklyn, N.Y.*—although I may be able to get along without it if it would be the least trouble. I have one clean outfit here in Wilbraham, & another awaiting me in Brooklyn—& the one I have on is good for 2 or 3 days more.

As for books—of course I shall have to practice some very drastic rearrangements when I adapt my new acquisitions to the shelves. A few more will come from Athol when Cook makes his next call. About the next forwarding address—use S H's shop—addressing mail % *S. H. Greene, 368 East 17th St., Brooklyn, N.Y.* I shall, of course, pause there to change valises; & will be able to pick up anything sent thither for me. Forward all letter mail, for I don't like to get too far behind in my correspondence. No—I haven't hurt S H's valise any. It is a brown leather suit-case costing $35.00, & still looks as good as new. For the owner of a 99¢ papier-maché affair, I have certainly been putting up an expensive false front lately!

As for my diary—Monday I read & wrote letters, & walked to Glendale church to see the antient churchyard. Tuesday I walked to Wilbraham village over the mountain, where Mrs. Miniter shewed me the sinister old cemetery (vide Dowe memorial) where her ancestors are buried. I also saw the brick Academy, built in 1825. The walk home was by a back road skirting the mountain, & I obtained some of the finest mountain panoramas imaginable—also seeing a *deer* cross the road. I had never before glimpsed a wild deer in its native habitat. Wednesday a large chicken dinner was served to guests— a couple from Springfield to see Mrs. Miniter, & the next-door neighbours, the Sandersons. In the afternoon I was taken on a motor ride by one of the guests, visiting Palmer & Monson. It is from Palmer that the Grand Trunk laid out its long-delayed line to Providence; & at this end one may see the same signs of half-completed work which are observed at the Providence end. Palmer is an ugly, dreary town. Today I have walked to the quaint & idyllically lovely old New England village of Hampden, four miles away—where the lower floor of the church is used as a grocery store. I am writing this in a corner of an icecream emporium, waiting for a summer shower to blow over, whilst a longmoustached rustic eyes me curiously. Hampden is a beautiful place—with fine old colonial houses, & a broad Old-England-like stream which winds through meadows & washes the backs of some of the village houses.

Further bulletins later. Send mail to Brooklyn until further notice, & await one-cent postcards. See you later.

Yr aff Nephew & obt Servt
H P L

Notes

1. Presumably a reference to a local performance of the opera *Elektra* (1909) by Richard Strauss (1864–1949).

2. The poem cannot be identified with certainty, but Sterling's "Evanescence" had appeared in *Harper's Monthly Magazine* 157, No. 1 (June 1928): 117.

3. George M. Cohan (1878–1942), composer of many musicals, was born on 3 July 1878 at 536 Wickenden Street in Providence.

[232]   [ALS] [HPL to LDC]

en route—
Poet's Seat, Greenfield
Saturday Evening, July 7. [1928]

My dear daughter Lillian:—

I take my pen in hand to continue the diary, last carried as far as Thursday's Hampden walk. I returned from that peregrination in somewhat dubious weather, but was amply repaid by the evening's marvellous *firefly display*—a spectacle equalling or even surpassing the earlier one about which I rhapsodised to you! Friday was devoted almost entirely to an examination of the old books in the Beebe attic—a collection of early New England material far surpassing that at Orton's place. Not a volume will ever leave Miſs Beebe's possession whilst she lives—she would sooner sell her soul to the devil! I literally saturated myself with the atmosphere of the past, & was reluctant to turn away, even to call on Mr. Sanderson & arrange my departure for the morrow. This morning I rose early & joined Mr. Sanderson at 9 a.m., being taken by him into Springfield, which I now observed for the first time in my life. It is a tolerably pleasant city, but mainly Victorian & undistinctive; so that I decided not to wait for the afternoon opening of the museums. Getting my clothes put in order for urban travel, & mailing home a package of some junk which I found I did not need in the valise, I took the trolley for Holyoke, there changing for Northampton, at which latter place I took the Greenfield coach. Holyoke is a large & busy manufacturing city, & therefore depressingly ugly. Between there & Northampton Mt. Tom rises majestically. I saw the base of the car line which goes to the summit, but did not pause to ascend. Northampton—Calvin Coolidge's home town—is fairly prepossessing, but not attractive enough to invite extended exploration. The coach ride to Greenfield is very fine—passing through archaick Deerfield, which I observed with perennial interest. I reached Greenfield at 4 p.m., too late for the daily coach to Albany. Since there is no good Y M C A here, I engaged a $1.75 room at the Mansion House—a Victorian brick structure by no means resembling our Golden Ball. I then proceeded to the *barber's*—my third away-from-home haircut of the year—& had an excellent job performed by a *real American* craftsman. My last haircut was June 8, & my locks were getting shaggy-looking. I have now ascended the lofty hill & tower outside the town known as "The Poet's Seat"—a place which A E P G knows well. Here I am enjoying one of the most lordly panoramas of distant hills, winding river, embowered village steeples, & so on, which it has ever been my good fortune to encounter. Tonight I shall read the new Weird Tales, (whose Eyrie is one continuous pageant of praise of myself, & which announces that my "Lurking Fear" won the vote as the most popular tale in the June issue)[1] & tomorrow I shall take my ease till the 2:15 coach for Albany leaves on its long & breathlessly scenic course over the Mohawk Trail. I shall, if all goes well, reach Albany Sunday evening at 6:45, stay over night, & proceed down the Hudson via the Day Line on Monday. I shall there exchange valises & pick up any mail which may be addressed or forwarded to me in Brooklyn. After that the southern tour, of which you may be sure you will receive ample bulletins.

The sun is now setting, so I will repair to the town once more. I enclose 2 Springfield cards which struck me as being of greater interest than the average. My real seeing of Springfield, however, will come next year; when I intend to go thither directly from Providence & continue on to Lenox,

Pittsfield, & North Adams in order to obtain a thorough familiarity with Western Massachusetts. I hope very much that tomorrow will be fair, & that I shall be able to get a decent seat in the stage-coach. The line is one running from Boston to Albany via Athol.

And so it goes. See you later. Hope all the packages will arrive home safely.

Yr aff Nephew & obt Servt

H P L

Notes

1. See Joshi, *A Weird Writer in Our Midst* 68.

[233]   [Souvenir folder] [HPL to AEPG]

[Postmarked Springfield, Mass.
7 July 1928]

[234]   [ANS postcard][1] [HPL to AEPG]

[Postmarked Greenfield, Mass.,
8 July 1928]

On the move again! Left North Wilbraham this morning, & look at the list of towns I have covered!

Springfield
Holyoke
Northampton
Greenfield.

I'm now in the *Poet's Seat* at Greenfield, enjoying a magnificent sunset. Tomorrow I take the 2:15 stage coach for Albany, arriving at 6:45 p.m. Monday I descend the Hudson on the Day Line & prepare for Philadelphia & the South. It's a gay round! Hope you're enjoying Boothbay Harbour. If you're having this sunset, you're in luck! Do you know the magnificent view from the Poet's Seat? Yr aff Nephew & obt Servt

H P L

Notes

1. *Front:* Massachusetts State Building, Eastern States Exposition, Springfield, Mass.

[235]   [ANS note on printed brochure: "Souvenir Folder of the Mohawk Trail, Mass."] [HPL to AEPG]

[Postmarked Albany, N.Y.,
8 July 1928]

Lately passed through *Shelburne Falls*. Great place! This trail contains the most magnificent scenery I've ever seen! Every plan matured finely—clear day, bus on time, & splendid front seat. Am now on highest point of trail, with a view beyond description. Just climbed an observation tower. Shall make Albany at 6:45, passing through Troy & other regions of Mr. Hoag's country.

Later (North Adams)

The western side of the Hoosac divide *infinitely* surpasses the eastern. The mountain view is breath-taking, & North Adams is one of the most picturesquely situated towns I have ever seen—deep at the bottom of a valley, with the precipitous Berkshires rising on every hand.

Latest—Albany

The landscape became less beautiful the moment we left old New England. Troy is a wretched dump, & Albany is Victorian & nondescript—State House on a hill at the head of an inordinately broad street. Y M C A charges $2.50 for non-members, so I'm stopping at the Hampton Annex $1.50.

Tomorrow morning I shall start down the exquisitely scenic Hudson via the Day Line—starting 9:00 a.m., & reaching 42nd St Pier 6:08 p.m. More later. Yr aff Nephew & obt Servt
H P L

[236]   [ANS [postcard][1] [HPL to AEPG]

[Postmarked Philadelphia, Pa.,
11 July 1928]

Well—here's Grandpa back in the Colonial Metropolis! Had a great ride down the Hudson, & found *Wandrei* domiciled in *Brooklyn* only 2 blocks from *169 Clinton St.!!!* Belknap & his family leave July 20 for Cape Cod, & Munn & I may meet them in Marblehead. Also—S H may come to Providence during a vacation which she is about to take. ¶ I left N Y after one day for Philadelphia, & shall now take the 2 p.m. coach for Baltimore. Then Annapolis & Washington. Philadelphia is a great old town! More later—Yr aff Nephew & obt Servt
H P L

Notes

1. *Front:* Independence Hall, Chestnut St., Philadelphia, Pa.

[237]   [ANS note on printed brochure: "Select Views of Baltimore, Md."]
[HPL to AEPG]

Did Philadelphia & hopped off for Baltimore. It's a pretty fair town—metropolitan but quaint. I'm about to digests [*sic*] the sights of both Baltimore & Annapolis with the aid of a rubberneck 'bus. Washington probably tonight.

[238]   [ALS] [HPL to LDC]

Philadᵃ, in His Majefties
Province of Pennsylvania
11ᵗʰ July, 1723. [i.e. 1928]

My dear daughter Lillian:—

As you may perceive, the southern part of my journey is now begun; its extreme limit (probably the Washington–Alexandria area) to be determin'd by the manner in which my cash holds out.

On Sunday last I retir'd early after mailing you the folder of Albany, & was up the following day in good season. The trip down the river, on the steamer *Alexander Hamilton*, was attended with every scenick delight, & I acquired an exceedingly festive coat of sunburn. Upon reaching the town of New-York, which lies at the foot of the river, I proceeded to 368 E. 17ᵗʰ St., where I exchanged valises with S H. We dined at the Sir Henry Restaurant in East 16ᵗʰ St; &, S H being without commodious living quarters at present, stopped at the Bossert in Montague St near Borough Hall.

The mail you forwarded contained one exceedingly interesting item— namely, the news that *Wandrei is in Brooklyn with permanent intent, & rooming with two other boys at 83 State St.*, **exactly two blocks from 169 Clinton St.!!!** It was wholly by chance that he happened to land in the dingy confines of Red Hook, & he was surprised to learn how near 169 Clinton was. He has come to N Y to seek an advertising position; & although he has not yet begun to look for it, his expectations are very high—as is the way of youth. He graduated with honours last month from the U. of Minn., & his book has gained him some very important literary recognition.

Tuesday morning I was up betimes, & made an engagement to go up to Sonny's for lunch. I then went around to Wandrei's, & found that he was out. When I reached Belknap's, however, I was agreeably surprised to learn that he had telephoned there—purely by chance—& that Mrs. Long had invited him to come over for lunch. It was indeed an impressive reunion. Wandrei looks immeasurably stronger & handsomer than he did last year, & he dresses vastly better. His manner, too, is less pensive & moody; & he is evidently in much better spirits. The afternoon was spent in abstract discussion—mostly about the 4ᵗʰ dimension—& we were sorry when Wandrei had to leave at 5 o'clock. I remained till six, & then went downtown to meet S H for dinner at the Milan. Belknap's party will leave on the 20ᵗʰ or 21ˢᵗ for Cape Cod & Marblehead, at which time I hope to cross their path with Munn.

The Milan dinner was as excellent as usual, & afterward S H & I attended a cinema at the Cameo in 42ⁿᵈ St. Upon its conclusion at 11:30 I accompanied S H home to her temporary quarters & prepared to depart southward. In a couple of weeks or so S H intends to take a vacation, during which she may come to Providence. If she does, she may be in Marblehead at the time of the projected general reunion.

Having proceeded to the Pennsylvania Station, where I had checked my 99¢ valise, I boarded the 1:30 a.m. train for Philadelphia & spent the journey in correcting some proofs (of Belknap's aunt's travel book—which reminds me that I met this aunt for the first time yesterday) for Cook; finishing the job before the train drew in. Arriving at the West Phila. station in the dark, I took a car for the Broad St. station & began writing letters in the waiting room. I am still there. Dawn has come now, & I shall begin sightseeing at once. I shall likewise investigate 'bus service to Baltimore, Annapolis, & Washington. I'll outline more of my programme in the next bulletin—for stage-coach schedules & prices, yet to be ascertained, will do much toward determining just how I shall apportion my time & distribute my attention.

But now antiquity beckons. I shall not be slow to follow, & broad daylight will find me deep in the antient town of Mr. Penn & Dr. Franklin. Look out for postcards!

Yr moſt aff Nephew & obt Servt
H P L

[239]   [ANS postcard][1] [HPL to AEPG]

[Postmarked Annapolis, Md.,
12 July 1928]

Greetings from antient Annapolis! Had a great time in Baltimore, where I saw Fort McHenry & the tomb of POE.

Now among the colonial reliques of a venerable seaport. Washington tonight.

Yr aff Nephew & obt Servt
H P L

[On front:] Erected in your honour, no doubt!

Notes

1. *Front:* St. Ann's Church, Annapolis, Md.

[240]   [ANS postcard][1] [HPL to LDC]

[Postmarked Alexandria, Va.,
13 July 1928]

Hurrah! God save the King! I meant to devote today to urban Washington, but Annapolis had so strongly drawn me toward the colonial past that I was obliged to proceed to antient Alexandria, in His Majesty's Province of Virginia. I am writing this in a tavern at the corner of *King & Royal Streets*. Alexandria is not quite so colourful as Annapolis, but it is a marvellous survival from the past. Brick Georgian houses on every hand—I've just been through the famous Carlyle Mansion, headquarters of Genl. Braddock in the French & Indian War. ¶ Found a magnificently cheap excursion ($2.50) to the *Endless*

Caverns at New Market, Va. for Sunday, & am going. This will eat into my home fare a bit, so I'll ask you to drop a 5 or 10 spot to 368 E. 17ᵗʰ St. Bklyn. This chance to see *real caves* was a little too good to miss!
Yr aff Nephew & obt Servt
H P L

Notes

1. *Front:* Christ Church, Alexandria, Va., Where Washington Worshipped.

[241]   [ANS postcard]¹ [HPL to LDC]

[Postmarked Washington, D.C.,
13 July 1928]

Annapolis was magnificent beyond description! The regular "Grey Line" tour did not even scratch the surface! When I started out on my solitary map-&-guidebook tour I uncovered a vaster wealth of archaick quaintness than I had thought to exist south of Marblehead & Newport! Quaint, narrow, curving streets & tangles of alleys, ancient brick houses dating back to 1694—I must see it again some time. ¶ Took the 8:15 electric train for Washington & arrived at 10 p.m. Y M C A does not accomodate non-members, but directed me to an excellent boarding house—where I obtained a small room for $1.00. It is now the lucky morning of Friday the 13ᵗʰ, & I am about to begin local explorations. I may try to locate Sechrist, who I find has no telephone. If he is in town, I shall probably be his guest. If not, waning cash will probably—yea, undoubtedly—send me back soon. Prepare, therefore, for my not remote advent after all these years! I have my return fare complete, but if you want to compete with A E P G in the banking business you might mail me a 5 or 10 spot—to Brooklyn—as a reserve for the home stretch. Of course, if Sechrist is here, I shall have no further room or food expense. More soon.
Yr aff Nephew & obt Servt
H P L

Notes

1. *Front:* Washington's Mansion, Mount Vernon, Va.

[242]   [ANS postcard]¹ [HPL to AEPG]

[Postmarked Washington, D.C.,
13 July 1928]

Annapolis was beyond all my wildest expectations! It is literally a close rival of Marblehead & Newport. The bus tour did not begin to scratch the surface—real sights started in when I started on my lone guidebook pilgrimage. I must

see it again—ROYAL street names—King George, Prince George, Duke of Gloucester, &c—everywhere! ¶ Came to Washington in the evening, & got a room for a dollar at a place recommended by the Y M C A. Am down to my last 10-spot except for return fare, but if Sechrist is in town I shall have no further board or food expenses. He has no telephone, so I'll have to hunt up his place in person. More later.
Yr aff Nephew & obt Servt
H P L

P.S.—I'm not far from your Powhatan![2]

Notes

1. *Front:* Washington's Mansion, Mount Vernon, Va.
2. Powhatan is the county seat of Powhatan county in central Virginia, named for the Native American leader Powhatan (1545–1618).

[243]   [ANS postcard][1] [HPL to AEPG]

[Postmarked Alexandria, Va.,
13 July 1928]

Old Alexandria in His Majesty's Province of Virginia! God Save the King! Am going on cheap excursion to the *Endless Caves,* New Market, Va. on Sunday. It will eat into my home fare, but I'm asking L D C to send a 5 or 10 spot to me in care of 368 E. 17th St. Brooklyn. This chance to see a real system of gigantic caverns is too much for any lover of the weird to miss. I've wanted to see a great cave all my life!
Yr aff Nephew & obt Servt
H P L

Notes

1. *Front:* City Hotel, Alexandria, Va.

[244]   [ANS postcard][1] [HPL to LDC]

[Postmarked Washington, D.C.,
14 July 1928]

Well—I returned from Alexandria & took a trip into the exquisite scenic region of Virginia which lies west of Washington; visiting the ancient hamlet of Falls Church. The old brick church, still standing in its shady churchyard, was built in 1734; & Gen. Washington was a vestryman. In the evening I tried to look up Sechrist, but found he was out of town—in Wyoming on government business. This morning—Saturday—I visited the great unfinished cathedral shewn on this card.[2] It is truly a magnificent thing, & I believe it surpasses New

York's St John the Divine in general delicacy & purity of line. Only the apse, with its airy flying buttresses, is at present complete. This afternoon I am hoping to visit Gen. Washington's plantation, Mt. Vernon, & after that shall observe the celebrated interior of the Library of Congress. That will finish Saturday. Then tomorrow comes the great trip to the *Endless Caverns*. Financially I am in an amusing state of slenderness, but am careful to save out my fare—*to New York*. If I find an enclosure of $10.00 awaiting me there, I shall be all right for Providence. You'll undoubtedly see me within a week.

Yr aff Neph & obt Svt

H P L

Notes

1. *Front:* Washington Cathedral Ss. Peter and Paul, Washington, D. C.

2. The Cathedral Church of Saint Peter and Saint Paul, known as the Washington National Cathedral, is a cathedral of the Episcopal Church in Washington, D.C. Construction of the cathedral, which began in 1907, was completed in 1990, although services began to be conducted in 1912.

[245]   [ANS postcard][1] [HPL to AEPG]

[Postmarked Washington, D.C.,
14 July 1928]

Took a great trip to the quaint village of Falls Church, Va.—in an exquisite scenic region—after my return from Alexandria, & later tried to look up Sechrist—but found he is in *Wyoming* on government business. Today (Sat.) have been to see new National Cathedral (splendid!!) & am now going to visit Gen. Washington the rebel, at his plantation of Mt. Vernon. Tomorrow I shall see a great *cave* system for the first time in my life—you'll receive reports of it. Am saving out only my return fare *to N.Y.*, since I've asked L D C to forward $10.00 to me at 368 East 17th St Bklyn. Altogether, I've made a very little cash go a darned long way—*what* a trip I've had, all in all!!! Hope the Maine coast hasn't begun to bore you.

Yr aff Nph & obt

H P L

Notes

1. *Front:* Lincoln Memorial, Washington, D.C.

[246]   [ANS postcard][1] [HPL to LDC]

[Postmarked Washington, D.C.,
15 July 1928]

Well—I fancy I need not write a travelogue for today, since the booklets I am sending under separate cover will tell you all about the stupendous sights I have seen. After all these years I have actually plunged deep into earth's black bowels—experiencing in fact what I knew only in fancy when I wrote "The Beast in the Cave" in 1905—23 years ago, just a year after moving into 598. (I had prepared the first draught of the MS. at 454) Read the booklets with care—they are my diary for today. The ride from Washington takes 4 hours, with a short 'bus stretch from sleepy, colonial New Market to the caves. The train trip is very lovely as soon as the Shenandoah Valley is entered—it is a hilly region like Athol & Templeton. The scenery is just like our own in New England except that the rivers (like the Potomac) are all yellow from the mud of the region. Virginia rail fences are omnipresent, although now & then I spy a homelike *stone wall.* But THOSE CAVES!! ¶ I don't know whether I'll start back tomorrow or Tuesday. You'll receive ampler bulletins—& anyway you'll see me before Saturday night.

Yr aff Nephew & obt Servt

H P L

Notes

1. *Front:* The Old Log Cabin.

[247]   [ANS postcard][1] [HPL to LDC]

[Postmarked Washington, D.C.,
16 July 1928]

Leaving for Philadelphia & New York at 3 o'clock this afternoon. Phila. at 10 o'clock tonight—N.Y. at dawn tomorrow. Hope you've sent my homeward fare to 368 East 17th. I'll send later bulletins from N.Y., & will see you at the end of the week or before.

Yr aff Nephew & obt Servt H P L

[On front:] Wish I had the cash to try this! I shall the next time.

Notes

1. *Front:* Fly in the New Ryan Brougham, Sister-Ship of Lindy's "Spirit of St. Louis" / Flying Daily over Washington from Washington Airport.

[248]   [ANS postcard][1] [HPL to LDC]

[Postmarked Philadelphia, Pa.,
16 July 1928]

Well—I had a fine trip by stage-coach from Washington to Philadelphia, & am now about to take the midnight coach for New York—arriving in the early morning. I shall kill time till 8 or 9 o'clock, & then begin to look people up. Shall be home very shortly now, even if I stop off at Hartford or New Haven, so I hope the precincts at #10 are in habitable condition. I mailed some things this morning by parcel post to relieve my satchel of excess weight. Just dump the package in my room beside the others, & I'll attend to it. I shall probably mail some more soiled linen from N.Y. rather than carry it in my bag. I have now seen Washington very thoroughly except for *interiors*. On my next trip I shall pay especial attention to them. I have also gathered data on sightseeing in Richmond, Williamsburg, &c. which will serve me in good stead when the time comes.

Yr aff Neph & obt Svt

H P L

Notes

1. *Front:* Carpenters' Hall, Philadelphia, Pa.

[249]   [ANS postcard][1] [HPL to AEPG]

[Postmarked Philadelphia, Pa.,
16 July 1928]

Heading back homeward at last, but still under the spell of those mystic & cryptical caves. Had a fine stage coach trip from Washington to Philadelphia, & am going on to N Y by night coach—arriving in the early morning. Will surely be home by the end of the week or before. It has been a record-breaking trip, & the Endless Caverns formed an appropriate culmination.

Yr aff Nephew & obt Servt

H P L

Notes

1. *Front:* Carpenters' Hall, Philadelphia, Pa.

[250]   [ANS postcard][1] [HPL to AEPG]

[Postmarked New York, N.Y.,
17 July 1928]

Well—back in this dump! Pretty dingy & foreign after Washington. The night stage coach blew in at 4:30 a.m., so I'm going to check my carpet-bag at the Pennsylvania Station & do some colonial exploring (probably Jamaica & Flushing) before calling anybody up on the telephone. The benches in the waiting room where I am are filled with sleeping citizens—one of whom just cried out very picturesquely in the throes of a nightmare! ¶ I have decided, after ample explorations, that *Washington* is my favourite among large towns.

It is the most American of any metropolis I have seen, & its climate & atmosphere seem quite ideal. The Virginia countryside near by is scenically exquisite, whilst reliques of the colonial past present themselves on every hand. However—I have not yet observed that finer, brighter colouring of the *sky* which so greatly impressed Henry Adams in contrast to the skies of his native Mass. More bulletins later—watch for the Providence postmark!

Yrs

H P L

[On front:] Summing up all my travels of this year, I find that *three* things stand out as high spots:

    (1) The wild hills, brooks, & glens of VERMONT;

    (2) The colonial vividness of ANNAPOLIS;

    (3) The weird mystery & beauty of the ENDLESS CAVERNS.

Notes

1. *Front:* Entrance to Canal and Bridge, Greenpoint, Brooklyn, N.Y.

[251]   [ANS postcard][1] [HPL to LDC]

[Postmarked New York, N.Y.,

17 July 1928]

Well—back in this poor old dump! Nothing makes N Y seem so garish & alien & common as seeing it directly after having been to another large city of higher grade. Washington is a white man's town, & to plunge from there into Manhattan is like going from Brown or Prospect St. to Camp St. or Atwell's Ave. All in all, I think I like Washington absolutely best of all *large* cities. If one must have a metropolis, that is the one. It even beats Philadelphia. As a straight-American city, it absolutely holds the prize for all places well up in the hundred-thousands. ¶ Shall indulge in some colonial exploration during the dawn hours before I can call up Belknap & S H. Think I'll go to ancient Jamaica, & from there to Flushing—(all nickle [*sic*] fares) thence back. The 'bus from Philadelphia passed through Elizabethtown—my good old colonial refuge in the nightmare period of Clinton St. I hadn't seen it before in three years. More later—& see you soon.

Yr aff Nephew & obt Servt

H P L

[On front:] Summing up all my travels of this year, I find that *three* high spots stand out:

    (1) The wild hills, brooks, & glens of *Vermont;*

    (2) The colonial vividness of *Annapolis;*

    (3) The weird mystery & beauty of the *Endless Caverns.*

Notes

1. *Front:* Entrance to Canal and Bridge, Greenpoint, Brooklyn, N.Y.

[252]   [ANS postcard (in envelope?)][1] [HPL to AEPG]

[No postmark;
17 July 1928]

Went on the antiquarian trip I planned, & also spent time in Prospect Park & Japanese Garden. Couldn't get in touch with S H in the morning, so went right up to Belknap's for dinner. Wandrei didn't come, so Sonny & I went to call on honest old McNeil, whom we left about 6:30 p.m. I then found S H at the shop, & received my mail—including three letters from L D C outlining the state of her health, which is infinitely more painful than I had imagined. S H also mentioned a letter from you advising my immediate return to Providence. Accordingly I have decided to take a second night on the road, & leave N Y on the 2:15 a.m. train, arriving in Providence about 7 o'clock. You will next hear of me from there. I was tremendously sorry to hear that L D C's new trouble is proving so considerable, & wish I had known of it in time to have been of more prompt assistance. L D C says that Dr. Cooke advises reëngaging honest Mrs. 'Arrison, but S H says she will gladly come to Providence during her vacation (ending Aug. 7) & serve in a nursing capacity herself, thus saving Mrs. 'Arrison's h'eight dollars per week. I am now in the Penn. Station awaiting train. I reënclose the $10.00 cheque—did not need it, since L D C sent a $10.00 bill herself. ¶ Yr aff n——H P L

Notes

1. *Front:* Montague St., Real Estate and Insurance District, Brooklyn, N.Y.

[253]   [ANS postcard][1] [HPL to AEPG]

[Postmarked Providence, R.I.,
18 July 1928]

Back home! Hope I'll find L D C resting in reasonable comfort. I'm waiting till about 9 o'clock before going up to the house, since I don't want her to be roused up too early, as she undoubtedly would be if she heard me coming in at 8. Providence is exquisite in the dawn's early light! Yr aff Nephew & obt Servt H P L

Notes

1. *Front:* Public Library, Providence, R.I.

[254]　　[ALS] [HPL to AEPG]

July 25, 1928

My dear Grandchild:—

　　　　　　　　I duly received both of your recent epistles, & am replying from a bench in the small memorial garden at Humboldt Ave. & Elton St.—where my beloved old ravine, the "Sewer Chimney Forest" used to be. This being Wednesday, the stores are closed; so instead of going downtown I am taking a walk through ancient scenes—454, Blackstone Park, Slater Ave. School, &c—in an effort to recall a youth long ago fled. By shutting my eyes I can still see the old ravine with its gnarled trees, steep slopes, & frog-haunted ponds. Would it were still there in fact! The grounds of the Friends' School are exceedingly beautiful today; but I was horrified to espy therefrom, close beside the stately Christian Science dome, the tall & intrusive tower of the new Industrial Trust Bldg. This is too much! Such things ought not to invade the vista of the ancient hill! I heartily wish they would take down 10 stories or so.

　　I suppose that you are by this time packing up for Ogunquit, hence I will direct the present letter thither. It is certainly too bad to have to move in the midst of a pleasant vacation, but after all I imagine Ogunquit is by no means an unattractive place. It looked pleasant enough to me when the 'bus took me through there nearly a year ago.

　　My trip was surely a marvel, & I can't say that it tired me; since I am always active & vigorous when given sufficiently piquant & varied imaginative nourishment. An echo of recent travels came day before yesterday, when all the Longs stopped here briefly en route for Cape Cod in the family Essex. Besides Sonny & his parents, the party included his aunt, Mrs. Symmes. I went down to see them at the Crown, & in the evening Dr. Long took everybody to a cinema show at the Rialto. They left town early the next morning.

　　L D C seems to have had much less pain during the past three days, although yesterday she felt some fatigue as a result of the warm weather. This same warm weather, on the contrary, is bracing me up—I was quite languid during the recent cool wave, & had to expend much effort in getting around; but since the mercury has mounted I am very spry again for a man of my years, & have conquered nearly all my accumulated correspondence. It has been hard work getting the alcove straightened out after its disarrangement, but I have done it at last. I have also finished reading all the accumulated papers & magazines. I make a daily trip downtown for supplies, & am arranging my usual reducing diet. Being at present 144, I must lose 4 lbs. in a single week in order to be 140 by Lammastide. L D C seems to eat as well as usual, her food being prepared by the nurse. I am hoping that she will soon feel able—or be authorised by Dr. Cooke—to eat some of her favourite Gibson's coffee ice cream. I feel quite guilty when indulging in my own vanilla brand of the same delicacy.

　　Both cheques safely arrived, & I at once returned the $15.00 I had borrowed of L D C. I have now begun my usual programme of economy, though a Bulletin bill took $1.75 the other day, whilst $1.15 has gone for a new straw hat. This latter—a conservative black-banded affair of my usual kind—I obtained at the new store where O'Gorman used to be, & it is certainly a bargain of the first water considering what I usually pay. Incidentally—I am having my new bargain blue suit pressed by the tailor in the Golden Ball Inn; the suave & swarthy successor of the *alterating* Mr. Bernstein.

L D C is sleeping quite tranquilly this afternoon, so that I have slipped out without disturbing her. I shall return presently—for the afternoon is waning, & the sunlight shines goldenly & glamorously over the scenes of my boyhood; casting long, mystical shadows & evoking many a ghost of vanished years. A pallid half moon gleams in the south—perhaps I shall get out my telescope this evening & complete the idyll of old-time 454-ish life. Heard from Cook today. He has traded his house in Athol for a 100-acre farm in the wild country east of the village, & expects to make a rather spectacular transition in the near future. More anon. Regards & best wishes.

Yr most aff Nephew & obt Servt

H P L

[255]   [ANS postcard][1] [HPL to AEPG]

[Postmarked Providence, R.I.,

26 July 1928]

Glad to learn from your card that you're enjoying yourself aquatically. I hope your rates as Maine guide are reasonable—I may want to employ you some day! Just had a card from Belknap telling how he & his family are enjoying themselves on Cape Cod. They expect to be in Marblehead in a week. My walk yesterday proved delightful. I ended up in the southerly colonial section—Dove St., Arnold & John Sts., &c—& proceeded north along Benefit. Repairs are progressing on the Stephen Hopkins house under Isham's direction. A colonial doorway (presumably a restoration of the original & forgotten one) has been cut in the broad side facing Hopkins St., & the whole fabric is being patched & overhauled. It will be a great place when it is done. Speaking of restorations—the slum houses in Benefit at the foot of Jenckes are being fixed & painted to guard against disintegration. The old gambrel roofer has received a coat of slate grey, whilst the Judge Durfee house has blossomed out in a vivid yellow. In Prospect St. the steel frame of the Sharpe house is going up—I hope the structure will be a good Georgian one. And so it goes. I intend to take a trip to Quinsnicket soon. L D C recd. your letter yesterday, & will reply later. Yr aff Neph H P L

Notes

1. *Front:* Manning Hall / Brown University.

[256]   [ALS] [HPL to AEPG]

Sunday, August 5[, 1928]

My dear Grandchild:—

Glad to hear that the "lost" mail matter was found so promptly. Thanks for the banking service—I might have done without the extra five, but am getting extravagant lately with all my numerous trips outdoors. I have secured ice cream nearly every time, & have twice spent 30 or 40 cents on a Waldorf Lunch dinner. I must begin putting on the screws in my programme of economy again!

It is certainly pleasant & appropriate that you have chosen a residential site so near my humble alma mater.[1] President Ave. isn't very far beyond the old place—indeed, I can't think of anything but open fields around there, for it is always the old landscape that lives in my mind. The ash-dump curve of Humboldt Ave. beside McKay's farmhouse & the Sewer Chimney Forest, the high vacant lot beyond Irving Ave. where we climb up the bank & cut across to Slater & climb down again right at the schoolhouse, the open view to the Boulevard in all directions, with Abbie's house[2] near the corner of President, the dark stretch of Cole's Woods to the north, with niggerville beyond, whence would troop Clarence Purnell & Asa Morse & the ash-cart Brannons, & the white-trash Taylors whose father tended the furnace at Slater Ave. & East Manning St. schools & whose most brilliant member founded The Jobbing Company—alas for the primitive & idyllick days! And the old scattered crowd—Chet & Harold, Reginald & Percival Miller, Tom Leeman & Sidney Sherman, "Goo-Goo" Coleman & Dan Fairchild the teacher's pet, "Monk" McCurdy[3] the rough guy whose voice had changed . . . . old days, old days! I shall look up your future abode with great interest, & shall surely be glad to assist you in settling there. I'll measure the mattress as soon as possible, though L D C tells me it is not now in a very reachable position. What sort of a bed is a Murphy bed? Is it one of the sort that folds into the wall as a mirror, pseudo-bookcase, or false door? It will take me a long time to get used to the neighbourhood as it is, for my mental picture is that of a quarter of a century & more ago. I shall drift about in quite a ghostlike manner!

Bless me, but I didn't think I'd neglected to thank you for the various literary offerings I found around #10! The set of Poe is magnificent—the illustrations alone are worth the price—& it is appropriate that an edition of this quality be in the library of one who specialises in the kingdom over which he ruled. I have not yet fitted it to my shelves—it takes more space than my cheap old edition picked up at Gregory's twenty years & more ago—but shall adjust it at my next general rearrangement.[4] Yet I shall never discard my old set. It grew old along with me, & is a symbol of the aspiring days of my youth, when its marvels seemed to unlock enchanted gates into realms of wonder & terror "out of space, out of time."[5] Poe is the one *first rate* literary figure America has yet produced, & it was with veneration that I gazed upon his grave in a slum-overtaken churchyard in Baltimore less than a month ago. The set of extracts from the classics of all literatures is a delightful anthology, & has been assigned a permanent place in my library. The volumes are of a convenient size for the pocket, & one or more shall be with me on many a trip to Quinsnicket or Blackstone Park. Some of the smaller items were delightful, too—& in general I feel that my modest collection has been very substantially enriched. It took me back to my youth to see the good old Webster of 1848. Old days! Lindley Murray's Readers, Webster's & Worcester's spelling books & dictionaries, "Peter Parley's" histories, Morse's Geography, Burritt's Geography of the Heavens, Greenleaf's Arithmetic, Comstock's Philosophy, Kane's Chemistry, Parker's Aids to Composition, Blair's Rhetoric, Cleveland's Compendia of Literature, the Geographical View of the World, Davies' Geometry, the Vestiges of Creation[6] .... & always the reliable Farmer's Almanack, past its 50th year & already using the word "old" on the title-page. Good old 1848! What a world of promise & simplicity, of naivete & classical polish! Pillared houses, the new Grace Church by Upjohn, the new rail-road station by the cove, & the new rail-road to Worcester, the quiet college of four buildings—including the new Rhode Island Hall—presided over by Dr. Barnas Sears[7]—the new Athenaeum & its group of literati—the circle of Mrs. Whitman, & that terrible man from Baltimore or Richmond or somewhere who *drinks*—Market Square crowded with teams—the old Coffee House—the Manufacturer's Hotel—the Franklin Building—the new-fangled gas-lighting system opened in December—the lately deserted East India wharves, with only Rufus Greene's barques from the Mozambique tied up beside them—the new Butler Hospital & Swan Point Cemetery, miles out in the country on the Neck, where the city will never spread—the new Historical Society Building—the Franklin Lyceum—the Mechanic's Library—the Greene St. school—the amazing spread of business across the bridge—half the houses in Westminster St. are given up to trade, & there's no hope of going back—Arcade is twenty years old—Weybosset is going over to trade, too—the Washington Hotel—the Manufacturer's & Farmer's Journal— heavens! what will Knowles & Anthony do next? .... they've installed a telegraph machine to get news for the Daily Journal!—Gladding & Proud's Bookstore—Camm's barber shop—Foster's Eating House & Oyster Saloon in Broad St—Perry Davis' Pain-Killer—Tripp the tailor—the new Quaker Meeting House—Wm. B. Wright's Improved Sky-Light Daguerrian Studio at 81 Westminster St., prepared to take Types of superior quality equally well in cloudy as in fair weather—Daniel Perrin's Bookstore & Circulating Library— Akerman the Bookbinder—Handy's Botanic Drug Store—Briggs, the undertaker near Hoyle Square, "has a new & elegant hearse, which cannot be excelled in this city, also a new style of coffins not found elsewhere"—Tyler's Temperance Eating-House in Market Square—Jones & Sisson's Oyster & Ice Cream Saloon, opposite the Museum in Westminster St.—Washington Row

Clothing Store—. . . . . . good old town, & good old 1848!

It is indeed too bad that L D C is having such a long siege of pain. Yesterday & the day before there seemed to be a return of some of the acuter back twinges—which she associated with possible pressure from digestive troubles. All in all, I fancy that rest & time are the things needed; & fortunately there is a very capable nurse on hand to see that the former essential is observed. This nurse is now evicted from her room because Miss Reynolds is occupying it herself—having rented an attic & a downstairs room to a new tenant—a Christian Science Healer named Mrs. Corrader or something like that. Being unable to sleep in the room with anyone else on account of nervousness, the poor creature is obliged to sleep on a cot in the hall near L D C's door, surrounded only by a screen.

I am glad the second half of your vacation is proving pleasant, & trust that in the end it may quite rival your Boothbay Harbour sojourn. No—I would not care for the frigid oceanic bathing! Weather here has just suited me—I think the Bulletin said it was 93 yesterday. As for East Greenwich—no, I did not pay any calls. The old town looked delightful—so much so that I am sure the inhabitants will but seldom climb to the hilly spot whence the Industrial Trust is visible.

You will certainly have an interesting time settling down next fall—but don't destroy too many things! What you don't want you can give to me. Yes—I shall be glad to get that 70-fish cheque. I am now working on a new tale—"The Dunwich Horror"—but on account of its extreme & utter hideousness I fear that W.T. will be reluctant to accept it. If it does land, it will mean a delectably ample cheque, for it will be of considerable length. I am now on page 29.

And so it goes. I'll measure that mattress for you shortly, & transmit the results by note or postcard. Now I shall return to my horror, & relate what Dr. Armitage of Miskatonic University did when It lumbered loathsomely & invisibly out of Cold Spring Glen.

Yr aff Nephew & obt Servt

H P L

Notes

1. AEPG's new residence at 61 Slater Avenue (corner of President Avenue) was two blocks north of the location of HPL's grammar school, the Slater Avenue Primary School (corner of Slater Avenue and University Avenue), which he attended in 1898–99 and 1902–3.

2. Abbie Anna Hathaway (1852–1917), the principal of Slater Avenue School, lived at 97 Blackstone Boulevard.

3. See Glossary for Chet and Harold (Munroe), Stuart Coleman, and the others. Percival Miller has not been identified. John McCurdy, Jr. (1884–1935) worked for a plumbing company as a bookkeeper.

4. The edition of Poe AEPG had given HPL is unknown. By "my cheap old edition" HPL evidently refers to a 5-volume set of the Raven edition of 1903.

5. Poe, "Dream-Land" (1844), l. 8.

6. HPL is discussing books that were popular in 1848, although few of them were first published that year. Some were in his library. "Peter Parley" is the pseudonym of the American writer Samuel Griswold Goodrich (1793–1860), who wrote a wide array of books on various subjects. HPL owned *Peter Parley's Arithmetic* (Boston: Charles J. Hendee, 1837; *LL* 389) and *A Pictorial History of England* (Philadelphia: Sorin & Bell, 1847; *LL* 390). For "the Geographical View of the World," see Bibliography under Sir Richard Phillips; for "the Vestiges of Creation," see Robert Chambers.

7. Barnas Sears (1802–1880), graduate of Brown (class of 1825) who served as its president (1855–67).

[257]   [ALS] [HPL to AEPG]

Saturday, August 11[, 1928]

My dear Grandchild:—

I appreciate the feline quotation very much, & congratulate you upon so graceful a literary achievement. It amply fulfils the promise displayed in "We have toil'd among life's reapers." The sentiments are precisely suited to my tastes, & I recited it last night to my old black friend Calef-kittie as I paused to exchange greetings with him beside a colonial doorway in Thomas St.[1] Calef-kittie grows younger as the years pass, & one beholds him higher & higher up the hill—& in greater & greater degrees of awakeness. I scarcely ever fail to see him now, & he knows the old gentleman very well; speaking to me in his own characteristic way as I pass toward down town & later pass back again. He & I are fellow-ancients—last reliques of 1848! I'd like to see one of those iron roof-cats you speak of. I vow, if I had one I'd entreat Miſs Reynolds' permission to place him atop #10 Barnes!

I enjoyed the warm weather greatly, though the mercury at no time ascended above 95°. The subsequent coolness is to me very depressing, & I don't wonder that the season seems quite over at Ogunquit. I'd abhor staying in any *one* summer place so long. When I travel, I like to *keep travelling*, & get a pleasing *variety* of scenic & antiquarian impressions. Thanks, by the way, for the King's Chapel card—which is the next thing to revisiting that archaick fane itself. I knew about the restoration of the Bulfinch State house, though I have not seen the result in actuality. I thought when I read of it how stupid it was to build marble wings when the central part could have been easily restored before—but there is no accounting for Victorian tastes.[2] Providence was commendably early in rectifying its nineteenth-century mistakes—it was aeons ago that University Hall & the old Market House lost their defacing integuments of stucco & yellow paint, respectively.

L D C still has more pain than when I wrote my letter before last, though less than when I wrote my last letter. Dr. Cooke was here yesterday morning,

& continued to enjoin time & patience—saying that the malady is essentially allied to rheumatism. She eats well, & the nurse seems very skilled in the preparation of satisfactory foods. Not yet, however, will she risk any coffee ice-cream from Gibson's.

I note all the points regarding 61 Slater, & will institute the necessary inquiries before the coming week is over. I am glad the powers in charge are such desirable ones—in contrast to the canny & frugal Meesder Frenk, who iss ah poor men, a'ready! I fancy there will be no difficulty in your occupying the place immediately upon your return, & a visit to the Glazen stable will surely furnish you with all the accessories you need. I shall be glad to attend to any details which may be within my power, & shall make inquiries concerning the proper procedure in gaseous & electrical installation. I will ask about the Murphy bed; & may meanwhile report that the mattress upstairs here, as measured a few days ago, is 76½″ long, 53½″ wide, & 4¼″ thick. Since the width of the bed is 48 inches, it is obvious that the mattress will have to follow my example of 1925 & practice some judicious reducing! I will request the sheets & towel, & am sure that L D C can furnish them. With these basic essentials you will certainly be able to camp out in some comfort until your ampler household adjustments are made. An' ob co'se, w'en de tahm comes, ah'll notificate Mr. Jackson of Medway St. an' git yo-all awn he waitin' liss' fo' p'ofessional extension. Ah reckins he willin' to subtend he sarvices ef de necessity ob de case be dissented to him in de right tackful manner.

Thanks as usual for the banking service. Incidentally—see why it's lucky I œconomised week before last, & didn't have to touch my cheque till the next came! I didn't spot the joker myself till after I signed it—but then I reflected that my own signature would not be quite enough to get me a *fife*, to say nothing of a full fife & drum! I have entrusted the 40-spot to L D C's care, asking her to present it to our benign hostess on Tuesday next.

My meals are all right—& I don't by any means limit my dinners to crackers & cheese! I usually have meat loaf & potato salad, with some cake for dessert; & sometimes choose baked macaroni. Then too, I have three times dined down town. But I must cut down these sybaritic rations, or I shall never be 140 by the equinox! For breakfast, of course, I uniformly have my favourite Downyflake doughnuts & cheese.

My new weird story is done, & I am now busy with the loathsome & prostrating task of typing it. It will probably come to 50 pages or so—which means an excellent cheque if it lands. It is a thing of most unutterable hideousness, & is called "The Dunwich Horror".

Had postcards today from two of my wandering children. Mortonius is hiking in the far New Hampshire wilds & has just paid his respects to the Great Stone Face, whilst Little Sonny & his papa & mamma are in an equally wild section of the Catskill region. The child wanted to stop at West Shokan & see Bernard Dwyer, but Pater Longus' constitutional impatience forbade such a delay. This is the second half of the Long tour. They returned from New England to N.Y. via Athol & the Mohawk Trail, stopping briefly to see Cook. Then, after a few days at home, they commenced the present westerly jaunt. Just had a long letter from good old Moe, who is in Madison collaborating with collegiate dignitaries on the editing of a 9th grade reader.³ Quite a pedagogue!

And so it goes. More later—& I'll attend to all the Slater Ave. details in due season. Have a good time & don't get frozen.

Yr aff Nephew & obt Servt
H P L

Notes

1. "Calef-kittie" is evidently HPL's name for the cat he later called "Old Man," who resided at "a market at the foot of Thomas Street" and lived to be at least twenty-two years old (see HPL to Duane W. Rimel, 22 December 1934; *Letters to F. Lee Baldwin* 243–45).

2. HPL refers to the Massachusetts State House in Boston, designed by Charles Bulfinch (1763–1844) and completed in 1798. The marble east and west wings were begun in 1895 and completed in 1917.

3. Moe was assisting Sterling A. Leonard and Harold Y. Moffett in the compilation of a series of books entitled *Junior Literature* (1930f.). Book Two included an extract from HPL's "Observations on Several Parts of America" entitled "Sleepy Hollow To-day."

[258]   [ALS] [HPL to AEPG]

The Recurrent 20th—1928
[20 August 1928]

My dear Grandchild:—

Oh—Oh—Ah—*Those doorways & houses!!* I refrained from opening the festive envelope—or rather, from undoing the festive wrappings—until the actual day of increased senility arrived; but now, at 9 a.m., I have unveiled the mystery. Hot dawg! But what a place good ol' Maine must be! That view de luxe of the rich Georgian porch & Palladian window above is surely a memorable masterpiece. I vow, it almost eclipses the architectural triumph designed by John Holden Greene for the late Truman Beckwith, Esq.! It is needlefs to exprefs the extent & sincerity of my gratitude. No more fitting remembrance of an old man's advance into the sunset could posfibly have been devised!

An' t'anks fer de fresh dope on me ol' side-kick Bossy, too. I seen a short spiel on de new scrap in de Bulletin, but dis is hot inside stuff what didn't get no publicity outside de Massachusetts countryside. Wot t'ell! An' so Bossy's ben wakin' up de livin' graveyard at State an' High! At dat, though, I gotta wit'draw me endorsement w'en it comes ter goin' dat fur. It's all right fer a guy to cut loose in a ord'nary neighbourhood; but w'en it gets so's he messes up a reel ol' Georgian backwater like State & High, dey's somebody gotta call

a halt & tell him w'ere he gets off! So dis time I'm wit' de mossback crowd—
an' I ain' gonna vote fer'm fer President, nuther—because if he started a fillin'
station on de W'ite House grounds he'd spoil one o' de classiest sections Wash-
in'ton has got. Al Smith's bad enough—but I draws de line at Bossy!¹

The reason I didn't raise that fife to fifty is merely because I hadn't practiced up on the signature. When I do get practiced, I shall raise one of those
fives to five million & take the next boat for South America. But this business
takes real finesse. The best I can do now is *A. E. P. Gamwell* [*signature*]—
which isn't much of a result from a truly professional standpoint.

Well—I think the L D C news this week is distinctly encouraging. Although she does not feel superabundantly strong or ready to dispense with the
nurse, her pain is now radically lessened—more so even than during the spell
of mitigation I described two or three weeks ago. She has lately been moving
about more independently & assuredly than at any other time since my return, & I would not be surprised if she were to write you shortly herself—
perhaps separately, & perhaps as an enclosure in an epistle of mine. Yesterday
she ate a fine lamb stew dinner prepared by the nurse, & she seems to be up
& about her room most of the time.

I shall consult the popular & important Mr. Jackson directly—asking him to
tender his professional services, if convenient to him, on the morning of Saturday, the 8ᵗʰ of September, preferably at nine o'clock. If he cannot, I fancy
there will be no difficulty in securing another transportation artist—either the
tenebrous & reliable Mistah Harold, neighbour of Delilah's, or the Caucasian
Mr. Redding so highly esteemed by our benevolent hostess Miſs Reynolds.

Meanwhile I have been making inquiries at 61 Slater, & find that I must
order the installation of the gas & electricity myself. Electric bulbs are not
furnished—but I will take the liberty of ordering three 60-watt lamps as a nucleus for whatever lighting system you may care to establish. This will give
you one light for every room. The apartment, I am told, will surely be ready
by the first of the month; & it certainly looks delectably inviting in its uncompleted state. The spring of the Murphy bed measures *3 ft 10 inches by 6 ft 6
inches*—reflect upon these figures, & pursue whatever course may seem advisable to you in the matter of mattresses. The present janitor—an 'ighly hintel-
ligent person with a slight Cockney haccent like Mrs. 'Arrison's—proved a
very affable informant, & took pains to let me know that he has seen better
days. He is a landscape painter by avocation! Unfortunately, this artistick soul
will not be your permanent janitor; for when furnace-time comes the work of
the four houses forming his present territory will be too much for one man,
& a colleague will be appointed.

It seemed homelike & old-fashion'd to be around in the old Slater Ave.
district again—I made two trips—Wednesday & Friday—since I did not find
the artist-superintendent at home upon the first occasion. The first time I
went to 454 & walked along my old route to school—Elmgrove & Hum-

boldt—except that I could not cut across the old high vacant lot between Irving Ave. & the schoolhouse. Afterward I walked to Swan Point & the river road, going from there to Pawtucket, where I visited Slater Park & saw the old Doggett house. Friday I followed the nearest route from Barnes St., across Cat Swamp; going through the Friend's School grounds to Lloyd, jogging up Arlington (past the most magnificent oak tree I have ever seen) to President, & along that to Slater. I afterward walked out President to the end—on the high bluff above the Seekonk—& noted the presence of benches, which will make that spot an ideal outing place for you in good weather. I think this property is part of Blackstone Park, for on the shore below are a row of "sewer chimneys" which seem to presage a future extension of the river road northward—across the creek to Butler Hospital at least, if not actually joining the Swan Point river road. This region formed one of the greatest stamping-grounds of our old gang in youth, & I wandered over it all with reminiscent eye. The creek, with the sandy bluffs about it, is absolutely unchanged except for the "sewer chimneys"; & I had hard work realising that all the years had flown. The flapping bottoms of my long trousers seemed strange to me, & I began considering the much-discussed plan of digging a pirate's cave in the great sand bank. But the afternoon was advancing, so I climbed the familiar path that came out between Coleman's house & the Thornley niggerville & prepared to set out for 454. Upon gaining the heights, I observed that after all the years *had* paſsed—so instead of going home I set out to find more unchanged places. The last house of niggerville is gone, & some magnificent neo-colonial estates are going up on the site of the old African settlement. Deciding that the grotto formed the least altered spot around, I looked about for the old entrance at niggerville, but found it boarded up. Proceeding, however, along Grotto Ave., I discovered that the next intersecting street—Lincoln Ave.—leads down to the spot where the old 'cross-lot path used to strike the ravine proper; so that it forms a new entrance which loses none of the scenic attractiveness of the old route. Entering, I walked north amidst the exquisite scenery of the ravine, finally continuing acroſs the hospital grounds to the bend of Rochambeau Ave., where the old brick farmhouse dreams amidst the harvest fields. I then proceeded to Swan Point, looked over the most ancient graves, & took another walk along the river road; emerging at the northerly end. I now began to explore that new thoroughfare connecting Pleasant St. with the end of the boulevard—Alfred Stone Road, which is half in Providence & half in Pawtucket. This I found to be a prodigiously pleasant street, lined with very tasteful houses on one side, & with only the stone wall & greenery of the cemetery property on the other. Upon arriving at the end of the Boulevard, I found a growing suburb where in my day was only open country; & I looked at the ancient junction point where once stood Mowry's Wheelmen's Rest with its long bicycle rack & its great "Phosa" sign. Alas—the spot is now occupied by a too, too modern drug store; but I stopped & had some ice cream in memory of old times—when I used to get ice cream at Mowry's whilst returning from Pawtucket wheel rides. It was now dusk, but I continued my walk back to the Swan Point new entrance, & along Elmgrove Ave., which is now quite cut through to the Boulevard. At Freeman Parkway I turned up to Morris Ave., & went thence to Barnes St. via the Friends' School grounds.

Thanks as usual for the banking service—though you didn't need to double the sum, since the œconomy was all accomplished & the programme made to come out even. Mariano has lately sent his semiannual remittance—& I shall get his cheque cashed today or tomorrow. I shall then be able to reciprocate courtesies, & plank down the deposits for you with the gas & electric companies if—as I have an idea—such deposits are customary.

So there are no cliffs on Cape Cod? Bless me, but what could that child have been thinking about? He ought to know a cliff when he sees it, for he's been all over the rocks at Magnolia. Sand dunes certainly can *not* be called cliffs—even earth & vegetation can form only *bluffs*. *Cliffs* are *rock walls* & nothing else but! I shall ask the little rascal what he meant—he ought to know the definition of *cliff*. Enclosed is a very pleasing feline card which he sent from the second half of his journey—also one from my fat grandson Mortonius, who is putting new wildness into the wilds of New Hampshire.

Enclosed is a death notice which L D C said might be of interest to you. As I conclude, I gaze again at those colonial cards & gasp with admiration & gratitude. Very shortly I hope to write that all gas, electric, & transportational matters are settled. ¶ Yr aff Nephew & obt Servt H P L.

Notes

1. HPL refers to Andrew Jackson "Bossy" Gillis (1896–1965), who was elected mayor of Newburyport, MA, in 1927. When he attempted to open a garage and gas station at the corner of State and High Streets without a permit, he was sent to jail, conducting municipal business from his cell.

[259]   [ALS] [HPL to AEPG]

Monday Night
[20 August 1928]

My dear Grandchild:—

Well—here's the Old Gentleman again, this time to report on sundry errands perform'd. The electric company is all fixed—no deposit, & the three 60-watt bulbs will be charged into your first bill. They promise to have things ready by the first of the month. The gas company will require a $5.00 deposit, & asks your signature—together with that of a witness—on the enclosed document. I fancy Miſs Ripley would do as the witness, since she is no doubt an old patron of the company & an honest payer of her bills. I fancy you had better send the application back to me, signed, & I will visit the company once more. They say they can install the meter at very short notice—as short as a single day, if necessary.

These details having been administered, I set out on foot for the ancient hill, resolved to combine my quest for the exclusive Mr. Jackson with an enjoyable walk in the late-afternoon sunlight. I climbed College Hill, traversed the grounds to the Roman Arch gate at Thayer & Manning, & proceeded up Manning to the more easterly region I was seeking. At the corner of Cooke St. a high-yaller gentleman of dignified maturity was watering the lawn & sidewalk of a terraced estate, & courteously turned his hose aside to accomodate my passage. Little did I fancy I should soon be in quest of him, & be addressing him by name! In due time I reached the sedate stable in Medway St. whose number proclaimed it the Jackson residence; & in response to my ring an urbane, coffee-coloured matron of later middle age appeared with the information that the gentleman of the house was to be found at 61 Cooke St., watering a lawn! Bress mah lawdy! An' ah des ben pas' a gemmun of colour a wat'rin' a lawn at des about de part ob Cooke St. dat 61 had orter be! Well—I trekked back to Cooke & Manning, & surely enough the high-yaller cavalier I had before remarked turned out to be none other than Mistuh Jackson! I address'd him with the buſineſs in hand, & he expreſs'd himself as pleas'd to undertake your commiſſion for Saturday the 8th of September at 9 a.m. I prepar'd him a suitable memorandum to retain, & trust that you will not find him absent from the appointed place at the appointed hour.

Buſineſs being despatch'd, I proceeded to beguile the remaining daylight hours with a walk through boyhood scenes. Going first to 454—for one must start from *home* in order to enjoy such a walk with proper perspective—I proceeded to Blackstone Park, where I read a copy of the Bulletin that I had extravagantly purchased down town. I then strolled out to the old creek, & later climbed the bluff to Grotto Ave., where I noted upon close analysis that *one* of the huts of Thornley's niggerville is still standing. The golden rays of the late afternoon sun gave a magnificently glamorous illumination to the chimneys of the new colonial houses thereabouts. I then sought the Boulevard & Cole Ave., desiring to ascertain just how much of the old Cole Farm is left. Here my discoveries were all pleasant, for there is really quite a bit of farm land still remaining—far more than appears from a brief glance at the Cole Ave. front. The farm extends back almost to the rear of the Keefe Surgery, & is diversified by pastures & orchards quite as of yore. After that I surveyed the Italian garden at Rochambeau & the Boulevard, & later walked down Elmgrove to Freeman Parkway, & thence home as on Friday's trip. Cat Swamp is surely a great place!

I enclose a couple of additional melancholy cuttings. Po' ol' Noah done git on de Hebbenly Ark at las'—& in Mrs. Chapman the kin of a genial & capable man of science perishes. L D C also encloses an item about some branch of your old friend Truman's family. Well—send back the gas blank soon if you want quick service!

Yr aff n——

H P L

[260]　[ALS] [HPL to AEPG]

Wednesday
[29 August 1928]

My dear Grandchild:——

I must apologise for my tardy acknowledgment of yours of the 23ᵈ, but recent accumulations of mail have thrown my schedule into something like total chaos. The gas application duly came back, & I shall try to get it into the office this very afternoon—in any case, you may depend upon it that both gas & electricity will be functioning at 61 Slater by the time you get there. I hope the mattress question may be adjusted with equal smoothness, so that you can at once take up your abode in the new & spotless haven now so near completion.

Thanks abundantly for the cliff. I didn't see the actual coast of Ogunquit when pafsing through last year, since the stage-coach stuck to the road. I have always understood, however, that it is highly imprefsive; with an observation-path along the top of the cliffs known as the "Marginal Way". I must ask that small child what he meant by talking about Cape Cod cliffs.

Bulletins of L D C assume a more encouraging tone this week. On Friday last, as I was bending over this desk, I heard a familiar intonation in the corridor—& soon perceived a well-known touch upon the door-handle. Turning, I beheld a surprising & heartening case of truancy—for in the nurse's absence (Friday being her day off, when her son comes to take her motoring) the patient had broken bounds & come down stairs for the first time since her illness assumed its acute phase! She did not stay long, but received the unstinted congratulations of all the denizens of the house whom she encountered. She seems none the worse for her adventurous jaunt, though she has not as yet repeated it. The pain is now uniformly less than during the peak of the illness; though naturally it still lingers somewhat, & shews its general tax on the system in the form of weakness & easy fatigue. I am enclosing a few cuttings which the patient thought might be of interest to one of your wide acquaintance & analytical erudition in the domain of Providence social history.

As for my diary—I find upon examining the records that I have neither done nor seen anything notable since last I submitted my report. The nearest approach to an outing was last night, when I had to kill an hour & a half waiting for a prescription, & spent the time in a trip to Roger Williams Park—where I saw the new statue of Bowen R. Church & read the Evening Bulletin on a bench. The statue is on a pedestal in the waters of the lake between the bandstand & the farther shore from the casino side. It faces this farther shore, thus turning its back to the decadent concert auditors of today, who are content to put up with the musick of lefser artists.

By the way—speaking of art, & its congener, literature—I was amused to learn yesterday that a small piece of my writing, signed with my name, is to appear in the 7ᵗʰ grade grammar-school reader which the Macmillan Co. will publish next year! Now don't you wish you were still teaching, so you could tell all the little Joe Merluzzos & Tony Rossis that your family wrote their schoolbooks! The source of this pedagogical publicity, as you may deduce, is good old Moe—who is assisting two U. of Wis. professors in preparing the new Macmillan reader series. He took a fancy to a passage in my long travelogue of spring & summer wanderings—the part describing Sleepy Hollow—& secured the consent of his academic colleagues to insert it in the reader containing Irving's immortal clafsick. Me & Wash Irving allus was important items of standard reading—though I don't see what's so great about Wash!

Well—more next time.

Yr aff Nephew & obt Servt

H P L

[261]   [ALS] [HPL to AEPG]

Sunday
[2 September 1928]

My dear Grandchild:—

I note with appropriate melancholy the advent of September, & hope I can get in at least a Newport trip before the outer world shuts down under the hellish power of the daemon Cold. I have made the final arrangements about your gas, & am assured that the meter will be connected before the 8ᵗʰ. There is a receipt for your deposit which I will keep for you—since there is no sense in mailing it merely for you to bring back. I hope the shipment of the mattress was successfully accomplished, & will take over the sheets & towel very soon. I have not seen anything hereabouts which resembles your Truman Beckwith cup & saucer, but I'll lend you the corresponding pieces from my collection of rare old Woolworth blue china if you'll promise not to break them. I don't blame you for anxiety to see the flat; & from what I saw on Aug. 17ᵗʰ, I don't believe you'll be disappointed. There is a "dining nook" in the kitchen with seats around the wall & an eating bench, & the view from the east window is splendid—though not so uninterrupted by foliage as is the corresponding view from across the hall in the northeast apartment. When the trees become bare you will have an opportunity to study East Providence.

Abundant thanks for the Kennebunkport cards—the next time I take a trip up the coast I must stop off & walk down to the ancient village. I have been saving that guidebook you sent me a couple of years ago. Too bad they don't emulate their coolly regarded rival Wiscasset, & give proper pictorial exploitation to their treasures. If Ogunquit is warm, I'm sure I'd like it. As autumn draws near my thoughts turn to the blue Caribbean, & the bale-laden wharves of sleepy towns along West-Indian shores. Jamaica—Trinidad—Martinique—Havana—Santo Domingo—ah, me! Why the deuce does New England have to be cold?

L D C has retained her comparative immunity from pain of the severer kind, though the general weakness of her condition makes the sojourn of the nurse a continued necessity. She is thinking of having Dr. Capron come over to provide her with new glasses if she cannot get out to see him in the reasonably near future. Naturally, it would be a great help if her eyes could be in perfect shape for reading—of which she will be doing more as her convalescence advances.

So Miss Ripley is one of those thunderstorm fearers? She reminds me of the poor old collie dog at the Beebe-Miniter farmhouse in Wilbraham, who whines & drools & crouches close to some human protector whenever the sky begins a pyrotechnical display. No—I couldn't undertake to stand a whole season at a summer hotel—unless it were near a Colonial countryside, & I didn't have to do anything but sleep in the place at night. Orton has virtually completed the purchase of a fine old brick colonial house (1770) & 140-acre farm in Vermont, about 2 miles from the one he is now leasing, & says he wants me to come up & spend a year! I'm telling him that he'll have to count the *winter* months out. Ugh . . . Vermont in *winter!!!*

As for my diary—on Thursday I went to Hunt's Mills by the same route we that took last autumn, & found the place still in its restored natural glory. The small Sayer store—where I was so anxious to get a job—appears to be closed, with all the shelves stripped bare. Another great industry fallen victim to New England's commercial depression! Friday I went to Quinsnicket & wrote letters there all the afternoon. I shall go again shortly—in fact, I shall take my work there often on good days until the weather gets cool. We never miss the water till the well runs dry—every fall, as good days become rare & limited, I begin an annual rush to crowd in some rustic outing! By the way—there has been a change in trolley schedules, & the Brown St. line has gone back to the custom of the golden nineties—ending at Brown & Olney Sts. All the Camp St. cars will be routed via North Main & Olney. Old days return! Now I want to see the little red Elmwood cars again! ¶ Yrs H P L

1929

[262]   [ANS postcard][1] [HPL and Samuel Loveman to LDC]

[Postmarked Boston, Mass.,
3 January 1929]

Greetings! Had a good trip to Boston, & spent the morning amongst the bookstalls. In the afternoon we secured a couple of rooms at the ancient United States Hotel, built in **1820**, which will form a very appropriate head-quarters for an antiquarian tour. This hostelry is in Beach St. near the South Station. After securing quarters, we went by subway to Cambridge, seeing Harvard Yard & Longfellow's House, & later attending a cinema at Harvard Sq. After that we returned to Boston, & have just obtained a good Italian dinner at the Florence Restaurant in Washington St., where Kirk & I dined in July 1926. We are now writing this card at that refectory. Later we shall devise a means of killing time until the theatre closing hour brings Loveman's friend—of whom he spoke last night. Possibly the interval will be filled by an electric-light tour of ancient Beacon Hill. We shall see. Tomorrow will also probably be a Boston day, & Saturday we shall visit Salem & Marblehead. More later. Will see you Sunday. Hope A E P G gets your muffins all right.
Yr aff Nephew & obt Servt
H P L

This has been a wonderful afternoon to me—with the most wonderful of guides. Sam

Notes

1. *Front:* Massachusetts Hall, Harvard University. Cambridge, Mass.

[263]   [ANS postcard][1] [HPL to LDC]

[No postmark;
3 January 1929]

Diary Continued—Thursday, Jany. 3. ¶ After leaving the Italian restaurant we explored Beacon Hill by electric light, then proceeding to the Hollis St. Thea-tre at 10:45 to meet that young friend of Loveman's—Gervaise Butler.[2] He proved very pleasant, & we all sat for some time over cups of coffee at a Child's Restaurant in Tremont St. We then dispersed, & I am now retiring late at the ancient U.S. Hotel. Tomorrow more Boston—probably the Art Museum—& we shall meet young Butler again in the evening. Saturday comes the climax—Salem & Marblehead. Loveman is very appreciative of the

737

colonial. Well—more later & see you Sunday. Yr aff Nephew & obt Servt
H P L

Notes

1. *Front:* Old South Church and Washington Street, Boston, Mass.
2. Gervaise N. Butler (1888–?), later a dance critic who served on the editorial board
of *Dance Observer.*

[264]   [ANS postcard][1] [HPL to LDC]

[Postmarked Boston, Mass.,
5 January 1929]

Well—here's a continuation of the diary for Friday, January 4th. We rose at 9
a.m., took breakfast at a Waldorf, & made another round of bookshops inter-
spersed with sightseeing. We saw the principal burying grounds, & explored
the interior of King's Chapel. At noon, after a Waldorf cup of coffee, we repaired to the Museum of Fine Arts, where Loveman was so enraptured by the
Greek sculpture & vases that we had no time to do the new period wing. I
shall do that alone Sunday. After closing time, we visited the ancient North
End, & saw all the ancient houses & alleys. We visited the site of Morton's
grandfather's birthplace & saw the bronze tablet, & thoroughly inspected the
Old North Church with its delightful steeple. After that, more Waldorf & a
cinema show; & at 11 we again met Loveman's friend Butler, & had coffee at
Childs'. Dispersing at midnight, we again sought rest—& I am now about to
retire at 2 a.m. Tomorrow we do Salem & Marblehead, & Loveman returns to
N Y in the evening. I shall stay over till Sunday & see the new period wing.
Will be home Sunday night.
Yr aff Neph & obt Servt
H P L

Notes

1. *Front:* The Old State House, Corner of Washington and State Streets, Boston, Mass.

[265]   [ANS postcard][1] [HPL and Samuel Loveman to LDC]

[Postmarked Marblehead, Mass.,
5 January 1929]

Marblehead!
Enough said!!
Yr aff Nephew & obt Servt

H P L

Sam L.

Notes

1. *Front:* Old Town House, Built 1727, Marblehead, Mass.

[266]   [ANS postcard]¹ [HPL to LDC]

[Postmarked Boston, Mass.,
6 January 1929]

I don't know which you'll see first—this card or me! If I get home early Sunday, you'll see me first. Otherwise, you'll see the card first on Monday morning. ¶ As for today's diary—Saturday the 5th—my cards from Salem & Marblehead have already apprised you of the main itinerary. We saw as much as time permitted, & Loveman was quite enraptured. In the afternoon we returned to Boston, dined at a Waldorf, & proceeded to the South Station, where Loveman took his N Y train. I then had my shoes repaired at a nearby cobbler's, for the day's walk had about finished them. They look very nice now. In the evening I went to the hotel, & have since been writing cards & reading in the three books I have just acquired. One is a treatise on *drawing*—which may give me some valuable rules in the art I so long to master.² Tomorrow I shall see the new museum wing, & in the evening I shall proceed homeward. It is now about midnight, & I think I will retire. See you later.
Yr aff: Neph & obt Servt
H P L

Notes

1. *Front:* Boston Common and Beacon Hill Section, showing State House, Boston, Mass.
2. Apparently Charles Lederer's *Drawing Made Easy.*

[267]   [ALS] [HPL to LDC]

Friday Apr 5. [1929]

My dear Daughter:—
                    I take my pen in hand to apprise you of the events of my visit, & to exprefs the wish that you are enjoying as good health as pofsible.
     My task of revision prov'd indeed an obstinate one; so that although I finish'd it superficially, I fear there is still more to be done upon it. At 9 a.m. yesterday I met Orton at his office in the tall Heckscher Building (the one with the golden rooster on top, in the antient Dutch manner) at 5th Ave. & 57th St., & learned that his liberty for the day had been suddenly curtailed, so that he would not be free until 5 p.m. I also learned that his wife's Vermont trip had been postponed, so that we would not have a bachelor freedom of

the house for ourselves. The family at Yonkers consists of Orton, his wife, little Geoffrey—who now walks, runs, & almost talks—& Orton's delightful grandmother, Mrs. Teachout, a Vermont gentlewoman above 80 years of age. Among the duties to be attended to by Orton yesterday was one very pleasant one—the purchase of a sumptuous & sedate Packard automobile, the first car he has ever owned except for a Ford years ago. This vehicle will be available tonight, & henceforward some delightful motor trips may be reckon'd as ingredients of the visit. Agreeing to meet Orton at the Grand Central (where I had checked my luggage) at 5 p.m., I at once telephoned my small grandchild Belknap (from whom a note was awaiting me in Orton's care) & was invited up to his house for lunch & for the day. Sonny is just recovering from a cold, & his mother is a still more enfeebled convalescent from an attack of grippe—her second this year. Yesterday was the first day that she sat up & ate at the family table. Felis & Dr. Long seem as usual, & of course I saw the new dog—which is a very languid & not especially healthy-seeming beast. Everyone in the household seems to be exceedingly fond of it, though Felis is not neglected on his account. My reception was marked by the most extreme cordiality, & the Longs are trying to persuade me to be their guest for a week after my Yonkers sojourn terminates—they say they will provide me a room in the same house, since the tenants in some of the other apartments rent rooms. It would be a great chance to visit with Sonny & explore the museums more thoroughly than can be done from a base as distant as Yonkers; but I told my hospitable inviters that I had promised not to protract my absence from home too long, since my coöperation is necessary to the maintenance of a good muffin supply. I might stay for a fractional period—just long enough to take certain expeditions which Belknap & I want to make; especially a cathedral-seeing trip to include St. John the Divine, St. Thomas's, & St. Patricks. The conversation yesterday was as congenial as usual, & Sonny & Grandpa disposed of most of the questions of art, literature, & science in one way or another. The usual lavish Long luncheon occurred at 1 o'clock—chicken a la King & multifarious accessories—but I took very frugal portions, mindful of my ambition to be 140 by Roodmas. At 4:30 I reluctantly took my departure—& without having been scratched once by Felis. Felis's temper is getting milder & mellower with age. Orton was on hand at the Grand Central, & we at once entrained for his home in the rural Grey Oaks district of Yonkers. The route lies through one of the loveliest countrysides near New York—the Bryn Mawr Park section, whose rolling & wooded topography so closely resembles New England, & which has had many park-like landscape improvements since last year. I had seen Orton's neighbourhood once before; when his uncle lived there, & we ended an all-night walk with a trip out to see him—but that was on a hellishly cold day in Feby. 1926, when the ground was one vast snowdrift & I was too frozen to think, see, or appreciate. Now, in the awakening glow of spring, I found a paradise which I could hardly believe I had ever previously beheld! It is most emphatically **not** a crowded real-estate "development" as I had so hastily assumed, but a genuine open countryside with wooded hills, lakes, farms, & glorious vistas. Few houses—no streets—just winding hill roads & meadows & woods & estates. Orton's house—a white gabled relique of about the 1830 period—is on a picturesque side hill with grounds, fence, grape-arbour, & all the appurtenances of a real farm. A rushing Vermont-like brook flows bubblingly beside the front gate, & the whole locale is absolutely antithetical to the New York atmosphere. It might easily be a stretch of country near Quinsnicket, so far as appearances go. Nor does Orton's house contain any jarring note. Flagstone walks, old white gate, low ceilings, small-paned windows, wide-boarded floors, white-mantled fireplaces, cobwebbed attic, rag carpets & hooked rugs, old furniture, centuried Connecticut clock with wooden works, pictures & decorations of the "God-bless-our-home" type—in short, everything that bespeaks an ancient New England hearthside. The guest room to which I am assigned is the best in the house—the gabled second story of the ell, with windows on *three* sides—looking north over meadows & ponds to the hills, south across the flagstoned yard to the front gate & shady country road, & east to the deep forest that runs down a slope toward the railway. Truly, at this moment I can't tell the difference from Brattleboro or Wilbraham! Orton's grandmother makes an ideal head of the household—he was her favourite grandchild, & she largely brought him up owing to the nervous semi-invalidism of her daughter—his mother. Now she is repeating the process with sprightly little Geoffrey as much as the latter's mother will let her. Geoffrey is lucky in having a living *great-grandmother.* Not many have that advantage, although I believe the son of our recent fellow-lodgers the Covells has. I may add that the house possesses steam heat, plumbing, & electricity as a concession to material comfort. Orton is exceedingly fond of it, yet talks of moving closer to town in winter on account of the trouble of furnace-tending & transportation. After an exploration of the house & an excellent roast beef dinner we settled down to conversation in the library—a fascinating haven with walls solidly lined with bookshelves. And there was plenty in that room to converse about! Orton has, next to Cook, the finest book collection of any member of the gang; & many of the items are valuable early-American imprints with the long ſ's I love so well. About midnight the session adjourned, & I retired in the ancient gable chamber overlooking the hills & meads & mysterious woods. Sleeping well, I did not arise today (Friday) until after Orton had left—& I have since been writing in the old gabled chamber, endeavouring to catch up with my correspondence. Now—3 p.m.—I am about to go to N.Y. to meet Orton at the Mercury office—plans for the evening being in his hands. I think he wants to take me to call on the authoress of that book whose title you noticed in the advertisement pages of the Times—"The Devil is a Woman". This lady—Mrs. Godfrey, who writes under her maiden name of Alice Mary Kimball—is an old friend of the Ortons & Teachouts, & an old-time Vermonter full of the folklore of that region. Her book is a collection of realistic narrative poems about Vermont life—Orton has asked me to skim it through before we call, so that I can discuss it. Speaking of books—Orton has seen Old De Castro's life of Bierce, & says that Sonny's preface *is* included. So the old boy is honest after all! Belknap doesn't know yet—he is too timid to go into a shop & ask to see the book—but I shall inform him very shortly. Whether or not I shall call on old De Castro I haven't yet decided—Orton advises me not to bother with him much, since his standing among authors & publishers is very doubtful. The son of Bierce's former publisher—Neale—is about to issue a really important biography of Bierce.[1]

Saturday Morning

Well—I met Orton yesterday at his office at 5, & was introduced to a very pleasant young man named Rothenburg, who was to be with us during the evening. Proceeding uptown to a garage, we obtained Orton's new Packard—which turned out to be a used one. It gave Orton trouble several times during the evening, but will probably come out all right—the trouble being with the battery system rather than the engine. Our destination—not the home of the authoress, it appeared, but the home of a friend of hers where she was to give a reading to a small group, was in Greenwich Village; so that we stopped for dinner at Hubert's Cafeteria in Sheridan Square—where you got the veal cutlet you didn't like, but where A E P G was well suited with the same material. In memory of those two visits, I ordered *veal* myself—a *veal goulash*—& found it splendid. The *quantity* served was the nearest thing to *Jake's* enormous portions that I've seen outside Providence! I had vanilla ice cream for dessert. We then proceeded to the scene of the reading in King St.—& I was delighted to find the house a *real colonial one*, with pillared doorway & panelled interior. There are fewer & fewer of them now, alas—you'd scarcely know Greenwich Village! The house was well filled with fairly intelligent people, to most of whom we were introduced & all of whom I forgot at once. Refreshments were served twice—once at an intermission & again at the end of the reading. I took a glass of lemonade the first time & a cup of coffee the second time—140 by Roodmas! Mrs. Godfrey read her longest poem very ably, & with every authentic shade of New England colouring. I would not call her work great or even notable, it being rather didactic, symbolic, & insensitive to sheer beauty. But it shews a profound insight into Yankee psychology, & in its detailed pictures & idioms is a truly vivid evocation of the Vermont scene. The gathering did not adjourn till after midnight, & on account of a rain Orton offered to take several of the guests to their respective homes or nearest subway lines. Accordingly he filled the new Packard like a Butler Ave. car at the rush hour, & consumed much time detouring around to various doors & subway entrances. Young Rothenburg, who proved exceptionally pleasant, came to Yonkers as an overnight guest, & is now reposing in the mysterious attic above me. We did not reach Orton's till 2 a.m., & it is now slightly later. I shall get a snatch of rest & rise again at 7, going into town with Orton & Rothenburg & leaving them at the Mercury office. I shall then spend the morning in my own way—probably looking up Loveman or Kirk or Sonny or all of them—& meet Orton again at noon, since he feels fairly sure he can get the afternoon off. What we shall probably do is to take a tour of colonial exploration in the new Packard—if it is fixed up by that time—covering a great deal of ground in a short time. We may see the old Schenck house in Flatlands, or perhaps invade Staten Island—or go over Long Island to Flushing, Jamaica, & Hempstead—but of that more later.

Sooner or later we shall have some gang meetings—Orton plans for one, & Sonny for another. I must get in touch with Morton, Talman, & Wandrei, too. Sonny & I plan to pay honest old Mac a surprise visit. Incidentally—you ought to see that little Belknap-imp in his new lowish-crowned *derby hat!* That & the moustachelet are enough to turn a grandsire's hair grey! He has lent me a new horror-novel—"Death in the Dusk", by Virgil Markham—but I've had no chance to read it yet.[2] By the way—I find that the fare from Orton's into N Y is even cheaper than I thought. A one-fare trolley ride—with a free transfer—takes one to the main centre (Getty Sq.) of Yonkers, & that transfer plus another nickel extends the trip to Van Cortlandt Park where the west side subway begins. Entering that for a nickel, one can go virtually anywhere; so that the whole fare from Orton's is only *15¢.* The railway fare, on the other hand, is *63¢.* I shall use the 15¢ route whenever Orton doesn't take me in in his new Packard. The running time is about 1½ hrs., whereas that of the train is 40 minutes.

But I will close this instalment here, & get a snatch of sleep before morning. More bulletins later, & a weight card as soon as I am down to 140. Hope your muffins are coming all right!

Yr aff Nephew & obt Servt

H P L

[On envelope:]

It was simply too good for words to see H.P.L. again. I anticipate another revival of my youth.

Sam Loveman

Saturday's Diary—

Went to town with Orton & Rothenburg in morning—stopped off at Loveman's (vide supra) & went out to lunch with him. He has had a marvellous new photograph taken of himself—by the famous photographer Arnold Genthe[3]—of which he will give me a copy. Now—noon—Orton has called at the Rowfant & we are going on a colonial expedition—the wavering Packard being put in shape at last. I am now at a one-arm watching Orton eat—&

with us is a friend of Orton's named De Kay, whose ancestry is the oldest Manhattan Dutch. I'm now writing postcards to all the gang—then Orton & I shall set out for the ancient Gracie Mansion at the foot of 88ᵗʰ St—built in 1813 & now housing the N Y City Museum.

Notes

1. The biography was written by Bierce's publisher, Walter Neale, not by Neale's son.
2. The novel, written by the son of the poet Edwin Markham, is in fact an offbeat detective story.
3. Arnold Genthe (1869–1942), German-American photographer, best known for his photographs of San Francisco's Chinatown and the 1906 earthquake and fire.

[268]   [ANS postcard within envelope][1] [HPL to LDC]

[7 April 1929]

MONDAY NOON—Well—here's a continuation of the diary! Saturday afternoon Orton & I found the old Gracie Mansion closed, but we went at once to the ancient Dyckman house, which we enjoyed exceedingly. A E P G has seen this, but I don't think you have. You must some time. We then went to the Van Cortlandt house—which you have seen—& enjoyed it no less. After that we returned to Yonkers, & in the evening (as I wrote letters) Orton went with the car to meet his other guest. This man proved to be one of the most delightful persons I have ever met—not a real Bostonian, as I had thought, but a genuine Englishman & Oxford graduate. He has been a professor as well as a clergyman, but is now working in a bookstall. His name is Troop—& he is not as young as I had fancied; being about my own age. His philosophy is, as one would expect in a former clergyman, more Victorian & idealistic than mine; but he is very broad & pleasant about it. Personally he is of the type I most admire—the true English gentleman, with all the mellowness & background of the ancient British civilisation. We exchanged addresses, & he may stop in Providence the next time he is in New England. He wants to spend his vacation in *Gloucester,* & I may go along & guide him—also shewing him Salem & Marblehead. Sunday was an idyllically warm day—as today also is— & we all went to ride in Orton's car, discovering some marvellous rustic scenes & vistas around Yonkers & Hastings which were as new to Orton as to me. The car developed more trouble, though, & is now in the repair shop again. In the evening Orton's parents & younger brother came over—they live in the Riverdale section where Orton used to live. After tea all hands read the Times & retired early. This morning Orton left before Troop & I rose. Guests arose at 9 a.m., & I guided Troop into N.Y. I then went to Loveman's bookshop—where I am now. I am now going to lunch with Loveman, & at 2 o'clock I shall meet Orton for an afternoon of exploration—on foot & subway, since the car won't be available. I shall call up Sonny also & see if he can go along. More soon—Yr aff Nephew & obt Servt H P L

[On envelope:]
P.S. There are several items in the new Times which I shall want to cut out. Note the article in the magazine section about the coming tragic demolition of Old Chelsea.[2] I shall visit the doomed section very soon. Incidentally—the Mrs. De Kay mentioned in the article is the mother of the young man I met at lunch Saturday. They still live at London Terrace, but will have to move shortly.

Notes

1. *Front:* Dyckman's House Museum—View from Garden.
2. Diana Rice, "The Tall City Marches upon Chelsea," *New York Times Magazine* (7 April 1929): 8–9, 16.

[269]   [ANS postcard within envelope][1] [HPL to LDC]
[9 April 1929]
Well—here's some more diary! Had lunch with Loveman & went to meet Orton at Times Square at 2 p.m. (Monday) We decided to visit the N.Y. Historical Society Museum at 79th St & Central Park West—which I think you have seen & which I know A E P G has seen. Having telephoned Sonny, we were met there by him—derby hat & all! Our session was highly congenial, & we soon adjourned to the Am. Museum of Nat. Hist., where we saw a marvellously arranged exhibit of the strange & sinister deep sea fishes discovered by William Beebe on his Arcturus expedition.[2] We then walked down to 72nd St.; where Sonny took a 'bus for home, whilst Orton & I went down to the Mercury office in 57th St. We saw De Kay there, & I sympathised with him regarding the approaching demolition of his home—see the article on Chelsea in the Sunday Times. Orton & I then set out for the uptown garage, but found the Packard still defective. It being too late to reach Yonkers for dinner, Orton telephoned his wife not to wait, & we went instead to his parents' flat near Van Cortlandt Park. The senior Ortons gave us a royal meal, & the younger son Carlton took us to Yonkers in his car. Arriving, Orton popped corn & the family retired at 10. I shall retire shortly, rising at 7 a.m. & having an indeterminate programme till evening, when Orton & I—or I alone if Orton can't come—will call on Loveman & arrange an evening with him. Thursday Sonny & I shall call on honest old Mac & surprise him—he doesn't know I'm here.

[On front:]

Hope you are prospering—with decent health & plenty of muffins. Have you improved these gorgeous warm days? Let's have a line of news—here's a card to use! Yr aff Nephew & obt Servt HPL

P.S. Loveman has presented me with 6 books, which I shall send home by parcel post.

[On envelope:]
    Retired 1 a.m., rose 7:30 a.m. Have helped Orton's grandmother wipe the dishes (the other Ortonii having gone to taown) & am now writing letters. Very soon I shall go exploring—possibly to the *Eastchester* which I have wished to see so long. You may recall that Morton only recently released me from my promise not to see it until he could guide me in person. There is a fine colonial church & churchyard I am anxious to see.
    ¶ I fear I've gained 2 pounds! Some Liggett scales gave me *144* yesterday! I must take drastick measures to get down to 140 by Roodmas! A E P G writes that she's been to Norton. You must work in a trip there during the summer. I think we could go by train if we knew the right hour to take it.

P.S. I find that my new acquaintance Troop has studied at Harvard as well as at Oxford. A great chap!

Notes

1. *Front:* The Beekman Family Coach / The New York Historical Society.
2. William Beebe (1877–1962), American naturalist and explorer. In 1925 he undertook an expedition to the Galápagos Islands and the Sargasso Sea on the steam yacht *Arcturus*.

[270]   [ALS] [HPL to LDC]

Friday Evening—
April 12, 1929

My dear Daughter:—
            I was indeed glad to receive yours of the 8th, & to learn that you & the muffin question are getting along well whilst Grandpa tarries on alien soil! I am certainly having a most marvellous time—surrounded by the most incredible cordiality & hospitality on every hand—& am kept in a round of pleasant activity quite antipodal to my habitual hibernation when at home! Not only do invitations come from my own old friends, but from the new friends I am now meeting through Orton. He says they have all expressed very flattering opinions of me—which is rather agreeable, since I have so far liked all of them exceedingly. Young Rothenburg, who is going to have me as a dinner guest a week from Sunday[*] after a motor trip of antiquar-

---

[*]Unless Orton takes me on a week-end motor trip to ATHOL & back. Cook has decided to stay on his new farm till he sells it, & is broadcasting all sorts of invitations.

ian exploration, is a Harvard man & the descendant of an ancient German family early domiciled in the New-Netherlands. De Kay—a nephew of the financially dubious president of our defunct Atlantic National Bank, who served a term in the Cranston state prison!—is about 35, although he looks vastly younger. He is a Harvard man also, & one of the most aristocratically descended persons in the United States—of the oldest Manhattan "400." His mother's miniature is in that collection at the N.Y. Hist. Soc. where A E P G found the miniature of her old Miss Abbott schoolmate Mrs. Iselin. You may also have noted the reference to her in that Chelsea article in last Sunday's Times Magazine. It is a pity that London Terrace is coming down—De Kay has lived there all his life, but is philosophically accepting the impending eviction. I expect to see Wandrei next Monday, but Talman & Morton are so busy that I don't know when I can get a glimpse of them. T. Everett Harré, the anthology-compiler who is using my "Cthulhu" & who asked me to call on him when in N Y, has gone to his old home in rural Pennsylvania, but says he may be back here on a visit before I go home. Meanwhile he has very thoughtfully given me a letter of introduction to the Asst. Editor of the Red Book Magazine—one Arthur M[c]Keogh[1]—who he thinks may soon consider using weird tales, & who (if he does) will pay a much higher rate than my present market. This editor may need other work done, too—in fact, Harré thinks he is a very profitable man for any writer to know. I would, of course, be avid to establish any business connexion permitting me to reside at home. Orton thinks he could get me a job at any time in New York as he did for Wandrei—but a job *in New York* is a very dubious substitute for a peaceful berth at the poorhouse in Cranston, or the Dexter Asylum! I have just written to M[c]Keogh, enclosing Harré's letter of introduction & expressing my availability for a personal call at the office at any time within two weeks. Not that anything important is likely to develop—but I wish it might. A new & high-priced market for weird material, plus a chance to do revision & special writing for the same magazine, would form a happy windfall of the first water. It could be undertaken with Providence as a base—for Harré is still doing it despite his return to his native Pennsylvania. I hope I can meet Harré next week—although his N Y trip is by no means certain. The M[c]Keogh interview is almost certain to occur—whether or not it leads to anything profitable. Orton is now attempting some writing—though of a popular & low-grade sort, for the Macfadden publications. (the same ones which honest Eddy's wife writes for.) He has only landed one story as yet—but I am helping him on a new one. He is weak in motivating incidents & eliminating artificial coincidences. I am glad to extend this free aid as a partial repayment of the marvellous hospitality he is giving me. Orton, by the way, is quite a friend of the editor & bibliophile John T. Winterich—that friend of Roy S. [*sic*] Morrish's to whom A E P G had me write in 1924, when he had just secured his editorship of the American Legion Monthly & might have had positions to offer.[2]

Now for my diary—which I believe I carried as far as Wednesday evening, when I took the subway for Yonkers after my call on good old Kirk. I reached my destination in safety, though the trip consumes a full two hours. One uses the west side Interborough Subway to the end of the line—Van Cortlandt Park—& then takes a surface car—2 fares, with free transfer on second fare—to the principal square (Getty Sq.) of Yonkers. The transfer is used on a Nepperham Ave. car, which goes almost to Orton's door. Of course seasoned commuters like Orton scorn this leisurely transportation & use the Putnam division of the N.Y. Central which takes only 40 minutes—but that is altogether too expensive for an impecunious visitor. Kirk, by the way, plans to commute on this division during the coming summer; having hired a place far up the river—1½ hours from the Grand Central. He wants to sub-let his Greenwich Village basement apartment till autumn. Well—Wednesday evening I spent with Orton devising a complicated plot for his coming story; & we retired at a late hour without having done more than a third of our allotted task. Thursday—the 11th—I rose at 11 a.m. & went down to Little Sonny's for lunch. In the afternoon the Child & his Grandpa went out to Astoria to see honest old McNeil—& right here I must acknowledge a piece of mightily poor prediction! You will recall my saying that, from my knowledge of Astoria, (the N.W. corner of Long Island—a few miles above Brooklyn & reached by the Queensboro subway from Times Sq.) I could not see how Mac's new move was any improvement on Brooklyn. Well—I was wrong for once! There *is* one half-decent corner of Astoria—along Ditmars Blvd. at the end of the subway-elevated—& Mac has miraculously stumbled upon it! He is on the ground floor of a really pretty apartment house at the corner where the boulevard meets the shore drive in the shadow of graceful Hell Gate Bridge, & his windows open directly on the drive, the boat-haunted river, the noble arches of the bridge, & the green meadows of Ward's Island. The apartment is as sumptuously modern & well-appointed as A E P G's, & has 2 rooms besides bathroom & kitchen alcove, yet Mac pays only 45 dollars per month. The locality is spruce, clean, & pretty, but rather unfashionable & remote from the subway-elevated. The real-estate company provides a *free 'bus service* to the station for tenants of the apartment. On the shore not far to the north are two ancient houses which I saw in the course of my last year's explorations—the Ditmars house (1820 with a 1719 part incorporated) & the Rapolye–Polhemus house (1749). The latter is a splendid Dutch cottage of the non-gambrel type, with lower walls of stone. Well—nice old Mac was properly surprised & delighted to see his fellow-ancient from Providence, & we all had a pleasant session—two old men & a small boy. Mac shewed the beginning of his new book, & Grandpa offered mild objections regarding the stilted pseudo-archaic conversation of the characters—Spaniards of the 16th century. Our honest friend cannot be made to see that romantic rhetoric has no place in seriously artistic prose.

This book deals with Cortez & the conquest of Mexico, & is the first tale of Mac's to have an adult hero. About 4:30 we all went for a shore walk to see the old houses, & at 5:00 Belknap & I set out for our return—Mac accompanying us to the subway-elevated station. It being a rush hour, progress was fiendishly slow—hence I did not reach Orton's till nearly eight. We spent that evening on Orton's tale, but did not finish the synopsis. Retiring at 11 p.m., I slept till 9 a.m. the next day. Friday the 12th I went down to the Mercury office to meet De Kay & Orton—De Kay having invited us both to lunch with him at the Harvard Club in 44th St. near 5th Ave. The day was cold & rainy, but all that was forgotten in the spacious & artistically stately clubhouse. Lunch was excellent, & De Kay proved even pleasanter on closer acquaintance than at our first meeting. He has a marked British accent, but it is *not* affected—for during his early years his father was American consul at Berlin, & sent him to fashionable schools in England. He is urbane & intelligent—& (to cap the climax of congeniality) is now *reducing*. He will always be heavy, though, for he is of the thick-set Dutch-Walloon type so common amongst the old Knickerbocker families. No 140-by-Roodmas for him, despite his dieting & his fencing exercises! After lunch we all discussed Orton's new plot-synopsis in the lounging room whose windows overlook 45th St., & after that we went upstairs to the club library, where we met a Vermonter named Walbridge whom Orton knows. About 3 o'clock we dispersed, & I went directly back to Yonkers to write letters. De Kay says he wants me to lend him some of my tales. I have seen none of his work as yet, save one book review. He—like young Rothenburg & Orton—works in the American Mercury office. The force of that company seem to be very cohesive & congenial. Well—in the evening Orton & I continued our plot discussion & reached a tentative conclusion. He retired at 10:30 p.m., but I am still writing at midnight. Tomorrow another friend of his—an Englishman whom I have not met—is coming out with him for the afternoon & evening, & some congenial discussions are expected. Sunday Orton intends to do gardening work, in which I may mildly coöperate. Monday I lunch with Wandrei. Tuesday I lunch & spend the afternoon with small Sonny. Wednesday night the gang meets at Kirk's—although I can't persuade Orton to go, on account of a silly feud with Kirk. All the gang feel that Kirk is more offish since he fell under the rule of his new wife, but Orton is the only one to refuse to visit him when invited. I myself found good old Georgius just as effervescently cordial as in the old 169 Clinton days! Thursday is open. Friday the Ortons & I may possibly start on a week-end trip to visit Cook in Athol—or if not, the date is open. Saturday is a possible Athol day, with Sunday as a day of return. If the Athol trip does *not* occur, Orton & I will spend Sunday the 21st with young Rothenburg—exploring colonial byways & dining at his house. Monday the 22nd will probably see the transfer of my visit to Little Belknap's—for the Child says it's altogether too incongruous for his grandpa to be in N Y with any headquarters other than 230 W. 97ᵗʰ St. After that will come the cathedral & museum trips, & aesthetic-scientific discussions of a type more abstract & more closely related to my own mental-imaginative life than is possible with the more practical, socially-minded, & out-in-the-world people of Orton's circle. Then finally my Philadelphia jaunt (if I get a revision cheque) & a homeward 'bus trip either through rural Connecticut or up the Hudson to include a day or two with Bernard Dwyer (at Kingston) & a crossing of the Mohawk Trail to Greenfield & Athol. Ancient New England! Blest haven to lend spice to a journey's end, & to serve as background for the appreciation of all else! The *cost* of my whole trip, except for such Philadelphian or other digressions as I may make, will be astoundingly close to *nothing*. As long as I am near N Y & the gang, it is virtually a free proposition both in board & food; hence I don't need any extra cash as yet. Such are the advantages of literary friends—but I wish to Pegāna they all dwelt in Boston or Philadelphia or Washington or some other attractive spot instead of in N.Y.! However— the place is not so hateful when one knows one is not chained to it, & has Providence to greet him when boredom supervenes. Actually, this trip is saving cash—for I'm spending less than I would be if at home & paying for food & laundry. Incidentally—Orton insists that I use his *stationery,* (of which this sheet is a sample) especially since he expects to make it obsolete in the fall by a cityward change of address on account of furnace & commuting difficulties. It is very sumptuous stuff—even outdoing my Christmas supply in style— though it is not as easy-writing as what I ordinarily use.

I was very glad to hear that your health has been decently stable, & hope you improved last Sunday & Monday by going out for walks to Prospect Terrace. It is good of Mrs. Hodgdon to mail letters—& I surely hope her physician will recover from his influenza. I don't believe I'll catch anything here— the epidemic is largely over, & the only victim I've seen (Sonny's mother) is well on the road to convalescence. Glad Mrs. Hodgdon is helping with the muffins—but I hope little Noyes will get his delivery soon.[3] By the way— speaking of mailing letters—an odd thing happened tonight. I went to the corner of Nepperham Ave. to mail a bunch of things, & found the letter-box stuck so that nothing could be inserted. A kindly old looking man waiting for a car observed my struggles with the mechanism, & volunteered to take my stuff along & mail it for me in Yonkers proper. I thankfully accepted his offer, for he seemed honest & amiable. Thus we have some vicarious mailing at both ends! I hope the local box will be repaired tomorrow. No—I don't sit up late writing anything I don't want to write. My hours bother nobody, for I never ask any meals out of season. As my diary proves, I usually have some outside invitation to lunch, & eat dinner at Orton's. Breakfast, of course, I never eat. 140 by Roodmas—although as you have seen by my Mt. Vernon missive, it is now merely a matter of *staying* 140 rather than *getting down to* 140. Sonnykins is 140, too, at present—exactly like his aged Grandpa, although *his* 140 does not wholly eliminate his incipient bay-window! The little rascal ought not to weigh more than 130, including all five hairs of his tender moustachelet; yet he is tragically regretful that he has lost as much as he has. He wants to be as broad as he is long! Grandpa's little Nero—I certainly must pick up an extra copy of that Nero novel ("The Bloody Poet" by Desider Kostolanyi) to give the child on his birthday! Loveman says he can pick me up one for a dime or so—but it must be before the 27th. On that date Sonny turns 27 . . . . I can't believe that the precious little imp is getting to be such a middle-aged man![4] Speaking of books—did I tell you that I found a complete Livy translation in 2 small-type volumes at Loveman's shop? I wanted to buy it, but he wouldn't take any pay! I shall have an enormous package of books—all free gifts!—to parcel-post home. What I may *buy* are some *Farmer's Almanacks* which a man has asked Loveman to sell for him. He will only sell the bunch as a unit—but if it's cheap I'll take it, duplicates & all, since it contains some dates I want most desperately, including *1798* & *1799*. Cook (whom I've notified) may go halves on the price, for there's as much in the batch which he will want, as there is of what I want. We hope for good luck.

I enclose a bookmark advertisement of Kirk's, & also a postcard which Belknap sent me—with a picture uncannily resembling honest old McNeil, even to the fact of his addressing a juvenile audience. This is a famous Ghirlandajo painting,[5] & is in one of the art books brought to #10 by A E P G—but it does look like good old Mac! Ask A E P G if she doesn't think so—for she has seen him.

Orton's second-hand Packard has been put in good shape at last, & he plans some notable excursions in it—especially the Athol one if all goes well. It is a great car, but takes a vast lot of gasoline. You may recall that when you were ill & moved from Waterman to Barnes St., Dr. Spicer advised you to select a Packard for the transportation—which accordingly was done.

Flowers & trees are coming out in Yonkers as well as in Providence—indeed, the graceful peach saplings around this farmhouse are in delicate full bloom! One hopes that the present cold spell may not destroy the blossoms & early leafage! Flowers in many places are delectably conspicuous—one whole terrace in Astoria being abloom with the massed splendour of some delicate lilac-coloured blossom that grows close to the vivid green turf. Another week will see still more lovely developments—indeed, I can well imagine what a feast of beauty Quinsnicket is preparing for my return.

Well—so it goes. This ends the diary for Friday the 12th, for I'm now retiring at 1 a.m. More later—either on the envelope of this missive (which isn't likely to be mailed till Saturday evening) or in a later communication. This is a great visit, & I only wish you & A E P G could be along to participate in the pleasure & see Grandpa in a more active role than he ever plays at home!

Keep healthy, get outdoors, & enjoy your muffins! More soon—& see you later! ¶ Yr aff Nephew & obt Servt H P L

[On envelope:]
P.S. *Saturday April 13*

Rose 11 a.m. & wrote letters. In afternoon Orton returned with guest—a prepossessing young Englishman named Ashley Belvin,[6] who is to collaborate with Orton in preparing short stories for the cheap magazines. Orton can write the prose, but has no plot ideas. Belvin has cheap ideas, but is bored by writing. Betwixt the two of them they expect to "make" low magazines of the Macfadden grade. During the afternoon we all started out for a ride in the supposedly reclaimed Packard, when lo! *More* trouble developed!! Radiator boiled over. Limping down past the Poe cottage to the now familiar Waterman Garage in Fordham, we interviewed the mechanics & were promised 48-hour service if Orton would bring the car in again on Monday. After that we returned to Orton's, had dinner, & indulged in some marvellously interesting philosophical discussion. This Belvin is delectably intelligent, though not quite equal to Troop, the guest of last week. On the whole, I think real Englishmen excel Americans in philosophic insight & powers of discussion. At any rate, I have more in common with them mentally. Belvin left at 10 p.m. Orton & I discussed till 11 p.m., & now I am writing letters. I shall retire soon after midnight—which ends the diary for Saturday.

SUNDAY, APRIL 14—Rose at 9 a.m. & spent whole day helping Orton about the farm. We cleared the grounds of leaves, changed the course of a brook, built 2 stone foot bridges, pruned the numerous peach trees, (whose blossoms are exquisite!) & trained the climbing rose vines on a new home-made trellis. Orton's father, mother, brother, & uncle (whom I met in 1926) called during the day, & the uncle invited us over to his place for dinner later in the week. But the greatest event of all was the acquisition by the household of a marvellously lovely little TIGER KITTIE—which I have been stroking ever since. Family now retiring—I shall write.

Card just recd. No—*I* haven't any library book out on your card! Ask A E P G about it!

[P.P.S.] Going to have dinner with Wandrei tomorrow (Monday)
FINAL P.S. New kitty is down cellar, & I am ending my writing & about to retire.

Notes

1. Arthur McKeogh (1890–1937), editor or associate editor of several popular magazines, including *Saturday Evening Post* (1919–23), *McClure's Magazine* (1925–27), and *Red Book Magazine* (1927–29).

2. For John T. Winterich and Roy A. Morrish, see LDC/AEPG 74n1.

3. Unidentified; but note a character named Noyes in "The Whisperer in Darkness" (1930).

4. See LDC/AEPG 23n3.

5. Perhaps *An Old Man and His Grandson,* by Domenico Ghirlandaio (1449–1494), Italian Renaissance painter.

6. HPL wrote about him, "the way this chap coolly analysed the needs of the Macfadden publications was enough to make an hippopotamus shrink. I'll own that I was hardly civil to him when he suggested that I try to reach this market—for my stomach was turned nearly inside out!" (HPL to Clark Ashton Smith, [25 December 1930]; *Dawnward Spire, Lonely Hill* 286).

[271]   [ALS] [HPL to LDC]

> April 20, 1929
> Address—% F. B. Long,
> 230 West 97th St.,
> New York, N.Y.

My dear Daughter:—

I was exceedingly glad to receive your letter of yesterday, & trust that its writing did not prove fatiguing. Great length is not necessary—the prime desideratum being a succinct bulletin of how you are & how the muffin supply is coming along. I regret that you allowed yourself to have a "belief" of a cold, & trust that the close of the frigid epoch has effectively checked the tendency. Too bad you didn't feel able to get out those marvellous two days a couple of weeks ago. When I get back, I'm going to drag you out by main force to Prospect Terrace & to a dinner at Brennan's—& later to Bristol, Newport, & other colonial places. If everything worth seeing in Providence is going to be torn down, one will have to spend most of one's time in Bristol, Warren, Newport, & such relatively unspoiled places!

As my card said, I shall be going down to small Sonny's with bag & baggage on Monday—arriving at noon for lunch. The Child has secured a room in the same apartment-house for his aged Grandpa, & the arrangement will seem very homelike indeed—for no matter where my own headquarters in N Y has been, that 96th St. Station neighbourhood has always been a focal point for visiting. I shall, of course, miss the rustic atmosphere of Yonkers; but the opportunities for constant congenial conversation with my grandson, & the easy proximity of the gang in general, will form notable compensating factors. I hope the weather may be decent, so that we may fill the week with exploration as originally planned. Just how the spring outing will end, I have not yet decided. If the Ortons make that postponed Athol trip next week-end instead of this, I may go with them; although I would like to be on hand at 230 a week from today for Sonny's birthday. It's hard to realise that the little imp is turning *27!* Also, I want desperately to see ancient *Philadelphia* & roam once more through the gorgeous Wissahickon valley. Orton & I may possibly make a side-trip thither in his new car—which seems to be behaving itself at last—for I shall still be in close touch with him despite my transfer of guestship. I'll let you know particulars & decisions in subsequent bulletins. Anyhow, I'll be seeing you & giving you an oral account of things before so very long.

If at this point my handwriting suddenly appears less legible, you may ascribe it to the self-invited presence of small tiger Hiram in his Grandpa's lap—for he has just jumped up there, & is trying to guide my pen with a velvet paw whilst he occasionally chews at the end of it between stentorian purrs. He is the friendliest little atom of fur & grace that I've ever seen in my life—indeed, he never enters the room without trotting straight to Grandpa & jumping up in the Old Gentleman's lap. When I am standing, he sometimes asks to be held, with a kind of amicable conversational mew. A great kitty—I certainly envy Orton the ability to harbour him. . . . Just now I heard the purring cease, & I find that the little rascal has fallen asleep. His head is on my right forearm, but I can move my wrist enough to write. Some tiger!

As for the fate of the Opera House—I simply lack words to comment! Hotel space indeed—when it is hardly possible to fill the hotels we have, & the Biltmore is said to be operated at a loss! Have any plans for another Opera House been made, or has Wendelschaefer decided to abandon all efforts to keep first-class drama for Providence?[1] A high-grade play really doesn't seem at home in any theatre but the Opera House—the Shubert-Majestic always had a false note when it was tried a decade ago. In Hoboken, where I was yesterday, there are two theatres of about the same age as the Opera House, & both are now used for revivals of old-time plays. The melodrama "After Dark" is at one of them, & "The Black Crook" is at the other.[2] When I saw their exteriors yesterday I smugly congratulated myself that we have something even better—& here I learn the very next day that ours is doomed! What a second home the old Opera House used to be to me! It was there, in 1896, that I saw Denman Thompson's "Sunshine of Paradise Alley", the first play I ever witnessed.[3] There, on Christmas Day 1897, I saw Margaret Mather in "Cymbeline"[4]—my first Shakespearian play. And now the old Opera House is doomed! Ah, me—but there's no place in this world for an old man! What am I living for anyway, now that the good old 'nineties have gone?

Hiram has just shifted in his sleep to a posture which makes writing more difficult, but I trust my epistle may still be read. Thanks immensely for the cuttings—& pray don't fail to keep all my papers intact & in a chronologically arranged pile—Bulletin, Sunday Journal, & Times. I don't know what's going on in the world—for all I see is the Sunday Times—& I shall want to spend a week stocking up on news when I get back. About *dishes*—I confine my collaboration to *wiping only*. Of course, all wiping is wholly needless; but Orton's grandmother follows an old Vermont tradition, & the quaintly obsolete process harmonises well with the archaick atmosphere of this ancient farmhouse. A week at Sonny's will reaccustom me to scientific efficiency, so that when I get home I shall be as strict as ever in enforcing my anti-wiping regulations! I shall not have work around my house!!! I saw the cat letter in the Times—

also the church pictures. Sonny & I plan to make a Gothick tour next week, inspecting some of the best examples of cathedral architecture. I haven't yet seen the latest progress on St. John the Divine.

Yes—A E P G sent a cheque, & I am expecting a small revision cheque also. Just as I was congratulating myself on my almost negligible expenditures, those glasses had to break & cost me $2.25! The case was 25¢, the lens $2.00—which of course indicates that my Putney job will cost about $2.00 when I get home. I shall have to guard my 140 lbs. very carefully when I get down to the Longs', for their table is something reminiscent of Apicius & Lucullus.[5] Two meals a day there for a week would menace any figure! Wednesday night, when Morton & I dined there, it was a circus to watch James Ferdinand gorge unashamedly on a second helping of everything after everybody else had finished & sat waiting for his performance to conclude.

(Hiram has just changed his position & dropped off to sleep again. The new position makes writing somewhat easier.)

My clothes—pressed yesterday—shew no signs of wear, & the new Regals behave magnificently. There are signs of rain today—& I vow I shall wear an old suit of Orton's if I go out, for I don't mean to ruin a fine 50¢ pressing. I have been sending my laundry with Orton's, & shall probably send it with the Long's [sic] next week. Holes are appearing in my *new* stockings—it seems as though hosiery can't be as substantial nowadays as it was when I was young. But these holes don't matter, for they are in the sole & can't be seen.

Glad you're having a pleasant social season, even if a less strenuous one than mine. Perhaps your *Butlers* are remotely related to the young Gervaise Butler whom I've been seeing—he has a tendency to stoutness also! Too bad you couldn't accept the motoring offer—I hope you can take some trips in the summer, both to colonial towns & to ancestral regions around Greene & Moosup Valley.

Hiram has waked up now & seems inclined to playfulness. The moving end of this pen arouses his interest most inordinately! No use talking—it takes a cat & an Old Farmer's Almanack to make a real home! I hope that client of Loveman's won't quote too high a price on his stack of almanacks— I'd give almost anything for those 1797, 1798, 1799 & 1808 numbers! Loveman, by the way, made me another present of a book last night—I shall have an enormous pile to parcel-post home to myself, & I fancy I shall need a couple of those little Boston Store bookcases right away!

Such, then, is which. Today—Saturday—I rose at noon & have been writing letters ever since. Orton has returned from town, & is cursing because the dubious weather discourages motor riding. Tomorrow there will be company—a young Vermont friend of Orton's, Henry Cheney of Rutland. Monday I shall transfer myself to Sonny's at noon, & at 3 p.m. pay my call on McKeogh of the Red Book. Wednesday the Child & I are going to Paterson to see Mortonius. Thursday night I'm going to meet Loveman at his shop at

9:45, & at midnight we shall both meet Talman at the Times Annex in 43ᵈ St. for an all-night session of antiquarian walks & loafings over coffee at cafeteria tables. That's as far as my absolutely set programme goes, but all the rest of the time will be crowded with other events. There will, for example, be another gang meeting at Belknap's, & we also want to get out to see honest old Mac again. His increasingly feeble aspect startles us—but he will not consent to see a doctor, since he naively believes all doctors to be pompous frauds. I wish Orton's kid brother—a medical student—could diagnose him & give him some remedy in an easy, informal way.

Well—more later. Saturday afternoon is wearing on, & I don't know yet what Orton will decide to do. I'm finishing this before the preceding card is mailed, hence will enclose the latter as an introductory chapter. Any later data will be added on the outside of this envelope. And so it goes. Don't do any work around my room—& I'll see you later.

Yr aff Nephew & obt Servt
H P L

P.S. Read the enclosed card *first.* Its mailing was delayed, so I am enclosing it herewith!

[On envelope:] 3:30 p.m. Going out in car with Ortons for errands & suchlike. Drizzling rain.

[No card enclosed]

Notes

1. The Providence Opera House (115 Dorrance Street), built in 1871, was closed in 1931 and demolished soon thereafter to provide parking space for the Narragansett Hotel. Felix R. Wendeschaefer was the manager of the opera house.

2. Dion Boucicault (1820–1890), *After Dark* (1868); *The Black Crook* (1868), written by Charles M. Barras, lyrics by Theodore Kennick, music by Thomas Baker.

3. Denman Thompson (1834–1911), *The Sunshine of Paradise Alley* (1896), co-written with George W. Ryer.

4. Margaret Mather (1859–1898), Canadian actress who played Imogen in *Cymbeline.* She died while playing that role in a theatre in Charleston, WV, on 7 April 1898.

5. M. Gavius Apicius (1st century C.E.) and L. Licinius Lucullus (118–57? B.C.E.) were noted gourmets in ancient Rome. HPL owned a book by Dick Humelbergius Secundus [pseud.], *Apician Morsels; or, Tales of the Table, Kitchen, and Larder* (New-York: J. & H. Harper, 1829; *LL* 480). Cf. also the character "Lucullus Languish," the protagonist of "The Poe-et's Nightmare" (1916).

[272]   [ANS postcard]¹ [HPL, FBL, and James F. Morton to LDC]

[Postmarked Paterson, N.J.,
25 April 1929]

DIARY FOR WEDNESDAY, APRIL 24, 1929

Rose at 11 a.m.—to a splendid warm day, thank Pegāna! Lunched with Belk-nap & walked with him whilst he aired his dog. We then started out for Pater-son, taking a surface car to the 125ᵗʰ St. ferry, crossing, & taking a trolley for Paterson. The ride was highly pleasant—finer by far than either train or 'bus ride—& I shall employ this route hereafter whenever I visit Paterson. The car line enters the town by a pleasanter route than I had ever seen before, passing close to the publick library & museum. We found Mortonius in accustom'd state, & he shew'd us obligingly over his splendid collection, of which Rhode Island minerals are the high spots. He then took us to the great rock falls—& this time the stupendous torrent was rushing in full force, forming a stupen-dously impressive spectacle of roaring foam & rising mist, with a delicate rainbow arching over the whole blend of scoriac crag & milk-white torrent. Aesthetically moved, we were loath to leave for dinner—but we finally ad-journed to the restaurant occupying the site of Mortonius' favourite old-time eatery—Westerman's . . . There Belknap & I were treated to a noble repast, & afterward we adjourned to Mortonius' pleasant & book-filled flat—where we wrote verse, heard a potent fear-poem by our host, & discussed the universe in general. Later in the evening Belknap & I reluctantly set out for N Y again—& I shall retire moderately early. Tomorrow is the big gang meeting, which we hope will be a success. More soon. Yr aff Neph & obt H P L

[On front:]

P.S. Talman & I have attended to the matter of writing nice old Mac's brother & friends.

Greetings from The Man from Genoa! Your nephew is really beginning to appreciate New York. And has grown disconcertingly stout.

They stole the space in which I was to have written something brilliant; so I can send only my greetings.

James F. Morton.

Notes

1. *Front:* Garret Rock, Paterson, N.J.

[273]   [ALS] [HPL to LDC]

Friday Evening
April 26, 1929

My dear Daughter:—

I take my pen in hand to say that I am well & hope you
are the same. My diary, I believe, last extended to Wednesday night, when
Belknap & I return'd from Paterson & retir'd early. The next day—Thursday
the 25th—I rose at 10 a.m. & did a few local errands before noon, then returning to 230 for lunch. In the afternoon a drizzle sprang up, hence I did not
go out at all, but remained in Sonny's den writing letters. Most of these epistles had to do with Cook's odd & perplexing failure to answer recent mail.
Though he blamed Loveman for doing much the same thing in connexion
with the "Hermaphrodite" edition, Cook is now neglecting all obligations in
the matter of the Bullen book "White Fire"—financed, as you may recall, by
the wealthy Chicago man Archibald Freer for the benefit of Bullen's family.
Orders from important bookshops remain unfilled, & he has not delivered
the second edition despite the fact that $350.00 has been advanced for it. Fre-
er & Mrs. Bullen are naturally worried & baffled, & are bombarding me with
inquiries about the delay on account of my original editorial connexion with
the venture. Freer, incidentally, is in an hospital—recovering from a sudden
operation. Of course Cook means to see the matter through, but his present
perplexities about a permanent residence & the future of the *Athol Transcript*
have made him so nervous that he evidently cannot attend to anything. He
does not even acknowledge Orton's latest letters—so that Orton has called
the week-end motor trip off. Freer is disposed to be magnanimous, & says he
would rather give Cook help than censure him for negligence; but Bullen's
mother is impatient to have something done quickly. Accordingly I have
sought once more to stir the delinquent to action, & have composed a letter
which ought to be quite a masterpiece of tactful insistence. This was the major task of Thursday afternoon. Orton had been invited to dinner, but at the
last moment found himself unable to come until 8 p.m., the scheduled hour
of the gang meeting. Accordingly the sumptuous chicken repast was consumed wholly by the Longs, Grandpa Theobald, Felis, & the night-black
were-hound. At 8 o'clock the members began to shew up, all but three
(Kleiner, Kirk, & nice old Mac) being present, to say nothing of two guests.
We had telephoned the hospital about Mac, & found that he was comfortable
though not spectacularly improved. The visitors arrived in the following order—Talman, Wandrei, Mortonius, Loveman & young Gervaise Butler, &
Orton & Ashley Belvin. Much spirited discussion & postcard writing occurred; & the non-members seemed greatly interested, though they did not
participate extensively in the conversation. Talman produced a news cutting
about Mac's illness which had appeared in the *Times*, & which we shall give to
Mac as soon as he is able to enjoy it. I also shewed Mac's latest book list,

(which came the same day) with its inclusion of "Tonty of the Iron Hand." All were vastly sorry to hear about Mac's misfortune. Welsh rarebit & coffee were appropriately served, & about 11:30 the meeting regretfully broke up. Wandrei & Talman, however, accompanied me upstairs to my room on the 7th floor—where we held the later meeting originally scheduled to begin at the Times Annex. Rain deterred us from making the session migratory. There was much to talk about—including "Jake's" restaurant in Canal St. & the menaced Opera House & South Water St. warehouses—& Wandrei did not leave till after 3 a.m. Talman stayed till still later—5 a.m.—discussing the inner workings of a newspaper office & speculating on the possibilities of my getting a position in one some time. After Talman's departure in a grey dawn which shewed many signs of clearing weather, I retired for a brief rest; rising at 9 a.m. Friday & joining the Longs for that all-day motor trip which a providentially warm & sunny day made possible. The dog, I may add, accompanied the party; sitting quietly on the rear seat of the Essex with Belknap & me. The route was one which we traversed a year ago on more than one trip—the exquisite Bronx River Parkway & the rustic regions beyond— Kensico, Armonk, Bedford, & the western fringe of Stamford, in His Majesty's Province of Connecticut. Most of the scenes were well remember'd by me, & it was with interest that I learn'd that Armonk (an idyllick elm-shaded colonial village) was the place where the Longs found their new dog—as a bewildered, apparently ownerless creature in danger of sudden assassination by passing motors. On this occasion Canis did not display any recognition or homesickness at the spot, hence it may be assumed that his naturalisation as a Long fixture has become an accomplished fact. Bedford I liked as well as usual—if you recall my letters of a year ago you will be aware of the white church, hillside burying ground, colonial houses, & triangular village green which give the village such a settled, delightful, & old-fashion'd atmosphere. Soon afterward we crossed the state line into Connecticut, & my heart swell'd with pride at the sight of old New-England . . . . . New-England with its rolling green hills, stone walls, white steeples, & cottage gables embowered in flowering valleys. We dined by the roadside in exactly the same spot where we dined a year ago—the time I sent you & A E P G cards from Stamford— at a picturesque junction of a new & an abandoned road, with a forest-fringed stream flowing through a ravine under two bridges. In the afternoon we covered more splendid country without entering the urban area of Stamford— returning to N Y past the Lake Katonah region. In reëntering the metropolis we followed the Sawmill River Parkway, catching a glimpse of Orton's house in the distance. Once more at 230, Belknap & I read miscellany & had dinner; & now I am penning these lines at 10 p.m., just before going upstairs to retire, whilst the Child reads in David Garnett's fantasy "Lady into Fox."

Tomorrow Sonny & I intend to do some shopping in town, & I shall probably inaugurate the first stage of my return by parcel-posting a vast bun-

dle of books & miscellany home to myself from Loveman's shop. Hope the
arrival of the package won't cause you any trouble. In the evening Sonny's
27th birthday will be celebrated—& I shall give him a 35¢ study of Swinburne
which I recently picked up as a remainder.[1] We may all go to the cinema,
likewise. Sunday we shall see the interior of St John the Divine in the morning, & take a motor trip in the evening. Monday I shall wind things up—
Museum & Mac, perhaps—& prepare for the southerly side trip which will
briefly presage my reappearance in my native plantations. ¶ Yr aff Nephew &
obt Servt H P L

P.S. Trust that you're well & that you've enjoyed "The Wind in the Rose-
bush".[2] I shall make you take some walks to Prospect Terrace shortly! ¶ Have
received a cordial invitation from Bernard Dwyer to stop a night or two at
Kingston with him on my way home, hence I probably shall choose the Hudson River & Mohawk Trail route. This means that I'll see Cook & Munn
briefly in Athol. Some trip! I'll have a full & inspired imagination to lend to
my summer's writing & retirement! See you later!

Notes

1. Possibly T[homas] Earle Welby (1881–1933), *A Study of Swinburne* (New York:
George H. Doran, 1926).
2. The celebrated collection of ghost stories by Mary E. Wilkins Freeman.

[274]　　[ALS] [HPL to LDC]

Sunday–Monday Midnight
April 28–29, 1929

My dear Daughter:—

As I take my pen in hand to continue my diary, I have
stark tragedy to report! Oh, for a black border to lend dignity to my mourning! *I have gained 8 pounds* since encountering the Siren-like enticements of the
sumptuous Long table, & now tip the scales at the monstrous & unmention-
able figure of *148!* Something, obviously, must be done! Here's Roodmas only 2 days away, & I'm 8 pounds above decent weight! And only a couple of
weeks ago I had made the grade! Bitter are my tears! From now on I am in
strict training; & if I don't shew a 140 weight-card by the time I've made my
southern & Kingston trips, I'll end it all in the broad, deep Hudson & never
come home at all! Sonny meanwhile tries to pile on as much weight as he
can—he is eating vast quantities of *yeast* to add to his already conspicuous
bay-window! The little rascal ought to lose 15 or 20 pounds—just as I ought
to lose 8. My motto is now *"140 by St. John's Eve"*.

As for my diary—I last wrote Friday night. Saturday I rose at noon & descended to take lunch at Sonny's. It was the young imp's 27th birthday, & we

decided to spend the afternoon in a round of shopping. First we stopped at Kirk's, where the Child took a look at De Castro's Bierce book with his preface in it. The result was something of a shock; for there were many grave misprints, & old De Castro had interpolated a whole section of a personal letter which Belknap wrote him in praise of the volume. Sonny intends, however, to buy the book eventually. It was a cheap trick of old De Castro's not to give us both free copies! Well—after Kirk's we began our shopping, Belknap getting collars for himself at Hearn's, a collar for his dog at Wanamaker's, a dog-license (renewed) at the S P C A near Madison Square, & so on. Our greatest splurge, however, was in *neckties,* of which some great sales are on all over town, & of which we both stood very much in need. You are aware how old & creased all mine are. Finding certain bargain lots at Wanamaker's (25¢) & Bloomingdale's (**19¢**) which were supposed to be odd or defective, but which had no visible flaws in many cases, we each laid in an *enormous* supply—my own naturally more conservative than Sonny's. You will see most of mine when my first homeward package arrives—for I'm only saving out two to wear—& I think you'll agree that I chose wisely. Very shortly I shall throw away many old ties which can no longer be made into a decent knot. Ties being bought, we went to Loveman's shop & found him in the throes of moving—so hampered that he could not mail home any of my things save books alone. Accordingly I had to take my miscellaneous stuff back to my room & arrange to mail it myself. This package—which I'll probably mail Tuesday—will contain my thinner nightshirt, which the Yonkers laundry split all the way down the back. I am now getting along by washing the good nightshirt myself & letting it dry daytimes. The package will also include one complete set of soiled linen for our American Hand Laundry to tackle—since the approaching end of my wanderings makes it no longer necessary to have so many extra pieces on hand. From now on, I shall mail home everything I discard—eventually arriving with nothing but the linen on my person, & with only one valise. Well—after Loveman's, Sonny & I walked in Central Park & finally took the subway for 230, where we had a sumptuous Long dinner. (I shan't need to eat again for a month after the Sybaritic feasts I've been confronting!) We then went across the street to a cinema show—dull as usual. After that we sought 230 once more, & celebrated the Child's birthday with ice-cream, a 27-candle cake, & some gift-presentations. I gave him the Swinburne book I picked up, & his mamma gave him a nice $3.75 Ingersoll watch—of small size, & with a radiolite dial. He was a very pleased small boy, it is needless to say! Finally I walked around the block with Sonny as he aired his dog, & set my watch for daylight time. You, I trust, have done likewise. I then went upstairs to my room, wrote letters, & retired at a moderate hour. Incidentally—during the course of this day I telephoned the hospital & found that nice old Mac is much better. It was not a visiting day, so we could not go to see him; but I shall go on Tuesday, my last day in N.Y.

The next day—Sunday the 28ᵗʰ—I rose at 9 a.m. & proceeded down to Sonny's. We then proceeded as a unit to the unfinished Cathedral of St. John the Divine, the majestick nave of which (about ¾ done) I saw for the first time. The structure is indeed marvellously impressive, & will undoubtedly rank among the great cathedrals of the world. On this occasion the Longs took me to the service, held in the choir & in the temporarily walled space which will eventually form the junction of nave & transepts. The choir is at present of Romanesque architecture, but will ultimately be Gothicised to harmonise with its fittings & with the final plan of the Cathedral as adopted by Ralph Adams Cram. You can get some idea of the whole edifice & its future shape from the set of postcards I bought—a set which will be in the package of material mailed home Tuesday. The service was quite picturesque in its Anglican ceremoniousness, though a Catholick service would doubtless have been quainter. This was the first church service I have attended since 1895. At 12 o'clock the congregation dispersed, & our party returned to 230 for another ponderous Long dinner—roast duck & all the accessories. Later we all set forth in the Long Essex, but our trip was cut short by a hot-box which necessitated repairs at a garage near the Dyckman cottage. Dr. Long has been having almost as bad luck as Orton with his car—his repair shop seems fully as incompetent & unscrupulous as the one on the Grand Concourse which I came to know so well a couple of weeks ago. When the Essex was finally patched up, it had begun to rain; so we abandoned the trip & returned to 230 to read the Sunday papers. About 7:30 Mrs. Long served the elaborate lunch which had been prepared for the ill-fated excursion, & after that Sonny & I discussed aesthetics, philosophy, the Arabic culture, & the future of Western civilisation. A great child—he & Morton are the only members of the gang who *never* fail to be informed & interesting. We then went out to air Belknap's dog, & at 11 p.m. I ascended to my room to write & retire.

As for the future—tomorrow (Monday) I shall descend to Sonny's at noon for lunch, & hope to meet as a fellow-guest a friend of Belknap's whom I have never seen before—the young Catholic Moran, who writes for the magazines. Later we all intend to go to the Metropolitan Museum & find the Casey tankard. Evening is indeterminate. Tuesday the 30th Sonny & I shall call on honest old Mac at the hospital—& either that night or the next morning I shall leave the metropolis behind me. First will come a jaunt to Philadelphia or as far south of it as I can arrange to get. Then—crossing back through N Y without stopping—I shall ascend the Hudson to Dwyer's, stop 1 or 2 nights, further ascend to Albany, & finally come home via the glorious Mohawk Trail & Athol. *Some trip!!* See you soon—

Yr aff Nephew & obt Servt

H P L

P.S. Expect 2 packages—one from the Rowfant Book Shop & the other directly from me.

[On envelope:] Your letter just received—will answer soon. Also had appreciated letter from A E P G. That package from Moe is his poetry book in MS.[1] I had a good letter from him. Did A E P G shew you the Journal letter about the old houses?

Notes

1. I.e., *Doorways to Poetry,* a book on poetic appreciation on which HPL had been assisting Moe. The book was never published, and the ms. does not appear to survive.

[275]   [ANS postcard][1] [HPL and FBL to LDC]

[Postmarked New York, N.Y.,
29 April 1929]

Greetings from a Roman Garden! S.P.Q.R. The gentleman on the other side is a special friend of mine, as you know. Belknap's friend didn't shew up for dinner, so we set out for the Museum via a 96th St. 'bus—stopping en route at the new Church of the Heavenly Rest (5th Ave. & 90th St.) which you may have seen illustrated in the Times Rotogravure Section recently. It is in a Gothic design, but with a very austere modern treatment. At the Museum we found the Casey tankard—which is splendid—& 2 other Casey pieces; a porringer & a creamer. We also did the American Wing & Minoan rooms, & have ended up in the Roman Garden. After this we shall take in some more sights & return to 230. This is next my last day in N.Y. I shall answer your letter shortly—& begin to expect packages soon. *Still address me in Belknap's care,* for I shall pick up mail at his house when I re-cross through N Y en route for Dwyer's & home. More soon.
Yr aff Nephew & obt Servt H P L

Best wishes from
The Man from Genoa

Notes

1. *Front:* Portrait of a Man, [Roman Bust] Roman, 1 Century B.C. The Metropolitan Museum of Art.

[276]   [ALS] [HPL to LDC]

Tuesday Morning
April 30, 1929

My dear Daughter:—

I was delighted to receive your letter, though sorry to hear that you have fatigued yourself working. Work is forbidden around 10 Barnes, & in a few days I shall be on hand to enforce the edict! Beware!

Glad you enjoy the visiting bulletins—you'll get 'em from more varied sources during the remaining few days of my absence, for tomorrow I shall be on the move—first southward, then back up the Hudson for a day or two with Bernard Dwyer & over the Mohawk Trail to Athol & Home. Mail can reach me, as I re-cross north, either at Belknap's or ℅ Bernard Dwyer, 177 Green St., Kingston, N.Y. I wonder what the delayed piece of Brooklyn mail is? It must be the card I wrote you at Talman's—perhaps held by a fussy clerk who thought I had put a letter's worth of writing on it! By this time you doubtless have the key to the mystery. The library business is queer indeed. That book by Christopher Morley is a very popular one—& I fancy the secret of the business is confusion of numbers.[1] My card will expire in May—hence I must have it renewed, as well as obtain a new stack permit. The express package, as I said on yesterday's card, is Moe's MS. of the text book "Doorways to Poetry" plus some school magazines he wants me to see.

Yes—I'll buy socks when I need them. Mine wear out so quickly (you ought to see that *new* pair which I donned when I bought my Regals!!) that I think I'll try some of those sold for a dime at Woolworth's. Sonny has had them, & says they aren't at all bad. I shall continue to get along on one night-shirt, washing it mornings when necessary. Weather seems to be better on the average. If it will keep decent for the kinetic & antiquarian part of my outing, I will pardon it for its bad behaviour during the visiting part.

I've given your regards to the Longs, & am instructed to transmit theirs to you. I don't think McKeogh of the Red Book can use my stuff, for the tone of his magazine is very different from mine. He has not seen any of my tales—& I'll probably send him one in a perfunctory way. As for Noyes—I shall look into this matter shortly! Has he given up his shop? And how do the Anderson muffins agree with you? Glad you've had some coffee ice-cream— I'm sure one indulgence won't hurt you! I can't get coffee ice-cream in N Y— it is, as you know, a wholly Novanglian institution. I didn't read of the fire at the Pier—indeed, I have read no papers save the Sunday Times, & am all ready to wade through a month's orderly accumulation of Bulletins & Sunday Journals. Trust Mrs. Pettis' visit was not too great a bore. Loveman is moving his shop today—his business will undoubtedly be on a sounder basis at the cheaper location. But he really wants to abandon it & return to non-worrisome salaried work. A wise plan.

As for my diary—after mailing your card at the Museum Sonny & I went down town in a 'bus & explored the magnificent Gothick interiors of St. Thomas's & St. Patrick's. We then had a session at the library & finally returned to 230 for dinner. In the evening Dr. Long took everybody to the cinema, & after that I ascended to my room, wrote letters, & retired at 3 a.m. Now I'm up again & ready for my final day in N Y—& my call on nice old Mac. More soon—Yr aff Nephew & obt Servt H P L

P.S. Thanks for the interesting cuttings.

Notes

1. Possibly an allusion to Morley's *Thunder on the Left* (1925), a novel that hints at time travel.

[277]   [ANS postcard]¹ [HPL and FBL to LDC]

[Postmarked New York, N.Y.,
30 April 1929]

Greetings again! I continue my diary from a bench on the Battery, facing the winds & foam of the eternal & immemorial sea! We visited honest old Mac this afternoon as per schedule, & were pleased to find him bright & *much* improved—though he is still of course quite weak, & probably won't be out of the hospital for a week or so yet. Someone else was there to see him—an old lady who went to school with his sister. We took him some oranges which Belknap's mother sent him. ¶ After our call we went down to the Battery & inspected the Aquarium—which I hadn't seen since 1922. Now we are seated on a bench absorbing the spirit of the sea & having our shoes shined by a small boy. Afterward we shall stroll about the ancient part of lower Manhattan—Trinity, St. Paul's, Fraunces' Tavern, &c—& finally return to 230 . . . . stopping en route at the Hotel Pennsylvania for guide leaflets & time tables to direct me in my coming antiquarian wanderings. More later.
Yr aff Nephew & obt Servt H P L

Howard has purchased an enormous, living sea horse (eighteen inches!) I sincerely hope that it lives to imbibe Providential atmosphere!
    F B L Jr.

[P.S.] I have purchased one of these & am bringing it home!

[On front:] [P.]P.S. 6 p.m. Have seen about tickets & found a *marvellously* cheap Washington 'bus excursion leaving N Y at 8 a.m. tomorrow. I shall take it—so that when you read this I shall already be en route. Washington tomorrow night—expect cards from there. At this rate of cheapness I shall probably be able to get to Richmond & Williamsburg. More soon.

Notes

1. *Front:* Sea-horse, New York Aquarium.

[278]　[ANS postcard]¹ [HPL to LDC]

[Postmarked Philadelphia, Pa.,
1 May 1929]

Ahoy! In old Philadelphia once more, though merely passing through. I've decided to cut out known places in favour of those I don't know, hence shall perhaps be able to take in Richmond after all. This line is *stupendously* cheap—its other routes as well as this one. I may use it some day in exploring the Middle West—only $20.00 to Chicago or St Louis! ¶ Queer day—sometimes rain, sometimes sun. Travelling is slow, as on all cheap lines. Many stops & delays—but it's worth it! From N Y to Phila. I had a slightly demented German as a seat mate. He muttered to himself about "letting his light shine", & now & then chanted "everything is lovely." Possibly he means to lecture on New Thought or something in Philada.² ¶ Rose early this morning, but Sonny was up too, & went to the subway to see his Grandpa off. Tonight I shall be in Washington. Some of the colonial villages & farmsteads along the route to Phila. are splendid, though not equal to New England. Princeton is a marvellous place—nearly all Colonial. I must explore it on foot some day. It surely is good to be out of N Y! Yrs H P L

[On front:] I have the right-hand front seat on the 'bus. Best of all!

Notes

1. *Front:* New York Aquarium, Battery Park.
2. HPL discusses this person further in "Travels in the Provinces of America" (1929; *CE* 4.34). HPL then used elements of this person's speech and mannerisms for the character Arthur Feldon in his revision of Adolphe de Castro's "The Electric Executioner" (1929).

[279]　[ANS postcard]¹ [HPL to LDC]

[Postmarked Washington, D.C.,
1 May 1929]

Hurrah! Have arrived in Washington at last—a golden paradise of sunshine & summer verdure! The latter half of the trip was glorious—Elkton, Havre de Grace &c. being splendid colonial towns, & the countryside being exquisite & expansive. Have decided I definitely prefer Washington to Philada.—nothing like the South except ancient New England. Left my overcoat with Sonny in N Y—it's so warm here that I think I'll leave off my vest! Have found marvellous bargain 'bus rates to Richmond, & shall proceed tomorrow morning at 6:45 a.m.—stopping over in archaic & colonial Fredericksburg. Have secured a delightfully neat room for $1.00 at the Senate Hotel opposite the Union Station near where the Richmond 'bus starts. All aboard for the Confederate States & the oldest British civilisation on this continent! God Save the King! Shall send you frequent bulletins. Washington is unbelievably beautiful! Am now about to write some cards & retire early. Have left orders to be waked at 5:45. Yrs H P L

Notes

1. *Front:* White House, Washington, D.C.

[280]   [ANS postcard]¹ [HPL to LDC]

[Postmarked Richmond, Va.,
2 May 1929]

DIARY FOR THURSDAY, MAY 2, 1929—PART I.

Rose early & caught the 6:45 'bus for Richmond. Very few on it, so I got the right-hand front seat. Day was variable—fog, & sometimes a bit of sun or sprinkle. The route to Richmond is very pleasant, though the scenery as a whole does not average up to the New England standard. We passed a few great plantations, & many typical Southern farmhouses—narrow, 2-story edifices with chimneys on each end & steeply pitched roof. Agriculture is more abundant than in N.E., & niggers & mules are omnipresent. All the natives are American, & now & then some highly quaint specimens appear. The soil is yellow & clayey, & colours all the numerous streams. Points of historic interest—both colonial & civil war—are carefully marked. I saw some of the most famous battlefields, including Spottsylvania Court House. Also old Pohick Church, which Washington attended, & in which eccentric Parson Weems (author of the cherry-tree myth) preached. Some of the rural crossroads or courthouse villages are quaint beyond anything we have in New England.
(continued)

Notes

1. *Front:* Old St. John's Church, Broad and 25th Sts., Richmond, Va.

[281]   [ANS postcard][1] [HPL to LDC]

[Postmarked Richmond, Va.,
2 May 1929]

DIARY—THU., MAY 2—Part II.

Quaintest of all is Falmouth, just across the shallow Rappahannock from ancient Fredericksburg. The half-crumbling brick houses & general irregular plan of the sleepy hamlet form the most *Marbleheadish* thing I have yet seen in Virginia. Fredericksburg itself is a marvellously colonial town—containing Kenmore, the home of Gen. Washington's sister. I shall stop off there on the return trip. I also passed through my old favourite Alexandria, but the 'bus did not stop. Scenery gets lovelier around Richmond—& now I have reached that busy city. It is rather varied—Victorian, Colonial, & modernly boulevardish being curiously mixed. I have secured a dollar room at the famous old Murphy's Hotel, & shall stop 2 or 3 nights—depending on the rather unsettled programme of the excursion management. This afternoon (it is now 12:30 noon) I shall do urban Richmond thoroughly. Then tomorrow come Jamestown, Yorktown, & Williamsburg. More soon. Yr aff n H P L

Notes

1. *Front:* Interior of Old St. John's Church, Richmond, Va.

[282]   [ANS postcard][1] [HPL to LDC]

[Postmarked Richmond, Va.,
2 May 1929]

THURSDAY, MAY 2, 1929—Part III

Before starting on my sightseeing I couldn't resist dropping a card to good old Harold Munroe, with whom I used to discuss *Richmond* as if it were holy ground. He & I were Confederates in sympathy, & used to act out all the battles of the War in Blackstone Park—using all the place-names whose originals I beheld today for the first time in reality. It will make H B M smile to receive a card from me postmarked at the *real* Richmond! ¶ Have been studying the dialect used in this hotel lobby. I find that the Southern accent is very marked. More soon. Yrs H P L

Notes

1. *Front:* White House of the Confederacy (12th and Clay Sts.), Richmond, Va.

[283]   [ALS] [HPL to LDC]

Thursday Evening, May 2nd 1929

My dear Daughter:—

I take my pen in hand to say that I am well & hope you are the same. Diary cards mail'd this noon have doubtlefs appris'd you of my safe arrival in Richmond; & I trust you have likewise receiv'd the packet of views sent under separate cover, so that you have some idea of the outward aspect of this famous place. I shall now relate the result of my afternoon's investigations—which indeed turn'd out very advantageously for me.

I began by a trip in the Grey Line sightseeing 'bus—an orientation tour to get the "feel" of the city, adjust my sense of direction, & learn what to see during later pedestrian tours. There were only two others on the 'bus—an old couple apparently from the Mid-West to judge by their rrrr...'s—& a genial, intelligent, & talkative lecturer (a real American Southerner with the usual accent) made the trip very pleasant & informative.

Richmond is a subtly delightful town of much poise & background, though with the languid negligence which prevents its shops & restaurants from being attractive or convenient. The aristocratic residential districts are magnificent—mansions, broad boulevards, & park-like grounds in the full bloom of summer—but the business section has an air of shabbiness & Victorianism. There is no one vast colonial district, though colonial houses are likely to be found anywhere near the river. A diligent searcher can find much to enthrall him architecturally, & of course a student of history could ask nothing more than this centre of Civil War operations. It is not as attractive a city as Washington or Alexandria, but is of the sort which grows on one. It is the most American city I have ever been in. Of a population of 200,000, about 30% are niggers & only 3% foreigners—the latter mostly Jews, who always swarm where money is to be had. The remaining 67%—forming indeed almost 97% of the white inhabitants—are pure-blooded English-Americans whose forbears have dwelt in Virginia from 300 to 325 years. It is this pure native stock which makes up all the crowds & controls all the functions of urban life. Everybody one speaks to is a regular American—hotel clerks, soda-fountain men, conductors, motormen, bus-drivers, & so on. And of course all the workmen & bootblacks & newsboys & elevator men are niggers. Niggers are not segregated as in the farther south, but move about as freely as in Providence. That is because they are not numerous—indeed, one sees fewer of them than in the upper part of New York. Oddly enough, the much more northerly city of Baltimore (which is, incidentally, hideously foreignised) has strict segregatory ordinances which are unknown in Richmond.

Richmond lies along the northern bank of the James River*, the oldest parts being naturally those nearest the water. Its ancient section was much

*which has the yellow colour—due to the clayey soil—common to all southern rivers.

decimated by the burning of the business district in 1865, to prevent valuable merchandise falling into the hands of the Yankees. The original town was built on seven hills like Providence & Rome—Church Hill, (containing ancient St. John's) Smith's Hill, Libby Hill, (now a park) Gamble's Hill, Oregon Hill, Hollywood Hill, & Capitol Hill (containing the fine old state capitol) corresponding to our Prospect Hill, Constitution Hill, Corky Hill, Smith's Hill, Federal Hill, Sky-High Hill, (Mt. Pleasant) & Neutaconkanut Hill; or to Rome's Palatine, Esquiline, Capitoline, Quirinal, Viminal, Caelian & Pincian.[1] It has tended, however, to shift westward—building up over the pleasant countryside & leaving the old eastern parts to a state of slumdom. The sections along the waterfront have long been given over to the tobacco industry, & possess at all times the pervasive odour of the weed. Richmond is the foremost tobacco town in the world. Parks are numerous & lovely—William Byrd Park on the western edge of the town being comparable to Roger Williams Park though by no means rivalling it. Forest Hills Park across the river contains woodland ravines almost equal to New England's. Richmond flora does not perceptibly differ from that of the north, though it perhaps grows in greater luxuriance. Several bridges connect Richmond with the opposite shore, using islands as stepping stones. Across the river is the dingy city of South Richmond, formerly Manchester—a sort of East Providence, as it were. The colonial houses of Richmond are small & made of brick, having resemblances to those of Philadelphia & Alexandria*. Peaked roofs with dormer windows seem to have been the rule—I have so far seen only *one* gambrel. The oldest house—preserved as a Poe shrine though Poe never inhabited it—dates from 1685; being a stone farmhouse antedating the urban settlement of the town. You now have a picture of this.[2]

Richmond—or the land it occupies—has been continuously known to the white man since the voyage of Captains Newport & John Smith in 1607—29 years before the founding of Providence, 23 before the settlement of Boston, & 13 before the Pilgrims landed on Plymouth Rock. I am thus at present in the oldest civilised region I have ever personally seen. A cairn & cross on Gamble Hill marks the spot where the voyages landed—their mission being to treat with the Indian Powhatan. The region & the town founded by Sir Thomas Dale was at first call'd *Henricopolis*, in honour of King James I's eldest son & heir-apparent Prince Henry; (who died, however, before succeeding to the throne, thus giving the crown to his younger brother, the ill-fated Charles I.) a designation which still survives as *Henrico County*, in which Richmond is situate. Henricopolis lay some distance southeast of the present town, & was destroyed by the Indians. In rebuilding, a safer site was naturally sought—hence the choice of the seven hills. Richmond proper was not estab-

---

*There is also a late-Georgian type quite peculiar to Richmond—square brick facade, & heavy Doric porch like that on our 1815-type houses.

lished until 1737, when a settlement was made by the great landed proprietor William Byrd, Gent., of Westover—direct ancestor of the present explorer Richard Byrd, & of his brother Harry Flood Byrd, now Governor of Virginia. William Byrd, a most versatile man, is also favourably known as a poet. In 1742 the village was incorporated as a town, & by 1779 it had so eclipsed the older town of Williamsburg (as Providence eclipsed Newport & Baltimore eclipsed Annapolis) that it was made the capital of Virginia. In 1782 it was incorporated as a city, & it has since remained the metropolis of Virginia, having a population of 200,000 against Norfolk's 160,000. It is a seaport—lying at the James's head of navigation—though it is content to leave chief maritime honours to Norfolk. In the Revolution Richmond sided largely with the rebels, & was harassed by Benedict Arnold after his transfer of allegiance to Great Britain. Arnold burned dwellings & tobacco warehouses, displaying as savage a spirit as when he attack'd the towns of Connecticut. On June 16, 1781, the town was enter'd without opposition by Lord Cornwallis on his way to the Yorktown peninsula—the Virginia government having temporarily removed to Charlottesville, a great distance westward.

The Civil War, however, brought Richmond its greatest & most tragick fame. As capital of the Confederacy, its capture was always the prime objective of the Federal Armies; & at two distinct periods it formed the focus of some particularly desperate fighting. Constantly in a state of siege, it developed defensive fortifications of the utmost effectiveness—some of which may still be seen as grass-grown trenches & embankments. I saw some in the western part of the town. It was around Richmond that the art of balloon observation first rose to prominence—the leaders in this procedure being none other than James & Ezra Allen of Providence, with whom the young German attaché Count Zeppelin took that first flight which launched him upon his memorable career. The battles around Richmond are too well known to old-timers to need description—Marye's Heights, Spottsylvania Court House, the Wilderness, Cold Harbour, Yellow Tavern, Williamsburg, Seven Pines, Mechanicsville, Gaines' Mill, Savage's Station, Frazier's Farm, Malvern Hill, Sharpsburg, Drewry's Bluff, &c. &c. Grant's "hammering campaign" finally made the city's abandonment necessary, & on the morning of April 3, 1865 (six days before the surrender at Appomattox) the defenders moved out. It was decided to destroy all the tobacco & supplies in the warehouse district along the river at the foot of the hills lest it prove of value to the Yankees, so sadly & reluctantly the whole section was put to the torch—just as the Yankee rebels in 1776 set fire to New York when forced to surrender it to His Majesty's lawful troops. The fire proved more extensive than had been planned—destroying Mayo's Bridge & obliterating nearly a thousand buildings. Reconstruction, however, was very rapid after the war; so that today all the structures in the burned district are old & dingy. Richmond will always remember the Civil War, & has erected some splendid monuments to Confederate heroes. Monument Avenue, a gorgeous boulevard with park centre strip & numerous landscaped circles at intersections, contains many noble tributes to vanished leaders—especially the great equestrian statues of Lee, Jackson, & Stuart, & the mighty Roman column, adorned by statuary & surrounded by a semicircular colonnade, sacred to Pres. Jefferson Davis. In Hollywood Cemetery here are buried Fitzhugh Lee, Stuart, Pickett, the oceanographer & naval officer Maury, & President Davis. On Libby Hill is another vast Roman column (modelled after the pillar of Pompeius) dedicated to all the Confederate dead.

Richmond's cultural life, like that of Providence, culminated in the 1830's & 1840's—the Poe period. It was then that the Southern Literary Messenger flourished, giving Philadelphia a close race for the cultural supremacy it was about to lose to Boston. Today the city has not a scholastic mood. There are no museums or art galleries or historical societies comparable to those of New England cities of equal size such as Providence, Worcester, Springfield, & New Haven. There are, however, signs of improvement in this direction—& a new publick library is under construction. There is one college—the University of Richmond. Murphy's Hotel, where I am staying so cheaply, (in an enormous barn of a room, shabby but clean) is one of the famous institutions of the town; & is very centrally situated about 2 blocks N W of the capitol building. I enclose a card of it, shewing the location of my room. This part of the town was semi-rural or suburban in colonial times—being on a height well back from the river.

Now as to the notable objects—the pictures I have sent you tell a great deal. The splendid State Capitol, crowning a grassy Acropolis-like height whose slopes are a park, was designed by the architecturally expert Thomas Jefferson, & forms perhaps the finest of early classic-revival specimens. Its foundation was laid in 1785, & it was finished in 1792. The two wings—of congruous design—added in 1902 are regrettable, but not as bad as one might fear. Within is a famous Houdon statue of Genl. Washington. The capitol grounds contain other things also—library & state office buildings, an old bell tower used as a powder-magazine during the war, a vast equestrian statue of Washington, & a fine Governor's mansion (now housing a true Virginia Byrd) built in 1811. It is a fine place to sit in the sun & read or write.

Jefferson Davis' Executive Mansion, not far away, is now a Confederate Museum. I have not yet explored its interior, but hope to do so Saturday. Another museum (old books, paintings, &c) is the Valentine Museum, which ought to be of interest to our Chortley kinsfolk. The Valentines are among the oldest aristocracy of Richmond—& it was the death of one of them which released for publication the Poe letters to his guardian John Allan about which so much has lately been written.[3] The house containing this museum was built in 1812. I hope for a chance to explore it. A third museum is the John Marshall house, residence of that famous Chief Justice of the U.S. from 1795 to his death in 1835. Most of the reliques are of Marshall himself, though there are

are [*sic*] a few of general nature. I plan to visit it Saturday. The town house of Gen. Robert E. Lee, occupied by the Virginia Historical Society, houses rare books, MSS. & reliques connected with the Old Dominion.

Of supreme interest to me, however, was the ancient stone house & its adjuncts lying in the easterly slum reaches of Main St. & now serving as a "Poe Shrine". This house, a farmhouse built in 1685 & overtaken by the growing town as our little Barnes & Prospect St. cottage was, is the oldest edifice in Richmond, & remains in a sound state of preservation. The space near it has been purchased by Poe-lovers & developed with great taste & ingenuity; an exquisite garden (supposed to represent symbolically that "enchanted garden" at Benefit & Church Sts., Providence, in which Poe glimpsed Mrs. Whitman, & of which he wrote so ably) lying in the rear, & the two adjacent houses on the street front being annexed as part of a three-building unit. Of these added houses that on the south is colonial, whilst that on the north is a fireproof museum built (like our Pendleton House) in imitation of the Richmond residence of John Allan, where Poe was reared as an adopted son. The ground plan of the unit is something like the accompanying diagram—the 1685 farmhouse being the central structure shewn in the views I have sent you. I spent an hour in this fascinating place, & saw all manner of Poe reliques—far more than are stored in the Fordham cottage I know so well. Poe's chair, desk, & various personal belongings are there, as well as many ar- chitectural details (mantels, a staircase, &c) from the two Allan houses & the Southern Literary Messenger building, all now demolished. One utterly magnificent feature is a gigantic model of the whole town of Richmond as it was during Poe's boyhood—about 1820—in a glass case occupying the entire ground floor space of the colonial house attached to the shrine. This model, made in natural colours & on a scale permitting even the smallest houses to be about an inch square, was constructed a few years ago with the utmost antiquarian accuracy & artistic skill; & is so vivid that one can almost imagine himself in a balloon looking down over the outspread colonial town. Never have I seen an ancient town so miraculously conjured out of the past—I wish someone would do the same for Old Providence! It gave me a short cut to Richmond's topographical & architectural history which at once places that venerable city among those I know best. What I had to worry out for myself in connexion with other colonial towns, has been all done for me in the case of Richmond. I never set eyes on the place till yesterday—yet today I know it like an old resident. I am convinced that models are the very best media for perpetuating the former appearance of old towns, & almost feel like writing to Chapin of the R.I. Hist. Soc. about it! Envy crept over me as I thought of how our ancient hill & 1st Baptist steeple & Great Bridge &c. would look if thus presented. There is much authentic data from which such a model could be made—the Henry R. Chase [*sic*] maps, the Francis Read drawings of

Westminster St. in 1824, the Harold Mason photographs & other pictures in the R.I. Hist. Soc. & Shepley Library, various accounts in books & MSS., oral traditions, & the structural evidence of buildings yet surviving. Providence really ought to have something like this!

It remains in this brief sketch to describe the most historic churches of Richmond. Richmond is full of churches, & I noted with interest that the pastor of the Broad St. Methodist Church—one of the most prominent in the south—is an old-time amateur & United poet with whom I used to correspond. I think I revised some of his poems—& now he is a prominent citizen written up in guide-books! This is *real* prominence—not the David V. Bush sort. He is the Reverend Frederick R. Chenault, D.D.[4] I don't believe I'll look him up, because I haven't corresponded with him for years & didn't know him *especially* well even when I did. But it is interesting to see how various old-time amateur acquaintances turn out. In his way, this chap has found a niche as definitely suitable & permanent as Mortonius's. But of course, it was the *older* churches of Richmond that captured my real interest. Of these, ancient St. John's is easily the foremost. This is a lineal successor to the original Church of England of Henrico Parish—the parish surrounding the first settlement made by Sir Thomas Dale at Henricopolis. A building was under construction at Henricopolis when the Indians destroyed it in 1622—& of this nothing remains but the baptismal font, which the savages carried off, but which was recovered from them in slightly damaged condition. This font still remains in the present church. After the founding of Richmond in 1737 it was decided to rebuild the church there, & land was given by William Byrd for the purpose. The region, "Church Hill," was then quite rural or suburban—on the eastern fringe of the town—though it is now of course urbanly engulfed. In 1741 a building was erected, part of which survives in the present edifice. You have a picture of the structure as it stands today in its ancient churchyard—the whole raised above the street level on a gentle mound & surrounded by an iron railing. The stones in the churchyard date back to 1751, & among the interments is the unfortunate actress-mother of Poe, who died in destitution in 1811. A fine monument to Mrs. Poe was set up a year or two ago by admirers of her great son. During the course of time St John's underwent such radical alterations & remodellings that almost nothing of the original church can be distinguished. What was once the nave, running east & west, is now the transept of a new nave running north & south—though a few of the old pews, & the ancient high pulpit & sounding-board, remain to this day. This church formed the meeting-place of Virginia delegates on March 20, 1775, during the early stages of the treason against His Majesty's lawful government; among them being Gen. Washington, George Mason, John Marshall, Thomas Jefferson, Patrick Henry, & other celebrated figures. On this occasion Mr. Henry, standing up in his pew, uttered those cheaply melodramatic words which have become such a favourite saw of schoolboys—"Give me liberty or give me death!" The pew from which he spoke is still preserved & marked with a tablet, but as a loyal subject of the King I refused to enter it. The whole ensemble of church & churchyard is marvellously captivating, & I mean to stroll thither again. A delightful mulatto sexton—very intelligent—shews visitors around the building. Another celebrated fane is the Monumental Church in Broad St. on the site of the old Richmond Theatre where Mrs. Poe acted & where the Convention of 1788 met to ratify the U.S. Constitution. The theatre was burned for the second time on Dec. 26, 1811—during the performance of a weird-horror play, "The Bleeding Nun", taken from Lewis' famous Gothick novel "The Monk". In this disaster, caused by the contact of an oil lamp with the scenery, 72 persons out of an audience of 643 lost their lives—among the victims being the Governor of Virginia, Wm. Smith, who escaped at the first alarm, but perished when he reëntered the building in an effort to save his small son. The magnitude of this calamity was an occasion of general mourning, & for four months theatrical performances were forbidden in Richmond. Jany. 1, 1812 was set aside as a day of fasting & prayer. At length it was decided to build a church on the site of the theatre, dedicated to the victims & forming a tomb for their mortal remains. The present edifice, finished in 1814, is a sightly structure with low dome & portico of two Doric columns *in antis*. Old St. Paul's near the capitol has a belfry tower & Ionick portico, & evidently belongs to the 1830–40 period although I cannot ascertain the exact date. It was here that Genl. Lee & Pres. Davis both worshipped—& here that Pres. Davis received, on the morning of April 2, 1865, the fateful telegram from Lee warning him that Richmond must be evacuated. The Lee & Davis pews are marked by tablets, & the memorial windows to Lee are the finest things of their kind in the U.S.

In Franklin St. near 19th is an austere old structure which would have interested Gramp—being the oldest Masonic hall in the U.S.—i.e., the oldest edifice built as such & continuously used for the same purpose. The corner stone was laid in 1785 by the chief Masonick dignitaries of Virginia, & the building has been occupied since 1787 by Richmond–Randolph Lodge, No. 19. In the War of 1812 it formed a military hospital, & Lafayette was entertain'd here in 1824.

Besides old buildings I have seen many historic sites—where famous structures have existed & passed away. Among these is the site of the dreaded Libby Prison near the waterfront. The building was originally a tobacco warehouse—& the hospital connected with it (probably a former dwelling-house) is still standing. The prison building existed until 1892, when it was taken down stone by stone to be reassembled & exhibited at the Chicago World's Fair. The intention was to return it later to Richmond, but somehow this plan was never carried out. I do not know whether the building still exists in Chicago or not.

Well—to return to my diary—after my orientation tour in the "rubberneck wagon" I did some pedestrian prowling-about myself, spending most of my time in the Poe Shrine, & writing some postcards in the golden afternoon sun that warmed the summer-like expanse of Capitol Park. I dined on sandwiches at a Liggett drug store, (for Richmond has no good one-arm joints like our Waldorfs & Thompson's, & no spaghetti places that I could find) & thereafter proceeded to the hotel, where I am now writing. I shall retire at midnight & rise tomorrow (Friday) morning, setting forth at 11 a.m. on the great all-day 'bus excursion which forms the climax & focal point of my entire vacation—the visit to Jamestown & Williamsburg, shrines of the oldest & greatest culture in the United States. Naturally you will receive ample bulletins of this event—including, if any are to be had, postcard views of the ancient regions visited. As you know, Jamestown was the original settlement founded in 1607—& is the real birthplace of the United States. It was burned by Nathaniel Bacon, who conducted a rebellion against the proprietors' government in 1676, & never rebuilt. I understand that nothing now remains of Jamestown but the old church—built in 1617 & now restored—& a few crumbling foundations. After the burning of 1676 the place steadily declined, & when the old State House burned down (accidentally) in 1698 the capital of Virginia was moved to Williamsburg. Williamsburg was founded in 1633 by Sir Francis Wyatt, & in 1699 became capital of Virginia. It was the cultural centre of the colony during its most important period, & is said to be one of the best-preserved colonial towns in America—whence the recent plan of John D. Rockefeller Jun. to restore it to its appearance of 1775. Here, in 1693, William & Mary College was founded—oldest in the country except Harvard. This college has a building directly designed by Sir Christopher Wren himself—the only one in the U.S. In Williamsburg is also old Brinton Church, built in 1715 & claimed by the natives to be the oldest house of worship, continuously used, in America. This claim of course must rest upon a challenge to the continuity-record of the Old Ship Church at Hingham, Mass., (1681) & the Dutch Church at Sleepy Hollow, near Tarrytown (1695). I shall also see—with a sigh—the village of Yorktown, where Lord Cornwallis surrender'd on Octr. 19, 1781. But all these things really belong in later diaries, & in the oral account I shall shortly give you. Be it sufficient to say that this is proving the greatest of all my trips—a thing to imagine & talk about for years to come! It is my first real saturation with the solid & ancient civilisation of the South—the only one I feel able to regard as equal to that of New England. Of later details I will apprise you more fully when I know more of the excursional possibilities of the next two days. I shall certainly stop in Fredericksburg & probably in Washington. Much depends on my purse, which I am naturally watching with care. I shall, if necessary, sacrifice the trip to see Dwyer in favour of additional Southern opportunities. Well—so endeth the diary for May 2nd. More soon.

Yr aff Nephew & obt Servt

H P L

[On envelope:]
Friday Morning
Bright & sunny. Cooler, but not uncomfortable if I wear my vest. Am now taking 'bus for the trip of trips!

P.S. Have just bought a June Weird Tales. The Eyrie is one continuous paean of praise to me & to my "Dunwich Horror," which won the popularity vote for April. Among the laudatory letters is one from Dwyer.[5]

[Postcard enclosure:][6]
Future plans
 Saturday—to visit occasional historic spots in Richmond on foot, also to sit in pleasant parks & read & write. *Possibly* to visit the barber's, since I need a haircut. Night at Murphy's.
 Sunday—to depart early for Fredericksburg, stop over there to explore the town & see Kenmore, home of Gen. Washington's sister, & then push on to Washington. Explore—& probably look up Sechrist. Night at Senate Hotel.
 Monday—undecided—depends on cash. May go directly north, but hope to diverge through Annapolis. Expect frequent postcard bulletins.

[On front:] my temporary headquarters

an elevated bridge, not shewn in this card, connects the annex where I am with the main hotel. There are chairs on it in which guests sit & survey the street.

Notes

1. In fact, the Pincian Hill (north of the Quirinal) is not regarded as one of the seven hills of Rome. HPL omits mention of the Aventine Hill.
2. Now the Edgar Allan Poe Museum at 1914 E. Main Street in Richmond. See HPL's discussion in "Homes and Shrines of Poe" (1934; *CE* 4.258).
3. See *Edgar Allan Poe Letters Till Now Unpublished, in the Valentine Museum, Richmond, Virginia*, ed. Mary Newton Stanard (Philadelphia: J. B. Lippincott Co., 1925). Hervey Allen used these letters extensively in his biography, *Israfel: The Life and Times of Edgar Allan Poe* (1927), which HPL owned (*LL* 27).
4. Frederick R. Chenault, pastor of the Broad Street Methodist Church (1915f.) and author of *The Broad Street Methodist Church, South and Community House* (Richmond, VA: Whittier & Shepperson, 1923). HPL discusses Chenault's poetry in various articles on amateur journalism during the years 1915–16 (see *CE* 1.66, 107, 123).
5. See Joshi, *A Weird Writer in Our Midst* 69–70.
6. *Front:* Murphy's Hotel and Connecting Annexes, Richmond, Va.

[284]   [ANS postcard]¹ [HPL to LDC]

[Postmarked Williamsburg, Va.,
3 May 1929]

All hail! Great trip! I'm now in the main room of an ancient colonial tavern in Williamsburg—looking out the window at the old court house shewn on this card. Some town! If you want to read about it, look at my files of cuttings in the kitchenette-alcove—the extreme right-hand pile next the wall. In the envelope marked "Washington & the South" you will find a full account of Williamsburg from the N Y Times.² ¶ The excursion duly set forth, though the trip from Richmond to Williamsburg was made in another 'bus—in which the ticket entitled one to passage. Now, at W'msburg, we shall pick up the regular Grey Line sightseeing 'bus. I fancy the return will be made in the same way. Going from Richmond we passed the picturesque Chickahominy River & Swamp, & saw some of the most famous Civil War battlefields. Also passed through the sleepy colonial villages of *Providence* Forge & Toano. W'msburg is sprawling, sleepy, & delightful—but less quaint than Marblehead because the streets are not narrow. More soon—
Yr aff Nephew & obt Servt
H P L

Notes

1. *Front:* Court House, Williamsburg, Va.
2. Possibly [Unsigned,] "Plan to Reproduce Colonial Capital," *New York Times* (8 January 1928): 1, about plans to restore colonial Williamsburg, spearheaded by financial contributions by John D. Rockefeller.

[285]   [ANS postcard]¹ [HPL to LDC]

[Postmarked Richmond, Va.,
4 May 1929, 2 a.m.]
[Written 3 May 1929]

Cradle of the Nation! Wait for my travelogue! Tremendously impressive to tread on soil once peopled by men of the Elizabethan generation. ¶ Williamsburg is magnificent—wait for my description! This is the most gorgeous day's trip I ever took! Yr aff Nephew & obt Servt H P L

Notes

1. *Front:* Jamestown Church Tower and Communion Service.

[286]   [ALS] [HPL to LDC]

Friday–Saturday
Midnight
May 3–4, 1929

My dear Daughter:—
                    Postcards have already made you aware of what I think
of Williamsburg, Jamestown, & Yorktown, & of the aspect of one or two
landmarks in these fascinating places. It remains for me to speak of my travels more fully, & to relate something of the spots I have seen. As I said, I
travelled by 'bus from Richmond over the old Williamsburg Road, or Nine-
Mile Road, to use another ancient name. This took me past some of the most
celebrated battlefields of the Civil War, including Seven Pines & the Chickahominy Swamp. The Chickahominy River was crossed on a new concrete
bridge, & presented an interesting swamp-like aspect with trees growing out
of the water far back from the open channel. This was the most Southern-
looking landscape I have yet seen—for Virginia is not really a Southern region except socially & politically. Climatically it is in the same approximate
zone as ourselves, as fauna, flora, & general atmosphere attest. It is in the
Carolinas & Georgia that the actual climatic South begins. At the sleepy little
Southern village of *Providence Forge,* in New Kent County, I was tempted to get
off & mail you a card for the sake of the postmark; but did not because the
driver told me the place is not a post-office! The card would have been postmarked "Toano" had I sent it. But anyway, I have seen a Providence outside
R.I.! Not long afterward, as if by coincidence, I saw a R.I. license plate—
25.116—on a passing motor! Evidently I am not the only wandering soul in
my native land. Providence Forge, according to the splendid guidebook I later
picked up at Williamsburg, was named from an old forge used in making
farm implements, set up there in 1770 by three men, one of whom was a
Presbyterian clergyman. It has given its name to the principal estate near by—
an 8-room colonial house of the farm type with dormer windows & a pair of
chimneys on each end. A stream, dam, & mill exist at Providence Forge, &
remnants of the old forge itself were recently found. Some distance beyond
this town I saw the small but famous old Hickory Neck Church, built in 1733
& serving as an academy for some time subsequent to 1825. It is a very small,
plain brick structure—like an enlarged dog-kennel—of a type fairly frequent
in Virginia. Toano next was reached—a straggling southern village without
distinctive features.
    At last came Williamsburg, where a change to the Grey Line sightseeing
'bus was made. This is one of the best-preserved colonial towns in America,
& amply justifies the Rockefeller plan for restoring it to its pre-revolutionary
state. Much restoration has been accomplished even now, but most of it is
still to come. In layout & atmosphere, Williamsburg resembles *Deerfield* more
than any other New England town—since it is largely concentrated along a

broad main street, & consists of houses widely spaced amidst their grounds. The central thoroughfare, Duke of Gloucester St., is well shaded with trees, & has a strip of turf down the centre. Houses vary from quaint peaked-roof* affairs of early date to fine Georgian mansions in the Southern style. I will shew you many pictures of representative specimens upon my return. One by one the non-Colonial buildings are being torn down, whilst plans are under way to re-erect the principal colonial structures on their carefully excavated foundations. Williamsburg, the oldest incorporated town in Virginia, began in 1633 with a palisade built by Gov. Wyatt as a defence against the Indians. It grew very rapidly, & with the decline & burning of Jamestown (1676) became the chief settlement in the colony. It was made the capital in 1699, after the burning of the Jamestown colony house. During the 18ᵗʰ century it was the centre of a brilliant life, as is attested by its many noble mansions. It likewise became the seat of William & Mary College, founded in 1693. The name Williamsburg was first applied in 1699—the former designation having been "Middle Plantations". It was made a city in 1722, & has always remained such, though it is scarce more than a village in population. As Richmond rose, Williamsburg declined; till at length (1779) it gave place to its younger rival as capital. This stagnation, akin to that of Newport, is what has preserved its colonial reliquiae so marvellously.

I can only describe a few of the sights of W'msburg—through which the Grey Line party was guided by a very bright young student from the college. Old Brinton Church, built 1710–15, is perhaps the high spot, & I was glad of a chance to explore it amply, crypt & all. It contains the ancient silver communion service from the early church at Jamestown, as well as other colonial reliques of the highest value. The churchyard is, bar none, the most hauntingly picturesque I have ever seen—with curiously carved granite monuments bearing coats-of-arms. William & Mary College, at the west end of Duke of Gloucester St., has for its original edifice the only building in America designed by Sir Christopher Wren. Newer buildings—including several still unfinished—all conform to the same type of design. The President's house, built in 1732, is of the steep-roofed Southern Georgian pattern. A chapel attached to the Wren building was erected in 1730, & another small building (donated by the eminent scientist Sir Robert Boyle for use as an Indian School) was built in 1723. In front of the Wren building stands the marble statue of the colonial governor Lord Botetourt, originally set up near the colony house, & removed hither in 1797. Botetourt himself lies buried beneath the chapel. At the east or opposite end of Duke of Gloucester St. the foundations of the colonial capitol are still visible—or rather, visible again after excavation. This building will rise again from these foundations—a perfect copy of the one erected in 1705, rebuilt after burning in 1750, & abandoned to de-

---

*a few gambrel specimens exist.

cay in 1780. The white-belfried colonial court house, built in 1769, is still in use as such, but will eventually become a public library. The old "Powder Horn" is a typical colonial powder house—like those at Marblehead & Somerville except that it is octagonal. It was built in 1715, & has since been put to a curious variety of uses—market house, Baptist church, dancing-school, Confederate arsenal, stable, & historical museum. Two interesting old gaols are shewn—the Debtors' Prison, built in 1748, & the Old Colony Prison built in 1705 with especially thick brick walls. In the latter were confined 13 of the pirate Blackbeard's men—who were subsequently hang'd nearby—as well as the royal governor of Detroit, Henry Hamilton, who was captured at Vincennes Ind. in 1779 by George Rogers Clark. Another interesting object is the pre-revolutionary apothecary shop, now in process of restoration.

The private dwellings of interest are too numerous to catalogue. Most famous perhaps is the George Wythe house in Palace Green, built in 1755 & inhabited by the famous statesman from 1779 to 1789. It was the headquarters of Gen. Washington in 1781. In 1927 this fine Middle-Georgian specimen became the Parish House of Brinton Church, & has been restored as a museum. I was glad to be able to give it a thorough exploration. The Paradise house is a splendid Georgian mansion built in 1760 & inhabited in 1788–9 by John Paradise, at one time a member of Dr. Johnson's literary circle in London. The Gov John Page house, (1710) a smallish wooden structure, is the scene of Mary Johnson's novel "Audrey." There are strange inscriptions scratched on two of its window-panes—"S.B. 1796 Nov. 23 O fatal day." & "A. Boush 1734". The Vest house is the largest brick mansion in W'msburg. The Galt house (1640) is the oldest in Williamsburg, & probably the oldest in Virginia. It is small, wooden, & steep-roofed. But the catalogue must end sometime. Besides the existing houses, there are many sites where houses will be rebuilt from surviving foundations—among them the Governor's house, the Masonick hall, & the famous Raleigh tavern. I must see W'msburg again when the restorations are complete—perhaps 2 to 5 yrs. hence. It will then form, without doubt, one of the most impressive evocations of the colonial past that America can display. One curious fact emphasised by this restoring work is the manner in which nature tends to give burial to the things which man has forgotten—a slow, subtle burial inch by inch as the dust of decades drifts & accumulates. It is thus that half the steps of Notre Dame have been cover'd up, & thus that classic Rome lies many feet below the level of the modern town. In Williamsburg the old foundation walls of vanished structures lie several inches below the present surface—& I noted with interest the lost brick driveway of the Governor Dinwiddie house, rediscovered only two or three weeks ago, which is fully a foot lower than the existing sidewalk.

From Williamsburg the 'bus drove over a lovely road to the island of Jamestown—birthplace of the British civilisation in America. En route we passed several lakes of clear blue, exempt from the general yellow mud colour of southern waters. The reasons for this differentiation are intricately geological—Mortonius could tell more about it than I can—& I was soon to find that the great York River shares the happy exemption. The James is yellow, but the York is blue! Incidentally, the whole area traversed in this trip lies between the York & the James, & has hence been termed "The Peninsula."

Jamestown is no longer a village, but simply a windswept grassy expanse overlooking the river & strown with monuments & melancholy reliques. Yet it is here that our nation took its rise in 1607—thirteen years before the Plymouth landing of the Pilgrims. The fateful expedition sailed from London on Dec. 30, 1606, in three ships—the "Sarah Constant" under Capt. Sir Christopher Newport, the "Goodspeed" under Capt. Bartholomew Gosnold, (who also explored our N.E. coast) & the "Discovery" under Capt. John Ratcliff. On May 13, 1607, the colonists landed at the spot which became Jamestown, naming their settlement from King James I. There were 105 of them in all—all men. First preparing a crude shelter for worship, they rendered thanks to Heaven according to the Church of England rite; & subsequently began building their crude village. The first church was rough & ugly, but a finer brick Gothic specimen was put up in 1638 (not 1617 as often erroneously thought), the tower of which yet remains in a ruined state, with a modern nave (1907) built on the excavated foundations of the old one. In 1608 Capt. John Smith became President of the Council, & used his distinguished ability in furthering the fortunes of the settlement. He had sailed up the James in 1607 with Capt. Newport & erected a cross at the falls & head of navigation where Richmond now stands. Indian troubles followed, as is well illustrated by the well-known incident of Pocahontas. In 1609 Smith was succeeded by Percy, & in that autumn came the great famine which left only 60 out of some 500 settlers. In 1610 the dissatisfied colonists all started back for England, but decided to stay when a fresh load of colonists (delay'd by shipwreck) arrived. Lord de la Warr now became governor & increased the general contentment, & to him Sir Thomas Dale ably succeeded. In 1619 wives were sent out for the colonists, & in the same year the first cargo of African blacks arrived. This was under the governorship of Sir George Yeardley. Industry & agriculture grew, silk culture & glassmaking being among the experiments. An Indian massacre in 1622 failed to kill off the settlement; & by the time of Bacon's rebellion against Governor Berkeley the colony had so grown that Jamestown's burning meant only a local loss—Virginia supremacy passing to Williamsburg, then called Middle Plantation. Many buildings of brick & wood were put up at Jamestown, including several notable Colony houses, the last of which was burned in 1699. After 1700 the town was gradually abandoned, so that fewer & fewer houses remained standing—the high winds destroying things rather readily. In the 1830's only one house—the brick Ambler house—existed on the island in addition to the ruined tower, & today even this has succumbed save for part of the walls. These reliquiae prove the house to have been of Gothick design—for it must be remembered that Jamestown was founded before the original Gothick period had wholly ended. The principal area of Jamestown is today owned by the Association for the Preservation of Virginia Antiquities, & is strown with monuments & excavated foundation walls. I cannot here attempt to describe these individually—save to say that the outlines of the old colony house were unearthed in 1903, together with those of four private dwellings in a solid block. The brick-paved cellar of one of the latter—Col. Philip Ludwell's house—has been completely excavated. The colony house here unearthed was that of 1686—whose burning led to the transfer of the capital to Williamsburg. There are two small museums in Jamestown, housing some small excavated reliques & some historical pictures. A sea wall has been built around the island to check the constant encroachments of the wind-lashed river. Part of Jamestown is privately owned & not open to the publick—some day it will yield up rich material. The real focus of interest is the ruined & ivied Church Tower of the 1638 edifice. Amidst its ancient brick-walled churchyard, & with its modern nave behind it, it well symbolises both the decay of the town & the permanence of the colony which sprang from it.

The coach now set out for Yorktown, a quaint colonial city celebrated as the scene of Lord Cornwallis's unfortunate surrender to the rebel armies of Genl. Washington & Marquis de la Fayette. This town, now sunk to a sleepy village, was once a port of very great wealth & standing, being a noted port of entry whose custom-house in 1749 recorded an annual trade of £32,000. It lies on land first patented by one Nicholas Martian, a Walloon, who came to Virginia in 1621. In 1691 Martian's grandson Benjamin Reade sold 50 acres of the tract to Mefsrs. Ring & Ballard to be settled as a town. The venture prosper'd, & in 1698 the new village became the seat of York County. In 1706 a brick custom-house, still standing, was built to accomodate its increasing trade. In 1781 the retreating troops of Ld Cornwallis reach'd this place, establishing a final line of defence some distance east of the town & surrendering on the 19th of October. This event, deciding the colonial rebellion in favour of the rebels, marked the virtual close of hostilities & signalised the practical separation of the colonies from their rightful government; hence is widely celebrated throughout America. The town & field are distinguish'd by monuments, & the place much visited by travellers. Some events of the Civil War also took place here, Genl. McClellan employing Yorktown as a Federal base in 1862. There is a cemetery & a monument dedicated to the memory of Union soldiers killed in battle & in an accidental explosion. Yorktown lies on the south bank of the broad blue York River—a stream curiously exempt from the yellowness of most Southern waters. A ferry connects it with Gloucester—which together with another ferry across the James from Jamestown to Surry forms a continuous route across the peninsula to the farther south. This is not, however, the main highway southward—the latter pafsing through Richmond & avoiding the peninsula altogether. Yorktown is 12 miles from the mouth of the York, 18 from Jamestown, & 12 from Williamsburg. En route from Jamestown, we re-pafs'd through Williamsburg, which I was very glad to see again, since I wish to imprefs it upon my memory. On the high road thence to Yorktown we beheld some Civil War & Revolutionary battlefields, & saw in the distance one or two famous colonial estates such as Carter's Grove, built in 1751 by Carter Burwell. We also pafs'd through the shabby whitewashed village of Lackey, which is apparently inhabited wholly by niggers. It is notable that the blacks are much more numerous on the peninsula than in Richmond. The Richmond–Norfolk 'busses require them to sit in the rear, & the stations around Williamsburg, Yorktown, & Lee Hall all have separate white & black waiting rooms. In Norfolk, of course, the colour-line is strictly drawn—for the place teems with niggers.

Yorktown proper is a kind of southern Marblehead, most of the houses being of colonial date. There are no sidewalks, & the only pavement is the concrete of the State Road. Its architecture is more typically Southern than that of Richmond, steeply pitched roofs & end chimneys being everywhere seen. The Grey Line 'bus pafs'd through it, view'd the battlefield, & then return'd to inspect the town at greater leisure. On the east edge of the compact part are the foundation walls of the Nelson house, used by Cornwallis as his headquarters till its destruction by shell fire on Oct. 11, 1781. These were excavated only last month, & will be very carefully preserved. The town as a whole is merely a double line of straggling brick, stone, or wood houses along the highway, & most of it can be seen from the coach. I was glad, however, when a stop permitted me to indulge in some pedestrian exploration.

The greatest mansion in Yorktown is the imposing Thomas Nelson house,—York Hall—a middle-Georgian structure shewing the Pennsylvania-Welsh influence in its architecture. This was own'd by the nephew of Secretary Nelson, owner of the demolished house. During the revolution it was held by His Majesty's officers, & to dislodge them the owner—himself serving as a rebel general under Washington—order'd his own mansion to be fir'd upon. Of this Spartan fusillade—which fortunately fail'd to destroy the splendid house—two cannon balls yet remain imbedded in the eastern gable end. I sent a card of this house to A E P G, who will doubtlefs shew it to you. A splendid garden adjoins the edifice. The oldest house in Yorktown, built in 1699, stands next to the Thomas Nelson mansion, & is a modest brick dwelling with ancient curb roof & colonial dormers. It was built by Thomas Sessions—perhaps related distantly to our R.I. Darius Sessions—& escaped injury in the revolution. Its present condition is excellent. Grace Church, built also in 1699 as York-Hampton Church, is also in a good state. It is very small but exceedingly tasteful, built of grey marl rock & having a modest white belfry. In the ancient churchyard are some interesting slabs. The small brick custom-house put up in 1706 is the oldest custom-house in the U.S., & is now a publick museum operated by the D.A.R. The Yorktown Hotel, put up in 1725, is still in continuous use for its original purpose; rivalling in that respect Sudbury's Wayside Inn. It is a small, steep, southern-looking building with end chimneys & dormers, & has been enlarged by a long rear extension which does not mar the original street facade. Other noted old Yorktown houses are the Cole Digges, (1705—small brick) the West, (1706—small wooden) & the Moore, a farmhouse of early but uncertain date near the village. This latter was anciently the abode of Gov. Spottswood, & in 1781 form'd the scene of Ld Cornwallis' conference with Genl Waſhington as to terms of surrender. It is on that account highly esteem'd by those who sympathise with the revolt against our rightful Sovereign.

I was very glad to have seen this village—& indeed, I reckon this day's explorations as among the most pleasant & striking I have ever made. From Yorktown the coach went to Lee Hall, a small town where it connected with the Richmond coach. The return trip to Richmond included one more welcome paſsage through Williamsburg, & a magnificently apocalyptic sunset seen over the Chickahominy Swamp. The scenery here has good spots, but is not equal to New-England in any respect. Probably no land but Old England has landscapes really comparable to ours. Reaching Richmond in the dusk of evening, I dined at Liggett's & repair'd to my room at Murphy's to write letters. I shall now retire—at midnight—& rise tomorrow (Sat.) morning for a day of Southern leisure—roaming Richmond with reading & writing materials in my enamel-cloth bag, & pausing in the pleasantest parks.

Yr aff Nephew & obt Servt

H P L

[On envelope:]

Saturday Morning

Glorious day! Warm again—absolute summer. Shall leave off vest. Up 10 a.m. & about to idle luxuriously about Richmond parks, reading & writing at intervals, & visiting the principal museums & antiquities. Expect small parcel post packages from time to time—I may send one today with miscellaneous cards, printed matter, & laundry.

¶ Have just found in a guidebook that the 1685 date of the Poe Shrine is disputed. It may be the Jacob Ege house, built in 1737.

¶ Have just found the kind of *pencil-sharpeners* we want, in a stationery store. Only 10¢ each—I've bought two. Will send you yours in my next package—or bring it in person. ¶ Now for the P.O. (near Capitol Park) to mail Package #1[.] My Virginia postcards & guidebook are in it—look at them if you like.

[287]   [ANS postcard]¹ [HPL to LDC]

[Postmarked Fredericksburg, Va.,
5 May 1929]
[Written 4–5 May 1929]

DIARY—SATURDAY, MAY 4ᵗʰ [vertically in margin]
Hurrah! Got weighed tonight for the first time since I was inflated to 148 by
the Long cuisine, & find that I have knocked off 6 pounds in 4 days! I weigh
just *142*, as tested by 3 different scales—which means that I'll touch the 140-
mark again before I reach the north. It's a science! Found a good place for
cheap meals in Richmond at last—a regular Jake's—the Park View in 9ᵗʰ St.
Hate to leave Richmond for the place grows on me day by day—feel as if I'd
lived there for years. Hard to realise that such a place as N.Y. exists except in
a nightmare, though Providence fits right into the picture—that is, the Providence of the ancient hill, not the foreignised West Side. It gives one an amazing sensation to be in a *really* American city in the year 1929. After all, the fact
is that the old America is not *dead,* but simply *contracted* to the South & to isolated oases like Vermont. This is the real old Richmond that William Byrd &
Poe & Jefferson Davis knew. Its great charm is its utter lack of "smartness"
& senseless bustle. Like the old-time New Englander, the Southerner has no
false front. Life is divested of affected excrescences, & kept to the main Anglo-Saxon stream. ¶ As for my diary—spent Saturday exploring on foot &
writing letters & reading in the various splendid parks. Retiring at midnight, &
shall set out for Fredericksburg & Wash'n tomorrow. More soon. Yrs H P L

[On front:] SUNDAY, MAY 5. Had intended to stop in Richmond another
day; but cloudy weather makes me decide to travel today. Shall start for Fredericksburg at noon, spend some time in Fredericksburg, & then go on to
Washington, arriving in the evening. Will drop you a card from Fredericksburg if I can get one.

Safe in Fredericksburg 1:30 p.m. Expect more bulletins!

Notes

1. *Front:* Old Saint John's Church, Richmond, Va.

[288]   [ANS postcard]¹ [HPL to LDC]

[Postmarked Fredericksburg, Va.,
5 May 1929]

DIARY FOR SUNDAY, MAY 5ᵗʰ, 1929, *continued*
    Arrived in Fredericksburg—a genial 'bus driver has given me all sorts of
booklets & information which will help me do it justice. This quaint old town

was charter'd as a town in 1727, & named from Frederick, Prince of Wales, father of George III. Falmouth, the still quainter village across the Rappahannock 1 mile north, is still older; having been laid out in 1720. Genl. Washington spent his childhood near here, & went to school both in Falmouth & Fredericksburg. Many of his relations also dwelt here—including his sister Betty, wife of Fielding Lewis, Esq., of the mansion of Kenmore. I shall see Kenmore presently, & send you a card of it if I can get one. The history of the region antedating the town is very ancient—it is said that white men glimpsed it as far back as 1570, & Capt. John Smith certainly reached it in 1608. I can see that this town is worth a long exploration & a travelogue—so you'll hear about it from me later. I expect to stop about 8 hours.
Yr aff Nephew & obt Servt
H P L

Notes

1. *Front:* General Hugh Mercer's Apothecary Shop, Fredericksburg, Va.

[289]   [ALS] [HPL to LDC]

Monday, May 6, 1929

On a bench in the park
between the White House &
Washington Monument,
Washington, D.C.

My dear Daughter:—

I take my pen in hand to apprise you that I am enjoying good health & hope you are likewise.

My last diary entry extended to yesterday (Sunday) noon, when thanks to a friendly 'bus driver I landed in Fredericksburg fully equipped with guidebooks & directions. And what a town it proved to be! Quaint & historic beyond my fondest expectations, it kept me busy for all of the 5 hours at my disposal; & made me wish I had 5 more in which to study its numberless antiquities & fascinating Old-Virginia atmosphere. For here is a quiet village which has slept unchanged through the centuries with its shady streets & colonial houses beside the green-bank'd yellow Rappahannock. The Civil War cruelly scarred it—it was, as you know, the scene of our Rhode-Island Burnside's rash exploits—but failed to impair its centuried charm & continuous tradition. There are very few foreigners—a mere handful of Greeks & Jews, & no Italians or Poles—& very few people of any kind whose ancestors have not dwelt there for centuries. Niggers are not numerous—indeed, they are by no means a conspicuous feature of the northern Virginia landscape. I was very fortunate in encountering a kindly, talkative, well-bred & scholarly old man who noticed my contemplative mien & frequent guide-book glances & who volunteered to guide me to the best colonial reliquiae. He was a connoisseur of Georgian architecture, inhabiting a colonial house himself & being something of a student of furniture, decorative detail, & early brick construction. Under his tutelage—& he tirelessly walked me through street after street, lean & alert despite his years—I absorbed dozens of sights & atmospheric touches which I would otherwise have missed, & he offered to shew me interiors on some later visit when I might have more time. This good old man—a Mr. Alexander—is quite typical of nearly everyone I have encountered in the south—including Mr. Strain, the genial 'bus driver. Without question, I find southern people more congenial than any other type I have so far met—despite my devotion to New England's landscape, architecture, & quiet ways. The Southerner reflects a civilisation of riper mellowness & higher graces than any other on this continent, & I wish this civilisation had a greater chance of spreading & leaving its impress on the culture of the nation as a whole. After a week in the south it will seem like wading through mud & putrescence to traverse the Manhattan region again, but thank heaven it will be a brief passing. Up the Hudson things become civilised again—& then over the Mohawk trail to ancient New-England! I dread hearing coarse New York voices in subway & on sidewalk—down here everyone talks in the mellow accent which characterises the young Corragher boy's speech.

To return to my diary—Fredericksburg indeed excelled all my expectations. I don't know but I'd rather live there than in Richmond, for this place is wholly of the past—a southern Marblehead. It straggles sleepily along the southern bank of the shallow Rappahannock at the original head of navigation, with the green unspoiled countryside (now in the full luxuriance of summer) drowsing exquisitely across the stream. Two bridges connect the town with the northern shore—one from the "civic centre" to the roads of the open country (Stafford Heights) & the other (the main Washington–Richmond highway bridge) from the extreme westerly fringe to the quaint & somnolent hamlet of Falmouth, which is seven years older than Fredericksburg. The centre of the town before the Revolution lay farther west, but a destructive fire during that period wiped out the business section & caused the residential streets farther east to turn to trade. The layout today is the same as in Civil War times. The town was named in honour of George III's father—Frederick, Prince of Wales, who died before succeeding to the throne. All the principal streets are named for members of the Royal family—Princess Anne St., Prince Edward St., Prince George St., William St., Sophia St., Amelia St., Caroline St., & so on. This is the kind of atmosphere in which my Tory soul revels—God Save the King!

The Fredericksburg region—to exclude all apocryphal tales—was first visited by Capt. John Smith with a crew of 12 men & Indian guide in 1608, on a trip during which he had a severe fight with a band of prowling Rappahannocks. Settlement—in the form of farms & gentlemen's plantations—was very gradual, but a fort was maintained near the falls of the river, & much sea-trade conducted—for the river was then broader & deeper than at present, & better adapted to navigation. In 1671 land patents were granted to Thomas Royston & John Buckner for the purpose of forming a settlement of 40 persons, but this did not prove lasting. The tiny hamlet of Falmouth, on the north bank of the river near the falls, was founded in 1720, & is the earliest continuous settlement. Falmouth still contains many decrepit, steep-roofed houses which must date back to almost the first decade of its colonisation. All these settlements reflect the desire of the neighbouring country-gentry for a town in their midst to serve as a trading-centre. Virginia was always rural by instinct, & even in 1700 Williamsburg was the only important town. Northern Virginians, wishing a more convenient centre of commerce, encouraged the trading class to settle around the Rappahannock region in urban fashion—then, realising the advantages of town houses for themselves, began to build mansions in the village & to develop a town social life in conjunction with their manorial existence. Fredericksburg, as a definite town, was incorporated & named in 1727. It was in this region that most of the Washingtons dwelt in the early 18th century—the "Cherry Tree" farm of Gen. Washington's father being just across the river from Fredericksburg. Young George & his brothers & sister went to school in Falmouth & Fredericksburg, & his mother always lived there. The sister, Betty, married Col. Fielding Lewis, who built Kenmore mansion for her. In later years Madam Washington lived in a cottage near Kenmore to be close to her daughter, & there she died in 1789. She is buried in the vicinity—I saw her tomb. The early houses of Fredericksburg are small, steep-roofed, wood & brick affairs with dormers & end chimneys—the regular southern type—built along the river-bank & sometimes forming solid blocks of 4 or 5. Later & finer dwellings are on the higher parallel streets farther back from the stream. Kenmore—really a country-seat—is very far from the Rappahannock, in what were open fields at the time of its building. Madam Washington's cottage was connected with it by a flower-bordered path. Both are standing, & in excellent preservation—I gave them a close & appreciative survey. The oldest real mansion, the Charles Dick house, was built in 1745 & is still standing in good shape. I view'd it with much interest. Another thing which impressed me greatly was the Rising Sun Tavern, built in the 1760's by Charles Washington, George's brother, & famous for having harboured most of the eminent southern statesmen of the 18th century. Still quainter is the little apothecary shop in Caroline St. kept by Col. Hugh Mercer, who was both a physician & a chemist, & who was killed in the Revolution. This has been fitted up exactly as it was in Mercer's day, with old-time jars, great brass scales, & all the appurtenances of a colonial pharmacy. Another cherished set of Fredericksburg associations is that connected with President James Monroe, who was born nearby & who practiced law there after the Revolution. His old office has been refitted just as it was in his day, so that it forms an admirable companion-piece to the Mercer shop. I am enclosing pictures of some of these things. Of great Masonick interest is the ancient brick home of Lodge N⁰· 4, where on Nov. 4, 1752, George Washington was initiated as a Mason. The Masonick order was very strong throughout colonial Virginia, & especially at Fredericksburg—where there is a special Masonick Cemetery.

But the chief charm of Fredericksburg is less in any one house than in its whole pervasive atmosphere of colonial Southernism—a culture which has certainly survived to a much greater extent than colonial New-Englandism. Fredericksburg doorways—while by no means equal to New England specimens—are famous throughout the South. The doors are generally double— that is, *vertically* double like those of Philadelphia—& above them is generally a *transom* of the colonial New York type rather than a *fanlight* in the New England & Philadelphia manner. The traceries on these transoms are often exquisite in the extreme, & are worthy of a special study. Only very late Georgian houses (circa 1825) have fanlights & sidelights. One or two of these have doorways very like those designed by John Holden Greene for such Providence houses as the Beckwith, Allen, Halsey, & Crawford mansions.

Kenmore deserves a chapter all to itself. This celebrated mansion was begun in 1752, on land surveyed on Feby. 20th of that year by young George Washington, brother-in-law of the builder. It is a splendid specimen of the plainer type of Middle Georgian architecture, & seems to follow northern or British models rather than the typical southern style. There is a portico & a garden in the rear, & the grounds are still spacious despite many ruthless subtractions from the original vast estate. The doorways & panelling are very notable, & the great recessed windows lend a charm of memorable poignancy. Massive locks & "Holy Lord" hinges form matters of importance to those interested in structural details. But the chief "show pieces" of Kenmore are, curiously enough, not parts of the original fabric but additions made more than twenty years later—viz., the marvellous stuccoed ceilings & overmantels. Most of these were done in 1774 & 1775 by the same Frenchman who did the stucco work at Mt. Vernon—& he has left a monument to his national loyalty in the dining-room, the centre of whose ceiling is the head of King Louis XIV, surrounded by solar rays typifying the monarch's boasted function as the bright sun of civilisation. In the "great room" the stuccoed overmantel is of different & perhaps more interesting workmanship. This was done during the Revolution by two Hessian prisoners taken at the battle of Trenton & quartered at Falmouth. When Mrs. Lewis learned of these artisans & what they could do, she decided to have them complete the stucco work at Kenmore, & wrote her brother Gen. Washington, asking for suggestions as to a good overmantel design. He thought that the Æsopic fable of the fox, the crow, & the piece of cheese would be a good thing to select for the place—both as a decoration & as a didactic lesson to his little nephews to beware of flatterers. Accordingly he sketched out a rough design for the artists to follow—a design in which the landscape & buildings are typical of the homely rural Virginia landscape. This suggestion was duly acted upon, & the result remains to this day in prime condition. I enclose a picture of it. Architects agree in praising it as a very fine specimen of its kind.

Col. Lewis, his health & fortune wrecked by his unceasing expenditure of money & strength on the rebel cause—for he was a leader in the intensive manufacture of muskets for the continental troops—died penniless in January 1782, & his widow was forced to open a school & sell portions of the estate. Throughout her trials she was ably advised by her illustrious brother, & in 1796 she sold Kenmore & went to live with a married daughter in Culpeper County, where she died March 31, 1797. She was greatly beloved & mourned by Gen. Washington, who was of about the same age, & whom she resembled so greatly that it was commonly said she could well pass for him if dressed in his clothes. She had a sprightlier disposition, however, & a greater sense of humour than either her brother or mother. Temperamentally she seems to have been largely a Washington, whilst the General took after the Balls in his disposition. Kenmore remained in good hands after its sale, till in 1914 its sale as a boarding-house was threatened. This peril gave rise to merited alarm, & an association was form'd to preserve it. Success happily crown'd the efforts of the association, & the house is today a publick museum of distinguish'd excellence & wide repute. I thoroughly explored the house & grounds, & accounted my time well-spent. Old Madam Washington's cottage is likewise safely preserv'd & open as a publick museum.

The Civil War history of Fredericksburg was of less interest to me, yet is dramatick in the extreme. Its strategick position can be understood when we realise that the whole crux of the war was really the capture of Richmond, south of it. The great battle—a futile & wasteful affair—was precipitated by the rashness of our Rhode Island Burnside & by the clamour of the Northern press. The Yankees were encamped on Stafford Heights across the Rappahannock, & began on Dec. 13, 1862, with a cannonade almost unparalleled in the annals of warfare prior to the Great War. The townspeople fled, & the Confederate defenders retired to Marye's Heights, which overlook the town on the south. Bridges having been burnt by the Confederates, Burnside's men crossed the river on hastily laid pontoon-bridges, & for a few hours occupied the town—not without some vandalism. Notwithstanding the obviously impregnable defences of Lee & Longstreet on Marye's Heights, the brave & reckless Burnside determined to attack the Confederate position; & led his men to what was virtually a wholesale suicide. What happened to Gen. Meagher's Irish brigade is a sample of what the whole charge was like. Of that unit of 1200 men, *937* were left dead on the field—one officer's body being found within 15 feet of the Confederate parapet. Utterly beaten, Burnside retired back across the river to Stafford Heights when night fell. He had killed the best part of his troops absolutely for nothing!

Earlier in the war Fredericksburg had been the scene of a more peaceful Yankee occupation—in the spring of 1862, when Gen. McDowell controlled the Rappahannock region. During that period Pres. Lincoln delivered an address from the steps of the (still standing) National Bank—framed in its exquisite colonial doorway. The Federal officer then in occupation was Gen. Marsena Patrick, whose kindliness & consideration won him many Southern friends. His correspondence with Mayor Slaughter (for Fredericksburg, small as it is, is a real *city!*) was of such courtliness that one historian has said that the letters "read like the extracts from the correspondence of diplomats."[1]

Fredericksburg is also quite near to many other noted Civil War battlefields—such as Salem Church, Chancellorsville, Spotsylvania Court House, & the Wilderness.

Returning to my diary—after a thorough survey of "urban" Fredericksburg I walked out along the main highway to quaint Falmouth—about a mile & a half, & across the long Rappahannock bridge. This hamlet is ineffably archaic & half fallen to ruin, & evidently houses a rather poor class of whites in addition to its niggers. It lies picturesquely on a curving hill road which ascends the northerly slope of the river-valley, & most of its houses are of the early 18th century. A few late-Georgian houses lie on the lower level near the river-bank—one of them, with a splendid fanlighted doorway, being labelled as the home of the "first millionaire in America." The interior woodwork of this fine house is announced as for sale—symbol of an increasing & very discouraging habit of stripping noble old buildings to enrich museums & the private homes of vulgar moneyed parvenus. In returning to Fredericksburg I did not follow the main highway, but ambled along the leisurely, unfrequented old road that skirt's [*sic*] the river's northern bank, crossing by the bridge from the foot of Stafford Heights to the centre of the town. It was now 6:30 p.m. & time for the last Washington coach, so I reclaimed my valise at the Princess Anne hotel & prepared for the journey. I duly obtain'd a seat, & after an uneventful trip landed in Washington at 8:30. This time, wishing to be nearer the centre of the town than I was last week, I stopped at the old Metropolitan Hotel in Penn. Ave. near 7th St.—antiquated & unpretentious, but clean & quiet—where I found a very good dollar room whose only fault is that the electric light bulb is feeble. After some reading & writing, I retired at 2 a.m. & rested well. This morning I rose at 10 a.m. & repair'd to a *barber-shop*, for my hair was getting too bad for publick view. After a truly excellent cut by an amiable Southern (pure American!) barber who owns & lives in a colonial house, I telephoned Edward Lloyd Sechrist, who was in Wyoming last summer when I passed through Washington. This time he was in town, & seemed delighted to hear from me. He is to meet me in the lobby of my hotel at 5:30 p.m. for a general aesthetick & antiquarian chat. Just before leaving town I shall have to telephone the good old lady amateur poet Miss Toldridge, who (though learned & interesting in letters) is probably a bore, but who would naturally be offended if she heard of my passing through without a word on the wire. I have spent this afternoon reading & writing in the park—where a trim detachment of boys from some military school are now drilling with magnificent effect on the broad training-ground before me. It is now 3:30, & in the 2 hrs. before I meet Sechrist I shall see some sights—about which my diary will tell in due time. Tomorrow—alas—I shall probably move northward; of that more anon. ¶ Yr aff Nephew & obt Servt H P L

[On envelope:]
P.S. Have just decided to spend the 2 hours at the Corcoran Gallery of Art—which I've never explored before.
Later—no—I shan't! Find this is a pay day, whereas tomorrow isn't. Shall tackle the Smithsonian Museum instead.

Notes

1. In Carmichael, 37.

[290]   [3 ANS postcards (within envelope?)]¹ [HPL to LDC]

[6 May 1929]

[1] *Diary for Monday, May 6, 1929—Continued*

Well—the Smithsonian Museum was great! Saw the first locomotives ever run in the U.S., & all sorts of interesting early automobiles dating from 1892 down, & including many of the good old 1900 period, which I recall so well from the days of my prime. Later I went over to the Library of Congress—a famously lavish building designed by a scion of the E. Greenwich Caseys,² which I had never entered before. Despite its excess of colour & ornateness it is not as bad as I had expected; & I found a wealth of interesting exhibits—including a set of splendid coloured photographs of the ancient parish churches of Virginia, which makes me wish I could stay in this region & view them all! Now, amidst gathering clouds which have at last produced a chilly drizzle, I have returned to the hotel lobby to meet Sechrist. The rain will spoil any walking—but there is plenty of talking to do. I shall continue this record tonight.

N.B. The rain did not last.

MONDAY–TUESDAY MIDNIGHT

Well—Sechrist shewed up on time, accompanied by a plain lady of much intelligence from Richmond, who turned out to be his fiancee. It seems that he has at last obtained the divorce he has been wistfully waiting for so long, & that he is about to embark on a second domestic venture based upon what he thinks is a congeniality ensuring felicitous permanence. Well—I wish him luck, & at that he may have it; for if he can stand such plainness, there must be some phenomenal mental sympathy of a solid kind! Sechrist & his bride-elect took me to dinner at the neighbouring National Restaurant—but I ate lightly for the sake of my reducing campaign. Scales gave me 141 this morning. After dinner [2] the future Mrs. Sechrist departed for some woman's club, & Sechrist took me out to the room in the N.W. part of the city which he is occupying until his wedding in July. It is in an old house, but rather carelessly & temporarily furnished—the most prized object being a *radio*, which through very expert installation has the most perfect & natural tone I have ever heard in connexion with such a thing. Our conversation was highly interesting; revolving around many phases of aesthetics, & finally centreing in prehistoric African antiquities. Sechrist, as you may recall, has lived in South Africa in the past. During the evening he shewed me many rare curiosities such as rare woods, rhinoceros-hide, &c. &c.—& especially a prehistoric bird-idol of strangely crude design found near the cryptical & mysterious ruins of Zimbabwe (remnants of a vanished & unknown race & civilisation) in the jungle, & resembling the colossal bird-idols found on the walls of that baffling & fancy-provoking town. I made a sketch of this, for it at once suggested a multiplicity of ideas for weird fictional development.[3] I also took notes on the topography, colour, & atmosphere of interior Africa, in order that my story may possess convincing verisimilitude. Well—discussion was so interesting that [3] our session did not break up till 11:30 p.m., & it is to be resumed at 8:30 tomorrow morning, when I shall meet Sechrist at the Smithsonian Museum an hour before the public opening time. It seems that he knows the curator & several under-curators of this important institution, & that he thinks I can secure better guidance & access to the vast collections if he introduces me personally. He is certainly most generous & considerate—it is not often that one is especially introduced at one of the greatest museums of the world! Well, at 11:30 I prepared to return to the hotel, Sechrist walking with me to the car. His neighbourhood is a shady, reposeful, & delightful one—like most Wash'n neighbourhoods—& has several houses of the 1825 period. Now—midnight—I am about to retire. I have left word with the clerk downstairs to ring me awake at 7:30 a.m., so that I may be on time for my Smithsonian appointment with Sechrist. Tomorrow—besides the Smithsonian—I intend to do the Corcoran Gallery of Art & possibly the Freer museum, together with as much outdoor sightseeing as possible if the weather is decent. May start north that night, but may possibly take another day for Wash'n. I'll let you know. This is certainly a great region, & I'm certainly having a great time. More later—& I shall see you before long! Yrrrs H P L

[note by HPL on front of card no. 1:] This library designed by our ineffably remote kinsman Edward Pearce Casey—of the East Greenwich line.

Notes

1. *Front:* 1) Second Floor Congressional Library, Washington, D.C. 2) Minerva, Library of Congress, Washington, D.C. 3) Lincoln Memorial and Japanese Cherry Blossoms, Washington, D.C.
2. Edward Pearce Casey (1864–1940), designer of the Library of Congress, was HPL's 6th cousin through common descent from Thomas Casey (1636?–1719?).
3. HPL subsequently wrote the poem "The Outpost" (26 November 1929) based on this image.

[291]   [ANS postcard]¹ [HPL to LDC]

[No postmark;
7 May 1929]

DIARY FOR TUESDAY, MAY 7, 1929—Well—I was duly up & met Sechrist at the Smithsonian at 8:30. The museum is not far from this hotel. It seems that Sechrist has a beekeeping exhibit on display there, & I was very much interested in seeing it. We also viewed the general collection more fully than I did yesterday—shewn about by men whom Sechrist knows. Among the most striking objects were the great stone images from Easter Island in the South Pacific—Cyclopean statues made by some unknown race of the forgotten past. After Sechrist had to leave, I went to the Corcoran Gallery of Art, whose most interesting feature was a set of models illustrating coming architectural developments in Washington—developments which will involve much demolition, though not the loss of anything as fine as our S. Water St. warehouses. After the Corcoran I went to the Freer gallery, which contains the famous "Peacock Room" by Whistler—a dining-room of an English mansion which he decorated, & which was saved when the owner died. After the Freer I took the car for the National Cathedral on Mt. St Alban, which I really think will eclipse St John the Divine in beauty. Upon my return I gave my duty telephone call to the old lady—Miss Toldridge—& she cordially insisted that I pay at least a brief call in person. She is a somewhat stately & intelligent gentlewoman living amidst family portraits & reliques in a pleasant apartment-house in Farragut Park. After a short call—less boresome than I had anticipated—I returned to my hotel & spent the later evening reading. At midnight I retired, & tomorrow I shall start north—at what hour I haven't decided. Next—Philadelphia! More soon. Yr aff Neph H P L

[On front:] Taking noon 'bus to Phila.—mailing another package home.

Notes

1. *Front:* Memorial Amphitheatre, Arlington, Va.

[292]   [ANS postcard]¹ [HPL to LDC]

[No postmark;
8 May 1929]

DIARY FOR WEDNESDAY, MAY 8, 1929

Well, I got the noon 'bus & had a delightful journey to Philadelphia under sunny skies. The farther north I come, the less I like the country; but I shan't go back on Old Philadᵃ· It surely has genuine charm, & a reposeful background that won't be spoiled for another generation. Have secured a fine room at the Y M C A—they still rent them to non-members in Phila. It is in the new part of the building, & has an unusual degree of freshness & immaculateness. Shall spend the twilight seeing ancient urban sights & retire early. Tomorrow I hope to see the museums—& ancient Germantown if possible. ¶ In my hasty packing this morning I did a careless thing—either mailed my diary & writing materials home by mistake or left them at the hotel. Shall drop a card to the hotel in case I did leave them there, though I think I must have accidentally slipped them in the home bundle. ¶ Shall move on to N Y tomorrow evening, probably getting the same room in Belknap's apartment house. Then up the Hudson Friday or Saturday, up to Albany & over the Mohawk Trail Monday, & home within a week. Some tour! More bulletins shortly.
Yr aff Nephew & obt Servt
H P L

Notes

1. *Front:* William Penn House, Fairmount Park, Philadelphia, Pa.

[293]   [2 ANS postcards (within envelope?)]¹ [HPL to LDC]

[9 May 1929]

[1] Well—here goes the diary to 4:30 p.m. Thursday, May 9, 1929! Rose at 9 a.m. & found the day too drizzly & raw for a Germantown trip—hence decided to devote the time to museums. First came the U. of P. with its marvellous Oriental antiquities, & after that (the rain having stopp'd) I walk'd out the Parkway to the new Art Museum—which is only partly finished & open. This is absolutely the most magnificent museum building in the world—a vast Greek temple group atop a high elevation (a former reservoir) which terminates the Parkway vista toward the Schuylkill; reach'd by vast broad flights of steps, flanked by waterfalls, & with a gigantick fountain playing in the centre of the great tessellated courtyard. A veritable Acropolis—I had seen it before, but had never ascended the steps or enter'd the place. Well— this time I did ascend & enter; & believe me, it was no disappointment! Colonial & British Georgian rooms in infinite profusion—not so many American rooms as in the new Boston wing or the Metropolitan's American Wing,

but much more British material than in either of those places. This card shews a room from the famous Powel house in S. 3ᵈ St., Phila., (still standing—I've just been to see it again) a smaller room from which you have seen in the N Y American Wing. A more unique feature is a pair of rooms from an 18ᵗʰ century Pennsylvania German house—the only things of their kind in any museum I know of. The furniture & paintings occupying these rooms are [2] as rare as the rooms themselves—including the best work of the corresponding periods. The pictures include Reynolds, Gainsborough, Romney, Raeburn, Gilbert Stuart, &c. &c. The wide assortment of English rooms presented enables one to form a very good comparative estimate of British & American Georgian styles; & curiously enough, I think I prefer the American. The American interiors are less lavish in scale & decorative detail, & thereby gain a classic austerity of tone which would be hard to surpass. That Powel room represents just about the high-water mark of domestic architecture.

Well—by the time I finished with the Art Museum it was too late to go to Germantown, so I decided to put in the 2 hours before the 4:30 'bus doing urban sightseeing. I must take that 'bus, else I shall arrive at Belknap's too late for the early hours kept by the Longs. I have now been over my favourite colonial routes, & find my liking for Old Philadelphia undiminished. At present I am sitting on a park bench in the shadow of the ancient colony house—popularly call'd "Independence Hall". God Save the King! At 4:30 I must embark for the N Y cesspool—more diary later.

Yr aff Nephew & obt Servt H P L

Notes

1. *Front:* 1) The Philadelphia Museum of Art: A Room from the Powel House, Philadelphia, 1768. 2) The Philadelphia Museum of Art: Fairmount.

[294]   [ALS] [HPL to LDC]

At Belknap's—
Thursday–Friday Midnight,
May 9–10, 1929

My dear Daughter:—
        To continue the diary which my last Philadelphia card carried to 4:30 p.m.—here I am at Sonny's in the old N Y dump again, after a sunny, pleasant, & uneventful journey. The ride from Philadelphia covers many fairly attractive spots—Princeton is a delightful colonial village, & it was like old times to pass through ancient Elizabethtown, my antiquarian refuge of the days of 1924 & 1925. Elizabethtown has obviously grown, & has some new buildings—but is basically much the same as when we bought the diary & filing envelopes at the Woolworth store there. Which reminds me that I must get some more filing envelopes. Well—when I got to Sonny's I

found the next stage of my journey all mapped out for me! More good luck & more cash saved! The Longs are going on a fishing trip to the trout-streams of the Catskills, & decided to make the date tomorrow—so that they could take me up to Dwyer's in Kingston! Naturally I accepted the invitation with alacrity, for this would have been the most troublesome stage of my journey in the absence of either 'bus service or (until May 30) Hudson Day Line boats. It would have meant a costly railway trip, or a night-boat trip delivering me at Kingston Point (some distance from Kingston itself) at an impossibly inconvenient hour. Now, however—with my characteristic good travel-luck—all is solved; & the trip will be made with ease without costing me a cent! I shall start with the Long party tomorrow morning at 8:30, & about 2 p.m. the faithful old Essex will deliver me directly at Dwyer's door—177 Green St. Dwyer will be out—at his work—but I can leave my valise with the landlady. It was certainly delightfully thoughtful of the Longs to facilitate my monumental outing programme in this way. For tonight I have a room in the same apartment-house—not the one I had last week, but a large transformed parlour in one of the 4th floor flats. Thanks to the interventions of just such happy accidents as this, my expenses have been virtually nil whilst in New York, & thanks to low 'bus fares & modest dining tastes, my road expenses have been far from heavy. I may be able to finish the trip without breaking into the extra cash A E P G sent me, for there will be no more lodging fees except very possibly a night at Albany. Cook insists that I stop off in Athol a day or two—& that means neither food nor rent bills. He is not ill, & has be-gun to discharge his duties at last. His delay was in part due to an effort to save Freer money—for he thought that returns from booksellers might pos-sibly obviate the need of a second edition of "White Fire." All told, this is proving about the most remarkable trip I've ever had in my life. Even the weather has not really been an adverse influence, because the great period of rain & chill occurred when I was not travelling but merely visiting with the gang. As soon as I hit the road in earnest, the weather duly improved in con-sonance—here's hoping it stays improved during the Kingston, Mohawk Trail, & Athol chapters of the epick! On the day you wrote—Sunday the 5th—you will see by my diary-letters that I had a sunny & genial afternoon in Fredericksburg, although it rained in the morning whilst I was on the coach from Richmond. I miss the South—it seems very strange & disconcerting to come out of luxuriant summer into the raw air & nascent leafage of a north-ern spring. For one thing I'm thankful—& that is that I shan't see much of N Y! There was only a misty twilight blur of Varick St. & lower 7th Ave. when the coach emerged from the Holland Tunnel, & then another vague blur of lights when I dodged out of the 96th St subway station into 230 W. 97. To-morrow I shall see only upper Riverside Drive & a ferry—then the wild domed hills, & not a sight of any town but venerable Kingston!

I was indeed delighted to receive yours of the 5th, & am glad that my sundry bulletins have proved entertaining. I trust that A E P G has shew'd you such chronicles as have been address'd to her. As for the cheque—I suppose it was wise to hold it for my arrival, though early cashing is a good rule to follow. It could have been sent for my signature, then I could have made it over to A E P G, & sent it back for her to cash. However, that would have saved only a week, for I'll be back ere that time has elapsed. You might give me just *one* more general forwarding of mail—% *W. Paul Cook, Box 215, Athol, Mass.* A good old New England address this time—there's something amusingly dramatick in edging home gradually in this way! One can trace my various temporary milieux as a sequence of colour-schemes established by the prevailing automobile license plates around me. First, after the Conn. white on red, came the New York black on orange, then a dash through the New Jersey white on black, Pennsylvania orange on blue, Delaware blue on orange, & Maryland blue on white, to the District of Columbia orange on black. Next came Virginia, with black on orange duplicating the New York scheme. Then a reëntry to the D.C.'s orange on black, & a rehearsal of the others in inverse order to N Y's black on orange again. This will remain over the week-end until I take the Mohawk Trail coach. Then I shall edge through a corner of *Vermont*, whose colours this year I don't know; & come at length upon the familiar Massachusetts white on blue—so frequently seen in our own Providence streets. That will last me through the Athol phase. Then—assuming that neither Cook nor Munn gives me a motor lift home—I shall take the Boston coach which cuts up twice across the *New-Hampshire* line, where the scheme is black on white exactly like ours. All told, I shall have entered the following states in the following order. Those distinguished by an overnight stop are marked with an asterisk. Those in which I have or shall have set foot outside a moving vehicle are marked with a dagger.

Connecticut	Maryland†
New York*	District of Columbia*
New Jersey†	Virginia*
Pennsylvania*	Vermont
Delaware	Massachusetts* } future
	New Hampshire.

Eleven commonwealths besides my own in one trip! Incidentally—I did not have to take that rabble-haunted Nevin 'bus line on my return journey. I found out in Washington that the more select Mitten lines (owned by the Philadelphia Rapid Transit Co., & patronised by me last year)[1] have brought down their rates in competition, so I rode both from Washn. to Philada. & from Philada. to N Y on a gasoline-electric (electrically driven by current from a gasoline-run dynamo) P.R.T. coach.

You must get outdoors more now that the weather is better—I shall make you take in Prospect Terrace when I arrive. As for my weight—as you have seen, it's now down to 140 again; & I certainly don't intend to get up to 148 again if I can help it! I'm enclosing the last two weight cards shewing how I finally trimmed down to the requisite figure. May 7 shew'd 142—but by the 9th I had struck my fixed goal of 140. Philadelphia is my principal reducing station—it was there, in Nov. 1924, that I first discover'd how to perform the miracle! If I were staying long at Belknap's my weight would be in peril again, but fortunately my only Long meal will be a lunch in the motor en route for Kingston. Still—one Long lunch is about equal to the average person's lunch & dinner for two days! Sonny gets fatter & fatter—I do believe the little rascal's bay window protrudes more than it did a week ago! And all the while his grandpa's wearing that Christmas belt in the last of the three holes punched to make it smaller. I trust that ere this the bundle of books has come from Loveman. If not, I shall have to get after him! By this time, too, you ought to have received two more bundles of linen & miscellany from me—one mailed from Richmond & another from Washington. I am making up still another one right now—with my sea-horse & your pencil-sharpener in it—which Sonny will mail from the 102nd St. station as soon as the family get back from this piscatorial week-end. Possibly still another will come from Kingston or Athol—I surely do know how to travel light! Today was so raw that I decided not to mail home my overcoat—I may need it as I progress northward. Open any package you like—you'll find interesting postcards & travel material in most of 'em. No—I haven't spent too much on postcards—I haven't sent as many to others as I have to you & A E P G, & they only cost 2¢ each to buy & mail complete. They give you a concrete, vivid idea of where I am & what I'm seeing.

As for reading—keep the piles intact—Bulletins, Sunday Journals, & N Y Timeses since & including *Thursday, April 4th*—& I'll wade through 'em somehow! I did not see the Times last Sunday, nor am I likely to do so next Sunday—but I'll spend a week keeping up with the news. Then of course I want to see all the copies of Time—the news weekly—& any Scribner's or Harper's which may have filtered in. I shall spend just about a week reëstablishing my routine & settling down for another year of inactive & stationary seclusion. I trust that nothing has disturbed the order of my china & silver in the dining alcove—& that no other upheavals or cleanings have convulsed my lair. I *will* not have work around my house!

Thanks for the cutting about the kittie—I saw the item in the Times & noticed it particularly. Wish I could see my little tiger friend Hiram again, but am passing through too swiftly for a call. Anyhow, I shall see Felis in the morning.

I telephoned the hospital from Belknap's this evening, & find that nice old Mac is much better, although still there. They want to get him all worked into his new diet before they turn him loose. I found a letter from his brother—Frederick McNeil of Long Beach, Cal.—awaiting me at 230. I had written him about the case, & he was very grateful for the information. The letter—which I'll shew you presently—was amusingly *illiterate*, which shews that Mac undoubtedly comes from a very crude & rugged rustic background—the un-furbelow'd[2] pioneer stock of primitive Wisconsin. I've dropped Mac cards from all along my itinerary—a sort of cheering influence, since he has shewn in the past that he appreciates such remembrances.

And so it goes. Trust you've missed none of my various bulletins. Those Philadelphia museums were certainly great—the memory of them haunts me. Look at this fine head of Akhnaton in the U. of P.! There is also a gigantic Sphinx there—& a superlatively fine diorite head of Rameses II, around which were clustered nearly a dozen art students copying it on canvas & drawing-paper. As for the Art Museum—the building alone is worth travelling leagues to see! Never have I dreamt of anything more utterly classick & majestick. And then those Georgian Rooms!

Well—tomorrow I shall see my artistic & literary correspondent Dwyer for the first time. So far, Wandrei is the only member of the gang who has met him personally. I feel sure I shall like him. Belknap is not yet sure whether he can arrange to see him or not. Meanwhile I must get a bit of sleep before starting. Tell A E P G I safely received her banking service & will answer her letter shortly. More soon—expect many bulletins from the wild domed hills!

Yr aff Nephew & obt Servt H P L

Notes

1 The Mitten Line was one of several transit lines operated by Thomas E. Mitten (1864–1929), president of Philadelphia Rapid Transit.

2. A furbelow is a gathered strip or pleated border of a skirt or petticoat.

[295]   [ANS postcard][1] [HPL to LDC]

[Postmarked Kingston, N.Y.,
11 May 1929]

Diary up to 2 p.m. Saturday, May 11, 1929

Well—at 6 p.m. last night I returned to 177 Green St. & met Dwyer at last. He is an absolutely delightful chap—6^{ft} 3^{in} tall, heavily built, & with an extremely handsome, open, & winning face which frequently breaks out into an infectious smile. A pleasant, deep voice, & a refreshingly pure diction & apt choice of words—& a phenomenally sensitive imagination. A true artist if there ever was one. His establishment is more of a separate household than I had gathered from his landlady—a whole wing or ell of the house, with 5 or 6 rooms & his own furniture. A very tasteful place, on the whole, & his sister appears to be a capable housekeeper despite outside employment. Dwyer insisted that I take all my meals with him, so one more expense is saved on this remarkable round of economical travel! Dinner last night was very fine—& I fear for my weight if I have many more meals there! In the evening Dwyer & I sat in the combination dining & living room & discussed art & literature till 2 a.m., at which time I returned to my part of the rambling house & retired. This morning—gloriously sunny—I have arisen at 11 a.m. & am exploring the ancient town as I did yesterday. A great place! I shall return to 177 Green & meet Dwyer at 2 p.m. More soon. Yrs H P L

Notes

1. *Front:* American Legion Memorial Building, 18 West O'Reilly St., Kingston, N.Y.

[296]   [ANS postcard][1] [HPL to LDC]

[Postmarked Kingston, N.Y.,
13 May 1929]

DIARY UP TO SUNDAY, MAY 12, 1929—6 p.m.
Well—I left off yesterday at 2 p.m. as I was about to join Dwyer for the day. I found him ready, & we strolled among ancient places discussing ancient things; finally settling down to write postcards in that idyllic country lane (which I find is call'd Noone's Lane) where I sat writing Friday afternoon. Finally we went to the Publick Library, where we spent the late afternoon & evening looking up Kingston antiquarian material & going over art books which Dwyer reveres—especially a fascinating Doré collection. At about 9:30 p.m. we dined at an excellent restaurant & returned to 177, where we found news of the Long party awaiting us. It seems that they had had no luck fishing, & that they had started on their return ahead of time. They were not surprised to find us gone, but said they would be back at 9 a.m. the next day, before taking the southward trail. Well, Dwyer & I discussed literature half the night & retired at 2 a.m. Rising this morning at 8 o'clock, we were dressed in time to welcome Sonny & his parents & to shew them around the antique part of the town. They left at 11, & I was thereupon treated to a noonday meal which work [*sic*] fearful havock with my 140 lbs. Then followed more literary discussion, & now I am about to look over some ancient streets while Dwyer takes a nap. At 6 we shall rejoin for dinner, & during the evening discussion will reign once more. Tomorrow, the rather uncertain weather permitting, I shall make the Hurley & New Paltz trips & go to Albany in the evening. Tuesday, the Mohawk Trail & Athol. More soon. Yrs H P L

Notes

1. *Front:* Kingston, N.Y., Birdseye View of Wilbur and the Bridge Looking up Rondout Creek.

[297]   [ANS postcard]¹ [HPL to LDC]

[Postmarked Kingston, N.Y.,
13 May 1929]

DIARY TO 6 p.m. Monday, May 13, 1929.

Well—last night I discussed the universe with Dwyer till 3 a.m., & at that hour retired, rising at noon today. The weather is mild & splendid; & perceiving that I shall not again want my overcoat, I have mailed it home—together with a set of linen I have just discarded. I am now wearing my last set of linen—hope I shan't have to buy more in Athol! I find that it will not be possible to make either the Hurley or New Paltz trip today, so fear I shall have to leave the exploration of these quaint Colonial villages till another trip. In lieu of these side-excursions, I have been through the ancient house shewn on this card (partly burned by His Majesty's troops in 1777 & now own'd by the D.A.R.) & am reading & writing in the idyllick country lane I recently describ'd to you. I shall later do some more exploring of Kingston's ancient streets—particularly in the old & now squalid section known as Rondout. At six I shall return to 177 Green St. to meet Dwyer & discuss various things throughout the evening. About 10 o'clock (unless I decide to stay over & see Hurley & New Paltz tomorrow) I shall proceed to the West Shore station & take a train for Albany—where I shall stop for the night & take a coach for ancient New England tomorrow. Then for the glorious Mohawk Trail—& His Majesty's Province of the Maſsachusetts-Bay! Expect to be in Athol about 3 p.m. tomorrow. More soon—
Yrs
H P L

Notes

1. *Front:* Old Captain Tappan House, now owned by Daughters of American Revolution, Kingston, N.Y.

[298]   [ALS] [HPL to LDC]

Mon.–Tues midnight—May 13–14[, 1929]

My dear Daughter:—

Well, here's a somewhat unexpected turn to the diary—for after all I'm staying over another day to do Hurley & New Paltz. It would be too great a shame to be right in this vicinity & not see these famous colonial towns, about which I'll tell you in my next diary. I hope to see both in the same day—then on to Albany, & over the trail to Athol Wednesday.

In continuing my chronicle from today's postcard, I must record a very provoking event in the form of a *robbery*. No—nothing as startling as the great Clinton St. cleanup of May 24, 1925, but irritating in a minor way, especially since it involved a bit of real carelessness on my part. The material stolen was my black enamel-cloth case; containing my stationery & diary, two copies of Weird Tales, my pocket telescope, & some postcards & printed matter of Kingston. I had left it for the merest moment in the idyllic lane where I sat reading & writing, & when I returned from that instant's uphill climb it was gone! That such an inconspicuous-looking outfit in such a peaceful rustic spot could be in peril of purloining was something which never crossed my mind—though in future I shall be more careful. The monetary loss is inconsiderable, for the spy-glass was an old & cheap one, but I rather hate to lose the 1929 diary with the record of all my spring travels & all my addresses written in it. However, I can reconstruct the diary from the letters & cards I have written home—provided I can find a 1929 issue still remaining at the ten-cent store. Upon discovering the loss I reported it at the proper police desk at the City Hall, though I have no great expectancy of recovering the property. I shall get duplicates of the *Weird Tales*, & have annexed a compensating bunch of stationery at the Van Ross hotel, which is the central 'bus terminal of Kingston. As for the black enamel-cloth case—I shall simply pick up my duplicate at Athol. You are aware that I purchased one last year when Orton had borrowed mine, & that it is among the still undelivered things which I left for Cook to bring to Providence in his car.

Well—I spent the evening discussing the universe with Dwyer, & am now retiring at 1 a.m. I shall arise at 8 a.m. & catch the 9:00 Hurley 'bus—heav'n grant that the weather may be decent. Hurley is a famous old Dutch town whose aspect has not changed since 1700 or so—I have seen models of its houses in the N.Y. Hist. Soc. It was to this town that the rebel inhabitants of Kingston fled on Oct. 16, 1777, at the approach of His Majesty's troops. New Paltz is a village of much the same characteristics, founded by French Huguenot settlers & having a plenitude of stone houses of 1700 & thereabouts.

Kingston itself is a great old place, as you may have inferr'd from my cards. The present city is a fusion of two once separate villages—*Kingston* proper, where Dwyer lives & which is about a mile inland, & the part of *Rondout* on the hilly Hudson bank, where the ferry from Rhinebeck lands & which is now a somewhat picturesque slum. The two were fused about 50 years ago when a municipal form of government was adopted.

The history of the region goes back to the decade of 1620–30, when the Dutch built a fort (*ronduit*) at the mouth of a creek on land called by the Indians *Ponckhockie*. The fort became the centre of a settlement called *Rondout*, & the creek received the name of Rondout Creek. About 1652 Kingston proper—the land then called Atkarkton, northwest of Rondout & inland along Esopus Creek—was settled by Dutchmen & Englishmen from Rensselaerwyck, farther up the river, after disputes regarding land titles had driven them from the latter place. In 1655 serious Indian Wars convulsed the locality, & in 1658 the Atkarkton settlers appealed to Gov. Petrus Stuyvesant for aid. "Old Silver-Leg" was disposed to grant the petition only on condition

that the colonists form their holdings into a palisaded village, & this require-
ment was duly & immediately complied with. The resulting stockaded town,
which was charter'd by Stuyvesant in 1661 under the name of Wiltwyck, was
embraced in the area bounded by the present Main St., Clinton Ave., North
Front St., & Green St. Streets were laid out, which correspond quite closely
to the streets of today. After the transfer of New-Netherland to His Britannick Majesty's domain, the name of Wiltwyck was chang'd to Kingston; & the
village prosper'd exceedingly. In 1695 the Rev^d. John Miller, Chaplain of His
Majesty's forces & Aide to the Governor of New-York, publish'd a book
with maps descriptive of the province & therein spoke of Kingston as a town
of the same area as Albany, but with half as many houses—i.e., as being 6 fur-
longs in circumference, & having an hundred buildings in its compaſs. Many
of those buildings are still standing today. Severe Indian warfare haraſs'd the
town throughout its early history—incidents not unprovok'd by the high-
handed seizure of lands & arbitrary & cruel treatment of Indians by the
Dutch settlers. When the unfortunate sedition against the lawful authority of
Great-Britain occurr'd, Kingston had well-nigh 200 houses, a market & brew
house, a church, an academy, (still standing) a court house, & two schools. As
a storehouse & source of supply for the rebel armies operating in its vicinity,
it was a highly dangerous menace to His Majesty's forces; so that in the autumn of 1777 its destruction by fire was found needful. Most of the rebel inhabitants, being forewarn'd, fled to the village of Hurley & other points, &
our troops enter'd the place without opposition; setting fire to all the edifices
save those inhabited by loyal subjects of His Majesty. This process consum'd
only the wooden dwellings, leaving the walls & great beams of the stone
houses scarcely damag'd. Accordingly the returning rebels later rebuilt their
homes, so that large numbers of the early structures still stand. At this time,
Oct. 16, 1777, the rebel Senate of New-York was meeting at the Ten Broeck
house in Kingston, (now pointed out as the "Senate House", & forming a
publick museum) & adjourn'd its sessions to the Van Deusen house in Hurley
when our troops burn'd the former. The city of New-York was the legal capital of the Province; but it was not at that time in the hands of the rebels,
hence their sessions at Kingston, which was the third town in importance in
the colony, Albany being second. In the compact part of Kingston not more
than one or two houses were left undamag'd by flame. Today the Van Steen-
burgh house, in Wall St. at the head of Franklin, (hardly in the village according to the limits of 1777) is pointed out as the only one which was not
touched. For this various reasons are assign'd—loyalty of the owner being the
most probable explanation. The tenure of Kingston by His Majesty's forces
was not of long duration, since powerful rebel forces under Genl. George
Clinton (a native of the region, & later Governor of N.Y. State for 21 years)
were observ'd to be advancing toward the town. Having destroy'd all possible
rebel supplies, the army evacuated without pursuit of the fleeing villagers; &

did not again enter. The rebel army soon arriv'd, & with its aid the villagers quickly reëstablished themselves in their accustom'd haunts. Local progrefs was by no means retarded, & in 1783 (being us'd to harbouring a legislative body) Kingston offer'd itself as a pofsible Capital of the United States—which offer was declin'd as the Federal City of Washington was plann'd. After the Revolution Kingston remain'd a very important town, tho' it did not grow as rapidly as many—Albany & New York City monopolising the activity along the Hudson. At the Bogardus Tavern, which stood at the corner of Fair St. & Maiden Lane, many persons of the first importance were entertain'd; & it was there that Aaron Burr, observing the clever chalk drawings of a stable-boy on a barn-door, resolv'd to send the lad to Europe for an art education, & thus produced the eminent painter John Vanderlyn. As the 19th century wore on, Kingston was more & more rivall'd by the river settlement of *Rondout*, on the Hudson at the mouth of the creek, which naturally obtain'd a great share of the region's trade. By the 1840's Rondout was greater than Kingston in population, & was heavily built up along its narrow, hilly streets in contrast to Kingston's straggling houses, broad streets, & level terrain. At the same time it was less select in population & less rich in traditions—a hive of traders & bargemen rather than a settled domain of hereditary agricultural magnates. In the 'fifties Rondout applied for a city charter, & seemed for a while about to get it—but vested & dignified Kingston intervened, & finally succeeded in disposing of its rival by engulfing it—i.e., securing a combined city charter for the villages of Kingston & Rondout *under the name of Kingston.* Thus Kingston became, by one sudden act, a city & a river port, with two distinct settled areas separated by a sparsely populated zone. So it has remain'd to this day; save that the sparse zone is gradually filling up with publick & private buildings including the railway station, P.O., publick library, city hall, hospital, & Y M C A. Kingston proper (or "uptown") has retain'd its social supremacy, & there may be found all the leading dwellings & shops. Hilly Rondout on the river has become a sort of South Main St. or Olneyville—distinctly declassé, & largely given over to foreigners, from whom Kingston proper is almost wholly free. The city is distinguish'd by a reposefulness highly pleasant to observe, & scarcely changes in population—having linger'd between 25,000 & 30,000 for the last thirty years. It has a single street-car line from the Day Line wharf at Kingston Point through Rondout to Kingston Proper—which still remains wholly two-man, still uses little single-truck cars, & still has *open cars* in season. I took several rides on the latter! Coach service also exists—both local, & to other towns including New York City. It must be a delightful place to live, save for its coldness in winter—for it has all the freshness, charm, & simplicity of a small village.

And so it goes. I shall hold this in order to add an account of Hurley & New Paltz, which I find I can easily see in a single day. A great region!

Albany, N.Y.
Tues.–Wed. Midnight
May 14–15, 1929.

Hades! I saw Hurley & New Paltz, but just now a disappointment has given me a temporary cast of sourness. I have found out that the Mohawk Trail 'bus, *although it continues to be cited in all travel folders,* **does not run except in summer,** & will not start this year till May 30th! That is cursedly provoking— for I had counted on the Mohawk Trail. It is really reprehensible in the extreme for the company to allow itself to be mentioned in tourist guides of winter & spring date as an operating factor, when in truth it is hibernating. Now I shall have to miss the dizzy mountain heights altogether & go by train through the Hoosac Tunnel, paying a dollar more than the 'bus fare to boot! Of all confounded anticlimaxes—just as I was planning my scenically triumphant reëntry to ancient New England! I'm hang'd if this doesn't make me angrier than yesterday's theft! Why *couldn't* the wretched company be honest enough to say in all tourist guides that it isn't running? The large Foster travel bureau in N Y City has no idea of this lapse, & might easily cause a person to go all the way up the Hudson to Albany for nothing. Fortunately I have not been "left" quite in this way, since I have really had what I went up the Hudson for—the Kingston visit—& want to see Cook in Athol independently of the Trail ride. But I did want the ride also, hence am properly furious. I have obtained my railway ticket, & shall take a train leaving Albany at 10 a.m., changing at Troy for the Hoosac Tunnel & Athol. My foreign travel is over— & at 1:30 p.m. tomorrow I shall feel the thrill of homecoming as I set foot upon the sacred & familiar soil of His Majesty's Province of the Maſſachuſetts-Bay. No more unfamiliar & remote names & narratives in my travelogues—the scene shifts in an instant from the exotick to the accustom'd. The pillar'd doorways of New-York, the steep roofs & dormers of the South, the marble steps & keystones of Philadelphia, & the old stone dwellings of the Esopus Valley—all these, & the centuried echoes of those who have known them, are about to vanish as if snapped off by an electric switch. Tomorrow my eyes & talk will be filled with known & neighbouring things—the eternal hills & stone walls of my native land, the oft-rehears'd legends of familiar tribes & settlements, the homely accents of Puritan speech, the white steeples & farmhouse gables of New England's countryside, the loved, ancient names of known places which look back only to English dreams & memories—Pownal, Vermont—Williamstown in the Maſsachusetts-Bay— North Adams—Zoar—Charlemont—Buckland—Shelburne Falls—West *Deerfield*—[what visions & memories that name evokes!] Greenfield—East Deerfield—Orange—& ATHOL! Home again! And on the threshold of ancient Providentium!

Well—to return to my diary & cover Tuesday, May 14th—I rose early & caught the 'bus to Hurley as plann'd, despite an unpleasant drizzle which persisted throughout the day. The road lay through an extremely fine rolling countryside; with green cultivated fields in a very unspoil'd & un-modern state, & the foothills of the Catskills as an eternal dominating background. In general, this territory is unchang'd since the colonial period; being still own'd & farm'd by the descendants of the original Dutch & Huguenot settlers. Hurley, some three miles northwest of Kingston, was not in any way a disappointment. It is a straggling village of ancient stone houses stretch'd along the highroad, with plenty of trees & diverging lanes, & the green fields & blossoming orchards stretching off on either side to where the purple mountains loom mystically. The houses are of Dutch masonry construction, some of them with wooden attics & lean-to's, & a few with projecting porches. All have the horizontally divided Dutch door with iron knocker & hinges to match, & the average date is from about 1700 to 1730. It is noteworthy that none of these Ulster County Dutch houses ever developed the gracefully curving roof-line or the gambrel arrangement so characteristic of the Dutch colonial architecture of *Southern* New York. Up here the plain peaked-roof tradition always persisted; so that the region is absolutely distinct from the Dutch region which Talman's family inhabits, (Rockland Co.) or the Manhattan & Long Island milieux which evolved the Dyckman & Lefferts cottages. The houses of Hurley have seen very little change in the more than two centuries of their existence, for the place is delectably slow & sleepy, with true Catskill conservatism. All the dwellings are tenanted by the same old families who built them—an Elmendorf still runs the single village store & post office—& the ancient Dutch Reformed Church still ends the vista at the bend of the road on the farther side from Kingston. The town is very famous among antiquarians—models of the houses being in the N.Y. Hist. Socy., & a large space being devoted to them in Eberlein's volume, "The Architecture of Colonial America." A Dutch diplomat has called it "more Dutch than anything left in Holland."[1]

Hurley, at first call'd merely the "New Village," was founded about 1660 by the overflow population of Wiltwyck, (Kingston) who desired to expand in the fertile untimber'd lowlands. A large proportion of the settlers were French Huguenots, though the Dutch element was very numerous. Land grants were made by Gov. Petrus Stuyvesant without consent of the Indians who form'd the original population; a circumstance which paved the way for considerable warfare & general harassment. On June 7, 1663, Hurley was burned to the ground by savages, & all the women & children were carried away into captivity. It was not until September that the pursuing forces of the Dutch succeeded in locating the unhappy prisoners—who had not been ill-treated, although they were later to have been burned alive in revenge for certain Indians who had been captured by the whites & sold as slaves to traders from Curaçoa [*sic*]. In the years that follow'd, Hurley prosper'd exceedingly, perhaps occupying a more important position in the life of the region than it does today. Its *cheeses*, milk, cakes, & other products were famous throughout the New-Netherland region, & became celebrated in more than one bit of Dutch doggerel folklore. One characteristick ballad of this sort can be found in Eberlein's "Architecture of Colonial America", which I possess. It was from Hurley that the settlement of New Paltz was made by Huguenots in 1677; & to Hurley that the fleeing people of Kingston repair'd just a century later, when the torches of His Majesty's troops menaced their homes. On that latter occasion the State Senate also fled to Hurley, conducting its delibera-tions in the old Van Deusen house, (1723) which is still standing & colonially furnished with a view to antique-selling. I enter'd & thoroughly explor'd the Van Deusen house, & will enclose a picture of the interior—which will shew the graceful staircase & hall-panelling, as well as the marvellously quaint door-hardware. There has been little change since the 18th century, & one may rec-ognise the atmosphere of the past on every hand. The oldest house in the vil-lage is the Elmendorf store, dating from about 1700—the proprietor of which gave me much valuable information. Having spent the morning in Hurley, I looked for the 11:20 'bus to connect me at Kingston with the 12:25 'bus for New Paltz—when lo! it was so late that I saw my programme was in peril. It was absolutely necessary to catch that 12:25 coach if I expected to make a round trip to New Paltz in a single afternoon. This being the case, I desperately adopted Wandrei's 1927 tactics & hailed the driver of a passing Standard Oil truck. He proved to be a good fellow, & to be bound all the way to Kingston—thus making my first attempt at "hitch-hiking" a 100% success! He got me back to the Van Ross (the hotel which serves as Kingston's gen-eral 'bus terminal) in ample time, so that 12:25 found me aboard a New Paltz 'bus & prepared for the oft-described antiquities of that quaint town.

New Paltz lies about sixteen miles south of Kingston, by the Wallkill & Shawangunk Creeks, & in the eternal shadow of the lordly & lovely Shawangunk Hills. It is a thriving village with shops, hotels, banks, a normal-school & a newspaper, quite in contrast to the scatter'd & sleepy Hurley; but the modern (i.e. post-Revolutionary) town lies some distance from the heart of the ancient settlement. This has tended to preserve the original area in its pristine, Hurley-like state; so that we may still see the place as it was in the early 18th century. To reach the old town from the modern town one has to walk a considerable distance, descending a steep hill & crossing the railway track. I had wished to see New Paltz ever since 1923, when an article about it in the N Y Tribune (which I still have in my files) attracted my notice. The day was dismal, but I appreciated the splendid unspoiled countryside none the less. Here is the old Hudson valley of Irving's day still unspoil'd—any one of these villages might have been the abode of Rip Van Winkle. Lovely val-leys abounded, & bends of streams in the lee of mountains produced a sce-nick effect hard to surpafs. I saw at least one old-fashion'd *cover'd bridge*—significant foretaste of the primitive part of New-England which I am about to enter. Finally the coach ascended a hill & deliver'd me at the principal tavern of New Paltz—the "modern" part, although even that is as quaint as East Greenwich, & far more untainted as to population. There are virtually no foreigners in this idyllick backwater, nearly all the population being descended from the original Huguenot settlers. Making judicious inquiries, I soon found my way down to the ancient section—Huguenot St.—& there revell'd in the sparse line of old stone dwellings which has given the town so great an historical & architectural fame. There are not many—perhaps a half-dozen at best—but their fine preservation & isolation from modern influences give them a magnified charm. One of them is fitted as a museum & open to the publick; others remain private dwellings, mostly in the hands of the families that built them more than two centuries ago. The museum—which is the old Jean Hasbrouck house built in 1712—is a large stone house of one full story & two attick stories under the immense sloping roof—an ideal storehouse for grain or other rural material. It is a fine type of early colonial construction under Dutch influence, (tho' Frenchmen built it) & I examin'd it with the utmost thoroughness & interest, visiting the attick & noting the maſsive expos'd beams. It is called the "Memorial House," & a boulder monument to the town's founders stands on the small triangular green opposite it. Nearby is the quaint burying-ground housing those 'rude forefathers of the hamlet'. The other houses—of varied types, & having features as unique as transoms with double rows of lights—stretch southward; the Du Bois, Elbing, Abraham Hasbrouck, Freer, &c. places. All are of about the 1700 period, as can be well seen from every detail of their construction. The interior of the "Memorial House" has some highly primitive features such as the great plank doors—some unpanell'd, & some single-panell'd. Oddly enough, there is just one of the ancient stone houses in the "modern" village—now us'd as a publick library. In the old times it must have been an isolated farmhouse on the hill.

New Paltz was settled by French Huguenots who had undergone a long & singular course of persecution & migration. Emigrating originally from France, they had settled at Pflalz [*sic*] or Paltz in the Protestant Rhineland; but had eventually been so harassed by French troops from across the border in their Catholick homeland that they reëmigrated to Holland. There, affected by that longing for a new world which sent so many religious refugees overseas, they took part in the general Dutch migration to New-Netherland—though sedulously retaining their French language & customs; a Gallick characteristick which we see today exemplify'd in our Woonsocket, Central Falls, & Pawtuxet Valley French-Canadians. Preferring the rural reaches of the upper Hudson to the crowded & cosmopolitan New-Amsterdam, this band of Huguenots (led by one Louis Du Bois, a pioneer of the utmost solidity & ability) selected Wiltwyck (Kingston) as an abiding place; but later transferr'd themselves to the New Village, (Hurley) which they consider'd more favourable to their retention of French speech & ways than the rather uncongenial

Dutch trading-post within the palisade. After the burning of Hurley in 1663, Louis Du Bois was much impress'd by the lovely countryside south of Rondout Creek, which was made familiar to him during his participation in the search for the Indian captives—amongst whom were his own wife & three sons. Especially did he relish the idyllick valley of the Wallkill, nestling amidst the Shawangunks & cut off from the bustling world which had treated him & his kind so ill. During the next fourteen years—a span mark'd by the transfer of the region from the Holland States-General to the authority of His Britannick Majesty—Du Bois interested many of his fellow-Frenchmen in a project for securing land patents & founding a new Huguenot village in the Shawangunk country; a project finally carry'd through with the aid of Abraham Hasbrouck, a young Huguenot having influence with His Majesty's Governor, Sir Edmond Andros—the same official who was so much hated in New-England because of his arbitrary exercise of power. Arrangements were also made to purchase the land lawfully from the Indians—a step which would have delighted Roger Williams—for the patentees were not insensible of the hostility created by the high-handed seizures of the Dutch. In May 1677 the Indians formally ceded the land in exchange for much assorted merchandise, & four months later His Majesty's Government granted the legal patent to the settlers—Louis, Abraham, & Isaac Du Bois, Abraham & Jean Hasbrouck, Andries & Simon Le Fevre, Pierre Deyo, Louis Bevier, Antoine Crispell, & Hugo Frère, ancestor of the *Freer* family. Homes were built the following spring—rude cabins on the site of the stone houses built during the next generation—& a few other settlers were admitted, including at least one Dutch family. A little stone Huguenot church, with services in French, soon adorn'd the village green—& the village was nam'd *New Paltz* in honour of that place in Germany which had first given the wanderers a haven.

With the years New Paltz attain'd a very comfortable agricultural prosperity, tho' remaining in that unspoil'd state which best suited its founders' wishes. Every effort was made to preserve the traditional piety & French ways of the forefathers, yet in the course of time the influence of the surrounding Dutch population could not help being felt. It became harder & harder to secure French-speaking schoolmasters & clergymen, & in the end the younger generation fell into the habit of speaking Dutch. Naturally the elders protested, & there is a well-known tale of a child sent to a relative to borrow some household utility, & refused it because she could not speak its name in French. This transition period was likewise mark'd by ecclesiastical schisms—some church members wishing to adhere to the Reform'd Dutch Church whilst others clung to a French Huguenot independence. By 1750 Dutch had definitely displac'd French as the language of New Paltz, & in 1752 the church commenc'd the use of that tongue. The village was now predominantly a part of the Dutch Hudson Valley, though still remembering its different traditions. Some of the pathos of the linguistick change is reflected in the will of Monsieur Jean Tebenin, the local schoolmaster who flourished in the early 18ᵗʰ century. He saw the gathering clouds; & when he left his French Bible to the church, provided for its sale for the benefit of the poor if the French language shou'd ever cease to be us'd thereabouts.

New Paltz in its Dutch-speaking period enjoy'd a steady growth, & that happy immunity from striking incidents which marks a peaceful community. Branches of its Huguenot stock were represented in the late unfortunate rebellion against His Majesty, yet the war itself left the town serene & unravag'd. As the 18ᵗʰ century drew to its close, time took its revenge upon the once conquering Dutch language by pressing it to extinction as French had formerly been press'd—the latest conqueror being the all-engulfing English. Signs of Yankee progress became manifest as an Anglo-Saxon population filter'd in, but the newer element built on the hill above old Huguenot St.; shifting the centre of gravity of the village & leaving the ancient part undisturbed to this day. In 1833 an academy was founded, which survives to this day as a State Normal School. Connected with these educational enterprises was the late Albert K. Smiley, *once head of the Friends' School in Providence,* who with his twin brother Alfred H. conceiv'd a vast liking for the region & develop'd a great estate at Lake Mohonk, in the neighbouring hills—where he founded a series of annual conferences on Indian affairs which endures to this day. New Paltz has erected a memorial gateway at the entrance of the Smiley estate—thus being linked the sleepy Shawangunk Valley & the Friends' School at the end of Barnes St., Providence, R.I.! Truly, a Providentian finds bits of home wherever he may go!

I was forc'd to do New Paltz in somewhat drizzly weather, so that my suit will need a tailor's attention when I reach Athol. The sightseeing was, however, extremely enjoyable; & I carry'd many an imprefsion of the greatest pofsible charm. Upon regaining Kingston, I at once proceeded to explore the interior of that ancient "Senate House"—the Ten Broeck homestead of 1676—which is now employ'd as a publick museum. I was not disappointed; for the interior is of the greatest conceivable interest, with low ceilings, hand-hewn beams, Dutch doors with ancient hinges, steps up & down caused by late 17ᵗʰ & 18ᵗʰ century additions to the original house, bulls' eyes in interior doors, & other typical earmarks of solid & conservative Dutch colonial craftsmanship. The Hist. Soc. is building a splendid new museum—in the exact style of a typical Old Kingston stone house—on the grounds west of the ancient house, into which the collection will shortly be mov'd. When this transfer is completed, the Ten Broeck house will be furnished as a colonial home; thus forming a sort of Pendleton House for the edification of Kingston. In the historical collection are some prodigiously interesting items—including the wooden sides of the farm wagon in which Genl. Burgoyne was convey'd away from the battlefield of Saratoga as a prisoner. I stay'd here until the 4:30 closing hour, after which I hasten'd to catch the 5:15 Albany train—there being no stagecoach service. The ride—despite an obscuring mist—was of considerable picturesqueness; involving many weird glimpses of the vapour-cloak'd Catskills. I reach'd Albany at 7:20, & made the disappointing discovery anent stagecoaches to Athol which I have already related. To console myself I did a little twilight exploring, seeing the graceful late-Georgian Albany Academy north of the State House, which I had never observ'd before. Albany is, however, an uninteresting city on the whole; with very little of the colonial left. Some time I shall look up the Schuyler Mansion there—tho' my programmes last year & this have not made such a procedure convenient. Still, Albany did give me my first definite touch of homecoming—for I dined at a **Waldorf Lunch!** The good old Waldorf chain—founded by one of the *Foster* Blanchards—has restaurants in only *two* cities outside New England—Newark & Albany. I saw the *sign* of a Waldorf last week as the Philada–N.Y. coach paſs'd through Newark, but could not stop to patronise it. This time, though, I *dined* at one; & encounter'd all the familiar appurtenances & atmospheric touches which I associate with the Waldorfs in Westminster St. & Market Square. In Washington I dined at a *Thompson* joint—one of the chain which includes our Providence *Thompson's* in Westminster St. next the Waldorf—but this has always been a nation-wide chain, hence gave no more thrill of home than a Woolworth's, a Liggett's, a Childs', or a United Cigar Store. But to dine at a good old *Waldorf Lunch* has something definitely Novanglian, Rhodinsular, & Providentian about it! Dinner over, I proceeded to the neat but humble Stannix Hotel near the station, where I had secur'd a dollar room. Here I have spent the evening writing, & shall now retire at 1 a.m., completing this chronicle tomorrow at ATHOL, in the good old PROVINCE OF THE MASSACHUSETTS-BAY.

> Athol, in the Pequoig Region of His
> Majeſty's Province of the Maſſachuſetts-Bay,
> in New-England. Wedneſday, May 15, 1929.

Home to New England at last!! I sit in a tailor's window in good old Athol, across the street from Cook's office, writing with a pair of strange trousers on whilst my grey suit is put in civilised form by one J. Jasins, Esq., to whom I am indebted for the redemption of that selfsame suit nearly a year ago, after its rough treatment amidst the wild domed hills of Vermont. Home—for the first thing I saw in Athol upon quitting the station was a *Rhode Island* truck—license X II.28—belonging to the Tar Products Corporation of *Providence!* I shall see Providence Friday or Saturday—& with me will come my present noble host, W. Paullus Culinarius, who is chafing for the sight of Eddy's Bookstore. Thus I shall import home with me an echo of that festivity which has characterised my long & widespread wanderings—shewing you, as it were, a sample of the social whirl out of which I shall shortly drop into my usual routine of desk & Weybosset Market & Kennedy's & Noyes's &

Quinsnicket. Cook will bring me in his car—a new one, I guess, tho' I haven't ask'd him about it yet—together with that enormous amount of material which I left in Athol last year for Culinary transportation at the *first opportunity.* This—ten months later—is that first opportunity! I'll let you know all details of the grand escorted homecoming—date & hour—as soon as I fully ascertain Cook's plans; though I fancy my room is ready enough to receive its tenant even though the party shou'd arrive unheralded. A E P G no doubt attended to that unpleasant financial detail which comes up on the 14th of each month, & which therefore was a timely topick of conversation yesterday. I imagine we shall come in the most direct way—Petersham, Barre, & Worcester, rather than the Gardner–Fitchburg–Leominster route which would revive memories of the summer of 1899. But whichever way it is, it's home soil now. On every hand are the near, familiar names which have been more or less on my tongue since my earliest days. This voyage has left foreign waters & is now near the harbour—for I now sit in the Province where my first conscious memories (Dudley 1892) took shape. I was properly awak'd at 8:30 this morning, & at once proceeded to the nearby station to catch the Troy train which connects for Athol & Boston. Troy seemed as dismal & nondescript as last year, & I was glad to get out of it in a quarter-hour. I experienc'd a thrill as I boarded the New England train, for I was at last on a system peculiarly Novanglian—the good old *Boston & Maine,* which I have known all my life, & which has no extensions outside N.E. except this one stub end at Troy. The feel of an old-fashion'd B & M coach was fair compensation for my disappointment at not traversing the Mohawk Trail. The ride through N Y State—the Mr. Hoag country—was not at all dull; for the landscape is very fine & includes many mountain vistas. At Valley Falls the train pass'd over the *very spot* where Mr. Hoag was born over 98 years ago—for he told me that his birthplace had been mov'd to make room for the railway. There are many delightful river vistas hereabouts, & Hoosick Falls is a town of considerable size.

Then the hills grew wilder & greener & more beautiful—yet less luxuriant in foliage as we receded from the warmth of the south. Finally I saw a station-name which made my heart leap—*North-Pownal, in His Majesty's New-Hampshire Grants, latterly call'd Vermont, in New-England!* God Save the King!! A town named for Tho: Pownall, Gent., Governor of yᵉ Maſsachuſetts-Bay! Home at last—tho' a second thrill occurr'd when we enter'd the Maſsachuſetts-Bay itself near Williamstown—the old Bay Province, where my first memories dawn'd, & which has always been a kind of home background looming just across the state line—Attleboro, Rehoboth, Seekonk, Swansea . . . . . Home stuff! Near North-Adams the Berkshires became highly impreſsive, & I regretted bitterly that I was to go under them instead of over them. Then came the Hoosac Tunnel, a long period of artificial night differing only in length from what we have betwixt North Main & Thayer Sts., & after that occasional exquisite glimpses of mountain & valley—Charlemont, Shelburne Falls, & so on. The landscape grew best near the end of the Berkshire region, when the lovely valley of the Deerfield River opened up in full sunny expansiveness. Then came the now-familiar Greenfield, & the picturesque run along Miller's River thro' Orange to *Athol*, where I once more set foot upon my native Novanglian sod. Cook was in his office & glad to see me, & says that young Munn will be around during the afternoon. The day being sunny, I decided to have my suit pressed—so here I am in the studio of the distinguish'd sartorial artist Jasins. A few minutes ago it clouded up & began to rain, which naturally rather nonpluss'd me in view of the object of my call; but fortunately the shower has already pafs'd—giving way to a blazing sky which will soon dry the benches in whatever park I choose as a loafing & postcard-writing place until Cook is free at 5:30. I shall probably choose *Phillips* Park in the upper village, my favourite haunt in both 1927 & 1928. Of later developments a later diary-instalment will tell you—if indeed there will be time for any postally transmitted matter to reach Providentium ahead of me. It has been a great trip, but I surely shall be glad to see 10 Barnes & the ancient white-steepled hill! God Save His Majesty's Colony of Rhode-Island & Providence-Plantations!

I found your card of yesterday at Cook's office, & he says he has some more forwarded mail for me at the farm. Sorry you've been feeling tired, for you'll have a lot of walking to do when I get back & drag you out to Prospect Terrace & Quinsnicket & Warren & Bristol & other interesting points! The summer is really all ahead—though it seems odd to think it when one has been in the south & had a foretaste of summer nearly a fortnight ago! Keep all the papers & magazines straight—for I shall be descending upon the ancient town very shortly! Now to get into my newly pressed suit & beat it for the open air!

Yr aff Nephew & obt Servt

H P L

Notes

1. The quotation is on p. 17 of Eberlein's book.

[299]   [ANS postcard][1] [HPL, H. Warner Munn, and W. Paul Cook to LDC]

[Postmarked Brattleboro, Vt.,
17 May 1929]

DIARY THROUGH THURSDAY, MAY 16, 1929.

Well—I duly met Cook at 5:30 p.m. Wednesday & we went over to Munn's flat where we saw him & his father. We then proceeded to Cook's car, where were waiting Mrs. C., her small grandson Alvin Smith, & an exquisite *new kittie* (very tiny) which the family has just acquired. The car, by the way, is the familiar old

Whippet refurbished for one more year—as you'll see soon. Having embark'd, we at once set out for the Phillipston countryside where Cook's new (but soon to be sold) farm is situate. And *what* a countryside it is! The very quintessence of ancient New England—rolling, stony hills, narrow, winding rutted roads, stone walls, ancient apple-orchards, & sparsely scatter'd white farmhouses. Cook's place is one of the latter—set on high ground with one of the most magnificent rural landscape effects conceivable—both foreground & far horizon of hills beyond hills. At one point a blue lakelet gleams among pines. No other house is in sight—just some stone walls, green fields, distant hills, & the rambling, scatter'd buildings of the farm. It is a poem in real life—but too remote & inconvenient to serve as a home, as the Cooks have discover'd. Having arriv'd, I inspected the place in the charm of a golden sunset, & was duly transported. After a marvellous dinner I play'd with the new kitten, & later Munn came over in his dignified new car for a period of card-signing & congenial discussion. After Munn left & Mrs. Cook & the grandson retired, Cook & I discussed literature till 3 a.m., when both retired. ¶ Thursday the 16th I rose at noon & went out for a rural walk with little Alvin. (OVER)

H. Warner Munn
       W. Paul Cook

[On front:] (THURSDAY, continued) The day soon grew unpleasant, however, so I return'd to the house (a typical colonial farmhouse with low ceilings & mystical attick) to read Krutch's work on Poe. The kitten spent much time in my lap—he is an exquisite atom only a few weeks old. Cook returned at 6, & dinner & discussion followed. After the family retired, I sat up reading till 3 a.m., when I turned in myself. My room is very pleasant, with a wide vista from the windows. Tomorrow we shall take a motor trip to Brattleboro Vt. & see Goodenough—& after our return we shall go to Leominster with Munn to see a congenial bookseller. More soon. Yrs H P L

Notes

1. *Front:* Public Library and Memorial Building, Athol, Mass.

[300]   [ANS postcard][1] [HPL to LDC]

                            [Postmarked Brattleboro, Vt.,
                                      17 May 1929]
Friday, May 17, 1929—Old Vermont again! Rose at 7 a.m. & started out with Cook in the old Whippet for Brattleboro. Splendid sunny day & fine ride. The old village looks just the same as last summer, & now we're going out to see Goodenough on his idyllick farm. We shall return to Athol in the afternoon, & in the evening Munn will take us through Gardner & *Westminster*

(shades of 1899—I shall try to see Moses Wood's old Harvard Cottage!)[2] &
Fitchburg to Leominster, where he wants to introduce Cook & me to a congenial bookseller named Hill—interested in the weird. Then—late in the
evening—we shall return to Cook's farmhouse; & tomorrow (Saturday)
morning we shall start for PROVIDENCE, accompanied by Mrs. Cook &
the small grandson Alvin, who are going to Norwich. I may—& probably
shall—see you before this card arrives; but thought I'd finish the diary in
style! Tomorrow night I shall do Eddy's bookstore, dine at the Waldorf or
Overland lunch, & sleep at 10 Barnes St!
Yr aff nephew
H P L

Notes

1. *Front:* Suspension Bridge, Connecticut River, Brattleboro, Vermont.
2. HPL "spent the summer of 1899 with my mother" (*Letters to Elizabeth Toldridge* 72)
in Westminster, a town in central Massachusetts.

[301]   [ANS postcard][1] [HPL, Arthur Goodenough, and W. Paul Cook to LDC]
[Postmarked Athol, Mass.,
17 May 1929]

Final greetings before my personal return! Here we are in the dreamlike Vermont landscape—amidst Goodenough's Arcadian acres on what has turned
out to be a gorgeously exquisite day. The charm of the place still lingers with
me—indeed, I've just seen back reaches of the Goodenough farm which excel anything I saw in 1927 & 1928! This is surely a glorious region! Now we're
about to return to Athol—then on with Munn to Gardner, Fitchburg, & Leominster for the evening. Shall look for Harvard Cottage at Westminster.
Tomorrow we start for PROVIDENCE; so that unless the mails are extraordi-
narily prompt, you'll see us before you see this! This Vermont scenery is absolutely beyond words—I vow, it almost effaces the memory of the rest of
my trip! It will be odd tonight to stroll in Westminster &c—the scene of my
aestivation of 1899. Just *thirty* years—& yet this northerly Novanglian terrain
has changed but little. Providence has sprouted 26-story skyscrapers &
Grandpa Theobald has become an old man, but still these green hills & winding roads dream on eternally. Well—see you later—or *before!*
Yr aff Nephew & obt Servt H P L

Arthur H. Goodenough

I will see you before you see this. If you do not get this let me know when I
see you. W. P. Cook

[On front:]

6 p.m EXTRA

Had a great dinner—real New England rustick profusion—at Goodenough's, & have now reach'd Athol after some delay due to changing a tire & encountering a bad stretch of road repairs. Now we're going to meet Munn & start for Leominster. Tomorrow when we descend on PROVIDENCE we shall blow in on the Louisquisset Pike & shall probably detour through Quinsnicket—appropriate return to my native village shades.

Yr aff Nephew & obt Servt

H P L

Notes

1. *Front:* Suspension Bridge, Connecticut River, Brattleboro, Vermont.

[302]   [ANS postcard]¹ [HPL to LDC]

[Postmarked Gardner, Mass.,
18 May 1929]

Well—here we all are at Leominster—Cook, Munn, & I—calling on a very discriminating bookseller in Haynes Court. Now we shall go back to Athol for a wink of sleep, & tomorrow Cook & I shall start for *Providence.* Munn's new Graham-Paige car is a magnificent affair—dignified, too. It made exactly a *mile a minute* on the best parts of the road! ¶ As we passed through Westminster we looked up Moses Wood's "Harvard Cottage" & all my haunts of 1899. *Nothing has changed.* Wood is dead, & so is old Mrs. Marshall who kept the gaol at the foot of the hill, but Wood's widow is still living. A man on the road gave me this information. I recalled every spot after 30 years, & guided Munn with perfect assurance to "Harvard Cottage"—only mistaking one house (of perfectly similar layout) for it before I hit on the right one. Look it up amongst the pictures in my table drawer. It was certainly interesting to leap back 30 years & recall the summer of 1899 when I was so bored with rusticity that I longed for the sight of a town! Well—I'll probably see you before you get this! Anyway, it was great to delve back into my forgotten youth!

Yrs

H P L

[On front:] P.S. Our bookseller-host has just made me a present of a delightful tiny almanack of 1834! It has some alluring *recipes* in it—which will interest you.

Notes

1. *Front:* Plaza Near Railroad Station, Brattleboro, Vermont.

[303]   [ANS postcard][1] [HPL, FBL, and Mrs. Frank Belknap Long to LDC]

[Postmarked New Bedford, Mass.,
13 August 1929]

New Bedford's Whaling Museum is magnificent! We've all been aboard this antient barque, & are debating whether to go to Cape Cod or go whaling! Good to see the House of Long again!

Yr aff Nephew & obt Servt
H P L

Mrs F. B Long's greetings.

This surpasses almost everything on the Cape—although I believe Howard still has some marvellous treats in store. F. B.

F. B. Long[2]

Notes

1. *Front:* The Bark "Lagoda," Jonathan Bourne Whaling Museum, New Bedford, Mass.
2. "F. B." is Frank Belknap Long, Jr.; "F. B. Long" is Frank Belknap Long, Sr.

[304]   [ANS postcard][1] [HPL and FBL to LDC]

[Postmarked Onset, Mass.,
14 August 1929]

Bulletin #2—Tuesday Night.

¶ As my former card appris'd you, I safely arriv'd in New-Bedford & gave the old town a thorough exploration—viewing the whaling museum & climbing all over the half-size whaling ship there exhibited. I then met the Long party, & conducted the masculine ⅔ of it over the museum I had so lately seen. All of New Bedford's waterfront is ineffably quaint. As we were about to hit the trail, Belknap jammed his fingers in the car door & had to have drug store repairs, but he's on the mend now—as I shall prove by making him sign this. The drive to Onset was exceedingly pleasant, passing through quaint & ancient Mattapoisett & Marion. Onset itself is a scenically well-situated shore spot of considerable liveliness, & Belknap has secured me a very pleasant upper room in a cottage around the corner from his. This evening we are writing cards & discussing things in general. Tomorrow the sightseeing begins—& look for more bulletins. Hope A E P G got the muffins all right. More later. Yr aff Nephew & obt Servt H P L

F. B.

Notes

1. *Front:* The King's Highway, Cape Cod, Mass.

[305]   [ANS postcard][1] [HPL to LDC]

[Postmarked Onset, Mass.,
15 August 1929]

All hail! Here's a diary for Wednesday Aug. 14—or up to the evening of that date. I arose bright & early at 8:30 a.m. in response to my grandchild's knock, & after a brief breakfast we all set out in the Essex for a tour of the lower part of the Cape—Provincetown being thought too distant for a leisurely day's travel. The plan was to follow the north shore to Orleans, then cut south to Chatham, & then to go to Hyannis via the south shore—thereafter returning to the N. shore & retracing steps to Onset. This we did—on a day in which sun & fog alternated. The only disappointment was the sea-mist at Chatham, which prevented Sonny from getting the spectacular marine panorama to which he had looked forward. I found the Cape delightfully quaint, with many fine old houses & villages, & a most extraordinary diversity of colonial *windmills*—there erected because (as on our island of Aquidneck) of a dearth of running streams for water-mills. The finest village, without exception, was *Sandwich*. On the whole, the Cape is not as spectacularly ancient & picturesque as its popular reputation would argue—but it is surely picturesque enough to be highly fascinating. More soon. Yrs H

Notes

1. *Front:* Old Cape Cod Mill, Built 1774, Cape Cod, Mass.

[306]   [ANS postcard][1] [HPL to LDC]

[Postmarked Onset, Mass.,
16 August 1929]

More diary! We had a good dinner Wednesday evening & went to see a cinema afterward. After that we sat discussing the universe in the parlour of Sonny's cottage till 11 p.m., when I returned to my cottage to write letters. Retired somewhat late. ¶ Thursday morning Sonny duly roused me at 8:30, & after a restaurant breakfast we all went in the Essex to Wood's Hole, traversing a countryside of considerable charm & quaintness & passing through drowsy old Falmouth. Wood's Hole is rather a neat & pleasant place—a typical high-grade resort, though rather colourless. Its principal feature is the government marine biological experiment station & museum—conducted by the U.S. Bureau of Fisheries. Fortunately the museum—or aquarium—was open, & we beheld a variety of exhibits of substantial interest. After this we returned to Onset, had lunch, & indulged in a rest period during which I read in Walter de la Mare's "Broomsticks" which Sonny has from the N.Y. Library. On the Wood's Hole trip we saw an excellent windmill, & a rather interesting Quaker meeting-house. Belknap's door-crushed fingers are improving finely, thanks to the odd kind of red-coloured dressing applied by the drug-clerk in New Bedford. In the afternoon Dr. Long & Belknap went in bathing whilst I sat on the bank & read De la Mare's "Broomsticks." Now—Thursday evening—we shall probably put in the time loafing about Onset & discussing the universe. More soon—& we'll all see you on Saturday. Yrs H P L

[HPL note at Onset:] where we are stopping [HPL note at Sagamore:] the prettiest spot we've seen [HPL note at Wood's Hole:] where we saw the Government marine-life aquarium [HPL note at Chatham and Orleans:] the limits of our exploration

Notes

1 *Front:* Auto Map[:] Cape Cod and the Pilgrimland.

[307]   [ANS postcard][1] [HPL to LDC]

[Postmarked Onset, Mass.,
16 August 1929]

Well—here's the final diary, for I shall see you before another bulletin could reach #10. Last evening (Thu.) we went to another cinema, & afterward sat on the steps of my quarters—the piazza at Belknap's cottage being preëmpted by some new arrivals. The Longs greatly prefer my cottage (which they had last year) to the one they have this year, & are going to make reservations there next year. At 10:30 the Longs returned to their quarters, & I read & wrote letters in my room; retiring at 1 a.m. This morning (Friday) Sonny awaked me at 8:30, & after a good breakfast decided to establish headquarters on the beach. Here we are reading, writing, & discussing art, philosophy, & the cosmos; whilst a blazing sun helps to give me more or less of a bronzed & formidable aspect. I fancy we shall spend the entire day rambling about Onset—if we add anything to the programme, I'll let you know. And tomorrow we'll see you—although the Longs can't stay over night in Providence. We hope to repass through New Bedford, & perhaps see some additional sights there. Well—more anon & see you later.
Yrs
H P L

Notes

1. *Front:* An Old Cape Cod House, Cape Cod, Mass.

[308]   [ANS postcard]¹ [HPL to LDC]

> [Postmarked Onset, Mass.,
> 17 August 1929]

Hurrah! Here's the best part of the whole recent diary! Found a hydro-aeroplane at the beach which took passengers on a splendidly long scenic ride—including the whole Buzzard's Bay & Cape Cod canal vista—for only $3.00—a far better value than any obtainable at a land airport. It was too good to miss, so I spread myself on it—though I shall arrive home wholly broke as a result. And believe me, it was great stuff! Far better than the balloon in which I ascended at Brockton in 1910. The landscape effect was that of a bird's eye view map—& the scene was such as to lend itself to this inspection with maximum advantage. Wish I could have gone up repeatedly! Well, we'll all see you tomorrow. This aeroplane ride (which attained a pretty good height at its maximum) adds a finishing touch to the perfection of the present outing. Sonny wants to look up the Lizzie Borden house when we come through Fall River!
Yr aff Nephew & obt Servt
H P L

Notes

1. *Front:* Old Cape Cod Mill. Built 1774. Cape Cod, Mass.

1930

[309]   [ALS] [HPL to LDC]

Bench in Capitol Park,
Columbia, S.C.,
Monday, April 28, 1930.

My dear Daughter:—

In reply to all questions concerning the location of Paradise, I now have one answer ready—it is the more southerly part of His Majesty's Province of South-Carolina, which I this morning enter'd for the first time—but a few hours after my first entry to North-Carolina. What can I say of such a region as it glows today under a June-like sun, & with such a vivid luxuriance of fresh verdure as I never before beheld? And remember that *even this* is not nearly as far south as I shall be by 2:30 this afternoon. Charleston, according to accepted reputation, is definitely subtropical; but Columbia is hardly such. I have seen but one palmetto; & although the great trees are of the flocculent, feathery-leaved & streamer'd sort peculiar to warm climates, they are not greatly cumbered with the vines & other parasitic growths of the really hot zone. But what a place! A *real civilisation*, with pure American people, a sense of leisure & repose, & a vast amount of very opulent (tho' not antiquarian) beauty. Why in Heaven's name does *anybody* live in the North—except from compulsion or from sentimental attachment? What a day! The song of the birds alone is worth the price of admission! Columbia is the capital of the state, & is a fine, mellow town with broad, sleepy streets & not enough modernity to spoil it. Niggers are numerous, but they never get in the way; & there appear to be no foreigners whatsoever. The accent of the population charms me—I shall be using it myself if I do not keep on guard! In tone & architecture this place is *not colonial* but rather *ante-bellum,* suggesting the last phase of the Old South—say 1850 as an average. I am glad to see it in some detail, although I would not have taken the time from Charleston if I had not been obliged to. As it was, there is a four-hour gap between coaches—which I am very glad to fill with this preliminary glimpse of South-Carolinian graces in a less utter & concentrated form. I enclose several cards shewing typical aspects of Columbia. Nothing can really convey the full charm—but the view of Gervais St. gives at least a hint of the luxuriance of the foliage & vegetation generally. What trees! What parks! What *gardens!* In short—what a region! No—there is no mystery about Paradise! It is in South Carolina!

And yet all this ecstasy, curious to relate, is *only an hour & a half old*—for my introduction to South Carolina at about 4 a.m. was a decidedly chill & discouraging one. As I told you in my card from Winston-Salem, it was a cold night; & of course this *interior* region (for the route from Richmond to W-S was *west* rather than *south*) could not have the geniality I had encountered in Richmond at 2 p.m. It would have been all right had the coach been heated properly, but the driver was a crank who would not turn on more than a trifle of the needed current; hence the chattering teeth & ague-shaken shoulders marking my entry into "tropic" South Carolina—"The Palmetto State"!

Indeed, the upland & inland parts which I first struck, are nothing like this blessed lower slope. Of course I could not see the North Carolina landscape through which the coach ploughed in the dark, but the headlights shewed me that it was a land of scrub pine woods & sandy soil, with hewn log cabins (having external end chimneys like the typical southern farmhouses) scattered thinly about & housing agricultural niggers. The villages—& this is true of upland & inland *South* Carolina also—are *ineffably* quaint & backward—vastly more so than even the Virginia hamlets I described yesterday. They seem never to have heard of the outside modern world, (what enviable bliss!) but build their latest buildings in the style to which they became accustomed about a century ago. Some of these styles are quite peculiar to the region, & their naively continuous survival (for there is no *re*vival or conscious antiquarianism in this conservatism) is worthy of serious attention. One may say if one wishes that these provincial whites are decadent—but in my opinion a bit of "decadence" is not too high a price to pay for the bland fixedness of personality & unchangedness of mood possessed by these farmers & villagers. As their great-grandsires lived in 1830, so do they live now—& long may they continue to do so!

But even so, one could not by any stretch of the imagination call their region other than weirdly ugly & repellent. It is exactly that—in amazing contrast with the geographically neighbouring paradise in which I am now seated. This inland Carolina is a high plateau of extreme flatness & sterility, with large empty surfaces broken only by sparse clumps of feeble scrub pines & oaks & other dwarfed or dwarfish trees, & with a barren, pale clayey soil not at all resembling the odd yellow clay of Virginia & Maryland. Occasionally there is a redeeming vista of great sweeps of distant landscape, but all too often the very windswept spaciousness has a repellent quality all its own. It suggests unholy linkages with forbidding outer planets—especially in the grotesque dawn when all the clumps of spare, anaemic trees take on curious & half-sentient shapes. All this expanse is sparsely strown over with nigger log cabins of the most squalid tho' not unpicturesque description. As dawn grew into day, some of the black peasants came out to work on their barren acres with antiquated ploughs & solemn, long-eared mules—forming a highly characteristic feature of the southern rural scene. The roads are poor & unpaved for the most part—cut through the surrounding clay, sometimes with visible embankments on either side, & maintained by forced convict labour. I saw one road-gang of convicts (all black) busily at work—clad in the horizontally striped prison uniforms which larger gaols long ago abolished. Once in a long while one sees an old plantation-house—usually in more or less of a state of decrepitude. At about this point one begins to note a change in the character of the vegetation—from the strictly north-temperate forms which we know in New England (& which Virginia & *North* Carolina share) to the more nearly tropical forms which begin in *South* Carolina. Just why this should be, I'm sure I don't know—for I was freezing, & shall always link the scene with Byrd's Antarctic Expedition[1] rather than with the lowland Carolinian paradise which I encountered less than three hours later! Probably the truth is, that in summer this vegetation does get doses of *continuous* heat which ours does not, & that in winter there is not much of the blighting hell-on-earth which we have to endure. So the leafage of these ugly uplands has one prophetic touch of the tropics to redeem it—a slight tendency toward the feathery, trailer-like forms which riot so exuberantly here in Columbia, & which I shall find even more gloriously dominant in ancient Charleston when I reach it at 2:30 p.m.

As for the route I covered since my last bulletin—the first sizeable town was Stateville, N.C., in which I beheld my first sight of the Latin-inspired *balcony* architecture of the farther south, of which Virginia has no specimens. Charlotte, N.C. is a sizeable modern city, not notable in any way. Lancaster, S.C. is an attempt to create a tasteful bungalow colony in a geographically repulsive milieu. Kershaw is depressing & squalid—but *Camden* marks the boundary between the ugly & the exquisite zones. It is itself very lovely—yet nothing compared to Columbia. And what will *Charleston* be? I can scarcely wait to see it—for it must have all the natural beauty & mildness of Columbia in still greater degree—*plus* a mellow *colonial* quaintness which Columbia lacks utterly. ¶ There go some tuneful & delectably lazy church chimes! I must walk amidst the warmth & greenery for a while ere I take the coach. ¶ More soon—
      Yrs H P L

P.S. Confound it! After all my praise, here's a cool breeze! But no worse than *we* have in June.
P.P.S. South Carolina motor license plates are almost like R.I. ones.

[On envelope:] P.S. Just as I am about to mail this, have seen *4 more* splendid *palmettoes!* But now for CHARLESTON!!

Notes

1. The First Antarctic Expedition of Admiral Richard E. Byrd (1888–1957) left on 28 August 1928 and returned to North America on 18 June 1930.

[310]   [ALS] [HPL to LDC]

Charleston, S.C.,
May 6, 1930

My dear Daughter:—

Well, for tardy deliveries, commend me to the Provi-
dence-Charleston service! Only *this morning—Tuesday, the 6th*—have I received
your welcome note & A E P G's postcard; both postmarked *Thursday, May 1st*
. . . . a lapse of *5 days* in transit! Have my bulletins been equally delayed in
their northward course? Note some of the postmarks when you receive them,
& compare the transmission rate.

But anyway, I was extremely glad to hear from you, & shall be equally
glad to receive the later letter which will be awaiting me at Sonny Belknap's. It
was all right to forward my mail to Belknap's instead of to Charleston, since
there couldn't have been anything important—all my correspondents being
aware that I am away. I received the forwarded missive from the Galpinius-
child just before starting south—he reiterates his design of coming East if
possible, but says that his intermediate stops in N.Y. & Providence will have
to be very brief. It is *after* his Peterborough sojourn that he hopes to arrange a
more leisurely triangular session with Belknap & me at some appropriate
point on the Massachusetts coast—probably Marblehead. We shall certainly
be glad to see the young rascal again after all these years! Send the Derleth
letter on to Belknap's—for it is now probably too late for me to receive anything in Charleston. My present plan, as outlined yesterday, is to break away
Thursday (the 8th) & commence the reluctant northward trek; though it is possible that I can't bear to do it even then! I am not hard pressed financially
now that I have definitely eliminated all elaborate stops between here & N.Y.
Expenses have not been great, & I have had only one batch of laundry done.
Last night I duplicated my Washington procedure of 2 years ago—washing
my shirt & undervest under the arms in the excellent Y M C A lavatory, &
allowing them to dry on chair-backs while I slept. The results are adequate—
for a four-in-hand tie covers any wrinkled crudity which the shirt-front may
display. I shall repeat this laundering just before I start north, leaving my
Charleston-laundered outfit untouched, & thus having *3* complete changes in
my valise when I hit New York. This will probably eliminate the need of your
sending any extra packages to N.Y. The present amateur-laundered outfit—
which will be good enough for a crumpling 'bus ride—will probably go to a
laundry in N.Y. with the Longs' weekly wash; & when I leave N Y for Kingston (as I think will be easily feasible) I shall mail my first batch of soiled lin-
en home—the outfit I shall have worn in N.Y. I shall then have 1 clean outfit
on, with 2 in reserve; & future events will decide whether I shall ask you to
mail the extra set to Kingston or Athol, or whether I can make the whole circuit on my original supply.

As to my northward trip—cards will keep you apprised of its various stages. The only stops, as now planned, will be at Richmond (for a Williams-burg side-trip) & Fredericksburg—besides, of course, the coach-change stop at Washington. Whether I can work in Annapolis is still debatable—& I shall decide the question of a Philadelphia stop when the time comes. With day & night travelling, it is likely that Richmond (& perhaps Philadelphia) will form the only overnight stop before N.Y. If Belknap's mother is not fully recovered, Loveman insists that I be his semi-guest for a week—stopping at his *former* boarding-place, the Laverty establishment which you remember so well. He is still on the best of terms with the Lavertys, despite the bookcase-fear which made them nervous about the safety of the floors when his shelves began to fill up. You ought, by the way, to see his *new* room at 130 Columbia Hts.! It is a marvellous, skyline-viewing eyrie, full of rare books & objets d'art from his original Cleveland den. He also has an excellent desk which Talman has just given him—Talman himself having obtained a genuine colonial desk to replace it.

As for food & postals—I am certainly not slighting the former, as you may see from the slowness with which I am getting down to *140*. I haven't quite made the grade yet—which is the reason I've sent no weight-cards hitherto. My breakfast is a large cheese sandwich, coffee, & ice-cream at a United Cigar Store lunch counter; & of late I have acquired the habit of eating a dinner as well. I have twice had splendid *spaghetti* dinners (35¢)—for there are 3 good Italian restaurants here despite the general scarcity of foreigners—& on two other occasions had, respectively, a sumptuous chicken course dinner (soup, chicken, [all white meat] potato, peas, dressing, salad, coffee, ice-cream, cake—all for 75¢!) & a marvellous roast beef dinner (potato, meat, peas, salad, coffee, ice cream—all for 50¢). This latter is the best food value I have seen outside *Jake's!* It probably beats your favourite Guernsey dinners because of the liberal *quantities* involved. But with plenty of brisk walking I'll reach 140 yet!! Now & then I indulge in ice cream—the best of which is uniformly 10¢ (yet as much as Gibson's 15¢) all over town.

No—there's no danger of the old man's overdoing! Bless my soul, but I didn't know there was so much energy left in the aged wreck! All the ills of winter have dissolved in the salubrious warmth of the subtropics, & I have unlimited stores of energy. I am never tired, even at the end of the most active days; & have such a surplus of force that I am always reading or writing when sitting down. Feet & ankles all right for the summer—no sign of swelling at any time now—& even the old *face* is behaving so pacifically that I hardly know what to make of it! Some of my new coat of tan is peeling off, but a very fair residue remains, so that the gang will probably note a healthy-looking change when I hit N.Y. Hope that some will be left by the time I get home—it probably will, since both Kingston & Athol will involve a very tolerable quota of outdoorness. But I'll never see as much of the sun up there as I'm seeing now in good old Charleston. Not a day in all this week & more, which has been other than consistently sunny. It is a climatic fact that Charleston has more fair days than any other American city except Los Angeles, Cal. The storms are largely confined to the late summer & autumn—Aug. & Sept.

Today I shall probably do some writing on my new Vermont story[1]—so that I can finish it before I start in motion again. I want it done by the time I get to N Y, so that I can read it aloud to the gang & get their opinion as to whether it's worth typing or not. That's the part I dread—for it's a novelette which will come to 60 pages or more when complete.

Yes—I certainly take care of my cash in the most approved fashion, & am not likely to lose any except by forcible robbery . . . . a thing not common in Charleston since 1718, when the pirate Capt. Stede Bonnet & 40 of his men were captured by Gov. Wm Rhett & hanged near the Battery! As usual, I keep in a separate compartment a full fare home from whatever place I may be at, so that the general fund may represent only spendable cash. My postal purchases are by no means extravagant, since it is only to 10 Barnes that I send the diurnal flood of material which may strike you as so abundant. Remember that these cards are only a cent apiece! This morning I came to the end of my original envelope resources, notwithstanding the supposedly good supply of Kirk charity envelopes I took along—so that I have had to lay in a nickel's worth of plain envelopes at Woolworth's. Fancy me *buying* envelopes, with a lifetime supply on my alcove shelves! But I had to do the same last year—indeed, I think I have some of those plain envelopes (from the Kingston Woolworth's) at the bottom of my desk drawer even now. I had then corralled a marvellous new free supply at the Philadelphia Y M C A—but this supply went in the Great Kingston Robbery. *This* year I shall keep a stern grip on my omnipresent enamel-cloth carryall, (which rests beside me at this moment) so that I hope I shall have no grand larcenies to report!

About the *Marshall* house—I suppose you refer to one of last year's *Richmond* cards, since I don't recall sending any Marshall house views from Charleston. I hope you're not permitting the slaves to work too much upheaval in my library, by the way!

I am now in Hampton Park again—on a bench surrounded by a quacking flock of friendly ducks from a nearby lake. They are looking wistfully at me, but I regret to say that I have no nourishment for them!

More soon—

   Yr aff Nephew & ob^dt Servt—

    H P L

P.S. I can imagine how vernally inviting R.I. is now getting to be. Kingston & Athol, on the other hand, must still be distinctly raw & chilly. N.Y. is always exactly the same as Prov.

Notes

1. "The Whisperer in Darkness."

[311] [ANS] [HPL to LDC]

[9 May 1930]

[Letter evidently lost. On envelope:]

P.S. I can see by the length of the twilight that I am once again in a relatively Northern clime. Here it is lingering as in Providence; whereas in Charleston it closed down quickly as in the tropics. ¶ Amusing how few darkies, as compared with Charleston, one sees in Richmond!

[312] [ALS] [HPL to LDC]

Midnight—May 9th 1930

My dear Daughter:—

Can't resist the temptation to add a final line to today's diary—after my researches anent Poe at the Richmond Publick Library. Note the new paper supply—almost as ample as the supply I picked up here last year but lost (together with the Philadᵃ· Y M C A paper) in the Great Kingston Robbery. The point is, that I have for the first time investigated the Mary C. [*sic*] Phillips life of Poe—the one published in 1926 just before the Hervey Allen biography which I purchased last fall. It has been generally conceded that the Allen book utterly eclipses the Phillips one—& indeed it does so far as good style & accurate scholarship are concerned—but I now discover that the eclipsed & forgotten book has some invaluable matter which the more standard work has not. The illustrations, for example, are voluminous; & cover virtually all the scenes of Poe's life. Then, too, there are maps shewing Poe's haunts in all the cities he frequented extensively—Richmond, Baltimore, Philadelphia, & New York. From this work I have drawn up a long table of Poe sites in Richmond which I intend to visit tomorrow, & I may stop off at Baltimore to see certain others next week. Tomorrow I shall see the old Allan home at 14th St. & Tobacco Alley, (still standing in decrepitude) the office of the Southern Literary Messenger, the place where Poe boarded when he returned to Richmond for the last time, & the pitiful brick hovel in Main St. near 23d. where his mother died in 1811. I shall see Shockoe Creek, where he used to go swimming as a boy, & the homes of many of his friends of later ages.

But in particular, I have made a *Providence* discovery in this book. It seems that Harry Lyman Koopman[1] of the John Hay Library has unearthed an old print of Earl's Hotel, opposite the foot of Thomas St. (69 N. Main) where Poe used to stop sometimes, & has had Halladay of the Journal make a copy of it for the Phillips book. It is obviously not now in existence, since the two buildings at the corner of Steeple & N. Main do not correspond with the drawing. It may have been removed without replacement in widening Steeple St. at some period. It was from a gold-crazed fellow-lodger there, during the early days of the California gold rush, that Poe obtained the idea of his "Von Kempelen and His Discovery." No question—I must ultimately own this book for the sake of its pictures & voluminous scenic & background data. It is in 2 volumes, like the Allen book, & may some day become similarly marked down.[2]

Richmond, as I said, grows on one. Franklin St., that leads to the library, is admirably stately; the great Doric-porched mansions (like those on the N. side of Washington Sq. in New York) looking rather odd in their Northern architecture as compared with the tropical, piazza-bearing mansions of Charleston. Richmond's residential districts make one think of Providence or Boston, for there is no concession to climate in any of the venerable buildings. The really hot zone begins considerably south of here. Since my last year's visit two or three rather tall buildings have gone up—though the general atmosphere is not spoiled as yet.

Hope you've been having some steadily decent weather in Providence, & that you've been able to get outdoors & enjoy it! ¶ Yr aff Nephew & obt Servt H P Lovecraft

[On envelope:]

P.S. Diary for
Saturday, May 10

Rose late after making up sleep for the preceding night of coach travel, & have so far spent all the time in good old Capitol Park writing cards, reading, &c. It is now 3 p.m., & I am going over to the Poe Shrine, which closes at 5. After that I shall explore various regions connected with Poe. But I *must* own that Phillips biography sooner or later! Am mailing an envelope full of odds & ends home to myself. The guide book of St. Michael's Church, Charleston, was given me free by a nice old lady at the Huguenot Church—otherwise it would have cost me 50¢. Read it when it comes. Also—you'll find the latest Weird Tales in this envelope*. I've read it all except the serial stories. Look at it & leave it for my permanent file. In the Eyrie you'll see Bernard Dwyer's flattering notice of my work[3]—I'll be glad to see Dwyer in Kingston in a couple of weeks. ¶ Richmond still grows on me—I shall hate to leave it! No question, the South is my natural environment except for Old Providence memories! More soon.

Notes

1. Harry Lyman Koopman (1860–1937), Librarian of Brown University (1893–1930)

---

*And also, those collars—which I can't seem to change. Arrow softs are almost abandoned & outmoded now. Nobody keeps 'em!

who supervised the building of the John Hay Library in 1910. He became president of the American Library Association in 1928 and also published several volumes of poetry.

2. HPL does not appear to have obtained the Phillips book for his library.

3. HPL refers to Dwyer's letter to *WT* in the June 1930 issue. See Joshi, *A Weird Writer in Our Midst* 72.

[313]   [ALS] [HPL to LDC]

Saturday–Sunday Midnight—May 10–11, 1930

My dear Daughter:—

As I take my pen in hand to continue my diary, I will begin by asking a favour. Will you please send me—in care of Belknap, of course—about a half-dozen of my *book-plates?* I have given away all of those which I had as specimens in my pocket case—since whenever I had occasion to shew the design in the course of architectural discussions with various curators & others in Charleston, the observer always begged for a copy in sheer admiration of Talman's delectable design. The last one went this afternoon to the old lady in charge of the Poe Shrine, hence I now have none to shew such gang-members in N.Y. as have not seen the thing. Accordingly, I would appreciate having a few awaiting me when I get to Little Sonny's. You will find the main pile wrapped in yellow paper on the rear of the top of my best glass-door bookcase—beside the smaller superimposed bookcase—or else hidden behind the vertical surface of the tip-table, perched atop the pile of Halde-man-Julius Blue Books which rest on the supporting pillar. Or you might take the specimens from my smaller sub-pile—under the paste bottle on the lowest shelf of the new small bookcase on the back of my table; said paste-bottle being at the extreme left of the shelf. Talman certainly created a little masterpiece when he designed that bookplate, as everyone who sees it agrees. Naturally, I mention him & give him full credit when I hear it admired. Grandpa'll make the kid famous yet! The old lady at the Shrine wanted an extra copy for a daughter who collects bookplates in an extensive & discriminating way.

Well—as for the diary—as I told you in my P.S. from Capitol Park, I started up at 3 p.m. to explore Poe sites & visit the Poe Shrine at Main & 19th Sts. The sites I visited were the actors' boarding house where Poe's parents used to stop when in Richmond; (bldg. still standing) the little brick house in the rear of this boarding house (Main & 23d) (also still standing) where Mrs. Poe died in 1811; the first Allan home at 14th St. & Tobacco Alley, where little Edgar was taken as a child of not quite three upon his adoption by Mr. & Mrs. Allan; (still standing, but abandoned & likely to come down) the site of the later Allan mansion (now demolished) at Main & 5th; the site of the Southern Literary Messenger office at Main & 15th, (now demolished) & several of the homes of Poe's friends, a fair percentage of which are still standing. When I registered at the Poe Shrine, the old lady in charge—a Mrs.

Traylor, widow of a prominent collector of Poeana who left his collection to the U. of Virginia upon his death a quarter-century ago[1]—volunteered much information about Poe, & finally offered to see if I could have an interview with the famous James H. Whitty of Richmond, foremost collector of Poeana in the world, & conceded to be the greatest living authority upon Poe & his work from a bibliographical standpoint.[2] I am rather sceptical about the ability or inclination of so eminent a man to spare time for chatting with an unknown & unprofessional Poe-devotee; but told good Mrs. Traylor that if by chance he does have a spare half-hour in the next 2 or 3 days, a telephone call to Murphy's Hotel will undoubtedly be taken & delivered to me on the evening of the day it is received. If such an interview does eventuate, I shall be able to match the good luck of Morton—who upon his Richmond visit came in touch with the venerable sculptor Edward Valentine, a Poe authority *who* **saw** *Poe in his boyhood.* Mr. Valentine, now much over 90, has not been in good health this spring, else Mrs. Traylor would have tried to secure me an interview with him.[3] At the Shrine everything is the same as last year, but a new descriptive pamphlet—which I annexed at once—has been issued by it. Incidentally—this pamphlet adopts the older theory as to the age of the stone building which forms the shrine's principal unit. You may recall last year that I reported a consensus of opinion as to this building's being the Jacob Ege house, erected in 1737 soon after the founding of Richmond as a town. New estimates, however—confirmed by no less an authority than Wallace Nutting[4]—throw the verdict back to the earlier & more common opinion that the house was built between 1685 & 1688 as a farmhouse before the town existed on this site. In any case there is very little doubt as to its being the oldest house in Richmond. Richmond, as you may see, (since it was founded in 1735) is not a very old city as colonial cities go. It is as much younger than Charleston as Charleston is younger than Providence. Providence was a century old, & Newport was a thriving & cultivated metropolis, when the first houses & streets of Richmond came into existence. *Williamsburg,* of course, was the Virginia capital & metropolis in those days. When Poe was editor of the Messenger in Richmond, it was almost as young a town as was Providence when Stephen Hopkins (nearly a century before) built his house at the corner of a steep lane in the Towne Street. Well—after my Shrine visit I continued my Poe-site exploration, had a veal-cutlet dinner at a modest refectory in Broad St., & spent the evening at the publick library reading in the Phillips biography of Poe. Truly—this work is a veritable mine of material despite its atrociously sloppy & sentimentalised style, naive italicisations, & uncritical handling of doubtful points. Its great advantage lies in its wholesale inclusion of interesting associational & anecdotal material which other biographies have excluded for lack of major relevance or literary significance. The prose is gossipy & execrable—but the facts it includes are often of the greatest dramatic interest. It goes deeply into Poe's ancestry & parentage, & traces all the dramatick appearances of his father & mother. One interesting point comes up in connexion with this matter—taking the reader as far north as Portland, Maine—a delightful old town to visit *in the summer.* It seems that, according to old New England diaries, a performance on Jan. 17, 1797 at the Portland Theatre was attended by a young gentlewoman of 18, by name Mifs Zilpah Wadsworth;[5] & that in the cast of the play—& therefore under the same roof—was a child of ten, one Elizabeth Arnold, daughter of the leading lady. It is improbable that the patrician Mifs Wadsworth ever spoke to the small stage prodigy, or ever mentioned her except with casual patronage—if indeed she ever remembered her enough to mention her at all—& it is equally unlikely that the child of the theatre ever noticed any one particular person, such as Mifs Wadsworth, in the audience of that night. But how curious it would have been if either could have looked ahead! A forward look of *fifty* years would have confirmed Mifs Wadsworth in her presumable feeling of superiority to a common stage person; but a perspective of *100* or *130* years would have been a different matter. For in the course of time Miss Zilpah Wadsworth was to be the mother of Henry Wadsworth Longfellow, whilst small Elizabeth Arnold was to be the mother of EDGAR ALLAN POE! It is further interesting to note that the Tubbs troupe of players (whose actor-manager Charles Tubbs was the 2nd husband of Elizabeth Arnold's mother) played in Providence (after a season at Newport) in the summer of 1797. The seat of the performances (evidently not high-grade enough for the elegant Providence Theatre at Westminster & Mathewson Sts.) was Mrs. Penrose's Hall in Cheapside, *at the corner of Church St.* There, at the bottom of the steep lane beside old St. John's, (the old steepled church of 1723, not the present 1810 one) acted the small Elizabeth Arnold; little knowing that a future son of hers would be a frequent caller, & a participant in a tempestuous & dramatic scene, at a house even then standing a few yards away in Benefit St. at the top of that steep lane . . . . . the house to which, in 1816, Capt. & Mrs. Nicholas Power moved with their children Sarah Helen & Anna; & which in 1848 was the home of Sarah Helen Whitman. The Phillips biography is full of this interesting (even if admittedly trivial) "side-light" stuff; & I must certainly add it to my library sooner or later. It is a pity the text could not have been revised & whipped into acceptable aesthetic shape by a competent stylist.

Tomorrow I shall continue my Poe-site exploration of old Richmond, & shall also read the N Y Sunday Times in some suitable park location. Therefore you may mark still another issue as "discarded", & omit it from the pile of papers saved for me. Incidentally—you might send me (% Belknap) any Wednesday pages & B K H's[6] which you may be through with, so that I can get them read in odd moments & off the programme before my return.

Monday I may possibly take the Williamsburg side trip, & Tuesday I may do the same with Petersburg—which I have never seen. Tuesday night I have half a mind to spend a dollar on a nigger-heaven seat[7] (free, however, from the race whence its sportive name is derived!) at the Lyric Theatre—at which will appear that same all-star production of Sheridan's "The Rivals", (with John Craig, Mrs. Fiske, Pedro de Cordoba, &c)[8] which I missed, but A E P G saw, upon its recent Providence appearance. The combination of Old Richmond—with its memories of theatrical productions in colonial days—& a real old Georgian drama like "The Rivals", which was repeatedly played in Richmond, Charleston, Baltimore, Philadelphia, & other American towns in the late 18th century, is almost too much for an antiquarian to resist! If anything could bring back old periwig days, it would be some sort of synthesis like that! I'll tell you whether I decide to go or not. With my specs, which are still unbroken, I could at least *see* the thing from the 3d balcony, even if my aged ears—a leetle mite hard o' hearing these days—didn't catch much. I know the text fairly well anyway! This may be one of the last chances to see a real play in ancient & traditional surroundings—for with the growth of the talking cinema, the actual drama is becoming extinct except in the garish metropolis now occupying the former site of poor vanished New-York.

Up to now the Richmond weather has been delectably warm—warmer than in Charleston, & a source of complaint amongst Richmondites who do not share my predilection for high temperatures. Tonight, however, a disconcertingly cold breeze is penetrating my windows—so that I fear my vest will have to come into service tomorrow. I recall that a year ago—at this same season—I had a few mild shivers in the Richmond area. ¶ Well—more soon. Wish I could stay in Richmond for weeks! ¶ Yr aff Nephew & obt Servt H P L

P.S. Have just done my laundry again—I shall be quite a competitor with Mr. Seagrave's establishment if I continue my practice in this art! Hope to make my present outfit last through to N.Y.

P.P.S. Study of Richmond foot-scrapers reminds me that *Charleston* has a very distinctive type—which I meant to mention whilst there. It is shaped like this: ⵖor ⵗ—& of course involves the fine wrought-iron craftsmanship for which old Charleston is famous. None of these scrapers occur in Richmond. Here, all are of the same type which we have in New-England.

[On envelope:]

P.S.—Sunday.

Rose late, & am enjoying the Times in Capitol Park. Am glad to note that Masefield is the new laureate.[9] Choice couldn't have been better. After finishing the paper & tearing out whatever I want to keep, I shall resume Poe explorations. Also—shall see if the library is open Sunday. Glad that Richmond is urban enough to leave its library open evenings, so that I don't have to waste precious Southern sunlight on it. Today isn't so cold as I feared it would be, but the vest is pretty welcome. Alas, there's only one Charleston!

¶ Times has some interesting stuff this week. Note the rotogravure pictures of the old house at Stockbridge, & the article on the new Chicago planetarium in the feature section. Also some more discussion on how to read the Sunday Times. There is also a very good article on the Stockbridge house in the magazine section. I must see Stockbridge some time—at present, Western Mass. is almost unknown to me.

4 p.m.

¶ Ugh! getting colder! Will cease reading & begin pedestrian exploration.

¶ Alas! find the publick library isn't open on Sunday! After all, modernity has its occasional redeeming features! Well—I shall spend the evening writing & planning the morrow's explorations. Ugh! but it's *cold!!* Me for indoors! Oh, that I were still in Charleston!!

Notes

1. HPL refers to Robert Lee Traylor (1864–1907), owner of one of the celebrated daguerreotypes of Poe. Mary Gavin Traylor (d. 1946), secretary of the Poe Shrine in Richmond, was Traylor's daughter.

2. James H[oward] Whitty (1859–1937), author of such works as *Discoveries in the Uncollected Poems of Edgar Allan Poe* (1916) and editor of *The Complete Poems of Edgar Allan Poe* (1911). His collection of Poe material is at the Harry Ransom Center at the University of Texas at Austin.

3. Edward Virginius Valentine (1838–1930), sculptor who designed numerous monuments in Richmond and elsewhere.

4. Wallace Nutting (1861–1941), Congregational minister, photographer, and antiquarian.

5. Zilpah Wadsworth (1778–1851), mother of Henry Wadsworth Longfellow.

6. Bertrand K. Hart, literary editor of the *Providence Journal* who wrote a long-running column called "The Sideshow."

7. The term "nigger heaven" referred to seats in church balconies reserved for African Americans, away from white members of the congregation.

8. HPL refers to a revival of Sheridan's play *The Rivals* (1778), featuring the actors John Craig (1868–1932), Minnie Maddern Fiske (1865–1932), and Pedro De Cordoba (1881–1950). This revival opened in New York (13 March 1930) at Erlanger's Theatre (246 W. 44th Street).

9. British poet John Masefield (1878–1967) was named poet laureate of the United Kingdom on 9 May 1930, following the death of the previous laureate, Robert Bridges.

[314]   [ALS] [HPL to LDC]

Tuesday–Wednesday Midnight—
May 13–14, 1930

My dear Daughter:—

As I once more take my pen in hand to continue my diary, I am happily able to report a relief from the cold of yesterday. Today—Tuesday—dawned warm & sunny, & I could not have asked for a better day.

Rising at 9 a.m., I decided after all to go to Petersburg, hence took the 10:30 coach over the old turnpike (which runs through a Rehoboth-looking countryside) & arrived at my destination within an hour. It gives me pleasure to state that Petersburg proved no disappointment, being one of the most fascinating small cities (pop. 38,000) I have ever beheld. It has absolutely no tall buildings, & its skyline appears to immense advantage from the heights over which one approaches it. Just ancient steeples, slant roofs, & chimney-pots—the traditional urban skyline of the elder America that is passing away. Upon entering the town, I was overwhelmed by the profusion of old brick buildings with slant roofs—exactly like our poor murdered brick row in South Water St.[1] There are literally *hundreds* of these venerable edifices in the lower part of the town—along the Appomattox River waterfront—whole streets & squares being lined with them. Even archaick Newburyport is outdone in this respect! The town is a quiet & sleepy one—exactly my style—& my only objection to it is its indifference to its own history & antiquities, as evinced in a total absence of obtainable maps or guide-books, & a very inadequate assortment of postcards. It is the very antithesis of Charleston in that respect—& is even worse than Newport, which at least has a city map. On account of my meagre & belated sources of information, I could not "do" urban Petersburg as thoroughly as I wished within the allotted time; hence I wish to revisit it on some future occasion. Having now a good general idea of it, I could do it justice in a second visit. This time, after a certain amount of urban exploration, I took a street-car for neighbouring Blandford; where I found & studied the celebrated old Blandford church, built in 1735, abandoned in 1800, & restored as a shrine of Confederate dead in 1901. It is in perfect shape, its massive construction having saved it from decay during its period of disuse. Around it is an exceedingly interesting rural churchyard, walled with brick & containing interments as far back as 1702. Around this churchyard has developed a more modern cemetery—just as in Tarrytown, N.Y., the Sleepy Hollow cemetery has developed around the churchyard of the ancient Dutch church—& this is one of the most attractive scenic regions on record. The land is high, commanding picturesque vistas of the neighbouring plains & hills & Petersburg steeples; & many of the slabs & tombs are overgrown with the lovely wild honeysuckle—a very common creeping vine in Virginia. In this region I met two old men of considerable information & loquacious bent, from whom I derived much valuable data concerning Petersburg. After this I proceeded onward along "Jerusalem Plank Road" to the site of the celebrated Battle of Petersburg with its memorable mine & crater—a site now open as a museum, & with the Yankee tunnel cleared out for visitors' access. The guide is a splendid Confederate veteran—Capt. Bishop—only 80 years old; his youth, for a Civil War veteran, being explained by the fact that he enlisted in 1864 at the age of *14*.[2] He does not look more than 60, but there is no question about his really being 80 & a veteran. He is one of the handsomest, most eloquent, & most impressive men I have ever seen—a true Virginia gentleman in every accent & feature, & as slender as a boy. He took the visitors over all the points of interest on the battlefield, & allowed us to traverse such parts of the Federal tunnel as are cleared out; delivering meanwhile the most vivid & anecdotal account of the battle (which he personally witnessed, although he was not allowed to go to the front line) that I ever heard. He is an historian of extreme accuracy & profundity—& is the real author of the descriptive matter in the enclosed folder, although another (D. V. Bush-like) bears the credit. It is clear from all evidence that the battle was one of the most stupid Yankee failures in the entire war, although the idea of the tunnel itself was a stroke of genius. From the Federal standpoint, it was a useless slaughter comparable to the Battle of Fredericksburg—Gen. Burnside's presence on both occasions arguing a sort of malign fatality connected with the rash & inept Rhode-Islander. From the Confederate standpoint it was one of the most glorious victories of the war—the almost incredible heroism of Genls. Mahone (a shrill-voiced little Scotch-Irishman who wore a **No. 2** shoe & had the fighting blood of an Achilles) & Gracie (of a Southern branch of the noted N.Y. family) being of the sort that epic balladists sing. I will not attempt to give any account of the battle, but will enclose a duplicate of the folder given me by Capt. Bishop.

As the afternoon advanced, I returned to Richmond in order not to be late at the performance of "The Rivals". I had a C 10 Centre balcony seat—for at the last moment I decided it would be silly to try to save a dollar by sitting in the 2d. gallery at a production of such importance—a play which in this age of transition may never be professionally enacted again, & which I have always wish'd to see. So I paid two fish & patronised the 1st balcony—confident that I could hear a good deal of the text from there. I shall make up the cash on meals—for I am getting overweight again . . . . 142 last night. The Lyrick Theatre is an institution much like our Opera House—& is dark most of the time in these days of declining drama, although it is going to try a summer stock co. beginning next week. The audience was exactly like a typical Opera-House audience—predominantly aristocratic, & with evening-clothes predominating in the parquet. In view of my shabbiness I was glad to be upstairs—though the accents of those even on that level proclaim'd them to be persons of cultivation. The play itself was magnificently staged & intelligently enacted; carrying out the true spirit of Mr. Sheridan in every particular. Tho' Mrs. Fiske was nominally the star, I believe the best acting was furnish'd by Mr. Mack (the one-time romantick Irish tenor, now grown fat & elderly) as Sir Lucius, & by Mr. Powers as Acres. Mr. Craig—who was leading man of the Albee Stock Co. in 1904—26 years ago—astonish'd me by the slightness of his aging in this lapse of more than a quarter-century.[3] His well-mark'd features were at once recognisable, & he has not grown fat at all. He looks young enough to be Mr. Mack's son, tho' they are both in all probability of the same age. In this performance Mr. Sheridan's text was very well-treated; only two extensive cuts being made so far as I can recall. As it was, the presentation lasted an even three hours. There were a few touches which I do not recall in the original text, & which may represent traditional accretions gather'd during the long history of the drama's popularity—especially as enacted by the late Joseph Jefferson.[4] I was glad to see that Richmond has not follow'd the parvenu modern custom of discarding theatre orchestras. The array of musicians was lamentably small, but it was present none the less. I will enclose a programme of this production—which was doubtless identical with the same company's Providence presentation as witness'd by A E P G. It was good to see an old play in an old town. I could well imagine myself at the old Richmond Theatre—which burn'd down in 1811—witnessing a company including Mr. & Mrs. David Poe. Had I heard an infant's cry from behind the scenes, I would have felt sure it was little Edgar—or perhaps his poor consumptive brother William Henry. Had I not seen, only two days before, the ancient boarding-house (now a nigger tenement) where the actors at the Richmond Theatre used to stop in the 1790's & early 1800's?

Well—after the performance I return'd to the hotel & devoted the next half-hour to some expert amateur *barbering*. I have used my patent hair-cutter to very great advantage—being greatly aided by the admirable light & mirror arrangement in this room. In the nearly 3 weeks since my journey's-eve cutting of Apr. 24, the back of my neck had become rather messy again, but it is now in spick & span shape for the second half of the outing, & will still be in good condition when I see the gang next week. I didn't have to bother the sides much, because I had rather overshot the mark in the cutting of April 24. The face behaves admirably, although a good deal of the Charleston tan is wearing off. I fear that neither you nor even the gang will see the lean, tropically bronzed old gentleman who was last week exploring the ancient byways of Charleston. With me, tan comes hard & goes easily. But it was impressive while it lasted. By the way—tonight's "Trimette" job saves me exactly *60¢*, which is what I would have to pay for a decent haircut in either Richmond, Washington, Baltimore, Philadelphia, or New-York.

I must start reducing again, now that I have gone up to 142. That Park View Lunch is a regular Jake's—I can't spend so *little* that they don't fill me up to capacity! Even a cheese sandwich (10¢) is a full meal with great slices of bread & enough cheese to make a welsh rarebit. The proprietor—a Mr. Kakoupopoulos, or some fine old Virginian name of the sort—is certainly imbued with true Southern hospitality. I have noticed that Southern cuisine emphasises different dishes as favourites—there being a much greater inclination toward pork, chicken, & ham than in the north. Potatoes are less taken for granted than in New England, the succulent *yam* being a frequent substitute. I have tried yams at the Park View—but while they're not bad, I think I prefer the commonplace 'tater. Another favourite Southern dish—in Charleston as well as in Richmond—is the Mexican stew or soup called *chili con carne*. This consists of a sort of Mexican bean, meat, (probably beef) & a very high & very palatable seasoning. I think this is becoming one of my favourite dishes— as, alas, the scales shew! 142 forsooth! I am also growing addicted to a kind of peach pie that the Park View has. One thing about the Park View—it can't be as rabbly as Jake, because the class which patronises Jake's has no counterpart in Richmond. All the rough stevedoring & unskilled trucking work is done by niggers—who of course cannot enter any lunch room in the centre of the town—& there are not enough foreigners in the city to line a good-sized counter. Whoever is white in Richmond is likely to be an Anglo-Saxon with the Anglo-Saxon's natural neatness & reasonable fastidiousness. There simply couldn't be a typical Jake clientele down here. ¶ Well—more later. Tomorrow will be devoted to Museum exploring—rain or shine. More later—this trip is certainly a 100% success so far! ¶ Yr aff Nephew & obt Servt H P L

P.S. The trip over the Crater battlefield was made doubly impressive by the presence—in addition to the Confederate veteran who did the guiding—of a Union veteran among the visitors—a fine old fellow of 87 from Massachusetts, who had been in the Battle of Petersburg & wanted to go over the old scenes again. It was a most unusual & felicitous coincidence to have representatives of *both sides* actually present in the flesh on the original scene. The Union veteran had a marvellous memory, & recognised many features of the terrain—also inquiring after other features which had changed or vanished.

Notes

1. HPL long campaigned to save the decrepit brick warehouses on South Water Street, built around 1815. After the warehouses were torn down, he wrote the poem "The East India Brick Row" (12 December 1929).
2. Captain Carter Richard Bishop (1849–1941), who became a banker in Petersburg after the Civil War.
3. Minnie Maddern Fiske (1865–1932), Andrew Mack (1861–1931), James T. Powers (1862–1943), and John Craig (1868–1932).
4. American actor Joseph Jefferson (1829–1905) frequently played Bob Acres in Sheridan's *The Rivals*.

[315]   [ALS] [HPL to LDC]

% F. B. Long, Jun.,
230 W. 97th St.,
New York, N.Y.,
May 20–21, 1930

My dear Daughter:—
          I was glad to find your note awaiting me—together

with the formidable pile of forwarded mail. I have not read all the latter as yet, but have merely opened such envelopes as looked important. The Weird Tales ones were proofs of my sonnets,[1] & the one from Simon & Schuster was a vaguely possible literary opening which is worth quoting here in full:

SIMON & SCHUSTER, INC.,
PUBLISHERS
OFFICE OF THE EDITORS

386 Fourth Ave.,

New York, N.Y.

Dear Mr. Lovecraft:—

The noted critic & anthologist, Mr. Edward J. O'Brien, has mentioned your name to us as that of a most promising & interesting writer.

It is probable that your labours thus far have been devoted mainly to the field of the short story. If you are contemplating any longer work of fiction, or if you would care to let me know anything of your literary plans in general, it will be a pleasure to hear from you.

Any manuscript with which you favour us is assured an interested reading.

Sincerely,

Clifton P. Fadiman,[2]

Simon & Schuster, Inc.

CPF/CFW

It surely flatters me to hear that O'Brien speaks so well of my endeavours, & the receptive mood of this company encourages me to try the full-length weird novel I have so long wished to write. However—it isn't likely that they'd care for my stuff once they saw a specimen. In answering the note I am saying that I hope to submit a novel some day—& that meanwhile I can let them have a set of short stories at any time.

Glad you had some good *warm days* up north—Belknap has been telling me about them—but sorry you didn't get outdoors to improve them. In about a couple of weeks or less I shall proceed to drag you out by force—if not to Newport or Bristol, at least as far as Prospect Terrace! During the warm weather the Long canine displayed signs of discomfort, so they had his shaggy hair clipped—which gives him a most singular & scarcely recognisable aspect. Sonny hates to take him outdoors now!

Glad to hear that the other sonnets were printed, & that A E P G has obtained extra papers.[3] If you haven't sent the Wednesday pages & B K H's as yet, you needn't bother to do so; for I fancy the answering of letters & the finishing of my revision job will take care of all the spare time I'll have during the residue of my outing. I cut out that Stockbridge material myself, but shall be glad of a duplicate. Pleased to hear that the Charleston & Richmond packages arrived safely, & hope the one from Philadelphia will do the same. I shall probably send still another from N.Y. before the week is over. Those Virginia pictures probably came from some member of that Poetry Circle branch in Washington—whose personnel persistently & rather inanely address me as "Judge" because I judged a poetry contest of theirs six years ago.[4] I shall be very glad to have the views—even though some of the places in question are remote from lines of public transportation & therefore inaccessible to me unless I can get somebody with a car to drive me around the Old Dominion some day. Of course I have seen all the Rockefeller restorations in Williamsburg. Thanks, by the way, for the additional bookplate supply. Talman certainly created a work of art when he finally hit upon that simple design!

A E P G spoke of her archaistic activities in connexion with "Old Meeting House Day", but did not enclose a programme. I shall be interested in seeing the official outline of the event. I'm telling her that I hope her costume was recorded in some sort of a photograph.

My laundry activities continue, & I think I can get through the entire outing without sending for packages A & B. Just before leaving Richmond I gave a complete laundering to all my underclothing—washing all of my outside shirt except the cuffs. I am still wearing the outfit on that laundering—thus having three full sets in reserve. My next task is to get my suit pressed—a process which will afford no trouble if I can get the loan of a pair of trousers from Sonny or his papa. My 1909 overcoat & I are now reunited—& although the past day has been decently mild, I fancy I may need it tomorrow, judging by the cold air now creeping in around a neighbouring window. This house, alas, isn't heated as well as the Philadelphia Y M C A—whose genial radiators saved my life Sunday & Monday!

Belknap & his mother are much better than last month, though Mrs. Long has discovered that much of her nervous strain came from an impaired vision due to incipient *cataracts*. These are not, however, considered grave; & nothing will be done about them at once except to provide new glasses. Even later, the operations for their removal will not be what the attending oculist considers serious. Just now the Child's worst trouble is his digestion—his mamma made him take some castor oil today!

Too bad the census men bothered you again. Did they collect the blanks of the original census which we so conscientiously filled out? One wonders what the population of Providence will turn out to be. As a general thing, increases are less than most theorists predicted.

As for my diary—naturally there isn't much to record since my final Philadelphia card. I had an uneventful coach trip, reaching N.Y. at 8:30 p.m., dining on macaroni & cherry pie at the Automat, & proceeding at once to Little

Belknap's; where I saw Felis, Canis, & all the family, & spent until 12:30 discussing anthropology & metaphysics with the Child. I then came up here, & have been writing ever since. I shall very largely make a night of it—getting important correspondence done up, & sorting out the rest to carry around in my inevitable black enamel cloth bag for piecemeal answering in odd moments. Tomorrow Sonny is to knock on my door at about 9:30, but our programme is undecided. During the day I shall probably get into telephonic touch with Loveman & Talman—& before the week is over there will in all probability be a gang meeting at Talman's. Further events will be chronicled in future bulletins. Belknap has a new story—his horrible novelette—just done, & I shall peruse it with appreciation very shortly.[5]

Ah notes wif int'rust de 'count ob de meetin' of dem 'Dustrial School folks. Anyhow, ah hopes dey keep up de ole buildin' right smart—though ah'd rudder de w'ite folks bought he back agin, & founded a new school in memory of the bygone Smithville Seminary. Speakin' ob dark folks—de Longs' new maid am a sight darker dan de Germans dey done use to hab—but 'pear to be all right fo' de job. Mis' Long done break her in awn de cookin' so's y'all kain't tell her dinners from de dinners dem German gals used to cook!

And so it goes. It was with genuine regret that I left antient Philadelphia, for despite its presence in the frigid North it undoubtedly belongs to the same solid area of old-American life which also contains the cities of the South. Many more of the old mansions in Fairmount Park are open, than were open when last I visited the place; & I made thorough tours of Mt. Pleasant, Sweet Brier, Cedar Grove, & Woodford. I enclose a printed account of them, with map, which the museum is distributing.

But the high spot of the trip was *Charleston**. That is the unique thing. As I look back, I can appreciate the completeness of its isolation from contemporary currents in American life. Geography is partly responsible; for it is situate on a peninsula remote from other thickly settled districts, & has consequently developed an active & highly differentiated individuality of its own. It is notable that very few motor licence plates other than the S.C. ones are ever seen in the streets of Charleston—& conversely, I haven't seen a single S.C. plate since leaving the state itself.

As dawn approaches, I fear tomorrow will be a coldish day—but now I have my 1909 overcoat to help defeat the onset of the frost-god.

Oh—I think I forgot to say that Galpin didn't win his Peterborough fellowship, hence can't come East as he had planned. Too bad—Belknap and I were much disappointed.

Trust you'll get outdoors as soon as the weather is better—& that your muffin supply has been adequate. ¶ And so it goes. More later, when I have some more events to record.

---

*With *Maymont Park* in Richmond next.

Yr aff Nephew & ob^t Servt
H P L

Notes

1. A proof sheet survives at JHL for the ten sonnets from *Fungi from Yuggoth* that *WT* published between September 1930 and April–May 1931.
2. Clifton Paul Fadiman (1904–1999), an American author, editor, and radio and television personality. He was at Simon & Schuster for ten years, beginning as a reader and ending as editor-in-chief, and became a judge for Book-of-the-Month Club. Following HPL's death, Fadiman was among the authors to whom *The Outsider and Others* was submitted for publication.
3. HPL refers to the publication of five sonnets from *Fungi from Yuggoth* published in the *Providence Journal:* "Nostalgia" (12 March), "Background" (16 April), "The Dweller" (7 May), "The Well" (14 May), and "Night-Gaunts" (26 May).
4. HPL had served as a judge for a poetry contest for the League of American Penwomen in 1924. A participant, Elizabeth Toldridge, wrote to HPL four years later regarding the comments he made then on her entry. The two remained frequent correspondents until HPL's death. Toldridge's friend Florence Radcliffe, a co-member of the American Poetry Circle, wrote Lovecraft several letters in the 1930s, sending the pictures referred to here. Both Toldridge and Radcliffe addressed him as "Judge."
5. Presumably the short novel *The Horror from the Hills,* in which FBL printed verbatim a long extract from a letter by HPL recounting his "Roman dream" of 1927.

[316]   [ALS] [HPL to LDC]

Wednesday–Thursday Midnight
May 21–22, 1930.

My dear Daughter:—

Again I take my pen in hand to present a diary of the day's events—Wednesday, May 21. I arose at 11 a.m., & descended to Belknap's to find a visitor on the scene—young Robert Randall, son of the well known ex-clergyman John H. Randall, Sr., & brother of the really eminent philosopher & Columbia professor, John Herman Randall, Jun.[1] The Longs & Randalls have known one another exceedingly well for many years, & Belknap used to play with the two boys when they were all small youngsters. The caller on this occasion contributed much interesting discussion, & departed around lunch time—12:30 noon. He is a chemist of great ability; who sometimes teaches the subject, & at other times employs his talent in the service of industrial corporations.

After a sumptuous lunch of the traditional Long sort, Belknap & I went out to the Roerich Museum at Riverside Drive & 103^d St. to see the strange & fantastic paintings of exotic scenes in mysterious Thibet which form its major contents. Possibly I have mentioned to you at various times my admiration for the work of Nicholas Roerich—the mystical Russian artist who has devoted his life to the study & portrayal of the unknown uplands of Central Asia, with their vague suggestions of cosmic wonder & terror—& perhaps I have pointed out illustrations of his strange & Clark-Ashton-Smithic paintings in the N Y Times.[2] Well—so distinctive is this artist that his admirers have erected this mighty, skyscraping museum for the sole purpose of housing his bizarre work, & presenting data on the remote & forbidden region whose weird aspect & singular soul he has so deeply absorbed & so well recorded for the benefit of the Western World. It is a large & commodious edifice, only recently finished & furnished, & so far as I know the only great museum in the world to be devoted exclusively to the work of one artist. Neither Belknap nor I had ever been in it before; & when we did see the outré & esoteric nature of its contents, we went virtually wild over the imaginative vistas presented. Surely Roerich is one of those rare fantastic souls who have glimpsed the grotesque, terrible secrets outside space & beyond time, & who have retained some ability to hint at the marvels they have seen. Roerich is a man of about sixty, with a long, grey Thibetan beard, & he is still producing large amounts of the work for which he is famous. At the museum we obtained several postcards, one of which I will enclose as an illustration of the Roerich manner & subject-matter.

Well, after that Sonny dragged Grandpa to a cinema show—which turned out to be a vapid Civil War drama whose redeeming feature was a splendid Southern mansion interior—a 3d phase Georgian type that made me pine for the Charleston & Richmond scenes behind me![3] No question, there is something hideously crude &.futile & unfinished about the North after one has seen the South! After this came dinner (alas for my *weight!*) & discussion, & at 8 o'clock I set out for Brooklyn to call on Loveman according to previous arrangement. I found his quarters as attractive as they were before, & his roommate Patrick McGrath was as pleasant as ever. Later in the evening another caller appeared in the form of Gervaise Butler—that young fellow to whom Loveman first introduced me in Boston during the Jany. 1929 visit, & whom I met again in New York a year ago. He was as breezy & pleasant as before, & surprised me by presenting me with a quaint book of children's verse of the 1830 period, entitled *Rhode-Island Tales*.[4] He had come across it some time previously, & was saving it for presentation on some such occasion as this. General discussion was varied & interesting, & the marvellous illuminated skyline across the river was suitably enjoyed. *That* is the one great asset & distinction of modern New York—the faery towers & pinnacles to which twilight & night give such an unearthly magic. Loveman gave me several things—prints, & a huge catalogue with some marvellous reproductions of 18th century French prints—which I shall shortly mail home to myself.

Well—the group dispersed about midnight, & I returned to 230 to begin this epistle. I think I shall hold it over till tomorrow in order to add another day's diary to it. The programme for tomorrow is open, though it will probably involve some form of museum-visiting.

Thursday–Friday Midnight

Well—today I rose at 11 a.m. & went down to Belknap's for discussion. After lunch we went over to the Metropolitan Museum & enjoyed the Roman sculptures, to say nothing of taking a look at Samuel Casey's tankard, porringer, & cream-pitcher in the silverware section of the American Wing. At the desk Belknap obtained a marvellous number of bargain pictures of various works of art for *1¢ each,* but I didn't find anything in the pile which especially interested me. I did get, though, some catalogues of reproduced objects in the museum—since sooner or later I want an Egyptian *cat* in plaster, plus a copy of my favourite Roman head—an old man of the vigorous Republican period. After a brief walk in Central Park we returned to 230 for discussion & dinner; following which the entire Long family dragged me to another cinema show—as uninteresting as the preceding day's, & minus the Georgian interior. The later evening was occupied by aesthetic discussion, & at midnight I came up here to do some writing before retiring.

Tomorrow the Longs go on one of their Friday motor trips, & I shall naturally be of the party. Of the route & weather conditions I will apprise you in my next bulletin. After returning from this trip at about 5 to 6 p.m. I shall see Talman—though whether by going over to his place or by his coming over here I'm not yet sure. Saturday I shall go over to Loveman's & partake of a dinner prepared by young McGrath, afterward exploring strange alleys & ancient regions with the two of them. Sunday comes another motor trip with the Longs, & Monday evening the gang meets at Talman's. Meanwhile much museum visiting will be pursued—my principal trip being to the Brooklyn Museum to see the new colonial wing there. In this collection, as I believe you know, there are not only many fine Dutch interiors, but a panelled Georgian room from the Joseph Russell house (later Clarendon Hotel & now district nurses' headquarters) in Providence. I have never seen this new wing, & look forward with keen expectancy to my first glimpse of it. At odd times I shall probably do considerable colonial exploring, & I may go to Paterson once more to see James Ferdinand. One more day's forwarded mail reached me, & I shall hope to see another batch tomorrow with a small cheque from *Weird Tales*—representing a slight royalty payment (maybe a dollar) on the Red Hook story in the Macy-Macius [*sic*] "Not at Night" anthology.[5] The reason I expect this is that a similar thing came for Belknap today, & I imagine they pay all their royalties at about the same time.

Haven't had my suit pressed yet, but must do so before the meeting. I must also stage a bonfire for these wretched 14¾ Arrow Tide collars, which bulge & gape & disarrange my tie worse than ever now that their buttonholes are getting more & more uncertain. It is a false economy to try to wear them—for they make me nervous, & the saving is only of a few cents anyway. Those which I don't burn, I shall place in cold storage or honourable retirement, as I have done with the 16¼, 16, 15½, & 15 reliques surviving from my corpulent period. Meanwhile I shall get a few new ones—bargain "seconds" if possible—of something like the right size—14¼, or perhaps an even 14. Little Sonny has just gone up from 14¼ to 14½—the little rascal now has two well-defined chins & a magnificent bay-window! I shall do my laundry once more, I think, & not have any professionally done in N.Y.

Today has been very decent in point of weather, & I only hope tomorrow will be likewise for the motor trip. Hope Providence skies have been genial, & that you have tried at least a short trip or two into the open air. Does the muffin system function properly?

Well—I guess I'll pause & get some sleep before the motor trip tomorrow. Best wishes, & see you later.

Yr aff Nephew & obt Servt
H P L

[On envelope:] P.S. You ought to see Belknap's Caproni mask of the young Roopman—I'm surely going to get one sooner or later! You remember that I took the catalogue number last winter.

Notes

1. John Herman Randall, Sr. (1871–1946), Baptist minister and author of such works as *A New Philosophy of Life* (1911) and *Religion and the Modern World* (1929). John Herman Randall, Jr. (1899–1980), longtime professor of philosophy at Columbia University (1920–67) and author of such works as *The Making of Modern Man* (1926) and books on Plato and Aristotle.

2. HPL was fascinated with the paintings of Russian artist Nicholas Roerich (1874–1947), and he would cite Roerich several times in *At the Mountains of Madness* (1931). The Nicholas Roerich Museum is now at 319 West 107th Street in Manhattan. The *New York Times* had several articles on Roerich in 1926–29, which included reproductions of his paintings; see, e.g., "Gods and Men in Storied India," *New York Times Magazine* (1 September 1929): 12–13, 19.

3. Probably *Only the Brave* (Paramount, 1930), a Civil War drama directed by Frank Tuttle; starring Gary Cooper, Mary Brian, and Phillips Holmes. The film is about a Union Army captain who enters Confederate territory as a spy with false dispatches to mislead the Confederate forces. He falls in love with the Southern woman who comes to his aid.

4. By Mrs. Avis C. Howland.

5. The Herbert Asbury anthology *Not at Night!* (Macy-Masius/The Vanguard Press, 1928) was later withdrawn from circulation because it was determined to be a plagiarism of the "Not at Night" anthologies edited by Christine Campbell Thomson and published by Selwyn & Blount.

[317]   [ALS] [HPL to LDC]

Saturday–Sunday Midnight—
May 24–25, 1930

My dear Daughter:—

I take my pen in hand to relate the events of the day in usual fashion—Saturday, May 24, 1930.

I arose at noon, had a lunch of the usual weight-imperilling Long pattern, & thereafter set out with Sonny for a second visit to the Metropolitan Museum—where we viewed the Havemeyer collection of Sino-Japanese objets d'art, & explored the Roman reliquiae more thoroughly than on Thursday's visit. After the sightseeing we repaired to the purchase desk, where Belknap bought a splendid reproduction of Roman Arretine pottery for $1.50—a terra cotta bowl with figures in high relief as in Wedgewood Ware. This was really the *most nearly genuine* of any of the reproduced material which he could have bought, since it was *cast in the original Roman mould actually made & signed about 100 B.C. by Tigranes, the apprentice slave of the great potter Marcus Perennius*. This is made possible by the fact that at Arretium (the modern Arezzo) there are discovered not only specimens of the old pottery itself, but *many of the actual moulds used by Perennius in making bowls & cups*. These are in as good condition as they were when Perennius & his slaves used them two thousand years ago; hence one can make an indefinite number of *new* bowls & cups in them, which will in every particular be the *exact* duplicates of what the original customers of Perennius had. This is not a mere matter of a cast made from an antique object, but the actual repetition of the antique process itself—giving the modern purchaser *just the same product* which the Roman purchaser received. What the modern purchaser receives is a direct impression from a given mould—& what the ancient purchaser received was *precisely the same sort of impression from that identical mould*. It is like the Paul Revere spoons which I obtained for you & A E P G—modern material from an ancient mould. If I am not broke when leaving N Y, I shall get one of these things myself, & have the museum ship it to #10. It is about the most Roman thing that one could well imagine. Some time, too, I shall take advantage of the system whereby the museum will make a photograph to order, for a nominal fee, of any object within its walls. Availing myself of this privilege I shall have a collective photograph made of the three objects fashioned by our collateral ancestor Samuel Casey (great-uncle of your grandmother Sally (Rathbone) Place)—the famous tankard, a splendid porringer, & a cream pitcher of infinite delicacy. The three pieces would make a splendid group of silverware. But all this pertains to some future trip when finances are less congested.

After the museum we returned to 230; whence, after a brief period of discussion, I set out for my evening engagement at Loveman's. We had meant to devote most of the time to outdoor exploration; but after a sumptuous dinner prepared by young McGrath we observed the approach of a rainstorm, hence cancelled this feature & spent the time in general discussion & the viewing of some of Loveman's literary treasures. About 8 o'clock the bell rang, & there appeared that tragically drink-riddled but now eminent friend of Loveman's whom I met in Cleveland in 1922, & once or twice later in New York—the poet Hart Crane, whose new book, "The Bridge", has made him one of the most celebrated & talked-of figures of contemporary American letters. He had been scheduled to speak over the radio during the evening; but a shipwreck off the coast (demanding the use of the ether for important messages) had cut off all local radio programmes & left him free. When he entered, his discourse was of alcoholics in various phases—& of the correct amount of whiskey one ought to drink in order to speak well in public—but as soon as a bit of poetic & philosophic discussion sprang up, this sordid side of his strange dual personality slipped off like a cloak, & left him as a man of great scholarship, intelligence, & aesthetic taste, who can argue as interestingly & profoundly as anyone I have ever seen. Poor devil—he has "arrived" at last as a standard American poet seriously regarded by all reviewers & critics; yet at the very crest of his fame he is on the verge of psychological, physical, & financial disintegration, & with no certainty of ever having the inspiration to write a major work of literature again. After about three hours of acute & intelligent argument poor Crane left—to hunt up a new supply of whiskey & banish reality for the rest of the night! He gets to be a nuisance now & then, dropping in on Loveman for sympathy & encouragement, but Loveman is too conscious of his tragic importance & genuine genius as a man of letters to be harsh or brusque toward him. His case is surely a sad one—all the more so because of his great attainments & of the new fame which he is so ill-fitted to carry for any considerable time. He looks more weather-beaten & drink-puffed than he did in the past, though the shaving off of his moustache has somewhat improved him. He is only 33, yet his hair is nearly white. Altogether, his case is almost like that of Baudelaire on a vastly smaller scale. "The Bridge" really is a thing of astonishing merit. In connexion with this poem—which is on Brooklyn Bridge—a very surprising coincidence was brought to light. It seems that the house in Columbia Heights where Crane lived in 1924 when beginning the poem (& which I visited with Loveman at the time, my first sight of the illuminated Manhattan skyline being from its roof!) turned out—*though he did not know it when he lived there*—to be the *old Roebling house,* where the builder of the bridge dwelt when construction was in progress; & furthermore, that Crane's own room (a shabby, $7.50 per week affair) was actually the room from which the crippled Washington A. Roebling watched & superintended the work with the aid of a telescope! And to heighten the coincidence, Crane swears that he finished the poem (while in Jamaica, knowing nothing of what was happening in the outside world) on the day that Roebling died at his final New Jersey home in 1926 . . . . which also happened to be Crane's own birthday![1] Personally, I think the matter of finishing the poem on that date is an imaginative exaggeration of Crane's, although his birthday is certainly the day on which Roebling died. The coincidence of the *house* is certainly genuine—& it amuses me because my own first glimpse of the bridge & skyline from a window was from Crane's window—undoubtedly the one which had been Roebling's! Crane, by the way, was interested to hear of my liking for *Charleston;* &, though he has never seen it, talked of going there himself as a refuge from a New York he has come to detest. But alas! I fear it would take more than Charleston to bake the alcohol out of him! After Crane's departure the conversation continued till a late hour—the rain meanwhile having stopped. I then return'd to 230 & began this epistle, which I shall not be able to finish tonight.

Sunday–Monday Midnight
May 25–26, 1930

Well—I rose today at noon, took an elaborate Sunday dinner at Belknap's, & set out with him for a second trip to that fascinating Roerich Museum. The usual Sunday motor trip of the Longs was cancelled because of a lumbago attack on Dr. Long's part, which made driving seem arduous & formidable. The Museum was as impressive as it was last Wednesday, & we stayed a long time imbibing the spirit of the strange exotic paintings. I obtained a catalogue containing black-&-white reproductions of several of the pictures,[2] which I will shew you upon my return. You will probably consider Roerich too modern to suit your taste, but his work certainly has that quality of phantasy which most appeals to me. After this visit we returned to 230 & spent the rest of the afternoon reading—Sunday papers, & stories by Clark Ashton Smith—following which came what the Longs call a "light supper", but which was equivalent to about two of my average dinners pieced together. At this moment I wouldn't get on a pair of scales for ten dollars! After supper I read my story aloud to Little Sonny, & was pleased to find him highly enthusiastic concerning it. He suggested 3 or 4 minor changes, most of which I shall adopt. Now that I feel assured the thing is worth typing, I shall not hesitate to put a new ribbon on the machine & settle down to the hideous ordeal of transcribing the MS. as soon as I get home.[3]

By the way—I must correct my original estimate of the importance of that Simon & Schuster letter which I so proudly quoted in a previous bulletin. Consider all the exuberant remarks as cancelled! It was the lynx-eyed young Talman who exploded the bubble by noticing a discrepancy betwixt the typography of the address or salutation & that of the text proper—a thing which proved it *no personal letter at all,* but a *mimeographed form letter* sent to *every* person on O'Brien's three-star Honour Roll! Therefore, O'Brien never even spoke to Simon & Schuster about my work! However, my reply—made in naive ignorance of the trivial nature of the original document—received a brief acknowledgment by the firm's editor, & this shews a fairly encouraging situation as regards the professional acceptance of weird novels. I still feel encouraged to make a try at the game—& to stage a revolt against revision in favour of original fiction-writing as soon as I get my present job off my hands. The text of the new Simon & Schuster note reads as follows:

May 23, 1930

Dear Mr. Lovecraft:—

Thank you very much for your letter of the 21st. I am afraid that you are right in that our interest in a collection of short stories would not be very vivid.

I hope, however, that you will buckle down & do that novel you speak of. If it is good, its subject matter [the weird] will be a help rather than a hindrance.

Sincerely yours,

Clifton P. Fadiman

Simon & Schuster, Inc.

Belknap & I were astonished to note the evidently expressed opinion that there is a demand for weird fiction of novel length, & I fancy we may both be trying our hands at the matter of novel-writing before the summer is over.

Having finished story-discussion with The Child, I came upstairs & proceeded to continue on this letter—after which I shall read the N Y Times & retire. One more Times which you can mark "discarded" & omit from my pile of papers!

Tomorrow I shall get my suit pressed—wearing an old brown one of Belknap's in the interim. I also hope to get some bargain soft collars of the right size & shape—perhaps at Hearn's, down in 14th St. In the afternoon I expect to go to the Brooklyn Museum & see the new American Wing which includes a room from the Joseph Russell house (Clarendon Hotel) in Providence—incidentally taking a turn through the Japanese Garden, which must be highly attractive at this time of year even though it be overshadowed by Maymont Park in Richmond. Then in the evening the gang meets at Talman's. Mrs. Long intends to invite Loveman to come up here for dinner before the meeting, though I don't know whether he'll be able to come or not. I shall probably see Morton at the meeting, since he said he would be present. Weather has been disconcertingly cool since the one warm day—Friday. Why on earth people build cities & try to live as far north as this is beyond me! I am still doing my own laundering, but shall shortly—since my tour is drawing toward its close—begin on the three complete fresh outfits in my valise . . . . though these include the shirt with the too-large neckband which I wore away, & which was laundered in Charleston. Haven't had time to answer much mail—but if tomorrow has decent weather I may take along some letters & answer them in the Japanese Garden. Clark Ashton Smith's new stories—one in particular—are splendid.

And so it goes. Will give further details of the week's programme in subsequent bulletins, & shall be turning up in person before long. Hope there has been some decent weather in Providence, & that you have managed to get out & enjoy a little of it. Now for some rest before the clothes-pressing expedition. Belknap has a tailor in 101st St. who presses suits for **35¢**.

Yr aff Nephew & obt Servt
H P L

P.S. I enclose an interesting article on Wedgwood ware from today's Sunday Tribune.

Notes

1. The Brooklyn Bridge is a suspension bridge spanning the East River, completed in 1883, from designs by John Augustus Roebling (1806–1869). After an injury to his foot left him incapacitated and led to his death, his son Washington Augustus Roebling (1837–1926) took over the project. Washington Roebling died on 21 July 1926, which was indeed Hart Crane's birthday. When Crane was writing *The Bridge*, he lived at the Roebling House at 110 Columbia Heights, Brooklyn. HPL visited him in 1924 (see LDC/AEPG 74).

2. See Bibliography under Roerich Museum.

3. In his memoir, "Some Random Memories of H.P.L." (1944), FBL records his impressions of hearing HPL read a draft of "The Whisperer in Darkness": "Howard's voice becoming suddenly sepulchral: 'And from the box a tortured voice spoke: "Go while there is still time—"'" (Cannon, *Lovecraft Remembered* 186). HPL significantly revised the story based on comments made by FBL and especially by Bernard Austin Dwyer.

[318]   [ALS] [HPL to LDC]

Tuesday–Wednesday Midnight
May 27–8, 1930

My dear Daughter:—

Your welcome letter arrived this morning, & I perused both text & enclosures with the keenest interest. Sorry to hear that you have been less well than usual of late, & hope that an early spell of good warm weather will dispel the trouble & enable you to get some healthy outdoor air. Delilah will no doubt be as useful as usual—but don't let her upheave my room too much, since I'll be back in it in less than a week! Yes—the small cheque came, but was for only 67¢. I can imagine the pile of 2nd, 3d, & 4th class mail awaiting me—also the papers since April 24! I have not had time to answer most of the mail which was forwarded here, but intend to take an afternoon in some park & dispose of it; so that I may have all my time for reading up the papers when I get home. Majority chances are for a direct trip by coach Sunday or Monday, though slight variations might possibly occur. Mortonius says the aëroplane fare has been cut to $14.00, & that he is going that way when he makes his visit next month. Wish I could do it—but it looks improbable this time. No further remittances seem necessary in order to complete the visit & return by direct coach. It surely has been a great trip, though the weather has not furnished much enjoyment since my return North. Today & the day before were barbarously raw—so much so Monday that I wore my overcoat. I shall, however, be mailing that venerable relique home before long; together with my oft-amateur-laundered outfit of underwear. Some items in the latter are so ragged that you may decide they are not worth a trip to Mr. Seagrave's establishment in Somerset St!

The enclosures are all extremely interesting—especially the programmes of the occasion when A E P G performed such valuable antiquarian service. I shall preserve this material for my files. B K H is as interesting as usual—I shall be eager to peruse the feast which his accumulated Sideshows since Apr. 24 will present. The variants of the old "mus cucurrit" rhyme[1] are interesting to observe—but I regret to say that the biblical riddle wholly stumps me. I might have a clue if I were still at the Charleston or Philadelphia Y M C A's, or at Murphy's Hotel in Richmond; all of which hospitable taverns had a neat & not at all used-looking bible reposing on the bureau of each room! I'll try the riddle on Sonny & James Ferdinand tomorrow. The item about the slightly elderly negress in North Carolina is a good testimonial to the healthfulness of the south—but what are her mere 121 years as compared with the *156* years of the old Turk whose picture appeared in last Sunday's Times rotogravure section? This old fellow—still spry & active—was born in *1774*, before these colonies revolted against His Majesty's lawful authority, & when the 1st Baptist steeple was still unbuilt! He was a definitely elderly man when Poe lived in the Fordham cottage & lingered around the alcoves of the Athenaeum in Providence . . . . yet here he still is! Long life to him![2] Speaking of the Times—there's no hurry at all about reading it. I have read all the issues, so that you can do just as you wish with the copies at home. I have cut out all the things I want, & have included them in the various packages mailed home to myself. Incidentally, there are splendid articles both on the South & on New England in the magazine section of last Sunday's issue.

Delighted to hear that your clock is going again—indeed, I had been advising that you have an expert come & fix it. Its delicate ticking & musical striking certainly lend a homelike quality to the atmosphere of any room. I doubt if mine would go without a considerable amount of repair, since it has been silent since the winter of 1925–26. It has never ticked a single tick at 10 Barnes St! Glad there has been a fire at #10 on the cold days—but depend on old Vulcan whether the furnace is operating or not! I'll wager there was a fire last night—for it grew viciously cold here. Monday was the coldest May 26th ever recorded since the N.Y. department of the weather bureau was established half a century ago. What a place the North is—only 2 months in all the year any good! Glad the muffin plan is working—but the chances are that Mr. Sherman will see "Mr. Clark" next Tuesday! For other ordering, the telephone is doubtless useful. I am getting my list ready for next week—cheese, downyflakes, grapefruit, pineapple, cup cakes, muffins, & nut bread, plus anything you may have to add when the time comes.

As for my diary—I rose Monday, May 26, at 10 a.m., & sallied forth in a borrowed suit of Belknap's to get my own pressed . . . . a matter of some 2 hours, during which I had my boots blacked & finished the N Y Times. After lunch—Belknap wishing to rest on the couch—I made a solitary trip to the Brooklyn Museum to see the new American Wing, & was utterly delighted by the splendid amplitude of the exhibit; which includes not only individual *rooms* of ancient houses, but whole *groups* of rooms in their original relationship, so that one may see them as they actually were in the old days. What it amounts to is displaying the *entire ground floor* of many of the houses in question—hall, staircase, & all the contiguous rooms. In some cases even the front door & a portion of the *exterior* are added—the arrangement being a clever system of corridors which isolates each group or section, one from the other. The apex of this kind of thing is attained in the presentation of the old Schenck house (Dutch 18th century) which I saw two years ago in Canarsie Park in the last stages of disintegration. This house has actually been removed in all entirety, timber by timber, to the museum, & set up again on the vast third floor just as it was—outside & inside—except that the peak of the gambrel roof had to be omitted on account of the museum ceiling. Naturally, each room or group of rooms—or *entire house* in the Schenck case—is furnished with the authentic furniture & accessories of its period, so that the illusion of antiquity is virtually perfect. It is astonishing how much more lifelike a *hallway & group of rooms* is, than a single specimen room. But of course there are many single rooms—in cases where groups were not obtainable; among these being the room which formed the chief object of my visit—the parlour of the Joseph Russell house (Clarendon Hotel—now housing the Providence District Nursing Association) in our own North Main St. I enclose a card shewing this magnificent object, & am pleased to say that it is regarded as the finest specimen of its kind in the whole exhibit, notwithstanding its relatively small size. Its panelling & decoration are exquisite & unique examples of middle Georgian architecture, in many details shewing a technique peculiar to Providence. The mantel is especially fine, & forms the frontispiece of the Museum Bulletin which describes the exhibit. Probably you recall what it looks like from illustrated articles which appeared last winter in both the Sunday Journal & the N Y Times, but the card will refresh your memory. The triangular pediment & pilasters are characteristically Providian. As you may know, this house was erected in 1773 by Joseph Russell, one of two brothers who had risen to wealth & prominence in the middle 18th century—first through a shop on Weybosset Point near the Great

Bridge, & later in the triangular trade of rum, niggers, & molasses. The Russells were a distinctly newer generation of rich Providentians than the Browns, Crawfords, &c., but were not at all inferior in taste. During the revolution this house formed the headquarters of Comte de Chastellux, & it is now (since the wanton destruction of the Nicholas Brown house in S. Main St. behind the Brick Row) one of only *two* Providence buildings which housed French officers at that time—the other being the Joseph Brown house (1774) with the cyma-curved pediment—now housing the Brown & Ives interests, & copied in the Gas Co. building. The interior of the Russell house is probably devoid of all original panelling by this time—since I hear that another room is now in a museum at Minneapolis. The other antiquarian items at Brooklyn include a group of rooms from a Maryland house of *1665* (with panelling added in 1720), a group from a 1758 house in North Carolina (with mantels of a type peculiar to certain parts of the South), a great dining hall from a mansion (1806) near CHARLESTON (i.e., from Summerville, a town in the midst of a moss-hung pine forest 24 miles inland, through which my coach passed), a pair of rooms (1820) from Irvington, N.J., & rooms & groups from Danbury & Wethersfield, Conn., & Springfield, Mass. All this besides the complete Schenck house. In general, this exhibit may be held to rival anything of its kind in the world—its uniqueness making comparison difficult. It is not equal in scope to the exhibit in the Boston Museum, & is perhaps arranged with less *educational* effect than the famous American Wing of the Metropolitan, where periods correspond to floors. In the matter of historic origins, the Philadelphia Museum surpasses it—on account of the rich array of British Georgian rooms. But many details of plan make the Brooklyn exhibit valuable & distinctive; hence I believe it belongs in the very front rank of its type. I obtained a full quota of illustrated booklets; which I shall soon mail home to myself, & which you will soon therefore see.

Having explored the museum, I started to visit my old-time favourite Japanese Garden—where we got lost, or rather shut in, in Dec. 1924—but found it temporarily closed for spring gardening work. However—it might have seemed very barren & pallid after glorious MAYMONT in Richmond. I then crossed over to Prospect Park, viewing the Lefferts Cottage & traversing some of my long-accustomed paths. This glorious park still holds its own—& has adopted a new plan of protecting its grass-plots by means of wire-netting fences near those entrances most infested by crowds. After the park I visited my old Flatbush barber—Signor D'Adamo—in Parkside Ave.; since I had to get a haircut for the meeting, yet have not a good light in this room for using my patent Trimette. The shop & its staff of artists looked much the same, though the district is more & more crowded & noisy. Sig. D'Adamo gave me a splendid cut—my first professional haircut since December—which blended well with the new-pressed suit & new-blacked shoes. Then, after a glance at my favourite Georgian steeple in Church Ave.—my first in 2 years—I took the B M T for Manhattan & proceeded to Hearn's to see about some decent collars. I found the Van York type (which I bought in Charleston) obsolete, but hit upon another similar type (called "Van Ince") which I like even better. The question of *size* is still a moot one—varying betwixt 14 & 14¼. I obtained the latter, but am almost sorry I did, since they seem distinctly too large for me . . . . despite the way Belknap's gift-collar fitted in Charleston. But one thing is certain—& that is that I can no longer wear those absurd 14¾ Arrow Tides. I think my neck must be smaller—must have actually contracted through some shrinkage of tendons—since those 14¾'s are now so bad that I can't keep my necktie in place with them. I shall either give them to Eddy or put them in retirement with other too-large collars. After my Hearn call I returned to 230 & had the usual excessive dinner with the Long household—then setting out with Sonny for the gang meeting at Talman's. Talman's new apartment on the top floor is exceedingly tasteful & colonially furnished. A good quota attended—Mortonius, Kleiner, Loveman, & McGrath,—though Kirk was unable to come. Our arguments covered all known subjects as usual, & the gathering dispersed at about 1 a.m. It was good to see old Kleiner again—& I am told that he is slowly drifting back to contact with the old crowd after a long period of invisibility. He even says he may get around to Providence one of these days! He does not age visibly except that his hair is rapidly turning grey—even greyer than my own few remaining spears. Otherwise he is still the same lean, languid Kleiner of other days. After the meeting I returned to 230, deposited The Child at his proper floor, & ascended to my 7th floor to write letters & eventually to retire. Tuesday the 27th I arose at noon, lunched excessively (why *will* they serve such irresistibly tempting stuff *twice* a day?) at Belknap's, & set out with that young cynic for a combined shopping trip & call on Kirk. At Hearn's I changed one of the 14¼ collars for a 14, (haven't tried it yet, but I think that will be my eventual size—old men get shrunken & withered) & bought three bargain ties which seem in every way superior to last year's "bargains" at Bloomingdale's. Sonny also stocked up on ties. We then proceeded to Kirk's shop in W. 8th St., & were pleased to find good old G K in his usual genial state. He wears that new moustache—as well as his hair—longer than I'd recommend, but outside of that he's all right! During the course of discussion he gave me two books—one a fine sidelight on colonial life at Princeton College,[3] & the other a variorum edition of the Rubaiyat which I wanted to send my correspondent Woodburn Harris—an Omar enthusiast. Nothing could make him take pay for either. He also gave Sonny Wells's Outline of History. Subsequently we took a 5th Ave. omnibus back to 230—following the same Riverside Drive route which I followed in April 1922, when I first called on Belknap. Arriving in good season, we overate as usual—& later the whole outfit swept me off to a cinema again . . . . . as mediocre a show as the rest I've seen on this visit! Despite the recent improvement in quality in some films—due to the new talking device—the majority are as inane & insipid as before; but the Longs go just the same, whether or not the performance is any good. I don't see how Belknap manages to keep awake—but it's all right when one is invited & doesn't have to pay the price of admission! After the show I ascended to my 7th floor, began preparing my superfluous paraphernalia for mailing home, & began this epistle . . . . which I shall hold over for the morrow.

Wednesday–Thursday Midnight
May 28–29, 1930.

Well—I rose Wednesday at noon & at once descended to Belknap's for overeating (what a tale the scales would tell if I dared get on them!!)—having as my fellow-guest that prince of all overeaters & scales-strainers, James Ferdinand Morton. It was a chill, drizzly day—but no day is dull when good old James Ferdinand is around & arguing, hence the time passed swiftly & pleasantly till he had to break away at 3 p.m. Sonny then proceeded to drag his aged Grandpa out to another of those eternal cinemas—perhaps as an antidote against Mortonian intellect—which carried the hour up to 6 p.m. Then some discussion & more overeating—& after that another discussion period extending to 10 p.m. At that hour I walked out with the Child whilst he gave Canis his nightly airing, & subsequently I ascended to my eyrie to write & eventually to retire.

Tomorrow (Thursday) Belknap will hold a gang meeting at 230—though Mortonius can't attend. Friday a motor trip will probably occur. Saturday I may get in touch with Kirk during the daytime, & at 6:45 I have a dinner-&-evening engagement with Kleiner & Loveman. Sunday I may start moving & may stay over. Monday I shall in any case be in motion. Just had a note from Dwyer cordially urging me not to omit the Kingston part of my schedule, but I fear it would take another five-spot to let me do it. I hate to call on the home bank for further funds—yet it would be glorious to see the old Catskill region, ride the Mohawk Trail, & descend on Providence through Athol & Worcester as originally planned! Incidentally—the last day for catching me with forwarded mail is the holiday Friday—so if you don't get this before then, send no more to 230. No delivery Sunday—& I'll be leaving Monday morning before the mail arrives. See you shortly, & hope you'll be feeling better by the time this arrives.

Yr aff Nephew & obt Servt
H P L

P.S. I think I'll send this by Special Delivery so you can get it Friday—in time to reach me if it is convenient for you to mail the 5-spot which would make the Kingston–Mohawk Trail return route possible. But don't try to do it if it would be any inconvenience—for there may be no one in the house to mail the reply on the holiday. See you later![4]

[P.P.S.] No—I'll send the special to A.E.P.G.

Notes

1. HPL refers to the macaronic rhyme "Mus cucurrit plenum sed / Contra magnum meum ad" ("A mouse ran full but / Against my big toe").
2. Zaro Aga (1777–1934) of Istanbul, Turkey, was of Kurdish origin. Allegedly aged 157 when he died.
3. By William Paterson.
4. HPL has crossed out the entire P.S.

[319]   [HPL to LDC]

[c. 10 June 1930]

[Letter nonextant. On envelope:] Hurrah! Rain has stopped—so my newly pressed suit is saved!

[320]   [ALS] [HPL to LDC]

451 Main St.,
Athol, Maſs.,
June 11, 1930
2 a.m.

My dear Daughter:—

I take my pen in hand to complete my diary for TUESDAY, JUNE 10, 1930—which ended with my emergence from Mr. J. Jasins' tailor shop in Exchange St., Athol, opposite the Transcript office. The rain which ended so providentially did not begin again, hence Mr. Jasins' handiwork has not suffered up to date. I also had my shoes blacked—a much needed measure.

After all these repairs I paid Cook another call, & subsequently took reading matter to a bench in Phillips Park (the triangular common of the upper village)—my favourite loafing-place in urban Athol. At five I rejoined Cook & proceeded with him to Munn's, the scene of my present visit, where Munn & his father gave us a cordial welcome. We then set out to see the new place to which Munn is about to move—a very pleasing house on a steep hillside just outside the settled district, & having many of the aspects of a country home. Returning to the present Munn home, (the apartment-floor above Woolworth's at 451 Main St., where Cook used to live 10 or 15 years ago) we found the new Mrs. Munn arrived from her work (she is employed at the Woolworth store underneath) & with dinner ready. After dinner we started forth on an expedition in Munn's car—a cheap second-hand Buick—to that rock waterfall & gorge in the deep woods (Bear's Den) which we visited in 1928. The ancient New England scenery along the route—narrow, wind-

ing, hilly road, stone walls, farmhouses & sheds, rocky rolling pastures, mysterious forests, &c. &c.—impressed me tremendously after my absence of a
month & a half from such things; & confirmed me in my belief that no other
region has natural landscapes even comparable to those of this favoured section. In balance of elements & weirdness of archaic suggestion, the New England vista stands alone. Bear's Den itself impressed me as much as it did two
years ago, & I marvel that it is so little known & visited. It stands unspoiled
today, just as it was when the first Indian to penetrate these forests beheld it
as a surprise & stood awed at its majesty. The rock cliffs of the gorge are
honeycombed with fissures & small caves—black orifices of a nether world
whose depths are yet unplumbed. Beasts of the wood make their lairs within
these openings—from the largest of which the place derives its name. After
seeing this natural wonder we cruised about the countryside absorbing colour
& atmosphere—visiting several spectral graveyards & pausing by the old
stone set up in 1777 to mark the passing of a detachment of Hessian prisoners taken by the rebels at the battle of Saratoga. These Hessians were later
quartered at Rutland, (the place where the R.I. Senators fled during the
Toupin legislative turmoil of 1924)[1] & more than half of them remained &
settled there—leaving descendants who still inhabit the region. Returning to
Munn's, we discussed general topics—& Munn shewed me the room I was to
occupy. Facilities are somewhat primitive, but I can make out very well with a
large washbowl. Munn's flat is a peculiar one, with many of the rooms on the
inside, destitute of windows save those opening on dimly lit corridors. Mine
is such an one—but that is no hardship to me, as you can well imagine. The
rent of the whole place—5 rooms—is only $12.00 per *month* (not week!).
Munn's plan of supporting himself wholly by writing did not materialise well,
so that he has returned to his old job of driving a nitroglycerine truck for high
wages. His wife also works at Woolworth's. With this steady income he now
feels justified in moving to better quarters—hence the newly rented house on
the idyllic rural hillside. He & Cook have each bought an aged & second-hand
Buick automobile, & it is amusing to hear them compare notes on their respective luck. Munn, being apt in a mechanical way, is faring better than
Cook—having spent only $1.50 (to Cook's $12.00) for repairs so far. You will
undoubtedly see both of these archaic reliques before the summer is over—
unless they shake to pieces first—since Cook & Munn each intend to come
to Providence on one or more occasions. They are of the old open pattern—
built about 10 years ago, I imagine, before closed types became so universal.

Well—after a time we adjourned to take Cook home in Munn's car.
Cook is boarding about two miles out in the open country—toward the farm
he owned last year—with a man who needs his rent money very badly. He
would rather live in town, but pities his destitute rural landlord so much that
he has not the heart to leave & deprive the fellow of his rent! That's good old
Cook all over! On a second inspection, I don't think Cook is in quite as bad

shape as I assumed at first glance. He was unshaven & in old clothes, & the dim light of the print-shop exaggerated the twist in his mouth. Munn says he is *prodigiously* better than he was in January, & that the steady upward curve of his health & equilibrium is such as to give ground for much optimism. But five months ago he was by all accounts a most alarming sight. Having deposited Cook at his lodging-place—a not very inviting farmhouse, so far as I could judge from the brief nocturnal glimpse I had—Munn & I returned to 451 Main for a final period of discussion. Munn brought out several samples of his recent work for criticism, & I shall read them at leisure—some here & some after I get home—giving him an opinion on them at a later date. One of them is an article on popular weird fiction for *The Recluse*—an issue of which is now partly on the press, though it may not appear for another year.[2] At 11 p.m. the Munn household retired, & I began writing letters in Munn's study, where I still am. He has a truly impressive library of weird & pseudo-scientific fiction, & it tantalises me to see on the shelves so many alluring volumes which I have no time to read. Munn & Cook are insisting that I stay over Friday, when they expect to have some leisure for long-term discussion & possible scenic exploration. I shall accordingly shew up at 10 Barnes around Saturday or Sunday—whether or not accompanied by Cook I can't yet say. Being lodged by Munn, I am all right financially even if I have to pay motor-coach fare. It will now be easy to get home by coach, since there is a direct Athol–Worcester line—via Petersham & Barre—which did not exist when last I was here. I shall have dinners with the Munn household, but will probably get my cheese-sandwich breakfast independently, in order not to be tied down to any set programme. I shall rise when I choose—probably being alone in the house at the time. Given a key, I can come & go as I wish. Munn is surely a cordial & generous host, & I highly appreciate his hospitality. His household consists of himself, his wife—a pleasantly undistinctive but doubtless sensible & congenial person—& his father, a small, kindly, gentle man of later middle age, whose diminutive physique contrasts oddly with the burly bulk of his athletic son.

Wednesday, June 11, 1930—2 p.m.

Well—I retired at 2 a.m. & slept till 11 o'clock. Then rising, I found the house deserted; so went out to get a sandwich & ice cream at Liggett's & pay a brief call on Cook at the Transcript office. After that—noting the occasional greyness of the sky—I proceeded to a bench on the lower common (nearer the centre of the town than my favourite Phillips Park in the upper village) to do my usual reading & letter-writing. I am still there, & shall remain there throughout the afternoon unless bad weather drives me to cover or good weather tempts me into an expedition to some of the rural spots I know—such as the hill across the bridge where the lordly Sentinel Elm still dominates the landscape as it has done since the settlement was founded in 1735. At 5 o'clock I shall drop around to Cook's office, & with him proceed back to

Munn's for dinner & another evening of trilateral discussion. Tomorrow's programme depends wholly on the weather. Given a good day, I shall take a solitary expedition to the wild woods & hills, & absorb more of that indefinable New England colour from which I have been separated for a month & a half. Naturally, you will receive more bulletins. ¶ Yr aff Nephew & obt Servt

H P L

P.S. One good old New England thing which gave me a thrill of homecoming was the sight of *white poles* along the still surviving Athol trolley line. This symbol for a car-stop does not exist outside N.E.

[On envelope? In RHB's handwriting:] Shower just set in—have retreated to the nearby Post Office to write. ¶ Shower stopped again—back to park!

Notes

1. In 1923, Felix A. Toupin (1886–1965), lieutenant governor of Rhode Island, and other Democrats introduced a series of progressive measures in the state legislature. After facing months of resistance from the Senate, Toupin conducted a 42-hour filibuster, leading to fistfights and the use of a bromine gas bomb in the Senate chamber. The senators fled to Rutland, Mass. The progressive measures did not pass, since the chamber now lacked a quorum. Toupin later became mayor of Woonsocket (1930–36, 1939–40).

2. No issue of the *Recluse* appeared aside from the first issue of 1927.

[321]   [ALS] [HPL to LDC]

Athol—
June 12, 1930

My dear Daughter:—

　　　　　I take my pen in hand to continue my diary for WEDNESDAY, JUNE 11, 1930 & extend it to the following day. At last reports I was dodging showers by vacillating betwixt Fish Park (the lower common) & the Post Office, & I am pleased to record that sunshine won over rain & gave the town a delectable late afternoon, with golden, glamorous light & a mystically lovely sunset afterward. After sending all my letters, I began reading up some of Munn's recent work—which I found excellent in content though lamentably slipshod in style. One tale of his—with a hideous submarine setting—could be a distinguished thing of its kind if he would polish it up—as indeed he intends to do. After finishing this tale I proceeded to Cook's office & was exceedingly pained to find him indisposed & about to go home instead of joining in a festive & literary evening. His old chronic appendicitis was troubling him again, & all he could do was to rest & abstain from nourishment. He ought to have his appendix removed; but so great is his dread of an operation that he prefers to limp along & take his chances without this relief. In view of this unfortunate development, we all piled into Munn's car & went out to the country where Cook has his lodging. The region itself is exquisitely beautiful—old New England in its most typical aspect—& from Cook's study window (he has two rooms on the second story of the farmhouse) there is a marvellously fine view of rolling meadow, deep woods, stone wall, & pasture bars. But the house itself is so squalid, & so overrun with the five unkempt children of Cook's needy landlord, that I do not see how Cook can stand such an environment. It would drive me mad in a couple of hours—but tastes & degrees of sensitivity obviously differ. Munn, though, vows that he could not stand it, rugged & hard-boiled though he professes to be. From Cook's preparations for settlement, I judge that his plan for moving into town is not as definite as I had gathered the night before. Doubtless his quarters will be less repulsive when he has them furnished & shut off from the lower floor over which the landlord's slovenly family are sprawled. This landlord is a sort of broken-down printer called "Shorty", who has lately taken—none too successfully—to farming. In the yard of this uninviting ruin I beheld Cook's new investment—the old Buick car which he bought when Munn bought his—& must amend my former statement that they are exact duplicates. Whilst Munn's is an open model of *1916*—fourteen years old—Cook's is a more modern closed car, probably not over four or five years old. It is not, however, in such mechanically good condition as Munn's antiquarian relique; so that the bargain-value of the respective purchases is probably about equal. But what interested me most of all at the farm were the *kitties*. The prettiest of them is a little tiger about ⅓ grown; but the most historically interesting is the full-grown cat which I saw as a tiny handful of fur last year when I visited Cook. You may recall my mentioning this specimen in my final bulletins from Athol on the former trip—Cook got it the very day I arrived, & it made its first trip to the old farm in my lap as I sat in Cook's old Whippet car. You may also recall how worried I was about its welfare when the Cooks accompanied me to Providence & left it locked in the house—& how relieved I was when Cook later wrote that he had called up Athol on the long distance telephone from Norwich to give instructions about its feeding. Well—little Togo (for so Mrs. Cook's 6-year-old grandson named him) is now a rather big Togo, but is still flourishing! He has had his accidents, though—including a 75-foot fall from a tree, which shook him up most painfully but did not injure him permanently. From his pleasant demeanour toward me I infer that he recognised the aged friend of his youth. Incidentally—my joy at finding Togo intact was somewhat offset by the news which Cook transmitted from the Beebe–Miniter farm in Wilbraham, where he visited last week. It seems that at least two of my seven furry friends there—the venerable Printer, born in 1911, & the scarcely less patriarchal Old Fats, who followed people about through the fields like a dog, having suc-

cumbed to the grim reaper's scythe at last. Eheu, fugaces![1] Old Printer was
the last of an elder civilisation, & knew secret passages through the walls &
up the chimney of the farmhouse (cf. my travel-letters, June 28–July 7, 1928)
which none of the younger cats could ever discover![2] But speaking of cats—
Munn has just obtained the most captivating little white kitten (with grey
touches on head & tail) that I ever saw in my life! This exquisite little atom of
purring & playfulness arrived on the very day that I did, (history thus repeating itself—since last year Cook got his kitten on the day that I arrived!) & has
ever since formed the centre of interest in the Munn household. Kittie realis-
es that Grandpa Theobald is very fond of his species, for he constantly makes
for the Old Gentleman's lap & sleeps or kicks or chews there during long
hours of reading, writing, & discussion. His adoptive family seem to appreciate him highly, & I trust he is destined for as long & honourable a life as
Printer of Wilbraham, who rounded out 19 well-spent years. Returning to the
main thread of the narrative—having bidden Cook a reluctant farewell, Munn
& I returned to 451 & had dinner, (heaven help my weight! According to the
Liggett scales it's almost 141, as against 139 on June 7th!) & afterwards began
the job of moving the Munn possessions to the new house on the suburban
hill. A young friend came over with his car to help in the process, & betwixt
the two vehicles a marvellous amount of stuff was transferred. I helped occasionally in details, & was impressed with the excellence of the new home. I
am sure Kittie will like it when he is taken over. At the present rate, Munn
ought to be all moved within a week. I did considerable rambling around the
hills behind Munn's new place. From the crest just above the house a magnificent view of plains & mountains—with the spires of Athol in the valley—is
obtainable. Going over that crest & descending to the ravine beyond, one encounters some incredibly glamorous old New England vistas—including a
stream, an old plank bridge, a waterfall descending over the moss-grown masonry of a long-vanished mill, & a sleepy old crossroads hamlet with two or
three crumbling colonial houses. The magical effect of such a scene in the
spectral twilight is almost beyond description, & confirms the fact that no
other region has even half the poignant landscape distinctiveness of New
England. Landscapes like this have a deeply ingrained character, & exude a
positive kind of antiquity. To enter one is almost like walking at will through
time & space, or climbing bodily into some strange picture which hangs on
the wall. I disagree with that Distaff article of Mrs. Allinson's in which it is
stated that New England landscapes lack the element of the weird & the macabre. To me they possess it as no other landscape does. Only in New England do I feel that odd undercurrent of sinister & unholy life in the brooding
fields & woods, & the little huddled farmhouses. Elsewhere I find *antiquity*,
but never *concealed terror*. Terror is the legacy of a long Puritan heritage with its
unnatural philosophy—the heritage of Salem, Endicott, & the Mathers—& only those visible symbols closely connected with this system possess the terror-

element to a complete degree. It is significant that I find this macabre atmosphere infinitely stronger in Massachusetts than in the comparatively non-Puritan Rhode Island. Well—returning to the diary—we returned to 451 at last, & Munn & I sat till midnight discussing weird fiction. After he retired, I read in Montague Summers' scholarly treatise on vampires till 5 a.m., then retiring myself. Through all these hours Little Kittie kept the Old Gentleman company—warding off any evil shapes of darkness which the perusal of so hideous a text might otherwise have evoked.

DIARY FOR THURSDAY, JUNE 12, 1930

Rose at noon & lunched at a one-arm diner. Then over to Cook's office & discovered that he is too indisposed to be at work today. Poor chap! Munn & I must go out this evening & see how he is. Probably this development will spoil all plans for tomorrow—when Cook had intended to go with me to Brattleboro to see Goodenough. Just now I am again writing in Fish Park—or the lower common—since the skies look almost as ambiguous as they did yesterday at this hour (2 p.m.) If it sprinkles I shall repeat my former procedure of retiring to the neighbouring P.O. As it is, I expect to write & read here till 5 o'clock, when I shall return to Munn's. In the evening—weather & circumstances permitting—Munn intends to drive me to some strange & glamorous waterfall in the mystical woodlands far from the paths of mankind.
More soon—
Yr aff Nephew & obt Servt
H P L

Notes

1. A quotation from Horace: *Eheu, fugaces* . . . / *labuntur anni* (*Odes* 2.14.1–2): "Alas, the swift years glide by."
2. It was probably around this time that HPL wrote a series of poems about Miniter's pets, entitled "Veteropinguis Redivivus" (*AT* 188–91).

[322]   [ALS] [HPL to LDC]

Friday the 13th
[13 June 1930]

My dear Daughter:—
Well—there's about a 50–50 chance that you'll see me on the same day that you receive this final bulletin; but I'll prepare it just the same in order to keep the record complete & save conversation for local topics upon my arrival. Let me, then, continue the diary for

THURSDAY, JUNE 12, 1930.

At the time of my last entry I was writing under doubtful skies in Fish Park. Well—it finally cleared as it did the day before, leaving a glorious late-afternoon & evening. At 5 p.m. I went back to 451 & met Munn, after which we went out to Cook's place in the ancient Buick. Cook was in his dressing-gown but up & around, & badly frightened at the prospect of having to go to the hospital & have the dreaded appendicitis operation. The doctor had called twice, & was scheduled to call again; but the application of ice-packs had vastly diminished the pain. After this call Munn & I returned to his house—but with the design of calling again on Cook later in the evening. After dinner Munn took me to see the scenic marvel he had promised—Doane's Falls, in the woods of Royalston, northeast of Athol—& I was utterly astonished at the breathless loveliness of this natural wonder—a thing wholly unknown to the world at large, though increasingly appreciated in Athol, & now set aside as a park reservation like Quinsnicket. The route to the falls involves some of the finest mountain vistas I have ever beheld—sights comparable to those of the Mohawk Trail itself—& when one reaches the reservation a detour through the woods is made; ending in a glen containing the picturesque ruined foundations of an ancient factory. To the left the roar of waters is heard; & upon approaching the sound one discovers a magnificent wooded gorge or cañon whose lower walls are of solid rock, & through which rushes the stream forming the various cataracts. Immediately within view is a splendid cascade about 15 feet wide & 5 or 6 feet high—& many uninformed persons (so Munn relates) mistake this for the main falls, & go away without penetrating the region any farther. This is, however, really a mere prologue to the main show; as one soon learns upon advancing along the edge of the gorge. The climax comes after about an eighth of a mile, when the eye beholds a mighty torrent in two tiers with a basin between—the first a narrow, raging flood easily 100 feet from brink to bottom, & the second a stupendous affair 30 or 40 feet wide & something under 100 feet in height—probably the greatest waterfall I have ever seen in my life, except the falls of the Passaic at Paterson, which are spoiled by their urban & mechanised setting—& perhaps the falls of the Blackstone at Pawtucket. Its nearest rival in my experience—Buttermilk Falls, in the woods near Paterson—was not in full splendour when I saw it in 1925, owing to dry weather. The closest thing to it which I have seen is probably one of the waterfalls in the woods near Brattleboro, Vt. We climbed all over the banks of the gorge—which are steep & rocky—& had the thrill of discovering the narrow upper cataract (which is concealed from the lower falls by a bend in the cañon wall bordering the intervening basin) after we had thought our sightseeing complete. There is still another cascade farther down stream, but this is a relatively minor one. As a scenic paradise, I am forced to admit that this great forest with its gorge & cataracts surpasses anything in my beloved Quinsnicket.

After this sight we returned to Cook's & found that the doctor had been there in our absence. He had advised Cook to go [to] an hospital at Montague—a suburb of Greenfield—for a more thorough series of tests; & this Cook had agreed to do on the morrow. He urged the operation as by far the most sensible course—for the trouble will always be a brooding menace until Cook has the inflamed appendix out—but Cook dreads the thing so that I doubt if he will consent. Cook was feeling much better, & talked on general topics as usual. He will drive to the hospital himself, & says he will probably join us again Friday evening. Indeed, he still harbours the plan of coming down to Providence with me tomorrow or Sunday—though I shall urge him to do this on the 'bus & avoid the strain of driving. Can he get a room at #10 if he does?

Well—upon leaving Cook, Munn drove the car for a moonlight jaunt along the Petersham road (which is also the road to Providence)—the great round moon being an ineffably glamorous sight over the stone walls & rolling fields of the ancient New England scene. It was as if some residue of the 1692 witchcraft were in the air, & I almost expected to see some bizarre & terrible form silhouetted against the mystical coppery disc which loomed hugely above the centuried farmhouse roofs & hoary New England elms. An ancient moon above an ancient land—to what greater extent can glamour & mystery be carried? At length we returned to 451 & spent much time in reading & discussion. Among other things we spoke of the splendid *artificial leather* manufactured by the company for which Munn does his nitroglycerine trucking. He is an enthusiast upon the subject of this product, & has always used it extensively in the binding of home made books—although its primary use is for the upholstering of furniture. Mention of this topic reminded me of your urging that I get some enamel-cloth for the repair of my decrepit books, & I asked Munn what the price of a moderate-sized square would be. In reply, he told me that he had in the attic a plethora of scraps & samples, of which I was welcome to take as much as I could use—free of charge—& at my signs of interest he led the way upward to the storage domain. The samples there displayed were truly alluring in their texture & variety; & I chose for a principal piece a rich brown surface admirably in accord with the tone & spirit of my library. But I could not resist annexing a few other scraps as well—including rich & exotic gold & silver fabrics which truly form a joint aesthetic & mechanical triumph. These latter are too gay for the uses of a sedate old man; but I fancy you may like them yourself for some purpose or other, since they cannot but appeal profoundly to your sense of harmony & colour. I am mailing these home to myself today—so that they will probably not arrive until after I do. I suppose I could have crowded them in the valise—but I hate to be any more burdened than I have to be.

After the family retired, I continued to read in the Rev. Montague Summers' hideous vampire book, whilst the little white kittie climbed up & down me & rolled about in my lap or on the nightmare pages before me. At 3 a.m. I retired—though little kittie shewed no signs of diminishing his liveliness as I left him to his own devices in the library.

FRIDAY, JUNE 13, 1930

Today—Friday the 13th—I arose at 11 a.m. & found Munn temporarily home from work. He induced me to return at noon for lunch, instead of patronising my usual one-arm diner; since his sister-in-law was visiting & cooking a somewhat elaborate meal for the family. For the brief pre-prandial hour I went to Fish Park to write; but after dinner I sought the open country—Munn taking me in his car to a rural spot toward Orange, which formed a good beginning for a ramble. I shall circulate about at will among the ancient New England woods & fields & winding roads, pausing to read or write whenever I come to a particularly inviting rock or grassy bank by the wayside. I am now in such a place, but shall shortly move along to get a glimpse of Lake Rohunta—& later of the old covered bridge toward Athol. Here & there I come upon melancholy sights—a bit of forest ruined by axemen, or a prosaic wire fence indicating where a stone wall has been sold to some rock-crushing company; but in the main the terrain represents venerable, brooding, rustic New England in its most typical phase. There is here a charm & glamour found nowhere else in the world—a settled, restful, elder atmosphere just now accentuated by the tinkle of a distant cow-bell.

Well—at 5 p.m. I shall return to Munn's—where I shall either find Cook or have a message from the hospital that he is not coming. I hardly know which would be the best for him—to have the operation over & done with now, or to wait (as he has many times done before, after similar attacks) until some time when his general health is better. According to Munn, his breakdown last January was much more complete than I had thought. He shook & twitched fearsomely, & came close to the border of having actual hallucinations. Once his threats of suicide seriously alarmed all his associates, & Munn's father thinks that his peculiar way of holding his mouth & talking (manifest only at times) argues some kind of incipient shock—or some tendency approaching that affliction. But his improvement during the last month or two has been steady, with the exception of the present attack of his chronic appendicitis.

As I said, there is an even chance of my reaching good old Providence tomorrow, (Saturday)—perhaps accompanied by Cook. We may be in his car, but I shall advise him to use the 'bus instead. Worcester busses leave Athol at 9:15 a.m., 1:15 p.m., & 5:50 p.m.—& of course the Worcester–Providence service is very frequent. ¶ Well—I'll see you very shortly! ¶ Yr aff Nephew & obt Servt H P L

P.S. Cook says that my "Shunned House" has been at the bindery in Boston since last December. It will be ready in a few months.

[323]   [ALS] [HPL to LDC]

[3–4 July 1930]
Diary for Thursday,
July 3, 1930.

Caught the 3:30 coach & had a delightful ride through old New England countryside. Wrentham & Dedham are my favourite villages. Reached Boston at 5:25 & secured a room at those Technology Chambers (near the Back Bay station) which advertise in the Bulletin. It is a place just like the Y M C A.[1] But—confound it—*I forgot my bath sandals,* so will have to wear my shoes at all times to the bathroom! After changing my collar I found it was too late to look up the amateurs before keeping my 6 o'clock engagement, so hustled right over to 40 Beacon St. I saw *Morton* on the street, but couldn't stop to get his attention. The club house at Beacon St. is, as I had known, a magnificent old Bulfinch mansion; & the interior is equal to the exterior. Curved wall lines correspond harmoniously with the bayed front, (like the Halsey mansion) & the mantels & decorations are fine late-Georgian work. The *staircase* is a poem—& I am about to get some postcards of it. Miss Peirce is a delightfully stately & academic old Boston lady, & with her were two friends—one the Miss Stuart with whom she lives, & the other a splendidly attractive young man named Fitzgerald—a Bostonian now teaching in a Brooklyn school. After an excellent roast beef dinner we all gave the house an architectural survey, & are now in the exquisite writing room at 8 p.m. Fitzgerald is writing a diary letter to his mother—for he has my diary habit—& I am doing my usual diary act. Will add another instalment later. We shall go over to the Peirce–Stuart abode in S. Boston, & later in the evening I shall proceed to the Statler & see how James Ferdinand & the convention are getting along. The new 14¼ collar is a fine fit!

Till later in the evening
—Yr aff Nephew
H P L

DIARY CONTINUED

Thursday, July 3, 1930

After dropping you the line from the colonial writing-room of the city club, I proceeded to obtain postcards of the place—two of which I enclose. It is truly a Bulfinch masterpiece.

Everyone—Miſs Peirce, Miſs Stuart, young William Fitzgerald, & myself—then adjourned to the Park St. subway & took a car for South Boston, where is situate the quiet backwater inhabited by the Peirce-Stuart duo. The house is neat & quiet, tho' the neighbourhood is going down hill. The Miſses Peirce & Stuart have an entire floor, & their parlour is a veritable library & museum. Seldom have I seen so many curios in a private home, & there was a mineral collection which would have made Mortonius' mouth water. A coin collection also adds interest. Mifs P. talk'd most entertainingly of ancient times, & most generously presented me with two books on weird themes—one a very old & scarce one. I shall mail these home to myself, together with some other volumes lent me. The whole place is a veritable citadel of the old Boston spirit, & I can see that Mifs P. must be an admirable teacher of the ancient school—indeed, her former pupil, young Fitzgerald, said as much after we left; which we did about 11 p.m. Fitzgerald is a highly interesting young man—½ Irish of good stock, & the other half old New England—the Beecher family, of which the line of Henry Ward Beecher[2] is a very close branch.

Upon bidding Fitzgerald farewell, I took the car for Boston & proceeded to look up the convention at the Statler. Finding very little information, I left a note for Morton—telling him of my whereabouts & bidding him telephone me the next day. I then return'd to Technology Chambers, wrote letters, & retired at 2 a.m.

P.S. Saturday's programme is varied, & will include a boat trip on the Charles.

Friday, July 4, 1930

I was awak'd at 9 a.m. by Morton's telephone call, & at 10 went over to the Statler for the convention session. I had not missed much by being away Thursday, since the gathering had not then been complete. On this occasion many notable old-timers were present—some I had never seen before, & others whom I had not seen in many years. The most interesting delegate was the youthful Official Editor, Helm C. Spink of Indiana, who was reëlected to his office after declining the Presidency. He is a diabetic invalid, & has to be under constant medical care, but is cheerful & active for all that. He looks like a child of 14, but is actually about 25 years old. His intelligence, cultivation, & taste are very great, & his manner singularly attractive. I had several discussions with him, & he may accompany me on my antiquarian sightseeing—including Salem & Marblehead. Cook was not present. Bacon was elected president, & St. Louis chosen as the next convention seat. After the session all hands were the luncheon guests of Louis C. Wills, a wealthy old-timer present, & after that there was a session of discussion about the formation of a National Alumni Association.[3] When this adjourned, Spink & I took an historical walk around Beacon Hill—returning to the Statler at 6 p.m. & thence proceeding to a restaurant for the official dinner. This was a notable event, & brought out a surprising crowd of the local old-timers. I saw Cole, Little Sandy, Mrs. Sawyer, Lynch, Wylie, &c. &c.[4] Some of the old crowd have changed tremendously in the 7 years since I last saw them. Cole is getting fat!! Everyone was astonished at the results of my reducing. Lynch has had a nervous breakdown, & is still very shaky. After dinner all readjourned to the

Statler for the speeches—& Morton had a fit of childish madness because people talked & smiled when he was trying to make a long, rambling address. Most adjourned at midnight, but Morton & I & a promising young Newark recruit named Francis Richardson stayed on till 1 a.m. I then returned to Technology Chambers, wrote letters, & am retiring at 5 a.m. ¶ More anon. Yrs H P L

P.S. Among the convention guests was an elderly Toronto lady—Mrs Saunders—who is the author of the famous old book "Beautiful Joe."[5]

Notes

1. HPL was attending the annual convention of the National Amateur Press Association.
2. Henry Ward Beecher (1813–1887), an American Congregationalist clergyman, social reformer, and speaker.
3. Edwin Hadley Smith founded an alumni organization consisting primarily of NAPA veterans. Charles W. Heins later founded a similar organization consisting primarily of UAPA veterans. Neither is to be confused with the Fossils, an organization of alumni of the amateur journalism movement, founded in 1904.
4. HPL refers to the amateur journalists Edward H. Cole, Albert A. Sandusky, Laurie A. Sawyer, Joseph Bernard Lynch, and Willard Otis Wylie.
5. The book is the purported "autobiography" of a dog.

[324]   [ALS] [HPL to LDC]

Monday Morning
July 6, 1930

My dear Daughter:—
                    I take my pen in hand to continue my diary to the present time. On Saturday, July 5, I rose at 9 a.m. & proceeded to a session of the convention at the Statler. It was the final one of the business meetings, & its ending was marked with considerable humour by Edward H. Cole. Cole is as interesting as in older days, despite his new avoirdupois; & he says he hopes to do some antiquarian exploring with me in September, after his programme becomes more free. I took lunch at a restaurant across the street with Mortonius, who insisted on paying the check. Then, in the afternoon, everyone proceeded to the Berkeley St. landing at the Charles River Basin & had an official group photograph taken. I am on the left-hand end, next to young Helm A. [*sic*] Spink. Spink, by the way, will be in Boston a week more for his medical treatments; & will probably leave by motor coach, stopping in Providence en route. Hope you will be able to see this prepossessing & intelligent youth if he gets around to 10 Barnes. After the photograph the whole crowd took a boat excursion up the winding Charles River, conducted by a

quaint benevolent old mariner named Capt. Charles H. Munroe, who has haunted the stream from boyhood, & who knows its folklore well. Capt. Munroe enlivens the trip (which is in a huge launch managed entirely by himself) with a flow of pleasing lecture material; describing the various objects in a naive, stately way, interspersing occasional flowery & sententious reflections, telling comic stories, & reciting long poems by the various bards of the Charles—chiefly the late Prof. Henry W. Longfellow. He is a delicious character, & is well beloved by all who know the river. On this occasion I beheld the graceful Boston skyline; now marred by several modern buildings, & eventually to be ruined by skyscrapers. It was still, however, delightful & London-like. Higher up, the splendid neo-Georgian college buildings on the opposite Cambridge & Brighton shores made a picture of rare beauty. I had never before seen them from the water, & I could think of nothing but a real scene in the tasteful 18th century. The school of business administration on the Brighton side is a magnificent series of colonial quadrangles, whilst the dormitories on the Cambridge side make a perfect Georgian group. Many of the gable ends duplicate that of the old Boston state house. The one flaw is the gaudy way in which the belfry of the new Harkness house is painted—but this can be soon rectify'd in a future age of better taste. Cambridge itself is a marvellous sight from those bends of the river immediately above it—its delicate spires rising above flat green river-pastures in a manner suggesting the best aspects of Old England's rural scenery. The trip extends as far as Sunset Bay, in the open Watertown country, where the lone tower of the Perkins Institute for the Blind stands silhouetted against the west. On the return trip the voyage was enlivened by the rescue of a drowning drunken man near the Harvard Bridge—a feat which proved the marvellous coolness & seamanship of the captain.

After a return to the Statler the convention party set out for the old, memorable Allston headquarters—the residence of Mrs. Sawyer at 20 Inrie Road, formerly Webster St. Here a bean supper & period of discussion were enjoy'd in an old-time manner vastly reminiscent of the festive gatherings of 10 years ago. There was also a wild tiger cat who would let me, but no one else, stroke him. On returning to the Statler, Mortonius, myself, & a latecomer to the convention (E. F. Suhre of St. Louis) sat up till 2 a.m. talking—punctuated by a visit to a Waldorf Lunch for coffee & ice cream. This day ended the official convention.

Yesterday—Sunday—was showery, hence I could not begin my antiquarian explorations. Morton & Suhre went on an early trip to Nantasket, & Lynch persuaded me to accompany him to the Kennedy home in Allston (opposite the Sawyer home) for a session of amateur discussion. We had dinner there, & afterward I returned to the Statler to join Morton & Suhre for discussion until 2 a.m. ¶ Today—Monday—I am arising at noon, & hope to take Spink & Suhre to Salem & Marblehead. Weather seems decent. We shall meet at 1 o'clock at the Statler—where Mortonius (returning to N.Y. by boat) will bid us farewell. ¶ Quincy probably tomorrow; home late Tuesday night or Wednesday. All told, it has been a surprisingly fine convention.

More soon—

Best wishes—

Yr obt Servt

H P L

[325]   [ALS] [HPL to LDC]

67 Prospect St.,
Onset, Maſs.,
Friday–Saturday Midnight
Aug. 15–16, 1930

My dear Daughter:—

I take my pen in hand to acquaint you with the events of my trip so far, & to assure you of its pleasantness despite the bad weather. It is still raining, & it looks as though I would have to wear the old blue suit another day. The grey coat suffered a trifle from being folded in the enamel-cloth bag, but is now on shoulders & may rectify itself. I have tried to smooth out the principal undesirable wrinkles—& anyway, it is better than it would have been had I worn it in the rain.

As for the trip—I caught the 1:45 coach without difficulty, & read the Bulletin en route. Thus the only papers I shall miss are Saturday's Bulletin & the Sunday Journal. The scenery was fairly good—though on account of the new straight road to Fall River it is not as good as one used to get on the ancient winding road in the days of the old "Snake Line." This new cement straight-line road is the one which B K H doubtless traverses each morning betwixt his Fall River residence & the Journal office. Fall River, seen from the heights across the river, didn't look half bad—for it is at least a city of old-time spires & roofs, without skyscrapers. Seen closely, of course, it is ineffably ugly & commonplace. The road from Fall River to New Bedford is broad & unpicturesque, though Westport Factory & North Dartmouth are attractive old-time villages. New Bedford was quaint, as usual, but I had no time for sightseeing. Instead, I hastened to the station—where I found the whole Long family in the Essex. They were all furious over the delay in my letter—which arrived in the same mail with the later letter I dropped them yesterday from New Bedford. There must have been a sidetracking or mishandling at the Onset P.O. Canis looked much as usual—& I properly rebuked his young master for the banishment of Felis! The drive to Onset was uneventful—though it was interesting to have Belknap point out a colony of *Fiji-Islanders* near Onset.[1] These Melanesians—probably imported in the old New Bedford whaling days—keep themselves distinct from actual negroes, & are to some extent treated by the community as non-negroes. Probably they have some actual negro blood by this time, but their puckered foreheads & frizzy (not woolly) hair testify to the persistence of the original Fiji strain even at this late date.

At Onset we proceeded at once to the cottage in which the Longs have their quarters, & in which they likewise secured me a room at $1.00 per night. We are all on the second floor, close together & near the bathroom, as in the accompanying diagram:

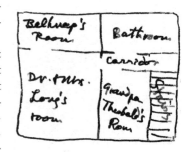

These quarters are very neat & pleasant, & are just across the street from the cottage at which I stayed last year. For a time we sat about & discussed various things—including the mail which I delivered. Sonny's letter from *Weird Tales* was an acceptance of his novelette, "The Horror From the Hills", for *$270.00*. Lucky child!

At length we adjourned to dinner, which was obtained at one of the small & inexpensive—but almost "Jake"-ishly generous—restaurants along the main street—a restaurant which we patronised considerably last year. I had chicken croquettes, coffee, & ice cream . . . . . but I must begin reducing again, since I weighed 144 in New Bedford! After dinner we attended a cinema show—the principal Long family diversion—& later the senior Longs retired whilst Sonny & I discussed anthropology, philosophy, & aesthetics on an unfrequented portion of the darkened piazza. At 11 p.m. the child decided to retire, so I ascended to my room & shall do some casual reading & writing until bedtime. I am looking through some new historical booklets from the Prov. Institution for Savings which came yesterday morning. You shall see them shortly—they pertain to Gov. Dorr, the Jencks family of Pawtucket, the Newport privateer John Dennis, & Mary Ann Angell of North Providence, second wife of Brigham Young.

As for tomorrow's programme—it depends largely on the weather. If the rain stops, we may take a boat trip around Buzzard's Bay; but if it doesn't, we shall doubtless continue the indoor & piazza discussions of today. Haven't had a chance yet to purchase my inevitable postcards—but tomorrow the mailing orgy will no doubt begin. More soon—& we'll all see you Monday—finding you in improved health, I trust.

Yr aff Nephew & obt Servt
H P L

Notes

1. HPL makes note of this colony in "The Shadow over Innsmouth" (*CF* 3.163).

[326]   [ALS] [HPL to LDC]

On Board Train in His
Majesty's Province of Quebec
August 30, 1930

My dear Daughter:—

Home to loyal soil at last! For the first time in my 40 years I am in a Dominion which still adheres to our rightful King & Parliament! But I could not tell when I enter'd it, for it was amidst the dense blackness of the night. Since the train was an excursion with a definite objective, there was no customs or immigration examination at the border—an official having inspected certificates shortly after we moved out of the North Station. A rain sprang up as we passed into New Hampshire, but it later ceased & gave place to a general mistiness. I wish I might have seen the old New England towns along the route, but of course the darkness forbade. After midnight we crossed the Connecticut River & entered Vermont—& before dawn Newport (Vt.) was passed—the last place of any size in the U.S. Dawn came at Sherbrooke, Quebec, where there was a long wait. This is a small city of very pleasing aspect, not unlike the average place of corresponding size in the U.S. Near the American border the towns are like those of N.E., but farther on the French element grows, & French signs & advertisements begin to appear. In aspect the country is often highly impressive, with great sweeps of rolling country affording magnificent vistas of wooded valley & river-bends. The vegetation seems sparse & bare as compared with ours—a thing I have noticed to a lesser degree in Vermont. Along the river-banks it is darker & thicker. This is a lumbering country, & for the first time I saw rivers jammed thick with logs. The atmosphere differs visibly from that of N.E. as one gets beyond Sherbrooke. There are absolutely no stone walls, but crooked rail fences of the ancient Virginia type. The *barns* are like ours, but the houses resemble our cheap Victorian cottages more than our farmhouses. This is doubtless because this part of Quebec was not settled *thickly* till the Victorian age—if indeed it can be called really thickly settled even now. There are great tenantless stretches, & not very much visible agriculture. We do not find here the much praised beauty & quaintness of ancient French cottages, as occurring in the older parts of the province, but merely a kind of squalor & dinginess much like that of foreigners in New England. There are, however, some pleasantly curious village churches built in a manner distinctly French—& another notable thing is the profusion of bright flowers, even around the most squalid hovels. The squalor reminds one of the barren sandy uplands of the Piedmont Carolinas—& indeed many of the French cottages are not much better than nigger cabins. There even [*sic*] a few *log* huts—& huts of half-hewn timbers. Sundry touches of the unfamiliar are supplied by certain of the telegraph or telephone poles—which are of a European type not seen in New England—& by the European railway custom of passing on the left-hand track. As the morning advanced, the mistiness began to dissipate, giving place to a day of utterly idyllic warmth & loveliness. The fantastic & ethereal forms of these morning mists, & the strange tricks they play with the sunlight as they churn & spiral upward from the horizon, form something I have never seen anywhere else. Another unique thing—to me—is the vast area of denuded forest land displaying endless reaches of withering stumps—a melancholy & almost sinister sight. Less dismal is the equally unique agricultural custom of making endless rows of *very small* haystacks—things which strike the eye at once upon entering this region. After a time we reached a grey & ugly terrain (Thetford Mine) containing the world's largest *asbestos mine*—a terrain wholly given over to this industry, & abominably depressing in consequence. It has the vastest *quarry-pit,* blasted in the solid rock, that I have ever seen—a thing which would excite Morton beyond words! Upon leaving these mines behind, we found ourselves in an *older part* of the province—the older parts naturally being those toward Quebec City. The landscape became extremely magnificent—involving in many places bold hills & glimpses of river valley like the Athol or Shenandoah regions, & in other places flattish expanses & gently rolling hills enabling the eye to span seemingly endless leagues of sunlit verdure & zigzag rail fences. This region is *rocky*—exactly like New England—but has singularly few *trees* of any sort; its bareness in this respect reminding one of Ohio.

Here, also, we begin to see typical old-time farmhouses—genuine outgrowths of the historic native building tradition. They are not the really *oldest* edifices, for the early farming land was on the north side of the St. Lawrence; but they probably date from the late 18th & early 19th century, & are authentic developments of the original style—made of wood instead of stone. Among the most distinctive features is the *curving roof-line,* which to the superficial eye suggests the Dutch curve which Talman loves so well. A representative survey, however, shews that most of them are differently proportioned—there being no gambrels, & the long downward sweep being perfectly straight except at the eaves—thus:
Now this was of extreme & especial interest to me, as you may recall if you read my *Charleston* letters—for this very feature is the distinctive mark of many Charleston houses of the early 18th century. Just as I suspected, it must be an essentially French form—probably brought to Charleston by the numerous Huguenots who exercised so much influence there. Charleston guide-books obstinately maintain that it is Dutch—picked up by the Huguenots during their stay in Leyden—but the evidence of Quebec is all to the contrary! Another distinctive French feature of these old houses is the type of window—especially in the gable ends. It is of the casement hinged type, & has the French horizontal divisions instead of the familiar small panes of our old houses. The trims & lintels, also, are distinctive. (see sketch) This window type

is *not* found in Charleston. Another typically French thing is the slender spire sometimes surmounting the old barns—which are otherwise quite like New England colonial barns. In general, these houses & farm buildings are arranged much like those of a New England farm. Were it not for the local & national idiosyncrasies above mention'd, & for the treelessness & absence of stone walls, one might well imagine oneself in New England when viewing one of the typical landscapes near Quebec City. Another thing—the eaves of these old houses all have a tendency to project—the roof overhanging the walls on all 4 sides.

Later—near the goal!

Pardon the style of this scrawled epistle—which I have been writing during the numerous & rather needless (it seems to me) waits of the train at various points along the route. I can't write at all when the train is in motion. We are now close to QUEBEC city itself, & I shall drop this letter in the first mail box I find—after getting Canadian stamps. As the St. Lawrence was neared, the scenery grew very picturesque—many slender French steeples revealing the presence of villages here & there. These steeples are very typical—unlike anything in New England. There is an especially fine group at Charny, the last village encounter'd before crossing the gigantick new bridge to the northern shore. *I have had my first distant glimpse of Quebec*—from the high ground between Diamond & Charny—& it promises untold wonders. Distant steep roofs & spires & battlements atop a Cyclopean promontory! Crossing the bridge was a great experience—the broad river is a marvel of impressiveness, & is marvellously set off by the tall, slim steeples of Sillery & Levis & Charny, the towns by the shore. The north bank looks more diversified & forested & New Englandish than the other side. Toward the north loom the purple Laurentian mountains. Quebec will be the next stop—& I look forward to strange elder wonders!

More immediately.

Yr aff Nephew & obt Servt

H P L

1931

[327]   [ALS] [HPL to LDC]

Y.M.C.A.,
Charleston, S.C.,
Tuesday afternoon—
May 5, 1931.

My dear Daughter:—

At last I take my pen in hand to produce a diary of my travels, so far, in the usual fashion. As A E P G has doubtless told you, I reached the Greyhound terminal in time, though somewhat fatigued from haste. The coach did not start, after all, till 11 o'clock; & by that time my headache had virtually vanished. Unlike the N.E. coach of last year, this Greyhound coach was admirably heated; so that I did not once regret the lack of an overcoat. The skies clouded some time after the Pawtuxet Valley villages were passed, but the loss of sunshine did not destroy the beauty of the typical New England scenery. Young tender leaves on ancient boughs, wistfully rambling stone walls, & apple blossoms in gnarled hillside orchards all appeared to mystical advantage through the filtering screen of a silver rain. At New London, where everybody lunched, I ate the remaining cup cake; & at Darien, Conn., the second lunching place, I disposed of some chocolate. Meanwhile A E P G gave me some cheese crackers & a banana—all of which please tell her were consumed with appreciation later on. Likewise, I may remark that the chocolate—now not quite half gone—is exquisite. I am not sure but that this Nestlé brand is beginning to rival Hershey's in my favour. The peanuts—now about half consumed—are delectable. So far, I have not bought any meals whatsoever! In proceeding to N Y I noticed with amusement how far our familiar First National Stores are spreading. Last year this peculiarly New England institution did not extend beyond Stamford, Conn— for beyond that the competition with New York chains—Daniel Reeves, James Butler, Gristede Bros. &c—becomes acute. Now, however, the "Finasts" have not only spread to the very New York line but have actually gone *beyond* it—being represented in Port Chester, N.Y. Hurrah for the good old Mayflowers! You will recall that the paper recently mentioned how Providence contains the greatest number of Finast stockholders.

Owing to daylight time the coach reached New York before dusk—going down the Grand Concourse to 138th St., then across to 5th Ave & down past the Museum to 59th, where it turned through to Columbus Circle & descended 8th Ave. Here I found a *brand new coach terminal* at 51st & 8th Ave.—the

"Capitol Terminal", a place as luxurious as a first class railway station, & the first thing of its kind I have seen which did not look like a makeshift joint. The "old" Penn terminal (which was, in its turn, new last year) is still used by the New England coaches, but now forms only a secondary stop for the Washington coaches—hence it was a very lucky accident which caused me to hit on the Greyhound Line. This is really the coming coach system of the whole United States. They have bought out the Philadelphia P.R.T. with its New York–Washington service, & have just acquired control of the Camel City lines in the south; so that I have reached Old Charleston without using any other company than that on whose coach I started at Fountain & Mathewson Sts.

Well—once at the Capitol Terminal I took out the stuff to be left at Sonny's, checked my paraphernalia, & set out by subway for 230 W. 97th. This Greyhound coach made better time than its New England rival, so that I was at the Child's door by 7:30 p.m. The household did not expect me so soon, & insisted that I share their dinner; which had only reached the dessert stage. They had steak—& gave some additional cooking to my piece, owing to my dislike of rare meat. This was a bad beginning for a *reducing* trip, but I could not politely refuse.* The Long household looks lacking without Felis— & I was furious to learn that the new mistress to whom Felis was presented is not a gentlewoman at all; but a German restaurant-keeper's wife who is a friend of the laundress! However, this person is a worthy old soul, thinks the world of Felis, & feeds him on the choicest products of the restaurant. He has killed two canary-birds since his acquisition, but has each time been freely forgiven. On the whole, I guess Felis is having an all-around better time than he had at the Longs'. When I get back to N Y—if I can bear to stop in that mongrel bedlam after being in this glorious Southern world—Little Sonny is going to take Grandpa to the restaurant where Felis now reigns. It will be good to see that regal scion of the jungle's lords once more. I can hardly think of N Y as existing without good old Felis! The human & canine Longs looked much as usual—the Child having perhaps an inch more on that expanding waistline, & 1¾ more hairs in the tenderly nurtured moustachelet. Now that the doctor has pronounced his heart better, his mother will let him be more active—but so fixedly sedentary have his habits become, that I fear it will take blasting-powder to get him as active as regular guys like Talman & Wandrei. His mother said he could even take a long coach trip like mine— but the prospect seems rather formidable to one who has never in his little life slept under a roof not housing mamma & papa! But time will tell. The fact that the coaches run on Standard Time the other side of N.Y. gave me an hour more than I expected—my Washington coach going at 12:10 midnight. I left Sonny's at 11:45, & was in good time at the terminal. In the four hours

---

*Also, I could not refuse coffee & cakes just before I left.

of the call we had a continuously interesting oral fight on various aesthetick topics—which will be continued upon my return (which I hate to think of) from the South. Having had a glimpse of typical New York mongrelism in the subway, I was glad to get into the terminal—where, of course, travellers from New England and the South preponderate. Home again, as it were, among the colonial American people! The Washington coach—now a Greyhound like ours instead of a P.R.T. Mitten Line affair—made an ideal trip, as my postcard from Philadelphia doubtless apprised you. The drizzle abated around Princeton, N.J., & from then on the nocturnal landscape (*wretched* by day!) was such a magically moonlit affair that I could not bear to drowse. Mrs. Long had loaded me up with cake, cheese sandwiches, banana, & pear; but I stored these in the bag-vacancy created by what I had left at Sonny's. Dawn came in Pennsylvania between Chester & that detestable factory waste called Marcus Hook—the ugliest place, bar none, I have ever beheld in my life. With the reddening east as a background, however, the miserable factory towers & chimneys acquired something of strangeness and beauty— suggesting the mystical minarets of some alien & forbidden city of multiple dimensions on another planet or in some other galaxy of infinite space. Full daylight came in Wilmington, Del.—where, also, I noted a slight thickening of the vegetation due to southward progress. At Elkton, Md., the beauty of a quaint southern town first struck the eye; & at equally quaint Havre-de-Grace, across the long Susquehanna Bridge, a breakfast stop was made at the ancient Lafayette Tavern. I, however, breakfasted on my Long donations— which both helped my purse & lightened the congestion in my enamel-cloth bag. Baltimore offered nothing of interest, but I revelled in the summery landscape south of it. Despite the cold day the *atmosphere* was of summer because of the vegetation. Washington looked exquisite in its advanced foliage, & I noted with interest the progress made on the new government buildings. Of course, I had missed the famous early-spring cherry blossoms—but there was enough else to delight the eye. After 20 minutes the coach for Richmond left—& I had a front seat, as on the Washington one. This ride was as delectable as usual, & I regretted that I could not stop off at Fredericksburg. Richmond was an exquisite & summery sight despite the rawness of the cold day—& the excellent 4th St terminal was finely heated. I wrote cards, bought the N Y Times, & entered the Winston-Salem coach as soon as it was ready. This, too, was admirably heated—in fact, the Greyhound Lines avoid all the trouble caused by the cold on lines otherwise controlled. One finds Southern life & folkways predominating for the first time, as one proceeds southward, on this Richmond–Winston line which has no direct link outside Old Southern territory. I noticed it last year, & this time it was even more accentuated. The ancient & homogeneous population of the South has created a civilisation of such depth & tenacity that one feels himself in a *real nation*—as he can never feel in the industrialised, foreignised, & quickly-changing North. The same condition—amongst the French—exists in ancient Quebec; but we have lost it in New England. On an inexpensive coach-line one sees how profoundly the old Southern attitude has affected even the lower middle classes—all of whose forbears, of course, have dwelt in Virginia for three centuries. There is an instinctive courtesy & friendliness of a sort unknown to the north, & the long trips are occasionally diversified by the conversational remarks—all civil & meant to be interesting—of utter strangers. In the north, such random conversation would be confined to foreigners, & would be of a totally vague, flippant, & valueless order. The few Anglo-Saxons would remain silent & contemptuous. Here, however, everybody on a coach belongs to one type of civilisation; & farmers talk of their plantings & exchange anecdotes of persons & places known in common. Jests are exchanged; & a positive merriment of the ancient American kind, without coarseness, not infrequently develops. On this occasion the passengers included two rustick musicians—a blind guitar player & a lean, gawky cross-eyed tenor-singer with a broad Virginia accent, who led his colleague about & participated in his performances. They were genuine folk products of the old Virginia rural scene, but had recently begun to make money by playing for radio broadcasting in various places. They probably had more money than either had ever seen at any one time before, hence stopped at the best hotels & made naive comments on their luxuries. Their dress & grooming, however, had not changed a bit—so that not even the subtlest visible touch differentiated them from the other old Virginia farmers around them. In the north, such a pair of minstrels would have been smartly & sportily dressed, & would have talked loudly & flashily on sporty topics while keeping their music for paid performances. Not so these honest, simple children of nature, who had been playing at Richmond & were bound for Danville (about ¾ way to Winston-Salem) on a similar mission. Hardly had the coach cleared the suburbs when the blind guitarist burst into carefree melody, soon to be joined by his angular & cross-eyed colleague—who sang exquisitely both the melodies of the present & the traditional folk airs of ancient Virginia. As they proceeded, various passengers began to join in the musick as best their vocal equipment allow'd—encouraged vociferously by the amiable minstrels, who had no prejudice at all against amateur crudity. The diversity & skill of their repertoire were positively astonishing—& they tried to refuse a collection taken up for them by a young man (a Southerner working in New York, who had sung with the crowd with much enjoyment) bound for Statesville, N.C. "We don' expeck any money, folks! We're having jes' as good a time (pronounced tahm) as you all!" In studying the response of the crowd to the invitation to join in song, one might note many culturally significant factors. In the first place, no one seemed to hesitate or feel foolish. These people are free from the silly Puritan reticence & pseudo-dignity of the corresponding Yankee classes. Secondly, *everybody*, young & old alike, knew the words of all the old folk songs. Even the youngest generation were at home amongst the melodies of their ancestors—which modern jazz has supplemented without displacing. No such total cleavage betwixt the older & younger people, as exists in the rest of the world, can be said to exist here. The present is the heir of the past in unbroken succession—for in tidewater Virginia & Carolina the original American civilisation still remains a living unit. The niggers in the rear of the coach did not intrude upon the merriment of their masters, though they would probably have sung if asked to do so at a time when the coachload preferred hearing to participating. They were gone long before Danville was reached—for of course the Piedmont south is practically niggerless. And to add a final tribute to the deep instinctive civilisedness of the rural Virginians—they did not shew any scorn or impatience toward the few more stolid Northerners or other strangers who failed to respond visibly to the prevailing mellowness. Song & jest of a less professional quality persisted long after the musicians left—& all of a simple, old-American type such as one hardly pictures as existing today. In the north, the only element which relaxes at all is a foreign element whose mirth is loud & crude & strident, & wholly out of harmony with the time-mellowed native tradition. This relaxation & mirth were all in the old main line of colonial folkways. Just how long the machine age will permit such a population to remain unspoiled, no one can venture to say. But at least it exists now, so that the traveller in Virginia may truthfully boast of having beheld a living part of the early American scene.

The wait at Winston-Salem was very brief, & at 11:15 I was again speeding through the night on a well-heated & drowsily filled coach. The occasional troubled moonlight shed magic over even the ugly pine barrens of the Carolina uplands; hence whenever I started awake & looked ahead (I had a front seat) I saw an enchanted scene which might have been a lunar or Saturnian landscape. Last year's time table was somewhat changed, so that a 2-hour wait at Charlotte, N.C. was introduced—from 2 to 4 a.m. Coaches being changed, I waited in the well-heated terminal on a vast leather easy-chair—finishing the Sunday Times & getting a cup of coffee to supplement A E P G's exquisite cheese crackers. I tore the Chesterton & Spanish articles out of the Times to send Belknap, since they touched partly on what we had been discussing Saturday evening.[1] At 4 a.m. the new coach forged onward, dawn coming around the new & colourless city of Lancaster, S.C. The typical feathery vegetation of the Carolina uplands now predominated, & the great red ball of the sun triumphed over threatening clouds. At Camden I again saw the thickening vegetation prophetick of the lowlands, & the long run down to Columbia was as delightful as last year. This time there was no long 4-hour wait—the Charleston coach leaving in half an hour & getting me to Charleston at 11:30 a.m. instead of 2:30 p.m. as before. I did not regret the improved service, for Columbia is not so very fascinating after one has seen Charleston. The day, besides, was wretchedly cold even in S. Carolina. I did, however, get a kick out of seeing *palmettos* for the first time in 1931. The Charleston coach—a smallish, old one—left on time, & after Orangeburg I was the only passenger. The ride was delightful, & the temperature definitely rose—for the coastal Charleston area is always warmer than the semi-upland where Columbia lies. The latter half of the ride—as I probably mentioned last year—is especially rich in really subtropical landscape effects; great forests of tall pines & cypresses with Spanish moss hanging from lofty limbs. Many were parts of swamps—recalling the colourful traditions & civil & military history of the region. I also began to see Southern live-oaks—one of my favourite trees. Summerville—the small city in the midst of one of these forests—was as welcome a sight as before—but the big kick came when the land opened out & revealed the scatter'd first houses of ancient & historick CHARLESTON. God Save the King!

That was at 11:30 a.m. Monday—only 48½ hours after I left the Rialto Hotel terminal at Fountain & Mathewson Sts. The day, alas, was cold—too cold to write outdoors—but it was not as bad as the north, & was amply good enough for sightseeing. I obtained an excellent room at the Y M C A for 2 nights—& am told that I can get one *for a week* at $4.75 on my return trip. I shall probably cut Florida short to take advantage of this offer—for after all, there's no place like Charleston. Not even Quebec. Quebec has, undeniably, more sheer beauty of line; but *nothing else* has the utter mellowness & 18th century survival that Charleston has. It does not shew off—it is not self-conscious. No shouting lecturers on rubberneck wagons—no tawdry souvenir "shoppes" catering to gaping outlanders. The old town of 1680 & 1730 & 1780 & 1830 & 1880 is still going about the same old business in the same old way. The only change during my absence is the new custom of painting street names on the vertical sides of the curbstones at intersections—supplementing the older bronze plates sunk in the sidewalks. No farther vandalism has occurred—the old Planter's House is still boarded up, but it is not torn down & may possibly be restored by some society. At the corner of Chalmers & Meeting Sts., where last year I mourned the demolition of a typical Old Charleston house to make way (ugh!) for a filling-station, the filling station is now built—&, delightfully enough, in genuine Old Charleston architecture. Even the Standard Oil Company has a gleam of taste once in a while! Yesterday I circulated around all my favourite spots like an old returned native—stopping at City Park or the Battery whenever it was warm enough to sit & write. The sun shone exquisitely through the rich foliage, & the ancient gardens glowed with unbelievable charm. No use—Charleston is pretty nearly the greatest spot on earth! Old tiled roofs—wrought-iron garden gates & step-railings—Georgian doorways—ancient steeples—grass-grown cobblestones in byways—how can one ever break away?

Well—at dusk I returned to the Y, wrote letters till late, & thereafter retired for the first time since last Wednesday after a peanut-&-chocolate dinner. Incidentally, I performed laundry work in the lavatory. This outfit which I put on for the Infantry Hall concert with Evans is going to see St. Augustine yet—though it may not last till next Christmas.

Today—Tuesday the 5th—I rose at 8 after a 9½-hour sleep & found the day chilly & cloudy. After some letter-writing I decided to devote the day to *interiors*—which I duly did, & to great advantage. The Old Exchange—erected on the shore of the Cooper River at the foot of Broad St. in 1767 as a custom house for the Province—was my first choice; & I did not regret the quarter admission I paid to see the ancient vaults below the edifice. It is now controlled by the D.A.R. This building—still perfectly preserved—was used by the rebels for publick assemblages in the 1773–1780 period, & Genl. Moultrie stored powder in a sealed chamber in the cellar. In 1780, when His Majty's arm'd forces under Sir Peter Parker & Ld Rawdon captur'd the town, the building & its vaults was us'd as a prison for military & civil offenders, many of whom were remov'd to St. Augustine, then under His Britannick Majesty's control, Florida having been taken from Spain (which had aided the French King) in 1763 after the fall of Quebeck & the ensuing peace negotiations. After the final victory of the rebels the building had much publick use, & was the scene of a ball at which Genl Washington was entertain'd in 1791. From 1818 to 1912 it was a government building—post office, lighthouse office, &c—& since then it has been owned by the D.A.R. It is a fine Middle-Georgian specimen of a design more British than locally Carolinian, & formerly had a vast portico on the seaward side. The interior has suffer'd much change, but the old vaults are just as they used to be—marvellously impressive. All the ancient waterfront near the Exchange is just as of yore—even the threat of a new summer hotel having faded for the time being. What a contrast to our lost opera house & wantonly ravaged South Water St!! My next visit was to Charleston's oldest surviving structure—the powder magazine of 1703, originally a bastion of the vanished city wall. This is one of the most impressive vaulted crypts I have ever seen—& now contains an historical collection presided over by the Colonial Dames. The ancient gentlewoman in charge—who must have been near 90, & who was full of recollections of Charleston in the plantation days before the Civil War—was exceedingly civil, & display'd many pictures of Old Charleston which I would not have seen but for her particular kindness. My next attempt was on the old Joseph Manigault house north of Marion Square, but I was here disappointed by finding it closed—as it was last year despite rumours that the D.A.R. were keeping it open. I now proceeded to the Charleston Museum, which I did more thoroughly than last year; seeing the impressive miniature model of young Poe standing on the lonely shore of Sullivan's Island during his military service here in the winter of 1828–29—a model whose photograph forms the frontispiece of one of the volumes of my best Poe biography—Hervey Allen's "Israfel", which I purchased in 1929. Upon leaving the museum I found an increasing rain in progress—which probably means a job for some St Augustine tailor! Under the circumstances I could not well prolong exploration, hence returned to the Y M C A to write. And here I am still—at 8 p.m., & with several hours of similar correspondence ahead. I shall try to get this epistle in tonight's mail, though.

Tomorrow—much as I hate to leave Charleston—I shall take the 11:45 a.m. coach for Savannah, reaching the old Georgia seaport at 3:15 p.m. From then till dusk I shall explore Savannah—which I expect to seem relatively tame after Charleston—& after dusk I shall write letters in some appropriate Savannah haven—probably the coach terminal. At midnight I shall take the Jacksonville coach—reaching the Florida metropolis at 6 a.m. Thursday the 7th. St. Augustine is only 1½ hours from Jacksonville, but I doubt if there is a coach before 8—hence scarcely expect to see the ancient Spanish capital before 9:30 or so. I have apprised Newton of my coming, & have also told Whitehead of Dunedin that I will be reachable in Newton's care at St. Augustine. This will be wholly new territory to me—yet I scarcely expect it to compete with either Charleston or Quebec. You will, as usual, receive bulletins from along the route, & at no infrequent intervals. I hope to hades it will get *warm* soon—so far the visible palmettos & live-oaks have been the only subtropical evidences at my disposal! But even so, I'm having a great time—for CHARLESTON is CHARLESTON. God Save the King! ¶ Hope you're not doing too much work in Grandpa's absence.

Yr aff Most Obt Servt

H P L

P.S. Have just bought a new pair of garters. Glad of the old hat in view of today's rain. Am posing as a tramp—unblacked shoes & all!

Notes

1 G. K. Chesterton (1874–1936), "Why Chesterton Likes America"; Clair Price, "Out of Old Hungers a New Spain Rises," *New York Times Magazine* (3 May 1931): 1–2, 16, and 4–5, 19.

[328]　　[ALS] [HPL to LDC]

Finished:

Sunday–Monday Midnight

—May 10–11, 1931.

written in
instalments

My dear Daughter:——

　　　　　Once more I take my pen in hand to continue the diary to date—though the folder mailed yesterday must have apprised you of my safe advent to the ancient Spanish provincial capital of San Augustin. When I

last wrote—Thursday morning—I was in commonplacely modern Jacksonville amidst glorious tropic sunshine, about to take the stage coach for the
older city. The trip was delightful, & I am glad I saved it for daylight performance. The road extends through many belts of splendid tropical woodland,
& at first the St. John's River is always gleaming through the trees or across
meadows on the right. St. Augustine itself, 37 miles to the southeast, & on
the coast, is in a splendid region of tropical luxuriance. Palms grow to a vast
height; lining all the avenues & creating a magical green twilight in conjunction with the massive live-oaks whose boughs bear opulent festoons of Spanish moss. Charleston's flora is northern as compared with this—this is the
real thing in tropical atmosphere, as A E P G will assure you! The effect of
the warmth upon me has been magical—like a tonic—so that I dread the
thought of encountering northern cold again. I am so active that you would
scarcely know me! St. Augustine lies on a narrow peninsular strip between the
narrow San Sebastian river on the west & the broad Matanzas River on the
east—the latter being at this point really a lagoon or bayou of the sea, since
only the long, narrow bulk of Anastasia Island separates it from the open Atlantic. A bridge—called the Bridge of Lions & flanked by twin marble statues
of Lions—connects the city with the island. My coach from Jacksonville approached St Augustine along the broad palm-&-live-oak-lined road called San
Marco Avenue—a truly tropical highway which even the commonplace Victorian cottages along the route could not spoil. At one point I saw a huge sign
pointing down toward the Matanzas River shore on the left & indicating the
site of Ponce de Leon's fabled Fountain of Youth—or more prosaically, the
estimated landing-place of de Leon, & the nearest visible spring. A second
sign on the same side points to the site of the first church in St. Augustine—
the Chapel of Nuestra Señora de la Leche,* erected in 1565 but subsequently
destroyed. On this site a memorial shrine has been erected—though there is a
rival site near the "Fountain of Youth" where another chapel has been built of
old stone blocks lying about—which the present builders claim are the stones
of the original demolished edifice. Some distance nearer the old centre of the
town, on the right-hand side, is the ancient Huguenot cemetery with its grotesque slabs embowered in tropic vegetation, & its gnarled, moss-draped,
overhanging live-oak branches. The atmosphere of this place is exceedingly
weird—though it does not equal the spectral Unitarian Churchyard in
Charleston. At length the coach approached the original part of the town,
where straight ahead loomed the massive city gates—dating from the 18th
century & forming the only surviving part of the ancient city wall. At this
point San Marco Ave. changes to the intra-mural name of St George St., &
narrows to a width of only 19 feet—for in the old part of St Augustine the
original Spanish street lines have been preserved unchanged. St. George St. is

---

*Leche = milk—i.e., milk of human kindness.[1]

still the leading business thoroughfare of the town, & preserves enough of its ancient Spanish houses to give it a very Marbleheadish or Newportly aspect. At this point, looking to the left toward the low-lying Matanzas River shore, one sees silhouetted against the sky the mediaeval masonry & corner turrets of ancient Fort San Marcos at the water's edge—the only perfect example of mediaeval fortification remaining in America. There was a wooden fort here as early as 1566; but the present stone one—built with Indian, negro slave, & convict labour—is a gradual growth, begun some time around 1638 & not finished till 1756. It suggests Morro Castle in Havana Harbour, & was used by the British & American* governments as well as by the Spanish. Its last governmental use was as a military prison in 1898, during the Spanish War. It is now owned by the St. Augustine Historical Society, & its multitudinous stone vaults, dungeons, casements, platforms, & watch towers are accessible to the public—parties being guided through. One set of dungeons was anciently sealed up by the Spanish & discovered only by accident by American repairers in 1835. There were chained skeletons & instruments of torture within—an excellent theme for imaginative fiction. In some of the old vaults historical booklets & cards are now sold, & in others a rudimentary museum is taking shape.

The coach did not—in fact, *could* not—pass through the ancient city gates†, but deviated to the left down Bay St along the Matanzas River waterfront—a palm-lined esplanade with frequent yacht-club piers, & with many winter hotels on the inner side. Across the broad sheet of water lay the low expanse of Anastasia Island with its dunes & spreading sea-beach, & with the tall lighthouse (painted like a barber's pole & marking the site of the ancient Spanish lighthouse destroyed in 1880) as a salient landmark. The graceful arch of the long Bridge of Lions, opposite the riverward end of the town's ancient plaza, added to the attractiveness of the scene. Close at hand, near the city gates, I beheld the great stone sphere recently placed to mark the beginning of the ancient Spanish trail across the continent—a trail extending from St. Augustine to San Diego, California, & linking the eastern & western parts of Spain's colonial empire. Another great circular stone marks the San Diego end. The stone of which everything is constructed—fort, ancient houses, sphere, curbings, pavements, &c. alike—is that conglomerate type known as *coquina*, & consisting of tiny shells pressed together through the chemical & physical forces of geologic action. This is a favourite building material in the

---

*The Americans renamed it "Ft. Marion" in honour of the rebel General Francis Marion of CHARLESTON.

†City gates are 10 feet square & 30 feet high, surmounted by pomegranate carvings. Each contains a sentry box with iron gates. Space between the pillars is 12 feet—formerly closed by heavy iron gate. City wall was of wood & earth, with line of bayonet spikes on top, & tidal moat surrounding it.

seaboard tropics, & occasional examples are found in Charleston. The stone used in St. Augustine is—& always has been—quarried on Anastasia Island across the Matanzas River.

Proceeding south along Bay St., the coach (which was bound ultimately for Miami) stopped at 9:45 a.m. (Thursday, May 7) at the terminal just beyond the Bridge of Lions & the riverward end of the Plaza—on the inner side of the esplanade at the corner of Ocean St., opposite the Municipal Yacht Pier & the low yellow Chamber of Commerce building which forms a lodge-like entrance to the pier. Also on the inner side of Bay St.—just across intersecting Ocean St. & therefore next the coach terminal—rose a wooden Victorian house of probable 1890 architecture, with a stone vaulted basement story, a balconied second story, & a tower chamber in the centre of the flat, railed roof. This, I knew, was the Rio Vista hotel or rooming house where my friend Newton lodged at such fabulously reasonable rates—his room being the tower chamber. As I alighted I saw Newton advancing to meet me—a pleasant, clean-shaven, well-dressed & well-groomed man of 60 or 65 years; born & reared in New York, well-read & widely travelled in Europe & America, acquainted with many persons of prominence & influence, & in the brokerage business before retiring on an income which the hard-time period has reduced to an alarming slenderness. He at once led me to Mr. & Mrs. Fryer, proprietors of the house, who let me have a magnificent river-fronting room on the 2nd floor with two long French windows opening on a balcony or piazza top as Gramp's southern window opened on ours. The view from these windows, or from the balcony if I choose to sit out there, is utterly magnificent—the river, Anastasia Island, the great lighthouse, the ocean horizon where the glorious eastern sun rises, & what not! And the incredible thing is that this room is only *$4.00 per week!* The house is a neat, prepossessing, & quiet one; & though my room has no running water, I am furnished with a washstand, bowl, & pitcher. The bathroom is just at the end of the hall, & if I do not wish to usurp it for laundry work Newton says I can do my washing in his magnificent tower observatory room—which has running water. The only trouble with the water in these pipes is a certain flatness, though in other parts of the city system it has an abominable (though reputedly healthy) tinge of sulphuretted hydrogen.

As soon as I was settled in my room—which I took for one week & may take for a second—Newton led me on a preliminary tour of some of the leading sights. Walking slightly inland & northward through the narrow streets & beneath the arcades of the public library, (which I shall shortly patronise & which is situate in an ancient Spanish mansion) we shortly reached the main civic centre or Plaza de la Constitución, on which front the Post Office, (in an ancient Spanish mansion built in 1591) the belfried old Cathedral (1793–1797) with its sweet & reminiscent chimes (one bell was cast in 1682), old Trinity Episcopal Church (over a century old), & the ancient market—an open affair of block pavement & massive roofed pillars now used as a band-stand, & as a gathering-place for the reposeful citizens of the town, who assemble languidly in every kind of sartorial disarray & indulge in endless games of checkers, cards, & dominoes at a long central bench. There are, it appears, sometimes two groups of these odd notables—the English-speakers toward the inland end & the Spanish-speakers toward the riverward end.* The latter come from the narrow lanes of the adjacent Spanish colony, but probably include more recent Cuban immigrants than actual descendants of the colonial Spanish Floridians. There are, however, some descendants of the Minorcans—from the Balearic Isles—brought in as indentured servants or labourers during the British period—1763–83. The general life of the place is that of a village about as large as East Greenwich or Warren—for the permanent population of the compact part cannot much exceed 5000. The shopkeepers & restaurateurs now & then leave their places of business to join in the checker games, & the single visible policeman is a grotesquely rural figure with uniform usually unbuttoned & hat askew. *Bicycles* are rather in evidence, & several horse-drawn vehicles—including a hansom cab with a spotted coach-dog running under it—cater to the tourist trade. The greatest activity is around the coach stations, for this is the end of the Florida tourist season. In midsummer the place is doubtless still quieter—& in midwinter it is likewise said to be quiet, since most tourists now prefer havens radically farther south. Though snow is almost never seen, the thermometer sometimes drops to 30° in January; the winter average being 60°. During St. Augustine's late-Victorian or Edwardian heyday a number of elaborate hotel buildings were erected—in what was then thought to be appropriate Spanish Renaissance architecture. For the most part, the most merciful description of them is tactful silence; though at sunset they really do present a glamourous, dream-evoking silhouette against the churning & rubescent west—their ornate Moorish towers & pseudo-belfries taking on a strangely fantastic quality, & losing the tawdry ostentatiousness observed by day. St. Augustine's skyline would be ideal—in such sunsets—but for one tallish rectangular building & one abominable metallic standpipe. The best place to survey it from is Anastasia Island—or the Bridge of Lions, or one of the yacht piers along the Matanzas River front. Florida sunsets are of proverbial magnificence—last night's being positively apocalyptic in its red-gold, many-rayed glory, with grotesque cloud-monsters revelling cryptically in a polychrome & ethereal ocean of light. This, with the fantastic skyline as a foreground, forms a breath-taking sight not soon to be forgotten. Between the old market & the river—at the entrance of the Bridge of Lions—is a modern plaza development promoted by northern millionaires, with a tasteful flagpole & an excellent new monument to Ponce de Leon. The narrow streets of St Augustine are no longer vexed with trolley

---

*They often mix, however.

tracks, though a line once existed. Some have proportionately narrow side-walks, (in part, or on one side of the street) whilst others have none. The main business street—St George—has many shops, including an A & P & a McCrory's 5 & 10¢ store. Card & souvenir shops abound, as well as Jake-like restaurants (no one-arms but many counter places) where food in vast quanti-ties is almost given away. These latter are so cheap that I don't think I'll both-er about importing package food to my room—10¢ gets a large breakfast of 2 huge doughnuts & coffee, & 25¢ gets a full-sized dinner. One Spanish place has a regular course dinner for 30¢. Amidst this network of narrow streets a really surprising number of ancient Spanish houses survive—some dating back to the 1500's. The usual type—set broad side to the street—is plain, with four sided red-tiled roof coming to a point like the typical Charleston roof & one type of Quebec roof—obviously a form common in Continental Europe. Ornate Georgian doorways do not, unfortunately, exist; though square-paned transoms & side lights are found. Lower stories are always built of coquina stone, & upper stories sometimes are—though wood figures largely in the latter. Doors & windows tend to be set at the inner surface of the thick walls, though with windows usage varies. Balconies over the street—mostly wooden—are very common; & some of the houses have win-dow blinds horizontally divided like those of Quebec. In common use, the lower halves are kept closed & the upper halves open—the precise opposite of Quebec usage. Windows are generally small-paned like our English Geor-gian ones—the Spaniards evidently not using the French casement type found in Quebec. Despite the balconies, large piazzas are by no means so common as in Charleston. This is perhaps because the Spaniards, accustomed at home to a warmer climate than the England & France whence Charleston's settlers came, did not feel any especial urge toward the open air. High garden walls occasionally appear—especially in the outlying parts W. & S.; but they lack the splendid wrought-iron gates typical of CHARLESTON.* ¶ In the midst of the plaza is the pyramidal or obelisk-like monument erected in 1813 in honour of the granting of a liberal constitution to Florida. When this mon-ument was erected, the work of chiselling the inscription was for some reason entrusted to an Englishman; & amusingly enough, he gave the Spanish word CONSTITUCIÓN the English spelling CONSTITUTION. The error occurred on all four sides of the monument, but on one of them an amateur hand has managed to re-chisel the offending letter into some semblance of its Hispan-ick equivalent. Over the whole plaza—which like all parts of the town is pro-fusely supplied with resting benches—broods an ineffably mystical green twilight supplied by the luxuriant overarching palms & moss-draped live-oaks. When this twilight is shot through by the magic golden light of very late afternoon, the effect is glamourous & imaginatively provocative beyond the

---

*circular stone walls abound, & little darting lizards are often seen in the ancient gardens.

power of the pen to delineate. It will be hard work breaking away from a place like this!

At the P.O.—the 1591 mansion—we found a highly welcome letter from A E P G as well as one of insistently cordial invitation from Whitehead of Dunedin. Whitehead would really be offended if I left Florida without seeing him, hence I shall make the Dunedin side-trip before starting back for CHARLESTON. At Whitehead's, of course, no financial food & lodging problem will exist. His health appears to be better after his "Sippy Treatment." I have looked up Dunedin bus schedules, & find that I can make the trip with two changes of coach—at Palatka & St. Petersburg.

Exploring the ancient streets only cursorily for the present, Newton & I set out almost at once for the ancient fort—of which you will learn more in the separate-cover folder. The charm of the massive moated masonry with its glacis, turrets, arch-supported ramp, casemates, dungeons, & sun-drenched parapet, is quite beyond words. A guide took us all through the interior, including the once-sealed cells & ultimate dungeons where immemorial blackness brooded. Osceola the rebel Seminole was confined here before his transfer to CHARLESTON'S Ft. Moultrie, where he died. The vast broad parapet overlooking the river has benches for visitors, & has already become a favourite haunt of mine—where I sit & write in an effort to pick up a coat of tan. The high lookout tower, containing a spiral staircase, affords the finest possible view of St Augustine's outspread roofs; & I shall make many ascents during my sojourn.

From the fort we proceeded northward along San Marco Ave. [named from Ft. San Mar*cos,* but given the Italian form Marc*o* through ignorance] past the Huguenot Cemetery to the ancient chapel site & the so-called "Fountain of Youth", which latter is provided with a decorative shelter of coquina & surrounded by a private park also containing one of the rival chapel sites. 25¢ admission is charged to this park & fountain, but Newton insisted on treating. The gatekeeper turned out to be an old Norwich, Conn. man who had worked for years at Brownell & Field's in PROVIDENCE, & was horrified to hear of the destruction of the Opera House & the South Water St. brick row. At the fountain I took an extra deep draught in an effort to get down below 12 years & be able to travel on the bus at half fare. So far no striking result has been observed, though I am steadily watching my shadow to see if it shrinks. Within this park—at the river's edge—is a coquina marker with a bronze plate commemorating the probable landing-place of Ponce de Leon.

On our return to town, Newton insisted on treating me to a 25¢ boiled dinner [heavens, my weight! How can I be 140 by St John's Eve?] at the Jake-like place in ancient St George St., after which we sat on a bench in the plaza & discussed miscellaneous topics. Subsequently Newton returned to the Rio Vista for a nap, whilst I rambled about the ancient streets & finally settled on a bench on the glacis of the old fort to write letters & postcards. This time I plastered the whole gang—though only with penny cards. I shall not send out any other equally expansive round during this trip. After admiring the magic of the town & the island in the golden light of late afternoon, I finally returned to the house & found Newton waiting on the piazza. We then went out to the end of the municipal yacht pier—virtually opposite the house—& admired the fantastic urban skyline against the sunset. Discussion was prolonged till shortly after nine, when Newton (an amusingly regular person in his customs) started to retire according to his usual schedule. I remained up, wrote in my room, & did my laundry in the bathroom; but after so full a day was drowsy enough to retire about 12:30 midnight.

On FRIDAY, MAY 8, 1931 I rose at 8 a.m. & accompanied Newton to a 10¢ breakfast at "Jake's." I think I shall depend on this place rather than buy more chocolate, since the latter melts troublesomely in the genial climate of antient San Augustin. Newton then returned to the house whilst I went out to the fort to sit on the sun-drenched parapet & write. At noon I returned to the house & accompanied Newton to the Spanish restaurant* in the section just south of the Plaza, where for exactly *30¢* I obtained the following dinner:

> splendid spaghetti with grated cheese
> Pork chops with French fried potatoes
> Coffee
> Banana

. . . . And I expect to be 140 by St. John's Eve!

After dinner I heeded a threat of rain & returned to the house to write; & at 6:30 accompanied Newton to his 10¢ supper at "Jake's". Here I tried for the first time the celebrated Mexican dish of *hot tamales*—small cylindrical pastry crusts stuffed with highly seasoned chopped lamb & immersed in a highly seasoned sauce of brownish colour. I like them very much, though not quite so much as the similar Italian dish called *ravioli*, which employs a tomato sauce like that used on spaghetti. Following this meal we went out toward the middle of the graceful Bridge of Lions [there are benches all along both sides. It is a toll bridge—1¢ for a pedestrian, 30¢ for a car. Its traditional arched-pier construction—not suspension—makes it more beautiful than our Mt. Hope Bridge] to see the gorgeously flaming sunset behind the fantastick urban skyline. Discussion—mostly about European travel, & London in particular—lasted till about 9:30, when Newton's conventional schedule started him off for bed. I returned to my room to write letters, & retired shortly after 4 a.m.

On SATURDAY, MAY 9, 1931 I rose at 8 a.m. & accompanied Newton to a 10¢ breakfast at "Jake's". I have now worked out a plan for accomodating my 2-meal programme to his conventional 3-meal one. In the morning I

---

*the old Spaniard who runs this place frequently goes out to join in the languid checker games at the riverward end of the ancient market.

shall breakfast with him, but when he gets his dinner at noon I shall merely take a cup of coffee. Then, at night when he gets his supper, I shall take my regular dinner. In the morning's mail was a letter from Small Sonny saying how much he liked his Grandpa Theobald's 115-page typed story.[2] The Child quite went into ecstasies about it—indeed, I think I'll send you his letter when I've answered it. I hope he's sent all the pages in good order to Wright—& that Wright will also look upon it with favour.[3]

Well—after breakfast Newton & I sat around the plaza—mostly at the old market—& I got considerable of my correspondence out of the way. At his dinner time I took coffee & ice cream, & after that he went back to the house to rest while I did some exploring around the quaint southern end of the town—where narrow streets, high coquina garden walls, old houses with balconies overhanging the sidewalkless roadway, & lush palm-tree vegetation give the perfect effect of an unspoiled Spanish colonial town. Here is the old Franciscan monastery—350 years old—which in 1763 became a barracks for His BRITANNICK Majesty's Garrison, & which is now the Florida State Arsenal. This vast & antient building is in a perfect state of preservation, & reflects the typical features of old Spanish construction. Near it—surrounded by a garden & now own'd by the St. Augustine Historical Society—is the reputedly oldest house in the U.S., which legend says was built in 1565 & subsequently used as an habitation for the earliest Franciscan monks of 1573, prior to the construction of the large monastery. After the latter was finished, tradition claims, the smaller house became the monastery hospital—being later sold as a private residence. The venerable edifice is of coquina & tabique (oyster-shell stone) construction, with wooden upper story & a balcony on the east gable end toward the river. It is of typical early Spanish design, & the pegged frame beams & shell-cement stone flooring are the original ones. Attached to an inner inconspicuous corner is a modern tower, & on the other inner corner the building is joined to a modern historical museum containing a diversity of traditional objects. The garden is highly attractive & full of statues, & in one place is a green bower in which various visitors leave their cards as a matter of custom. At another place I saw a small lizard or chameleon dart into a graceful pile of rocks—such quaint little saurians being rather typical of Florida. The rear of the old house is lined by a modest arcade, with which the tasteful loggia of the museum building forms a right angle. In the grounds is an ancient circular stone well, reputedly blessed by the monks & today figuring in folklore as a "wishing well." I went through this house with much thoroughness, reflecting upon the singularity of its age so far as my previous experience is concern'd. It is—granting it a date of 1565—67 years older than the oldest surviving English building on this continent—St. Luke's Church (1632) in Isle of Wight County, Virginia—& 71 years older than the Fairbanks house at Dedham, Mass.,[4] oldest surviving English dwelling on this continent. It was 71 years old when Roger Williams first landed at the Spring on the shore below 10 Barnes St., & *177 years old when the Stephen Hopkins house, oldest authenticated surviving building in Providence,* first arose on the Town Street south of the Market-Parade over-against Obadiah Brown's wharves. Before leaving, I purchas'd at the souvenir desk two samples of coquina stone—so typical of all St Augustine construction—at a nickel each. Of these one represents the more compact form, whilst the other represents the looser form in which individual shell-particles are clearly visible. In returning to the Rio Vista I noted another old house near the oldest one—the so-called "Don Toledo house", whose interior is said to be furnished in the old Spanish manner. This establishment—privately controlled—advertises itself rather ostentatiously & puts up deceptive guide signs calculated to make the tourist mistake it for the *oldest* house; yet in spite of all this cheap exploitation is undoubtedly a highly important relique & eminently deserving of exploration. On this occasion I had not time to explore it, but shall do so very shortly. At 5 p.m. I return'd to the Rio Vista to meet Newton & accompany him over the bridge for a walk on Anastasia Island—crossing the latter in order to walk on the oceanward tropick beach—a thing which would delight Belknap beyond words. The region just across the bridge—called Davis Shores—is one of those melancholy "developments" started in the late Florida "boom" & abandoned when the crash came. Lots & streets are staked out, aimless bits of curbstone & sidewalk are laid, & here & there will be found a vast pile of concrete building material which was to have gone into houses & business blocks. Great heaps of unused sectional piping of every size—sewer & water mains that were never laid—rise at many points; & feeble lines of wilted & anaemic palms shew the contemplated course of ambitious boulevards. Amidst all this desolation just *two* buildings exist—both in a complete state, & one inhabited. The large one—evidently an apartment-house, has all the grace of a sausage-factory & is mercifully empty. The smaller one is a single dwelling of nondescript pseudo-Spanish design—the sort of commonplace thing with which unaesthetic architects promiscuously plaster the landscape in Florida, California, & the Southwest, or wherever the dominion of Spain once extended. For these amorphous dumps but little excuse exists. They belong to an imaginary Spain which never was & (thank Pegāna!) never will be. With the exercise of just a little intelligence architects could study the *real* types of building evolved by the Spaniards in different parts of their colonial Empire, & produce duplicates harmonising as well with the genuine local tradition as our new Court House & Providence National Bank harmonise with the hereditary Providence tradition. A typical *St. Augustine* Spanish house is not the concrete hash that passes for Spanish in real estate offices, but is a distinctly local adaptation of Spanish urban (not hacienda) design—lower parts of coquina stone, upper parts wood, four-sided red-tiled roof coming to a single point in centre, & balcony (wooden) overhanging the street. Why cannot modern St. Augustine architects build edifices like this? Anastasia Island, as you will see from the accompanying map, is very narrow; so that it took no great walk to bring us to the farther or oceanward shore. Here we found a wide, flat beach of the fine, white calcareous sand peculiar to the South, & well adapted to motor driving—this form of shore locomotion being greatly esteemed, as one may gather from reports of races & speed trials at Daytona & other Southern beaches. Shallowness of water here prevents bathing, hence no obstructing crowds exist. The sea air is here more devoid of its typical salty smell than in the north. The whole spectacle of the wide, white lonely tropic beach with its curious southern shells, the chalk-white, sedge-spotted dunes of nearby Vilano Island across a wide strait, & the tall barber-pole lighthouse & red buildings of the alligator-ostrich-turtle farm to the south, is something not soon to be forgotten. Looking backward, across the Matanzas river, the fantastic skyline of St Augustine appears to immense advantage. After a brief period here, the rising of some dark clouds led Newton to fear rain & suggest a return. Only a few drops fell, but we abandoned further wanderings & partook of an evening meal—hamburg & onions, 25¢, on my part—at "Jake's." After that we sat in the ancient market & discussed literature (of which Newton knows more than I had suspected, despite his Victorian bias) till 9:30—Newton then retiring & I writing in my room till midnight.

On SUNDAY, MAY 10, 1931, I rose at 7 a.m., wrote a bit, & accompanied Newton to "Jake's" at 9 o'clock. I took only coffee, since I am finishing up the peanuts & chocolate I had on hand. I haven't yet decided whether to keep the little boxes for further use. Both are greasy, but they are infinitely convenient. After some discussion in the old market, Newton returned to the house whilst I remained in the market to write letters. Plans were to meet at noon for a dinner (chocolate so far as I am concern'd) & discussion of the afternoon's plans. The designated objective was the ostrich-alligator-turtle farm on Anastasia Island, & the discussion was to concern the question of whether one or both should make the trip—Newton having seen the place before. Well—this brings the diary to the present moment, for I am still in the old market at 11 a.m. with the 1682 bell of the 1793 cathedral pealing close at hand. This bell has an ineffably sweet & glamourous sound, & makes one wish one could hear the many bells & chimes of Old Spain itself.

At this point it is appropriate to take some notice of the origin & growth of the antient town wherein I am sojourning. The European discoverer of this region, as well as of all Florida, was Juan Ponce de Leon, of Leon, in Spain, who accompany'd Columbus on his second voyage to the New World. Being in command in Porto Rico, he heard Indian tales mentioning Bimini, a northward land of abundant gold & of rivers & springs which would restore youth to anyone who bathed in them; & in response to this allurement led an expedition of three caravels in search of the blessed region. On March 27, 1513, de Leon sighted the mainland coast; & just a week later, on Easter Sunday, he landed inside the Matanzas River inlet near the shore of a cove or creek since call'd Cano de la Leche—the probable spot now being mark'd, as previously mention'd. In honour of the festival day—Pascua Florida or Flowery Easter—de Leon gave the new realm the appropriate name of *Florida*. Planting a cross & taking possession of the territory in the Spanish King's name, he look'd about him & observ'd the proximity of an Indian village by the name of *Seloy*. Upon attempting exploration, & vainly trying the virtue of the rivers & springs in restoring him from the oppression of his 52 years, de Leon found nothing but weariness & Indian hostility; & left without forming a permanent settlement. The pioneering & temporary nature of de Leon's expedition, & the long period of relative neglect (punctuated by such things as De Soto's expedition) which follow'd it, remind one of Verrazzano's voyage along the Rhode-Island coast in 1529—or much more strongly of Jacques Cartier's expedition of 1535, on which Quebeck was discover'd & claim'd for the French King. Likewise, of John & Sebastian Cabot's exploration & claim of the New-England, Nova-Scotian, & Newfoundland coasts in behalf of His BRITANNICK Majesty in 1497.

The second—& first permanent—phase of Floridian history begins in the 1560's, when European eyes began to be cast on American shores as places of possible colonisation. In 1562 the Huguenot Jean Ribaut attempted unsuccessfully to found a colony in what was later to be His Maj^{ty's} Province of South-Carolina, & in 1564 his fellow-Frenchman Rene de Laudonmére [*sic*] surveyed the Ponce de Leon country around Seloy & named the Matanzas River the River of Dolphins; finally establishing a fort & settlement—Fort Caroline—near the mouth of the River of May—now the St Johns River. This colony met with vast hardships, & would have been abandon'd but for help extended by that great British navigator SIR JOHN HAWKINS, who saw the lookout tower & brought food—finally leaving the colonists one of his ships. On Aug. 29, 1565, Jean Ribaut return'd to the New World in an effort to promote the French colonial enterprise—bringing 7 ships & 300 colonists.

Meanwhile Spain, sensible of the foothold secur'd by the French on soil officially claim'd by Ponce de Leon in his Hispanick Majesty's name, determin'd to send an expedition to dislodge the intruders & found a true Spanish colony. For the leadership of this enterprise there was selected the most eminent Spanish seaman of his time—*Pedro Menendez de Aviles,* of the town of Aviles; whom his country has never ceas'd to honour, & who wou'd have had command of the great Spanish Armada in later years but for his death just after his appointment. Menendez had left Cadiz, in Spain, with a fleet of 34 vessels & 2640 men including priests, armourers, artisans, & seamen. A storm at sea destroy'd ⅔ of this formidable fleet, but the remaining third safely arriv'd at Porto Rico. Sailing up the east coast of Florida, & observing the colony of Ribaut at the mouth of the St John's, Menendez landed at Seloy on the 28th of August, 1565, the feast-day of Saint Augustine; there announcing the founding of a new Spanish town to be named after the saint—*La Siempre fiel*

Ciudad de San Agustin—the Ever-Faithful City of St. Augustine. Unfurling the flag of Castile & Aragon, & sounding cannon & trumpet, Menendez planted a cross & took possession in the Spanish King's name—claiming a coast-line that extended from Labrador to Mexico. Peace being made with the Indians, Menendez fortify'd the Indian Council House at Seloy by means of a ditch & 24 brass cannon—a defence less than a year later to be replaced by a real fort farther south at the entrance from the sea to the bay or river, called at first San Juan de Pinos & subsequently Castle San Marcos. In due season the priests with Menendez celebrated a Catholick Mass at the new settlement— the first to be celebrated on this continent—on a spot later known as Nombre de Dios; a chapel called Nuestra Señora de la Leche being soon erected, & the name Cano de la Leche being apply'd to the neighbouring cove.

Thus was founded, in 1565, the antient town of St. Augustine. Immediately subsequent events were of the most cruel & sanguinary description; & have made Menendez as great a fiend & enemy in the folklore of Carolina Huguenots, as he is a founder & hero in the eyes of St Augustinians. Ribaut having attempted to attack St Augustine, a storm dispers'd his ships & cancelled the expedition. Soon afterward Menendez with 500 men attacked Ft. Caroline after an arduous wade through the swamps—surprising the garrison & massacring every man save de Laudonmère & 2 others. Meanwhile 200 of Ribaut's men had been shipwreck'd below Seloy, near the south end of Anastasia Island at what is now Matanzas Inlet. Menendez, returning, demanded & received their unconditional surrender; whereupon he had them murdered in squads of 10 behind a hill—the fate of each squad being hidden from those about to undergo the same fate. Later another shipwreck'd party of 150 men including Ribaut himself was similarly dealt with. This murderous baptism of St Augustine is perpetuated in the name apply'd to the river— *Matanzas,* which signifies "Place of Slaughter". Tradition records that Menendez, when he hang'd the garrison at Fort Caroline, set up a placard reading: "I do this not as to Frenchmen, but as to hereticks."

History records the revenge of the French. In 1568 the Catholick Frenchman Dominique de Gourges [*sic*] proceeded with 3 ships to the site of Ft. Caroline, now the Spanish Fort San Mateo, & made an alliance with neighbouring Indians. With his new allies he next descended upon the fort & put all of its garrison to the sword except 45. These 45 he hang'd from trees, placing by them a caustick retaliatory reply to Menendez earlier proclamation: "I do this not as to Spaniards, but as to murderers."

Meanwhile the city of San Agustin, & the Spanish colony of Florida (ultimately divided into Florida Oriental, or East Florida, with the capital at St. Augustine, & Florida Occidental, or West Florida, with the capital at Pensacola) remain'd & prosper'd in a moderate way. Pirates, mutinies, & foreign & Indian attacks harrass'd the people & garrison, but could not put an end to the enterprise. Negro slaves were imported, & the Franciscan missionaries began to arrive after 1573. The centre of the settlement shifted rapidly southward, so that the present Plaza has been a prime focus throughout St Augustine's history. Houses of surprising ambitiousness—with balconies & walled gardens—were quickly built, & after Menendez came a long line of Governors of equally noble birth & high civil & military reputation. The title of the Governor was *Adelantado*. City walls & gates were constructed, & in 1690 the first sea-wall was built along the Matanzas river front. Indian hostility & humid climate retarded progress, & at times the fort fell into grave disrepair. In 1572 an attack of 3 of His Britannick Maj^{ty's} vessels was repuls'd, & later French privateers gave much trouble. On May 28, 1586, SIR FRANCIS DRAKE with a fleet of 26 vessels & 2300 men attack'd St. Augustine but did not at once take the fort, to which the townspeople fled. He then burn'd the town & captur'd the fort; seizing therein a treasure of some £2000. GOD SAVE THE KING!—or rather, QUEEN, for it was under Her glorious Majesty ELIZABETHA REGINA that men of our race first trod the narrow lanes of St Augustine as Conquerors. In 1593 the population of St Augustine mutinied against the Adelantado, Gutierrez de Miranda, & set up Capt. Francisco Salazar in his place. Lack of wages to the garrison was the prime cause. For this act the leaders were taken to Havana, drawn at the tails of 4 horses, hang'd, & posthumously beheaded—their heads exhibited on the city walls. Salazar was sentenc'd to be beheaded, but was pardon'd after an appeal to the King. In 1597 the Indians, oppress'd by restrictions impos'd upon them, conducted a concerted massacre of the Franciscan missionaries in different places; so decimating & disorganising them that their influence languish'd till more were sent from Spain in 1612, 1613, & 1633. The influence of the Franciscans was at its height from 1650 to 1675, & extended north into territory later Georgian & Carolinian. It was somewhat retarded by the founding of Old CHARLES-TOWN in 1670, & when His Britannick Majesty took over Florida in 1763 the order was forc'd to withdraw, their Indian converts being afterward known as the Seminoles. In the Franciscan heyday, the brown-robed, sandall'd, tonsur'd priests were one of the most characteristick sights in St. Augustine—like the black-rob'd Jesuits of antient Quebeck.

The founding of CHARLESTON open'd intermittent local hostilities betwixt Spanish & English, & soldiers, citizens, & convict labourers were imported from Mexico to aid in the town's fortification & defence. At this period—1670 et seq.—old Fort San Marcos was developing in its present form. French as well as English fleets also harass'd the coast.

In 1686, a group of Scotsmen having settled at Port-Royal in His Maj^{ty's} Province of Carolina, the Spaniards of St. Augustine sent a force of 3 vessels & massacred them. In revenge, in 1702, Govr Moore of Carolina order'd an attack on Fort San Marcos; Colonel Daniel going by land & pillaging the town whilst Moore himself came with the fleet & bombarded the fort. The townsfolk fled to the fort with 4 months' supplies, & upon Moore's arrival the church was made the army's headquarters. Hope of taking the fort being finally abandon'd, & 2 Spanish ships being seen close by, Moore rais'd the siege after 3 months, burn'd the town, & departed—taking the church plate, according to some.

In 1725 Col. Palmer of Georgia, with 300 militia, likewise captur'd the town but not the fort. He obtain'd much pillage, including the silver plate of the chapel of Nuestra Señora de la Leche. The Spaniards themselves later demolish'd this chapel for fear we might capture it & use it as a base in conducting operations against them.

In June 1740 Gov. Oglethorpe of Georgia led a land force of 2000 & a fleet of four ships against St Augustine, capturing outlying forts & forcing the townsfolk to crowd once more within the fort—which was oblig'd to shelter 3000 persons including a garrison of 900. Planting batteries on Anastasia Island, we gave a heavy bombardment which was made ineffective by the way in which our shots sank into the soft coquina of the walls without producing any breach. The Spaniards were nearly starved out when a supply ship from Cuba broke through our blockade & reconditioned them. At last Gen. Oglethorpe abandon'd the siege, left all his artillery, ships, & supplies behind, & return'd to Georgia. In reprisal, the Spanish fort commander Monteano pursu'd Oglethorpe with a force of 53 ships & 5000 men; encountering our small force of only 625 on St. Simon's Island. Here, in the open field, our ENGLISH valour prov'd itself; for Oglethorpe kept the Spaniards at bay for 15 days & finally drove them back to St Augustine. GOD SAVE THE KING! In 1742 Oglethorpe again attempted to take St. Augustine, this time by surprise, but was frustrated in the end. He besieg'd the city walls for 2 months, meanwhile laying waste the neighbouring region, but ultimately had to retire. The city walls were completed, & their present impressive gate constructed, in 1743. In 1756 the completion of the fort, as attested by an inscription, was accomplished.

We were now in the throes of the Old French War, with Spain fighting us on the side of France. In 1759 the glorious victory of the immortal WOLFE on the Plain of Abraham turn'd the scales in our favour, & in 1762—as announced by the first printing job ever turn'd out in Providence by John Carter at the Sign of Shakespear's-Head; the broadside "Morro Castle taken by Storm"—the Spanish town of Havana fell into our hands. God Save the King! At the peace negotiations of 1763, in settling with Spain, we exchanged this important capture for the whole of Florida—which thus came under the banner of His BRITANNICK Majesty, George the Third!

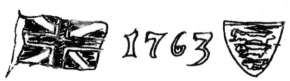

St. Augustine being now the capital of His Britannick Majesty's Province of East-Florida, the Spanish official clique with their families mov'd out, & were supplanted by many English planters from Barbadoes. There were left, however, a large number of Spaniards; so that the place must have been very largely bi-lingual. At Mosquito Inlet the planter Dr Andrew Turnbull brought in a horde of indentured labourers from the Mediterranean, naming his grant "New Smyrna". Of these 1500 men—Greeks, Italians, & Minorcans from the Spanish Balearic Isle—the Minorcans by far predominated; thus adding a fresh element to the Spanish character of the Province. Being dissatisfy'd on the indigo & sugar plantations, they soon revolted; but were quickly reduc'd to submission. In 1776 they again revolted, fled to St. Augustine, & receiv'd a legal discharge from their indenture—whereupon they settled down as inhabitants & are to this day represented amongst the population by descendants.

About this time the late unfortunate revolt against His Brittanick [sic] Majesty's rule was begun by the 13 colonies to the north; but the Floridas, like that other newly-acquir'd province of Quebec, remain'd faithful to our lawful Sovereign & Parliament. Many loyal gentlemen from Georgia & Carolina took up abodes on Floridian soil, & there was continual border strife betwixt the rebel guerillas of Georgia call'd the Liberty Boys, & the loyal Florida Rangers. At one time the rebel Genl. Charles Lee plann'd an attack upon loyal St. Augustine, but was stopt at the St. John's River. When His Majesty's troops captur'd rebellious Savannah & CHARLESTON in 1780, many men of St Augustine—including Minorcans—were among the captors. At this time 61 rebel leaders of CHARLESTON were arrested & sent to St. Augustine; all but one accepting parole & being sent north, whilst Christopher Gadsden, Esq., who refus'd parole, was confin'd in the antient fort. These prisoners, before leaving CHARLESTON, were kept in the dungeons beneath the Old Exchange at the foot of Broad St., which I explor'd on Tuesday last.

Before the close of the war Spain was rang'd with France & the rebell'd colonies against our rightful Sovereign, & in 1783 an expedition from St. Augustine captur'd the then Spanish town of Nassau, in the Bahamas. Spain, meanwhile, held Jamaica. During the general peace of 1783 His Maj^{ty's} representatives return'd Florida to Spain in exchange for Jamaica; thus restoring the pre-1763 status & bringing back the Spanish official group whilst our loyal English planters found refuge in the West-Indies. At this period—in 1793–7—the great Cathedral was built.

But the ferment of rebellion had been set in motion, & during the ensuing decades Florida shar'd in that general agitation amongst Spanish-Americans which finally sunder'd the whole of Mexico & South-America from the Crown of Castile & Arragon. In the course of this agitation—1812—the Spanish Cortes granted to Spain & her colonies liberal constitutions; & ordered that each colony erect a publick monument in honour of the event. The response of Florida Oriental to this order is the still existing obe-

lisk in the Plaza de la Constitucion. When the constitution was shortly re-
vok'd, the several monuments were order'd demolish'd; but upon the plea of
the St. Augustinians this one was allow'd to remain on condition that the in-
scrib'd tablets be remov'd. These tablets were carefully sav'd, & in 1818 were
replaced without opposition. This is the only monument of its kind in existence, since Spain's other colonies destroy'd their entire monuments according
to orders.

At this period, also, border troubles with the turbulent young republick
of the United States began to develop; so that at one time Florida was invaded by Genl. Andrew Jackson. American settlers also tried to set up a "Republic of Florida" in 1812. Amidst the ensuing turmoil a treaty was negotiated, &
in 1819 the United States formally purchas'd both East & West Florida. Two
years later—in 1821—the transfer of sovereignty was actually accomplish'd.
Castle San Marcos became Fort Marion, & Florida was added to the states of
the American nation.

St. Augustine, however, was slow in losing its reacquired Spanish character. In 1821–3 it served as the American capital of Florida, but after 1823 Tal-
lahassee officially supplanted it. The Spanish garrison & official group, plus
many private families, emigrated to Cuba; though a large number of Spaniards remained, became Anglicised, & have descendants today among the
population. But of course Anglo-Saxon blood poured in, so that the ultimate
transition to an American town was inevitable from the first. In 1836 the re-
fusal of the Seminoles to accept transportation to the Indian Territory along
with the other Indian nations of the southeast precipitated the memorable
Seminole War. During hostilities the two chiefs Osceola & Coacoochee came
to St. Augustine to confer with the American general Hernandez, but were
imprisoned in spite of the flag of truce under which they came. They were
confined in a casemate of the fort, whence Coacoochee escaped by fasting till
he was thin enough to squeeze through the single ventilator 18 feet above the
floor.* (140 by St. John's Eve—& lo! I have made the grade already! Look at
the enclosed card—which another, to be sent to Belknap, confirms!) Osceola
could have done likewise, but refused on a point of honour. After confinement here for 2 months, he was removed to Ft. Moultrie in CHARLESTON,
there dying in a month—it is said—of a broken heart. I saw his cell & grave
at Moultrie last year. When he died—on Jan. 30, 1838—his passing must
have been noted with more than ordinary interest by Edgar Allan Poe, who
had serv'd at Fort Moultrie in the winter of 1828–9.

After the Seminole War Florida became more & more American, receiving a filtration of Anglo-Saxons from Georgia & other neighbouring commonwealths, & becoming quite thoroughly a typical Southern slave state. The
hamlet of Cow Ford, renamed Jacksonville in 1822, rose to the dignity of an

---

*also, he had to drop 25 feet to the moat outside

attractive town; & it was clear that the compact civilisation of the United States would soon override all traces of Hispanic civilisation. Of course, only the northern part of Florida was populated in any true sense. The great bulk of the peninsula was left to swamps & desolation, & remained for future cold-shunning generations to develop.

In the Civil War Florida adhered to the Confederacy, but was constantly overrun by Federal troops. St. Augustine & Ft. Marion were surrendered to a Union commander in 1862, & the fort was garrisoned by Federals throughout the balance of the war. At that period the town was unmistakably becoming American in aspect & language. The coquina sea-wall of 1690 had been supplanted in 1837–43 by another, also of coquina & built by the state from the fort to the southerly edge of the old town at St. Francis St. The old city wall, which had run from the great gate to both rivers, along the San Sebastian to the southern edge of the old town, & thence east to the Matanzas, was removed—except for the still surviving gate.

St. Augustine remain'd a delightful & somnolent village till the late Victorian aera, when the hotel enterprises of the late Henry M. Flagler, Esq. develop'd it as a winter resort.[5] It then acquired that slightly unfortunate air of showmanship, & that profusion of baroque pseudo-Spanish modern architecture, which present observers notice. Northern men of wealth have done much for the town, though at the cost of a lamentable loss of old Southern atmosphere. Florida is not in any sense the Old South that the Virginia & Carolina regions are. Many unduly ambitious plans were develop'd during the late Florida "boom", & one recent tall building (7 stories—a skyscraper for St Augustine—erected by the now defunct 1st Natl Bank) sorely mars the skyline. The present depression has greatly checked such expansion, & the development of areas farther south has caused the place to wane as a winter resort. It is now devoted chiefly to transient tourist traffick bound to or from such tropical resorts as Miami & Palm Beach. The town is unique in every way, & would be more keenly appreciated in an age less obtuse & democratic than this. Its low prices, genial hospitality, delectable climate, prodigious quaintness, genuine beauty, & many conveniences recommend it to every sort of visitor, & anyone wishing slight expenses amidst ideal conditions would do well to think of it for permanent residence. It is—except for a slight Spanish element—absolutely American; foreigners being virtually unknown. Its typical diversions—checker-playing, horseshoe-pitching, fishing, hunting—stamp it as still belonging to the naive early-American scene; whilst its ingrained reposefulness suggests the best of European cultivation. Once a year—each April—a stately historical pageant is enacted by the townsfolk; persons being chosen by vote to represent such leading characters as Ponce de Leon, Pedro de Menendez, & the Queen of Spain. The survival of historick feeling is well attested not only by institutions like this, but by the activities of the St. Augustine Historical Society. The city's recent invitation to King Alfonso to spend his exile here is quite characteristick.[6] An excellent publick library—housed in a 1775 Spanish Mansion with walled garden—exists; & such facilities as schools, hotels, amusements, fire protection, shops, clubs, transportation, &c. &c. are admirably supplied. The city water has an unfortunate sulphurous taste, but spring-water is cheap & universally distributed. Fires are rather prevalent because of the fatty, combustible nature of the local timber—but this is being rapidly remedied by better construction methods. The city is the county-seat of St John's County, & the cathedral is the head of the Catholick diocese of St Augustine.

Well—such is antient San Augustin—a town I can scarcely bear to think of breaking away from. Its healthful qualities seem to me virtually miraculous—for my degree of strength, comfort, activity, & good spirits astonishes me as much as it would astonish you & A E P G could you behold it! But to continue my diary—left off Sunday noon in the antient market.

At 12:15 I return'd to the house, met Newton, & accompany'd him to "Jake's", where he had a roast beef dinner whilst I took only coffee. By this time lowering clouds had arisen, cancelling plans for outdoor trips & dictating indoor activities. Accordingly we sought the Rio Vista again—where I wrote letters at length whilst a picturesque tropick thunderstorm rag'd outside. By evening it had clear'd, so that Newton & I again sought "Jakes". This time I got a pork chop & French-fried potato dinner for 35¢. Afterward Newton return'd home whilst I strolled around the antient streets in the mystick twilight. At dusk I returned to the Rio myself, had an interesting chat about Florida history & southwestern antiquities with the proprietor—Fryer—& sought my room to finish this epistle. Here I am still—& shall retire about 1 a.m. Tomorrow's programme is still unsettled—but it cannot help being interesting & delightful. I shall get the Sunday Times, & vary my letter-answering with a brief spell of reading. Have just heard from A E P G, who describes mail which has come for me. I want the envelope from London, which probably contains a small cheque.

Don't work—& don't let any sable cleansing agent upheave my crowded quarters too violently! And get out for some brief walks if the temperatures up north are in any way civilised! ¶ More soon—& don't forget to keep the Bulletins & Sunday Journals stacked up!

Yr aff Nephew & obt Servt

H P L

[HPL's annotations on verso of leaf IV:]

[~~Bonita~~ (Rio) Vista Hotel] renamed because the original title sounded too much like the neighbouring Buena Vista Hotel.

[Mr. and Mrs. J. T. Fryer, Props.] very worthy people from Texas, in late middle life.

Notes

1. HPL is in error. The title refers to a common Catholic image of the Madonna nursing the infant Jesus.

2. *At the Mountains of Madness*, the 115-page T.Ms. of which HPL finished on 1 May, just before he departed for his Southern trip.

3. In fact, Wright rejected the story for *WT*. See LDC/AEPG 333.

4. See HPL's essay "An Account of a Trip to the Antient Fairbanks House, in Dedham, and to the Red Horse Tavern in Sudbury, in the Province of the Massachusetts-Bay" (1929). In *CE* 4.

5. Henry Morrison Flagler (1830–1913), American industrialist and a co-founder of Standard Oil. Beginning in 1885, Flagler funded the construction of numerous hotels in St. Augustine, including the Ponce de Leon Hotel, as well as Florida East Coast Railway.

6. Alfonso XIII (1886–1941), king of Spain (1886–1931), fled the country on 14 April 1931 upon the establishment of the Second Republic. He eventually settled in Rome.

[329]　　[ALS] [HPL to LDC]

May 30, 1931

My dear Daughter:—

I was delighted to hear from you, though sorry to learn that you have had one of those nerve-racking chills. Don't over-exert, but get out for brief walks in the sunshine whenever possible—for I assume that even up north there is a little decent sunshine by this time of year! Glad the general health average is about as usual, but hope the summer will put it above the usual mark. When I get back I'm going to drag you out for a boat trip to Newport, a railway trip to Warren & Bristol, & other ventures of a salubrious & not too taxing quality.

Glad my diary cards have been arriving. The Tampa item for which you were requested to send postage is probably a postcard with rather meagre address space. As you know, one or two fussy postmasters sometimes object to my economical methods—Morton having just reported a similar holdup. Possibly I had better be a little less economical in my diary programme if I hope to get the instalments to you in proper order & without delays & technicalities! Trust the package I mailed home to myself from St. Augustine safely arrived. Within a week I shall probably be making myself a similar shipment from Dunedin. Glad the views are of interest. Really, they are not in the least exaggerations! So the picture of the St Augustine shrimp fleet caused you to eat shrimps! Since then I have sent a view of the Greek sponge fishing fleet at Tarpon Springs—which has no doubt caused you to discard facecloths in favour of sponges!

Interested to hear that Evans called up. I wasn't sure about how we left the telephoning business, and that accursed typing job erased nearly everything else from my memory. I have dropped Evans one or two cards from along my route.

Florida is certainly the greatest place I've ever struck for climate. Not in years have I even begun to feel so well. At last I have succumbed to Whitehead's insistent offer to lend me a white drill suit of the West Indian sort, & I find it infinitely comfortable & becoming. It is as perfect a fit as if made to order by a tailor! As I have just remarked to A E P G, I have never looked less offensive since 1900 or 1901—my heavy coat of tan & miraculous freedom from face trouble coöperating with the tropical raiment to produce an effect vastly unlike the accustomed Theobaldian exterior. My idea of solid comfort is to have the temperature always high enough to permit of the wearing of white drill. In the evening, of course, I find my own woollen coat & vest necessary. To get any great number of hot evenings, one would have to be farther from the seacoast.

Of the beauty of the scene I have already spoken. Sky, sea, tropical vegetation, & exotic birds all combine to produce an atmosphere of dreamlike loveliness. Dunedin's absence of old houses & quaint byways, however, would bore me after a while; so that I think I'd choose St. Augustine for anything like stable habitation. For a visit, though, the ideal climate, delectable scenery, & fascinating conversation of Whitehead are more than enough to keep an old man entertained. CHARLESTON, naturally, surpasses all these places in interest; & I intend to stop there a full week on my return trip—perhaps accompanied by the bright young Grayson fellow whom I have previously described. In selecting a Southern residence I would indeed hate to pass over Charleston—though undeniably it is colder than Florida. Some hibernation would be necessary in almost any place—that is, a relinquishment of outdoor reading & writing—but the amount of such hibernation would obviously vary in different places. Charleston well knows what a sprinkle of snow looks like, St Augustine sees snow perhaps once in every 5 or 10 years, & Dunedin has never had a snowfall. Decent weather apparently begins in Charleston some time in April; though as I remarked, it can be temporarily very chilly in May when it chooses to be. So, for that matter, can it be in St. Augustine; though there I was seldom driven in by the cold till evening. It is very good there from March onward. In Dunedin it is never too cold to write in the open at this time of year if one has a good coat & vest. It is sometimes hard to choose between physical comfort & imaginative contentment—so that the race betwixt Charleston & St Augustine is very close. Charleston is *incomparably* the more captivating & fancy-satisfying place—since it is the very heart of the ancient colonial civilisation of the South, & has preserved an unbroken heritage from the 18th century onward. Only on the score of *climate* could St. Augustine or any other place in Florida be even in the running with Charleston. *Charleston & Quebec* have a magic possessed by no other towns on this continent.

I note the heron item with interest. In Dunedin the profusion of exotic wading birds is very striking, & would sooner or later make one an ornithologist in spite of himself. There are also fascinating land birds—some of them oddly crested—& a species of whippoorwill with a trilling, liquid note much more elaborate than that of our New England whippoorwills. The tapping of woodpeckers is always heard in the offing, & all these feathered denizens are encouraged by frequent bird houses on the broad lawns of the sightly cottages. If this isn't a close approach to the fabled paradise, I don't know what is.

I have spoken of the unearthly & alluring glamour of sunset beyond the low outlying key, & of the mystical bridge of light that a white, hanging moon builds across the tranquil gulf waters to some unknown & fabulous land in the ethereal west. These things powerfully affect not only myself but my poetic young fellow-guest & possible fellow-traveller Allan Grayson; so that when he asked me to write something in his autograph album I could not refrain from dropping into the following quatrains:

To A Young Poet in Dunedin

You haunt the lonely sand where herons hide,
    And palm-framed sunsets open gates of flame;
Where marble moonbeams bridge the lapping tide
    To westward shores of dream without a name.

Here, in a haze of half-remembering,
    You catch faint sounds from that far, fabled beach.
The world is changed—your task henceforth to sing
    Dim, beckoning wonders you could never reach.

One thing I note both here & in St. Augustine is that the sea does not have the salty smell it has in the north. Whitehead says it is just the same in the West Indies. Only once in a while does a stray whiff remind one that the neighbouring water is not a lake. Another local asset is the presence of many delightful *cats*—especially a black & white one in the Clearwater Piggly-Wiggly where Whitehead trades. This shop, by the way, keeps a kind of cheese superior to any other I have ever tasted—so that I am going to see if our local Piggly-Wigglies in Thayer St. & Elmgrove Ave. have it after I get back.

Hope you haven't let that dark substantial shadow disarrange too many of Grandpa's paper-filled nooks & corners—& also, I trust you have not let your own personal labours extend beyond the directive stage!

Yes—Whitehead is certainly a great guy, & I find him one of the rare few to whom I can talk at length without running out of topics. He is about as far from the stereotyped clergyman—even intellectually—as anyone could well be; & he recognises that even his assumption of a deity is only a guess suggested by tradition. He seems to be the idol of everyone in Dunedin, & especially of the small boys—whose psychology he understands very minutely as a result of long experience in directing boys' summer camps. He has written boys' stories for years—though not as a main line as good old Mac used to write them—& is about to have a juvenile novel published by Putnam's—an account of which in the Dunedin paper I recently sent you. His health is improving, though he still has to be very careful & rest each afternoon. In generally fascinating personality I can find no better comparison for him than the Edward F. Gamwell of 1895–6–7. His spontaneous generosity is so vast that one has actually to be careful about admiring anything of his, lest he offer it as a present! When I leave in about a week I shall bear away as gifts a jar of West Indian cherry marmalade, a copy of Paul Morand's "Black Magic", & a copy of Wakefield's weird collection, "Others Who Return." [*sic*] Whitehead is negotiating for an automobile—trying to get one in exchange for the royalty rights on his new book—& in the meantime is given all sorts of free rides by his generous neighbours. These neighbours are incredibly accomodating—especially a delightful old couple from Detroit named Metzen; who have a fine little estate on the shore a trifle north of Whitehead's, & who urge me to spend any amount of loafing, reading, & writing time in their tastefully landscaped seaward garden.

About the old hat—which would clash hideously with my borrowed white finery—I solve the problem by not wearing any; this being customary even among elders in Dunedin. Whitehead has lent me a white belt to go with the suit, & would have lent white canvas shoes except that his are too large for Grandpa. As for retiring—I never do so till I can sleep, but sleeping is easier here than in the north. Also—one feels more rested after a sleep than in the north. Everyone says my aspect of health has improved prodigiously since arriving in Dunedin—though I was already tanned & free from face ploughings before I arrived.

As for my diary—last carried through Thursday the 28th—I rose on FRIDAY, MAY 29, 1931 at 8 a.m., tried out the white suit, talked with H S W, did some reading & writing in a favourite summer-house (or arbour, or lodge-gate) on the shore at the entrance of the walk to an unoccupied cottage called "The Birds' Nest", had a *welsh rarebit* lunch with H S W, (he is an expert in rarebit-construction) talked & wrote on the shore in the afternoon, & returned to dinner at 6. A very pleasant man named Hancock was a guest for the evening, & shortly after dinner the boys began to arrive for their regular Friday night meeting—an institution they vastly cherish. Mr. Hancock was inducted as an honorary member of the secret society, & the usual story-telling programme was then followed—during the course of which I read my reprinted "Outsider" from the new Weird Tales, whilst Whitehead read his "Hill Drums" from the same issue.[1] After the gathering dispersed, the bulk of the household retired—whilst I read & wrote till about 3 a.m. Today—SATURDAY, MAY 30, 1931—I rose at 8, breakfasted with H S W & Grayson—plus a couple of small boy visitors—& did some reading & writing on the shore. Then lunch & more writing & reading. For the evening a dinner guest—a Mrs. Grant—is scheduled; & afterward the usual reading & writing programme will doubtless end the day. Moon is full now—an utterly glorious spectacle! ¶ Best wishes & more soon—

Yr n——

H P L

[P.S.] Current weird tales [*sic*] has items by Whitehead, Belknap, Clark Ashton Smith, & myself. I shall get my copy & mail it home. Eyrie gives me quite a little mention.

Notes

1. Both stories were published in *WT* (June/July 1931). The other stories cited by HPL in his P.S. are FBL's "The Abominable Snow Men" (verse) and Clark Ashton Smith's "The Venus of Azombeii."

[330]   [ALS] [HPL to LDC]

Miami—
Wednesday Midnight
[10 June 1931][1]

My dear Daughter:—

After mailing my 2 diary cards for today I have done some evening sightseeing, examined some local views, & come to the conclusion that I did Miami an injustice in my first estimate. The place seems to be better than I thought—having some really splendid tropic vegetation even if it is artificially planted. And I infer that there are areas out of the business section in which really notable groves & gardens are to be found. When I get back from Key West I may stop an extra night & take a sightseeing tour of the surrounding region. The vegetation is unmistakably more tropical than that of either St. Augustine or Dunedin—although I can't say that I find the apparent climate any warmer than the latter's. The chill I felt in Bayfront Park is not apparent farther back from the water—indeed, it is delightfully warm here at the Hotel Alexandria. I have a fine room with running water for only a dollar, & there are some excellent-looking rooming houses where the summer rent is only **$3.50** per WEEK.

The town as a whole is extremely spruce & modern—actually metropolitan in atmosphere, & looking larger than its officially enumerated population (year round) of 110,514. It is larger than Tampa (100,910) & smaller than Jacksonville (129,682). Flagler St.—the business centre—looks like Worcester's Main St. Despite numerous semi-skyscrapers, the architecture preserves a touch of the old subtropical tradition—including balconies or canopies supported over the sidewalk on pillars, presumably to afford shade for pedestrians. Miami is distinctly more prepossessing than Tampa, & far less prosaic than Jacksonville. I think it would tend to grow on one with time—& most certainly, its climate is one of the most healthful & stimulating in the world. But the general rural landscape between here & West Palm Beach is certainly about as poor as any I have seen—except perhaps New Jersey & the Carolina highlands. I miss the live-oaks & Spanish moss which were with me from Charleston to Dunedin. As a permanent thing, I'd rather live in St Augustine & stay indoors during January & February than live in Miami & have a constant June climate.

Really, this place is tremendously far south; being in the same latitude as the Bahama Islands. I enclose a folder with map illustrating my various stops in Florida. This is the most southerly city on the *mainland* of the U.S., & is *1758* miles from Providence. Key West is 156 miles to the southwest—on one of the remote Florida Keys. You will be glad to hear that Miami (like Tampa & Jacksonville) has retained its street-car system.

I fear my borrowed white suit is going to prove a kind of white elephant—for it will not stay clean in motor coaches. I have just given some of the worst spots an expert laundering, but fear I shall have to repeat the process after each day's ride. I'll be glad to get the old grey back in St Augustine. What I *would* like to own is a *dark* Palm Beach suit—but not a white outfit. They are no good unless one owns half a dozen & has them washed constantly as Whitehead does.

Trust all goes smoothly at #10. From Friday morning onward my trip becomes a *return* one—albeit a somewhat leisurely return if cash holds out. I shiver at the thought of going north—yet by this time Quinsnicket's mystical hills & groves must be getting very attractive!

More soon—

Yr aff. nephew & obt
H P L

P.S. As for *real tropic heat*—I've decided that none exists in the U.S. What Florida gives is simply a *long, steady, & dependable* succession of genial summer days about the same as the *best* summer days of Providence.

Notes

1. Date written on the ALS by RHB.

[331]   [ALS] [HPL to LDC]

Thursday–Friday Midnight
June 11–12, 1931

My dear Daughter:—

Continuing my diary for THU., JUNE 11, 1931, I may report that I am in Key West at last. I am 1914 miles from Providence, & 839 miles nearer to the Panama Canal than to Exchange Place! This is the most southerly point in the United States, & the *only* city in the U.S. *which has never had a temperature below the freezing-point of 32°*. I have struck the real tropics at last. All the houses are without furnaces, & even the best hotels have no steam heat. The average temperature for *January* is **77°**—although on account of the sea the summers are not correspondingly hot. The highest monthly average temperature is for August, & amounts to 84°—which, paradoxically enough, is less than *Quebec's* August average! The nearest other city is Havana, Cuba, which is only 87 miles away—less than the distance from Providence to Hartford or New Haven. And not far west are the keys of Dry Tortugas, which belong to the Central American republic of *Honduras* . . . . surely a close approach to the tropical heart of Latin-America!

As utterly isolated from the populous part of the world as Block Island or Nantucket, Key West has retained an unique provincial character differing vastly from that of any other place. It is simple & village-like, & extremely frugal & primitive in all things. Spanish influence is everywhere observable—Cubans being about as thick as French-Canadians in Fall River or Jews in New York. One of the two cinema theatres (both owned by a Spaniard) has its films in the Spanish language. There is, however, no Spanish newspaper. Vegetation is thick, splendid, & tropical—including great trees & surpassing that of any of the other keys. There is, however, no Spanish moss so far as I can see. Under cultivation, the greenery assumes an unbelievable luxuriance in gardens. Cocoanut palms are frequent.

Unlike Dunedin & Miami, this is an *old* town with a *natural* growth; & it is certainly refreshing to be back in such a place. The town was founded under the Spanish regime—though not, I think, till the early 1800's. The original name is *Caya Huesco,* (Bone Key) which American usage soon corrupted into the present title of *Key West.* Early in the American regime it became an army post, & it has always since remained a military & naval station of importance; because of its strategic control of the entrance to the Gulf of Mexico. In the Civil War it pursued the anomalous course of supporting the Federal side despite the secession of Florida as a state. In the Spanish war it was a great naval base & hospital centre. The harbour is of exceptional depth & convenience, & many steamship lines—to Tampa, New Orleans, Havana, &c—converge here. The principal industry—employing most of the Spanish population—is the manufacture of cigars. Next come fishing, sponge-fishing, ship supplies, & fruit growing—the latter accomplished largely on the adjacent keys.

Houses are largely small wooden cottages set in fenced-in gardens, recalling the old America of the 1840's. Tropic balconies are frequent on both residences & shops, & the latest buildings (though not many new ones are built) have them as well as the old ones. Some shops have folding doors of many sections, which can be so opened as to throw the entire front open to the street—forming a sort of open-air bazaar, as it were. This is especially true of drug stores & soda fountains. In the residences, most front doors have auxiliary doors with shutters like those of blinds—a fashion which also existed in New England during the late Georgian period, & which is well exemplified by [the] fine hillside colonial house at the corner of Angell & Congdon. Some of the houses have window blinds hinged at the top, which open outward like awnings & are propped with sticks. A distinct Latin touch pervades everything. *Chimneys* are very rare, & roofs tend to come to a central point or ridge like those of most far-southern towns. It is a relief to be in a really *old* & naturally developed town once again. Miami & all it represents seems in another world—for Key West is one with Charleston & Providence & Salem as a representation of pre-machine-age America. The city has a population (1930) of 12,613; being therefore about the size of Bristol, & somewhat larger than Athol or N. Attleboro. Its size is almost identical with that of my favourite village of Hempstead, Long Island. It is the seat of Monroe County, which includes all the keys. Up to 1911 or 1912 its isolation from the world was even more profound than at present; but at that time the Florida East Coast Railway completed its causeways & opened service from the mainland. Lack of *highway* access continued to keep it semi-isolated, but in 1928 the present motor route (interrupted by two 2-hour ferry trips) was opened. But for the business depression, these ferries would have been eliminated by this time— but lacking money, the state has not been able to construct the desired causeways. This delay is probably all that saves Key West from tourist invasion, standardisation, & self-conscious showmanship. As things are, the town is absolutely natural & unspoiled; a perfect bit of old-time simplicity which is truly quaint because it does not know that it is quaint. There is only one luxurious winter hotel, & one first-class city hostelry like our Biltmore. I am stopping at the latter—because the poor business season has caused them to quote fine single rooms with hot & cold water at only $1.50. It is the Key West Colonial—owned by the same chain which owns Charleston's palatial Ft. Sumter Hotel on the Battery. There is a widely advertised roof garden with a magnificent view of the whole city & surrounding keys & ocean, which I intend to investigate tomorrow morning. But my own room has a fine enough view.

The coach drew into Key West at sunset, when the whole tropic scene bore an aspect of ineffable glamour. This approach was along a wide seaside boulevard; & betwixt the observer & the mystical westward gulf there rose a low, picturesque line of old-fashioned roofs & steeples which even the tall skeleton masts of the wireless station could not spoil. On the farther side one could note great ships tied up at the docks—messengers from Caribbean realms of still more enchanting glamour. In reaching the hotel—which is also the bus station—the coach passed through a large part of the town; so that I formed an excellent general impression at the very outset. With the coming of daylight, I shall do further exploration on foot—as well as consulting books in the local library. So far I have studied only the few Chamber of Commerce

leaflets procurable at the hotel desk. The local Cubans are very picturesque—
& not even nearly as squalid as our Federal Hill Italians. They are addicted to
sporty clothes of a flamboyant striped pattern. Most of the younger ones, locally educated, speak fluent English.

Well—more soon. Now I'm retiring.

Yr aff Nephew & obt Servt—

H P L

[332]   [ALS] [HPL to LDC]

St. Augustine, in His
Majesty's Province of
East-Florida
—June 16, 1781.

My dear Daughter:—

Delighted to find your interesting note awaiting me up-
on my return to the ancient capital. I surely did signify my appreciation of
Whitehead's hospitality, & he would not let me depart without many a solemn promise to visit him early & often. A delightful character—& I surely
wish him a speedy & complete restoration to perfect health!

Glad the postcards have proved of interest. By this time you are aware of
my Key West expedition, & of how marvellously enchanting I found this one
glimpse of the full tropics. Still—I am tremendously glad to see St. Augustine
again; for the ancient houses, narrow streets, & live-oak vegetation have an
imaginative appeal overbalancing the relative coolness of the climate & the
sulphur tinge in the city water. It is now slightly warmer than last month,
though not nearly so hot as in Dunedin or Miami or Key West. I am able to
keep on wearing the soiled white suit (which is quite all right for informal St
Augustine) & save my newly-pressed old grey for the next stage of the trip.

St. Augustine is exquisite amidst its tangled foliage under the June sun, with
the old fort looming up & the sweet bells (1682) of the old Spanish church
sounding drowsily across the ancient Plaza. I am doing my writing around in
my favourite haunts of last month—all the more attractive now that the last
trace of tourist life has vanished for the summer. My meals are once more taken
at the cheap Jake-like place in St George St.—a procedure which I fear will
soon annul the result of my spectacular 10-lb reducing of last week. But I'm still
136 in the white suit this morning. I think I'll only take one meal at Jake's, & let
the other be ice-cream. Last week I grew so fond of an ice-cream diet that I
often substituted a second plate for a sandwich. Of course, one can't get coffee ice-cream outside New England; but I alternated betwixt vanilla & chocolate. I hope I shall manage to be not over 140 by St. John's Eve. Then my
goal will be 140 by Lammas. I am continuing to go hatless—for now that I
have the new cheap straw I don't like to wear it out. The indoors barely

knows me—indeed, the open air is an ideal habitat in any decently warm climate. Of course I shall make for the woods & fields every decent afternoon after I get home—just as I have done for the last five years. I can imagine how exquisite Quinsnicket's ancient elms & stone walls are getting, & shall surely be glad to encounter them in their fullest glory! Your windows are surely a splendid vantage-point—as indeed I told you before you moved in! But on some of those warm days you'd better try a few pleasure-walks in front of the house, in preparation for the trips I'm going to drag you out to when I get back! Don't forget Warren, Bristol, & Newport—& the 27 varieties of ice cream at Maxfield's. A E P G says she stopped in at Maxfield's the other day.

Thanks for the forwarded letters—& don't imagine for an instant that your own are commonplace! That from Weird Tales was not a communication from the magazine at all, but from a young man in Pittsburgh—J. Vernon Shea, Jr.—who likes my stories and wants to discuss them with me. So far, the fate of my long & painfully typed novelette still hangs in the balance—probably on account of Wright's uncertain health. He has also shewn delay in passing on a recent tale of Little Belknap's.

Sonny & Galpin had some good conversations in N.Y., though there was no opportunity for a gang meeting in Alfredus's honour. Galpin has not changed even a trifle in the last five years according to Belknap—& he still goes hatless, with long hair now & then falling into his eyes. I was certainly sorry to miss seeing him—but the charm of the tropick South overrides everything else. I may possibly miss seeing Mortonius, too, since he will be taking trips to Boston & Nova Scotia during the coming month. But it may be that he will be in Providence about the time I get home. His elaborately foreplanned schedules make me laugh—for I wouldn't have more than a shadow of a kick from any trip whose moves were perfectly known in advance. The whole thrill of travel lies in the element of *surprise & unexpectedness*—suggesting as it does the quality of adventurous liberation. Half the fun of my Key West extension came from the fact that I didn't know till a late date whether or not I could take it. My next large trip—1932 if I live through another cursed winter—will have *Havana* as its primary goal . . . . whether or not I can ever get that far.

As for my diary—as I said last night, I safely reached the ancient capital over Anastasia Island & the Bridge of Lions, & secured my old room at the Rio Vista for 4 fish—one week. I don't think I'll have to make any further calls on my banker—especially if I cut out the trip up the Hudson as I may regretfully do at the last moment. I ate an enormous 25¢ beef stew at "Jake's"—my first meal other than sandwiches & ice cream since Tuesday, June 9th (6 days)—& sat around the Plaza reading my voluminous mail & talking with Newton. After Newton retired I wrote letters in my room & retired at 2 a.m.

Today—TUESDAY, JUNE 16, 1931—I arose at 9 a.m. & took some ice-cream, after which I sat in the Plaza writing letters & talking with Newton.

In the afternoon I strolled about the ancient, narrow streets—stopping to write at various favourite points, especially the massive old fortress of San Marcos. Then another Jake dinner, discussion, writing, & retiring. I shall do some historical research at the library after catching up with my voluminous correspondence. St. Augustine is still the same delicious old place—with the same groups of American & Cuban checker-players in the ancient market house. Now & then the drowsy chimes peal out, as they have pealed down through the long, unchanging centuries . . . . .

Tomorrow—despite the imperilled 136—I shall probably obtain some spaghetti at the Spanish place in Charlotte St. They only had it Fridays last month, but now Newton tells me they also have it Wednesdays. I shall be starting northward next Monday evening (June 22) at 9:30, (unless they take the night coach off) arriving at Jacksonville 10:55 p.m., & at Savannah 6:00 a.m. Doing Savannah in one day, I hope to get a late afternoon coach to CHARLESTON & reach there Tuesday evening—one week from tonight. Thus my address for an *immediate* batch of mail will still be St. Augustine, but after Saturday or Sunday will be % Y M C A, CHARLESTON, SOUTH CAROLINA. How glad I shall be to see the old English South again!

Well—more soon.

Yr aff Nephew & obt Servt

H P L

[On envelope:]

Today has turned out delightfully hot—everybody else is complaining, & I'm in my element! Many in Florida—especially around Key West & Miami—wear amber-tinted sun-glasses* on account of the tropical radiance, but I have not found this necessary. Incidentally, that tugging at my left eye has *entirely vanished.* I don't yet know whether the cure is due to the better general health of tropic air, or to the fact that I've read absolutely no newspapers of late. The very last faint signs of the trouble were in Dunedin the first few days. Not a trace since. When I get home I'll see whether newspapers bring it on again. Aside from the absence of tugging, my general left-eye vision is vastly more distinct. I have worn glasses only at cinema shows.

[333]   [ALS] [HPL to LDC]

St Augustine—
Last Day—June 22, 1931

My dear Daughter:

Well—things are well timed, for I have received both your & A E P G's notes on this very last day of my San Augustinian sojourn!

Confound that wretch Wright for turning down the tale I half killed my-

---

*they sell at 25¢ & 50¢ at all the drug stores

self typing! The accursed cheap skate!! The package cannot well be anything else—& if it looks small, it is because what you saw was the whole double stack of leaves together—original & carbon copies. If it isn't too much trouble, I wish you'd open the package & take out whatever *letter* is in it—sending me this letter *in care of F. B. Long, 230 West 97th St., New York City*. It will be some consolation to be able to talk it over with one who has suffered likewise—we will think up new joint insults to fling at Wright, & will curse his name in chorus, & with appropriate variations.

Yes—Key West has a Whitehead St., & I dropped H S W a card about it. Glad it's decently warm up north, & hope a cold wave doesn't come by the time I get there. Tampa is certainly a cheap town—measuring the writing on all the post cards! I'm trying to allow a little more space now, as a general rule—but I'm sure St Augustine isn't so finical about measurements! Glad Mortonius is enjoying himself at Harvard. I shall probably see him in Providence shortly after my own arrival—perhaps before I get my stack of Bulletins & Sunday Journals read up! He will then be returning from a trip to Nova Scotia.

I'm reading the Times this afternoon—for I can get it in St Augustine. My eyes still function perfectly—no sign of the tugging at the left one—& I may not need new glasses at all. I will go to some optometrist, however, before getting duplicate lenses for my gold bows—then if any change is indicated, I'll get a new pair of lenses instead of repeating the old prescription. Possibly a daily paper reading would bring the trouble back.

Did quite a bit on a new story yesterday—but am so disgusted over Wright's latest rejection that I can't do a thing in that line today.[1] But probably the Times will keep me busy the rest of the afternoon. I'm now at the old fort.

At 9:30 tonight I shall take the coach for Jacksonville—most reluctantly, for it's like pulling a tooth to leave old Florida behind! If all goes well, I shall catch the midnight coach for Savannah—once more entering the ancient English South, & arriving at the town of Genl. Oglethorpe at 6 a.m. Plans then depend on conditions. If the town does not seem interesting, I shall stay only an hour & a half, taking the 7:30 a.m. coach for CHARLESTON, & reaching that ancient seat of civilisation at 11 a.m. If, however, Savannah looks very promising in an antiquarian way, I shall stay until 2 p.m. & reach CHARLESTON in the evening. Waning finances will sadly abbreviate my stay in CHARLESTON, but I hope to get at least a couple of days. It would not, however, be safe to try to catch me with a letter there. Or if I do try to stay longer, I will drop you word to that effect. It is possible that I simply *can't* bear to leave CHARLESTON after a day or two. My Richmond stop will be of the briefest—as will also be any pause in Philadelphia. Note, by the way, B K H's allusion to a hurried & worried trip to the ancient city of the Friends. At Sonny's—where the expenses go down—I shall spend at least a week, & it is there (unless I send word otherwise) that my next mail should be forwarded. That will probably be my last stop, since finances do not favour the Catskill detour. Miami & Key West rather strained my purse—but they were worth it, & I think it was the part of good sense to put the bulk of the trip in the far South once I was down there. Before mid-July I shall be back among Rhode-Island's ancient elms, stone walls, & white steeples, & dragging you out to Warren, Bristol, & Newport. Hope you're getting out around Barnes & Prospect Sts. on the good sunny days! ¶ More soon—

Yr aff Nephew & obt Servt

H P L

Notes

1. It is unclear what story HPL is referring to. His next completed story, "The Shadow over Innsmouth," was not begun until November.

[334]   [ALS] [HPL to LDC]

Charles-Town, in His *Britannick* Majeſty's
Province of *South-Carolina.*

GOD SAVE THE KING

Midnight, June 23–24, 1731.

My dear Daughter:—

Home to Charles-Town! Back in the old ENGLISH South with Georgian steeples & fanlighted doorways & railed double flights of steps & Palladian windows & flaring lintels & pineapple gateposts & herds of niggers & unbroken memories of a proud Anglo-Saxon life of 250 years! God Save the King! Florida is all right, & has the best climate in the U.S.— but home is where Old England's blood & language & ways have always existed dominantly & unbrokenly! CHARLESTON!!

Well—as I said in my last postcard bulletin,[1] I duly reëntered the Old South in the night when the coach reach'd His Majesty's Province of Georgia, & at dawn—5:30 a.m., half an hour ahead of schedule—was duly deposited in the ancient seaport of *Savannah.* Having two hours before the first Charleston coach, I check'd my portmanteau at a tavern & prepar'd to observe all the archaick sights in rapid but comprehensive order. The previous study of maps & guide literature enabled me to thread the streets like an old resident, without wasting time in inquiries or losing my way; hence I may report complete success in mastering the salient points of the older or colonial parts of Savannah. My only hardship was in not being able to purchase postcards—the shops being still clos'd at 7:30 a.m., when my coach left for Charleston.

The Province of Georgia, as all in these colonies are sensible, was charter'd by His Majesty George the Second in the year 1732; on behalf of a company of gentlemen philanthropically desirous of producing a refuge for worthy persons opprest by debt. Of these philanthropick gentlemen, the greatest & most active was Genl. James Edward Oglethorpe, whose military genius & indomitable courage were of the highest importance in ensuring the success of the venture. His Majesty favour'd the enterprise as a means of checking the Spaniards of Florida in their aggressions against South-Carolina. On account of the humble quality of the first colonists—opprest debtors—this province did not gain the proud & civilis'd tone of the Carolinas & Virginia, & has always been somewhat look'd down upon by Charlestonians of the old planter stock. It became a harbourage for fanatical religionists of dissenting sects, & early encourag'd the nasal Methodistical preachments of John Wesley & the muddled emotionalism of George Whitefield. (who lyes bury'd in antient Newburyport, in the Province of the Massachusetts-Bay) It was in Georgia that there first develop'd that backward lowland type of peasant-yeoman (now overlapping into Florida) locally known as the "cracker".

Genl. Oglethorpe personally accompany'd his first unit of colonists, & on the 12th of February, 1733, founded a town beside the southern bank of the Savannah River, some 16 miles from the open sea. This he call'd "Savannah" after the river—the name being held to come from the neighbouring tribe of *Sawanno* Indians. Like Philadª & Charleston, it was plann'd in advance; & was to have broad shady streets intersecting at right angles. One principal street was to stretch back south from the river front, & at every intersection there was to be a sightly park .... a system which, it is pleasing to record, has been perfectly liv'd up to. In physical actuality, this plan was first put into effect by the expert surveyor & civil engineer William Bull; after whom Oglethorpe courteously nam'd the principal street. The first square near the river was nam'd Johnson Square, after his Majtyˢ governor of South-Carolina—Robᵗ Johnson, Gent., who had greatly help'd in the promotion of the Georgia enterprise. Oglethorpe carefully plann'd this square, intending it to serve as a model for all the other small intersectional parks of his future system. The arrangement of streets was push'd back only a few blocks from the river—ending at the present line of Oglethorpe Ave., (then call'd South Broad St.) where planks were nail'd to the trees—painted red on the side toward the interior & white on the side toward the town—to shew the boundary line betwixt the red men & the white men. Genl. Oglethorpe acquir'd the land through peaceful negotiation with the noble & intelligent Tomo-Chi-Chi, mico or chieftain of the Yamacraws—though later on the local Indians were to prove a serious menace under the secret incitation of the Spaniards at St. Augustine, whose Franciscan missionaries had vast influence with the redskins. Genl. Oglethorpe twice sought to punish the Spaniards for their aggressions; leading expeditions against St Augustine in 1740 & 1742; but he was never able to capture the impregnable Fort San Marcos—on whose glacis & terreplein, strange to say, I sat writing but yesterday! He planted batteries on Anastasia Island, but his cannonades simply sank into the soft coquina stone of the fortress's walls without doing any damage whatever. To-day Savannah has a great monument to Genl. Oglethorpe, shewing him in his smartly cock'd hat & short, full-bottom'd wig. There is also a boulder dedicated to the dusky, faithful, & honourable Tomo-Chi-Chi.

With the years Savannah prosper'd & expanded, being the capital of Georgia till long after the revolt against our lawful sovereign. It was a great seaport in the 19th century when Genl. Sherman's Yankee thieves & ruffians descended upon it; & after the war it throve commercially at the expense of Charleston as the lower South's great point of export. Most of the colonial edifices have succumbed to change, but a good deal of typical Civil War Savannah is left. It is today a modern metropolis with a population of 87,714, though Atlanta has gone far beyond it as the chief city of Georgia.

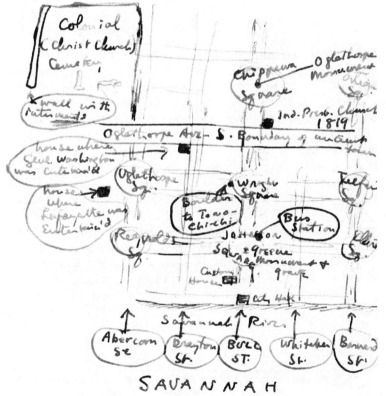

The coach deposited me in antient Johnson Square, in whose centre is the imposing monument to that gifted & capable rebel against his lawful king—Genl. Nathanael Greene, of Potowomut, King's County, & Coventry, Kent County, in His Majesty's COLONY OF RHODE-ISLAND AND PROVIDENCE-PLANTATIONS. As you have been lately appris'd by the current Bekes,[2] Genl. Greene mov'd to his Georgia lands after the close of the war & after his financial difficulties; dying of sunstroke in middle age. The

present monument to his memory is over a century old, its cornerstone having been laid by Genl. Lafayette in 1825. The General was originally interr'd in Colonial Cemetery, Savannah; but in the year 1902 his mortal remains, together with those of his son, George Washington Greene, Esq., were transported to Johnson Square & deposited in a vault beneath the venerable obelisk. The memorial is severe & harmonious in design, having fortunately preceded the Victorian aera of tasteless extravagance.

Monument to Gen[l] N. Greene of POTOWOMUT, RHODE-ISLAND in Johnson-Square, Savannah, Ga.

Being already familiar, through maps & guides, with the general topography of Savannah, I now proceeded to cover the antient district by walking south along Bull St., diverging when necessary down the side streets. The town in general is marvellously attractive, having a drowsy & beautiful atmosphere all its own, & being utterly different from CHARLESTON. According to Genl. Oglethorpe's original plan, the streets are extremely broad; & all are heavily shaded by those luxuriant trees which the genial climate favours.* The palmettos grow much taller than in Charleston, but after seeing Florida I can realise how *very little* of real subtropicality there is about the whole Georgia-Carolina region. Palmettos are really exotic to the locality—growing mainly under cultivation—while the ordinary verdure has only the live-oak & Spanish moss to distinguish it from that of the north. The zone is essentially the North Temperate one—with only the faintest suggestion of that real subtropical belt which Florida represents. In a word—Savannah & Charleston are more like Providence than like Key West in their general landscape values. There is nothing exotic or foreign about the Old South.

---

*Some fine *mulberry* trees—especially around Bay & E. Broad Sts.—attest Oglethorpe's early attempts to introduce silk cultivation.

The whole effect of Savannah is that of one vast sleepy park. Sidewalks are of brick, as are most of the houses, especially of the middle 19th century. The architecture is wholly unlike that of Charleston, yet has one point of parallelism—i.e., the fact of its having been relatively little vitiated by the vile taste of Victorianism. This is doubtless due both to the healthy conservatism of Southern taste, & to the economic stress following the Civil War, which prevented extensive building operations during the worst architectural period. The Savannans evidently lacked the highly developed taste of the cultivated Charlestonians; for we look in vain for the splendid gardens, garden walls, & wrought-iron gates which are the glory of CHARLESTON. A few cases of quasi-Charlestonian architecture exist—especially the fine house (circa 1800) in Oglethorpe Sq., where Genl. Lafayette was entertain'd in 1825. This house has a double flight of railed, curving steps in the best Charleston manner. In Perry St. near the Colonial Cemetery are some very ancient wooden houses which must go back to the very first days of the settlement—small & steep-roof'd, & one having dormer windows & a high stoop over a basement. The average Savannah house, as developed during the early 19th century & crystallised about the time of the Civil War, is tall, square & box-like in outline; & shews the architectural influence of northern cities (Richmond, Baltimore, Philadelphia, New York) to an extent unheard-of in CHARLESTON. Brick is the dominant material, & a *high stoop* is the dominant characteristic. The steps usually descend laterally to the sidewalk over a basement arch, & the doorway is almost invariably broad, with transom & sidelights. The door is often vertically divided in the Philadelphia fashion. Roofs are flat. Some of the older houses—perhaps 1820—are essentially Georgian; with a sloping roof, (tho' the flat roof sometimes goes back even before the Revolution) colonial doorway with fan & sidelights, (flanked by *columns* in the New York Georgian manner) high stoop, six-panelled single door, & steps descending straight out & down so that they project over the sidewalk. In these houses the extreme *width* of the door & doorway is as manifest as in the later houses. This feature may have its source in England, where wider doorways than in the colonies

Typical Savannah House circa 1850–60.

Savannah—late Georgian house—circa 1820

were usual. Georgia's late settlement prevented the growth of an anterior local tradition. We have *one* such doorway in R.I.—that of Bishop Berkeley's
"Whitehall" near Newport—fashioned in 1731 in the overseas manner. The
general Savannah tendency was to build houses in more or less solid blocks
with gardens in the rear. Stables—as in N.Y.—were in the rear in rows parallelling the houses, & opened on narrow alleys or "mews" (like our Fones Alley, which discharged a similar function for Angell & Waterman Sts. below
Hope) instead of upon the same streets as the houses. This was directly opposite to the old Charleston practice, where each great house had a high-
walled garden *beside* as well as behind it, with wrought-iron carriage gates on
the same street as the house door. Horse-blocks in front of house doors are
very frequent in Savannah; & they accord very well with the wide, shady,
brick sidewalks. I cannot say how vast a surge of homelike feeling I experienced upon beholding old Georgian fanlights & other English characteristics
again after the Spanish & pseudo-Spanish architecture of Florida. Savannah is
without a doubt the most southerly of our real Anglo-Saxon colonial towns—
just as Halifax, Nova Scotia, is the most northerly. It is *1033* miles south of
Providence, & 129 miles south of Charleston—Charleston being 904 miles
from Dorrance & Westminster Sts.

Classic columnar architecture—as represented by Christ Church in Johnson Sq. & the custom-house on the Bay St. waterfront—is fairly common in
Savannah; though by no means so universal as we find it amongst the publick
buildings of CHARLESTON. Of the ancient & lovely *Georgian steeples* of Savannah, only one specimen remains; (as restored in 1891 after a destructive fire)
but this is so magnificent, & so completely dominates the general Savannah
skyline, that it impresses one as strongly as a whole forest of inferior steeples
might. It is interesting to compare the surviving number of pure Georgian
steeples in various American towns. Providence has 2—the 1st Baptist &
Unitarian—& Charleston is just even with St Michael's & St. Philip's. Richmond has none at all left. Philadelphia has 2—Christ Church & old St Peter's—though the latter is not very typical. New York has 2 also—St Paul's &
St Mark's-in-the-Bouwerie—or three if one counts in the old Flatbush
church, & four if the old church in Jamaica be included. Or even 6 or 7 if certain *late* specimens (Brick Presb. Ch. in 5ᵗʰ Ave, Bushwick Lutheran, &c) be
included. Boston has 3—Park St., Old South & Old North—of the original
type, & 4 if the late Arlington St. specimen be included. Newport has one—
Trinity—but Marblehead, Salem, & Portsmouth have none left. Elizabethtown, N.J., has one—& so on, & so on. Well—Savannah's specimen, the Independent Presbyterian at Bull St. & Oglethorpe Ave. is one of the tallest,
slenderest, & finest I have ever seen. It is in the last & most delicate Georgian
manner, & has of course received the usual bungling & ignorant comparisons
to Wren's work & to St. Martin's-in-the-Fields. Naturally, it is very distinctive
& magnificent. It has three stages of column—the lowest Corinthian, the next

Ionick, & the topmost of a mixed order—& a needle-like spire of infinite grace. I cannot say, at the moment, just how much of the present steeple is original & how much due to the restoration of 1891. The church was built in 1819, & is a splendidly design'd edifice of stone with a parish-house of congruous architecture. In this building—or rather, the parsonage thereof— Woodrow Wilson was marry'd to his first wife, a Miſs Axson of Georgia. This splendid 1819 steeple form'd my first sight of a Georgian spire since my entrance to Florida; hence I view'd it with appropriate sensations of homecoming. God Save the King! I bitterly regretted that the clos'd state of the shops forbade my obtaining a postcard of it—tho' I have its picture, torn from the N.Y. Times, in my files at home. Much as I prefer Charleston, I must admit that neither of its Georgian steeples can bear individual comparison to this Savannah specimen. Both of PROVIDENCE'S specimens, however, almost undoubtedly *surpass* it—the 1st Baptist being indeed the finest in America & probably in the world.

Unlike Charleston, (indeed, 'tis hard to imagine that these two different worlds—so utterly antipodal in atmosphere & architecture—are only 129 miles apart!) Savannah did not follow the old custom of churchyard burials. The antient cemetery attach'd to Christ Church is situate at a great distance from that edifice; south of Oglethorpe Ave. (the old city limit) & two squares east of Bull St. It may have been for sanitary reasons in a warm climate that burials were thus made outside the compact town. This old church burying-ground was enlarged & made a publick cemetery in 1789, & in 1853 was clos'd against further interments. It was taken over by the city in 1872, & is now kept as a park under the name of "Colonial Park." It is here that Genl. Greene & his family were originally bury'd—the dust of Rhode Island added to the dust of Georgia. Of all antient graveyards I have ever beheld, this is the

most utterly unique. In the first place, many of the tombs are of the same odd general cast as those observed in the antient Spanish cemeteries—Tolometo & Nuestra Señora de la Leche— of St Augustine. Compare the accompanying sketches with those I have made in earlier St

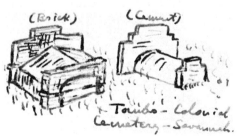

Augustine letters, & note the rough similarity. Evidently these graves follow some sort of general subtropical tradition—although *Charleston,* with its tenacious Old-English fashions, has nothing of the sort. Any interment in any of the Old Charleston churchyards might well be in London, Providence, Boston, Portsmouth, Salem, New York, Philadelphia, or Richmond, so far as tombstone designs & workmanship are concern'd. Indeed, many of the stones in Charleston were quarried & carved in the North. Did I not mention in a former travelogue that one of the stones in the Congregational church-yard was carved by one Jonathan Bull of Newport, R.I.?

But the most spectacularly exotick feature about Savannah's antient burying-ground is its eastern wall of stucco-carv'd brick—prodigiously thick, & pierced by regular tiers of oven-like vaults or graves for above-ground interments. This was the universal custom in old New Orleans cemeteries—the soil being unfit for inhumation there—as you may recall from the postcard Morton sent last year. In New Orleans, the French *rented* the above-ground graves, so that corpses

(Brick & stucco wall—marble slabs)

East Wall of Colonial Cemetery, Savannah—
Shewing oven-like above-ground interments.

were evicted after a decade or so to make room for others; the bones then being transferr'd either to some private ossuary or to a common charnel heap. This was also much the custom in France; & still is, I believe, in Cuba. I had never heard of any above-ground wall graves in the English world, hence was astonished to come across this arrangement in old Savannah. I don't believe Morton saw it at all—for he called Savannah "uninteresting" (fancy!!) & prattled naively about the "uniqueness" of what he found in New Orleans. In Savannah the wall interments appear to be permanent; tiers of old marble slabs being affixed to the wall in very solid fashion. As may well be imagin'd, I study'd this singular arrangement in most minute detail! The earliest known grave in the cemetery (not a wall one) dates from 1762, but the majority seem to be of the early 19th century. Marble is the leading material for slabs. The grounds are finely landscaped—in a funereal, 18th century way well harmonising with the date & nature of the place.

My general walk, as I have said, was out Bull St. & along certain necessary lateral courses. I saw the principal parklike squares with their historical names & monuments, & paused reflectively by the Oglethorpe statue in Chippewa Square & the boulder monument to dusky, honourable Tomo-Chi-Chi in Wright Sq. I also view'd the fine late-Georgian house (stucco) with the Charlestonian steps where Lafayette was entertain'd, as well as the brick house where Washington visited. My walk lay beyond the scope of the sketch-map in this letter, for I follow'd Bull St. to its end in Forsyth Park, where there is an imposing Confederate monument & a fountain of Tritons copy'd from that in the Place de la Concorde, Paris—where Galpin probably is at the present moment. I likewise looked westward to Telfair Square, site of the local art gallery. Altogether, I obtain'd so broad & comprehensive a view of Savannah that it is hard to realise I was there but two hours in all! Of course, I walk'd with extreme rapidity, & concentrated my attention very minutely whenever I paus'd to observe any specifick object. I check'd my valise at the Hotel Savannah—near Genl. Greene's monument, & just across from the coach station (which was not open when I arriv'd at 5:30 a.m.)—hence was wholly unencumber'd in my progress. I took a cheese sandwich & cup of coffee at 7 a.m. in a Greek counter lunch—the only place that was open. Whilst not many were on the streets at so early an hour, I gain'd the impression that Savannah is as predominantly pure-American as most other Southern cities—as Providence used to be in 1850 & before. Niggers are more numerous than in Florida, but not as thick as in Charleston; since the Savannah people were not as opulent as the Charlestonians, & could not afford to maintain such extensive black retinues. Wide streets—conservatism—green shadiness—brick sidewalks—high stoops—broad doorways—brick facades—tall palmettoes—classick columns—parklike squares & monuments—extensive vistas—the slender 1819 spire—these are the salient impressions I carry away from Old Savannah. As the coach enter'd the town I had a chance to see the ancient publick market area—still throng'd & busy, even at that early hour, & replete with ebony visages.

DIARY FOR TUESDAY, JUNE 23, 1931.

Began the day exploring Savannah. Caught the 7:30 Charleston coach & had a gloriously sunny ride. At last the antient spires of CHARLESTON loom'd hazily out of the distance across the noble Ashley River—& I knew I was "home" at last in the absolute heart & nucleus of 18th century colonial America. God Save the King! With what elation did I tread once more the now familiar streets with their endless fanlighted doorways & ancient garden walls! I put up at the Y M C A, & regretted bitterly that I could not stay a full week. Since the cost was only 25¢ a day more, I took a room with private shower bath— thus being in luxury while I *am* here. I can afford only 2 nights—but this gives me 3 full sightseeing days in Charleston . . . . . Tuesday from my arrival at 11 a.m. till dusk, all of Wednesday, & Thursday till the Columbia (Richmond-connecting) coach leaves at 5:45 p.m. I shall get to Richmond Friday noon, & shall try to see Maymont Park & the Poe sites the same day—in order to have to stop only one night. Saturday morning I shall (probably) leave Richmond for Fredericksburg,* stopping off there all day & going on to Washington in the evening. Then comes the big jump—for I shall make no stop, but take a night coach & be in the chilly & foreigner-infested North (ugh!) on Sunday morning. Hades—I can hardly picture myself in the north!!

---

*assuming that I cannot afford a Petersburg digression

If my cash is about gone, I shall have to make the unbroken & nauseating leap to N.Y.—sickening as that mongrel dump will seem after two months in a real American milieu. I hope fervently, though, to break the shock by a brief pause in *Philadelphia;* which although northern, has a persistent historical aura & elusive suggestion of imaginative richness not shared by any other place north of Maryland & west of New-England. I hope I can get a good day in Germantown & the exquisite Wissahickon—you will recall how cold, rotten weather cheated me in this respect last year. But it does seem foolish to try to live in the north. Actually, the past stretch of nearly 2 months has formed the only long period of really *unbroken physical comfort* which I can recall in my decaying span of 41 years! There has been no day too warm, & even the cool days have not been nearly so bad as the average northern cool day at the same time of year. And as for *winter* . . . . !!! * * * ¶ + + ... Today it is glorious in Charleston—I wore no coat at all in the inland streets, & was not too cold with my coat on along the Battery. And I am still going hatless—though custom will force me to don my new straw purchase when I get as far north as Richmond.

Well—I spent Tuesday floating around amongst my favourite Charleston sites, & writing letters & postcards here & there—mostly on the Battery or near William Pitt's 1770 statue in ancient City Park at Broad & Meeting Sts. over-against St. Michael's Church (1757) & churchyard. My nourishment has consisted of ham & cheese sandwiches, coffee, & ice cream at a United Cigar Store lunch & soda counter. This counter serves the finest vanilla ice cream that I have ever tasted except at Gibson's & Maxfield's—& it is only 10¢ per generous portion, too! At dusk I return'd to the Y M C A, where I have since been writing. I will leave this epistle unseal'd in order to add tomorrow's diary; posting it tomorrow evening—Wednesday the 24th. Good old Charleston! Well—I have at least 2 more days to drink it in!

DIARY FOR WEDNESDAY, JUNE 24, 1931.

Rose 9 a.m. & spent morning writing in antient City Park in the shadow of Pitt's statue. In the afternoon I visited The Dungeon Studio, occupy'd by the artist R. B. Abbott-Smith, Esq.,[3] formerly of Montreal, Canada, & displaying a sign that the publick might inspect, free of charge, some odd mural paintings about a century old; lately discover'd beneath a coat of whitewash on the half-ruin'd ground floor. These paintings turn'd out to be of no mean workmanship; consisting largely of French military scenes & portraits of Napoleon. It is conjectur'd that around 1830 this building was us'd as a tavern, & that the proprietor—a Frenchman—took occasion to remind his patrons of the greatness of his native land. They have surviv'd surprisingly beneath the concealing whitewash, & needed but little restoration upon discovery. The artist Abbott-Smith occupies the upper part of the house—for which he plays only

$25.00 per month rent. Getting into conversation with me, he shew'd me many of his fine water-colours of Old Charleston—& it irk'd me that I could not buy any, for he is a veritable Henry J. Peck in colour! He says Charleston is the finest place on earth to live—& very cheap, also. His own Montreal has such winters that he could not expect to get through many more—hence he migrated permanently to Charleston. February, he says, is the only bad month—& that is no worse than a Quebec or New England November or March. He appears to be of almost my own age, & is evidently of much taste & cultivation. He has never seen Providence, & I promised to send him some pictures of the Baptist steeple & other antiquities upon my return. He knows & loves *Old Quebec,* & we talked at length of it. He agrees that the view from the outer works of the Citadel is absolutely the loveliest sight on this continent, & is as fascinated as I by the magical silver spires & belfries of the French churches. Also—he clearly perceives the architectural similarity of Charleston & Quebec. He has drawn & painted Quebec extensively, & well knows all those byways on St. Famille hill, & the steep lanes ascending from Rue St Jean outside the walls, which so poignantly fascinated me last year.

Quebeck! Would that some magick could enable me to see that *& Charleston* at the same moment! And over Quebeck hangs the hellish tragedy of the *cold*—two months of summer loveliness, then the dismal autumn, the white hell, & the slow painful spring—with ice in the St. Lawrence till April or May! But I wish I could see it at this moment—quaint Rue Couillard, the old Basilica, the Ramparts, narrow Rue Sault au Matelot, tunnel-like Rue Sous-le-Cap, the frowning mediaeval arsenal at Port du Palais, the lordly height of Cape Diamond & the Citadel—& over all the glorious colours of His Britannick Majesty—still triumphant, & never lower'd in treacherous rebellion since that supreme 13th of September, 1759, when WOLFE, victorious in death, destroy'd the power of Gaul in the New World. God Save the King!! Would that the glory of Rhode-Island's Nathanael Greene were that of loyal service to his King instead of able but misguided service in a rebel cause which will ultimately wreck our civilisation! Ah, me—only this afternoon I look'd wistfully at the still unchang'd residence of Sir William Campbell in Meeting-St., last lawful governor of South-Carolina by Royal Authority. He was menac'd by lawless mobs of ruffians, who invaded his home much as the Newport mobs invaded the homes of loyal citizens at the same time; till at last he took refuge on one of His Majesty's arm'd vessels in the harbour. Across the street lived W: Bull, Esq., the Deputy-Governor; but he sided with the rebels & was not mistreated. His house, too, is still in fine condition—& is occupy'd by his descendants. 1775–1931—156 years, though in *Charleston*, where time does not exist, it seems but a day. The same people—the same ways—the same houses—in spite of everything, Colonial America has this one final living stronghold!!

But I digress. After leaving Abbott-Smith's studio, (which is in Broad St. near the park with William Pitt's statue) I proceeded next door to the Chamber of Commerce, (housed in a colonial building) where I laid in a supply of the latest free booklets on Charleston. There is one splendid map—though I am rather beyond the stage of needing maps now. Later I strolled through my favourite haunts & did some writing on the ancient Battery. At 6 p.m. a rain threatened, so that I had to return to the Y M C A & spend the evening writing. I shall continue to write till midnight, when I shall retire in preparation for my final Charleston day. I hope it won't rain—if it does, I shall stay another day even if I have to relinquish all hope of a stop in Richmond or Philadelphia!

I duly receiv'd the letters forwarded here. The Weird Tales one is merely another forwarded query from a reader—a soldier at Ft. Benning, Georgia.[4] Odd that I should have passed through his state only yesterday! My next forwarding address will be % Long, 230 W. 97th St., New York City.

And so it goes. I'll probably see you within a fortnight or so, hence prepare to be dragged out to Warren, Bristol, Newport, & similar places. I'll wager the ancient elms, white steeples, & stone walls of New England make a pretty tolerable sight right now! ¶ More soon.

Yr aff Nephew & obt
H P L

Notes

1. Nonextant.

2. HPL wrote that *Bekes* was "our local colloquialism (based on the sketchy phonetic value of the signatory initials) for the diurnal columnar essays of Bertrand Kelton Hart, Esq." (MFB 7).

3. Reginald B. Abbott-Smith (1894–1978), Canadian veteran of World War I who became an artist in Charleston.

4. This was RHB's first letter to HPL. (HPL's reply mentions that RHB's letter had

been double-forwarded: from *WT* to Providence, and from Providence to Charleston.) RHB was not, of course, a soldier, but his father, Col. Everett D. Barlow, was stationed at Fort Benning.

[335]   [ALS] [HPL to LDC]

Thursday–Friday Midnight
July 2–3, 1931

My dear Daughter:—

As I said on my card, my hosts have kept me so busy that not a second of writing leisure has remained! It is amusing that I always receive the most effusive & engulfing welcomes in the least interesting of all cities! I duly received the forwarded Wright letter, & indeed recognised the pink paper. I have a piece of it in my pocket now—a list which I did not have time to attend to before departing on the present voyage. As you will probably deduce from the chirography, I am writing with a new fountain pen. When I took my old one into Waterman's it was pronounced hopeless— point worn out—so that I could do nothing with it but get a new gold pen for it at a cost of $2.75. This I did not care to do, since it would be far better to put in a little more cash & get a new pen than pay so much for a mere patching of the old one. Later, however, I found a shop in Fulton St. where the dealer would take my old pen in exchange for a new one, allowing me $2.50 value on it. This seemed a sensible proposition to take up—giving me the whole new pen, yet making the old one count heavily. Accordingly I paid *$2.62* & turned in the old hulk; receiving in exchange an excellent specimen only a little smaller than its predecessor, & of the same old-fashioned black finish now so hard to obtain. It rather disturbs my financial programme to have to pay out so much—but I think I can patch through in view of the extra cash recently sent by my banker. As I write this epistle, it occurs to me that I may have chosen too *fine* a point—but since this is a new pen, I have the privilege of exchanging it at the Waterman offices until suited. I shall give it a trial between now & Monday—& if it still seems to me too fine, I shall then exchange it. One can never judge of a new pen till one has written considerably with it.

As for my diary—the last entry was made in Philadelphia last Sunday— June 28—as I took the coach for New York after a day of delectable exploration. The ride was sunny & excellent, & N Y was reached in the twilight. Even from New Jersey I saw the new Empire State Bldg. (tallest structure in the world) on the horizon, & greatly disliked it because of the tasteless cylindrical shaft surmounting the edifice proper. The whole N Y zone seemed repulsive & chaotic in contrast with the settled & American South & even with Philadelphia. Losing no time, I proceeded to Sonny's, but found that all the rooms in that 7th floor apartment were taken. Accordingly, after a discussion-period lasting till 1 a.m., I proceeded down town to the vicinity of the Pennsylvania Station, where I obtained an excellent $1.50 room at the Penn Post Hotel—a modest but neat establishment which I knew because my old correspondent John Russell of Clearwater, Florida stopped there in 1925 when he was bound for England & had me shew him N Y en route. The light in my room was so good that I gave my hair a trimming—knowing that I would not be likely to get such a light anywhere else. I also did a good deal of laundry & retired late.

On *MONDAY, JUNE 29, 1931* I rose at 11 a.m. & reëngaged my room for another night in expectation of having to hunt extensively elsewhere. However, when I got up to Sonny's I found that the Longs had been able to get me a dollar room across the hall on the same floor—with a new family including two delectable grey *cats!* This was virtually as good as being right in the Long flat. Since Mrs. Long had engaged the room beginning with that night, I made an effort to cancel my second night's reservation at the Penn Post; but found they would do no more than issue a credit slip good for a night's lodging at any future time. I took this, & shall use it either at the end of this trip or next year. At any rate, I transferred my things to 230 at once. That afternoon, after lunch, Sonny & I went on an expedition—beginning with a call on Talman at his office on the 18th floor of the tall Chrysler Bldg. at 42nd St & Lexington Ave. Talman was very cordial, & shewed me the issue of the Texaco Star with his belated Providence article. Next Monday he will hold a meeting of the gang at his home—having as a guest that popular Weird Tales author Seabury Quinn (of Brooklyn) whose personal acquaintance he recently made. Later he insists on having me visit him for a week after my visit to Belknap terminates—his new flat having an occupiable couch in the living-room. I wish I had such a cordial group of insistent hosts in Charleston, Richmond, or Key West!! Talman shewed us the new Weird Tales with my "Whisperer", & with some great praise for Sonny's "Horror from the Hills" in the Eyrie. I have since purchased my own copy. Later in the afternoon the Child & I visited the Museum of Peaceful Arts in another new skyscraper in 42nd St.—a place containing valuable scientific material including a vast revolving globe in the lobby. Among the exhibits were models of ships, locomotives, &c. in every stage of development. We then tried to look up Loveman & Kirk at their respective shops, but found both out. Returning then to 230, we had dinner & indulged in philosophic discussion. Meanwhile Loveman had telephoned that he was working at the bookshop till 10 p.m., & would like to get in touch with me at that hour. I therefore proceeded downtown at the designated time, finding him & his roommate McGrath ready to leave the shop. We boarded the subway to Columbia Heights, & I was pleased to see that Loveman's room is even more of a library & museum than ever. He brought in some ice cream, & we had a very congenial time discussing & viewing the magical skyline across the river till 1:30 a.m., when I proceeded back to 230 & retired.

On *TUESDAY, JUNE 30, 1931,* I rose at noon, imperilled my weight by consuming another Long luncheon, & set out to do museums with the Child. We first visited the Roerich Museum (Riv. Drive & 103ᵈ St) with its mystical Asian paintings of mountain wonders, & later went over to Sonny's favourite, the Am. Museum of Natural History. After the closing hour of five we sat around Central Park & ultimately returned to 230 for dinner. In the evening Belknap had a very small meeting whose guests included Talman, the immortal James Ferdinand Morton, & Whitehead's young friend (whom I met in Dunedin, but who turned out, through coincidence, to be one of Dr. Long's patients) Allan Brownell Grayson. I was surely glad to see good old Mortonius again. He will pass through Providence, returning from Nova Scotia, on or about July 21, & wants me to have 2 or 3 paper cartons (not exceeding 12 × 18 inches each) ready for his confounded minerals. I suppose I'll try to rake 'em up when I get back—anyhow, he promises to pack & address his own junk this time! The older members took to Grayson quite readily, & I imagine the youth will develop into quite a gang member eventually. After the visitors left I argued with Belknap till 2 a.m., then retiring.

On *WEDNESDAY, JULY 1, 1931,* I rose at 11 a.m., lunched at Belknap's, & greeted young Grayson at 2 p.m. when he came over to do the museums with us. We went first to the Roerich, where Grayson seemed moderately impressed, & later to the Metropolitan, where Sonny has unearthed some new paintings of great mystical power—that is, new *acquisitions,* for the pictures are all Renaissance specimens averaging 1500 as a date. After the museum closed we sat around Central Park a bit—& then Grayson went home (he lives at 701 West 178th St.) by bus, while Sonny & I strolled back to 230 for dinner. In the evening, as per an insistent invitation of Monday, I went down town & met Loveman & McGrath in Times Square. Loveman had insisted on treating me to Gilbert & Sullivan's "Pirates of Penzance"[1] (which I had never seen before) while he & McGrath attended another play which I would not care for. My seat was in the balcony, but the view was good & most of the words & music audible. As you are doubtless aware, the "Pirates"* is a grotesquely brilliant satire on the mawkish Victorian "sense of duty", through whose pompous & ponderous hypocrisy Gilbert so clearly saw. The present production seemed to me admirably adequate, though it was presented (at the Erlanger† Theatre in 44th St.) by a Gilbert & Sullivan Stock Co. (last week was "Patience" & next week will be "Iolanthe")[2] whose prices are by no means high. Prominent in the cast was the comedian Frank Moulan,[3] who was in the musical comedy stock company which played at the Providence Opera House in the summer of 1917, & at the Shubert-Majestic (then under

---

*produced 1880
†named after Abe Erlanger, the famous producer whose rapacious theatrical trust caused so much trouble for Felix R. Wendelschaefer & our Opera House.

Wendelschaefer's management) in the summer of 1918. It was curious to see again one whom I have seen in dozens of Victor Herbert or Pixley-Luders[4] roles—& I don't see that the intervening thirteen years have changed him much. After the show I met Loveman & McGrath again in Times Square, & we all proceeded to a very quiet basement Automat a little south along Broadway, where we discussed things in general till after midnight. Loveman insisted on my taking, as his treat, some of my favourite old-time Automat standbys—coffee, cherry pie, & vanilla ice cream—hence I fear my weight is already hopelessly beyond 140! Finally we dispersed, & I returned to 230 to retire. My next engagement with Loveman—probably an exploring trip in strange places—is for Wednesday, July 8, & will be arranged Monday.

On *THURSDAY, JULY 2, 1931* I rose at 11 a.m. & had the usual weight-imperilling luncheon at Little Belknap's; after which we entered upon a long afternoon of urban exploration beginning with the Aquarium at the *Battery*. Alas—the name makes one homesick for CHARLESTON'S Battery of live-oaks, waving palmettos, & Georgian mansions with glamourous walled gardens! We later followed a route of quaint sights—old churchyards, waterfront areas, Chinatown, Five Points, &c.—which Sonny had compiled from a series of newspaper articles, & on which he needed his old Grandpa's expert guidance. I could steer him without difficulty, & we covered everything on the programme. The lower Manhattan skyline is vastly changed by the addition of new towers, but the main sights & general impressions are just as of old. The Washington St. Syrian colony is thinned by migration to Brooklyn, & the long-projected Nassau St. loop of the B-M.T. subway is actually complete & in use. During this exploration I attended to the fountain pen business. We tried to explore the vicinity of the Fulton St Fish Market, but the odour quickly drove us away . . . . as it was, I nearly lost the contents of my stomach. Ending up at *old* St Patrick's (1809) in Mott St., we returned to 230 by subway & had the usual avoirdupois-breeding dinner. Later all hands attended a local cinema—the dullest show, without exception, that I have ever yawned through. Thank Yuggoth I didn't pay admission! Then the present writing period—to be followed by retiring around midnight.

Tomorrow I shall awake at 7:30 a.m. & accompany the Longs on their trip to Asbury Park (or Ocean Grove—I forget which, or both) over the week-end. I don't think the region will be in the least interesting, but it would probably offend the Longs if I proposed staying behind—& of course one never tires of arguing about science, philosophy, & aesthetics with Little Sonny. More bulletins will follow.

Trust all flourishes at #10—which I shall see inside of a fortnight. Here are some Bekes. Don't forget to keep the piles of newspapers intact. What a job of reading lies ahead of me!!!

Yr aff Nephew & obt Servt

H P L

Notes

1. The musical was running at Erlanger's Theatre (246 West 44th Street), 29 June–24 October 1931. It was performed by the Civic Light Opera Company.
2. *Patience* (15–29 June) and *Iolanthe* (13 July–9 January 1932) both ran at Erlanger's.
3. Frank Moulan (1872–1939), American actor.
4. Victor Herbert (1859–1924), Irish-born American composer and performer. He wrote dozens of operettas from 1894 to 1924. Frank S. Pixley (1863–1926), an American librettist, and Gustav Carl Lüders (1865–1913), a German composer, collaborated on many musicals in the early 20th century.

[336]   [ALS] [HPL to LDC]

> Back in Old Flatbush—
> Vale of Cashmere, Prospect Park.
> Wednesday, July 8, 1931.

My dear Daughter:—

Well—once again the overwhelming cordiality of my hosts has kept me too busy for writing! I have not written a single letter except to you & A E P G since striking N Y—& from the number of epistles forwarded, you may judge of the desperate state of my correspondence. My last diary was mailed from Asbury Park Saturday night—July 4—& meanwhile I have duly received yours of June 30th, remailed (as your P.S. states) after its return by the P.O. I am now visiting Talman in Flatbush—at 2215 Newkirk Ave., one station south of Cortelyou Road & 4 stations beyond Parkside Ave. The general region is the same homelike one of green lawns & shade trees which I described in travelogues of 1928, though the number of apartment houses is gradually increasing. Talman is in a new & attractive apartment house called The Davenport; which has an ornate lobby with doorman, & a system of *self-operated* elevators in which the passenger reaches his proper floor by closing the gate & pressing suitable buttons. Talman's apartment, though, is on the second floor; so that he always uses the plain, honest, old-fashioned stairs. His place has two large rooms plus hall, kitchen, & alcoves. I am using a couch in the living room, which is well isolated by corridors & with easy access to the bathroom. The walls are of white finish—imitation Colonial panelling—& the furniture is all of a delightful Georgian cast. Upon awaking, the first thing I behold is the scroll-&-urn top of a splendid secretary! In order to be out of the way, I have to arise at 7 a.m. with the household; but this is no more than I did at Dunedin with Whitehead. I am invited to all meals, but other invitations of the same sort will limit my acceptances to about half. The Longs urge me to take as many as possible with them—but I am carefully watching my weight! I have cut down to 143, but hope to shed 3 lbs. more before long. I shall be at Talman's till the end of the week, when his brother is due to visit him. Then I shall avail myself of the credit slip on the Penn Post Hotel issued to me a fortnight ago. I still have a few explorations to make, but by next week shall be returning to stone walls, Georgian steeples, & the ancient hill. Between now & then I shall mail home another large package of booklets, soiled linen, &c—which reminds me that I hope the first package from N Y has duly arrived. This has all my Charleston & Richmond material, &c. I shall from now on begin to use up whatever spare linen is in my valise, so as to have nearly nothing to carry home. My laundering operations are highly successful—being now developed to such a pitch that I can radically cut down my valise-filling quota of linen on future excursions. Which reminds me, though, that I shall probably have to get a new 99¢ valise next year. This old standby of 1928 is getting shaky around the bottom, & I am beginning to fear its fate in the hands of the careless niggers who throw it around on coach tops & in stations. Another item in need of early replacement is my Regal outfit. The uppers are now becoming riddled with cracks, whilst the pre-Quebec taps are loosening at their rear fastenings. However, they have worn well for $6.60 shoes; their date of purchase being April, 1929. A minor tragedy this morning is the sticking-together of my postage stamps, due to the damp weather. Almost 25 are so affected—but I shall save them for home use; soaking them apart & attaching them to letters with the Cico paste whose smell you dislike. It was, by the way, here in Flat-bush that I first adopted Cico paste! Fountain pen news is more cheerful, since I think I have hit upon a good point after 2 changings. I discover, though, that these Cavalier pads (whose cheapened quality I remarked to you when I got this one in Clearwater) are very poor as writing surfaces. It is a pity, for they used to be magnificent. I shall have to desert Woolworth's for this item, & look about elsewhere for a better dime's worth. Fortunately this one is almost gone. One thing I have done in honour of my new pen is to throw away the last dregs of my current ink supply (thick & ill-flowing) & purchase a new 10¢ bottle at my old Flatbush drug store—Reed & Snyder's.

But the best piece of news is the one made manifest by the principal en-closure—which you may have seen for yourself by this time. I was over at Kleiner's last night, & discovered to my delighted astonishment that his old song book was one of the very few things of his which had **not** perished in his general upheaval of 1926–27. His failure to copy "Roll On, Silver Moon" for you was merely another instance of Kleinerian lassitude, so marked in lat-ter years. Well—*this* time I put no reliance in promises, but sat down at once with my new fountain pen & a piece of paper borrowed from my host. The result is before you—legible, I hope, though scarcely neat or artistic. I have copied a skeletonic account of the man who in 1842 first correlated the old (& presumably anonymous) words & music, & have also made an effort to reproduce the musical notes of the air—though this latter is purely a piece of blind copying, without intelligent comprehension of musical notation. It was quite a job, but that was the only way to get the thing. Hope you'll be able to form an idea of the tune—otherwise you'll be in the same position as Little Sonny, who has a copy of his poem "Prediction" as set to music by Galpin, but can't find anybody to play it, hence doesn't know even remotely what it's like! In regard to this matter, I tell the Child that he ought to have made Alfredus hum or whistle the tune while he was in N.Y.—but the little rascal never thought of that . . . . . or else he didn't want to admit to Alfredus that he didn't know anybody who plays the piano. Well, anyhow, here's the good old "Silver Moon" nailed down at last. I find some departure from the words of the chorus as I recall them, & wonder whether our version of the tune is equally incorrect. The book containing this song is really a valuable bit of American folklore, & I don't wonder that Kleiner clung to it when the rest of his library was engulfed by disaster. It was published by Holt as recently as 1909, & may possibly be obtainable from the publishers even now. Certainly, no better repository of our early XIXth century minstrelsy is in existence! Incidentally, it was like old times to see so much of Kleiner; & I hope I can see him again before I leave. He has not changed at all in aspect, save that his hair is a trifle greyer each year.

Thursday, July 9, 1931
—Prospect Park again.

I had to cut short yesterday in order to get over to Sonny's in time for lunch. In the old days I always used to miscalculate about the time consumed on the subway betwixt Flatbush & 96th St., but now I have the schedule down pretty fine. This is another dull, grey day; but at least it is not raining, & Prospect Park (like Roger Williams) is attractive in any weather. When I come home you may very possibly see me in an unfamiliar summer suit of virtually Palm Beach weight & excellent fit, for Talman is very intent on making me a present of an old one of his, for which he has now grown too stout. The way it fits me is positively uncanny, & I am almost on the point of deciding to take it & have it cleaned & pressed at the local tailor's. What makes me hesitate is the fact that it has a pattern, & is thus possibly too youthful for an old man. It is a medium-darkish greyish-brown, & Talman likes it on me exceedingly. There are worn places, but it would last *me* for aeons. The sleeves ought to be shortened a trifle, & the turned-up trouser-bottoms ought to be removed. My principal misgiving is that the tailor may not find the latter procedure practicable. But even if the reclamation is not feasible I may accept the thing just the same—to wear exactly as it is around Quinsnicket on very hot days. It would cost only the presumable dime for parcel post, & would make an excellent adjunct to the old blue. You'll see in my next bulletin what I decide.

Glad your health continues up to the best recent average, & hope you'll be able to get out on some moderate trips—like Warren, Bristol, & Newport—even if you can't attempt anything really ambitious. I suppose the wedding across the street was an active & conspicuous spectacle from your windows—& I hope the nice yellow kittie will remain in the neighbourhood till I get back to see him. Trust A E P G enjoyed her Newport excursion. The garden exhibition idea is really an excellent one.

As for my diary—I think my last entry was made in Asbury Park, covering Saturday, July 4. I expected to have to leaf through another day of relative ennui at that unpicturesque spot, but fortunately Dr. Long decided to drive home early Sunday in order to avoid the heavy road traffick of afternoon. He parked the family Essex outside the corporate limits of Ocean Grove in order to comply with the local Blue Laws regarding automobiles on the Holy Sabbath. On SUNDAY, JULY 5, 1931, all hands arose at 7:30 a.m., had breakfast at the usual place, & started back for N Y not much after 8 o'clock. The day was fine & the ride excellent—a different route being taken in order to include a glimpse of the sumptuous & park-embowered country-seats along the Rumson Road. We reached 230 W. 97th at noon & had a light lunch, after which Little Belknap & Grandpa went up to see the George Gray Barnard cloisters, (an old church & colonnade brought over from France stone by stone & set up amidst exquisite garden surroundings on an eastward-facing cliff along Ft. Washington Ave. beyond 181st St.) now owned by the Metropolitan Museum. He, Morton, & I had surveyed them amidst a November Twilight in 1922, but they were not then quite completed. On the present occasion they were ineffably glamourous in the full blaze of a July sun, & I could hardly tear myself away from their subtle & archaick spell. Sonny—a confirm'd little mediaevalist—linger'd breathlessly over the ecclesiastical images & altars of the interior; but it was the garden & landscape setting which got the old man excited. At last we departed—continuing north & bending down to Broadway over the semi-rustick course of Ft. Washington Ave. This region is still relatively unspoiled, though the great stone castle (once a residence of Boss Tweed) which was such a landmark in 1922 has vanished—as warehouses, opera houses, & Angell St. stables vanish. All the region below the cliff, east & north, is overrun by a mushroom growth of cheap flats whose earliest beginnings we noted in 1922—so that the once-stupendous vista from the cloister garden is now seriously impaired. At Dyckman St. we took the subway & proceeded all the way down to the Child's favourite resort—the American Museum of Natural History, whose recent acquisitions we had mastered only in part on the preceding Tuesday. After this we walked in Central Park, returned to 230 for dinner, & discussed philosophy & aestheticks till far into the night.

On MONDAY, JULY 6, 1931, I rose at noon, took lunch at Belknap's, discussed aestheticks with the Child, & subsequently went down town for errands. I changed the fountain pen—though one more change was to be necessary before the selection of the present effective specimen. Later I called in at Kirk's book shop & found him there. It was certainly good to see G K again—& I was delighted to observe that he has got rid of the ugly, bristling moustache which defaced him last year. He looked like the real old Georgius once more—not aged a bit since I first saw him in Cleveland in 1922—& he says he will not grow the ghastly deformity again. From there I went over to Loveman's shop—accompanying him to a restaurant to watch him eat dinner, though I was myself scheduled to gorge at the Long table. (Oh, my weight! I began a reduction at Asbury, but now I'm going up again!) After the gorge Sonny & I set out for Talman's Flatbush abode (which I had not previously seen) in order to attend the gang meeting, at which the Weird Tales celebrity Seabury Quinn was scheduled to be present. For me an added attraction was the presence of good old Arthur Leeds; whom I had not seen in five long years, but who is now back in N Y & working in a bookshop at Coney Island. We reached the scene in good season, & found Quinn already there. He is a quiet, baldish, increasingly stout fellow of 44—very pleasing & well-bred, & with a mellow voice whose accent is unmistakably Southern (it made me homesick for Richmond & Fredericksburg!) despite his Brooklyn residence. His hair is dark, & he sports a closely clipped moustache. Conversation revealed him as exceedingly tasteful & intelligent; though he is primarily a good business man, catering to closely studied markets, rather than an individualistic aesthete with anything urgent & serious to say. Sonny & Loveman found him too self-contained & casual to suit their tastes, though I liked him very much. Leeds was a very welcome sight after five long years. Contrary to Sonny's opinion that he has aged terribly, I found him just the same as in the old days—not a bit older-looking. He has, though, added a dandified (& probably wax-induced) uphilt to his once short & bristling moustache. Wish he'd shave the thing off as Kirk [h]as done! Another welcome sight was good old Kleiner, who somehow seemed more like his earliest self (as on his Providence visits in 1918–19–20) than he has done in recent years. Discussion was spirited & diversified, centreing more in weird fiction than in anything else. Little Sonny went home early, & Loveman did not arrive till after his departure. Everyone was present except Morton, who is in Nova Scotia. At length departures began to occur—Quinn, Loveman, Kirk, Kleiner,—until Leeds & I were the only ones left. As of old, Leeds hung on as long as possible; & then we proceeded to the B M T subway—he to go home to Coney Island, & I to proceed uptown for my final night at 230 W. 97. I got in late, but was welcomed by one of the exquisite grey kitties, with whom I talked for some time before retiring. He is one who makes friends slowly, but is very purr-ful & amicable once he admits an outsider to his circle of acquaintance.

Manhattan—Central Park near 97th
St.—Friday, July 10—A E P G's birthday
Well, bless my soul! Kind hosts simply won't give an old man time to write letters! Here it is the 3d day, & still on the same epistle. But to continue

the diary. On TUESDAY, JULY 7, I rose at noon, had lunch at Belknap's, & was dragged by the Child to one of his beloved cinemas. One thing of interest there was a news picture shewing Solomon Island cannibals—obviously of mixed negrito & australoid race, & without exception the most bestial entities I have ever beheld under the nominal category of homo sapiens. In the late afternoon I went down again about my fountain pen—getting the present one, which I think is as satisfactory as any could possibly be. Thence I proceeded to Talman's in Flatbush—arriving for dinner, as invited, & settling my belongings for the coming visit. In the evening I went over to Kleiner's as previously mentioned—indulging in much old-time conversation, & copying "Roll On, Silver Moon". I did not leave till about 1:30 a.m., but had the key to Talman's flat, & retired without disturbing the family. The place really accomodates a guest with admirable ease despite its phenomenal compactness.

On WEDNESDAY, JULY 8, I rose at 7 a.m., breakfasted at Talman's, & set out for Prospect Park under grey, sticky skies to begin this letter as indicated on p. 1. Flatbush is still the most pleasing & homelike place in Greater New York, & has not radically changed in the last 2 or 3 years. There is a new cinema theatre beyond Albemarle Road, some of the business blocks along the avenue are being replaced, a grating has been put up at the end of Albemarle Arcade to keep people out of Albemarle Court, & the edges of the grass in Prospect Park have been fenced in near the Parkside Ave. entrance with wire netting. Also, a new small entrance to the park has been cut a short distance down Ocean Ave. But the general atmosphere of the place is much the same. The city water still has a flat taste, & the ancient Church Ave. steeple still rears its Georgian height above the Dutch-inscribed gravestones of the rambling churchyard. Most of the street cars are still 2-man, though a few one-mans are now operated during the rush hours. On this occasion I sat & wrote in the Vale of Cashmere till dampness made writing impossible—whereupon I packed up & took the Interborough for Sonny's. After lunch the Child & I went over to Coney Island (via Sea Beach B M T Express) to see Leeds at his bookshop; & found him apparently very contented & well-placed. He is still writing stories & getting them constantly rejected, but never loses hope & resiliency. In his shop—The Half Moon, in Surf Ave., the principal street—I found a copy of the ancient Saxon epic of Beowulf (in a good school translation) for 10¢; hence purchased it, since I have always wished for a copy of my own. It is only a thin volume, & will be included in the package I am about to mail home. After Little Belknap had a look at his cherished ocean, we returned to town—he going home, & I stopping off at 14th St. to keep an engagement with Loveman at his shop at 5:45 p.m. Being a little early, I tarried among the second-hand bookshops of 4th Ave.—obtaining for 10¢ a fine little copy (Harpers 1842) of Gilbert White's famous "Natural History of Selborne", which I have previously possessed only in a 2-volume paper-covered edition—Cassell's old National Library. Reaching Dauber & Pine's, I found

Loveman all ready to go; hence we set out at once for his seaward eyrie. Young McGrath was there—busy copying Loveman's "Sphinx" on the typewriter, since a chance for its publication as a small book seems to have developed. All three now set out for dinner—at the old Bristol Dining Room in Willoughby St. near Fulton, next door to the now defunct John's, which was my Brooklyn headquarters for spaghetti in the old days. Joe's is too expensive for steady use—though it still flourishes as vigorously as when you were there. Loveman insisted on treating me to a stupendous gorge—the effect of which on my weight is woeful to contemplate! Whilst in the Bristol we accidentally encountered a friend of Loveman's—a pleasant chap from Cleveland named Leonard Gaynor. He is now connected with the Paramount cinema firm, & expressed great interest in my work when Loveman described it to him. However—in cold fact nothing of mine could ever be suitable for his purposes. Cinemas want *action*—whereas my one specialty is *atmosphere*. After dinner Loveman & I took McGrath out to see Union Place—that ancient & spectral courtyard which inspired one of my "Fungi from Yuggoth."[1] It was just the same as ever—though we were there just too early to catch the most ghoulish note in its sequester'd & mouldering personality. It is, as I may have told you, wholly hidden from the street proper—reached by an archway & long passage. Returning to Loveman's place, we discussed philosophy, aesthetics, & old times till a late hour—incidentally taking coffee & cake (oh, my weight!) & listening to a radio which very opportunely played some of the familiar musical comedy airs of the 1890's & early 1900's. A typical old man's session! At 12:30 midnight I broke away, returned to Talman's, & retired in due season. I have not yet been around the 169 Clinton neighbourhood, but am told it is rapidly going down—invaded by Syrians through the overflow of the Atlantic Ave. colony. Squalid Red Hook! 169 itself is said to be at present in a very decrepit condition. I may take a look at it before returning to civilisation.

On THURSDAY, JULY 9, I rose at 7 a.m. & wrote letters under grey skies in Prospect Park as previously indicated. At noon I went up to my small Child's for lunch; & afterward Sonny & Grandpa went over to the Brooklyn Museum for a long period of aesthetic & scientific contemplation. This museum is really a great place. Its American wing has a panelled room from PROVIDENCE, & shews most of these features in such lifelike coördination (rooms in groups, with hallways & even exterior fragments) that their educational value is prodigiously enhanced. Other items are commensurate in merit—the collection of Chinese cloisonné being, according to common report, the finest in the world. When the museum closed, we adjourned to that exquisite Japanese Garden so close to it—where you & I got lost in December 1924, & could not find an open exit. This time it was in the marvellous full bloom of summer, & its charm was as poignant as of old—even though it cannot even begin to compare with Maymont in Richmond. Subsequently we strolled through Prospect Park to Parkside Ave., & Belknap decided to stay in

Brooklyn for the evening—coming out to Talman's, where I was to take dinner & confabulate with my host. This was a remarkably independent thing for the Child to do, for he almost never takes a meal away from papa & mamma. Now that he is in better health, his old Grandpa is encouraging him to be more independent & active! But he would not invite himself to Talman's for the meal—so Grandpa shewed him a nice cheap place along Flatbush Ave. where he could supply himself. Then I went on to Talman's & took dinner with him—small Sonny shewing up at 7 o'clock. The evening was very pleasant—questionnaires (like those each night in the Bulletin, which I occasionally spring on A E P G Fridays) forming the main diversion. Sonny & Talman made astonishingly low scores—indeed, I don't know what the education of the younger generation is coming to! The Child left early, but Talman & I kept up the questionnairing till after midnight. He also got a trite & inane weird story over the radio. Then retiring.

Incidentally—during the day I finally decided to take the suit Talman wanted to give me. Even though it has a pattern, the *cut* is sober & conservative enough for an old man; & the local tailor agreed to clean it, shorten the cuffs, & remove the trouser turn-ups all complete for only $1.50. It will be ready Saturday—& we shall see how the thing looks on Grandpa!

On FRIDAY, JULY 10, 1931, I arose at 7:30 a.m. & proceeded up to Sonny's at 9:30 for the usual Friday motor trip. The day was a curious alternation of sunlight & showers, & the region chosen was Westchester County in the vicinity of the great Croton Dam. When we drove over this piece of cyclopean masonry—which holds a titanick reservoir in check—the view southward down the mighty valley that it crosses was magnificent beyond description. Vivid green slopes, fantastic clusters of trees, blue threads & patches of water, & great lines of outspread hills from the green eminences close at hand to the faint, half-fabulous purple peaks on the far horizon. Lunch—of the usual Long elaborateness—was served in an exquisite rural spot; & all along the route were unfolded scenick panoramas of the utmost loveliness. Some of the territory was familiar to me, whilst other parts (including the vast dam) were seen for the first time. I don't know that I ever took a day's trip averaging a higher percentage of first-rate scenery. Beyond doubt, the landscape of the northeastern United States is superior to any other in the country—what a pity it can't be joined to the climate of Florida! Well—we returned to 230 in the mid-afternoon, & I set out to write letters in Central Park while Little Sonny took a nap in the house. At 6:30 I am to be back for dinner, after which the Child proposes to drag Grandpa to another of his precious cinema shows. Then I shall return to Flatbush, chat with Talman if the household is still up, & in any case retire earlier than I have been retiring for the last few days. Tomorrow I am due up at the Child's for lunch at noon, after which I shall take him back to Talman's (who has Saturday afternoons off) for a sort of informal conference at which Kleiner is expected to be present. I shall also get my charity suit at the tailor's & see what it looks like after renovation. Talman is so nearly my size that he might well do as Miss Ripley[2] does with A E P G in the matter of keeping apparel in circulation! Likewise—tomorrow I shall use up my credit slip at the Penn Post Hotel because of the sojourn of Talman's brother at the flat. This will, however, be for only one night; since the brother will immediately move onward, & Talman absolutely insists that I re-instal myself Sunday for a few more days. Sunday evening at 6 I am due to meet Loveman at his house for a session of discussion & exploration. Home in about another week—& will send advance bulletins.

Dwyer regrets not being able to see me in West Shokan, & says he may be able to get down to Kingston for a week-end session of discussion if I can manage to get up there. In view of the new fiver just sent by A E P G, I am almost tempted to try it—but we shall see!

Shall be sending a package of soiled linen & miscellany soon, for at this stage I don't need much in reserve. I hope to hit Providence with a very light valise.

Hope the shelf-painting hasn't caused a vast upheaval around #10. Don't be over-active, but take a stroll now & then to get in training for the trips I shall soon be dragging you on. Glad most of my postcards arrive safely & semi-legible. I transmitted your greetings to the Longs, & they reciprocate with the utmost heartiness. I am still using Belknap's address for mail, hence no change in forwarding procedure will be necessary.

Here are some Bekes—& more to come soon. Received the epistle from Galpin, who is enjoying life in Paris preceding an excursion into Germany. I also enclose something about *meteorites* which I picked up at the Am. Museum.

More soon—& will see you in person before long. Best wishes—& happy returns for A E P G.——

Yr most aff Nephew & obt Servt

H P L

P.S. Whitehead's great story "The Black Beast" will be in the next issue—July 15—of *Adventure*[.]

Notes

1. "The Courtyard" (*Fungi from Yuggoth* IX).
2. Apparently Alice Maud Ripley (1873–1962).

[337]　　[ALS] [HPL to LDC]

Japanese Garden, Bklyn
Thursday, July 16, 1931

My dear Daughter:—

　　　　　Though you'll see me in a couple of days after receiving

this, I thought I'd bring the diary a bit nearer down to date than last Friday. The days pass so swiftly that I can hardly realise the passage of almost another week!

On SATURDAY, JULY 11, 1931, I rose at 7 a.m. & mailed my large package home at a substation near Newkirk Ave. Hope it arrived safely. I then did some writing in the Vale of Cashmere, & went over to Sonny's at noon for lunch. Early in the afternoon the Child & I went over to Talman's for a look at his famous file of cuttings—& on the way I stopped into the tailor's & got the suit Talman had given me. Dry-cleaning had made the brownish surface seem somewhat lighter than it had formerly seemed, but even so it did not look quite too ridiculous for an old man. The fit, as I said before, is uncannily good—& with the sleeves shortened & trouser turn-ups removed, it comes close to absolute perfection. It is a genuine Palm Beach suit, & is quite close to what I might have bought of my own volition. In use, its worn-ness is not obtrusively apparent. Arriving at Talman's, I put the new suit on—& have been wearing it ever since. When I shew up on Sunday or thereabouts you will see me in it. I wish it were a bit darker & without the checked pattern—but for a gift it surely hits the mark very tolerably. Its *comfortable* quality is beyond description. Extravagant or not, I shall nevermore be without a suit of this weight if I can help it. As you know, I have long been planning to get one cheaply at the end of some season. Talman had a light-grey winter overcoat which he also wished to give me, but I finally decided against it. It was so youthful that its appearance on me would have been even worse than that of my present archaeological reliques—hence I let Little Belknap take it. It looks very well on the Child—& indeed, I think Talman is very rash to let it go. He tires easily of clothing, & discards things long before they are really worn out. Well—the first thing Talman did after the change of clothing was to take a set of snap shots of Grandpa & Sonny. I enclose two representative specimens herewith. These give some idea of my new charity suit, & also shew how astonishingly the old man has aged since even last year. Wrinkled face, thin grey hair, &c. &c. You can't see my coat of tan in the pictures, but the close-up shews how marvellously well my face has been behaving— no vast scars & ploughed-up areas such as would ordinarily shew in an untouched picture of equal closeness. Sonny looks well in the pictures, because the glare of the sun conceals his lip-fuzz. His suit is rather sloppy because (emulating his Grandpa's œconomy as manifested in home laundering) he tried to press it himself after a rain-exposure.[1] There are more pictures of this series which I'll shew you on my return.

Well—after the session over Talman's file Sonny & I returned to 230 W. 97, had dinner, & attended a cinema with the family. I then went down town to the Penn Post Hotel, where I used up the credit slip previously issued to me—Talman's brother being at 2215 for the night. This brother—whom I did not meet—is a missionary in China, & is a pious fanatic of the most ridiculous sort. In preparation for his brief advent, Talman had to hide all the cigarettes & gaudily covered magazines in the house lest his stuffy clerical decorum be violated. I had a good sleep at the Penn Post, & (taking advantage of the marvellous light & mirror arrangement) gave my thin grey locks an exhaustive & artistic Trimetting. Poor Fernando King—to think I should desert him after a lifetime of faithful service!

On SUNDAY, JULY 12, 1931—Orangeman's Day, sacred to the victory of King William's troops at Boyne Water in 1689—I rose at noon & went up to Belknap's for dinner. After the gorge the Child & I went out to Central Park to stroll & loaf—stopping to explore the Am. Museum of Nat. Hist. midway in the ramble. I don't see how Sonny can endure Central Park—it is so much more seedy & moth-eaten than Prospect! After a second gorge I proceeded back to Talman's for the evening, & found Kleiner there. My previous engagement with Loveman had been postponed till Tuesday. General conversation of an interesting nature ensued, & after Kleiner's departure all hands retired. On MONDAY, JULY 13, 1931, I rose at 7:30 a.m. & proceeded to the nearest cobbler to have my almost disintegrated shoes fixed. They are about at the end of their rope, but for 45¢ I got the soles nailed back & the worst cracks patched. Also, a pair of new strings. I then looked up an ancient Flatbush house at E. 25th St. & Ditmas Ave. which Talman discovered last year, & which is not listed in any guidebook. It is a fine specimen of the curved gambrel, though rather late in date if the Georgian doorway be a good clue. (circa 1815?) Its condition is magnificent, since the neighbourhood is still residential & undecayed. A small bay-window on the corner gable is the only Victorian defacement which the fine old structure has suffered. It is obviously in well-to-do private hands. In this locality I met a delectable little tiger kittie perhaps 3 months old, & paused for half an hour to converse & play with him. After that I sat around Prospect Park & gave Sonny's latest tale (just rejected by Wright) a critical reading. It is not up to the Child's best standard, & marks an unfortunate tendency on his part to cultivate certain rather vacuous artificialities of style. At noon I went up to Belknap's for lunch, & afterward we went down to the Heckscher Bldg. in 59th St. (where Orton used to work for the Am. Mercury) to see the Museum of Modern Art which occupies the 12th floor. The collection did not greatly impress me. After this we proceeded to the Central Park menagerie, where are exhibited two recently acquired young *gorillas*—the only living specimens now in captivity. For some reason or other, gorillas are very hard to keep alive & healthy away from their native habitat; hence very few people outside Africa have ever seen one. This was a first glimpse for both Sonny & myself. They were in an exceedingly large cage, with plenty of scaffolding to give them an opportunity to climb & swing about. Though only half-grown, they had all the familiar traits peculiar to their species—including the odd habit of resonantly drumming on their chests with their fists. It was distinctly thrilling to behold—alive & active—a type of being known formerly only through books & pictures! Certainly, the gorilla is a sinister-looking customer; & very close to mankind. After the gorilling we adjourned to a well-placed bench, where Grandpa gave the Small Boy a severe scolding about his newer theories of fictional style. Sonny didn't get mad, but will probably write along exactly the same as before! That evening, Mrs. Long being indisposed, Sonny & his papa were scheduled to dine out—hence I sent the Child home at the proper hour & adjourned to Prospect Park to complete my day's writing. I sat in the Vale of Cashmere & old-fashioned garden—having taken an ice-cream dinner at Reid & Snyder's. After dusk I adjourned to Talman's & convers'd with him till a late retiring hour. Talman has 2 books for me—which I had long wanted—which his wife had picked up for 33⅓¢ each at a Womrath Library sale. They are de la Mare's "Riddle & Other Stories" (containing the famous & sinister "Seaton's Aunt") & Machen's "Three Impostors." (my old copy of which perished in Dwyer's fire last year) I shall either mail them home to myself or carry them in my valise.

On TUESDAY, JULY 14, 1931, I rose at 7:30 & wrote & read in Prospect Park. I am re-reading Vanderbilt's "Social History of Flatbush"—a splendid antiquarian volume which I came near to purchasing in 1924–5. I then went up to the Child's for lunch—& afterward we jointly welcomed young Grayson for a literary conference. Meanwhile letters & telephone had brought some rather dismal though by no means unexpected news from G. P. Putnam's Sons. Neither my stuff nor Belknap's (who sent a collection in 2 weeks after I did) is wanted in its present form, hence both our MS. packages are being returned. Shiras—who called Sonny on the telephone & wrote me in some detail—hems & haws & talks of changes he would like to see & plans he would like to make after the lapse of a few months. Sonny & his Grandpa, however, know a polite letdown when we see one—hence have dismissed the entire matter from our respective minds. Thus bursts the great Putnam bubble—just as I said it would in the first place. Still, it was well not to let the chance go by untested.[2] The discussion with young Grayson was pleasant, & after his departure we had dinner. I then went down town to meet Loveman, who wanted to take me to a cinema show. After this show—dull as most of them are—we adjourned to his eyrie in Columbia Heights, where we discussed aesthetics & looked over books till 1:30 a.m. I then returned to Talman's & retired.

On WEDNESDAY, JULY 15, 1931 I rose at 7:30 a.m. & proceeded to Prospect Park for reading & writing. On this occasion I explored places I had not visited in 6 years, but found them wholly unchanged. At noon I took the subway for a long uptown ride—to Grayson's flat in 178th St., (not far from the George Grey Barnard cloisters) since he had invited me for a motor ride in the afternoon. Grayson's neighbourhood is rather shabby & upheaved with preparations for an approach to the new Hudson River Bridge,[3] but the flat itself is a good one. His mother, who drove the car, is a school-teacher of great affability & competence—a stout gentlewoman of middle years & undistinguished aspect, descended from line [*sic*] of actual German nobility. The father, now deceased, was a Grayson of Alabama, & uncle of Admiral Cary T. Grayson, Woodrow Wilson's personal physician. Grayson's grandmother, who lives with them, was absent, but I beheld the family canine—Jerome Napoleon Bonaparte—& a very pleasant young neighbour named Joseph something or other—both of whom participated in the ensuing ride. The ride itself was of vast interest & pleasure, insomuch as it covered several regions of extreme scenic beauty never before seen by me, tho' close to town in Westchester County. Betwixt the Boston Post Road & the Sawmill River Road lies a vast area of hills now under development as a residential community, & the views therefrom are magnificent beyond description. In Hartsdale the houses are all new, & mostly of Georgian or Tudor design; built along the brink of a titanic bluff, & facing away from it so that their rear gardens (all exquisitely landscaped) look out over a breathless & dizzying vista of green valley & rolling wooded countryside. From this region we proceeded across to Ardsley—on the Hudson above Yonkers—where a cousin of the Graysons has an exquisite estate. This cousin—a now elderly gentlewoman—has become a sort of semi-recluse & eccentric as a result of excessive parental supervision in youth; it having been her father's design to keep her closely secluded till he could find her an husband among the German nobility. This latter he did not succeed in doing—hence died leaving a browbeaten & no longer attractive daughter in middle age, unfitted for the world by reason of early seclusion. After this death, the daughter was promptly married, for her money, by a commonplace, semi-rustic, & none too grammatical neighbour—& there the couple now live; elderly & eccentric, in the midst of scenic loveliness & architectural opulence. They keep no servant, & have closed all but three rooms of the great house—dwelling like campers & wearing the most shapeless & nondescript apparel. The grounds, however, are still cared for; & present an admirable appearance with trees, lawns, walls, brooklet, & waterfall. We stopped there for some time, observing the landscape & seeing the owners—who are of a pleasant, tranquil cast despite their eccentricity & diverse degrees of cultivation. Finally my hosts bade me farewell at the 137th St station of the subway, & I proceeded downtown for some macaroni & cherry pie at the Automat—thence returning to Talman's & conversing till midnight.

Today—THURSDAY, JULY 16, 1931,—I rose at 7:30 a.m. & gave my old grey suit to the tailor to be pressed & mailed to 10 Barnes St. I then sought the open for letter-writing—first Prospect Park & now the good old Japanese Garden near the Brooklyn Museum. This afternoon I shall do some suburban exploration & perhaps visit the old Convict ship "Success" (which I saw in Providence in 1911) which lies at the 79th St. dock, & for which Talman has given me a ticket obtained through his oil co. I dine at Talman's at 6, & in the evening I have an engagement with Loveman. Tomorrow I look up Sonny again—his family leaves for their summer vacation Sunday—& shall dine with Talman. Saturday I think I shall start homeward—though I don't know just how directly. It depends on my cash—& probably I can't take the northward loop. I may, though, go by way of *Hartford*—perhaps stopping overnight if necessary. I shall probably shew up at #10 some time not far from Sunday. ¶ Best wishes—

Yr aff neph & obt Servt
H P L

P.S. If I do stay on one day beyond Saturday I'll drop you a line. Tomorrow will probably decide the question.

Notes

1. The photo on the frontispiece of *SL* 3 is probably one of those taken by Talman at this time.

2. At the request of Winfield Shiras, an editor at G. P. Putnam's Sons, HPL had submitted about 30 stories for possible book publication in late March 1931. But Shiras ultimately rejected the collection. His letter to HPL is nonextant.

3. I.e., the George Washington Bridge, a double suspension bridge that spans the Hudson River between Washington Heights (around 181st Street) in New York and Fort Lee, NJ. The bridge was begun in 1927 and dedicated on 24 October 1931.

[338]   [ALS] [HPL to LDC]

Old-Fashion'd Garden,
Prospect Park, Bklyn—
July 17, 1931

My dear Daughter:—

In this—my probably final bulletin before seeing you—I dedicate the new Kresge pad which I have adopted since the decline in quality of the Woolworth article. It seems to me rather good,* & I fancy I shall keep on buying it until it begins to deteriorate.

It is probable that I shall stay over Saturday night & take a Sunday stagecoach direct for Providence—although I may decide at the last moment to try to include Hartford. The swing up the Hudson is quite out of the question. I ought to be around 10 Barnes St. Sunday evening or Monday—the latter in case I finish the journey on a night coach. I shall have mailed one more small package to myself, & will stop down town to get whatever I need for the next day's breakfast; (Riley's Delicatessen being open Sundays) so that you need

---

*LATER—No! Surface does not agree with my new pen.

take no pains to provide any advance material for the larder. A day or two after my arrival you will witness an echo of my now-concluding active period in the form of a visit from James Ferdinand Morton, Esq.—on his way back from Nova Scotia, & avid for some more minerals from the quarries of Signor Mariano de Magistris. Which means, of course, that my first act upon homecoming must be to secure some cartons somewhere for the cursed stuff! Incidentally—if I do return through Hartford, you will probably receive a last-moment postcard to that effect.

It surely has been a great trip, & I dare say the habit of activity implanted in me will last for several days. I shall drag you out to Newport & other places before it subsides—that is, if I ever conquer the file of newspapers awaiting me. Hope they're all carefully saved. The hustle in which my kindly hosts have lately kept me has prevented me from reading the last two issues—July 5th & 12th. It is amusing how completely one can run the gamut of activity—veering suddenly from a state of complete seclusion & inertia to one of extreme gregariousness, & vice versa!

I shall surely be glad to see the ancient hill again, & trust that no old houses or steeples have been torn down during my absence. The loss of the barn is bad enough! Most of my work will, as is now my fixed summer custom, be done in the open air—& I may even take piles of papers to Blackstone Park for reading & discarding. So far as the world is concerned, my coördinated information ends with May 1st. I am trying to get the worst of my correspondence disposed of here—in Prospect Park or the Japanese Garden—so that I can attack the massed newspapers with a mind relatively free from other responsibilities. Wonder if A E P G still gets the Literary Digest from any source? Bless my soul, but I'll never catch up with the times!

As for my diary—I concluded yesterday noon—THURSDAY, JULY 16, 1931—as I left the Japanese Garden to do errands & explore suburbs. My errands were all at the 42nd St. Woolworth's, & primarily concerned a new collar supply. The other day a collar wilted hopelessly in the course of a ramble, & I had to seek a sudden cheap replacement. The nearest Woolworth's being out of 14½ Parkdales, I had to purchase a 2 for 25¢ substitute at McCrory's—& felt myself rather cheated because of the poor fit. I can't get a tie to stay above the collar button with them, & believe I'll throw them away—reckoning the quarter spent in bitter experience. Well—anyway—my immediate object yesterday was to get a couple of Woolworth collars for a reserve; & while at the counter I noticed the inviting profusion of *10¢ ties*. I have seen these before, in Providence & elsewhere, but have hitherto refrained from purchasing because of my belief that they would not make good knots—this being the case with all the cheap ties I have ever had. On this occasion, however, I was tempted beyond all resistance by a display of dime cravats of **exactly** my favourite pattern—black with white spots—hence took a chance despite all my long-standing misgivings. My current collar & tie being unsatisfactory, I paused at the Grand Central Station to change to the new Woolworth outfit—& fancy my pleased surprise at discovering that the 10¢ tie actually forms a *splendid knot!* I still have it on, & no one could possibly guess that it—as well as the collar—cost only 10¢. This really opens up an entirely new tie policy on my part; for if I can get new ties for a dime, I certainly shall not wear the old frayed junk I have been in the habit of wearing. Of course, the dime ties will get creased sooner than good ones—but even so, it will be cheaper to throw them away & get fresh new ones than to buy dollar ties & cling to them through long periods of decline. Better cheap & immaculate than sumptuous & seedy. And with new ties costing $\frac{1}{10}$of the usual price, there will be a genuine net economy. I have bought another 10¢ tie—black with another sort of white dot—& shall continue to replace my stock with this type. Woolworth's is surely becoming my one universal emporium—for food, clothing, & stationery as well as for less staple articles. As I continue to use this Kresge paper—which does not suit my pen very well—I am not sure but that I shall return to Woolworth's for my note paper. Look at the array of things which I now buy regularly at Woolworth's

Food	*Clothing*	*Stationery*	*Sundries*
Catsup	collars	typewriter paper	candlesticks
Chili Sauce	ties	note paper	decorations
Pickles	socks	carbon paper	pocket mirrors
Relishes		Waterman Ink	
Worcestershire		postcards &c	

This reminds me—I have at last obtained my long-wished brass hand candlesticks! You will recall that Sonny & I saw some in this same 42nd St. Woolworth's last year, & that I refrained from buying them because I thought the Providence Woolworths would have them. Then, upon my return, I found to my dismay that our local Woolworths do *not* carry such items. Well—the 42nd St. shop still had its supply, hence I purchased two. I am carrying them in my valise—wishing to take no mailing chances on such bendable material. You will, I am sure, find them fascinating—& I'll let you have one if you wish it.

Resuming the diary—I proceeded from the Grand Central to Flushing by subway, & found that ancient town still American & old-fashioned despite the lapse of 3 years since my last previous sight of it. New York atmosphere has not yet touched it, though many apartment houses (with lawns, like those of Providence) are going up in certain districts. I mourned the passing of several Colonial houses I had known, & shed a tear for old St George's church; (1812) which—though superseded in 1850 by a stone Gothick structure—still remained intact & in use as a parish house. It was still there in 1928—but yesterday I found a new brick Gothick parish house on its site, with a cornerstone dated 1930. Eheu, fugaces! Opera Houses, warehouses, stables, churches . . . . . it's about time Grandpa passed along, too! However—the Bowne house of 1671[1] & the Quaker meeting house of 1694 are still intact. Flushing is a delightful place—much as Flatbush probably was about 1885 or 1890. From Flushing I proceeded by trolley to Jamaica—a village still having many quaint sections, though farther advanced toward metropolitan absorption than Flushing is. After a brief survey I hastened back to Flatbush for dinner, & conversed with Talman till 9 o'clock, when I went down to Dauber & Pine's to meet Loveman. Meanwhile I received a note from Sonny telling of his mother's sudden acute (though not dangerous) illness; a thing which will probably set the household in a turmoil & prevent my seeing the Child again on this visit. It may also postpone the Longs' New England trip. Well— I duly met Loveman & accompanied him to his eyrie for discussion. With him was a very brilliant young Bostonian—a new protege of his named Robert Thompson, who has been to sea & is now seeking to adopt literature as a career. Leaving at 12:30, I returned to 2215 & retired. Today—FRIDAY, JULY 17—I am writing in the park, & shall later explore sights. Tonight I shall behold Seabury Quinn again, since he is due to dine at Talman's. ¶ Well—see you later.

Yr aff Nephew & obt Servt
H P L

Notes

1. In other letters (see, e.g., LDC/AEPG 130), HPL correctly dates this house to 1661.

[339]   [ALS] [HPL to LDC]

Final Bulletin—
Sunday noon—July 19 [1931]

My dear Daughter:—

At the moment it looks as if I would arrive *Monday night*—the evening you receive this—at about 11 o'clock. But don't stay up on my account. Heaven knows I'll have enough around my room to keep an old man busy! Packages—papers—!!!!!

Invitations piled up so thickly that I simply *couldn't* get away yesterday or today, & Talman insisted that I stay over till Monday. He & his wife have gone to Spring Valley for the week-end, hence I have the flat all to myself— sleeping as late as I wish. I shall leave it in a neat & securely locked condition.

I last wrote on Thursday, from the Japanese Garden—or no—pardon me!—I sent another bulletin Friday telling of my Flushing-Jamaica trip & Woolworth candlesticks & neckwear.

Well—Friday noon, at Loveman's earnest recommendation, I went to a cinema to see the film of "Trader Horn"—& for once I was *not* disappointed.[1] It is really a marvellous production, with the feel & atmosphere of cryptic Africa in every inch of it. The scenic glimpses & depictions of authentic savage life are tremendous—*sounds* as well as *sights* being introduced. Hellish negro war & torture rituals are reproduced with poignant verisimilitude & authentic detail—so that one really feels disquietingly close to the soul of the Dark Continent. With this film & the gorillas of last week, I ought to be quite an African authority! "Trader Horn" came to Loew's State in Providence before my departure, but I let it slip by. Very glad to have had this belated opportunity to witness it. After the show I went up to the 79th St docks to see the ancient convict ship "Success"*—built of Malabar teak about 1780 as a merchantman & used around 1840 & 1850 to transport convicts to Botany Bay. It is a fine old square-rigger, & has been on exhibition in different parts for a quarter of a century. I saw it in Providence—docked near the Crawford St. bridge—exactly 20 years ago, in 1911, & it has not changed since then. The general antique lines of the ship (thought to be the oldest afloat) interested me even more than the special convict features. On this occasion the presence of 2 other sailing ships at the dock (one a square-rigger) added vastly to the illusion of old sea days. After this I returned to 2215 for dinner, & in the evening Seabury Quinn came over. Really, he is a delightful chap, & improves on further acquaintance. He likes my article on the weird tale, which Talman lent him, & I intend to send him one of my extra copies to keep. On SATURDAY, JULY 18, I rose at 7:30 a.m., bade the Talman household adieu, & set out to write in Prospect Park. But alas! In the early afternoon a drenching rain got me suddenly in the open, completely soaking everything I had on, & spoiling one of my new 10¢ Woolworth ties![†] I then returned to 2215 to dry off—restoring my new charity suit to shape the best I could by stretching the coat with my hands & laying the trousers flat beneath the mattress of the bed. I learned of the latter trick years ago in a comic picture, but never tried it till now. It worked so well that I shall try it again at home. At 8 o'clock I went over to Loveman's for an evening of discussion, & later we went out for a late lunch—eating at the most homelike of places—a real **WALDORF LUNCH!** Shades of Foster, Westminster St., & Market Square!! Yes—at last the good old Providence chain has invaded the metropolis with several one-arms. After this we walked around to 169 Clinton—the same old dump—& I shook my fist at the cursed joint. Then back to 130—& finally back to 2215 & retiring. Today—SUNDAY, JULY 19, I rose at noon & am writing in Prospect Park. Later I may explore some colonial sights, & I may

---

*for which Talman gave me a cut-rate ticket
†I shall get another Monday at the same store, in case our Prov. Woolworth's don't carry the pattern.

dine at the good old Milan. At 7:30 I meet Loveman at the Paramount for some cinema. Tomorrow I shall see Kirk again—& then the stage coach for home, seeing you at 11. ¶ Yr aff Nephew & obt Servt

H P L

P.S. One more pkg. coming—Loveman having given me a couple of Civil War books. I mailed the last previous pkg. yesterday.

Notes

1. *Trader Horn* (MGM, 1931), directed by W. S. Van Dyke; starring Harry Carey, Edwina Booth, and Duncan Renaldo. Based on the book by Alfred Aloysius Horn and Ethelreda Lewis.

[340]   [ANS, on envelope from thje Athol Transcript Co.] [HPL to LDC]

[27 September 1931]

Good Morning!

We pretty nearly bought Eddy out last night—you ought to see Cook's car! And I got an old Atlas of Burritt's Geography of the Heavens to replace the lost one![1] Now Grandma's set is complete again!

Today I'm taking the last (possibly) of my autumn outings. Am guiding Cook on his way to Norwich, & shall leave him at a point slightly west of Thornton, prepared to ascend Lippitt Hill. Shall be knocking about the countryside all day, & am not decided whether I'll take dinner downtown or here. Looks like a good day—I'm wearing the old brown suit.

See you later—

Yr aff Nephew & obt Servt
H P L

Notes

1. The atlas was lost c. March 1926.

1932

[341]   [ALS] [HPL to AEPG]

230—Dec. 27–8[, 1932]

My dear Grandchild:—

Well—I've had my first fountain pen session, & this is the result. So far it appears excellent—but it may not, of course, prove so good after I've written more with it. It is the coarsest of all the *non-stubs*, & does not have that troublesome hitch in writing which the outright stubs have. As you see, it is coarser than what I used to use—coarser than the pen you have—but the Waterman man (a splendid chap who preserved ideal patience while I tried pen after pen with Little Sonny looking wearily on from a neighbouring settee) tells me that the finer points are never made with such a free feed. The E. L. Freeman clerk was right in saying that the feeds are not adjustable. Each different point comes in two lines according to feed, but beyond that there is no variation. This is of course the freer of the two feeds furnished with this style of point—being in fact the freest feed obtainable for any Waterman short of an actual stub. It is pretty good, but not quite as free (with my light touch) as the stub I returned. Notice how I have outrun the feed in writing this page—free & heavy at the top, but fainter as my hand races along & uses up more ink than the existing feed will replace. Of course, if I bear on more, or write more slowly, the flow speeds up; but my whole object is to get something which will *not demand* such pressure & slowness, since I cannot write effectively unless I can go along rapidly & pressurelessly. I don't like this coarseness of point, either—though I'll forgive it if the feed will behave. It certainly doesn't offer the obstacles to writing which the real stub offered. I shall give it a good trial, & if it doesn't stand up under the test I'll go in again Thursday or Friday. Hope the clerk's patience (if I get the same fellow again) will hold out.

Leaving my favourite subject of pens—I rose today & [*sic*] noon & had lunch at Sonny's. After a session of argument we went down town in a drizzling rain—my first trip down town, since the coach from the Fountain St. New England terminal took me directly to 97th St. I bought a new pair of shoe laces at Frank's in 14th St (mine broke this morning) & also a 1933 diary, since my sojourn here laps over into the new year. We then proceeded to Dauber & Pine's, & almost knocked Loveman over with surprise. He at once invited me over for the evening. After that we repeated the surprise with Kirk. A telephone call to the Paterson Museum revealed that James Ferdinand will be out of town till next Tuesday, so that I shall have to miss him. Tough luck! We then proceeded to the Whitney Museum of American Art (in 8th St. near Kirk's) & viewed a boresome exhibit of modernistic junk. After that came the momentous trip down to the Waterman office in Broadway—

951

just across Dey St. from ancient St. Paul's & its churchyard. Then back to 230 for a turkey dinner as colossal as yesterday's—Ædepol, but what will become of my weight!—& after dinner a period of discussion. At 9 o'clock I took the subway to Loveman's new apartment at 17 Middagh St., not far from Columbia Heights. It is a trim apartment house of recent date, although there is an ancient Colonial gambrel-roofer just across the street. The apartment has two rooms & kitchenette, & Loveman & McGrath have fixed it up magnificently. It is a veritable museum with its endless array of Egyptian, Greek, & other antiquities, Chinese & Japanese objects, early American paintings, &c. &c. It is on the 5th floor—& the absence of an elevator gives one a healthful climb. Loveman played his radio—transmitting a programme from the opening night of "Radio City".[1] Did WJAR or WEAN give any parts of this? The numbers on Loveman's dial are *not* like yours—& Belknap's differs from both. Loveman did some ether-fishing (an old game of his long before your new-fangled contraption reduced me to this degree of childishness), & among the things we got was **MEXICO CITY**—La Vieja Ciudad de Mexico—with a suave announcer pattering in Spanish, & mellow-voiced singers carolling in the same mellifluous tongue. At last I have thus completed the triad of American civilisations—French on the north (our good old 75) & Spanish on the south! Loveman's radio is indubitably much more powerful than yours. He has had both *Charleston* and La Vielle Cité de *Quèbec*, [*sic*] though he could not land them tonight because he had not remembered the numbers. He finds more fascination in ether-fishing when he does not know exactly what to expect—as I did when I began the sport. Mexico City is a very powerful station—so powerful that other stations complain of its interference. It comes at *30* on Loveman's dial, though that is no indication of where it would come on yours. After the "raddio" session—about 11 p.m.—Loveman & McGrath further aggravated my excess weight by forcing me to eat a toothsome supper whose nucleus was *turkey*. This was my *4th* turkey meal since day before yesterday—first at the Pheasant, then at Long's yesterday afternoon, then at Long's again this evening—& finally this Lovemanic meal—which McGrath cooked. And there may possibly be turkey again at Sonny's tomorrow noon! Add to this list also a 25¢ turkey dinner which I got at the Waldorf last week

 . . . . never before was Grandpa so saturated with his favourite fowl! Well—at 1 a.m. I broke away from Middagh St. & returned to 230 . . . . bearing with me two valuable antique gifts which Loveman insisted on my accepting. Wait till you see them! One is a very primitive & prehistoric idol of stone—about 4 inches tall, & meant to lie on its back—found in Mexico, & probably made by the Mayas before their rise to civilisation 4000 or 5000 years ago. The sketch on the left gives an idea of its general nature. The other antique is an equally primitive flint chisel in an ivory handle—from *Africa,* & perhaps a relique of tribes forgot

ten by all the world. Both items were the property of poor Hart Crane, & were given by his mother to Loveman. Loveman ought not to be giving them away—but who can stop that generous soul when he sets out to exercise his generosity? By the way—*Loveman almost came to Providence Monday to surprise me!!* What a disaster that would have been, with me at the other end of the route! A narrow escape— caused by his lack of funds. He may come briefly during the winter.

The Flint Chisel

Well—now to write another letter & hit the hay. If you're over to #10 Friday or before, you might forward all 1st class mail % *Long, 230 W. 97th St., New York, N.Y.* Tomorrow Sonny & I are going museuming, & we expect to drop in at Talman's office. Thursday night I meet Loveman at 10 for a late-evening session. Friday evening the gang meets at Sonny's. Wandrei hasn't been seen lately, but I think I'll try to look him up. ¶ Am reading a library book—Pitkin's History of Human Stupidity—lent me by the Child. Surely a vast subject! ¶ Well—I trust that all flourishes at #61. Did you get a second Christmas dinner at the Ripley abode? ¶ More soon, & see you later. ¶ Yr aff: Nephew & obt Servt—H P L

P.S. Sonny likes his tie immensely. His mamma agrees with me that the sale of his books was a foolish & needless thing. Happily he hasn't sold them all—but his old Grandpa won't ever give him any more!

Notes

1. The Radio City Music Hall in Rockefeller Center, New York City, opened on 27 December.

[342]   [ALS] [HPL to AEPG]

230 W. 97—
Dec. 30–31, 1732

My dear Grandchild:—

Delighted to hear from you! This is still the same pen, about which I can't seem to make up my mind entirely. It doesn't hold me up like the real stub, but I do wish it were finer. However, we'll see. I'll wager you wrote your note with Tom West's bank pen & ink!

Rose today—or technically yesterday—at noon, had lunch at the Child's, & spent the first half of the afternoon discussing psychological values with the little imp. He does have the vastest amount of information inside that bushy young head! At 3:30 Sonny led Grandpa forth to a cinema—which was not at all bad, one of the features being a film including highly instructive views of the island of Bali. We then returned for dinner (& what a gorge!) &

prepared to receive the guests for the gang meeting. It was not a very large one, only Wandrei, Leeds, Loveman, & McGrath showing up. Leeds has a new job which he hopes will be permanent—in a place in Coney Island where second hand correspondence-school courses are sold by mail. He doesn't change at all from year to year—just the same breezy & debonair fellow you saw in 1924. About midnight everyone but Leeds went, but he & Sonny & I stuck together till 2:15 a.m. discussing bolshevism—from which Leeds & I did not, alas, succeed in weaning the child. We then dispersed, & between now (2:30) & 5:30 a.m. (my retiring time, in order to have 7 hours of sleep before the established rising time of 12:30 noon) I expect to finish the library book lent me by Sonny—Pitkin's History of Human Stupidity—& possibly read a story of Leeds's which he wished me to look over.

Tomorrow Sonny & I expect to do some museum haunting, & in the evening Loveman wants me to come over to his place to see the old year out. (good riddance to 1932, a dismal enough twelvemonth!) Among his other guests will be young Richard Morse—that Amherst professor's son who has corresponded with me since I met him here last May.

I really have more on my programme than I can do in a single week, yet I don't wish to presume on the hospitality of the Longs for too protracted a period. Very possibly I *may* stay over if I can do so independently—without depending on the household even for meals—but I'll see in the course of the next three days. One reason—in addition to James Ferdinand Morton—that I'd like to stay over is that Brobst's friend Carl Strauch (the young poet who visited Providence last September) will be in New York on Sunday, Jany. 8th—taking advantage of a cheap excursion from Allentown. If I do stay, I'll duly notify you & ask you to forward first class mail. Otherwise I'll be return-ing Monday night—getting in Tuesday morning (the same morning you re-ceive this, since I assume that the technical holiday Monday includes postal elimination) & calling you up Tuesday night. Hope I'm not swamped with mail. I shall get another Times Sunday, so that my total newspaper reading due Tuesday will be 1 Sunday Journal & 7 Bulletins.

I have duly transmitted your regards to Sonny's Mamma, & am instruct-ed to transmit her reciprocal regards to you. Don't let the old ladies overwork you! Trust you've duly forwarded the Rathbun will to Mrs. Lawton, late of Washington Square. If my homeward coach passed through Norwich I'd stop & see her brother Edgar Balckom ¶ More soon—

> Yrs
>
> H P L

P.S. The writing of this pen does *look* like that of a stub!

1933

[343]   [ANS postcard][1] [HPL to AEPG]

[Postmarked New York, N.Y.,
3 January 1933]

DIARY FOR MONDAY, JAN. 2, 1933

Rose 10 a.m. & had breakfast at Sonny's. The Child & I then went down to
the new Museum of Modern Art at 11 W. 53d St. (near 5th Ave.), where the
famous Whistler portrait of his mother (lent by the Louvre) is temporarily on
exhibition. The picture—so often seen in reproduction—is indeed a splendid
piece of quietly effective art. We also saw the notable collection of crude
"American Primitives" (like those recently exhibited at the Prov. Art Club) on
the top floor. Many are of great folklore value, while some have a striking
merit as unconscious art. We then returned on the elevated to 230. Orton telephoned, but we could not arrange a meeting today. He will be passing
through Providence soon, & you'll see him. Loveman also telephoned. Dinner was a marvellous turkey & mince pie feast—& I overate so heavily that I
can't mount the scales for a week. In the evening we attended a cinema, &
have now returned to 230, where Sonny & I shall argue till 11:30—at which
time I shall go down to the Penn. Terminal for the 'bus. In Providence 7 a.m.
Jany. 3—& shall call you up soon. Had a great time, all in all.
Yrs
[H P L]

Notes

1. *Front:* Gilbert Stuart / First Minister for Spain / Metropolitan Museum of Art, New
York.

[344]   [ALS] [HPL to AEPG]

℅ F. B. Long, Jun.,
230 W. 97th St.,
New York, N.Y.,
Dec. 25–6, 1933.

My dear Grandchild:—
                                        I take my pen in hand to acquaint you with the events
of the first day of my journey. I duly caught the midnight stage-coach, & after
a pleasing, drowsy journey reached the borders of New-York almost before I
knew it. Olneyville, North Scituate, South Foster—& then, after a few intervening villages, Fordham & Harlem. The coach was vastly ahead of time, so

that I could not well go directly to Little Sonny's. As it happened, the route into town this time lay along 5th Ave. instead of Broadway—so that I could not have gone straight to the Child's door as I did last year, even had I wanted to. Reaching the Penn. Station at 6 a.m., I at once proceeded up to the Times Bldg., bought a Times, & read it in the subway till time to start for the Long mansion. Reaching the latter at 7:30 a.m., I found the family still asleep—only the servant being up. They had all been aroused at 4 a.m. by a violent telephone call—which they thought might have some bearing on my arrival, but which turned out to be from some muddled person looking for a physician. Afterward they made up sleep. I finished the Times, & at about 8:30 the household appeared. They all radiated the usual cordiality, & Canis appeared to remember Grandpa quite well. A canary has now been added to the menagerie. He is young, & does not yet fully sing; although he chirps in a way indicating future musical possibilities. But the main acquisition is Little Belknap's aquarium of tiny, grotesque *tropical fish*—a very prevalent fad nowadays. They are of many odd varieties, & do not average much larger than ordinary insects. Like me, they require high temperatures; the water being kept heated by means of an electrick toddy-iron of the sort you used at the Truman Beckwith mansion. At present this iron is out of order, so that Sonny is experimenting with the immersion of electrick-light bulbs. He loves his aquarium, & spends as much time over it as other children do over their stamp albums or mechanical trains. Well—as soon as Belknap had shew'd Grandpa his new toys, he gave the Old Gentleman a present in a nice Christmas box—a blue knitted tie (of the kind he is fond of, though I never wear them! I'll wear it tomorrow, though, to please the child.) & a pair of delightful little black kittie statuettes—wrought in a bizarre technique possibly meant to be "modernistic" but strongly suggesting the Egyptian. Thus: 🐈🐈

Breakfast was serv'd in the usual dining-living room—an apartment lavishly bestrown with Christmas decorations & candles of every sort—including the enormous crèche filling a whole corner. We then adjourned to the Child's study (from which the little rascal has banished ALL books!) for a heated session of argument—fighting several hours over bolshevism & allied subjects. Early in the afternoon we went over to Loveman's—finding him & his companion McGrath at home, & indulging in a series of spirited arguments. His new Greek head is really exquisite, & McGrath has mounted it in an electrically lighted niche where it can be seen with marvellous effectiveness. The whole place is a fascinating museum-library—though as a home I vastly prefer the colonial hearths of 66 College. On this occasion Loveman overwhelmed me with a gift of incredible delightfulness—a real Egyptian *ushabti* (like the one you gave me) *almost a foot long*, cryptically hieroglyphed, & fashioned of wood covered with bitumen. The fascination of this thing is almost beyond description—its battered, greenish-black surface suggesting its uncanny age with potent vividness. It is probably 4000 or 5000 years old—more than a thousand years old when that little Greek tomb-vase was fashioned (1000–600 B.C.). What hands made it in that dim twilight of civilisation's dawn? And to think of the living cells of that remote age which formed the tree whereof it was carved! Incidentally, Loveman was greatly interested by my Greek jar—of whose authenticity he says there can be no doubt. He, in turn, shewed me some early Greek coins which I envy. Also—he gave Little Sonny as [*sic*] scarabaeus-sphinx about 4 inches long & 3″ high—a delightful imagination-stirrer. My newly acquired *ushabti* harmonises curiously with the tall squatting black cats which Belknap gave me, & I shall find some place to form a group of all three against a light background—with the cats on each side of the cryptic image, gazing enigmatically at it. The whole group—so typical of Egypt's millennial mystery—is now set up in Little Sonny's study for the benefit of such visitors as may appear during the ensuing days. Loveman gave me some invitations which commenced the congestion of my visiting programme. Wednesday afternoon he wants me to attend a weird play called "The Double Door", & based on the fortunes of the strange Wendel family & their gloomy, shuttered mansion in 5th Ave.[1] And on New Year's eve he wants me to attend a gathering at his place as I did last year. One of those present will be the mother of the unfortunate Hart Crane. I met her—& Crane's grandmother also—in Cleveland in 1922.[2] This gathering, I fear, will tend to be something of a bore; but I can't politely evade it.

Well—at 5 p.m. Sonny & I returned to #230 for a magnificent Yuletide gorge parallelling yesterday's offering of Friend Fadden. The turkey had a marvellous flavour, & my plate was simply loaded with white meat . . . . & dressing . . . . & everything else! The dessert was a huge plum pudding—ignited in traditional fashion & served with an exquisite sauce. Alas, alas—how far from 140 shall I stray! I offered some of my candy & peanuts, but was in turn offered other candy & salted almonds.

During dinner I was twice called to the telephone—once by Wandrei, & once by the Sutton–Morgan[3] family (who invited me to N.H. last August, & from whom I'm concealing my Quebec trip). Wandrei wants a gathering at his place Wednesday evening—among those present being his younger brother Howard (an artist of real genius) & the editor of *Astounding Stories*—Desmond Hall. The Sutton-Morgans want me to call tomorrow evening. Altogether, a rapidly filling programme—& I may stay over longer than Monday . . . . in which case I'll ask you to forward more mail Saturday. [sentence deleted] James Ferdinand Perkins-Morton will be back on New-Year's, & will take dinner at Sonny's. Good luck!

After dinner came the inevitable cinema show—mediocre stuff through most of which I dozed. We then returned to 230 & held a session of argument till 11 p.m.—after which I ascended to my room on the sixth floor. This room is in a flat whose position corresponds to that of the Longs. It is conducted by an elderly German woman who speaks with a strong accent, & whose roomers seem to be excellent, quiet fellows. She runs both this & the adjoining flat—which have been thrown together by the removal of a partition; the single outer door being that of the flat I'm not in. The room is small but clean & comfortable, & has a neat closet with running water. The bath in the bathroom (next door) is a *shower*, which I like very much. Electric lights adequate. Incidentally—the Broadway ground-floor frontage of this apartment-block (which does not, of course, spoil the residential entrance-lobby in 97th St)—formerly occupied by a branch of the spectacularly exploded Bank of the United States—now harbours a de-luxe *saloon* where beer & perhaps more ardent stimulants are offered over a sumptuous bar. No swinging doors, though—the whole palatial interior being displayed through plate-glass windows. I now joke the Child about living over a bar-room!

I am now coping with my mail—though I doubt if I shall complete more than this one epistle before retiring. Drowsiness supervenes—hence I guess I'll retire early & rise around 9 a.m., getting some letters off before joining the Long household at noon.

Tomorrow's programme includes a round of calls downtown—Kirk, Loveman, Talman—plus a little shopping & perhaps fountain-pen changing. In the evening comes the Sutton-Morgan call. Wednesday afternoon the weird play, & Wednesday night the gathering at Wandrei's. Sunday night the gathering at Loveman's, & Monday James Ferdinand over to dinner at 230. Other events not yet dated are Loveman & McGrath as dinner guests on one evening, & Wandrei & Desmond Hall on another. I may possibly meet T. Everett Harré, who edited "Beware After Dark"—the anthology containing my "Cthul[h]u". Doubt if I shall see Neil Moran,[4] for he is in financial difficulties & has not appeared lately. No one has track of poor Leeds now—though Loveman heard reports of him some months ago, to the effect that he is losing his mind. A tremendous tragedy if true—& undoubtedly the fruit of hardship & worry. But he always did have an occasional tendency to *ramble*. You met him once, you'll recall. By the way—Mrs. Long is quite on her feet again; though, like you, she feels a lack of energy & becomes easily fatigued.

Well—I hope all goes well on the ancient hill. Don't be in a hurry to disperse the presents, & keep the greens till Twelfth Night. Hope the new fire-irons aren't rusting! Regards to Spotty, Mr. Osterberg, & the boys of the K.A.T.[5] When I get back a biology student will be permanently & unaccountably missing! ¶ Best wishes—more anon. Yr aff Nephew & obt Servt H P L

Notes

1. Elizabeth McFadden (1875–1961), *Double Door* (Ritz Theatre, 21 September 1933–January 1934), directed by H. C. Potter; later published as a book (New York: Samuel

French, 1934) and made into a film (Paramount, 1934). For the Wendel family, see LDC/AEPG 146n1.

2. Crane's mother was Grace Edna Hart Crane (1876?–1947). His maternal grandmother was Elizabeth (Belden) Hart (1840–?).

3. HPL refers to Mayte Sutton and her daughter Margaret Morgan.

4. A writer for the pulp magazines, chiefly detective.

5. For the K.A.T. "fraternity," see Introduction. Count Magnus Osterberg probably belonged to the Osterberg family living at 51 Waterman St., next to The Arsdale. See further MFB 2n2.

[345]   [ANS postcard][1] [HPL to AEPG]

[Postmarked New York, N.Y.,
27 December 1933]

DIARY FOR TUESDAY, DEC. 26, 1933

Rose 9 a.m. & got some letters off. Snowstorm raging—as was no doubt the case on our ancient hill. I'll bet Mr. Osterberg wasn't out! Down to Sonny's at noon—heavy lunch—debate—& then (the storm having abated) downtown on a round of calls. Stopped at Kirk's a while, & then over to Loveman's shop—where we met a very pleasant young fellow (a critic of some note) named John Birss, who knows of my tales & wants to read more of them.[2] Next to Talman's office, where we had a pleasant chat. While we were there we met the ship captain whose nice kittie ("Aussi") was portrayed in the recent Texaco Star (I shewed it to you). Talman is coming over to dinner Friday, & afterward Belknap thinks he'll try to call a meeting after all. Then back to 230—dinner—more debate—& finally my departure for the Sutton-Morgan call. This was not the bore I had expected it to be. Old Mrs. S. is very pleasant & cordial, & the daughter Miss Morgan is highly intelligent, learned, cultivated, & acute in debate. Her political & economic views are socialistic, but she does not duplicate Sonny's total bolshevism. They are both enthusiastic antiquarians. I shall call again—if possible, with Sonny & Wandrei, whom they want to meet. They had a *wood fire*—but no irons! Back to 230 at midnight, & now some writing. Tomorrow—Loveman's matinee, & in the evening the gathering at Wandrei's. ¶ More anon. Regards to the boys of the K.A.T.
Yr aff Neph & obt Servt
Asaph[3]

[On front:] Yrs just recd.—also mail. I'll never catch up with it! Hope Miss Sheppard[4] didn't ridicule Grandpa's hearth decorations. Her candles must have been impressive. All the House of Long sends its collective regards. Beastly cold this morning, but the subway helps out. Am borrowing an overcoat from my youthful host. More anon. Yr aff Nephew & obt Servt

Asaph

[P.S.] Thanks for the Beke!

Notes

1. *Front:* Hotel Belmont, Grand Central Terminal, New York

2. John H. Birss (1907–1994), Melville bibliographer and author of *English Underworld Slang* and "Additional Circus Expressions." HPL's sole surviving letter to him is at Harvard, but the enclosure to that letter—a list of stories—is held by JHL.

3. A nod to HPL's great-great-grandfather Asaph Phillips (1764–1829) of Foster, RI.

4. HPL refers to Alice Sheppard (1870–1961), HPL's downstairs neighbor at 66 College Street. She taught German at Classical High School (see HPL's later reference to "Fraulein Scheppard" [LDC/AEPG 348]).

[346]   [ANS postcard]¹ [HPL to AEPG]

[Postmarked New York, N.Y.,
28 December 1933]

DIARY FOR WEDNESDAY, DEC. 27, 1933

Rose at 10 a.m., & discussed plans with Belknap. Cold day, but not below my danger-point. Borrowed a winter overcoat of Sonny's—one with sleeves which happen to be long enough. Went down to Loveman's shop after lunch & arranged for the play he wanted me to see—& thence up to the play itself—"The Double Door", at the Shubert Theatre in 44ᵗʰ St. The thing was really very good—not supernatural, but with a dark, pervasive atmosphere of brooding hate. It reminded me of that novel which you've probably read by this time—"The Lady who Came to Stay".² It is really based on the history of that odd Wendel family in lower 5ᵗʰ Ave., whose gloomy mansion still survives. After the play I returned to 230, & soon after that Loveman & McGrath arrived for dinner. We ate, sat around, & discussed till 9 p.m., & then started out for Wandrei's—although Loveman felt so ill of indigestion that he & McGrath eliminated the call & went on home. Sonny & I arrived at Wandrei's & found quite a gathering there—including the editor Desmond Hall & his wife, & Wandrei's artist brother Howard. Wandrei's brother showed some of his drawings—all weird—& he certainly has a vastly greater talent than anyone else in the gang. I was astonished at their sheer genius & maturity. When the name Wandrei first becomes known, it will probably be through this brother instead of Donald. We returned to 230 at 2 a.m., & I am now retiring at once. Tomorrow's programme is left entirely open—to be decided in the morning. Friday we have a gang meeting at Sonny's. Saturday the Sutton-Morgan call with Sonny & Wandrei. Sunday night at Loveman's. Monday Morton & Wandrei to dinner at 230. ¶ More anon.

Yr aff Nephew & obt Servt
H P L

Notes

1. *Front:* Porte St. Louis, Quebec, Canada / St. Louis Gate, Quebec, Canada.
2. See Bibliography under R. E. Spencer.

[347]   [ANS postcard][1] [HPL to AEPG]

[Postmarked New York, N.Y.,
29 December 1933]
DIARY FOR THURSDAY, DEC. 28, 1933.

Rose 11 a.m., wrote a bit, & went down to Sonny's for lunch. Cold day, but not below danger-point with Belknap's winter overcoat. In the afternoon we went down to the Aquarium to satisfy Belknap's constant craving for fishes—after which we took separate courses, he to do some errands & I to see about my fountain pen. I found a point I liked (am writing with it), but the feed was not free enough. They said they could amplify the feed—but now that I'm giving the thing a fair trial I find it is not free enough. I shall have to go in again unless the flow limbers up decidedly. What a job! Well—after a monstrous gorge at Belknap's I begged off from the dull cinema trip which followed, & am spending the evening in my room vainly trying to catch up with my piled-up correspondence & giving the new Waterman a fair demonstration. Shall retire around midnight. Tomorrow's daytime programme is unsettled, but the evening is provided for. Talman will come to dinner, & at 8 o'clock the gang as a whole is due. Devilish cold, but in N.Y. that really does not matter on account of the subway. More anon.
Yr aff Neph & obt Servt
H P L

[On front:] The Longs hear Lowell Thomas & Amos 'n' Andy every night—it's hard to think I'm not at 66 College listening from the next room! / Hope Mr. Osterberg & The Boys endure the cold weather well. / Coming 🐻 back from Wandrei's last night I met a delightful tiger kittie.

Notes

1. *Front:* Reform Church, Tappan, N.Y.

[348]   [ANS postcard][1] [HPL to AEPG]

[No postmark;
30 December 1933?]

DIARY FOR FRIDAY, DEC. 29, 1933

rose [*sic*] 11:30 a.m. & read your welcome note of the 28th. Don't worry about the cold—for with the present subway system one can get almost anywhere without being in the open for more than 2 blocks. It is perfectly safe to cover that short distance in *any* temperature, with handkerchief at nose & mouth. That is N.Y.C.'s *one* advantage. I couldn't visit anywhere else in this weather, but I can here. Incidentally, I shall be staying over into next week—so forward mail Saturday. No rubbers needed. ¶ Today we stayed around 230 & discussed the universe, going out only once—to a cinema 2 blocks away—in the afternoon. I kept my handkerchief up & walked briskly—no harm done in either direction. One of the films was by no means bad—a satirical comedy called "Three-Cornered Moon".[2] Talman's cold kept him home in Spring Valley, so that there were no guests to dinner. In the evening we had a gang meeting, but no one came save Kleiner, Leeds, & a friend of the latter. I was glad to see Kleiner—for the first time in a year & a half. Leeds was in fine shape—all reports of his disintegration were clearly exaggerated. We talked over old times & had a splendid meeting—which dispersed at 1 a.m. Now I'm upstairs coping with my correspondence. ¶ Glad the K.A.T. boys are staying out of the cold, & that guests approve our Yuletide decorations. That episode of Fraulein Scheppard & the red package must have been tame indeed!!! ¶ More tomorrow.
Yr aff n—
Asaph

Notes

1. *Front:* Notre Dame de Victoire, Quebec.
2. *Three-Cornered Moon* (Paramount, 1933), directed by Elliott Nugent; starring Claudette Colbert, Richard Arlen, and Mary Boland. Based on the play by Gertrude Tonkonogy.

1934

[349]   [ANS postcard][1] [HPL to AEPG]

[Postmarked Brooklyn, N.Y.,
1 January 1934]

DIARY FOR SATURDAY, DEC. 30, 1933

Yr. New Year greeting duly recd. Glad to see from the picture that you have discarded your cane! Keep it up! I must get in touch with Koenig. Will have to change my room Monday—new tenant coming in here—but am staying over at least a little. Will merely have another room at 230. Trust the good old Brown U. steam kept 66 uniformly hot during the icy spell. ¶ Rose today at noon—lunch at Sonny's—then up to Am. Ind. & Hispanic Museums. Weather steadily warmer. In the late afternoon we returned to 230 to meet a couple of boys—editors of a little magazine like The Fantasy Fan—who wanted to interview us.[2] They proved very affable & pleasing—though I don't know what they'll print about us. Dinner followed. Sonny & I then went down to 23d St. to meet Wandrei & make the Sutton-Morgan call. All were very cordially received—but Wandrei had to leave at 10:30 p.m. Sonny & I stayed till 1 a.m. discussing philosophy with our hosts. Mrs. S. is rather blindly orthodox, but Miss M. is keenly analytical & intelligent—more so, I must admit, than Little Belknap himself. They are invited to 230 for dinner Tuesday evening. Upon returning to 230, I at once proceeded upstairs & have been writing ever since. Tomorrow's programme unsettled till 8:30 p.m., when I go over to Loveman's to watch the old year out. Monday Morton & Wandrei come to dinner. Tuesday I must change my fountain pen again. ¶ More soon.

Yr aff Neph & obt Servt
H P L

Notes

1. *Front:* The Newburyport Turnpike, Newburyport, Mass.
2. Charles D. Hornig and Conrad Ruppert, respectively editor and publisher of the *Fantasy Fan.* No interview of HPL or FBL appeared in the magazine.

[350]   [ANS postcard]¹ [HPL to AEPG]

[Postmarked New York, N.Y.,
1 January 1934]

DIARY FOR SUNDAY, DEC. 31, 1933.

Rose at noon—lunched at Sonny's—then went with him to the Am. Museum of Natl. History, where the new Hall of Oceanic Life is partly finished & open. Got a distant view of that coral island reproduction which we saw described in the Sherwood lecture at Metcalf Laboratory in 1929, but could not get close to it. The upper parts are still uncompleted. Later we returned to 230—Sonny taking a nap & Grandpa going upstairs & reading the N Y Times & the new Weird Tales. Down at 6:30 for a meal, then discussion with a guest of Sonny's & a start for Loveman's at 8 o'clock—for his New Year gathering. Weather vastly warmer—so much so that in going to the museum we took a stroll in snow-covered (but rapidly melting) Central Park. The guest whom I saw prior to my departure for Loveman's was a young writer named James Niles—very bright & pleasant. He knows the weird author A. Merritt, & wants me to look him up, although I doubt if I shall. Later in the evening I started for the New Year gathering at Loveman's, which was attended largely by the same group that was there last year. The mother of the late Hart Crane was present—looking vastly older than when I met her in Cleveland in 1922. At 2 a.m. this gathering dispersed, & I returned to 230, where I am writing letters & finishing the Times. Tomorrow Morton & Wandrei will be here for dinner & discussion. More anon. Yr aff Nephew & obt Servt—Asaph

Notes

1. *Front:* Lago di Como—Menaggio.

[351]   [ANS postcard]¹ [HPL to AEPG]

[Postmarked New York, N.Y.,
2 January 1934]

DIARY FOR MONDAY, JANUARY 1, 1934.

Rose at noon & cleared out of my lodgings on the 6th floor. Have a new room—very good—in a place on the same floor with the Longs, where a good many college students board. Have taken it for 3 days—it is barely possible I'll stay over even that. Anyhow, forward mail Wednesday. ¶ Well—Mortonius arrived at 3 o'clock & we had a great round of discussion. Mostly genealogical—& with an amusing tale of 3 card-sharps whom Morton encountered last week on the Boston boat. At 5:30 Wandrei arrived, & a marvellous turkey & mince pie dinner was served at once. Wandrei called our attention to a mention & illustration of his brother's batik work in the decora-

tion column of yesterday's Times Magazine. Look it up for yourself on p. 12—bottom of column 1. In the illustration, Wandrei's brother's piece is shewn hung on the wall—the 3d piece from the right.[2] Wandrei had to leave early, but the Longs dragged Mortonius & me to a cinema of Lewis's novel "Ann Vickers".[3] Rather mediocre, & J F M couldn't wait for its finish. He took his rocks & the Eliot picture—with appropriate gratitude. Finally the rest of us returned to 230, & I am writing letters & finishing the Times book review before retiring. Tomorrow shopping &c—fountain pen changing—expected guests can't come to dinner. Wednesday unsettled. I may see Talman & Harré. Thursday I shall visit Paterson—either alone or with Sonny. May come home that night, but may stay over. See you later—regards to K.A.T. Weather delightfully warm. ¶ Yr aff n—
Asaph

Notes

1. *Front:* View of Mohawk Trail Near Model Forest Nursery, Mass.
2. HPL refers to the photograph accompanying Walter Rendell Storey's article "Hand-Weavers Show Their New Fabrics," *New York Times Magazine* (31 December 1933): 12, about an exhibition at the Decorators Club. Storey writes: "Increased facility in the use of the difficult batik technique . . . is indicated in several hangings. Especially successful is one by Howard Wandrei picturing a mermaid and an octopus."
3. *Ann Vickers* (RKO Radio Pictures, 1933), directed by John Cromwell; starring Irene Dunne, Walter Huston, and Conrad Nagel. Based on the novel by Sinclair Lewis.

[352]   [ANS postcard][1] [HPL to AEPG]

[Postmarked New York, N.Y.,
3 January 1934]

DIARY FOR TUESDAY, JANUARY 2, 1934.

Rose at noon & lunched at Belknap's. In the afternoon we went downtown for errands, calling on Loveman at the shop & disposing of other things. After a walk through the colonial parts of Greenwich Village I left Belknap & went down to the Waterman offices to see about the pen. This time I got results! Indeed, I don't know but that the present feed-adjustment is too free, if such a thing be possible. But I'd hardly dare have it tightened up, for then it probably wouldn't be free enough. At 5 I returned to 230, & at 7 dinner was served. The expected guests did not come—on account of a heavy cold. Tomorrow Wandrei & I dine with T. Everett Harré at 6:30, & after dinner all hands will adjourn to Belknap's, where H. Koenig, James Niles, & possibly Loveman will be assembled. I learn that A. Merritt has heard of me & wants to get in touch with me—possibly we'll arrange something tomorrow. Thursday (unless it gets too cold) is dedicated to Paterson. ¶ Am writing with the newly fixed pen. It certainly flows super-freely—but I don't know whether I ought to change it. Well—I had planned (after learning that the guests would not be here) to go to Kleiner's tonight, but found he had an engagement. Accordingly Sonny & I sat around & talked—& at 9:30 I sought my room to get some reading & writing done up. One thing I did that afternoon was to get my electric light fixed—new battery & adjustment. Works magnificently now. ¶ More anon. Regards to Mr. Osterberg & Spotty—will be seeing you all soon. ¶ Yr aff N & obt

Asaph

[On front:] Where I wish I were. / P.S. Staying over till Monday—send mail up to & including SATURDAY. / Mortonius returned my Finney book. A bit the worse for wear—glad I have another copy. / Shall dine with A. MERRITT Monday!

Notes

1. *Front:* A Beautiful Lake Scene, Florida.

[353]   [ANS postcard][1] [HPL to AEPG]

[Postmarked New York, N.Y.,
4 January 1934]

DIARY FOR WEDNESDAY, JANUARY 3, 1934.

Rose noon, lunched at Sonny's, & thereafter accompanied him down to the flat of the people (Mrs. Sutton & Miss Morgan) who were to have been to dinner last night. He wanted to take them some old andirons which he had promised during our call of last Saturday—for they have a fine fireplace. The andirons are not colonial, but late-Victorian brass. Not at all bad, on the whole. We found Mrs. S. in, & the andirons look splendid in place—although the lack of a set of fire irons & bellows like yours is regrettable. According to present plans, Mrs. S. & Miss M. are coming to dinner here Saturday evening. At 3:30 I left Sonny & went up to the Museum of the City of N.Y.—5th Ave & 103d St.—where some new historical groups are on display. Very fine. I then walked across Central Park in the twilight to 230 & arranged about a room for the rest of the week. I may have to change again—because of a permanent roomer coming Saturday—but that will be a minor detail. At 6 o'clock I went to the Paris Hotel near Belknap's to dine with T. Everett Harré—Wandrei being also invited. A third party was a boy named Ralph Simpson. Harré is a genial soul, but hopelessly pickled in alcohol. AND HE HAS A MARVELLOUS CAT NAMED WILLIAM. We had a fine dinner downstairs, & were joined by young Niles. At last all but Harré & Simpson adjourned to Belknap's, where our new friend Koenig had just arrived. Koenig

is GREAT. A blond, boyish looking German of absolutely delightful qualities. He gave me a full catalogue of his library. Wandrei left first & at 12:30
the meeting broke up. After some reading & writing I am now about to retire.
Paterson tomorrow.

Yr aff

H P L

Notes

1. *Front:* Delta Dam—Donkey Market.

[354]   [ANS postcard]¹ [HPL to AEPG]

[Postmarked New York, N.Y.,
5 January 1934]

DIARY FOR THURSDAY, JAN^Y· 4, 1934.

Rose at noon & lunched with Sonny—then proceeded to Paterson via Fort
Lee ferry & trolley line. New Jersey has kept several of the interurban car
lines, although the *local* service in Paterson is now all busses. Mortonius was
his usual hospitable self, & shewed me all the new features of the museum—
including a set of fluorescent minerals which shine with strange colours in
ultra-violet light (a machine for which he has) & emit a whitish glow in the
dark after exposure to light. This is in the attic, but will be brought down to
the ground floor as soon as a dark booth can be provided. Also saw the ter-
rapin shell donated by Price. At 5 p.m. we adjourned to a restaurant, &
thence to Mortonius' flat—where we discussed genealogy, economics, & everything else till a late hour. We have a new ancestor for you to remember—
MICHAEL GATER, father of Judith, wife of John Perkins.² Morton gave
me a lot of single tax booklets which I read on the return trip—but they have
not convinced me. Sonny did not participate in this trip. I returned to N.Y. at
11 p.m. & am now reading & writing preparatory to retiring. Still undecided
about having this pen feed changed. Morton advises me to let well enough
alone. Tomorrow 's programme undecided. More anon. Hope you & Spotty
& the K.A.T. are flourishing. What a colleague for Messrs. Randall & Osterberg Harré's cat William would make!

Yrs

H P L

Notes

1. *Front:* Venezia—Ponte dei Sospiri.
2 John Perkins (1583–1654) and Judith Gater Perkins (1588–?) were HPL's great-
great-great-great-great-great-great-grandparents.

[355]   [ANS postcard]¹ [HPL to AEPG]

[Postmarked New York, N.Y.,
6 January 1934]

DIARY FOR FRIDAY, JANᵞ· 5, 1934

Rose at noon & lunched with Sonny. Then went downtown with him for various errands. Rainy—but I borrowed an old coat & hat of Dr. Long's. Stopped in to see Loveman & made an evening engagement with him at his house. Then back to 230. Sonny broke his beloved aquarium trying to wash it in hot water, but papa fixed it up for him with cement. Did some reading in a queer book about the lost Pacific continent of Mu which the Child has from the library.² After a heavy dinner (I won't mount a pair of scales for a month!) I went over to Loveman's for the evening—finding only him & McGrath. Very interesting discussion, & Samuelus gave me *two more* objects for my museum. I shall certainly have to clear a new museum space on the top shelf of my secondary glass-doored bookcase. These new objects are an ancient Mayan stone image about 4 × 2 inches in area & ½″ thick (see sketch) , & a tiny carved monkey (wood) from the East Indian island of Bali. This object (see sketch) has its eyes covered with its paws & is probably an ornament broken from a larger fabric. You'll see all these things next Tuesday. Back to 230 at midnight, & am now reading some tales of Leeds's on which he wants my opinion. Some are really rather good. Programme for my remaining 3 days is crowded, but I mean to snatch some time for the Metropolitan Museum. More anon.
Yrs
H P L

Notes

1 *Front:* Firenze. Museo Nazionale. Bruto (Michelangelo).
2. Probably Col. James Churchward (1852–1936), *The Lost Continent of Mu, the Mother-land of Man* (1926).

[356]   [ANS postcard]¹ [HPL to AEPG]

[Postmarked New York, N.Y.,
8 January 1934]

DIARY FOR SATURDAY, JAN. 6, 1934

Rose at noon, lunched at Sonny's, & then went with him on a shopping tour for aquarium supplies in the Bronx. Warm, springlike day—hope it was the same in Providence. The child bought a new *15-gallon* aquarium which I helped him get home . . . . also some new fish. In the evening Mrs. Sutton & Miss Morgan came for dinner, & much interesting conversation followed. At

11 p.m. the guests left, but a sick fish in the aquarium kept the Longs up till midnight. (It was one of the new acquisitions—he is now recovering.) Finally I went up to my new room—in a nice place on the 5th floor—& am now disposing of reading & correspondence. Tomorrow afternoon Sonny, Loveman & I are going to do the Metropolitan Museum—seeing the new Assyrian collection. Later we shall dine at Wandrei's. Monday partly unplanned, but dinner with A. Merritt in the evening—& then the coach for home. Home Tuesday morning—so don't forward any more mail. Shall be glad to see you, 66, the ancient hill, & the boys of the K.A.T. Hope the warm weather continues. ¶ Yr aff Neph & obt Servt
Asaph

Notes

1. *Front:* Woolworth Building. New York City.

[357]   [ANS postcard]¹ [HPL to AEPG]

[Postmarked New York, N.Y.,
8 January 1934]

DIARY FOR SUNDAY, JANʸ· 7, 1934

Rose at noon & went down to Sonny's. Found that the ailing fish had died after all. Immense turkey dinner, & then off in a drizzle to meet Loveman at the Met. Museum. Sonny stayed home to fix his new aquarium. Saw some magnificent new things at the museum—Assyrian, Etruscan, Egyptian, &c. Got some printed matter which I'll show you. S L & I then walked across the park & down to Columbus Circle, getting coffee & ice cream at an Automat. I then went to Wandrei's, where the Child had preceded me. Interesting conversation—& Wandrei took our pictures—I don't know how they'll come out. Later we returned to 230 & discussed the universe. At midnight I came upstairs to wind up my correspondence. There is an *exquisite* tiger cat in the lobby of this place—I wish I could persuade him to come home with me & join the K.A.T.! Tomorrow miscellaneous errands & dinner with Merritt. Shall go up to Sonny's in the evening, (Wandrei coming too) & take the midnight coach for home. See you Tuesday morning. Regards to Mrs. Osterberg & everybody. Yr aff Nephew
H P L

Notes

1. *Front:* The [American] Museum of Natural History—New York City.

[358]   [ANS postcard]¹ [HPL to AEPG]

[Postmarked New York, N.Y.,
8 January 1934]

DIARY FOR MONDAY, JANY. 8, 1934

Rose 10 a.m. & proceeded to Sonny's. Helped him do some more goldfish shopping. Lunch at the Child's, & then Brooklyn Museum. After that I called on A. Merritt & had dinner with him at the Players Club in Gramercy Park. He is genial & delightful—a fat, sandy, middle-aged chap, & a real genius in the weird. He knows all about my work, & praises it encouragingly. Is Asst. Ed. of the Hearst Sunday Supplement. At 8 p.m. we adjourned, & I went briefly down to Loveman's shop for a book & a call. At 9 I returned to Sonny's, where Wandrei was also a guest. Mrs. L. served ice cream. W. had to leave early, but I stayed till 11:30. Now I am departing for the midnight coach, on which I have reserved a seat. Mrs. L. has provided me with sandwiches for the trip—which I may save till I get home. I'll see you before this card arrives, but the record must be completed! Regards to Spotty & Mrs. Osterberg & all the K.A.T.
Yr aff Neph & obt Servt
H P L

Notes

1. *Front:* Washington Bridge and Speedway, New York City.

[359]   [ANS postcard]¹ [HPL to AEPG]

[Postmarked New York, N.Y.,
31 December 1934]

DIARY FOR MONDAY, DEC. 31, 1934

Well—I got to the station alive! Kept my handkerchief to my nose & mouth all the time, so avoided acute lung pain & stomach sickness. But the cold got at my heart action rather badly, so that I was forced to pant for some time. Apparently the cold affects my heart in a general way—not dependent on breathing. Nice & warm in the station. Have time to burn—it's only 12:30. Hope coach will be heated!
NEW HAVEN—4 a.m. Bus heated magnificently! Fine trip—front seat, & nobody next me. Went through Pontiac, Arctic, Hope Valley, Westerly, & New London. Just thought—I've left my new 1935 diary at home—on the shelves at the right of my chair. But I can keep notes on loose paper & copy them in when I get home. Due in N.Y. 7:30 a.m.
DARIEN, CONN.—5:15 a.m. Last stop before N.Y. Most of the crowd is out imbibing nourishment at a holdup joint that charges double what any-

thing is worth. Heat continues to be ideal—hope it will be as good on the homeward trip. Stars have been brilliant all night—have been watching Mr. O'Ryan edge along toward the west. A waning crescent moon is also present. Dawn will probably come somewhere near New Rochelle.

PENN. STA. N.Y. 7 a.m. Bum guess! It's still rather dark, & no dawn signs appeared till 110th St. 40 minutes ahead of time . . . & nearly an hour to kill. Shall try to get hold of a Sunday Times. Wish I were waiting for a Washington–Richmond–Charleston coach! Weather outside still bad, but I've only one short walk to go in the open. ¶ I miss the Christmas tree! Haven't eaten my chocolates—saving room for Long breakfast. Will cover the residue of the day in a later bulletin. Blessings—

Yr aff n—

Asaph

[On front:] Trip made in 5 h. 50 m.—10 m. faster than the *train* used to make it in 1922–1926 days. Regular streamline stuff! Got in just as early as I did on the *12* o'clock coach a year ago. No ice on roads.

Notes

1. *Front:* Hotel Times Square, New York City.

1935

[360]   [ANS postcard]¹ [HPL to AEPG]

[Postmarked New York, N.Y.,
1 January 1935]

#2 DIARY FOR MONDAY, DEC. 31, 1934.

Reached Sonny's safely at 8 a.m. & read Times magazines until family was up. Then the usual cordial greetings from all. Mrs. Long was all right, & the maid was nearly so. This maid is a middle aged negress who comes in for the day. The old maid's room has been taken as a reception room for patients, & all three corner rooms next the office have been devoted to family uses—thus: This means that the household have one more room to use. Dr. Long has found that he has a mild case of *diabetes*, hence is having to cut down sweets & arrange a special diet—a fearsome hardship for him! ¶ Bobby Barlow came over at 1:30 p.m.—after lunch—& I was surely

glad to see him. I took a stroll with him while Sonny rested, & saw his quarters at the Clendening in 103ᵈ St. He gave me some new drawings, & 2 fine new photographs of himself. Then back to Sonny's, & all three down to the art department of the publick library. Then with Barlow shopping at art stores in 5ᵗʰ Ave. Then back to 230. Barlow is not getting his meals at the Longs', tho' he is invited to the New Year turkey dinner tomorrow. After dinner Barlow came over again & we went to the inevitable cinema. Rather poor. Then everybody back to 230—discussion, cider, welsh rarebit, &c—& seeing the old year out. Sonny retired at 1 a.m.—then Bobby & I went up to my room & discussed various literary & artistic matters till 3 a.m. On Bobby's departure I retired. More bulletins shortly. Regards to the K.A.T. Hope the tree is looking its best!
Yr aff Neph
Asaph

[HPL's note on front:] Tomorrow we shall have a great turkey dinner at 4 p.m.—little Bobby being invited. Wednesday night the gang will meet at Sonny's. Haven't seen Loveman yet—he is reported in poor health & spirits.

Notes

1. *Front:* Hotel Times Square, New York City.

[361]   [ANS][1] [HPL to AEPG]

[Postmarked New York, N.Y.,
2 January 1935]

DIARY FOR TUESDAY, JANUARY 1, 1935.

Rose noon. The nice old German landladies sent in some coffee & toast, so I had breakfast before descending to the Belknapian regions. Barlow soon arrived, & after some interesting discussion we all walked across Central Park to the Metropolitan Museum—where we devoted the entire afternoon to the Egyptian Wing. Then back to 230, where we had one of the finest turkey dinners I ever ate. Both mince pie & plum pudding for dessert—I chose the pie as usual. Quite up to Brother Leslie's standard. After dinner—while Sonny drowsed—Barlow & I went up to the Clendening & back. Then all hands visited the inevitable cinema—mediocre throughout. Upon our return to 230, the Longs retired at once, but Barlow & I went up to my quarters & revised a story of his—an excellent one—till 3 a.m.[2] I then did some writing & turned in around 5 a.m. Tomorrow the gang meets at 8:30 p.m., & we hope as many as possible will be present. We shall also do some museum visiting &c. in the afternoon. Weather remains relatively mild, though I've so far worn the old winter overcoat. Have 4 of Louis' chocolates left. There is a mammoth Christmas tree in this flat—the Germans surely do excel in all Yuletide phenomena! Forward letters till Friday. At present, I doubt if I'll stay over the single week. I'll keep you posted. Every good wish—
Yr aff Nephew
H P L

Notes

1. *Front:* Hotel Times Square, New York City.
2. Possibly "The Summons." Probably not "'Till A' the Seas,'" as in his letter to Barlow of [15 January 1935], HPL suggests that he is seeing the ms. of the story for the first time (*OFF* 201–2).

[362]   [ANS postcard][1] [HPL to AEPG]

[Postmarked New York, N.Y.,
3 January 1935]

DIARY FOR WEDNESDAY, JAN. 2, 1935.

Rose at noon & had lunch at Sonny's. Barlow soon came over, & some interesting discussion ensued. Belknap then decided to do some writing while Barlow & I went to a really good cinema down town at the Cameo—a version of "Don Quixote" with the eminent basso Feodor Chaliapin in the title role.[2] It was really a magnificent piece of art, justifying all that Prof. Damon said of the cinema as a serious aesthetic medium.[3] I then returned to 230 for dinner, after which came the meeting. This latter was extremely fine—the best, perhaps, the gang has ever had. Every invited guest came—Barlow, Kleiner, Leeds, Talman, Morton, Kirk, Loveman (with a friend named Gordon), Koenig, both Donald & Howard Wandrei, young Phillips[4] & a friend named Harry—*15* persons in all, including Sonny & Grandpa. Fine refreshments, good conversation—an ideal gathering. Talman took pictures of us when we weren't looking—with one of his new sensitive cameras—& we hope the results won't be too libellous. Little Bobby was enraptured to meet so many of the giants he has long admired. As one feature, we all wrote a round robin letter to Clark Ashton Smith.[5] After midnight the gathering gradually dispersed, but Leeds & Barlow lingered longest—talking with me in the vestibule till 2:30 or 3 a.m. I then did some writing & am retiring at 5 a.m. More anon. We shall assemble at Loveman's Friday.

Yrs

~~

[On front:] Read in the N.Y. Sun of the delightful coup d'etat put over on the pompous & predatory Republicans of our independent commonwealth. Hot dawg! Now they've got a taste of their own medicine! Viva Don Teodoro Francisco![6]

Notes

1. *Front:* Hotel Times Square, New York City.

2. *Adventures of Don Quixote* (Nelson Film, 1933), directed by G. W. Pabst; starring Feodor Chaliapin Sr., George Robey, and Oscar Asche. Based on the novel by Miguel de Cervantes. Chaliapin (1873–1938) was a prominent Russian opera singer.

3. S[amuel] Foster Damon (1893–1971), professor of English and curator of the Harris Collection of American Poetry and Plays at Brown University. He was a scholar on Blake, Amy Lowell, Thomas Holley Chivers, and other authors. In December 1935, HPL heard a lecture by Damon on the cinema as an authentic art form. The address was followed by a showing of *All Quiet on the Western Front* (1930). Presumably Damon had delivered an earlier lecture on the same subject. See also MFB 11.

4. Dean P. Phillips, a friend of Samuel Loveman. HPL describes him as "a young chap who has professionally studied trick photography, art photography, retouching, &c., &c., & has a real artist's zeal in the matter" (*OFF* 151). In the summer of 1934 he was "making a statuette of Pickman's Model" (*OFF* 168).

5. Nonextant.

6. HPL refers to the fact that governor Theodore Francis Green and lieutenant-

governor Robert E. Quinn instituted a recount of the ballots relating to two Republican state senators; a committee of three senators determined that Democrats had actually won the seats in question, thereby granting control of the State Senate to the Democrats. The conservative *Providence Journal* compared the act to a Central American coup d'état.

[363]   [ANS postcard][1] [HPL to AEPG]

[Postmarked New York, N.Y.,
4 January 1935]

DIARY FOR THURSDAY, JANUARY 3, 1935

Rose at noon & lunched at Sonny's. Barlow soon arrived, & we all went over to call on Koenig at the Electrical Testing Laboratories. A fine chap! He cashed a cheque for R H B & shewed us all over his establishment. The place is used for various processes testing the durability of electrical devices—how long lamps will burn, how much wear & tear insulated cords will stand, &c. &c. Some of the testing devices—simulating the average processes of household usage—are odd & ingenious indeed. We then walked across Central Pk & took the subway to the Pub. Lib., where we looked things up in the art department. Then R H B left for shopping while Sonny & Grandpa returned to 230. Dinner & discussion—About 8 p.m. R H B blew in with some newly-purchased dry point etching materials & began making a weird copper plate. Then young Phillips appeared, & general discussion ensued. He, like Sonny, is a communist—& Barlow is getting to be almost one. Then out for a walk & to Automat—later more walking & dispersal. I am now writing letters & shall retire soon. ¶ Pleased to get your card & forwarding material. It has not been very cold here, though the papers threaten a cold snap. Expect to be home Tuesday. Sunday night we're going over to Phillips's. ¶ Tomorrow night Loveman's. ¶ I'm eager to see how the poor old Journal will froth at the mouth over the new Democratic coup d'etat. Long live Green & Quinn! ¶ Yr aff Neph & obt Servt
Asaph

Notes

1. *Front:* Columbus Circle, New York.

[364]   [ANS postcard][1] [HPL to AEPG]

[Postmarked New York, N.Y.,
5 January 1935]

DIARY FOR FRIDAY, JANUARY 4, 1935.

Well, what the hades! Your card of Jany. 3 speaks of not hearing from me,

whereas I've mailed a diary card *every day!* What sort of delay has been afflicting the postal system! ¶ Rose 9:30 & am [*sic*] & went up to meet Barlow at Clendening. Bitterly, hideously cold—but an handkerchief at nose & mouth made travel safe. Automat, & over with R H B to Metropolitan Museum. Saw Graeco-Roman stuff—paintings—casts, &c. Then back to Automat & Clendening, where we revised a story of R H B's. Then over to 230— dinner—R H B arrive—& all hands over to Loveman[']s. Both Wandreis there. We had a great time—discussing a new forthcoming book of Loveman's verse, looking over various art books & objects, & going through Loveman's collection of Clark Ashton Smith's drawings. Barlow was utterly enchanted. Incidentally, Loveman may shortly leave Dauber & Pine & start up a high-grade book business of his own. We broke up around 1 a.m., & Loveman & McGrath accompanied us to the Plymouth cafeteria near the subway, where we had coffee & discussed some more. Then back to 230, a little writing, & retiring at 4 a.m. We shall see Loveman again at the Museum Sunday. And I'll see you on Tuesday. Hope the hellish cold abates, but the subway is a great protection. More anon.
Yr aff Neph & obt Servt
H P L

Notes

1. *Front:* East View of Lower New York As Seen from Woolworth Tower.

[365]   [ANS postcard][1] [HPL to AEPG]

[Postmarked New York, N.Y.,
6 January 1935]

DIARY FOR SATURDAY, JANUARY 5, 1935.

Well—I hope the cards have begun to come through! Wonder if any rascal in the P.O. held up some of the earlier ones because of small address space! ¶ Rose 11:30 a.m., wrote a bit, & went down to Sonny's for lunch. Barlow was there—& he'll be at Sunday's dinner. Sonny decided to stay home & write, so R H B & I decided to light out for the whole afternoon & evening. We visited Kirk's shop, & also Dauber & Pine's—seeing Loveman at the latter. Afterward we browsed around all the various downtown bookshops—largely in 4th Ave. In one of them we came unexpectedly on good old Leeds—who has a part-time job there. At this place I got a cheap copy of the old Gothic horror tale—"The Monk", by M. G. Lewis—written in 1795. We dined at the 14th St. Automat & then looked at some westward bookshops—finally taking the subway up to Barlow's lodgings at the Clendening. We then discussed things in general, & worked on a revision of one of R H B's tales. After that I returned to 230, & have since been reading & writing. ¶ Tomorrow R H B & I dine at Sonny's, & all hands will meet S L at the Metropolitan Museum. Then a session at Wandrei's & then one at young Phillips's place in Brooklyn. Home about Tuesday. ¶ Now for some sleep.

Yr aff Nephew

~~

Notes

1. *Front:* Public Library & 5th Ave., New York.

[366]   [ANS postcard]¹ [HPL to AEPG]

[Postmarked New York, N.Y.,
7 January 1935]

DIARY FOR SUNDAY, JANUARY 6, 1935.

Rose 11:30 a.m. & went down to Sonny's. Barlow had some digestive trouble, so called off both the Loveman & Phillips engagements. Also, Sonny decided not to keep any but the Wandrei engagement. After dinner I went over to the Metropolitan Museum to meet Loveman, & we had an interesting 2 hrs. in the Graeco-Roman & Egyptian collections. We then walked over Central Park to Columbus Circle & down to 42nd St.—where I took the subway for Wandrei's new place in Greenwich Village. I found Donald & Howard Wandrei both at home, & Sonny & Bobby arriv'd before me. Interesting discussion, & at 7:45 the guests adjourned. Sonny had lunch at a "Bohemian" cafeteria in Greenwich Village, but Barlow & I waited till later. We then went up to 103ᵈ St., where R H B & I dined at the Automat. All hands then adjourned to the Clendening for discussion. At 11:30 we saw Sonny home, & R H B & I went down to the Penn Station to see about coach tickets. He leaves for Washington at 11:30 a.m. tomorrow—I leave at midnight tomorrow night—seeing you Tuesday morning. Then uptown. I returned to 230, & will retire after a bit of writing. Tomorrow up early—all hands assemble at Belknap's at 9:30 a.m. After Barlow's departure there will be other events in which one or more Wandreis will participate. Blessings—& see you soon.

Yr aff

~~

Notes

1. *Front:* Skyscrapers from East River, New York.

[367]   [ANS postcard]¹ [HPL to AEPG]

[Postmarked Providence, R.I.,
8 January 1935]

DIARY FOR MONDAY, JANUARY 7, 1935.

Rose 9 a.m. & went down to Sonny's. Had coffee. Barlow overslept, but blew in at about 10:30. Belknap & I accompanied him back to the Clendening & helped him check out, & then took him down to the coach . . . . . seeing him off at 11:30. This coach gets into Washington at 8:45 p.m. Sonny & I then went to the public library & looked over John Martin prints, after which we returned to 230 for lunch. Misty rain ensued, & we stayed in & discussed various things. At 3:30 Wandrei came, remaining a couple of hours. Dinner at 7, & then more discussion. At 9 Sonny & I went down to Dauber & Pine's & bade Loveman adieu. Then over to Wandrei's, where both Donald & Howard were assembled. We talked till 11, when Sonny went home. At 11:30 the two Wandreis saw me to the Penn Station—my coach leaving at 12:01 a.m. Rather good trip—well heated. Arrived in ancient Providentium half an hour late— abt. 6:35 a.m. Am writing this in terminal preparatory to ascending the ancient hill to #66. Mrs. Long gave me two sandwiches, one of which I consumed at New Haven, & the other of which I shall consume here—perhaps at the Waldorf with a cup of coffee. See you before you see this.
Yrs
~~

Notes

1. *Front:* Washington Bridge—New York.

Annie Emeline Phillips Gamwell

1936

[368a]   [ALS] [HPL to AEPG]¹

Home Again on St. Patrick's
[17 March 1936ff.]

My dear Grandchild:—

In case you can read before you can see visitors I will begin this diary—to keep you fully informed of the progress of things at the Garden House. By the time you receive this I hope you will be rid of all drastic procedure & well started on the gradual (though I hope not unduly long) convalescence.

DIARY FOR TUESDAY, MARCH 17, 1936

Had a bit of delay finding the elevator—& the latter was a long time coming after that. When I finally reached the lobby I enquired about finances & the clerk said a bill would come to the house in a day or two. Evidently Kingman² didn't consolidate the hospital fee in his bill. I will draw cash & pay the hospital when the bill arrives, unless I receive orders to the contrary from you or your authorised representatives.

Walked home over Point St. Bridge—quite like the old days of '33. Met Miss Sheppard in the hall, & she was most cordial & solicitous in her enquiries. I told her I'd keep her informed of all the stages of your recovery. She took the butter, but couldn't use either the roquefort or the mayonnaise.

After reading the paper—in which there was no major news (I'll save it for you)—I proceeded to get dinner, but varied somewhat from the programme previously adopted. I decided that the soup might keep till tomorrow, so got rid of the milk with a cracker-&-milk meal. Coffee was still good. For dessert I ate the residual cake which you ought to have finished—covering it with orange marmalade made in Rumford, R.I. Great stuff! I'll get rid of the roll in the morning—using it instead of a dog-nut.³ Thrift! Now I'm wrestling with correspondence & will retire at a moderate hour. I'll be calling up your hostess Mrs. Brown⁴ tomorrow afternoon—& hope meanwhile that Lucius & his allies will fix you up in fine shape. By the way—about 9 p.m. Frederick T. Guild⁵ called up & asked after you—saying that his wife had just received a letter telling of your advent to Mrs. Brown's boarding-house. I told him I'd give a report to his household tomorrow evening—when I also report to Miss Bonner & Fraulein von Scheppard.

DIARY FOR WEDNESDAY, MARCH 18, 1936

Rose at noon & found that Nichols—the darned fool—*had left milk again!* I shall have to rearrange my schedule . . . . soup now (with the roll) & another cracker & milk meal tonight. Bill also left, & it comes to *$6.23* for Jany. & Feby. It seems that the smaller bill we had was for February only, & that January had not been paid. Only 17 qts. (= 1.36) are charged for March, so it would appear that today's pint is a present from Mr. Nichols . . . "one on the house." I will prepare the bill for payment at once. You had left 4.00 for it, on my guess that it would be of that amount, & to this sum I last night added the 19.00 which you sent home. That made 23.00—from which I now deduct 6.23 . . . . leaving a balance of *16.77* on hand. ¶ Soup was all right, & I also ate that pickled peach. It was very good—like the sweet pickle from watermelon-rind—& I surely don't see why you dislike it. Also took some postum[6]—using the top of the new milk with it. Very good. ¶ No mail for you except an advertising card. I'll bring or send any letters which arrive. ¶ Enquired of Aunt Jane Brown how you were, & was told that you were doing splendidly, but that you wouldn't want me to call for 2 or 3 days. Good work! I shall duly inform your friends—in fact, I *have* just informed Miss Sally Wilcox, who called up not long after I received my information. Now to get at my correspondence. It's raining like blazes, but I don't believe I'll have to go out (save to the letter-box) at all. ¶ Am dropping a line to Shelburne Falls with the news. ¶ Fraulein von Scheppard just enquired about you, & was immensely glad to hear that all was coming along well. She said that she was almost as nervous about your case as you were yourself—indeed, her solicitude & sympathy are obviously genuine, & she will welcome your early return despite the prospect of enduring the hideous racket of Mr. Thomas & the boys from 6:45 to 7:15! Incidentally, she had a real dose of din last night, for the boys at the fraternity house conducted some sort of ceremony with wild & deafening shouting until after 4 a.m.! According to the paper it was incidental to a freshman-sophomore conflict—one of the details of which was a false fire alarm rung on the deserted Brown campus around 2 a.m. ¶ Have wound both your clocks to make sure they won't run down. Will water the plants tomorrow. ¶ Paper duly arrived. Principal news is of great floods in Pittsburgh & western Pennsylvania generally. ¶ Mailed letters & called up Miss Bonner & Guild as promised. Both were delighted to hear of progress. Miss B. will relay news to others at boarding-house, including Miss Staples, Spotty, Johnny Perkins, & Gilbert John Murray Kynymond Elliot.[7] ¶ Cracker & milk dinner—orange juice dessert—& Postum. Just as I was finishing, Mrs. Carpenter called up to enquire how you are, & was duly pleased to hear of good progress. ¶ Retired 10:30 p.m. & slept 15 hours without a break[.]

DIARY FOR THURSDAY, MARCH 19, 1936

Rose 1:30 p.m. & enquired about your progress. Told it was satisfactory. Keep it up! Took regular dog-nut breakfast with orange dessert. Made Postum with the small can of evap. milk you obtained some time ago. Good. Am keeping it in closet under inverted tin. Attempted some correspondence, read the paper (floods throughout New England, including Blackstone & Pawtuxet Valleys), received & answered enquiries from Miss Sally Wilcox & Fraulein von Scheppard, & continued wrestling with correspondence. Later Miss Ripley called up—& was especially solicitous & detailed in her enquiries. She had also called up the hospital earlier in the day. ¶ Had a good dinner of corned beef hash & did some more writing prior to retiring. ¶ Retired 1:30 a.m.

DIARY FOR FRIDAY, MARCH 20, 1936

Rose 10:30 a.m. Almost simultaneously I received an enquiry about you from someone whose name I could not catch. She was pleased to hear of progress, & will call up later today to learn the most recent developments. Had usual breakfast—finishing the oranges. Enquired at your Lockwood St. residence & found you were still improving—& that you might possibly be ready for a caller Sunday. Also that you might be ready for a letter tomorrow—so that I'll mail this diary when I go down for errands this afternoon. Will now proceed to wrestle with correspondence. This is the first day of spring—the sun entering Aries at about 2 p.m. according to the Old Farmer's. Temperature—appropriately—is around 60°. Now hurry up & get well or semi-well in time to enjoy the new foliage of next month!

All good wishes, & sympathy for the current ordeal—

Yr most aff: Grandsire & ob[t] Serv[t]

Aſaph Phillips[8]

[368b] [HPL to AEPG]

DIARY FOR FRIDAY, MARCH 20, 1936

Continuing from where I left off—went downtown for errands—paid Nichols bill by money order—got myself some rolls & cheese—obtained 3 copies of *Astounding* with final "Mts. of Madness" instalment—& finally returned to 66. Found Miss Angell[9] at the door. She had come to invite you to "Artists' Night" at the Art Club, & was extremely sorry to learn that you weren't in shape to go. She invited me in your stead, but I declined with thanks—both because I wanted the time to work in, & because I'd have felt rather like an outsider at a gathering designed primarily for members only. Just before Miss A. left, Fraulein von Scheppard appeared in the alleyway, & I took occasion to give her the good report I had received from Aunt Jane Brown. Miss A. then decided to make a call on die Fraulein, & I excused myself to mount to the upper regions. Read the paper (floods in R.I. receding, but Haverhill partly under water) & had a good dinner of chile con carne. This time I experimented in *heating* it, & found (as I had half expected) that some of the solid matter liquefies with rise of temperature. Dessert—a chocolate bar & postum. Then wrestling with correspondence. ¶ Miss Sally Wilcox called once again, & was glad to hear of progress. She said that several had enquired through her, & that by getting frequent reports from me she was able to spread the tidings at second hand—thus avoiding a constant calling of either myself or Aunt Jane Brown. The woods are certainly full of enquirers—indeed, I doubt if public characters like Brother Clarence[10] received a wider range of queries & good wishes while sojourning at the popular South Providence hostelry! ¶ Retired at 1:30 a.m.

DIARY FOR SATURDAY, MARCH 21, 1936

Up in good season & enquired about your progress. Found I could call tomorrow between 1 & 2 p.m., which I'll do. Read paper, & found that flood at Hartford has become very serious. Bulletin has been full of dramatic flood pictures for several nights, all of which are duly saved. I'll bring all Bulletins to your temporary residence if you like. Incidentally, your Cambridge Tribune came this morning. Do you want to see it now? ¶ Fraulein von Scheppard has just enquired about you, & is pleased to hear that you'll be receiving your first caller tomorrow. ¶ Just saw Johnny Perkins & Gilbert John Murray Kynymond Elliot around the fence near the clubhouse. Hope they intend to join the Kappa Alpha Tau. ¶ Have just secured Gilbert John as a guest—he is busy devouring catnip from the *new* box—but I can't for the life of me capture the Big Black Bum! The rascal is too agile for an old man! ¶ The 4th Earl is extremely companionable, & has just rolled over in his catnip as Big Brother used to do. And *what* a big boy he is getting to be! You must have him for a guest when you get back. ¶ Gilbert just asked to go, so Grandpa let him out. He has a full-throated mew wholly unlike Big Brother's little "ew". Hope he'll call again! ¶ The two brothers are now cavorting around the back garden. If I weren't going out for po'k & beans I'd try to catch that Big Black Bum again! ¶ Got my bek bin—*with* pork. Upon my return I found that good old Spotty had joined her sons, & was calling piteously to Gilbert John to cease his explorations of the clubhouse's interior. Gilbert is evidently a hard boy to manage! ¶ Watched lights come on—Industrial beat the court house by 15 or 20 minutes. ¶ Had a good bek bin dinner, & did some writing. ¶ Retired around midnight.

DIARY FOR SUNDAY, MARCH 22, 1936

Rose 10 a.m. Telephone enquiry from Miss Sally Wilcox, who told me to tell you that the brother of the family is now with them in Providence, being driven from his own place in or near Nashua, N.H. by the prevailing floods. These floods are certainly a formidable thing, & I wonder how good old Try-out is getting along. His place in Groveland St. Haverhill is not very far from the raging Merrimack. ¶ Read part of Sunday Journal & have set out for Aunt Jane Brown's in a high wind.

[368c]   [HPL to AEPG]

DIARY FOR SUNDAY, MARCH 22, 1936

Went out of Aunt Jane's via the south door, & found that this parkward side is indeed the main facade—& a very pleasing Georgian facade, at that. Home via Point St. Bridge & Benefit St., & then proceeded to write the promised notes to Miss Bonner & "Aunt Enda" [sic].[11] Went to deliver Bonner epistle, & ran into a virtual convention of 55's inhabitants—Miss Bonner being outward bound as I arrived, & Misses Johnson, Fenner,[12] & Staples appearing successively on the scene. I told them all the good news from Lockwood St., virtually duplicating what I had written in the note, & they were all appropriately delighted; each one sending you her most especial regards & good wishes for a quick recovery & return. As the convention began to disperse, the Big Black Bum & Gilbert John Murray Kynymond Elliot began racing through the porch space, & I finally tried to help Miss Staples catch the elusive Earl of Minto . . . . although it was she who really got the little divvle in the end. He is a great boy—with a face of remarkable beauty when one comes to analyse it. I then mailed the Brookline epistle[13] & returned to 66—where Fraulein von Scheppard at once made her usual enquiry. She, like the rest, was overjoyed to hear of your progress. ¶ I now started the 20-minute eggs to boiling—continuing the Sunday Journal as I waited—& later combined these with the short end of the bek bin to form a sumptuous repast. Then finishing the Sunday Journal & wrestling with correspondence. By the way—the sugar from Aunt Jane's very nicely sweetened one cup of Postum! ¶ Finished an epistle to Clark Ashton Smith & retired 4 a.m.

DIARY FOR MONDAY, MARCH 23, 1936

Rose 11 a.m. Heard racket downstairs which I hoped—at first—was of men fixing the front door, but it was only Miss Gayton with mop & pail. Note from Miss Bonner in the door thanking both you & me for care of her "woodland lot". So much credit was unduly assigned to me that I felt obliged to disavow it in a brief note. Your friend Mrs. Watrous[14] called up to enquire about you, & I told her of your present whereabouts. You will probably hear directly from her. I called up Aunt Jane—as you are aware—& duly received your transmitted instructions. Will be over tomorrow at 2 p.m. with the desiderate 42 bucks. I guess I'll draw 50 this afternoon, & add the 8 fish residue to your local fund of $16.77—bringing the latter to $24.77. Have just written note to Miss Ripley as directed, thanking her for letter, flowers, various messages, &c., & containing reports on your condition to date. By the way—there was another "Presented" note in the door for you, presumably from the amiable Mr. Peck. I'll bring it along when I come tomorrow. ¶ Went down for cash & errands. Got some Vienna loaf & potato salad—the 2nd of my experiments with different kinds of meat loaves (pressed corned beef was the first). Chocolate creams from Frank's (20¢ per lb.) for dessert. Returning home, I read successively in the N.Y. Times & the Bulletin. Picture of flooded Haverhill on the Bulletin's front page, shewing a place I know well (the main square in front of the P.O.) under water. ¶ Excellent sunset. From my desk window the sun now sets just north of the northerly tower of Memorial Hall. ¶ Had a good dinner—the Vienna loaf is good, though not up to veal. Evaporated milk has begun to thicken & become immiscible, though the taste remains all right. Shall open Challenge (the old reliable!) tomorrow. ¶ Now to wrestle with correspondence. ¶ Later finished *Weird Tales* for March & retired 1 a.m.

DIARY FOR TUESDAY, MARCH 24, 1936

Rose 10:30 a.m. Found the *unopened* can of Challenge Milk spoiled—gelatinously hard & brown. Wonder if there could have been an imperceptible leak? It had been kept 3 years, but exploring expeditions often keep condensed milk & other canned goods that long. Wonder how other long-unopened products are—Zocate potatoes, L D C's Protose,[15] the Hatchet canned brown bread, & some of the pickles? Emptied the hardened milk into a garbage bag & washed the can. Fancy I can dispose of the mayonnaise in the same way if necessary. ¶ Then proceeded to coördinate correspondence, & am now starting out for Aunt Jane's.

Yr affec: Grandsire & ob^t Servt

Aſaph Phillips[16]

[368d]   [HPL to AEPG]

DIARY FOR TUESDAY, MARCH 24, 1936

Home via What Cheer, where I got a can of Challenge.[17] Find I have 522 coupons now . . . guess I'll look at the premium office in Cranston St. & see what they have. If you'd save your Welcome Soup wrappers you'd get something good, too! Didn't get any hamburg because it was marked up to 17¢, but may succumb later. Didn't get fancy dessert because it was too far from meal time. ¶ Read paper, & received an enquiry from Miss Sally Wilcox—who was delighted to hear of progress. I gave her your thanks for the 1st Baptist flowers, but she said a Miss Margaret Rose of the flower committee was the one to thank. Couldn't find any such person in the telephone book, so let the matter drop. If you want thanks sent, it can be done later. Possibly you know the address of the person in question. ¶ Wrote a note of thanks to Mrs. Carpenter. ¶ Had a great dinner—the Protose was better than I thought it would be, & not at all spoiled. I ought to have changed it after all! It is really great with catsup! After all, I ate half instead of the expected third. Will finish it with Worcestershire tomorrow. May try the Zocate 'taters soon. But evidently not all canned goods are as perishable as condensed milk. Perhaps, indeed, there was some defect in the can. Used my new Challenge with Postum, & it was excellent . . . though I took too much, being used to the relatively thin evaporated milk. It was quite like old Barnes St. days using Protose & Challenge . . . & incidentally, Protose & Postum all in one meal certainly make an intensive health-food diet! I ought to feel new waves of health coming over me! ¶ After dinner I read the Times magazines & wrestled once more with correspondence. ¶ Duly wound your 8-day clocks—so swiftly does a week fly by! ¶ Retired 2 a.m.

DIARY FOR WEDNESDAY, MARCH 25, 1936

Rose 10:30 a.m. Telephone enquiry from Miss Maud Robinson, who was very glad to hear of progress, & who sent you her choicest regards. You will probably hear directly from her ere long. She had called several times before, but had failed to receive a response. ¶ Postum with the *right* amount of Challenge (1 good spoonful to the large-sized cup) was splendid. Actually, Challenge beats both natural & evaporated milk as an ingredient of coffee-like drinks. ¶ Enquired at Aunt Jane's, & found that you had been sitting up an hour. Good work! Made an engagement to call tomorrow at 2 p.m. ¶ Wrestled with correspondence as usual, though I don't get very far. No letters today, thank Yuggoth! ¶ Read the paper—which reminds me that I tore out a page last night because of a new weekly series of articles on the various arts (by Brown professors) analogous to the series on the sciences a year ago. I'm saving these—so you can read them as well as the rest of the paper as soon as you feel like it. ¶ Had a good dinner of Protose—this time with Worcestershire. Finished up the can . . . & now for the Zocate 'taters! Tried an experiment & found I can get rid of your Roquefort! On your new salty crackers the rotten taste is virtually killed, only a rather pleasant cheese flavour remaining. Thus I can both dispose of the cheese, & keep your crackers from getting mouldy! Smelled of the mayonnaise, & it still seems all right. May try to utilise that somehow. I might use it for a salad with the canned 'taters . . . that & some of my Armour's hot dogs would make quite a banquet! ¶ Now wrestling again with correspondence. DIARY FOR THU., MARCH 26 ¶ Rose noon. Paralysing lot of mail, including a line from Shelburne Falls which I bring along. Miss Bonner is quite shocked that I didn't forcibly prevent you from tending the miniature garden during her absence. ¶ And now to start for Aunt Jane's.

[368e]   [HPL to AEPG]

DIARY FOR THURSDAY, MARCH 26, 1936

Proceeded downtown from Aunt Jane's & did sundry errands—all connected with nourishment. Then up to 66 & across to Miss Staples' with the *Times* magazines & your thanks. Spotty & the Big Black Bum were on hand, so that I could thank them in person, but the little Earl of Minto was nowhere to be seen. After some conversation with the family—during which they all sent you their best regards & hopes for an early recovery—I returned to the Garden House & read the paper . . . finding no news of especial interest. ¶ I now proceeded to experiment with the mayonnaise & the Zocate 'taters—having obtained a quarter-pound of hamburg loaf (the third of my experiments) to furnish the meat element. Both spuds & dressing were in fine condition, & I cut the former up to salad-size fragments, mixing them well with the mayonnaise & adding a sprinkling of sodium chloride. Finding the mayonnaise a bit lacking in taste, I added a slight touch of catsup—which made an absolutely perfect & highly appetising blend. I shall furnish the murphys tomorrow, but will endeavour to find other uses for mayonnaise until the can is used up. I notice that it is made in Westerly, R.I., & that this brand (like Hershey's Chocolate & Borden's Milk) was carried on the Byrd expedition.[18] The hamburg loaf was excellent. Tomorrow I may get some other sort of loaf—or else try my hot dawgs. Among the supplies I have laid in are new catsup, Postum, cheese, & sugar. I think I'll risk the rats & use sugar from the bag in my old convenient way. I'll keep the bag inside a large paper bag, & only a corner is open anyway. The whole thing, set high up on top of the red canister, won't attract the rodentia very readily. ¶ After dinner I tackled the thanking job—completing all the notes (Gamwell,[19] Guild, Rose, Thomas) in time for the 9:45 collection. Then a wrestle with my own correspondence— which is complicated by a set of "Innsmouth" proofs to be read & returned at once.[20] I'll have to shelve something somehow—for my tasks are more than I can handle! ¶ Found your dresses in front of the fireplace, & have done them up for the cleaner. I see that the Penn outfit near the What Cheer (where I have my stuff done) is advertising dress-cleaning for 19¢, so I may take the material there. One is probably just about as good as the other. ¶ Retired 3:30 a.m.

DIARY FOR FRIDAY, MARCH 27, 1936

Rose noon & enquired at Aunt Jane's. Told you are steadily gaining each day. Made appointment for 2 p.m. tomorrow. Wrote Little Mr. Sterling a letter, transmitting your understanding sympathy.[21] ¶ Then down with your garments, the cleaning of which at the Penn (other places didn't offer 19¢ dress rate) will come to 60¢ in all. The condition of some of the seams of the dress was such that they could not be guaranteed to hold, but I presume you can Bernstein them back to normal without much difficulty. Articles will be ready on Tuesday. Went to bank, & to avoid bothering with frequent visits drew 200 bucks—which covers your second nurse bill & leaves a residue. Have put $145.05 & $42.00 in separate envelopes—& will pay the first at the desk tomorrow & bring the second next Wednesday when it is due. After the subtraction of hospital bill, nurse bill, & cleaner's 60¢, $12.35 remains of the 200. This I have added to the 24.77 already on hand, giving a total of *$37.12* remaining on hand. It is simpler to draw *even* sums & let the residue mount gradually—then, when the residue is enough to pay some necessary bill, it can be used without an extra drawing. ¶ Got veal loaf for my dinner. ¶ Back to 66 in the rain & read the paper—which contained no striking news. ¶ Telephone enquiry from Miss Alice Wilcox—who said she brought you flowers in person the other day, but was so late that she didn't ask to see you. I thanked her & told her you'd let her know when you could see visitors. ¶ Good dinner. Finished Zocates. They make fine salad, but I can see why L D C thought them underdone for general use. ¶ Found ants on the kitchen shelves, & traced them to your Johnnycake flour. Destroyed hundreds, but was able to salvage a bit of the flour, which I've put in an empty Maxwell House tin. ¶ Am using up the caked sucrose in my old Barnes St. bowl. All right after 3 years. ¶ Read "Innsmouth" proofs a bit, & a little after 8 p.m. I went down the hill in the rain (on this & the previous occasion I wore pants instead of trousers, but carried no umbrella) to increase my neglected education by hearing a lecture at Memorial Hall by Prof. Alan J. B. Wace of Cambridge University, the well-known classical scholar & archaeologist.[22] As I entered the hall a button came off my 1909 raincoat. Prof. Wace's subject was "The Archaic Ivory Trade in the Mediterranean", & it contained important hints regarding the influence of the Orient on prehistoric Greece. By tracing ivory objects of a certain technique, Prof. Wace draws the conclusion that Early Greece was (through Phoenician mediation) greatly influenced by Assyria, & that ivory-producing elephants once existed in Syria as well as in India & Africa. ¶ Later finished proofs, wrote letter, & retired around 3 a.m.

DIARY FOR SATURDAY, MARCH 28, 1936

Rose 10 a.m.—elec. light bill—coördinated correspondence—set out for Aunt Jane's—paid bill at desk—proceeded up to 332.

[368f]   [HPL to AEPG]

DIARY FOR SATURDAY, MARCH 28, 1936.

¶ Left Aunt Jane's & proceeded to look up the gasometer. The street just opposite your window is not CRARY but CLAY. CRARY ST. is parallel with LOCKWOOD on the other side of the cyclopean dome. The enclosed map

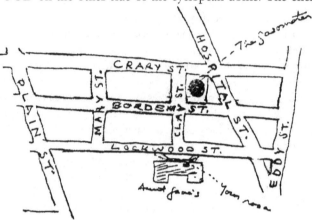

gives an idea of things—& incidentally reveals the fact that the street *behind* the hospital grounds is PLAIN. OCEAN does not start until Public St. is reached. Well—the monstrous ruin is tremendously impressive at close quarters. Its sheer bulk is staggering, & its architecture (clumsy Doric triglyphs are outlined in the brickwork just below the dome) has a sort of crude picturesqueness. It is situate on a high plateau, raised by a stone bank wall above the surrounding streets; but the floor is a basement—that is, at the street level, but far below the level of the plateau. The great door on the Crary St. side—probably cut when the place was used as a garage, opens level with the street & involves a deep breach in the bank wall. The entire place is distinctly ruinous, & a few holes have appeared in the great dome. The dark, overawing bulk of the edifice on its high, black, masonry embankment forms a curious contrast to the commonplaceness of the surrounding slums, & suggests mystery, alienage, & even potential terror. The vast archway is only imperfectly boarded, & I stepped inside the spectral abyss—a mere dot in the midst of utterly empty shadowy immensity. The situation carried with it some obscure & inexplicable grain of horror, & I was glad to emerge quickly into the golden afternoon sunlight. Certainly, this structure is a highly curious & fascinating thing, & I regret its impending demolition. I do not know the date of this spectral ruin, but imagine it must be of about the Civil War period. According to the new historical booklet the dome is 136 feet in outside diameter—that of St. Peter's in Rome being 148. The ribs of the dome are wooden—formed of large beams spliced together—& the workmanship is reputed to be of exceptional excellence. You must get out to see it before long—the spacious interior would make a good wheeling-rink for one of those chairs! ¶ I now proceeded down town via Eddy Sts. [*sic*] & did my modest marketing. No dognuts or po'k & bek bin at What Cheer, so got 'em at Arnold & Maine's. While there I was tempted by a nickel jelly roll & got it for dessert. Got a stamp at the P.O. & mailed Shelburne Falls epistle. Then up to 66 to read the paper—no striking news. Had a good dinner—& got rid of quite a bit of mayonnaise with the bek bin. The jelly roll was great—I shall probably indulge again. ¶ Then got your thanks letters written—Robinson, Ingalls,[23] Watrous, Sweetland[24]—& proceeded to wrestle hopelessly with correspondence. Retired 1 a.m.

DIARY FOR SUNDAY, MARCH 29, 1936

Rose 10 a.m. Enquiry from Miss Sally Wilcox. Read Sunday Journal. Enquired at hospital & made appointment to call tomorrow. Finished Sunday Journal. ¶ I now made an attempt to go on with the one revision job which I have not yet returned—in the hope that I might be able to perform at least part of it & receive remuneration therefor. Results remain doubtful, since the more original parts will need leisure & concentration. It is a text-book on English usage by Mrs. Renshaw—& most of my time today was spent in straightening out historical & mythological errors in the section where certain familiar allusions are explained.[25] ¶ Had a good dinner of bek bin & mayonnaise—& decided on an experiment to see if I could use up the Chase & Sanborn dated coffee which is otherwise going to waste. Got out your pot & added to some boiling water a goodly quota of the aromatic grain—then allowing the mixture to simmer whilst I eat my bek bin. The result—with Barnes St. sucrose & a spoonful of Challenge—was not at all bad—though I think I prefer Postum now that I'm used to it. However, I shall use up this Chase & Sanborn before it spoils. Don't know which is the cheaper. Postum costs more, but I use less of it. Probably about 50–50. Chocolate bar for deezort. ¶ I now resumed the revisory labours, continuing till 5 a.m. Just a bit of progress, but I still doubt my ability to finish the job before May 1st—the limit set.[26] Too many other things—like "Innsmouth" proofs—clamouring for immediate attention. At last I retired for a rest of undetermined length.

DIARY FOR MONDAY, MARCH 30, 1936.

Awaked 9 a.m. by bell—Mrs. Rausch calling. She was tremendously sorry to hear you are ill. Is moving back to #67.[27] Later Miss Bancroft called to invite you to her house for a cup of tea—& was extremely sorry to hear that—& why—you will be unable to accept. ¶ Brobst telephoned, & will call tomorrow. And PRICE may be here in May.[28] ¶ Now downtown to hosp.

[368g]   [HPL to AEPG]

DIARY FOR MONDAY, MARCH 30, 1936

Home via Point St. Bridge & Benefit. Wrote Mr. Peck a cordial note, & in delivering it ran into Miss Bonner. Usual regards sent, & she is anxious to know when she can call. Returning to 66, I ran into Fraulein von Scheppard, who sent similar regards & congratulations on good progress. Read paper & Bernstein'd a couple of moth holes in my trousers without taking them off. Oy, you shood see how I've voik oudt ah vay I kin feegs it ah moth-hole a'ready so yah kent tell vhere it vas! ¶ Then wrote Rausch & Sisson[29] notes & mailed them. ¶ Then dinner. Had hot dawgs (cold), biscuits, & mayonnaise. Very good. Made coffee very successfully—but, alas, broke my last Turner Centre milk jar . . . a link with early Barnes St. days. No—it was *not* through my method of washing. It was through pouring coffee fresh from the pot. Next time—adopting one of the three remaining Nichols jars—I shall let the fluid cool a bit before pouring. But when I use up the Chase & Sanborn I shall return to Postum. Coffee is too darned much bother—& really doesn't taste as good as Postum. ¶ Telephone message from Mrs. Carpenter. She is eager to call on you, but I told her you were not *quite* ready. However, you'll probably enjoy Mrs. Rausch's call so well that you'll thereafter want others. ¶ Read N.Y. Times & wrote a bit. Retired 4:30 a.m.

DIARY FOR TUESDAY, MARCH 31, 1936

Rose noon. Cleaned both my rooms & your living-room—with Brobst's impending call as an incentive. Also swept hall. ¶ The Turner Centre bottle crack—which I examined very carefully as I breakfasted—does not extend very far; hence I shall continue to use the vessel. ¶ Telephoned Aunt Jane, & find you wish to see me tomorrow afternoon, & Misses Bonner & Staples in the morning. Prepared & delivered a note of invitation. ¶ Went down town for your clothing at cleaner's. Got it, & put it in front of your fireplace whence it came. Shall I take it out of the box & attempt to hang it up somewhere? Brobst called, & we had some interesting discussion. He says he is coming again Thursday unless notified to the contrary. After he left I read the paper. Italians capture Gondar, which is near the source of the Blue Nile & therefore of significance in connexion with Anglo-Egyptian irrigation projects. Hope no international complications will ensue.[30] ¶ Had a good Boiardi dinner in honour of the Italian victory. Made coffee very successfully, but Turner Centre bottle cracked further—even though I let the coffee cool quite a bit before pouring. Reluctantly put it on the retired list & took a Nichols bottle. Then proceeded to wrestle with correspondence. Retired 3:30 a.m.

DIARY FOR WEDNESDAY, APRIL 1, 1936

Awaked at 2:15 p.m. after nearly 11 hours' slumber. Hustled like the devil for Aunt Jane's!

[368h]   [HPL to AEPG]

DIARY FOR WEDNESDAY, APRIL 1, 1936

Home via Point & Benefit. Read paper & had fine dinner of chile con carne & crackers. Made coffee (I'm an old hand at it now!) & didn't break any bottles. Hung up your suit & dress, & annexed the row of small jelly-jars. Thanks! Wrote invitations to Mrs. Carpenter & Fraulein von Scheppard. Around 9 p.m. had a telephone call from Big Mr. Sterling in Pawtucket.[31] He says that Little Mr. Sterling is now doing very well, & that he sent both you & me his best regards. Big Mr. Sterling has been in N.Y. all the time during the dangerous part of his heir's illness, & has only just returned to R.I. I invited him over for some evening, but he says he is now staying in at the Y every night in order to receive a long-distance call from his wife concerning Little Mr. Sterling's progress. Mrs. Sterling is spending all her time at the hospital with the young patient. This illness will undoubtedly blast the little sage's plan to enter Harvard in the fall, but for the present his parents are letting him think he can make up the lost time somehow. Big Mr. Sterling sent you his most solicitous good wishes for a quick recovery—& I transmitted your best wishes for the Young Biologist's speedy restoration to health. I am informed that my recent letter duly reached the Infant Sage, & that it was heartily appreciated. ¶ Proceeded to wrestle with piled-up correspondence, & retired late.

DIARY FOR THURSDAY, APRIL 2, 1936

Rose noon—raw, rainy day. Brobst telephoned that he couldn't come—feels bad & fears a touch of grippe. Received a package from Koenig containing among other things 3 mimeographed copies of my Charleston guide letter to him. Full of errors—it took virtually all the afternoon to correct them.

Fraulein von Scheppard rang the bell to say that she'll probably be over to the hospital some time next week—perforce in the afternoon, but on one of those afternoons (probably Monday or Wednesday) when you have no other callers. She is only just recovering from a bad bronchial cold, & fears she might give it to you now. Next Thursday she is going to Newport to spend several days. She had a card all ready to send you, but lacked stamps—so I am bringing it along. I offered her stamps, but she said she would have to get a supply tomorrow anyhow. Telephone call from Miss Robinson of Slater Ave., who has only just heard of your illness. She sent her profoundest sympathy—& congratulations on your improvement. She wants to call at the hospital, but I was a bit indefinite about the date, since she was not on your list of permitted visitors. ¶ Had good dinner of Heinz Macaroni, & finished up the Chase & Sanborn. Crackers & jelly for dessert—that stuff in the small jars is great, but each jar is good for only one meal! ¶ After dinner read an Easter Island article & others in magazines (published by Am. Museum) sent by Koenig, & wrestled with correspondence. Retired 2:30 a.m.

DIARY FOR FRIDAY, APRIL 3, 1936

Rose noon—coördinated correspondence. Set out for Aunt Jane's.

[368i]   [HPL to AEPG]

DIARY FOR FRIDAY, APRIL 3, 1936

Downtown through the slums. Raw, cold day—with a few actual flakes of snow. Errands. Up to 66 & read paper. Dinner of meat balls & spaghetti from the What Cheer—they had no po'k & bek bin left for the day. Got rid of some mayonnaise on rolls. Made Postum. Telephone enquiry from Miss Sally Wilcox, who was glad to hear of progress. I told her the lid on callers was off, but advised preliminary telephoning. Then wrote & mailed notes of thanks to Miss Angell & Big Mr. Sterling. Feeling fatigued, I retired at 8:30 p.m., but was soon aroused by the telephone—Frederick T. Guild enquiring about you. He was vastly pleased to hear of progress—& of the removal of the ban on callers. ¶ I then retired for good.

DIARY FOR SATURDAY, APRIL 4, 1936

Rose 8 a.m. Mail brought a bewildering tangle of stuff requiring immediate attention. Among less insistent things was a dictated epistle from Leedle Meestah Stoiling, who is gaining rapidly, eating everything & (as in the gravest part of his illness) interested in everything. After a bit of coördination I felt so tired that I was compelled to rest instead of going to the bank as I had planned. A rest—almost solid sleep—from 10 to 3 considerably refreshed me. Found 70¢ gas bill—which I'll defray in full. Fraulein von Scheppard appeared in the hall & bade me say that she hopes to call at Aunt Jane's on *Monday* at about 4 p.m. ¶ Read paper & observed that Edmund Sullivan has died. Now only the baby—the artist J. Banigan Sullivan—is left.[32] ¶ Wrestled with correspondence. As I was returning from the box I met Miss Bonner, who had come to bring some vernal branches for you—trophies of the first Field Naturalists' expedition. I shall bring them with me when I call tomorrow. ¶ Had good dinner of chile con carne—was a bit too tired to make the trip down for bek bin. ¶ Wrestled with correspondence & retired 2:30 a.m.

DIARY FOR SUNDAY, APRIL 5, 1936

Rose noon, glanced at Sunday Journal, & set out for Aunt Jane's.

[368j] [HPL to AEPG]

DIARY FOR SUNDAY, APRIL 5, 1936

Home via Point & Benefit. Finished Sunday Journal. Good dinner of Campbell's vegetable soup—watered & heated, with hardened rolls broken in. Read new Weird Tales so that I could furnish a report to Leedle Meestah Stoiling. Wrestled with correspondence. Retired 2:30 a.m.

DIARY FOR MONDAY, APRIL 6, 1936

Rose 10 a.m.—read part of Times—rested 1–3 p.m.—down town for cash & groceries—back to 66—read paper & continued with Times. Good dinner of meat balls & spaghetti from What Cheer—with fresh rolls. Finished mayonnaise. Telephone message from Miss Maud Robinson, who enquired solicitously & was glad to hear of progress. Read Times magazines. Telephone message from yourself—quite a surprise—making appointment for 3:30 tomorrow. Enquiry from Fraulein von Scheppard—who enjoyed her call on you—about best way to send rare books to California. I advised ensured parcel post. Finished Times magazines & struggled with correspondence. Retired 5:30 a.m. after a bit of Sam Singing.[33]

DIARY FOR TUESDAY, APRIL 7, 1936.

Rose 2 p.m.—tried to coördinate correspondence—started out for Aunt Jane's.[34]

Current finances

	Previously on hand	$33.80
	Drawn April 6	150.00
		183.80
Hosp 63.10	⎤ ——spent April 7	105.10
Nurse 42.00	⎦	
	On hand April 7	78.70

[368k] [HPL to AEPG]

DIARY FOR TUESDAY, APRIL 7, 1936

Entered #66 & set the new plant with its kindred in the dining apartment. Undid the ink & will bring it over when I come. I don't see why you didn't take it over directly. Found some Easter cards from nice old Miss Toldridge in Washington, which she thought you might enjoy using. Will bring them over. Read paper & tore out the Tuesday art page—which, oddly enough, is this week devoted to *history*. By the way—there will be a lecture on Greek sculpture at Faunce House tomorrow night which (in addition to the Edman lecture Friday) I shall probably attend. Telephone call from Miss Staples, who had called the hospital & had been told you had gone home. She was glad to hear of your emergence, even though it did not involve your instant return. She & the Perkinses sent their regards—& incidentally, I saw the Big Black Bum out in the yard. Wound clocks & watched lights come on. At 6:48 the court house floodlight sprang up, & almost instantly afterward—as if taking the signal—the Industrial crown of stars appeared. Attempted some correspondence & had a good chile con carne dinner. Telephone message from Miss Sally Wilcox, who rejoiced to learn of your transfer. I now attempted work on the Renshaw revision job—the time limit of which has very kindly been pushed ahead. Retired 5 a.m.

DIARY FOR WEDNESDAY, APRIL 8, 1936

Rose 2 p.m. headache. Rested. Started out for Russell Goff's house.[35]

[368l] [HPL to AEPG]

DIARY FOR WEDNESDAY, APRIL 8, 1936

Back to #66 via 454. Note that the ivy arch is down. Met Fraulein von Scheppard in hall—she may come to see you next week. Is going to Newport tomorrow, & asked me to use her milk if the man leaves it by mistake. ¶ Left black bag & went to lecture in Faunce house—by Prof. Charles A. Robinson, Jr. of Brown, an archaeologist who spent last year excavating in Athens.[36] He was introduced by the suave & Vandyked Prof. Potter,[37] & illustrated his lecture with lantern slides. His theme was the Greek sculpture of the late archaic period—ending with the period of the Parthenon—& he handled it splendidly, dwelling on basic characteristics & explaining many significant aesthetic principles. His slides included many of statues very recently discovered—especially a magnificent bronze Zeus found only last year at the bottom of the sea. I'm certainly glad I didn't miss this. Attendance, however, was very slight. The speaker looked about 20 years old, but he must be more than that in order to be a professor. Friday night comes the Edman lecture—& a week hence is one by Prof. Taylor of Brown on Mexican art.[38] ¶ Back to 66 & read paper. Then a bin zup dinner. Then wrestling with correspondence. Looked up articles to bring, & find we have only 3 & 5 grain cascaras[39] . . . . & no rubbing alcohol. I'll get both. Have packed towels, Pepsodent antiseptic, & stationery for transportation. ¶ Retired 6 a.m.

DIARY FOR THURSDAY, APRIL 9, 1936

Roused 11:30 a.m. by bell. Was Miss Stafford delivering mis-sent mail from 10 Barnes & intending to call on you. She was sorry to hear of your illness but glad to learn of your good progress. Asked if you could see callers, & I told her the proper hours. Almost simultaneously a telephone message came from Miss Maud Robinson, who was glad to hear of your transfer & took your new Boulevard address. Rose for good at 2 p.m., feebly struggled with correspondence, & went down town for errands. Rubbing alcohol has gone down sensationally in price—the accompanying bottle costing only *12¢.* Hall & Lyon do not carry 1-grain cascara tablets, but Blanding's had them. They were 35¢. This total expenditure of 47¢ brings the current fund down to 78.23. Back to 66, read paper, & struggled with correspondence. Then meat ball & spaghetti dinner—milk not being left at Fraulein von Scheppard's. More struggles with correspondence. Retired 6 a.m.

DIARY FOR FRIDAY, APRIL 10, 1936

Rose at noon. In getting lunch, I experimented with my 10-year-old Rich's Cocoa & found it deteriorated. Has acquired an earthy taste. However, I shall use it up somehow. It had, of course, been opened. Hope my Hershey's Cocoa Syrup (also from Barnes St. but never opened) is all right. ¶ Struggled with correspondence & set out for Russell Goff's.

[368m] [HPL to AEPG]

DIARY FOR FRIDAY, APRIL 10, 1936

Back to 66—read paper—out to Edman lecture at Metcalf Lab. on Philosophy & Poetry. Excellent address, though holding nothing especially new. The speaker pointed out meeting places of philosophy & poetry—the essentially poetic content of many philosophic expositions, & the poetic expression (as of Lucretius, Dante, & Milton) evoked by strong emotion born of philosophic ideas. The introduction was effected by Prof. S. Foster Damon. Edman is a shortish, smooth-faced man of middle age, so blond (& probably greying) as to convey an almost albino effect to my dim & senile vision. He has an impediment of speech (mainly perceptible as a sort of semi-lisp) which forces him to speak very slowly, & occasionally with curious oral motions. It is probably psychological, since once—in an aside—he spoke rapidly & clearly. Edman is the author of many philosophic works, & of one volume of verse. He is professor of philosophy at Columbia, & a frequent book reviewer for the Times & Tribune.[40] The audience was of fair size, but was so tardy in assembling that the lecture did not begin till nearly 8:30. The auditorium was abominably cold—so much so as to induce drowsiness. ¶ Back to 66 & ate fine chili con carne dinner with your small cake & spoiled cocoa for des[s]ert. Then struggles with correspondence. Got out your dress & paper-cutter & wire shoulder ready for transportation. Will get stamps tomorrow if all goes well—leaving you a balance of $77.73. Retired 5 a.m.

DIARY FOR SATURDAY, APRIL 11, 1936

Roused 11:30 a.m. by telephone message from Miss Sally Wilcox, who was glad to hear of your progress & wished to know about the conditions of telephoning to Russell Goff's. Rose for good at 4 p.m., coördinated correspondence, & went down town for errands. Noticed that much of the upper part of the ancient Franklin House is removed—which arouses my apprehensions. Possibly structural considerations made rebuilding necessary—but I hope all the bricks are numbered & will be replaced in their proper positions. Around 5:30 p.m. some flowers were delivered for you. I've put them in your cold closet for safe keeping, & hope I'll remember to bring them over tomorrow. Duly obtained your stamps. ¶ More demolition in N. Main St.—corner of Steeple—but the houses concerned are Victorian, hence there is no loss. ¶ Read paper & had a good po'k & bek bin dinner—with spoiled cocoa. I wonder how the canned brown bread from Barnes St. is keeping. ¶ Then embarked on a long struggle with correspondence. ¶ By the way—I note a card in your handwriting in Fraulein von Scheppard's rapidly growing pile of mail! ¶ Retired late.

DIARY FOR SUNDAY, APRIL 12, 1936

Rose 3 p.m.—glanced at Sunday Journal—over to Russell Goff's.

[368n] [HPL to AEPG]

DIARY FOR SUNDAY, APRIL 12, 1936.

Out to Wayland Square. Hall & Lyon had only *5-yard* packages of gauze—they don't sell by the pound. 54¢. Tape 25¢. When I got home I weighed the gauze & found it was only ½ lb. I'll get another carton on my way over tomorrow. 54 + 54 + 25 = 1.33—which, subtracted from 77.73, leaves *76.40*—the current balance. ¶ Finished Sunday Journal. Searched out & assembled the articles to be carried to Russell Goff's—adding the Sunday Journal section describing the Carrington House. ¶ Home dinner of bek bin & Barnes St. canned brown bread. Latter was still good. Rabbit cookie for dessert—& finished spoiled cocoa. Shall soon experiment with Hershey's Cocoa Syrup. ¶ Struggled with correspondence. ¶ Retired 5 a.m.

DIARY FOR MONDAY, APRIL 13, 1936

Waked noon, but too tired to rise. Rose 2 p.m. Explored top shelf of kitchen to get Hershey's Cocoa & found a nearly full cylinder of salt (from Barnes St.) & a can of Hatchet diced carrots. Have placed these in the common larder. Price's curry powder was also there. Maybe he can use it if he comes next month. ¶ Coördinated correspondence & set out for Russell Goff's. ¶ Young Moe returned the books he borrowed a year ago—& felt very guilty in having kept them a year.[41] To atone for this delay he said he wished to present me with a book—but not knowing what to select, enclosed a five-buck money order instead. Certainly graceful & generous of the young rascal! He & his pa may get here next summer, when good old Moe comes East for a vacation & a course at the Bread Loaf Writers' Conference in Vermont. ¶ Made visit & returned to 66. Read paper & N.Y. Times. Had good dinner of chile con carne & brown bread, with mouthful of cake for dessert. Read Times magazines & retired 12:30 midnight. ¶ Awaked 2:30 & was unable to sleep again. Up 4:30 & struggled with correspondence. Retired again 8 a.m. Roused 11:30 a.m. (Tuesday) by Fadden, who called to ask me to let him have the rent *in person* when I paid it. I paid him on the spot from your general fund (noting 20.00 owed by me), leaving a balance of $36.40 on hand. He later left a receipt. About the same time Brobst telephoned—& sent you the regards & best wishes of himself & wife. I then retired but could not sleep. Rising, I was too weak & drowsy to do anything. Saw the Big Black Bum at play in his garden. Rested again & dropped off to sleep some time after 12:30 noon.

DIARY FOR TUESDAY, APRIL 14, 1936

Rose 5 p.m. feeling perfectly refreshed. Read paper—including art page. Modern art explained by Hezekiah's friend John.[42] Am saving sheet with others of series. Had fine hash dinner—& for dessert I succumbed to repeated temptation & consumed ⅓ of the Ayama peaches. This is positively the most delicious dessert conceivable except ice cream. Made cocoa with Hershey syrup from Barnes St., & it was perfect. Not very cheap, though, for one of those dime cans won't make more than 3 or 4 large cups. Now proceeded to wrestle with correspondence. Miss Sally Wilcox called up under the impression that you might be home. She sent regards. Retired 5:30 a.m.

DIARY FOR WEDNESDAY, APRIL 15, 1936

Awaked 10 a.m. & unable to sleep more. Delighted to receive your letter & learn of the outing. Assembled material to bring. Have a sort of prickling throat cold, but not sore throat. Struggled with correspondence. Finally set out for Russell Goff's. Intermittent rain.

[368o] [HPL to AEPG]

DIARY FOR WEDNESDAY, APRIL 15, 1936

Back to 66—out again to lecture on Mayan ruins at Faunce House by Prof. Taylor. Speaker was elaborately introduced by the Vandyked Prof. Potter, & gave an excellent illustrated address. Slides were exceedingly graphic, & included views of *new* excavations I had never seen illustrated before. The speaker also described many principles of Mayan architecture which had hitherto been vague to me. He illustrated the differences between the buildings of the Old Empire (up to 500 A.D.) in Guatemala & adjacent parts, & those of the New Empire near the tip of Yucatan whither the whole people suddenly migrated en masse. He also shewed the coming of Toltec influence when the northern invaders conquered the Mayas. Taylor is a good speaker, but makes occasional slips—such as *1684* for *684*. The audience laughed when he spoke of something ancient as happening in *1967*. Auditorium well heated. ¶ Back to 66 & read paper. Death of Rev. Gibbs Braislin, Jimmy Pyke's brother in law, aged 88.[43] Oldest living graduate of Class of 1880 at Brown. Had been retired since 1917. Died in Haddonfield, N.J. ¶ Good chile con carne dinner with fruit dessert. Struggled with correspondence. Retired midnight.

DIARY FOR THURSDAY, APRIL 16, 1936

Awaked 4 a.m.—unable to sleep—rose 5:30 & wrestled with correspondence—Rested again when unable to continue—about 8 a.m.—& dropped off to sleep some time before 10:00. ¶ Awaked again 3:30 p.m. feeling quite well though hoarse. Downtown for errands—though too late for bank. Paid telephone bill & got my groceries. Back to 66 & read paper. Fine dinner of spaghetti & meat balls. Wrestled with correspondence. Retired 10 a.m. Friday—official N.A.P.A. stuff engulfed me.

DIARY FOR FRIDAY, APRIL 17, 1936

Tenth anniversary of my return from N.Y. & advent to Barnes St. Rose 3:30 p.m. Hustled for Russell Goff's.

[368p]   [HPL to AEPG]
DIARY FOR FRIDAY, APRIL 17, 1936

Back to 66—read paper—good chile con carne dinner—struggled with that confounded N.A.P.A. official matter till 6 a.m.—breakfasted & retired. Around 9 p.m. F. T. Guild called up to enquire about you.

DIARY FOR SATURDAY, APRIL 18, 1936

30th Anniversary of San Francisco earthquake. I was out in my piano-box "New Anvik" beside 598 when the Bulletin announcing the disaster in bold headlines arrived. It was a warm, golden afternoon . . . as indeed are all the afternoons of one's youth as compared with those of the grey elder years. Skipping down three decades—rose 4 p.m. A Miss Blinkhorn[44] telephoned to enquire about you, & was glad to hear of progress. Your Cameron letter came back again, although addressed % Mrs. Bowen, 22 Wesleyan Ave., in the Ripleian handwriting. There was no further postmark, & since I fancy there may have been a P.O. misunderstanding I put it in a fresh envelope with 2¢ postage, addressed it properly, & mailed it again. Now we'll see what will develop. My own return address is on the envelope. ¶ Read paper & had good bin zup dinner. Struggled with correspondence. Sam-sang my handkerchief & got out some of the ink with my ink-eradicator. By the way, Frank[45] now sells eradicator for 10¢, & it seems to work all right. Guess I'll patronise him in future, since the other costs 15¢. Retired 9:30 a.m. Saw Mr. Perkins Sr. in the alleyway.

DIARY FOR SUNDAY, APRIL 19, 1936

Rose 4 p.m.—over to Russell Goff's—discussed various topics—back to 66—hash dinner—read Sunday Journal—Retired midnight.

DIARY FOR MONDAY, APRIL 20, 1936

L D C's birthday. Awaked 4 a.m. & unable to sleep. Rose 5 a.m. Struggled with correspondence. Dressed 7 a.m.—but all for nothing, since Fraulein von Scheppard left a note saying that Miss Gayton was indisposed & could not come till the following day. Read Bekes & corrected a section of "Innsmouth" proofs. Struggled with correspondence. Down to bank & What Cheer. Return. Saw good old Spotty in garden. Over to Russell Goff's—discussed return of patient—back to 66—home dinner—read paper—retired 9 p.m.

DIARY FOR TUESDAY, APRIL 21, 1936

Rise 6 a.m.—read Bekes—Miss Gayton arrive & clean—tel. from Mrs. Thomas—will not be able to aid transportation—tel. from A E P G—read N Y Times—ancient Place Bible arrive—cleaner lv—A E P G arrive—place flowers—conversation—finish Times & read Bulletin—dinner, writing, retiring, & end of diary.

Notes

1. Note appended by AEPG: "Howard's diary the five weeks I was away from home. I went to Jane Brown March 17 & from there to Dorcus House April 6 & to 66 April 21."
2. Lucius Collinwood Kingman (1878–1958) was a surgical specialist and later served as president of the Rhode Island Medical Society in 1940–41.
3. I.e., a doughnut.
4. HPL's jocular reference to Jane Brown Memorial Hospital (now part of Rhode Island Hospital), then at 44 Lockwood Street, where AEPG had undergone a mastectomy (and where HPL himself would die on 15 March 1937).
5. Frederick T. Guild (1868–1941), Registrar of Brown University (1891–1938).
6. Postum was a caffeine-free coffee substitute in powdered form created in 1895 by the Postum Cereal Company (predecessor to General Foods). HPL was probably using the "instant" version created in 1912.
7. The latter three are cats belonging to the Kappa Alpha Tau fraternity.
8 HPL has added a large flourish underneath the signature.
9. Probably Louise M. Angell (1858–1949) of 42 College Street, proprietress of the Handicraft Club art shop, Truman Beckwith House, at the corner of Benefit and College streets.
10. Clarence H[erbert] Guild, Jr. (1875–?).
11. A joking reference to Edna Lewis (1868–1955), AEPG's cousin and joint heir (with Ethel Phillips Morrish) of AEPG's estate.
12. Doris Elizabeth M. Johnson (1904–2004), a library assistant at the Providence Public Library, and Eleanor H. Fenner (1875?–1942). Both were living at 55 Waterman Street.

13. To Edna Lewis.

14. Ralph C. Watrous (1866–1939) and Susan A. (Aldrich) Watrous (1870–1947) of 76 Elmgrove Avenue were members of the Providence Art Club.

15. Protose was a meat substitute (made mostly of wheat gluten and peanuts) manufactured by several different food companies. The product and the term were invented by John Harvey Kellogg.

16. This signature also features a large flourish below it.

17. Perhaps the What Cheer Hall at 643 North Main Street.

18. Presumably Admiral Richard E. Byrd's Second Antarctic Expedition (1933–35).

19. Either Edward F. Gamwell's brother Irving Henry Gamwell (1871–1963) or sister Helen Sears Gamwell (1874–1938).

20. HPL refers to the edition of *The Shadow over Innsmouth* (1936) issued by William L. Crawford's Visionary Press.

21. Kenneth Sterling had required an operation for an abscess of the colon.

22. Alan J. B. Wace (1879–1957), British archaeologist. At this time he was the Laurence Professor of Classical Archaeology at Cambridge (1934–44). Among his books are *An Approach to Greek Sculpture* (1935).

23. Perhaps Fannie T. Ingalls of Wayland Manor, 500 Angell St. (apt. 601).

24. Perhaps Louisa A. Sweetland (1871–1942), Wayland Manor, 500 Angell St. (apt. 315).

25. HPL refers to his work on Renshaw's *Well Bred Speech* (1936). Much of his original work was not included in the published book. The omitted chapters can now be found in *Letters to Elizabeth Toldridge and Anne Tillery Renshaw* 403–38.

26. HPL did not finish the revision of *Well Bred Speech* until mid-September.

27. Bertha (Mrs. Anthony) Rausch and AEPG were neighbors on Slater Avenue. Mrs. Rausch moved back to the latter address in 1936.

28. E. Hoffmann Price did not in fact visit HPL at this time.

29. Charles Peck Sisson (1890–1947) & Margaret A. (Gifford) Sisson (1888–1980) of 117 Elmgrove Avenue were members of the Providence Art Club.

30. HPL refers to a city in Ethiopia that was captured by Italy in the course of the Second Italo-Ethiopian War. The war was over by May, resulting in Italy's control of the country until 1941.

31. HPL had become friends with not only Kenneth Sterling but also his father, Lee Welvan Sterling (1890–1980?).

32. Edmund James Gibbons Sullivan (1893–1936), brother of J. Banigan Sullivan (1905–1970) of 281 Waterman Street joined the Providence Art Club in 1934. They were the sons of Dr. James E. Sullivan (1849–1920) and Alice Margaret (Banigan) Sullivan (1866–1909).

33. I.e., laundering. HPL refers humorously to the Sam Sing Laundry at 121 North Main Street. It closed in 2002 after about 90 years of operation.

34. At the bottom of the page AEPG has written: "Pouring rainy day. Mrs. Carpenter made me a nice call bringing gay flowers Called up Norma asking if she could bring us over & she did. Howard—the Primrose—Miss Burns & me. Miss B. waited & put me to bed. Couldn't have lived without her."

35. Dorcus Home for Convalescents, a private convalescent home at 32 Blackstone Boulevard (1.5 miles east of 66 College Street), to which AEPG had been transferred on 7 April. The house apparently belonged to Emma E. Dorcus (1872?–?). It is unknown why HPL referred to it as "Goff's house," seemingly referring to Russell E. Goff (1892–1970). Census records for 1940 show persons with the Dorcus surname at 32 Blackstone. Perhaps Goff was a personal acquaintance of HPL or AEPG.

36. Charles A. Robinson, Jr. (1900–1985), professor of classics at Brown University (1928–65) and author of many books on Greek history and culture.

37. Apparently Albert K. Potter (1864–1948), professor of English at Brown (1898–1935).

38. Will S. Taylor (1882–1968), professor of art at Brown (1926–53).

39. A purgative made from the dried bark of an American buckthorn.

40. Irwin Edman (1896–1954), professor of philosophy at Columbia University and author of many books on Plato, Schopenhauer, and other philosophical subjects. His book of poetry is *Poems* (New York: Simon & Schuster, 1925).

41. Robert E. Moe, son of HPL's correspondent and amateur friend Maurice W. Moe. Moe had visited HPL by car in Providence in 1935.

42. For Hezekiah Anthony Dyer, see LDC/AEPG 99n3. His friend John is unidentified.

43. Gibbs Braislin (1850–1936), longtime pastor at the Baptist church of Rutland, VT. In 1886 he married Jennie C. Pyke, sister of James Tobey Pyke (1858–1935), Congregational minister and poet whose work HPL published in his amateur journal, the *Conservative*. See also the essay "Introducing Mr. James Pyke."

44. Cecelia A. Blinkhorn (1872–1954) of 577 Public Street. (A D. P. Blinkhorn lived in an apartment at 183 Benefit Street, two doors away from the Horace B. Knowles Funeral Home, where HPL's funeral was held.)

45. I.e., F. W. Woolworth.

To Nelson Rogers

[1]   [TLS, in private hands]

598 Angell St., Prov., R.I.

Feb. 15, 1912.

Dear Mr. Rogers:—[1]

I wish to express my great regret at having been unable to see you last Saturday when you called at our house.

So much had I heard of you from my mother, that nothing save the ill health from which I am at present suffering would have caused me to miss your visit. As it unfortunately happened, I was not sufficiently well to be awaked from the sleep which I was taking, for I had not slept previously for two nights.

I sincerely hope you will at no distant time be here again, that I may have the opportunity of meeting personally one who is through my mother so well known to me.

Lamenting, therefore, the circumstance which prevented me from making your acquaintance at your late stop in Providence,

I am,

Yours truly,

H. P. Lovecraft

Notes

1. For Nelson William Rogers (1878–1951), see Kenneth W. Faig, Jr., "Clergymen among Lovecraft's Paternal Ancestors," *Lovecraft Annual* No. 9 (2015): 176–77.

[2]   [ALS, in private hands] [Sarah Susan Lovecraft to Nelson Rogers]

February 17th 1912.

My dear boy Nelson.

Howard Phillips L. wrote a note to you a few days ago. I asked him to keep it until I could put in one also. I cannot tell you how much I appreciated your call upon me one week ago today. I have wondered so often where you were, and many times have felt like writing to you.

But thought maybe that you might have forgotten .. you were so young when I saw you the last time. I was introduced to you when you were about 6 or 8 months old and have loved you dearly ever since. I was nineteen yrs. old I remember.

You gave me a beautiful & complete surprise last Saturday. It was lovely of you Nelson and so fortunate I was home. You really look just the same as my little boy of long ago. How we all loved you. Do you remember that Father would have your chair close beside his at the table? He did appreciate your visit and after you left us father used to say it was lonely and wished I had kept you longer.

Howard P. has heard so much about you says you seem like his older brother. It does seem hard to completely lose track of you again. would you care to take trouble to write to me a line once a year at least, to let me know of yourself & my one time friends? I may die and you would never know, or vice-versa. You see old memories reassert their claim since your call. I hope you are very happy and contented. Of course I would love to see you any time. Our lawn extends to the street where you stood waiting for a car. All that in summer is lovely we have such huge elm trees and one apple tree, also a pear tree. Back of the house I have flowers. They were fathers and I moved them here. Do you remember how he loved flowers? Always a bo[u]quet on table, and his yard full. I wonder if you saw our old house as you went down street.

Please tell me of your wife and family. I can't realize you are married, your wife is Carrie. Oldest son Thomas and the two younger ones. I do not think their names were mentioned. I did not catch the name of your mother's street, but will direct to Dansville—she will receive it no doubt.

We have talked of Howard attending an Institute in Brooklyn. If he does so in a year or two we shall be nearer to you.

Did you *invent* this year? You spoke of your office at home. Seems to me I heard you did something like that. Perhaps I am mistaken. H. has a laboratory here down stairs. If we build after we know where he will settle, he will have one up stairs tiled[?] and light. Good night my beloved boy.

Will love always

598 Angell St.   Susie Lovecraft

Letter to Bertha Rausch

[1]   [ALS, JHL]*

March 30, 1936

Dear Mrs. Rausch:—

I visited my aunt at the Jane Brown Hospital this afternoon, & she was greatly interested in your coming return to Slater Avenue. She has thought of you very often, & when I mentioned your call she announced quite suddenly that she would really enjoy & appreciate seeing you, despite the fact that she has hitherto been seeing no one but myself. Hence to you comes the compliment of being the very first person she has invited since her advent to the hospital!

Any day that you can get over to the hospital she would be delighted to see you. If you would telephone in advance, she would be sure to have her schedule arranged in readiness for your call. Probably her best time for receiving a visitor would be about *11 a.m.*—but any time after that would do if it were more convenient for you. Her early mornings are taken up with exercise & treatment.

I really believe that a visit from you—whom she esteems so highly—would be a very cheering & encouraging thing for her, so that I hope you will be inclined to drop in at the Jane Brown in the near future. She wishes me to send you her very best regards—to which I most cordially add my own.

Yours very sincerely,
H P Lovecraft

---

*Addressed to "Mrs. Anthony Rausch, 159 Prospect St., Providence, R.I." On the envelope AEPG has written: "The letter my dear Howard wrote to Mrs. Rausch when I was ill—She was so pleased with it & saved it & brought it to me after my beloved Howard's death."

Letters to Mayte Sutton

[1]   [ALS, JHL]

[H. P. LOVECRAFT
66 COLLEGE STREET
PROVIDENCE, R. I.]

66 College St.,
Providence, R.I.,
Novr. 2, 1933

Dear Mrs. Sutton:—
          I have not yet heard from Long as to the date of my
Manhattan visit, but will let you know the moment I do. As I may have mentioned, it depends on the rate of his mother's recovery from a bad case of food poisoning. Very possibly circumstances will push the event farther into November than we had anticipated.

I will do my notifying by mail, & hope there will be no slip-up this time. If there is any occasion to get quick word to me telephonically after my arrival, my hosts may be reached by telephone—Riverside 9-3465. I think I mentioned the name & address—F. B. Long, 230 W. 97th St.

My aunt's recovery now progresses steadily.[1] The other day she used a street-car for the first time—with my assistance—& yesterday she repeated the process alone. The doctor encourages activity on her part, & is about to prescribe some arch-supporters for her shoes which may enable her to dispense with a cane before many weeks.

Autumn weather has been remarkably genial hereabouts, so that my rural walks have continued right up to the present—& *future*, for that matter, since I plan to take one this afternoon if I can wind up my duties in time. It is astonishing how many absolutely new byways of unexpected attractiveness one can unearth in one's native region. Only yesterday I traversed the *whole length* of a suburban road whose *ends* I had known half my lifetime, & was rewarded by a series of westward landscape vistas (outspread hills & stone-walled meadows, distant woods, a glint of sunset-litten river, & a steepled village in a northward valley) of surprising & breath-taking beauty. Adding to the almost eerie charm of the scene was a great round Hunter's Moon which climbed above the eastern slopes as soon as the twilight was thick. Tonight ought to afford a roughly comparable spectacle.

Negotiations seem to be under way for the publication of my "Colour Out of Space" as a separate booklet before many months elapse. The other day I carefully corrected the manuscript for the prospective publisher—one F. Lee Baldwin, of Asotin, Wash.[2]

I surely hope that no hitch may develop in connexion with the coming visit, for I want exceedingly to pay that much-postponed call. If you do not find me a wearisome & intolerable bore (in these latter years I have made some efforts to check a natural loquaciousness, though I am still apt to get most monotonously voluble on my favourite subjects!), I think it is very likely that I might get over more than one evening during my metropolitan week. I appreciate the invitation keenly.

With every good wish to you & your daughter,

I remain

Yrs most sincerely,

H. P. Lovecraft

[Enclosure: two photographs, one of HPL standing in the doorway of 66 College St., the other of Annie E. P. Gamwell in the doorway.]

Notes

1. AEPG had broken her ankle shortly after she and HPL moved into 66 College Street in May 1933; her convalescence was very slow.

2. The project never came to fruition.

[2]   [AHT]

66 College St.,

Providence, R.I.

August 6, 1936

Dear Mrs. Sutton:—

[. . .]

The hot spell of mid-July was certainly welcome, and I really think it saved me from a sort of general breakdown, nervous and digestive. I was just about "all in" from the exhaustion of cold weather when the life-giving heat struck Providence on July 8. In two days I was in splendid shape—fatigue vanished, nerves relaxed, and digestion rapidly cleared up. In the 6 days of really hot weather I accomplished more than in all the six *weeks* preceding. When the heat waned, my extra vigour and alertness declined—but I have not fallen back into quite the morass I was in before. I am certainly an idiot to continue living in this subarctic climate—but that's what attachment to native and ancestral soil will do! My aunt (who likes cold as well as I do heat) continues to improve in a very satisfactory way.

[. . .]

H. P. Lovecraft

Letters to Marian F. Bonner

[1]   [ALS, JHL]

[H. P. LOVECRAFT
66 COLLEGE STREET
PROVIDENCE, R. I.]

March 22, 1936

Dear Miss Bonner:—

I called on my aunt at the hospital for the first time this afternoon, & she wished me to drop you a particular line of thanks for the many works of consideration extended—the pansies which arrived almost simultaneously with herself, the flowers arriving since then, & the bottle of eau de cologne, all of which were profoundly appreciated.

My aunt was in excellent spirits, & seemed to be making a fine recovery. She had just had an adequate duck dinner, & was completing the ice cream dessert when I arrived. Of course the whole experience is not a pleasant one—there has been pain (although the etherisation, conducted under modern conditions, was wholly free from unpleasantness & nausea), & there is still discomfort from the constant reclining in a fixed position; but everything is progressing according to schedule, & Dr. Kingman—whom I called up the other day—considers the case very satisfactory. My aunt finds the Jane Brown Hospital extremely restful, in contrast with the R.I. Hospital where she was three years ago. Before long she may be able to receive other callers than myself, & when that stage arrives you will certainly be at the head of the invitation list! Meanwhile she sends her most select regards—& her most enthusiastic thanks for the many cheering tributes.

Adding my own most cordial appreciation, I am

Very sincerely yours,

H. P. Lovecraft

P.S. I remained at the hospital for two hours, chatting on various subjects, & my aunt did not seem unduly fatigued. Her appearance is excellent—I would scarcely take her for a patient!

[2]   [ALS, JHL]

[H. P. LOVECRAFT
66 COLLEGE STREET
PROVIDENCE, R. I.]

March 26, 1936

Miſs M. F. Bonner,
        The Arsdale, 55, Waterman Str.,[1]
              Providence, (Brown Station), R.I., U.S.A.
Dear Madam:—
                Unaccustomed though I am to elaborate attempts at self-
exculpation, I am impelled to present at least a shadowy suggestion or instance or two in reply to the formidable charges (relative to the management
of the microcosmic park) contained in your communication of present date.

I. A not wholly irrelevant question. Have you ever, by any chance, attempted to stop the present patient from doing anything she was determined to do?

II. An extremely homely & utilitarian semi-parallel. The defendant wishes
that the prosecution might witness the perennial struggle (unabated during the
period of malady, though then usually resulting in the defendant's victory) within the Garden House over the laborious honour of washing dishes and utensils
after (or during) one of the defendant's meals. The present patient, being (base-
lessly, I assure you) dissatisfied with the defendant's technique, goes to the
length of snatching articles from him before he can wash them—a procedure
which he combats & occasionally circumvents only by darting suddenly
through the bathroom door with the articles in question & washing them in
the bowl while the present patient is still lurking watchfully by the kitchen
sink. The defendant must sadly add, that even in this case the present patient
often secures an ultimate technical victory by washing over again the articles
thus washed. During the present patient's illness the defendant's apparent victories were doubtless caused less by his own skill than by said patient's absence
from the immediate scene during the defendant's periods of nourishment.

In the present case the defendant would urge that the prosecution carefully consider Points I & II, correlating them both with each other & with the
matter of the fractional forest. Whether or not the indictment is quashed, said
defendant feels confident that these considerations would not be without influence before an adequate & impartial jury.

The defendant may add that he has twice visited the present patient since
Sunday—on the afternoons of Tuesday, March 24th, & of today (Thursday,
March 26th). He finds her condition improving, according to all authorities;
although sleeplessness & discomfort still exist, while nervousness & worry
over general affairs (signs, really, of convalescence) combine to make the days
less than pleasant. She now sits up a short time each morning, & today was
wheeled out to the sun-porch, where she enjoyed the unaccustomed view of
the hospital's park-like grounds.

The present patient sends her best regards to the prosecution, & begs to say that the many cheering messages from that quarter have done much to lighten the tedium & oppression of these dismal days. She was also delighted to receive an encouraging floral tribute from the furry inhabitants of #55—Mrs. Spotty Perkins, John Perkins, Jun., & Gilbert John Murray Kynymond Elliot, 4th Earl of Minto.[2]

With this presentation of evidence & transcript of current information, the defence rests.

Accept, Madam, the renewed assurances of my high consideration.

Yr oblig'd ob^{dt} Servt.,

H. P. Lovecraft

Notes

1. The Arsdale at 53–55 Waterman Street was later renamed the Hopkins House of Brown University (for Chancellor Stephen Hopkins) and used as a student dormitory. It was later razed.

2. HPL refers to some of the cats of the K.A.T. fraternity. "Gilbert John Murray Kynymond Elliot, 4th Earl of Minto" was "named by an old lady at the boarding-house who spends her summers in New-Brunswick" (HPL to Helen V. Sully, 18 May 1936, *Letters to Wilfred B. Talman and Helen V. Sully*, 459). The woman is Evelyn M. Staples. See MFB 3. The 4th Earl of Minto (1845–1914) was governor-general of Canada (1898–1904) and viceroy and governor-general of India (1905–10).

[3]   [ALS, JHL]

[H. P. LOVECRAFT
66 COLLEGE STREET
PROVIDENCE, R. I.]

March 31, 1936

Dear Miss Bonner:—

At last the Hermit of Lockwood St. becomes accessible! When I telephoned this noon my aunt said that she would very much appreciate a call from you—& from Miss Staples, if you can persuade that gentle ailurophile to accompany you—*tomorrow morning* (Wednesday, April 1st—but the invitation is *not* an April Fool stunt!) around 11 o'clock. You will, I imagine, be the first non-blood-kinsfolk to be invited to invade her sanctum—an honour which I trust you will duly appreciate!

Please do not regard the invitation as quasi-compulsory—like a summons to a royal audience—if you have other plans for tomorrow. It is merely that the patient would appreciate seeing you if you find it entirely convenient to drop around.

With best wishes, & much appreciation of the cheer which your messages have afforded the patient,

Yr obt hble Servt
H. P. Lovecraft

[4]   [TLS, JHL]

The Garden House,
#1, Ely's Court,
over-against John Hay Library,
66, College Street,
Providence, R.I., U.S.A.,
1st April, 1936.

Miss M. F. Bonner,
The Arsdale,
55, Waterman Str. (East Side Station),
Providence, R.I., U.S.A.,

Dear Miss Bonner:—

Being in receipt of your enquiry and correction of recent date, I take pleasure in attending to the various topics in order of presentation.

First, regarding the term by which the undersigned's aunt was described. Observation of said aunt's coiffure this morning has doubtless apprised you of the erroneousness of the *Haircut* interpretation. To this I may add that the actual word was *Hermit*—a designation often applied to persons in extreme seclusion, as the individual referred to has been up to this morning. The word is an interesting one, being derived (through the French *hermite*) from the Latin *eremita,* meaning a religious recluse; this term in turn being a transliteration of the Greek ἐϱημίτης—which itself comes from the word ἐϱῆμος, meaning a desert or solitude, and perhaps alluding to the desert environment of the typical early anchorite. Further and less elementary information could probably be gleaned in the appropriate department of the Providence Public Library. The word *eremite* represents the same etymology in purer form.

Second, regarding the term by which your kindly and delightful fellow-inhabitant of The Arsdale was described. The word was *ailurophile,* and signifies one who, like myself, possesses an extreme fondness for the feline species. It is, of course, derived from the Greek αἲλουϱος, a cat—this term meaning literally "wag-tail", from αἰόλος, quick-moving or changeable (cf. Αἴολος—Lat. Aeolus—the God of the Winds), and ὀυϱά, tail. (If it be objected that the felidae are not habitual tail-waggers, except in anger or disapproval, I respectfully refer you to Mr. John Perkins of The Arsdale, whose eloquent caudal appendage is in a constant state of gentle vivacity even when he is most contentedly rounding out a catnip gorge.) I cannot guarantee the presence of this word in Webster (I have no edition later than 1890, and this gives only the word *ailuroidea,* a zoölogical term signifying the general catlike group of carnivora), but it has in the last twelve years been greatly popularised by the amiable and innocuous Professor William Lyon Phelps in his "As I Like It" column of *Scribners* (vide periodical room, P.P.L.);[1] this eminent Victorian being himself enthusiastically ailurophilic.[2] The coinage of the word follows the most regular laws of philology—α ἲλουϱος, cat, and φιλέω, I love. Whether any single word α ἲλουϱόφιλος exists in Greek to signify "cat-lover" I am frankly ignorant. It is not, however, in the tattered unabridged Liddell and Scott which I inherited from my uncle. But if it did not exist in the classic Attic speech, this surely signifies a grave oversight on the part of the ancients. Professor Phelps' employment of this word took my attention most keenly when I first noticed in [*sic*] in 1924, since I had myself, through independent coinage, been habitually using it for years. Incidentally, I may remark that the word α ἲλουϱος figures in the name of the *Kappa Alpha Tau* fraternity of sleek old Toms which meets on the shed roof in the ex-Randall yard across the garden from my west windows.[3] Whilst the superficial tend to give a commonplace phonetic interpretation to the initials K.A.T., I always correct this error by informing them that the name really signifies Κομψῶν Αἲλουϱῶν Τάξις—i.e., a band or company of elegant or well-drest felidae. The dense ignorance of the majority is surprising and discouraging!

Third. The magnifier enclosed in my recent epistle was there by intention, not by mistake. I was acting upon a recent suggestion that such devices are necessary in decoding my ciphers, and shall probably include them in all outgoing non-typed mail. Most certainly, it was meant for permanent retention. I regret most profoundly that it did not prove efficacious in identifying *hermit* and *ailurophile*, and would suggest that a more powerful instrument be employed. Enclosed is an advertisement of an instrument which can scarcely fail to give satisfaction, and which may be obtained for the low price of only £6, 15s. from Messrs. James Swift & Son, 81, Tottenham Court Rd., London. With double nosepiece and extra eyepiece (15s. as quoted) and 0.1" oil immersion objective (£5), this device is guaranteed to unriddle even my postcards.

Fourth. I am extremely grateful for the correction of my humiliating error regarding the postal affiliations of The Arsdale. I had fancied that the village pust-office sarved all edifices belonging to the university corporation, but I now perceive my mistake with the utmost embarrassment.

Fifth. In writing fiction I employ a script similar in size to that in my epistles (as distinguished from postcards).

Sixth. I trust that the legibility of the present communication is above reproach. I have just cleaned the type of this venerable junk-pile (purchased July 6, 1906, as a rebuilt machine), and believe the ribbon still retains some pigment. I regret profoundly the absence of Greek letters from the keyboard, which perforce throws me back now and then upon the sputtering Parker.

In conclusion, I may add that my aunt enjoyed most profoundly the visit from you and Miss Staples this morning—a visit whose encouraging influence was perceptible when I called this afternoon. She appreciated particularly the floral tribute, which so admirably blended the elements of aesthetic appeal and salubrious nutrition.

With profoundest apologies for past cacographical offences,

Believe me, Madam,

Yr most oblig'd & obdt Servt,

/a/ H. P. Lovecraft

/t/ (H. P. LOVECRAFT)

Notes

1. I.e., the Providence Public Library.

2 See LDC/AEPG 93n7.

3. The Samuel N. Gerard house at 58 College, once owned by R. F. Randall. The Randalls had a black and white cat whom Lovecraft referred to as President Peter Randall, Esq., and a tiger-striped brother he called Stephen. When the Randall family moved, the cats did as well. Other members of the "fraternity" included a tiger, Vice-President Count Magnus Osterberg (whom Stephen Randall succeeded as vice-president), Peter Randall's successor, President Johnny Perkins (who would come to call on HPL), his brothers Vice-President Gilbert John Murray Kynymond Elliot, Earl of Minto, and Little Sam Perkins, and their mother, Mrs. Spotty Perkins.

[5] [TLS, JHL]

Dear Miss Bonner:—

The K. A. T. Executive Office is in receipt of your recent communication, and takes pleasure in replying to various points contained therein.

First: there *is* a word *hermitess,* which has been employed by no less illustrious a writer than the late Samuel T. Coleridge. It is, however, relatively rare; the preferred usage being to let *hermit* cover both genders—like the word *poet,* whose scope includes both sexes despite the parallel existence of the word *poetess.*

Second: [¶] The K.A.T. Educational Board extends no academic demerits for failure to identify *ailurophile,* since knowledge of the word is necessarily largely accidental. The Board is itself only a very intermittent follower of Grandma Phelps's[1] cheerful and well-bred column—and the word in question would not have stuck in its consciousness save that it happened to be the first printed occurrence of a coinage which the Board had devised on its own account during the first decade of the century.

Third: this Board disclaims all imputation of being a collector of "firsts". Indeed, no one could despise mere editions *as editions* more than said Board. We accumulate volumes for what is recorded in them—not for the date somebody happened to print them. Of all obtainable editions of a book, we would choose not the first but the last—which had the benefit of all the additions and revisions the author chose to make. In many cases bibliophily and literature are not merely unrelated but actually antagonistic—and I am among the keenest appreciators of Mr. Addison's 158th *Tatler* (for Thursday, April 13, 1710), wherein he gently ridicules the title-page pedantry of Tom Folio the Book Broker. The Board acknowledges with gratitude your invitation to inspect the attic shelves of the Arsdale, and hopes to be able to do so at no distant date. The Hoppin volume referred to, we imagine, is "Recollections of Auton House".[2] In our executive offices we have the original (and probably only edition) of Greene's "Old Grimes" (Sidney S. Rider, 1867) with *illustrations* by Augustus Hoppin.

Fourth: the ex-hermit or hermitess of Lockwood Street (whom we visited yesterday afternoon) retains the pleasantest recollections of your call of 1st inst., and wishes to extend particular thanks for cards received since then—notably the ichthyic specimen of yesterday. Nerve-shock has undoubtedly played a part in her case, but I think the tension is now greatly relaxing. I shall make renewed observations tomorrow.

Fifth: this board has not perused Mr. Walpole's "Inquisitor"—having been too congested with other business when the volume lay on the centre-table of the adjoining parlour. Indeed, we have virtually abandoned any attempt at contemporaneousness in our literary knowledge. Our correlated reading extends, perhaps, up to the middle 1920's. Some time we hope to compile from adequate sources a list of the really significant volumes issued since 1925—a list which would include such new figures as Thomas Wolfe, and the sociological novelists like Albert Halper[3]—and thus touch the high spots without wading through the underbrush.

Sixth: the Board probably will take in Professor Edman's lecture—the last of a notable series, of which the performances of Profs. Savery and Rothschild seem to have been the most brilliant to date.[4]

Seventh: congratulations on your debut in King Lear. As Regan you will be able to present some very unctuous hypocrisy. In my youth I was very fond of heavy and villainous parts, Richard III being beyond comparison my favourite.

Eighth: Anent the art of vessel-cleansing. No—most emphatically—accumulation is the *precise and antipodal reverse* of my lifelong policy. On the contrary, I cannot endure dealing with more than one item at a time, or using any medium save running water direct from the faucet. As fast as one vessel or implement is used, I cleanse it for re-use—never having in the house any soiled item except that from which—or with which—I am taking nourishment. Thus I use but one plate, one fork, one knife, one spoon, one cup, one saucer, and so on . . . . . washing and reëmploying as needed. This I consider the only civilised policy in the absence of a proper staff of servants—for a sink full of used and engreased objects is anathema to me. As once remarked, my policy is not uniformly endorsed at #66—but I nevertheless persist in it as far as possible. Thus, while appreciating in the extreme the philanthropick offer of yourself and the Chief Ailurophile to coöperate in an Augean-Stable ordeal, I am happy to state that the non-existence of any accumulation makes it needless for the Board to impose on your joint generosity. At this moment—and indeed at all moments save during meals—there is not a soiled dish or article of cutlery in the upper half of the Garden House!

Ninth: We extend congratulations on your first pedestrian tour as a Field Naturalist—though we ourselves would not relish the Great Outdoors quite so early in the season. 80 to 90 Fahrenheit is our optimum range, and below 70 we find progress distinctly uncomfortable. When we are not able to escape to more genial climes, Mid-May marks the opening of our river-bank and Quinsnicket season.

Tenth: the Board presumes you have duly ordered the "Discovery" microscope from Messrs. Swift & Son—but since the order is probably not yet filled, we are dictating the present bulletin to our staff of typists.

With the season's compliments we beg to subscribe ourselves
Most faithfully yours,
The Board of Education, Kappa Alpha Tau.
Per   /a/ H P Lovecraft /t/ (H. P. Lovecraft),
3d Assistant Under-Secretary.

Notes

1. HPL once described Phelps's speeches as "bland," hence the epithet used.

2. But see MFB 6.

3. Albert Halper (1904–1984), novelist and playwright, author of *Union Square* (1933), *Foundry* (1934), and *On the Shore* (1934) among others.

4. For Edman, see LDC/AEPG 368n40. William Briggs Savery (1875–1945) was a professor of philosophy at the University of Washington (1902–45) and a follower of George Santayana, William James, and John Dewey. Edward Francis Rothschild (1903–1937), Assistant Professor of the History of Art at the University of Chicago, was author of *The Meaning of Unintelligibility in Modern Art* (1934).

[6]   [ALS, JHL]

1, Ely's Court, Providence,
April 9, 1936

Dear Mifs Bonner:—

In acknowledging your bulletin of the 7th we wish to append the following bits of information concerning the current patient.

(a) We delivered to her on the 5th inst. the vernal boughs entrusted to us for that purpose—carrying them boldly through the following public thoroughfares: College, Benefit, Transit, South Main, Cent, Point, Eddy, & Lockwood Sts. No small boys jeered at us, being probably impressed with the punitive possibilities of our aesthetic burthen. The patient was properly delighted, & wished me to apprise you of that fact.

(b) On Tuesday, April 7, at 4 p.m., the patient left the gas-house district by motor to complete her convalescence at Dorcus Convalescent Home, 32, Blackstone Blvd. (cor Irving Ave.) (Tel. PL 3485), an extremely prepossessing private retreat whose domestic atmosphere & favourable situation ought to aid greatly in promoting rapid recovery. After a trial of a ground-floor room (which proved too noisy) the patient is now settled in a really delightful second-floor room at the front of the house, with a door leading out upon a screened private porch which commands a fine view of the boulevard. The edifice is a relique of the 1890's, but makes up in comfort what it lacks in taste. The patient, though missing the detailed & instantaneous service provided by the hospital, is getting to like it better & better—& indeed finds the cuisine even superior to Aunt Jane Brown's. When I called yesterday afternoon she seemed in fine shape indeed, & ate her dinner at a table while seated on the edge of the bed. She continues to welcome callers—the best hour being in the morning at any time after 10, & the second-best being in the afternoon betwixt 3 & 4. The mid-day period is devoted to a siesta—a habit she ought to continue after her return to the Garden House.

The K.A.T. Educational Board is pleased to note your stand on purely technical bibliophily, & takes pleasure in getting ahead of the P.P.L. in the matter of No. 158 of *The Tatler*. Despite non-membership in the K.A.T., no inhabitant of our President's home ought to be wholly deprived of our library privileges—& besides, if we recall aright, at least one representative of the rival institution has been notably generous in extending the latter's facilities to relatives of one of our under-secretaries. Hence, with unparalelled magnanimity, we have gone to the prodigious trouble of reaching up to Shelf vii, Case D, &

extracting the volume in question—which we herewith proffer as a loan, albeit
without any of our rival's chronological restrictions. No fines for overdueness
in case you are tempted to peruse more than the single account of Tom Folio.
We regret exceedingly that this tome includes only Mr. Addison's contributions to the *Tatler* & *Guardian*. Some time we hope to acquire complete sets of
both papers (we have *Spectator, Rambler, World,* & *Looker-On* complete, & possess an odd volume of *The Idler*),[1] since the essays of Sir Richard Steele are not
less fascinating than those of his celebrated contemporary. One of the objects
of our infant reading was an illustrated (by Hugh Thomson) book of Addison–Steele selections called "Days With Sir Roger de Coverley" (still on our
shelves), which probably did much toward giving us an 18th-century bias.

Your correction regarding the identity of the Hoppin item is accepted
with gratitude & belated recognition. To be sure A E P G let me see it—& I
now recall it well . . . . the annals of the whiskered Victorian beset by hay-fever,
who tried everything once, including aëronautics! My memory needs jogging
now—it isn't what it was back in the 90's! This volume is certainly a rare em-
bodiment of its age, & is worth guarding as an heirloom. I would surely never
part with my "Old Grimes"—which was given me by my late elder aunt some
years ago after an extremely clever renovation by a local bookbinder (W. E.
Horton,[2] 681 Westminster St.); it having been nearly ruined by mould whilst
in storage. I was then staying in Brooklyn, N.Y., & acknowledged the gift in
some lines whose anticlimactic spirit was suggested by the text itself:

Old *Theobald** for an elder Scene   To lovelier Scenes it leads his Feet,
   This garish Age is dropping;   By *Seekonk's* ſhady Rill;
The Verſes are by *A. G. Greene,*   For fixing up the Leaves ſo neat
   Cuts by *Auguſtus Hoppin.*   There muſt be quite a Bill!

His Gratitude no common Song   Thus ceaſing, left with ſoaring Aims
   With fitting Grace may found;   His thankful Throat ſhall burſt,
The Book, tho' muſty, ſtill is ſtrong,   He vows that *Horton* well reclaims
   And very well rebound.   What *Rider* publiſh'd firſt![3]

My mother used to *sing* "Old Grimes" to me 40 years ago, to the tune of
"Auld Lang Syne". Regarding early Rhodinsularia in general—the K.A.T. library also has Job Durfee's epic "What Cheer", & his son Tom's "The Village
Picnic & Other Poems"—both written in the still-standing colonial house at
the southward corner of Benefit & Jenckes Sts.[4]

Regarding the difference betwixt "mystery" & "fantastic" fiction, as these
terms are commonly used—I believe that by the former only *detective* tales &
their close congeners are usually meant. Some striking event or situation of
unknown cause, but with a natural explanation deductively reached, is the

---

*a pseudonym of mine, based on the "hero" of Pope's "Dunciad".

usual so-called "mystery" pattern. On the other hand *fantastic* fiction involves the impossible & incredible, admitting supernatural causation of every sort. It is, in its purest form, simply *the projection or crystallisation of a certain type of human mood.* Its truth is not to objective events, but only to human emotions. In this genre the greatest masters—in addition to Poe—are Algernon Blackwood, Lord Dunsany, Arthur Machen, Montague Rhodes James, Walter de la Mare, William Hope Hodgson, & to some extent the present incumbent of Lord Minto's erstwhile vice-regal seat at Ottawa.[5] Many of the finest specimens, though, are the work of writers who do not specialise in this field—for example, "The Turn of the Screw" by Henry James, & "The King in Yellow" by the late popular hack Robert W. Chambers.

As for *towers*—they do form a delectably appropriate setting for secluded scribblers of supernatural shockers, though their harmony with the architecture of the Garden House is distinctly doubtful. The only typical turriform structures of the Georgian age are *windmills* & *steeples.* I might emulate Henry Ford & import a windmill from Cape Cod or Aquidneck to set up in the garden beyond Ely's Court—& if I do so I shall certainly secure an owl or raven. Whether I could *keep* the latter would depend on how well he might get along with the K.A.T. boys.

Many thanks for the tip anent last Monday's *Time.* I'll try to get a look at it. If you like *words,* I presume you've read Trench's now venerable classic on the subject.[6]

With the hope that your "Discovery" microscope has arrived in time to untangle the foregoing hieroglyphs, I remain

Yr most ob[t] h[ble] Serv[t]

H P Lovecraft

Notes

1. HPL refers to some of the famous periodical essayists of the 18th century: Joseph Addison (1672–1719), Sir Richard Steele (1672–1729), et al., *The Spectator* (1711–14); Samuel Johnson (1709–1784), *The Rambler* (1750–52); Edward Moore (1712–1757) et al., *The World* (1753–57); William Roberts (1767–1849), *The Looker-On* (1792–94); Samuel Johnson, *The Idler* (1758–60). HPL had two different editions of *The Spectator* (see *LL* 11 and 12), along with a volume of selections edited by Thomas Arnold (*LL* 7). He had the complete *Rambler,* ed. Alexander Chalmers (1812 [4 vols.]; *LL* 517) and Vol. 1 of *Idler* (1803 [2 vols.]; *LL* 513). In the multivolume series *The British Essayists,* ed. Alexander Chalmers (1855–57 [38 vols.]; *LL* 131), HPL had Vols. 22–24 (*The World*) and 35–37 (*The Looker-On*), both published in 1856.

2. Walter Eugene Horton (1854–1938) worked as a bookbinder in Providence as early as 1878.

3. Published in *AT* as "[On *Old Grimes* by Albert Gorton Greene]."

4. See *The Case of Charles Dexter Ward*: "Farther and farther down that almost perpendicular hill he would venture, each time reaching older and quainter levels of the ancient city. He would hesitate gingerly down vertical Jenckes Street with its bank walls and colonial gables to the shady Benefit Street corner, where before him was a wooden antique with an Ionic-pilastered pair of doorways, and beside him a prehistoric gambrel-roofer with a bit of primal farmyard remaining, and the great Judge Durfee house with its fallen vestiges of Georgian grandeur."

5. John Buchan (1875–1940), 1st Baron Tweedsmuir, whose *The Runagates Club* and other weird works HPL admired. He was governor-general of Canada (1935–40).

6. See MFB 7.

[7]   [ALS, JHL][1]

April 17, 1936

Dear Mifs Bonner:—

Sight of the patient, up, dressed, around, & alert is surely a heartening thing—& the homelike atmosphere of the Dorcus promotes the effect. I may add with pleasure that on Tuesday the 14th—when there was a bit of sun—she took her first *outdoor walk*, looking up Slater Ave. & reorienting herself to the outside world. She will probably be home next week—an event welcomed equally by the K.A.T. & by herself.

The fraternity is greatly flattered by your commendation of its second issue of stationery, though it entertains no extravagant illusions concerning the artistic value of the designs. So far as drawing goes, we consider the drawing of regular pay a far rarer & less easily attainable feat in this age! We are, however, glad that Pres. Perkins & the chief Ailurophile were given an opportunity to inspect the work.

We duly appreciate the distinction betwixt *fines* & *charges* (as betwixt *penalties* & *sanctions*, or betwixt *barber-shops* & *tonsorial laboratories*), but are happy to repeat that our library imposes neither. Mr. Addison is at your complete disposal for an indefinite period, & I can lend you more of him if you like—including a set of his miscellaneous works (poems—the play "Cato", &c.) published in 1774. He surely did have ideas as well as style, & a perusal of all his essays will disclose more than one apparently modern notion! I surely regret the loss of your paternal library, & wish you could have managed to retain it. Some volumes have been eliminated from the books I have inherited, but there is a certain nucleus to which I adhere more tenaciously than to any other possessions. Durfee's poems ("Village Picnic" &c) & Trench's "Study of Words" are at your disposal at any time. The latter is something of a classic—& the Garden House contains at least two copies, one in the K.A.T. library & the other in the patient's. You must indeed examine the bibliotheca some time, for it may contain many an item worth borrowing. Not but what its marble rival next door—or its granite rival a square down the hill[2]—or very possibly the P.P.L.—could parallel a good many of its items—but we at least allow the unique privilege of overdueness without *charges*.

Let me thank you most abundantly for the "Bekes"—to use our local colloquialism (based on the sketchy phonetic value of the signatory initials) for the diurnal columnar essays of Bertrand Kelton Hart, Esq. I always peruse these with extreme pleasure when they are passed down to me—& I, in turn, pass them along to a learned friend of mine in the distant metropolis of Milwaukee. He—a teacher of English in the West Division High School—uses many of them as a basis of classroom exercises, saves many in a scrap book, & constantly carries a pocketful for reading in odd moments. He has come, after many years, to measure distance by "Bekes". Thus the trolley trip from his home downtown is 2 Bekes. The train ride from Milwaukee to Chicago is 10 Bekes, &c. He is coming east next summer, & I expect to see him in person after many years. When he does I shall ask him the distance in Bekes from Milwaukee to Providence. I shall use my judgment about letting the patient read this batch—or rather, I guess I'll use *her* judgment. Since she recently looked over 3 weeks of N.Y. Times Supplements, & is now perusing Santayana's "Last Puritan", I fancy a mere month of Bekes might not be very formidable. But she shall herself be the arbiter of that point.

That cutting on *locality words* is highly interesting. I have noticed marked local differences of phrase, vocabulary, & speech-rhythm in different parts of the country—& sometimes within relatively narrow limits. Popular versions of quotations vary locally. In the Middle West Burke's famous phrase "chip of the old Block" (applied to the younger Pitt) is commonly rendered "chip *off* the old Block", &c. In New York any ordinary large cheese of the old-time non-tinfoil sort is called "*store* cheese" by dealers. &c. &c. Rhode Island is the most conservative of all the states of the Union in retaining original usages. Nowhere else in America does "Intelligence Office" still signify an exchange for the securing of domestic servants . . . . & we alone habitually pronounce correctly such names as Greenwich, Warwick, & Olney. Even in Massachusetts one repeatedly hears *War-wick, Öl-ney,* &c.

The address of Prof. Edman was very well editorialised—despite the proofreader's determination to place a superfluous *r* in the speaker's name. I enjoyed the event, even though half-frozen by the auditorium's defective heating. Other recent addresses of interest were those of Prof. Robinson on late archaic Greek art, & of Prof. Taylor on the Mayan ruins.

Why did I traverse *Cent St.* in reaching Aunt Jane's from here? Atmosphere? Not at all. The reason is extremely prosaic. It is the *shortest cut* from S. Main to the Point St. Bridge for the southbound pedestrian! This I soon learned in 1933, during my first period of habitual travel to South Providence.[3] Congratulations on your hardihood in public hat transportation. I, too, have conveyed grotesque loads in my day—yet am none the worse for it.

Aye, it is indeed lonely without ex-President Peter Randall—& his tiger brother Stephen, who so closely resembled the late Count Magnus Osterberg. Even now I occasionally forget their departure, & look expectantly at the clubhouse roof to see if any of my old friends are there. Old Peter was always like me—never visible in cold weather! He, by the way, was the first living being I ever saw in these ancient gardens, when exploring them three years ago with a view to future tenancy. In those days he fled at my approach—but in time he came to know & tolerate the other old gent, & would purr & roll over when Grandpa drew nigh . . . still imbued with some sportive recollection of his long-vanished kittenhood. And *what* a kitten he must have been, with that white spot at the tip of his tail!

You surely ought to see the ancient Durfee house at Benefit & Jenckes—fallen though it is from its once high estate. That eastward-running blind alley is surely fascinating—as is, indeed, the entire street. I wish it might be reclaimed as John St. was a decade or so ago—or as, at an earlier period, Pinckney St. in Boston was. Yes—& Stoll's Alley & parts of Church St. in Charleston. One of the issues of *The Netopian* (late publication of R.I. Hospital Trust Co.) had an excellent illustrated article on Benefit St.—which our library has at your disposal if you wish to consult it.[4]

Pray congratulate Pres. Perkins upon his delineation of the 3d Asst. Under-Secretary. He remembers more of my history than you do, for when I was the approximate age of the portrait I actually *did* wear glasses continuously (I wear 'em *now* for continuous middle-distance gazing, as at an illustrated lecture or theatrical performance). It was only about a decade ago that I discovered I could leave them off without acquiring (as formerly) headache & dizziness—& I promptly took advantage of that discovery, since the confounded things always were a nuisance. In these latter days my sight isn't what it used to be, & I keep fearing I'll have to go back to continuous four-eyedness. But I'll stave it off as long as I can! Oh, yes—& tell Mr. Perkins that I always heed the admonition subjoined to the portrait.

I am now starting out for 32 Blackstone, & will duly convey your regards to the patient. Incidentally, if you noticed the architecture of her present habitat (I prefer *not* to notice the architecture of Victorian structures), you will realise that she is now living in the next room to a *tower* even though not in the stately Norman turret itself. Around 1890 American architects thought there was nothing smarter to do than to put into small wooden houses the lines which were meant to belong to monumental stone chateaux—& to mix & debase those lines until only a keen & tolerant observer could recognise the lineage! Fortunately this seigneurial pile is a merely temporary residence—for, as previously mentioned, a few days will bring the objective realisation of your recent dream.

Extending the most appropriately urbane purrs,

I have the Honour to fubfcribe my felf,

Madam,

Your moft oblig'd, moft obᵗ Servt.

H. P. Lovecraft

Notes

1. The images on this "stationery" were designed by R. H. Barlow.

2. The marble edifice is the John Hay Library, the granite the Providence Athenaeum at 251 Benefit Street.

3. The Jane Brown building (1922) of Rhode Island Hospital is on the grounds at 593 Eddy Street.

4. The *Netopian* 10, No. 7 (January 1930) contained "Looking Backward through the Years on Benefit Street" (7, 10–11) and "On Benefit Street, Providence, May Be Found Some of Rhode Island's Most Characteristic Colonial Architecture" (8–9).

[8]   [ALS, JHL]

Dear Mifs Bonner:—

The fraternity indeed rejoices at the return of the Garden House's long-absent chatelaine, & will welcome the time when the recent ordeal shall have retreated to the domain of the fabulous & half-forgotten.

Meanwhile it reiterates its appreciation of the part played by your cheering messages in sustaining the spirits of the ex-patient.

Turning to recent topics in logical order—pray extend my sincerest gratitude to Pres. Perkins for his appointment of me as Official Limner of the local K.A.T. chapter. I shall proceed with the initial task—the portraits of all the members—just as soon as I can induce the latter (including the restless executive himself) to grant me suitable sittings. The list of suggested poses has been very carefully filed, & is most profoundly appreciated. Some are capable of very diverse treatment—thus *cat-a-comb* may signify either something like the Canal St. Station of the B.M.T. subway in New-York, or some process like that which my Florida friend Barlow applies to his Persian companions Cyrus & Darius when their acquisitive interest in entomology seems excessive. Regarding our letter-head #3—this same Barlow, rather than the local limner, must be held responsible for its pictorial designs; the latter being impressions of linoleum cuts fashioned by his skilful young hands. As you infer, the right-hand panel consists of hieroglyphs interpretable only by members of the fraternity. The *lettering* involves the resurrection from my autobiographical museum of two rubber-stamp alphabets which formed my pride & joy some 40 years ago. Many of my earlier works—such as "Wilkes's Explorations" (1902), "Ross's Explorations" (1902), "Antarctic Atlas" (1903), & "Astronomy" (1903),[1] have title-pages printed from these old reliable devices, & I never could bear to discard them. To the best of my knowledge, the recent letter-head forms the first impressions made from these alphabets since the year 1904. In order to anticipate questions regarding the awkward outlines of the *K*, let me state that this letter was perforce formed by the superimposition of *I* upon the western half of *X* . . . a makeshift necessitated by the regrettable loss of *K* from the font at some unknown period. (cf. the humorously-intended sketch by Poe,* entitled "X-ing a Paragrab")[2] Incidentally—whilst in the disclaiming business—let me state with sorrowful candour that I am *not* the designer of my bookplate. Would that I *could* draw like that! The artist in this case is my young friend Wilfred B. Talman, Esq., of Spring Valley, N.Y. (who, by the way, has studied here at Brown & the School of Design)—now assistant editor of a group of four trade papers (does the P.P.L. handle such things as *The Texaco Star* &c.?) for the olefic Texas Co., & having an office on the 18th floor of Manhattan's Chrysler Bldg.

Turning to the next point: (a) I have used exclamation-points several times during a long life. (b) *confounded* is by no means a strong word for me to use once I am involved in a really vigorous argument. Under suitable provocation, the K.A.T. vocabulary is the very reverse of lacteal . . . . as strange fe-

---

*whilst we think of it, pray convey our thanks to your colleague Mr. Sherman, whose thoughtful postal regarding the article in *Am. Lit.* was duly received & hope to act upon.

lidae & canidae used to discover when they rudely invaded the fence-top isolation of the late Count Magnus Osterberg.

Regarding the possible transmission of my recent 'Beke' remarks to that sprightly essayist himself—I'm sure I have no possible objection . . . nor do I think that Maurice Winter Moe, Esq., of Milwaukee, would object in the least to the identification of the scene of his labours. The outline of your Bekeward note seems eminently adequate—the signature supplying the needed touch of sprightliness. Incidentally, the erudite Zythopolitan[3] himself—in contributing to R. H. L.'s (formerly B. L. T.'s) "Line o' Type" in the *Chicago Tribune*[4]— signs with the compact trisyllable *Mawimo*. Such is the brevity of human memory—among the busy—that Beke is not likely to identify Mawimo from the present allusion, though as a matter of fact he has heard directly from him. Back in 1929–31 I exchanged a few letters with Beke myself, in the course of which I mentioned Moe's interest. Later—during a period when Beke was discussing folk balladry *in extenso*—Mawimo sent him several specimens current in pioneer Wisconsin, though those were neither printed nor acknowledged. By this time Beke has doubtless forgotten both Moe & myself. For a while, though, I was one of The Sideshow's prominently noticed freaks— as you may gather from the accompanying cuttings[5] (all of which please return some time). These yellowed parchments of yesteryear speak for themselves— telling of how I butted into a discussion of weird fiction, & how (in connexion with my tale "The Call of Cthulhu") a really amazing coincidence developed.[6] My aunt was very grateful for the recent bunch of Bekes, all of which she devoured with avidity. She informs me that your adventurous pedestrian organisation will invade the bibliotaph's aestival country-seat during the ensuing months—a report indeed confirmed by his own 'colyum'.

As to the manner in which I used to rant & rave through such passages as

> "What! fhall th' afpiring Blood of *Lancafter*
> Sink in the Ground? I thought it wou'd have mounted!
> See how my Sword weeps for the poor King's Death!
> O, may fuch purple Tears be alway fhed
> From thofe that wifh the downfall of our Houfe!
> If any Spark of Life be yet remaining,
> Down, down to Hell, and fay I fent thee thither!"[7]

. . . . I believe I dwelt more upon the metrical form than the moderns are accustomed to encourage. I was a heavy tragedian of the old school, & verse was verse so far as I was concerned. I was not insensible of the demands of the meaning, yet the *rhythm* would never leave my subconsciousness. Not that I made a real pause after each line (Lancaster, shed, &c), but that I realised the pause myself so fully as to make a microscopic difference in the rendering. I also gave the pronoun *my* its old-fashion'd value "me" or "mih" when it did not call especial attention to the quality of possession—as recommended in Walker's (18th cent.) Rhetorical Grammar. Thus in the above, I would ironically & leeringly whine

"See how *mih* Sword weeps for the poor King's death!"

Ah, me—tragedy isn't what it was when I was young! Nowadays we hear young whippersnappers preaching quiet, realistic technique, & frowning on the vigorous, orotund delivery that Booth, Barrett,[8] & I used to sling from the stage of Forbes' Theatre, Swarts Hall, Harrington's Opera House, & the Providence Opera House!

"Hence, babbling Dreams! Ye threaten here in vain!
Confcience, avaunt—*Richard's* himfelf again!
Hark! the fhrill Trumpet founds—to Horfe, away!
My* Soul's in Arms, and eager for the Fray!"[9]

I am astonished to hear that the newer generations in Rhode-Island are forgetting the proper pronunciation of *Warwick*—but I suppose I would en-counter the error if I saw more of the public. In my day, a person who would say *War-wick* would be likely to say *Gay'-no* Street—or *West-min-i-ster*—or *El-lumgrove Ave*. But alas

—"Dociles imitandis
Turpibus et pravis omnes sumus."[10]

Possibly I mentioned that one of the features of a revision job I am doing is the compilation of a list of 100 or more words commonly mispronounced.[11] A little reflection revealed many score more than could possibly be used! My own guide to pronunciation is generally Stormonth—the dictionary used by my father.

My aunt pointed out your old home yesterday, when we took a walk to see the Carrington house.[12] That locality is a favourite of mine, & I share your rejoicing in its restoration during the past decade. No part of Providence is more delightful & unspoiled, nor could one guess from the immediate envi-ronment that a large city stretched around that idyllic village scene. The Car-rington estate is extremely fascinating. We went into the inner courtyard—quaint & cobblestoned—where I had never been before. It is a veritable world apart, surviving from the great maritime age. I am eager for the public opening of the house as a museum—which really ought to be speeded up in order to coincide with the tercentenary celebration.[13]

---

*mih

Yes—my general ocular trouble is short sight, coupled with a muscular maladjustment in the left eye. I hope fervently that I shall not again be driven into the full-time wearing of spectacles.

Under separate cover—or rather, under no cover at all—I am lending the two volumes recently mentioned . . . Trench on the Study of Words, & Tom Durfee's "Village Picnic". No hurry about return—& no fi—er—*charges* in case of retention beyond some theoretical time limit. ¶ Extending the most respectful Compliments, I am, Madam,

Your moft obᵗ hble Servt—

H P Lovecraft—3d Aſst Under-Sec K.A.T.

Notes

1. HPL refers to some of his early scientific works. The first three are small treatises; they are nonextant. *Astronomy* (sometimes combined with *The Monthly Almanack*) was a monthly magazine of which seven issues survive (Aug. 1903–Feb. 1904).

2. Clarence Edgar Sherman (1887–1974), who succeeded William E. Foster as head librarian of the Providence Public Library in 1930, after Foster had served in that position for fifty-three years.

3. Denizen of "Zythopolis," HPL's coined Greek word for "Beer-town," or Milwaukee.

4. "A Line O' Type or Two" was a popular column in the *Chicago Tribune*, edited by Bert Leston Taylor (1866–1921) until his death, followed by Richard Henry Little (1869–1946).

5. B. K. Hart, "The Sideshow," *Providence Journal*. The clippings HPL provided are unknown, but likely are of the following columns: 101, No. 280 (23 November 1929): 2; 101, No. 281 (25 November 1929): 2; 101, No. 286 (30 November 1929): 10.

6. Hart had read HPL's "The Call of Cthulhu" in *Beware After Dark!* and was struck by the fact that the Fleur-de-Lys building at 7 Thomas Street in Providence, which Hart himself had once occupied, was where the artist Henry Anthony Wilcox lived in the story.

7. Shakespeare, *3 Henry VI* 5.6.61–67.

8. HPL refers to the celebrated stage actors Edwin Booth (1833–1893) and Lawrence Barrett (1838–1891).

9. The text derives from the 1699 adaptation of Shakespeare's *Richard III* by Colley Cibber (1671–1757), at the end of Act 5, Scene 5.

10. Juvenal, *Satires* 14.40–41: "We are all inclined toward imitating base and wicked things."

11. Anne Tillery Renshaw, *Well Bred Speech*.

12. Edward Carrington House (1810; 1812), 66 Williams Street. John Corliss built the

original two-story part of the house in 1810. In 1936, Margarethe Dwight, a descendant of Carrington, gave the house and many of its furnishings to the Museum of Art, Rhode Island School of Design, as a museum showing the influence of the China trade in New England. It was sold to private owners in 1961.

13. HPL refers to the tercentenary of the founding of Rhode Island (1636–1936).

[9]   [ALS, JHL]

> The Garden House,
> 1, Ely's Court,
> Providence-Plantations
> 4th May, 1936

Dear Mifs Bonner:—

The K.A.T. takes pleasure in acknowledging yrs. of 1st inst. with enclosures, as well as the safe return of archaic Bekes (thanks for repair material thoughtfully enclosed) & of Tho: Durfee's "Village Picnic". We likewise appreciate the marked article in the *Atlantic* on the exclamatory style[1]—an article of added interest by reason of our having met Mr. Devoe (then a somewhat affected youth with important-looking rudimentary side-whiskers) in New-York in the year 1928.

We rejoice that the early Bekes proved of interest, but regret to say that the K.A.T. anthology of horrors still remains unedited. As for a bibliography—we do indeed keep a record of such *stories* as we think good enough to remember, but of nothing else—since all our verse & other minor mewings may at once be classed as negligible. We would, indeed, be well-nigh willing to pay blackmail to keep such miscellany out of the sight of the keenly critical. Every now & then we go over our list of tales & strike out such as we are no longer willing to recognise. The last deletion left some 47 in the catalogue, but about ten of these will probably succumb very shortly to the growing critical severity of the author's old age. We strive never to forget the sound advice given by Mr. Q. H. Flaccus a couple of millennia ago—

"Vir bonus et prudens versus reprobandet inertes;
Culpebit duros; incomptis allinet atrum
Transverso calamo signum . . . ."[2]

No—our macabre metrical reply to Beke's spectral threat is not to be found in the rival institution across the fence . . . . indeed, we are one of the few American poets *not* represented* in the justly celebrated Harris Collection.[3] Regarding your projected epistle to Beke—we really see no reason why it should not be sent. Beke probably recalls neither Mawimo nor ourself—& even if he did, he would be unlikely to connect the idea of Bekes as a linear unit with two nebulous figures of the dim past. In these sunset years we have about given up the habit of bombarding 'colyums' with communications; so that unless the contemplated note goes forward, the public is likely never to learn of the metric system's potential successor. Regarding the columnar announcement of your coming pilgrimage—permit me to reverse the order of donation & enclose the item you overlooked. We appreciate most heartily the invitation to accompany the erstwhile patient & your genial band on the Joyeuse Garde[4] expedition, & trust that nothing (unless some miracle sends us Charlestonward or Floridaward) may prevent us from accepting. No—the K.A.T. has never been there (although last week we were driven along the so-called "Drift Road" near Westport Point & told that Joyeuse Garde lay at some undetermined point betwixt the highway & the sea), nor has it ever met Beke in person. As to the tale of mine referred to by Beke but not named—I can't exactly place the reference, but if you mean the praise so charitably given in the column discussing De la Mare's anthology,[5] I must confess that I don't know what tale drew it forth. I really have not the least idea how many things of mine Beke has read—but I doubt if he can have seen many. Under separate cover, as per request, is "The Outsider" (in an issue of W T)—which can be returned at your leisure. I don't think much of this early attempt, for it is deplorably melodramatic & mechanical—but it happened to please the youth who drew up one of the lists for Beke.† This youth (August W. Derleth), by the way, is now making headway as a serious author—getting ahead of the old gentleman whom he once so kindly commended! Concerning the spontaneity of Bekes, ancient & modern—I fancy the 1929–30 specimens had a fresh vitality & enthusiasm, & a certain authenticity of substance, which isn't so often met with in 1935–6. No fountain can be perennially inexhaustible; & if Beke's sprightliness & anecdotage seem now & then a little forced & unctuous in recent years, I can say only that he is, at his worst, a darned sight cleverer than I could ever be at my best!

---

*except, perhaps, by junk in magazines which the collection has.
†I'll wager Beke has never seen the story himself. If he had, he wouldn't think much of it.

Does the K.A.T. Library have a Dept. of Fantasy? (I don't know of any word on the order of "Americana" or "Shakespeariana" which quite covers the broad field including supernatural horror-fiction and its penumbra[.]) Yes—in a measure, it does. Not so much a deliberate collection as a spontaneous growth—but enough to catalogue, anyhow. It is, indeed, the only section of John Hay's competitor which *is* catalogued*—this listing being for the benefit of distant members of the "weird fiction gang" who wish to borrow spectral volumes not obtainable in their home-town bibliothecae. Enclosed is a copy of the list[6]—any item on which is at your disposal if your interest & curiosity run in this direction. You will recognise many titles as standard classics—"Udolpho", "The Monk", "Melmoth", &c. Regarding our own attempts—there is no single rule of composition. Some are 'dashed off', some are mentally planned ahead, & some involve endless correction & pen-chewing. The more laboured they are, the worse they generally turn out to be. No—we are never scared of the dark *now*, though we used to be prior to 1895 or '96. Our grandfather cured us of this tendency by daring us (when our years numbered approximately 5) to walk through certain chains of dark rooms in the fairly capacious old home at 454 Angell. Little by little our hardihood increased—& by the time we graduated from the fully-inhabited 2nd floor to the merely servant-&-store-&[-]guest-room-occupied *3d* floor, we were reasonably hard-boiled so far as the Amorphous Entities of Shadow were concerned. *Actual nightmares*, though, were another story. We still have 1 or 2 per year—though even the worst is pallid beside the real 1896 product. I invented the name of NIGHT-GAUNTS for the Things I dreamed of in '96 & '97.[7]

Concerning old Providence street-names—we are likely to blunder as badly as the average sap, though in the '90's we were an assiduous devotee of the contemporary Sampson-Murdock & Pabodie products.[8] Assuredly, we are far from formidable—& indeed, were a list of the books we *ain't* read to be compiled, we would lose whatever residual aura of grim authoritativeness may still cluster around our pompous facade! ¶ We used to like "Swiss F. R.", though hopelessly overawed by the unfailing competence of the castaways. At one time we had the much inferior sequel "Willis the Pilot"—but this seems to have disappeared from the shelves in the course of repeated eliminations.[9] ¶ I shall surely welcome the temporary accessibility of 'the most elegant private mansion on this continent', and only wish it were permanent![10]

Yr. moſt oblig'd & obt. Servt ¶ H. P. Lovecraft—
3d Asst. Under-Secy.—K.A.T.

---

*That is, catalogued *now*. Between 1903 & 1911 I tried to maintain a *general* catalogue of my library.

P.S. The list of words frequently mispronounced is part of a school text-book—"Well Bred English"—which I am revising & expanding for the author. If I ever get it done, it will probably be published in the autumn or winter. I picked up a fine acquisition for the list the other night at that Edman lecture—when a man behind me said *sŏn'-o-rous*. It occurred to me that I had heard that before from reasonably educated persons—hence I set it down as sufficiently typical. A correspondent has just suggested *ev-i-dent'-ly*—but I'm not sure how typical this is. Another part of the job is a list of 50 current *stock phrases* to be avoided.

[P.]P.S. The idea of a course in Franklin is surely interesting, although there was always something a bit bourgeois & tradesmanlike about the thrifty sage. I've never read Mather's "Essays to do Good", although I have an hereditary copy of his famous "Magnalia Christi Americana" printed in 1703. I've also read his "Wonders of the Invisible World"—which, as well as the Magnalia, has some fair source-material for weird tales. My "Unnamable" was founded on a passage in the Magnalia. ¶ Have never seen Byron's verses on Pitcairn's Island[11]—such not being in the family copy.

Notes

The coat of arms that HPL has drawn is based on his own, which had instead of cats' heads three foxes' heads.

1. Alan Taylor Devoe, "The Exclamation Point Style," *Atlantic Monthly* 157, No. 5 (May 1936): 581–82.

2. Horace (Q. Horatius Flaccus, 65–8 B.C.E.), *Ars Poetica* 445–47: "A friendly Critic, when dull Lines move slow, / Or harshly rude, will his Resentment show; / Will mark the blotted Pages, and efface / What is not polish'd to its highest Grace" (tr. Philip Francis).

3. The Harris Collection of American Poetry and Plays at the John Hay Library, one of the world's greatest collections of such material.

4. "Joyeuse Garde" was Bertrand K. Hart's home at 787 Pine Hill Road, built in 1820 and also known as Buttonwood Farm, in the town of Westport, MA. The John Hay Library of Brown University possesses a hand-drawn Christmas card by Hart depicting his house, with verses beginning "From Joyeuse Garde, now waiting snow . . ." The reason he adopted the epithet for his home is not known, but the Chateau de Joyeuse Garde is a ruined castle in Brittany associated with the Arthurian legend.

5. In discussing *They Walk Again: An Anthology of Ghost Stories* (1931), ed. Colin de la Mare (son of Walter), Hart concluded, "What has become of my mentor in these matters, up in Barnes street? I want his verdict on the wisdom and probity of this selection." "The Sideshow," *Providence Journal* (10 November 1931): 14.

6. "Weird &c. Items in Library of H. P. Lovecraft" (printed in *LL*). Other roughly similar lists appear in letters to Robert Bloch, Clark Ashton Smith, and others.

7. Mentioned in *The Dream-Quest of Unknown Kadath* (1926–27) and *Fungi from Yuggoth* (1929–30).

8. Sampson-Murdock was publisher of the standard Providence city directories. C. A. Pabodie & Son published maps.

9. Johann David Wyss (1743–1818), *Der schweizerische Robinson* (1812), first translated into English as *The Family Robinson Crusoe* (1816) and subsequently titled *The Swiss Family Robinson* (1824f.). *Willis the Pilot: A Sequel to The Swiss Family Robinson; or, Adventures of an Emigrant Family Wreck* (1858), is probably not by Wyss.

10. John Quincy Adams's description of the John Brown House at 52 Power St. HPL visited the house in June 1936.

11. "The Island" (1823).

[10]   [ALS, JHL]

Κ ομ ψ Ω N
Α ι λ ο υ ρ Ω N
Τ α ξ ι ς
Εἰς τὴν Βιβλιοθήκην

May 22, 1936

Dear Miſs Bonner:—

Permit me to acknowledge with utmost gratitude, on behalf of the Historical MS. Dept. of the K.A.T. Library, the Providence street notes so kindly transcribed. These settled a long-standing controversy in the 3d. Asst. Under-Secretary's household (& in said 3d A.U.S.'s favour) regarding the inclusion of *S. Angell St.* in the line of the original *Angell.* The limited length of Thayer St., the location of the "North Pumps", the former name of the avenue on whose Angell St. corner I was born, the date of Prospect Alley's naming—all these things proved of the keenest interest. But the library regrets to say that its staff has so far been unable to identify *Friend St.* Could it be *Hope?* I cannot be sure at the moment when the latter was named, or whether its entire length always bore the same name. Part of it was always a path or road, originally forming (with Meeting, Angell, & S. Angell) the Indian route from the bay to the Seekonk—& also forming the rear boundary of the settlers' long, thin home lots.

Another failure of our sadly inefficient staff relates to the often-referred-to poem of Mrs. Whitman on the busts atop the John Brown gates in Power St. Our edition of Mrs. W's poems—a posthumous one issued in the 1890's & said to be the fullest single collection in print[1]—contains nothing of this kind, & we have at the moment no clue to its discovery. When the coming of a little leisure permits me to enquire at other libraries, we may be able to solve the mystery. But at present we are stumped.

Adverting to matters described as "amazing"—we may say that our non-personal-acquaintance with B.K.H. is merely a typical example of our traditional policy of unobtrusiveness. The canidae bark & fawn & slobber over eminent persons on every possible occasion—but we felidae keep to our policy of non-encroachment, & continue to walk our fence-tops independently & unexcitedly until we have some definite & specific reason for exchanging purrs with the King Toms of the neighbouring fences. Certain young friends of ours[2] have written to dignitaries like H. G. Wells, Machen, Dunsany, &c., & have spent good postage mailing copies of their first books (usually printed at their own expense) to Santayana, the late Mr. Kipling, the late George Sterling, H. L. Mencken, & other high lights—including the book departments of all the leading newspapers & magazines. Not so the members of the Kappa Alpha Tau. We appreciate the great, but we are sceptical of their possible interest in our crude attempts. It is wiser, we think, to keep our minds on those attempts themselves. Time enough to know the great when our work speaks for itself & spontaneously attracts their notice . . . & if it never does that, we are just as well off in our merciful obscurity.

No—weeding out poor work is not a very painful process. Far more painful is the ordeal of beholding a stilted, bombastic piece of junk & being forced to admit that one wrote it oneself. Now & then the magazine *Weird Tales* drags out some early atrocity which I have long since repudiated, & reprints it for the benefit of a gaping yokelry. I can't stop them—for they own the copyright. But in such cases I thank the dark gods Nyarlathotep & Yog-Sothoth that relatively few civilised persons ever see *Weird Tales!*

The modernity—or, rather, the timelessness—of Mr. Flaccus is assuredly a striking phenomenon. It is not a matter of chance that he has been more quoted, parodied, & imitated in all ages than any other poet of antiquity. Though he dealt much in surfaces—thus appealing more to the urbane than to the intense—he had that *curiosa felicitas* which instinctively prompted him to choose such surfaces as are most universal, & most persistent amidst mutations & metamorphoses. That first satire against misers is assuredly as timely in 1936 as in B.C. 36—for both ages represent an economic crisis in which the concentration of wealth has produced an impasse requiring new & drastic remedies & a readjustment of perspective & ideology.

Congratulations are due you for your recent dramatic achievements, & I trust that critics hailed your Regan with suitable respect. Poor old Lear! The elder gals gave him a raw deal, but one cannot refrain from thinking that he was a bit naive to expect them to live up to their protestations.

The library list came safely back—& any of the items on it are at your disposal if they seem to promise interest. Many thanks for the additional orthoëpic boners—*tex-tyle* & *ävvyation*—both of which I have appreciatively entered on the list. Someone else recently suggested *e-quit' -a-ble* & *con' -trast* (as a verb)—but I am in doubt as to the *typical* nature of these slips. Regarding *sŏn'-o-rous*—I have not been able to find any authority for it, either in Stormonth or in the columns of variant pronunciations prefixed to my 1890 Webster. Other dictionaries might yield different results. At any rate, this pronunciation seems to possess a wide unofficial currency.

Stock phrases are hackneyed or "bromidic" expressions . . . . . "wend one's way", "the psychological moment", "all Nature rejoices", "easier said than done", "trip the light fantastic", "wee, small hours", &c. &c. &c. Their elimination is one of the first necessities of a good style. No—the term does not signify syntactically *incorrect* phrases. I presume the meaning is that such expressions are cheap, common, ready-made devices always kept in *stock* for the use of the unoriginal & the unimaginative.

I duly conveyed your sympathy to the dental victim—but perhaps she has had a chance to apprise you that her ordeal has not as yet been unduly formidable. Her activity increases. We have been to see the Old Providence pictures by Henry J. Peck at the Art Club, & have walked around the more southerly portions of the ancient hill in quest of the scenes of some of them. Peck catches the spirit of Old Providence as cleverly & consistency [*sic*] as any artist I can think of, & I have been an admirer of his work since his first exhibition in 1928.[3]

[Marginal note:] Many thanks for Bekes enclosed. My elder aunt was a Trollope devotee. I shall probably read "Honey in the Horn"[4] in 1946 if living.

The K.A.T. president & vice-president seem to bear up well despite the absence of the Chief Ailourophile—indeed, they are sometimes so lively in their garden gambols that it's rather hard for an old man to catch them! They both paid me a visit not long since—indeed, I wish they might decide to adopt #66 as one of their major clubhouses!

As for the *casual* mention of Florida*—we have learned with the years to regard all things casually. One is then less disappointed when they fail to materialise . . . as the spoken-of Florida trip will probably fail. In my youth I regarded a journey to the end of the Dyer Ave. car line (I recall the white cars that exchanged the grip for horses at the foot of the hill—& the transformation of those cars to electric power & dark green hue in 1894. The old open horse cars were spliced together—1½ of them making one of the rebuilt open cars numbered from 101 to 115 & used on Dyer Ave. & Plainfield St. routes. The closed cars of '94 on these lines were new—first a series numbered from 7 or 8 to the late teens & having no iron posts from dasher to hood, & then [these being transferred to Governor & Brook Sts.] a series with iron posts numbered from the late 20's through the 30's. All this equipment remained in use till the opening of the tunnel in Aug. 1914) as an event. In middle age a ride to East Greenwich or Buttonwoods or Taunton seemed about the same . . . as did a trip to Boston. By 1922 or 23 it took a trip to

---

*from which, if we ever reach it, we shall surely send a typically overcrowded card.

New Hampshire or New York to impart a sense of adventurous exploration. And now I never feel really started till I have reached Washington or Newport, Vt., or some such place. As I go southward, Olneyville & New York coalesce into a single (& not very favourable) impression, & Philadelphia is what Cranston Print Works used to be. Richmond is like Buttonwoods, & Charleston or Florida is like the end of the old Sea View line . . . through Narragansett Pier & Peacedale & Wakefield. Alas that the economics of transportation have called a halt to this progressive expansion of orbit & ideas! ¶ With renew'd expressions of gratitude for the street list &c., Yr most obt Servt

    H P Lovecraft 🐈

Notes

The epigram in the drawing means "In the library."

1. HPL refers to the poem "A Bunch of Grapes," which can be found in Whitman's *Poems* (Boston: Houghton, Osgood & Co., 1879), 178–80.

2. HPL has in mind in particular August Derleth and RHB.

3. Henry J. Peck (1880–1964) published *Glimpses of Providence: From Crayon Drawings, with Notes* ([Warren, RI: Henry J. Peck, n.d.]). HPL once met Peck in person.

4. H. L. Davis, *Honey in the Horn* (New York & London: Harper & Bros., 1935).

[11]   [ALS, JHL]

        June 9, 1936

Dear Miſs Bonner:—

        From an edifice with well-nigh 130 years to its credit, the K.A.T. commiseratingly returns the greetings from your painfully modernistic abode! It must seem strange to inhabit such a mushroom growth of merely 75 years' standing . . . . though come to think of it, our librarian did not until 1933 have the pleasure of tenanting anything of pre-Civil-war date. Some inhabitants of the Garden House allude nostalgically to such late-19th-century gadgets as cord-&-weight windows—though the present writer is not among these. For our part, we yearned for small-paned & archaic windows over a period of more than 40 years—hence, having at last achieved them, we profess ourselves satisfied! As for waxed floors—our one regret is that the southwest study at 1, Ely's Court is encumbered with an intrusive hardwood surface, as contrasted with the wide boards we prefer. However—everyone to his taste . . . & I presume Victorian structures at least afford warmth & shelter! The absence of horological chimes must be a genuine deprivation—though I assume that the loss is not complete. But despite all possible objections, I presume that 156 has many advantages over the declining Arsdale.[1] The only reason the higher officials of the K.A.T. remain at the latter is that it affords convenient access to the clubhouse & its roof. I regret that the quadrupedal population at 156 is of a merely canine variety.

And speaking of regrets—the K.A.T. yowls dolefully over the dispensation of fate whereby the 13th lives up to its infelicitous reputation. For as the Parcae would have it, events have made it impossible for us to be represented in the coming Joyeuse Garde invasion! On Saturday last we received word that the first of our many expected visiting delegations of the summer had lit upon the following week-end for its advent—so that the long-awaited Ides must perforce be dedicated to the sundry rounds of historic & antiquarian sightseeing expected by the pilgrims. This is not the Milwaukee pedagogue who measures distance in Bekes (he is expected in August), but a pair of brothers (one of N.Y. & the other just on from the home town of St. Paul to join him) in the weird-fictional & (in the case of the Twin City one) weird art line.[2] Their itinerary virtually precluding any change of dates, I must relinquish purely local activities in order to play the perfect (or approximately so) host! Alas for the irreconcilabilities of schedules independently conceived . . . . . & let my appreciation of the Joyeuse Garde invitation be no less abundantly manifest because of this unforeseen plan-wrecker! To make matters worse, the Quondam Patient also has doubts of her ability to be on hand—not that she has to entertain my guests, but that she is anxious not to overtax her newly regained strength with trips of any degree of strenuousness. However—she'll speak of that herself if she has not already done so. Eheu!

As for the K.A.T. policy toward celebrities—we could name quite a few contemporaries who share it. So far as our long recollection goes, we have been actually introduced to only one celebrity of the first rank [except the magician Houdini, for whom we did some revision work in 1924–6 . . . but he was an idol of the crowd rather than one of the solid achievers of the age]—this being the late astronomer Percival Lowell, who lectured here in 1907. We didn't butt in on him—but having arrived early at Sayles Hall, we were espied amidst the prematurely gathered handful by Prof. Upton; who, knowing our devotion to celestial science, most considerately hailed us & made us known to the eminent Martian discoverer. Dr. Lowell no doubt remembered our existence fully five minutes after his courteous handshake.[3]

Yes—a K.A.T. delegation visited the Tercentenary House on the Mall (which is *not* a good specimen of early R.I. architecture, but rather of a northeastern Massachusetts type) on May 18, but found no state maps (of the sort described in the "These Plantations" column of the Bulletin) available. If the maps *are* now ready, we shall have to send another delegation for a supply . . . to outfit the library as well as to present to visitors. According to J. Earl Clauson, the tercentenary map is quite a work of art & antiquarian scholarship combined—shewing small rural roads (the only kind worth traversing) as well as the ugly motor highways.

How do we pronounce *ate?* Well—as a matter of personal usage, especially before strangers, we employ the conventionally ultra-modern *ayt*—which also seems to have been customary in the family for two generations behind us. *But*—let me assure you that the *ĕt* sound was not only deemed perfectly correct up to a relatively recent date, but was recorded by Stormonth as the *only* permissible pronunciation . . . this in the 3d quarter of the 19th century! A learned friend of ours, born in 1870 & the son of a Baptist clergyman & academy principal in Massachusetts & New Hampshire,[4] habitually says *ĕt*— & with an apparent bland unconsciousness that anybody says anything else. The ultra-modern Webster of 1890 lists *ĕt* as "obsolescent & colloquial"—but old Noah always was a radical! Incidentally—one might add that the past & participial form pronounced ĕt is not properly *spelled* "ate". It is spelled *eat*— thus in the lacteal Mr. Tennyson

> —"The island princes overbold
> Have *eat* our substance."[5]

And more—even the now comically regarded *"het"* (= heăt) for *heated* was correct in Elizabethan times. Shakespeare says "the iron, though *heat* red hot".[6] My teacher in the Slater Ave. Primary & Grammar School 38 to 33 years ago used to say "het"—she (Abbie A. Hathaway, a daughter of the contractor heading the Waterman St. firm of Hathaway & Douglas) having probably been born in the 1840's. It was certainly a common New England ruralism up to the Civil War period. Stormonth, however, does not sanction it. Hervey Allen, in his life of Poe entitled "Israfel", makes some interesting speculations as to the type of pronunciation prevalent in various American cities in the 1830's & 1840's. The Georgia poet Chivers (a favourite object of study with our neighbour Prof. Damon)[7] rhymed *Yuba* with *ruby*—thus affording a clue as to the handling of a final *ă* a century ago even in circles of considerable cultivation. [short final ă was probably *y*—as "Ezry", "Elviry", &c., whilst long ā was just that—in the English sense—as "Americay", "Floriday", &c.]

Many thanks for the extremely apt verses quoted from the Library Journal. We are going to exhibit these, in a spirit of respectful reprobation, to a couple of all-too-bibliophilic (as distinct from literary) acquaintances!

Once more wishing you a congenial settlement in your up-to-date quarters—
& reiterating regret at the development which precludes Joyeuse Garde*—

I have the honour to remain

Yr most oblig'd obt Servt

H. P. Lovecraft—Lib'n K.A.T.

Notes

1. See letter 12 regarding MFB's change of address.

2. I.e., Howard Wandrei the artist and Donald Wandrei the writer. It does not appear as if they visited HPL at this time.

3. HPL refers to the noted astronomer Percival Lowell (1855–1916) and to Winslow Upton (1853–1914), astronomer and professor at Brown University. See HPL to Rheinhart Kleiner, 19 February 1916: "As to celebrities—one experience of mine had to do with . . . Percival Lowell. . . . He lectured in this city in 1907, when I was writing for the *Tribune,* and Prof. Upton of Brown introduced me to him before the lecture in Sayles' Hall. . . . I never had, have not, & never will have the slightest belief in Lowell's speculations; & when I met him I had just been attacking his theories in my astronomical articles with my characteristically merciless language. With the egotism of my 17 years, I feared that Lowell had read what I had written! I tried to be as non-committal as possible in speaking, and fortunately discovered that the eminent observer was more disposed to ask me about my telescope, studies, &c., than to discuss Mars. Prof. Upton soon led him away to the platform, & I congratulated myself that a disaster had been averted!" *Letters to Rheinhart Kleiner* 53.

4. I.e., James F. Morton.

5. Alfred, Lord Tennyson (1809–1892), "Song of the Lotos-Eaters," ll. 75–76.

6. Shakespeare, *King John* 4.1.61.

7. For S. Foster Damon, see LDC/AEPG 362n3. Damon wrote the biography *Thomas Holley Chivers: Friend of Poe with Selections from His Poems: A Strange Chapter in American Literary History* (New York: Harper & Brothers, 1930).

[12]   [AN, JHL; a condolence note within a mourning border.]

[June 19, 1936]

Miſs M. F. Bonner,

156, Gaol-Lane,[1] Proſpect-Hill,

near yᵉ Beacon-Pole,

Providence, in Rᵈ: Iſland.

The Providence Chapter of the Kappa Alpha Tau desires to expreſs to Miſs Bonner its most sincere appreciation of her meſsage of sympathy regard-

---

*the excursion to which I surely hope will—for those who can make it—be pleasant & weather-favoured!

ing the recent dual bereavement; a paralysing blow which has necefsitated the complete reorganisation of the Chapter, & has left the garden oasis in a state of unrelieved desolation.

The Chapter also transmits the appreciative acknowledgments of Mr. & Mrs. John Perkins, Sr., parents of our late officers. Mrs. Perkins has just returned from her pedagogical duties at Brown University, where she acted as an Afsistant Profefsor in the Department of Psychology.[2]

19th June.   Per the 3d Afst. Under-Secretary

Notes

1. MFB had moved to 156 Meeting Street (formerly Gaol-Lane).
2. See HPL to RHB, 13 June 1936: "I have lost my best friends—& the local chapter of the Kappa Alpha Tau staggers under a crushing blow. This week both Mr. John Perkins (black—b. Feby. 14, 1935) & the Earl of Minto (black & white—b. Oct. '35) succumbed to some malady which is afflicting all the felidae of the neighbourhood—a thing which may be an obscure epidemic, yet which may be the malign activities of some contemptible poisoner. The sad end of the brothers seemed connected with some digestive disorder, & recalled the equally sad fate of their bygone brother—little Sam Perkins (May–Sept. '34)—of whom you have heard. If this *is* the work of some wretched neo-Borgia, I hope to hell somebody feeds him a poison a thousandfold more painful than that with which he has subtly supplied his innocent furry victims!" (*OFF* 345).

[13]   [ALS, JHL]

EXECUTIVE COMMITTEE
K . A . T .
ELY'S COURT AND DE FOE PLACE,
PROVIDENCE,
R. I.

November 23, 1936

Mifs Marian Bonner,
    156, Gaol-Lane, Providence,

Dear Madam:—
              Replying to your enquiry of 22nd inst. regarding the posthumous action of the Kappa Alpha Tau on the recent tragical heroism of Senhora Caterina Almeda of 496, Back-Street,[1] we beg to inform you that a memorial fund was collected at our last meeting (in the vacant stable at Prospect Alley & De Foe Place), to be used in providing a dozen catnip mice apiece for the surviving children of the deceased—Senhorita Inkspot Almedia, Senhor Manuel Almedia, & Senhor Rodrigo Braganza Almedia. A memorial of this practical nature was deemed advisable, insomuch as the

symbolic & decorative side was so well covered by our human colleagues of the N.Y. Anti-Vivisection Society. We have also extended invitations to the young Senhoras Almedia to become members of our sadly depleted chapter upon their attainment of their majority, & to Senhorita Inkspot to become affiliated with the Ladies' Auxiliary.

With appreciation of your interest in the activities of our organisation, we beg to remain

Most faithfully yours,
The Executive Committee, Providence Chapter,
Κομψῶν Αἰλουϱων Τάξις

Per: Thomas Broadbeam-Blackman, Pres't[2]
[elected at Sabbat of Oct. 31 to succeed Mr. John Perkins, Sr. Mr. Perkins' non-attendance at recent meetings militated against him, & prejudice concerning Mr. Broadbeam-Blackman's dour temperament & bluff mannerisms was easily overcome.]

Dan'l Defoe Vice-Pres't   White Stubtail Congdon, Secy
  Mrs. Spotty Perkins,   H. P. Lovecraft, Librarian &
     Pres. Ladies' Auxiliary   3d Asst. Under-Secy.

Notes

1. I.e., 496 Benefit Street.
2. HPL mentions this cat and those named below only in letters to MFB.

[14]   [ALS, JHL]

Providence Chapter   Καππα Αλφα Ταυ

1, Ely's Court,
                                     Decr 9   1936

Mifs M. F. Bonner,
    156 Gaol-Lane, Profpect-Hill,
        Nr. the Beacon-Pole.

Dear Madam:—

        The K.A.T. authorities, pausing for a moment from their grateful contemplation of newly acquired almanacks, wish to acknowledge with appreciation the message from Pres. Emerson Thoreau Cornell of the

Framingham Chapter, in the Province of the Maſsachusetts-Bay, as kindly transmitted through you. We are keenly interested in his clever & original lounging-place, & in his sportive gambols with his diminutive testudinate friend. The latter, we are certain, must feel honoured at his choice as boon companion of the snowy & scholarly Pres. Cornell; whilst the strenuousness of the sport cannot but form a salutary influence in combating the natural sluggishness of the reptilian disposition. Messages from Pres. Cornell will always be welcome—& he may rest assured that the picture enclosed in his letter (a view of us when confronted by a long revision job or a volume of Victorian fiction) does *not* represent our attitude in hearing from him.

Nor does it typify our sentiments toward the Hon. James O'Flaherty McCarthy,[1] at whose delicatessen (even in the ould days phwin it was a branch av Riley's) we have purchased many a pound of cheese & many a slice of veal loaf. Mr. McCarthy's rough exterior would not weigh against him with us—for is not our new chapter president, Thos. Broadbeam-Blackman, Esq., a bit brusque & negligent of the amenities? I am sure that Mr. McCarthy would be a welcome addition to any K.A.T. enterprise! Larng loives to 'im intoirely!

We have indeed seen the new *Harpers* (thanks, I believe, to the Chief Ailurophile) & perused "The House of the Laburnums",[2] which is a clever bit of spectral horror though by no means original in plot. The idea of ghosts of *future* events is a fairly old one, & has had notable exemplars as far back as Wilkie Collins's "Dream Woman".[3] A later specimen with the same general idea is W. F. Harvey's "August Heat" (1910), to be found in the first "Omnibus of Crime".[4] This Downes story is notable chiefly for its atmosphere—& I rather fancy that *Harpers* (normally unsympathetic toward the weird) took it more because of the author's established status than because of any particular intrinsic merit. However, it is undeniably pretty good as the milder sort of spectral fiction goes.

As orally expressed before, we rejoice that you have located "The Witch-Cult in Western Europe"[5] & have thereby become familiar with Sabbats, Estbats, Covens, & all the other attributes of the festering horror which brooded over mediaeval & renaissance Europe & perhaps over colonial Salem. And we apologise that our nominated guide Sir Walter failed to mention Sabbats at all—as he really should have done, since the term was well-known from constant repetition at witch-trials long before the actuality of any subterraneous cult was suspected.

Pray consider all the facilities of our Chapter, including the bibliothecal, perennially at your service, & accept our renewed expressions of gratitude for the additions to the almanack department of our archives.

Madam,

   Yr moſt oblig'd & obt Servts.
   K.A.T., Providence Chapter

per:

    T. Broadbeam-Blackman, Pres't.

    Dan'l Defoe, Vice-Prefident

    H. P. Lovecraft, Lib'n & 3d Afst. Under-Secy.

Notes

1. Probably James F. McCarthy (1906–?). "O'Flaherty" is HPL's joke.

2. Mollie Panter-Downes, "The House of the Laburnums," *Harper's* 174, No. 1 (December 1936): 42–45; rpt. *The Ash-Tree Press Annual Macabre 1997*, ed. Jack Adrian (Ashcroft, BC: Ash-Tree Press 1997). Panter-Downes (1906–1997) was a British writer and author of the bestselling novel *The Shoreless Sea* (1923).

3. Wilkie Collins (1824–1889), "The Dream Woman," first published in *Temple Bar* (November–December 1874) and collected in Collins's *The Frozen Deep and Other Stories* (1874).

4. Ed. Dorothy L. Sayers. The story first appeared in Harvey's *Midnight House and Other Tales* (1910).

5. By Margaret A. Murray.

Appendix:
Letters by Whipple V. Phillips to H. P. Lovecraft

[1]   [ALS, JHL]

[The Paxton
Ralph Kitchen, Manager.
Omaha, Neb.]

June 19th 1894

My dear Howard

I have a moment before I take the train for Deluth [*sic*] and I will occupy the time writing to you. I will not attempt to tell you all about my journey through the wild west and of the many things that has [*sic*] happened since I left home, but only speak of a few points that will be most interesting to you. Well I saw the black Butes [*sic*] where there are so many Antelopes and other places of much interest but the greatest of all I have seen was Little Shorty and the black Pigs.

Shorty is a Dog just the color of a Leyon [*sic*] and they have sheared his hair all but his head and shoulders and the tip of his tail. He looks just like a little Leyon and is a cunning little fellow. His legs are so short that they call him Shorty on this account

Shorty goes in the water to swim and chaces [*sic*] the cats and Jack Rabits [*sic*] all about the House and lawn He is a great smoker, and eats plenty of good food, everything except Quaker Oats. I forgot to tell you he likes to play with the black Pigs

We have about thirty black Pigs. Some of them have a little white on them Some are speckeled [*sic*] and others are as black as nigros[.] Some of them are just wee bits of Pigs and some are medium sized pigs[.] Others are quite large Pigs and their Mothers are very large Pigs, so you see we have all sizes, but they are nearly all black Pigs

Well one day one of the little Pigs got his head into a tomato can and he could not get it out and he ran all around the yard and made lots of fun for the other pigs. All of these Pigs are so gentle that they will eat out of your hand and we have to keep a board at the door to keep them out of the House when the door is open. I think on the whole you would have a great time if you could play with Shorty and the Pigs. I will tell you more about what I have seen when I get home if you are a good Boy and *wear trousers*.

Give my love to Grand Mama Mother and all the rest of the family

Yours truly

Grand Papa

[2]   [ALS, in private hands]

[Office of
Owyhee Land and Irrigation Co.
W. V. PHILLIPS, President and General Manager.
A. J. WILEY, Chief Engineer.]

[EASTERN OFFICE,
48 CUSTOM HOUSE ST.,
PROVIDENCE, R. I.]

[Grand View, Idaho,] Oct. 17th 1895

Dear Skimper

I got a letter from you Annie & Grandmama so I will write to all of you in this letter, for you can tell them all about it. I think your letter was very nice and I was much pleased with your expression. It was out of sight.

I and Mr Wiley are running the gold machine and doing good work. The gold begins to show up on our burlap and in our concentrates. We are doing lots of work here now in every direction, but I hope I can get home about the first of november and then we will have a real Gramp day.

I went down the Valley this morning and I saw a big Coyote. Dick was with me. My stars and garters how Dick went for him, he has caught lots of them, and has lots of fights with Badgers. I will tell you all about it when I get home

You and Dumplin Mama must keep the Barn shut every night and take care of Nig.

Tell Ant Annie and Grandmama to write again and dont forget Ant Lillie[.] Kiss them all for me and be a good Skimper. B. Doodles

Gramp

[3]   [ALS, JHL]

Grand View Feb. 20th 1899

Dear H. P. L

I have just written to Lillie and as I have a few moments to spare I will tell you of some things that have happened in the last few days

There was a man drowned in Snake River 10 miles above us. Yesterday a large band of Horses swam acros[s] the River in front of our House, and to-day we had three big fish for dinner that we caught on the apron to the dam on the Bruneau. We also started up the mining plant today.

I saw a man out here that looked some like John Rathbone Well you see he looked like your picture, and I immagined [*sic*] he had gotten straight away out here[.]

You must look after things while I am gone, and don[']t say a word about that *fear* Ten Shakes just the Same

Gramp

Whipple Van Buren Phillips

[4]   [ALS, JHL]

[Hotel Jermyn
Absolutely Fire-proof
F. S. Godfrey]

[Scranton, Pa. <u>Oct. 27 [18]99</u>]

Dear Punky

Just 10 tonight I have been to supper and while I am waiting for Dr Hill to call on me I will drop you a line

Scranton is a fine place and this Hotel is the nicest I ever saw—everything is perfect, even the bill of fare is up to the Dulcatine Temple's spread. I went to the theatre last evening with Dr Hill and his wife they are splendid

Well how about the pears, and all other matters at 454. You must look well to things in general and learn the manly art so you can nock [*sic*] out some of them bad boys

With love to all and 10 as above written

Yours truly

Gramp

P.S. I may be home next week for a few days

Glossary of Frequently Mentioned Names

Baird, Edwin (1886–1954), first editor of *Weird Tales* (March 1923–April 1924), who accepted HPL's first submissions to the magazine. Also editor of *Real Detective Stories.*

Barlow, R[obert] H[ayward] (1918–1951), author and collector. As a teenager he corresponded with HPL and acted as his host during two long visits in the summers of 1934 and 1935. In the 1930s he wrote several works of weird and fantasy fiction, some in collaboration with HPL. HPL appointed him his literary executor. He assisted August Derleth and Donald Wandrei in preparing the early HPL volumes for Arkham House. In the 1940s he went to Mexico and became a distinguished anthropologist. He died by suicide. HPL's letters to Barlow have been published as *O Fortunate Floridian* (2007).

Bierce, Ambrose (1842–1914?), American author and journalist. His collections of horror and Civil War tales, *Tales of Soldiers and Civilians* (1891; later titled *In the Midst of Life*) and *Can Such Things Be?* (1893) are landmarks. He was also the author of *The Devil's Dictionary* (1906 [as *The Cynic's Word Book*]) and enormous quantities of journalism, chiefly for the Hearst papers.

Bishop, Zealia Brown (Reed) (1897–1968), HPL's revision client. HPL ghostwrote "The Curse of Yig" (1928), "The Mound" (1929–30), and "Medusa's Coil" (1930) for her based on her slim plot synopses.

Blackwood, Algernon (1869–1951), prolific British author of weird and fantasy tales whose work HPL greatly admired when he read it in 1924.

Braithwaite, William Stanley (1878–1962), literary editor for the *Boston Transcript* and of the *Anthology of Magazine Verse . . . and Year Book of American Poetry.* Recipient of the Spingarn award from the NAACP.

Brobst, Harry K[ern] (1909–2010), late associate of HPL who moved to Providence in 1932 and saw HPL regularly thereafter.

Bullen, John Ravenor (1886–1927), amateur poet from Canada. HPL edited his poems, *White Fire* (1927), for posthumous publication.

Bush, David Van (1882–1959), prolific author of inspirational verse and popular psychology manuals, many of them revised by Lovecraft.

Campbell, Paul J[onas] (1884–1945), amateur journalist and editor of the *Liberal* and other amateur papers.

Coates, Walter J[ohn] (1880–1941), amateur journalist, printer, editor of *Driftwind,* and staunch advocate of the literature of Vermont.

Cole, Edward H[arold] (1892–1966), longtime amateur associate of HPL, living in the Boston area. Editor of the *Olympian.*

Coleman, Stuart Tiepke (1892–1969), boyhood friend of HPL.

Cook, W. Paul (1880–1948), publisher of the *Monadnock Monthly*, the *Vagrant*, and other amateur journals; a longtime amateur journalist, printer, fifty-third president of the NAPA, and lifelong friend of HPL. He first visited HPL in 1917, and it was he who urged HPL to resume writing fiction after a hiatus of nine years. In 1927 Cook published the *Recluse*, with HPL's "Supernatural Horror in Literature."

Crane, Hart (1899–1932), eminent American poet who met HPL sporadically in Cleveland (1922) and New York (1924–26, 1930). HPL admired his work, especially *The Bridge* (1930), on which HPL saw him at work in 1924. He died by suicide.

Daas, Edward F[rancis] (1879–1962), joined the UAPA within a year of its founding in 1895; was elected President in 1907 and served as Official Editor in 1913 and 1915. Recruited HPL to the UAPA in 1914.

Davis, Edgar J. (1908–1949), young amateur journalist with whom HPL explored Newburyport and other locales in New England.

de Castro, Adolphe (Danziger) (1859–1959), author, co-translator with Ambrose Bierce of Richard Voss's *The Monk and the Hangman's Daughter,* and correspondent of HPL. HPL revised his "The Last Test" and "The Electric Executioner."

Dench, Ernest A[lfred] (1895?–?), British-born Brooklyn amateur, author of *Making the Movies* (1915) and other books about the cinema.

Dowdell, William J. (1898–1953), amateur journalist who abruptly resigned as president of the NAPA in late 1922, leading the executive judges to appoint HPL as interim president.

Dryden, Wheeler (1892–1957), half-brother of Charlie Chaplin (they shared the same mother), and himself an actor and film director. In 1945 he informed Sonia H. Davis of HPL's death.

Dunsany, Lord (Edward John Moreton Drax Plunkett) (1878–1957), Anglo-Irish writer of fantasy tales whose work notably influenced HPL after HPL read it in 1919.

Dwyer, Bernard Austin (1897–1943), weird fiction fan and would-be writer and artist, living in West Shokan, NY; correspondent of HPL.

Eddy, Clifford M[artin], Jr. (1896–1967), pulp fiction writer for whom HPL revised several stories in 1923–24 and who also worked with HPL on ghostwriting work for Harry Houdini in 1926.

Evans, Thomas S. (1885–1940), a friend of HPL in Providence. A self-employed cosmetician who worked from his home at 145 Medway Street.

Fadden, Leslie B. (1896–1982), proprietor of The Arsdale, the boarding house at 55 Waterman Street across the back garden from 66 College Street, where HPL often directed visitors from out of town to stay. He and Annie Gamwell often ate meals there.

Fairchild, Daniel (1891–1938), boyhood friend of HPL.

Fritter, Leo (1878–1948), lawyer and member of the Woodbee Press Club. HPL supported Fritter's campaign to be President of the UAPA (1915), which Fritter won. (HPL was First Vice-President.)

Galpin, Alfred (1901–1983), amateur journalist, French scholar, composer, and protégé, then longtime friend, of HPL. He lived in Appleton, WI.

Gamwell, Phillips (1898–1916), HPL's cousin, son of Edward F[rancis] Gamwell (1869–1936) and Annie E. Phillips Gamwell (1866–1941). Edward was editor of the *Cambridge* (Mass.) *Tribune*, which published HPL's "Elegy on Phillips Gamwell, Esq."

Goodenough, Arthur H[enry] (1871–1936), amateur poet who resided in Brattleboro, VT. HPL visited him there on several occasions.

Grayson, Allan Brownell (1913–1967?), young friend of Henry S. Whitehead who, like Whitehead, became an Episcopal clergyman, serving in New York and New Jersey. HPL met him when he visited Whitehead in 1931.

Greene, Sonia Haft (1883–1972), HPL's wife (1924–29). Born Sonia Haft Shafirkin in Ichnya (near Kiev), in the Ukraine. Settling in the United States, she eventually joined the amateur journalism movement, publishing two lavish issues of the *Rainbow* and becoming president of the UAPA (1924–25). After her divorce from HPL, she moved to California and married Dr. Nathaniel Davis. Her memoir of HPL has been published as *The Private Life of H. P. Lovecraft* (1985; rev. 1992).

Hall, Desmond W[inter] (1911–1992), associate editor of *Astounding Stories*.

Hamlet, Alice M. (1888–1967), amateur journalist who introduced HPL to the work of Lord Dunsany.

Harré, T[homas] Everett (1884–1948), American novelist who edited the horror anthology *Beware After Dark!* (1929), containing HPL's "The Call of Cthulhu." HPL met him on a few occasions in New York in the 1930s.

Harris, Woodburn Prescott (1888–1988), correspondent of HPL living in Vergennes, Vermont.

Hart, B[ertrand] K[elton] (1892–1941), literary editor for the *Providence Journal.*

Haughton, Ida C. (1860–1934), amateur journalist with whom HPL had a bitter feud in the early 1920s. He directed the pungent satirical poem "Medusa: A Portrait" (1922) at her.

Henneberger, J[acob] C[lark] (1890–1969), founder of *College Humor* (1922f.) and the original publisher of *Weird Tales.*

Hoag, Jonathan E[than] (1831–1927), amateur poet for whom HPL regularly wrote birthday poems from 1918 to 1927; upon Hoag's death he wrote the elegy "Ave atque Vale." HPL was the chief editor of *The Poetical Works of Jonathan E. Hoag* (1923).

Houdini, Harry (stage name of Ehrich Weiss, 1874–1926), celebrated escape artist and opponent of spiritualism for whom HPL ghostwrote the story "Under the Pyramids" (1924; published as "Imprisoned with the Pharaohs") and for whom he did other revisory work in 1926, just prior to Houdini's death.

Houtain, George Julian (1884–1945), amateur journalist who established the semi-professional humor magazine *Home Brew*, for which he commissioned HPL to write "Herbert West—Reanimator" (1921–22) and "The Lurking Fear" (1922).

Jackson, Winifred Virginia (1876–1959), poet and amateur journalist who worked extensively with HPL during the period 1918–21; she was rumored to have amorous designs on HPL.

Kamin, Martin, a business colleague of George Kirk. Kirk lived with Kamin and his wife, Sara, at 617 West 115th Street in Manhattan before establishing his own bookshop at 317 West 14th Street.

Kirk, George [Willard] (1898–1962), member of the Kalem Club. He published *Twenty-one Letters of Ambrose Bierce* (1922) and ran the Chelsea Bookshop in New York.

Kleiner, Rheinhart (1892–1949), amateur poet and longtime friend of HPL. He visited HPL in Providence in 1918, 1919, and 1920, and met him frequently during the heyday of the Kalem Club (1924–26).

Koenig, H[erman] C[harles] (1893–1959), late associate of HPL who spearheaded the rediscovery of the work of William Hope Hodgson.

Kuntz, Eugene B. (1865–1944), Prussian-born poet, Presbyterian minister, and amateur journalist. HPL edited Kuntz's slim collection of poems, *Thoughts and Pictures* (Haverhill, MA: "Cooperatively published by H. P. Loveracft [*sic*] and C. W. Smith," 1932), probably revising the poems in the process.

Lazare, Edward (1904–1991), colleague of Hart Crane in Cleveland and later the editor of *American Book-Prices Current*.

Leeds, Arthur (1882–1952?), an associate of HPL in New York and member of the Kalem Club. He was the author (with J. Berg Esenwein) of *Writing the Photoplay* (Springfield, MA: The Home Correspondence School, 1913; rev. ed. 1919).

Leeman, Thomas Francis (1890–1948), boyhood friend of HPL.

Long, Frank Belknap (1901–1994), fiction writer and poet and one of HPL's closest friends and correspondents. Late in life he wrote the memoir, *Howard Phillips Lovecraft: Dreamer on the Nightside* (1975).

Loveman, Samuel E. (1887–1976), poet and longtime friend of HPL and Hart Crane, and associate of Ambrose Bierce, Hart Crane, George Sterling, and Clark Ashton Smith. He wrote *The Hermaphrodite* (1926) and other works.

Lynch, Joseph Bernard (1879–1952), amateur journalist and member of the Hub Club.

Martin, Harry E. (1887–1972), amateur journalist and official editor of the NAPA during the period of HPL's interim presidency (1922–23).

McGrath, Patrick (1906–1978), a friend of Samuel Loveman. At a New Year's Eve party at Loveman's apartment in Brooklyn Heights on 31 December 1933, McGrath supposedly spiked HPL's punch, so that HPL began speaking very volubly (as told in Loveman's "Lovecraft as a Conversationalist").

McNeil, Henry Everett (1862–1929), author of historical and adventure novels for boys; member of the Kalem Club.

Merritt, A[braham] (1884–1943), writer of fantasy and horror tales for the pulps. His work was much admired by HPL in spite of its concessions to pulp formulae. His late novel *The Dwellers in the Mirage* (1932) may have been influenced by HPL.

Miller, Reginald (1890–1964), boyhood friend of HPL.

Miniter, Edith (1867–1934), amateur author who also professionally published a novel, *Our Natupski Neighbors* (1916) and many short stories. She was the President of the NAPA (1909–10). HPL was guest at her home in Wilbraham, Massachusetts, in the summer of 1928.

Moe, Maurice W[inter] (1882–1940), amateur journalist, English teacher, and longtime friend and correspondent of HPL. He lived successively in Appleton and Milwaukee, WI.

Morse, Richard Ely (1909–1986), poet, librarian, and late correspondent of Lovecraft.

Morton, James Ferdinand (1870–1941), amateur journalist, author of many tracts on race prejudice, free thought, and taxation, and longtime friend of HPL. His brother is Nelson Glazier Morton, an amateur journalist.

Munn, H[arold] Warner (1903–1981), contributor to the pulp magazines, living near W. Paul Cook in Athol, MA.

Munroe, Chester Pierce (1889–1943), boyhood friend of HPL.

Munroe, Harold Bateman (1891–1966), boyhood friend of HPL.

Newton, Dudley C[harles] (1864–1954), HPL's elderly guide to St. Augustine, FL, in 1931. He was a resident of the Hotel Rio Vista, where HPL stayed on his trip.

Orton, Vrest [Teachout] (1897–1986), a late member of the Kalem Club. He was for a time an editor at the *Saturday Review* and later the founder of the Vermont Country Store. He compiled an early bibliography of Theodore Dreiser, *Dreiserana* (1929).

Parker, Charles A. A. (1880–1965), amateur journalist and editor of the little magazine *L'Alouette*, chiefly devoted to poetry.

Price, E[dgar] Hoffmann (1898–1988), prolific pulp writer of weird and adventure tales. HPL met him in New Orleans in 1932 and corresponded extensively with him thereafter.

Quinn, Seabury (1889–1969), prolific author of weird and detective tales to the pulps, notably a series of tales involving the psychic detective Jules de Grandin.

Renshaw, Anne Tillery (1890–c. 1945), prolific amateur journalist and professor. She met HPL during the latter's visit to Washington, DC, in April 1925. In 1936 she commissioned HPL to revise a textbook of English usage, *Well-Bred Speech* (1936), although much of the work HPL did for it was excised and remains unpublished.

Russell, John, an Englishman residing in Tampa, FL, who engaged with HPL in a controversy in verse, conducted in the letter column of the *Argosy* in 1913–14.

Sandusky, Albert A[ugust] (1896–1934), amateur journalist whose use of slang amused HPL. HPL met him frequently during trips to the Boston area.

Sawyer, Laurie A., amateur journalist. HPL alluded to her in "The Prophecy of Capys Secundus" referred to her as "Ouija" in his poem "Theobaldian Aestivation."

Sechrist, Edward Lloyd (1873–1953), amateur journalist and beekeeper. HPL met him on several occasions, especially during visits to Washington, DC.

Shea, J[oseph] Vernon (1912–1981), young weird fiction fan from Pittsburgh who began corresponding with HPL in 1931.

Sherman, Edwin Sidney (1890–1977), boyhood friend of HPL.

Smith, Charles W. ("Tryout") (1852–1948), longtime amateur journalist, editor of the *Tryout,* and friend and correspondent of HPL.

Smith, Clark Ashton (1893–1961), prolific California poet and writer of fantasy tales. He received a "fan" letter from HPL in 1922 and corresponded with him until HPL's death.

Spink, Helm C. (1909–1970), printer and Official Editor of the NAPA in 1930 and again in 1935 (with O. W. Hinrichs). He printed HPL's *Further Criticism of Poetry.*

Staples, Evelyn M. (1860–1938), born in Barrington, RI, had lived for a time in New Brunswick, Canada. She settled in Providence and taught at the Charles Street School (291 Charles Street) no later than 1910. By 1930, she was residing at 55 Waterman Street, in the same boarding-house as Marian F. Bonner. She continued to live there through 1938.

Sterling, George (1869–1926), California poet and early mentor of Smith.

Sterling, Kenneth (1920–1995), young science fiction fan who came into contact with HPL in 1934. They collaborated on the science fiction story "In the Walls of Eryx" (1935). Sterling later became a distinguished physician.

Strauch, Carl Ferdinand (1908–1989), friend of Harry Brobst and correspondent of HPL. He later became a distinguished professor and critic.

Suhre, Edward F. (1879–1939), editor of the *Missourian* and *Occasional Press,* and forty-fourth president of the NAPA.

Swift, Dr. Edwin B. (1859–?), editor of the *Hyperion* (1890–02), twenty-first president of the NAPA, and member of the Fossils.

Talman, Wilfred Blanch (1904–1986), correspondent of HPL and late member of the Kalem Club. HPL assisted Talman on his story "Two Black Bottles" (1926) and wrote "Some Dutch Footprints in New England" for Talman to publish in *De Halve Maen,* the journal of the Holland Society of New York. Late in life he wrote the memoir *The Normal Lovecraft* (1973).

Toldridge, Elizabeth (1861–1940), invalid poet living in Washington, DC, who corresponded with HPL from 1928 to 1937. He coached her extensively on her poetry.

Tucker, Gertrude E., editor of the Reading Lamp, evidently a literary agency. She also edited the *Reading Lamp*, a literary journal for which HPL wrote at least one review (not located).

Upham, Ronald Kingsley (1892–1968), boyhood friend of HPL.

Wandrei, Donald (1908–1987), poet and author of weird fiction, science fiction, and detective tales. He corresponded with HPL from 1926 to 1937, visited HPL in Providence in 1927 and 1932, and met HPL occasionally in New York during the 1930s. He helped HPL get "The Shadow out of Time" published in *Astounding Stories*. After HPL's death he and August Derleth founded the publishing firm Arkham House to preserve HPL's work. For their joint correspondence, see *Mysteries of Time and Spirit*.

Wandrei, Howard (1909–1956), younger brother of Donald Wandrei, premier weird artist and prolific author of weird fiction, science fiction, and detective stories; correspondent of HPL.

Whitehead, Henry S[t. Clair] (1882–1932), author of weird and adventure tales, many of them set in the Virgin Islands. HPL corresponded with him and visited him in Florida in 1931. HPL wrote a brief eulogy of Whitehead for *Weird Tales*.

Wright, Farnsworth (1888–1940), editor of *Weird Tales* (1924–40). He rejected some of HPL's best work of the 1930s, only to publish it after HPL's death upon submittal by August Derleth.

Wylie, Willard Otis (1862–1944), of Boston, noted philatelic editor and writer. Editor of *Our Compliments*, and member of both the NAPA and UAPA.

Bibliography

A.   Works by H. P. Lovecraft

Books

The Ancient Track: Complete Poetical Works. 2nd ed. Edited by S. T. Joshi. New York: Hippocampus Press, 2013.

The Annotated Supernatural Horror in Literature. 2nd ed. Edited by S. T. Joshi. New York: Hippocampus Press, 2012.

Charleston. [New York: H. C. Koenig, 1936.] Text in *CE* 4.

Collected Essays. Edited by S. T. Joshi. New York: Hippocampus Press, 2004–06. 5 vols.

Collected Fiction. Edited by S. T. Joshi. New York: Hippocampus Press, 2015, 2017. 4 vols.

Dawnward Spire, Lonely Hill: The Letters of H. P. Lovecraft and Clark Ashton Smith. Edited by David E. Schultz and S. T. Joshi. New York: Hippocampus Press, 2017.

Letters to Alfred Galpin. Edited by S. T. Joshi and David E. Schultz. New York: Hippocampus Press, 2003.

Letters to Alfred Galpin and Others. Edited by S. T. Joshi and David E. Schultz. New York: Hippocampus Press, 2020.

Letters to Elizabeth Toldridge and Anne Tillery Renshaw. Edited by David E. Schultz and S. T. Joshi. New York: Hippocampus Press, 2014.

Letters to F. Lee Baldwin, Duane W. Rimel, and Nils Frome. Edited by David E. Schultz and S. T. Joshi. New York: Hippocampus Press, 2016.

Letters to J. Vernon Shea, Carl F. Strauch, and Lee McBride White. Edited by S. T. Joshi and David E. Schultz. New York: Hippocampus Press, 2016.

Letters to Rheinhart Kleiner and Others. Edited by S. T. Joshi and David E. Schultz. New York: Hippocampus Press, 2020.

Letters to Maurice W. Moe and Others. Edited by David E. Schultz and S. T. Joshi. New York: Hippocampus Press, 2018.

Letters to Wilfred B. Talman and Helen V. and Genevieve Sully. Edited by David E. Schultz and S. T. Joshi. New York: Hippocampus Press, 2019.

Letters with Donald and Howard Wandrei and to Emil Petaja. Edited by S. T. Joshi and David E. Schultz. New York: Hippocampus Press, 2019.

O Fortunate Floridian: H. P. Lovecraft's Letters to R. H. Barlow. Edited by S. T. Joshi and David E. Schultz. Tampa: University of Tampa Press, 2007.

Selected Letters. Edited by August Derleth, Donald Wandrei, and James Turner. Sauk City, WI: Arkham House, 1965–76. 5 vols.

The Shadow over Innsmouth. Everett, PA: Visionary Publishing Co., 1936. Text in *CF* 3.

The Shunned House. Athol, MA: Recluse Press, 1928 (printed but not bound or distributed until 1959–61). Text in *CF* 1.

Fiction

At the Mountains of Madness. Astounding Stories 16, No. 6 (February 1936): 8–32; 17, No. 1 (March 1936): 125–55; 17, No. 2 (April 1936): 132–50. In *CF* 3.

"Beyond the Wall of Sleep." *Pine Cones* 1, No. 6 (October 1919): 2–10. *FF,* 2, No. 2 (October 1934): 25–32. In *CF* 1.

"The Call of Cthulhu." *WT* 11, No. 2 (February 1928): 159–78, 287. In *Beware After Dark! The World's Most Stupendous Tales of Mystery, Horror, Thrills and Terror,* ed. T. Everett Harré. New York: Macaulay, 1929. 223–59. In *CF* 2.

The Case of Charles Dexter Ward. In *CF* 2.

"The Cats of Ulthar." *Tryout* 6, No. 11 (November 1920): [3–9]. *WT* 7, No. 2 (February 1926): 252–54. *WT* 21, No. 2 (February 1933): 259–61. In *CF* 1.

"Celephaïs." *Rainbow* No. 2 (May 1922): 10–12. *Marvel Tales* 1, No. 1 (May 1934): 26, 28–32. In *CF* 1.

"Cool Air." *Tales of Magic and Mystery* 1, No. 4 (March 1928): 29–34. In *CF* 2.

"The Doom That Came to Sarnath." *Scot* No. 44 (June 1920): 90–98. *Marvel Tales of Science and Fantasy* 1, No. 4 (March–April 1935): 157–63. In *CF* 1.

"The Dunwich Horror." *WT* 13, No. 4 (April 1929): 481–508. In *CF* 2.

"Facts concerning the Late Arthur Jermyn and His Family." *Wolverine* No. 9 (March 1921): 3–11; No. 10 (June 1921): 6–11. *WT* 3, No. 4 (April 1924): 15–18 (as "The White Ape"). *WT* 25, No. 5 (May 1935): 642–48 (as "Arthur Jermyn"). In *CF* 1.

"The Festival." *WT* 5, No. 1 (January 1925): 169–74. *WT* 22, No. 4 (October 1933): 519–20, 522–28. In *CF* 1.

"From Beyond." *FF* 1, No. 10 (June 1934): 147–51, 160. In *CF* 1.

"He." *WT* 8, No. 3 (September 1926): 373–80. In *CF* 1.

"Herbert West—Reanimator" (as "Grewsome Tales"). *Home Brew* 1, No. 1 (February 1922): 84–88 ("From the Dark"); 1, No. 2 (March 1922): 45–50 ("The Plague Demon"); 1, No. 3 (April 1922): 21–26 ("Six Shots by Moonlight"); 1, No. 4 (May 1922): 53–58 ("The Scream of the Dead"); 1, No. 5 (June 1922): 45–50 ("The Horror from the Shadows,"); 1, No. 6 (July 1922): 57–62 ("The Tomb-Legions"). In *CF* 1.

"The Horror at Red Hook." *WT* 9, No. 1 (January 1927): 59–73. In *You'll Need a Night Light,* ed. Christine Campbell Thomson. London: Selwyn & Blount, 1927. 228–54. In *Not at Night!,* ed. Herbert Asbury. New York: Macy-Masius (The Vanguard Press), November 1928. 27–52. In *CF* 1.

"Hypnos." *National Amateur* 45, No. 5 (May 1923): 1–3. *WT* 4, No. 2 (May–June–July 1924): 33–35. In *CF* 1.

"In the Vault." *Tryout* 10, No. 6 (November 1925): [3–17]. *WT* 19, No. 4 (April 1932): 459–65. In *CF* 1.

"The Lurking Fear." *Home Brew* 2, No. 6 (January 1923): 4–10; 3, No. 1 (February 1923): 18–23; 3, No. 2 (March 1923): 31–37, 44, 48; 3, No. 3 (April 1923): 35–42. *WT* 11, No. 6 (June 1928): 791–804. In *CF* 1.

"The Moon-Bog." *WT* 7, No. 6 (June 1926): 805–10. In *CF* 1.

"The Music of Erich Zann." *National Amateur* 44, No. 4 (March 1922): 38–40. *WT* 5, No. 5 (May 1925): 219–34. In *Creeps by Night: Chills and Thrills,* ed. Dashiell Hammett. New York: John Day Co., 1931. 347–63. In *Modern Tales of Horror,* ed. Dashiell Hammett. London: Victor Gollancz, 1932. 301–17. *Evening Standard* (London) (24 October 1932): 20–21. *WT* 24, No. 5 (November 1934): 644–48, 655–56. In *CF* 1.

"Nyarlathotep." *United Amateur* 20, No. 2 (November 1920): 19–21. *National Amateur* 48, No. 6 (July 1926): 53–54. In *CF* 1.

"The Other Gods." *Fantasy Fan* 1, No. 3 (November 1933): 35–38. *WT* 32, No. 4 (October 1938): 489–92. In *CF* 1.

"The Outsider." *WT* 7, No. 4 (April 1926): 449–53. *WT* 17, No. 4 (June–July 1931): 566–71. In *CF* 1.

"Pickman's Model." *WT* 10, No. 4 (October 1927): 505–14. In *By Daylight Only,* ed. Christine Campbell Thomson. London: Selwyn & Blount, 1929. 37–52. *WT* 28, No. 4 (November 1936): 495–505. In *The "Not at Night" Omnibus,* ed. Christine Campbell Thomson. London: Selwyn & Blount, [1937]. 279–307. In *CF* 2.

"Polaris." *Philosopher* 1, No. 1 (December 1920): 3–5. *National Amateur* 48, No. 5 (May 1926): 48–49. *FF* 1, No. 6 (February 1934): 83–85. In *CF* 1.

"The Quest of Iranon." *Galleon* 1, No. 5 (July–August 1935): 12–20. In *CF* 1.

"The Rats in the Walls." *WT* 3, No. 3 (March 1924): 25–31. *WT* 15, No. 6 (June 1930): 841–53. In *Switch On the Light,* ed. Christine Campbell Thomson. London: Selwyn & Blount, 1931. 141–65. In *CF* 1.

"The Shadow over Innsmouth." Everett, PA: Visionary Publishing Co., 1936. In *CF* 3.

"The Shunned House." Athol, MA: W. Paul Cook (The Recluse Press), 1928. [Printed but not bound or distributed.] In *CF* 1.

"The Statement of Randolph Carter." *Vagrant* No. 13 (May 1920): 41–48. *WT* 5, No. 2 (February 1925): 149–53. In *CF* 1.

"The Temple." *WT* 6, No. 3 (September 1925): 329–36, 429, 431. *WT* 27, No. 2 (February 1936): 239–44, 246–49. In *CF* 1.

"The Terrible Old Man." *Tryout* 7, No. 4 (July 1921): [10–14]. *WT* 8, No. 2 (August 1926): 191–92. In *CF* 1.

"The Tomb." *Vagrant* No. 14 (March 1922): 50–64. *WT* 7, No. 1 (January 1926): 117–23. In *CF* 1.

"The Tree." *Tryout* 7, No. 7 (October 1921): [3–10]. In *CF* 1.

"The Unnamable." *WT* 6, No. 1 (July 1925): 78–82. In *CF* 1.

"The Whisperer in Darkness." *WT* 18, No. 1 (August 1931): 32–73. In *CF* 3.

"The White Ship." *United Amateur* 19, No. 2 (November 1919): 30–33. *WT* 9, No. 3 (March 1927): 386–89. In *CF* 1.

Essays

"Introducing Mr. James Pyke." *Conservative* 1, No. 4 (January 1916): 1–2 (unsigned). In *CE* 1.

"Observations on Several Parts of America." In *Marginalia*. Sauk City, WI: Arkham House, 1944. 238–67 (as "Observations on Several Parts of North America"). Extract (as "Sleepy Hollow Today") in *Junior Literature: Book Two*, ed. Sterling Leonard and Harold Y. Moffett. New York: Macmillan, 1930. 545–46. In *CE* 4.

"The Omnipresent Philistine." *Oracle* 4, No. 3 (May 1924): 14–17. In *CE* 2.

"The Poetry of John Ravenor Bullen." *United Amateur* 25, No. 1 (September 1925): 1–3, 6. In *CE* 2.

"Travels in the Provinces of America." In *CE* 4.

Poetry [all in *AT*]

"The Cats." Not published in HPL's lifetime.

"The East India Brick Row." *Providence Journal* 102, No. 7 (8 January 1930): 13.

Fungi from Yuggoth.

　　　IX. "The Courtyard." *WT* 16, No. 3 (September 1930): 322.

"A Garden." *Vagrant* [Spring 1927]: 60.

"Hallowe'en in a Suburb." *National Amateur* 48, No. 4 (March 1926): 33 (as "In a Suburb"). *Phantagraph* 6, No. 2 (June 1937): 3–4. *WT* 44, No. 6 (September 1952): 9.

"The House." *National Enquirer* 9, No. 11 (11 December 1919). *Philosopher* 1, No. 1 (December 1920): 6 (as by "Ward Phillips").

"In Memoriam: Oscar Incoul Verelst of Manhattan." HPL to George Kirk (2 August 1926). In *Letters to James F. Morton* (without title) p. 111. Cf. also *Lovecraft Studies* No. 28 (Spring 1993): 15.

"My Favourite Character." *Brooklynite* 16, No. 1 (January 1926): 1 (as "My Favorite Character").

"Nathicana." *Vagrant* [Spring 1927]: 61–64 (as by "Albert Frederick Willie").

"Nemesis." *Vagrant* No. 7 (June 1918): 41–43. *WT* 3, No. 4 (April 1924): 78.

"October." *Tryout* 10, No. 7 (January 1926): [3–5].

"On a New-England Village Seen by Moonlight." *Trail* No. 2 (Summer 1915): 8–9.

"The Outpost." *Bacon's Essays* 3, No. 1 (Spring 1930): 7. *Fantasy Magazine* 3, No. 3 (May 1934): 24–25. *O-Wash-Ta-Nong* 3, No. 1 (January 1938): 1.

"The Poe-et's Nightmare." *Vagrant* No. 8 (July 1918): [13–23]. *Weird Tales* 44, No. 5 (July 1952): 43–46 ("Aletheia Phrikodes" section only).

"Providence." *Brooklynite* 14, No. 4 (November 1924): 2–3. *Brooklynite* 17, No. 2 (May 1927): 1. *Californian* 5, No. 1 (Summer 1937): 26–27.

"Solstice." *Tryout* 9, No. 11 (January 1925): [8].

"To a Dreamer." *Coyote* No. 16 (January 1921): 4. *WT* 4, No. 3 (November 1924): 54.

"To Alan Seeger." *Tryout* 4, No. 7 (July 1918): [1–2]. *National Enquirer* 6, No. 20 (15 August 1918): 10. *United Amateur* 18, No. 2 (November 1918): 24.

"To an Infant." *Brooklynite* 15, No. 4 (October 1925): 2.

"To George Willard Kirk, Gent., of Chelsea-Village, in New-York, upon His Birthday, Novr. 25, 1925." *National Amateur* 49, No. 5 (May 1927): 5.

"To Jonathan Hoag: (Upon His 95th Birthday)." *Troy* [NY] *Times* (10 February 1926): 8, col. 3 (as "The Poet at Ninetyfive"). *Brooklynite* 16, No. 1 (May 1926): 1.

"To Mr. Hoag on His Ninety-fourth Birthday, February 10, 1925." *Troy* [NY] *Times* (10 February 1925) (as "To Jonathan Hoag of Greenwich: Upon His Ninety-fourth Birthday, February 10, 1925"). *Tryout* 9, No. 12 (March 1925): [3–4].

"To the Rev. James Pyke." *United Official Quarterly* 1, No. 1 (November 1914): 1.

"To Zara." *SL* 1.164–65 (in a letter to Maurice W. Moe misdated January 1922 [actually probably September 1922]).

"A Year Off." Not published in HPL's lifetime.

Revisions and Collaborations [All fiction in *CF* 4]

Bishop, Zealia. "The Curse of Yig." *WT* 14, No. 5 (November 1929): 625–36. In *Switch On the Light,* ed. Christine Campbell Thomson. London: Selwyn & Blount, 1931, pp. 9–31. In *The "Not at Night" Omnibus,* ed. Christine Campbell Thomson. London: Selwyn & Blount, [1937], pp. 13–29.

de Castro, Adolphe. "The Electric Executioner" [orig. "The Automatic Executioner"]. *WT* 16, No. 2 (August 1930): 223–36.

———. "The Last Test" [orig. "A Sacrifice to Science"]. *WT* 12, No. 5 (November 1928): 625–56.

Eddy, Jr., C. M. "Deaf, Dumb, and Blind." *WT* 5, No. 4 (April 1925): 25–30, 177–79.

Greene, Sonia. "The Horror at Martin's Beach." *WT* 2, No. 4 (November 1923): 75–76, 83 (as "The Invisible Monster").

Hoag, Jonathan E. "Alone." *Tryout* 10, No. 7 (January 1926): [7]. In *AT*.

Houdini, Harry. "Under the Pyramids." *WT* 4, No. 2 [May–June–July 1924]: 3–12 (as "Imprisoned with the Pharaohs"; as by "Houdini"). In *CF* 1.

Jackson, Winifred V. "The Green Meadow." *Vagrant* 15 (Spring 1927): 188–95 (as by "Elizabeth Berkeley and Lewis Theobald, Jr.").

Talman, Wilfred Blanch. "Two Black Bottles." *WT* 10, No. 2 (August 1927): 251–58.

B. Works by Others

Addison, Joseph (1672–1719). *The Miscellaneous Works, in Verse and Prose, of the Right Honourable Joseph Addison. With Some Account of the Life and Writings of the Author,* by Mr. [Thomas] Tickell. Dublin: Printed for T. Walker, 1773. 3 vols. (*LL* 5)

————. *The Tatler and The Guardian.* Ed. George Washington Greene. Philadelphia: J. B. Lippincott Co., 1876 or 1878. (*LL* 8)

Addison, Joseph, and Sir Richard Steele (1672–1729). *Days with Sir Roger de Coverley.* Illustrated by Hugh Thomson. London: Macmillan, 1886.

Allen, Hervey (1889–1949). *Israfel: The Life and Times of Edgar Allan Poe.* New York: George H. Doran Co., 1926. [HPL owned the 2nd. ed. of 1927.] (*LL* 27)

Apuleius, Lucius (123?–180?). *The Golden Asse of Lucius Apuleius.* Translated out of Latin by William Adlington, anno 1566. Ornamented by Martin Travers. London: Chapman & Dodd, [1898]. (*LL* 48)

Arlen, Michael (1895–1956). *The Green Hat.* New York: George H. Doran, 1924.

Atherton, Gertrude (1857–1948). *The Conqueror: Being the True and Romantic Story of Alexander Hamilton.* New York: Macmillan, 1902.

Austin, John Osborne (1849–1918). *The Journal of William Jefferay, Gentleman . . . A Diary That Might Have Been.* Edited [i.e., written] by John Osborne Austin. [Providence: Press of E. L. Freeman & Sons,] 1899. (*LL* 63)

————. *Philip and Philippa: A Genealogical Romance of Today.* [Newport, RI: Newport Daily News], 1901. (*LL* 65)

Bacon, Dolores [pseud. of Mary Schell Hoke Bacon] (1870–1934). *Old New England Churches and Their Children.* New York: Doubleday, Page & Co., 1906. (*LL* 67)

Barbey d'Aurevilly, Jules (1808–1889). *The Story without a Name.* Translated by Edgar Saltus. New York: Bedford & Co., 1891. 179 pp. *or* New York: Brentano's, 1919. (*LL* 74)

Baring-Gould, S. (1834–1924). *The Book of Were-wolves: Being an Account of a Terrible Superstition.* London: Smith, Elder, 1865.

————. *Curious Myths of the Middle Ages.* London: Rivingtons, 1866. (*LL* 75)

Beckford, William (1759–1844). *The Episodes of Vathek.* <1912> Translated from the Original French by Sir Frank T. Marzials. Boston: Small, Maynard & Co., [1922?] or [1924?]. (*LL* 83)

————. *The History of the Caliph Vathek.* <1786> Printed Verbatim from the First Edition, with the Original Prefaces and Notes by [Samuel] Henley. New York: W. L. Allinson, [1868?] or [188-?]. (*LL* 84)

Beers, D. G., & Co. *Atlas of the State of Rhode Island and Providence Plantations.* Philadelphia: D. G. Beers & Co., 1870. (*LL* 88)

Benson, E. F. (1867–1940). *Visible and Invisible.* New York: George H. Doran, 1923. (*LL* 90)

Bible. *The Holy Bible: Containing the Old and New Testaments.* Translated out of the Original Tongues, and with the Former Translations Diligently Compared and Revised, by His Majesty's Special Command. Edinburgh: M. & C. Kerr, 1795. (*LL* 96)

Bierce, Ambrose (1842–1914?). *Can Such Things Be?* <1893> New York: Boni & Liveright (Modern Library), 1918. (*LL* 98)

———. *In the Midst of Life: Tales of Soldiers and Civilians.* <1891/1909> Introduction by George Sterling. New York: Modern Library, [1927]. (*LL* 99)

———. *Twenty One Letters of Ambrose Bierce.* Edited with a Note by Samuel Loveman. Cleveland: George Kirk, 1922. (*LL* 101)

Birkhead, Edith (1889–1951). *The Tale of Terror.* New York: E. P. Dutton, 1921. (*LL* 105)

Bishop, John Peale (1892–1944), and Edmund Wilson (1895–1972). *The Undertaker's Garland.* New York: Alfred A. Knopf, 1922.

Biss, Gerald (1876–1922). *The Door of the Unreal.* New York: Putnam, 1920.

Blackwood, Algernon (1869–1951). *Day and Night Stories.* London: Cassell, 1917. New York: E. P. Dutton, 1917.

———. *The Empty House and Other Ghost Stories.* London: Eveleigh Nash, 1906. New York: Alfred A. Knopf, 1917.

———. *Incredible Adventures.* London: Macmillan, 1914. New York: Macmillan, 1914.

———. *John Silence—Physician Extraordinary.* London: Eveleigh Nash, 1908. (*LL* 107)

———. *The Listener and Other Stories.* London: Eveleigh Nash, 1907. New York: Vaughan & Gomme, 1914. New York: Alfred A. Knopf, 1917. [Contains "The Willows."]

———. *The Lost Valley and Other Stories.* London: Eveleigh Nash, 1910. [Contains "The Wendigo."] (*LL* 110)

———. *The Wave: An Egyptian Aftermath.* London: Macmillan, 1916. New York: E. P. Dutton, 1916.

Blair, Hugh (1718–1800). *Lectures on Rhetoric and Belles Lettres.* <1783> With a Memoir of the Author's Life. To Which Are Added, Copious Questions, and an Analysis of Each Lecture, by Abraham Mills. Philadelphia: J. Kay, Jun., and Brother; Pittsburgh: J. I. Kay & Co., 1829. (*LL* 113)

Bloomfield, Robert (1766–1823). *The Farmer's Boy: A Rural Poem.* Ornamented with Elegant Wood Engravings by A. Anderson. The 5th American, from the 6th London ed. New York: Printed by Hopkins & Seymour, and Sold by G. F. Hopkins, 1803. (*LL* 117)

Boyd, Ernest (1887–1946). *H. L. Mencken.* New York: Robert M. McBride, 1925.

Brucker, Johann Jakob (1696–1770). *Historia Critica Philosophiae a Mvndi Incvnabvlis ad Nostram vsqve Aetatem Dedvcta.* 2nd ed. Lipsiae [i.e., Leipzig]:

Weidemanni et Reichii, 1766–77. 6 vols. [HPL had only Vol. 4, parts 1 & 2.] (*LL* 137)

Bulfinch, Thomas (1796–1867). *The Age of Fable; or, Beauties of Mythology.* <1855> Edited by J. Loughran Scott. Rev. ed. Philadelphia: D. McKay, [1898]. (*LL* 142)

Bullen, John Ravenor (1886–1927). *White Fire.* Athol, MA: The Recluse Press, 1927. (*LL* 143)

Bulwer-Lytton, Edward (1803–1873). *A Strange Story; The Haunted House* [*sic*]; *Zanoni.* <1862; 1859; 1842> Boston: Desmond Publishing Co., [18—?]. (*LL* 145)

Burritt, Elijah Hinsdale (1794–1838). *Atlas Designed to Illustrated Burritt's* Geography of the Heavens. A New Edition, Revised and Corrected by Hiram Mattison. New York: Mason Brothers, 1856. (*LL* 150)

————. *The Geography of the Heavens, and Classbook of Astronomy: Accompanied by a Celestial Atlas.* A New Edition, Revised and Illustrated by Hiram Mattison. New York: F. J. Huntington, 1853. (*LL* 151)

Burton, Warren (1800–1866). *The District School as It Was.* By One Who Went to It. Edited by Clifton Johnson. Boston: Lee & Shepard, 1897. (*LL* 152)

Byrne, Donn (1889–1928). *Messer Marco Polo.* New York: Century Co., 1921.

Cabell, James Branch (1879–1958). *The Eagle's Shadow.* New York: Doubleday, Page, 1904.

————. *The Line of Love: Dizain des Mariages.* <1905> With an Introduction by H. L. Mencken. New York: Robert M. McBride & Co., 1921.

Cannon, Peter, ed. *Lovecraft Remembered.* Sauk City, WI: Arkham House, 1998.

Chambers, Robert (1802–1871), ed. *Vestiges of the Natural History of Creation.* From the 3d London ed., Greatly Amended by the Author. New York: Wiley & Putnam, 1845. (*LL* 181)

Chambers, Robert W. (1865–1933). *The King in Yellow.* New York: F. Tennyson Neely, 1895. (*LL* 184)

Carmichael, Virginia. *Porches and Portals of Old Fredericksburg, Virginia.* Richmond, VA: Old Dominion Press, 1928.

Cleveland, Charles Dexter (1802–1869), ed. *A Compendium of English Literature, Chronologically Arranged from Sir John Mandeville to William Cowper.* Philadelphia: E. C. & J. Biddle, 1848. (*LL* 195)

Colman, George (1762–1836). *The Heir-at-Law: A Comedy in Five Acts.* Dublin: T. Burnside & George Folingsby, 1798.

The Colonnade. Volume XIV: 1919–22. New York, 1922. [Part II contains *The Poetical Works of John Trumbull,* reprinted from the original edition of 1820.] (*LL* 211)

Comstock, J[ohn] L[ee] (1789–1858). *A System of Natural Philosophy.* Hartford, CT: D. F. Robinson, 1830.

Conrad, Joseph (1857–1924). *Lord Jim.* Edinburgh: William Blackwood & Sons, 1900. New York: McClure, Phillips, 1903. (*LL* 1082)

————. *The Point of Honor: A Military Tale.* New York: McClure Co., 1908. [First published as "The Duel: A Military Story," *Pall Mall Gazette* (January–May 1908); as "The Point of Honor," *Forum* (July–October 1908).]

Cooley, John C. (1819–1903). *Rathbone Genealogy.* Syracuse, NY: Press of the Courier Print Job, 1898.

Cowan, Frank (1844–1905). *Revi-Lona: A Romance of Love in a Marvellous Land.* [Greensburg, PA: Tribune Press Publishing Co., 188-?]. (*LL* 217)

Crane, Hart (1899–1932). *The Bridge.* New York: Liveright, 1930.

Darwin, Erasmus (1731–1802). *Beauties of The Botanic Garden.* New York: D. Longworth, 1805. (*LL* 236)

Davies, Charles (1798–1876). *Elements of Descriptive Geometry.* Philadelphia: H. C. Carey & I. Lea, 1832.

Davis, Owen (1874–1956). *Icebound: A Play.* Boston: Little, Brown, 1923.

Davis, Sonia H. "Four O'Clock." In *CF* 4.615–20.

De Casseres, Benjamin (1873–1945). *The Shadow-Eater.* New York: Albert & Charles Boni, 1915. New York: American Library Service, 1923.

de Castro, Adolphe (1859–1959). *Portrait of Ambrose Bierce.* Preface by [Frank] Belknap Long. New York: Century Co., 1929.

de la Mare, Walter (1873–1956). *Broomsticks and Other Tales.* London: Constable, 1925. New York: Alfred A. Knopf, 1925.

————. *The Riddle and Other Tales.* <1923> New York: Alfred A. Knopf, 1930. (*LL* 244)

Dennie, John. *Rome of To-day and Yesterday: The Pagan City.* 5th ed. New York: G. P. Putnam's Sons, 1914. (*LL* 246)

Doyle, Sir Arthur Conan (1859–1930). *The Lost World: Being an Account of the Recent Amazing Adventures of Professor George E. Challenger, Lord John Roxton, Professor Summerlee, and Mr. E. D. Malone of* The Daily Gazette. <1912> London: George Newnes, 1921 or 1925. (*LL* 275)

Dunsany, Lord (1878–1957). *Alexander and Three Small Plays.* London: G. P. Putnam's Sons, 1925. New York: G. P. Putnam's Sons, 1926.

————. *A Dreamer's Tales and Other Stories.* Introduction by Padraic Colum. New York: Boni & Liveright (Modern Library), [1917], [1919], or [1921]. [Contains *A Dreamer's Tales* (1910) and *The Sword of Welleran* (1908).] (*LL* 290)

————. "Explicit." *Saturday Review of Literature* 1, No. 27 (31 January 1925): 489. *New York World* No. 23,175 (1 February 1925): 3E.

————. *Fifty-one Tales.* London: Elkin Mathews, 1915. New York: Mitchell Kennerley, 1915. (*LL* 291)

————. *The King of Elfland's Daughter.* London: G. P. Putnam's Sons, 1924. (*LL* 294)

————. *Plays of Near and Far.* New York: G. P. Putnam's Sons, 1923. (*LL* 297)

Durfee, Job (1790–1847). *What Cheer; or, Roger Williams in Banishment: A Poem*, rev. ed. by Thomas Durfee. Providence: Preston & Rounds, 1896. (*LL* 302)

Durfee, Thomas (1826–1901). *The Village Picnic and Other Poems*. Providence: George H. Whitney, 1872. *LL* 302.

Dyer, Walter Alden (1878–1943). *Early American Craftsmen*. New York: Century Co., 1920. (*LL* 305)

Eberlein, Harold Donaldson (1875–1964). *The Architecture of Colonial America*. Boston: Little, Brown, 1921. (*LL* 308)

Edkins, Ernest A[rthur] (1867–1946). *Amenophra and Other Poems*. Detroit: Edwin B. Hill, 1889.

Elliott, Charles Wyllys (1817–1883). *The Book of American Interiors*. Boston: James R. Osgood and Company, 1876.

Erckmann-Chatrian [Émile Erckmann (1822–1899) and Alexandre Chatrian (1826–1890)]. *The Man-Wolf and Other Tales*. London: Ward, Lock, 1876. [Also available in Julian Hawthorne, ed., *The Lock and Key Library* (q.v.).]

Ferber, Edna (1885–1968). *So Big*. Garden City, NY: Doubleday, Page, 1924.

Flaubert, Gustave (1821–1880). *Salammbô: A Realistic Romance of Ancient Carthage*. <1862> Tr. J. S. Chartres. London: Vizetelly, 1886. (*LL* 341)

Forbes, Allan (1874–1955), and Paul F. Cadman (1889–1946). *France and New England*. Boston: State Street Trust Co., 1925–29. 3 vols.

Frank, Waldo (1889–1967). *City Block*. Darien, CT: Waldo Frank, 1922. (*LL* 350)

Freeman, Mary Eleanor (Wilkins) (1852–1930). *Giles Corey, Yeoman: A Play*. By Mary E. Wilkins. New York: Harper & Brothers, 1893. (*LL* 353)

———. *The Wind in the Rose-Bush and Other Stories of the Supernatural*. By Mary E. Wilkins. New York: Doubleday, Page & Co., 1903. (*LL* 354)

French, Joseph Lewis (1858–1936), ed. *The Best Ghost Stories*. New York: Modern Library, 1919.

Froissart, Jean (1338?–1410?). *The Chronicles of England, France, Spain, etc.* <1400?> (*LL* 359)

Galsworthy, John (1867–1933). *The White Monkey*. New York: Charles Scribner's Sons, 1924.

Garnett, David (1892–1981). *Lady into Fox*. London: Chatto & Windus, 1922. New York: Alfred A. Knopf, 1924.

Garrett, Edmund Henry (1853–1929). *The Pilgrim Shore*. Boston: Little, Brown, 1900.

———. *Romance and Reality of the Puritan Coast*. Boston: Little, Brown, 1897.

Gautier, Théophile (1811–1872), and Prosper Mérimée (1803–1870). *Tales Before Supper*. Told in English by Myndart Verelst [i.e., Edgar Saltus] and Delayed with a Poem by Edgar Saltus. New York: Brentano's, 1887. (*LL* 368)

Gemmill, William Nelson (1860–1930). *The Salem Witch Trials: A Chapter of New England History*. Chicago: McClurg, 1924.

Gessler, Clifford (1893–1979). *Kanaka Moon*. New York: Dodd, Mead, 1927.

Gonzales, Manoel [pseud.]. *London in 1731.* <1745> London: Cassell, 1888. (*LL* 387)

Greene, Albert Gorton (1802–1868). *Old Grimes.* Providence: S. S. Rider & Brother, 1867. (*LL* 401)

Greenleaf, Benjamin (1786–1864). *The National Arithmetic, on the Inductive System.* Boston: R. S. Davis, 1839.

Griswold, Rufus Wilmot (1815–1857), ed. *The Poets and Poetry of America.* With an Historical Introduction. Philadelphia: Carey & Hart, 1842. (*LL* 406)

Haldane, J. B. S. (1892–1964). *Daedalus; or, Science and the Future: A Paper Read to the Heretics, Cambridge, on February 4th, 1923.* London: Kegan Paul, Trench, Trübner & Co., 1924 *or* New York: E. P. Dutton, 1924. (*LL* 413)

Harrison, James A. (1848–1911). *George Washington: Patriot, Soldier, Statesman, First President of the United States.* New York: G. P. Putnam's Sons, 1906. (*LL* 427)

Hart, Mara Kirk, and S. T. Joshi, ed. *Lovecraft's New York Circle: The Kalem Club, 1924–1927.* New York: Hippocampus Press, 2006.

Hawthorne, Julian (1846–1934), ed. *The Lock and Key Library: Classic Mystery and Detective Stories.* New York: Review of Reviews Co., 1909. 10 vols. (*LL* 428)

Hawthorne, Nathaniel (1804–1864). *Dr. Grimshawe's Secret: A Romance.* Boston: J. R. Osgood, 1884.

———. *Mosses from an Old Manse.* <1846> New York: Lovell, Coryell & Co., [189-]. (*LL* 433)

Hazard, Caroline (1856–1945). *Thomas Hazard, son of Robt Call'd College Tom: A Study of Life in Narragansett in the XVIIIth Century.* Boston: Houghton Mifflin, 1893.

Hearn, Lafcadio (1850–1904). *An American Miscellany.* Ed. Albert Mordell. New York: Dodd, Mead, 1924.

Hergesheimer, Joseph (1880–1954). *Balisand.* New York: Alfred A. Knopf, 1924. (*LL* 445)

———. *Java Head.* New York: Alfred A. Knopf, 1922.

Herodotus (fl. 5th c. B.C.E.). *The Ancient History of Herodotus.* Translated from the Original Greek by Rev. William Beloe. With the Life of Herodotus by Leonhard Schmitz. New ed., rev., & cor. New York: Bangs Brothers, 1855. (*LL* 446)

Hervey, James (1714–1758). *Meditations and Contemplations.* <1746–47> The Sixteenth Edition. London: Printed; New York: Re-printed, by H. Gaine, 1778. 2 vols. in 1. (*LL* 448)

Higginson, Henry Lee (1834–1919). *Life and Letters of Henry Lee Higginson.* Boston: Atlantic Monthly Press, 1921.

Hoffmann, E. T. A. (1776–1822). *The Serapion Brethren.* Tr. Alex. Ewing. London: G. Bell & Sons, 1892–1908. 2 vols.

Holliday, Carl (1879–1936). *The Wit and Humor of Colonial Days (1607–1800)*. Philadelphia: J. B. Lippincott Co., 1912. (*LL* 456)

Holmes, Oliver Wendell (1809–1894). *Elsie Venner: A Romance of Destiny*. Boston: Ticknor & Fields, 1861.

———. *The Guardian Angel*. Boston: Ticknor & Fields, 1867.

Hoppin, Augustus (1828–1896). *Hay Fever*. Boston: J. R. Osgood & Co., 1873.

———. *Recollections of Auton House: A Book for Children*. Boston: Houghton Mifflin, 1881.

[Howland, Mrs Avis C. (1795–1842)]. *Rhode-Island Tales, and Tales of Old Times*. By a Friend of Youth of Newport, R.I. New York: Mahlon Day, 1839. (*LL* 474)

Hutchinson, A. S. M. (1879–1971). *If Winter Comes*. Boston: Little, Brown, 1921.

Huysmans, Joris-Karl (1848–1907). *Down There*. Translated by Keene Wallis. New York: A. & C. Boni, 1924. (*LL* 484)

———. *En Route*. <1895> Tr. C. Kegan Paul. London: Kegan Paul, Trench, Trübner, 1896.

Hyde, Edna. *From under a Bushel: A Book of Verse*. Introduction by Samuel Loveman. Saugus, MA: Charles A. A. Parker, 1925.

Ingram, John H. (1842–1916). *Edgar Allan Poe: His Life, Letters, and Opinions*. London: J. Hogg, 1880. 2 vols. (*LL* 488)

Irving, Washington (1783–1859). *A History of New-York, from the Beginning of the World to the End of the Dutch Dynasty*. New York: Inskeep & Bradford, 1809. (*LL* 493)

Jacobs, W. W. (1863–1943). "The Monkey's Paw." *Harper's Monthly Magazine* (September 1902). In Jacobs's *The Lady of the Barge*. New York: Dodd, Mead, 1902.

James, Henry (1843–1916). *The Two Magics: The Turn of the Screw; Covering End*. <1898> New York: Macmillan Co., 1911. (*LL* 498)

James, M. R. (1862–1936). *The Five Jars*. London: Edward Arnold, 1922. New York: Longmans, Green, 1922.

———. *Ghost-Stories of an Antiquary*. London: Edward Arnold, 1904. (*LL* 499)

———. *More Ghost Stories of an Antiquary*. London: Edward Arnold, 1911. (*LL* 500)

———. *A Thin Ghost and Others*. <1919> London: Edward Arnold, 1925. (*LL* 501)

———. *A Warning to the Curious and Other Ghost Stories*. London: Edward Arnold, 1925. (*LL* 502)

Johnson, Clifton (1865–1940). *The New England Country*. Boston: Lea & Shepard, 1893. (*LL* 507)

———. *What They Say in New England: A Book of Signs, Sayings and Superstitions*. Boston: Lee & Shepard, 1897. (*LL* 508)

Johnston, Mary (1870–1936). *Audrey*. Boston: Houghton Mifflin, 1902.

Joshi, S. T., with David E. Schultz. *Lovecraft/s Library: A Catalogue.* 4th ed., rev. and enl. New York: Hippocampus Press, 2017.

————, ed. *A Weird Writer in Our Midst: Early Criticism of H. P. Lovecraft.* New York: Hippocampus Press, 2010.

Kane, Robert (1809–1890). *Elements of Chemistry.* New York: Harper & Brothers, 1842.

Kimball, Alice Mary (1886–1982). *The Devil Is a Woman.* New York: Alfred A. Knopf, 1929.

Kimball, Gertrude Selwyn (1863–1910). *Providence in Colonial Times.* Boston: Houghton Mifflin, 1912.

[Kinglake, Alexander William (1809–1891).] *Eōthen; or, Traces of Travel Brought Home from the East.* New ed. New-York: G. P. Putnam, 1850. (*LL* 533)

Kipling, Rudyard (1865–1936). *The Mark of the Beast, and The Head of the District.* Girard, KS: Haldeman-Julius Co., [19—]. (*LL* 536)

Kirk, William (1880–?), ed. *A Modern City: Providence, Rhode Island and Its Activities.* Chicago: University of Chicago Press, 1909. (*LL* 538)

Kleiner, Rheinhart (1892–1949). "At Providence in 1918." *Conservative* 5, No. 1 (July 1919): 8.

Kosztolányi, Dezsö (1885–1936). *The Bloody Poet: A Novel about Nero.* By Desider Kostolanyi. With Prefatory Letter by Thomas Mann. Translated out of the German by Clifton P. Fadiman. New York: Macy-Masius, 1927. (*LL* 542)

Krutch, Joseph Wood (1893–1970). *Edgar Allan Poe: A Study in Genius.* New York: Alfred A. Knopf, 1926.

Lederer, Charles (1856–1925). *Drawing Made Easy: A Book That Can Teach You How to Draw.* <1913> Chicago: Hall & McCreary, 1927. (*LL* 556)

Levi, Eliphas (pseud. of Alphonse Louis Constant, 1810–1875). *Histoire de la magie.* Paris: G. Ballière, 1860. Tr. by Arthur Edward Waite as *The History of Magic.* London: W. Rider & Son, 1913.

Lewis, Matthew Gregory (1775–1818). *The Bleeding Nun; or, Raymond and Agnes.* London: Printed by Kemmish & Son, [c. 1800].

————. *The Monk: A Romance.* <1796> London: Brentano's, [1924]. 3 vols. in 1. (*LL* 567)

Lewis, Sinclair (1885–1951). *Main Street.* New York: Harcourt, Brace & Howe, 1920.

Lewisohn, Ludwig (1882–1955), ed. *A Modern Book of Criticism.* New York: Modern Library, 1919.

Liddell, Henry George (1811–1898), and Robert Scott (1811–1887). *A Greek-English Lexicon.* <1843> (*LL* 569)

Lippitt, Charles Warren (1846–1924). *The Battle of Rhode Island.* Newport: Newport Historical Society, 1915. (*LL* 572)

Livy (T. Livius) (59 B.C.E.–17 C.E.). *The History of Rome.* Translated from the Original, with Notes and Illustrations, by George Baker. London: Jones

& Co., 1830. 2 vols. (*LL* 575)

Long, Frank Belknap (1901–1994). "Dr. Whitlock's Price." *United Amateur* 19, No. 4 (March 1920): 70–73. In *The Eye Above the Mantel and Other Stories.* Ed. Perry Grayson. West Hills, CA: Tsathoggua Press, 1995. 13–15.

———. "The Eye Above the Mantel." *United Amateur* 20, No. 4 (March 1921): 53–56. In *The Eye Above the Mantel and Other Stories.* Ed. Perry Grayson. West Hills, CA: Tsathoggua Press, 1995. 16–20.

———. *The Horror from the Hills. Weird Tales* (January and February/March 1931). Sauk City, WI: Arkham House, 1963.

———. *A Man from Genoa and Other Poems.* With a Preface by Samuel Loveman. Athol, MA: W. Paul Cook, 1926. (*LL* 581)

———. "The Marriage of Sir John de Mandeville." In *A Man from Genoa.* In *In Mayan Splendor.* Sauk City, WI: Arkham House, 1977. 36–39.

———. "An Old Wife Speaketh It." In *In Mayan Splendor* 61–62.

———. "Prediction." In *In Mayan Splendor* 26.

Lossing, Benson J. (1813–1891). *The Pictorial Field-Book of the Revolution; or, Illustrations, by Pen and Pencil, of the History, Biography, Scenery, Relics, and Traditions of the War for Independence.* 2 vols. New York: Harper and Prothers, 1859.

Loveman, Samuel (1887–1976). "Dolore." *Bacon's Essays* 1, No. 1 (Summer 1927): 8.

———. *The Hermaphrodite: A Poem.* With a Preface by Benjamin De Casseres. Athol, MA: W. Paul Cook, 1926. (*LL* 593)

———. *Out of the Immortal Night: Selected Works by Samuel Loveman.* Ed. S. T. Joshi and David E. Schultz. New York: Hippocampus Press, 2004.

———. *The Sphinx: A Conversation.* [North Montpelier, VT:] W. Paul Cook, 1944.

Lowell, Amy (1874–1925). *John Keats.* London: Jonathan Cape, 1924. Boston: Houghton Mifflin, 1925.

Lucretius (T. Lucretius Carus) (98?–50 B.C.E.?). *De Rerum Natura Libri Sex.* Recognovit Iacobus Bernaysius [i.e., Jakob Bernays]. Lipsiae [i.e., Leipzig]: Sumptibus et Typis B. G. Teubneri, 1879. (*LL* 600)

———. *On the Nature of Things: A Metrical Translation.* Tr. William Ellery Leonard. London: J. M. Dent; New York: E. P. Dutton, 1916.

[Ludlow, Fitz Hugh (1836–1870).] *The Hasheesh Eater: Being Passages from the Life of a Pythagorean.* New York: Harper & Brothers, 1857. (*LL* 601)

Macaulay, Rose (1881–1958). *Told by an Idiot.* New York: Boni & Liveright, 1924.

Machen, Arthur (1863–1947). *The Canning Wonder.* New York: Alfred A. Knopf, 1926. (*LL* 614)

———. *Far Off Things.* New York: Alfred A. Knopf, 1923. (*LL* 615)

———. *Hieroglyphics: A Note upon Ecstasy in Literature.* London: Grant Richards, 1902. New York: Mitchell Kennerley, 1913. New York: Alfred A. Knopf, 1923. (*LL* 616)

————. *The Hill of Dreams*. London: E. Grant Richards, 1907. Boston: Dana Estes, 1915. New York: Alfred A. Knopf, 1923. (*LL* 617)

————. *The House of Souls*. <1906> New York: Alfred A. Knopf, 1923. (*LL* 618)

————. *The London Adventure: An Essay in Wandering*. New York: Alfred A. Knopf, 1924. (*LL* 619)

————. *The Secret Glory*. London: Martin Secker, 1922. New York: Alfred A. Knopf, 1922. (*LL* 620)

————. *The Shining Pyramid*. London: Martin Secker, 1925. (*LL* 621)

————. *Things Near and Far*. New York: Alfred A. Knopf, 1923. (*LL* 622)

————. *The Three Impostors*. <1895> New York: Alfred A. Knopf, 1930. (*LL* 623)

McFee, William (1881–1966). *Casuals of the Sea: The Voyage of a Soul*. New York: Doubleday, Page & Co., 1916.

Mackenzie, Henry (1745–1831). *The Man of Feeling*. London: T. Cadell, 1771. (*LL* 625)

McNeil, Everett (1862–1929). *The Lost Nation*. New York: E. P. Dutton, 1918.

————. *Tonty of the Iron Hand*. New York: E. P. Dutton, 1925.

Mann, Henry (1848–1915). *Our Police: A History of the Providence Force from the First Watchman to the Latest Appointee*. Providence, 1889. (*LL* 638)

Mansfield, J. Carroll (1896–1957). *Highlights of History*. Indianapolis: Bobbs-Merrill, 1925.

Markham, Virgil (1899–1973). *Death in the Dusk*. New York: Alfred A. Knopf, 1928.

Marquand, John P. (1893–1960). *Lord Timothy Dexter of Newburyport, Massachusetts*. New York: Milton, Balch & Co., 1925.

Mather, Cotton (1663–1728). *Essays to Do Good*. Boston: Lincoln & Edmands. 1808.

————. *Magnalia Christi Americana; or, The Ecclesiastical History of New-England, from Its First Planting in the Year 1620, unto the Year of Our Lord, 1698*. London: Printed for T. Parkhurst, 1702. 7 parts in 1. (*LL* 645)

————. *Wonders of the Invisible World*. Boston: Benjamin Harris, 1693.

Melville, Herman (1819–1891). *Moby-Dick; or, The White Whale*. <1851> Boston: Dana Estes & Co., 1892. (*LL* 651)

Metcalfe, John (1891–1965). *The Smoking Leg and Other Stories*. London: Jarrolds, 1925. Garden City, NY: Doubleday, Page, 1926.

Miner, Lilian Burleigh. *Our State: Rhode Island*. Providence, RI: Oxford Press, 1925.

Miniter, Edith (1867–1934). *Our Natupski Neighbors*. New York: Henry Holt & Co., 1916. (*LL* 659)

Morand, Paul (1888–1976). *Black Magic*. Translated from the French by Hamish Miles. Illustrated by Aaron Douglas. New York: Viking Press, 1929. (*LL* 677)

Morrow, W[illiam] C[hambers] (1854–1923). *The Ape, the Idiot and Other People.* Philadelphia: J. B. Lippincott, 1897.

Morse, Jedidiah (1761–1826). *Geography Made Easy: Being an Abridgment of the American Universal Geography.* <1784> 8th ed. Boston: I. Thomas & E. T. Andrews, 1802. (*LL* 684)

Mumford, Lewis (1895–1990). *Sticks and Stones: A Study of American Architecture and Civilization.* New York: Boni & Liveright, 1924.

Munro, Wilfred Harold (1849–1934). *Picturesque Rhode Island.* Providence: J. A. & R. A. Reid, 1881. (*LL* 694)

Murray, Lindley (1745–1826), ed. *Introduction to the English Reader; or, A Selection of Pieces, in Prose and Poetry.* Philadelphia: Daniels & Getz, 1800.

Murray, Margaret A. (1863–1963). *The Witch-Cult in Western Europe.* Oxford: Clarendon Press, 1921.

Neale, Walter (1873–1933). *Life of Ambrose Bierce.* New York: Walter Neale, 1929.

New York Walk Book. New York: New York–New Jersey Trail Conference, 1923.

Omar Khayyám (1048–1131). *Rubáiyát of Omar Khayyam: A Variorum Edition of Edward FitzGerald's Renderings into English Verse.* Ed. Frederick H. Evans. London: Privately printed, 1914.

Ovid (P. Ovidius Naso) (43 B.C.E.–17 C.E.). *The Heroycall Epistles of the Learned Poet Publius Ouidius Naso, in English Verse.* Set Out and Translated by George Tuberuile. London: Henry Denham, 1567. (*LL* 725)

Parker, Richard Green (1798–1869). *Aids to English Composition, Prepared for Students of All Grades.* Boston R. S. Davis; New York: Robinson, Pratt & Co., 1844. (*LL* 738)

Parsons, Thomas William (1819–1892). *Poems.* Boston: Ticknor & Fields, 1854. (*LL* 741)

Pater, Walter (1839–1894). *Marius the Epicurean: His Sensations and Ideas.* <1885> New York: Boni & Liveright (Modern Library), [1921]. (*LL* 742)

[Paterson, William (1745–1806).] *Glimpses of Colonial Society and Life at Princeton College 1766–1773.* By One of the Class of 1763. Edited by W. J. Mills. Philadelphia: J. B. Lippincott Co., 1903. (*LL* 743)

Paul, Elliot H. (1891–1958). *Indelible: A Story of Life, Love, and Music, in Five Movements.* Boston: Houghton Mifflin, 1923.

Pearson, James Larkin (1879–1981). *Pearson's Poems.* Boomer, NC: Published by the author, 1924. (*LL* 745)

Pepys, Samuel (1633–1703). *The Diary of Samuel Pepys, from 1659 to 1669, with Memoir.* Edited by Lord Braybrooke. London: F. Warne, 1825. (*LL* 751)

Percy, Thomas (1729–1811), ed. *Reliques of Ancient English Poetry.* <1765> London: J. M. Dent; New York: E. P. Dutton (Everyman's Library), [1906]–[1932]. 2 vols. (*LL* 752)

Petronius (T. Petronius Arbiter) (fl. 1st c. C.E.). *The Satyricon of T. Petronius Arbiter.* Burnaby's Translation, 1694. With an Introduction by Martin Travers. London: Simpkin, Marshall, Hamilton, Kent, [1923]. (*LL* 754)

Phillips, Mary Elizabeth (1857–1945). *Edgar Allan Poe, the Man.* Chicago: John C. Winston, 1926.

[Phillips, Sir Richard (1767–1840).] *A Geographical View of the World, Embracing the Manners, Customs, and Pursuits of Every Nation.* By the Rev. J. Goldsmith [pseud.]. 1st American ed., rev., corr., & improved by James G. Percival. New-York: E. Hopkins & W. Reed, 1826. (*LL* 756)

Phillpotts, Eden (1862–1960). *The Grey Room.* New York: Macmillan, 1921.

———. *The Red Redmaynes.* New York: Macmillan, 1922.

Pitkin, Walter B. (1878–1953). *A Short Introduction to the History of Human Stupidity.* New York: Simon & Schuster, 1932.

Poe, Edgar Allan (1809–1849). *Marginalia.* Edited, and with an Introduction by Isaac Goldberg. Girard, KS: Haldeman-Julius, [1924]. (*LL* 766)

———. *The Narrative of Arthur Gordon Pym of Nantucket.* New York: Harper & Brothers, 1838.

———. *The Works of Edgar Allan Poe.* The Raven Edition. New York: P. F. Collier & Son, 1903. 5 vols. (*LL* 769)

———. *The Works of Edgar Allan Poe.* The Cameo Edition. With an Introduction by Edwin Markham. New York: Funk & Wagnall's, 1904. 10 vols. [HPL had only Vol. 9: *Essays and Philosophy*, which contains, among other things, *Eureka.*] (*LL* 770)

Powys, John Cowper (1872–1963). *The Art of Happiness.* New York: Simon & Schuster, 1935.

Providence Sunday Journal. *Half a Century with the* Providence Journal. [Providence, RI:] The Journal Co., 1904. (*LL* 780)

Ransome, Arthur (1884–1967). *Oscar Wilde: A Critical Study.* London: Martin Secker, 1912. New York: Mitchell Kennerley, 1912.

Read, Francis (1811?–1896). *Westminster Street, Providence, As It Was about 1824* from drawings made by Francis Read and lately presented by his daughter, Mrs. Marinus W. Gardiner, to the Rhode Island historical society. Providence: Printed for the Society, 1917. (*LL* 791)

Richman, Irving Berdine (1861–1938). *Rhode Island: A Study in Separatism.* Boston: Houghton Mifflin, 1905. (*LL* 804)

Robbins, Charles Henry. *The Gam: Being a Group of Whaling Stories.* New Bedford, MA: H. S. Hutchinson, 1899. Salem, MA: Newcomb & Gauss, 1913.

Roerich Museum. *Catalogue.* Eighth edition. New York: Roerich Museum, 1930. (*LL*)

Rohmer, Sax (pseud. of Arthur Sarsfield Ward, 1883–1959). *Bat Wing.* Garden City, NY: Doubleday, Page & Co., 1921.

———. *The Romance of Sorcery.* London: Methuen, 1914.

Saintsbury, George (1843–1933), ed. *Tales of Mystery.* New York: Macmillan Co., 1891. (*LL* 824)

Saltus, Edgar (1855–1921). *The Lords of the Ghostland: A History of the Ideal.* <1907> New York: Brentano's, 1922. (*LL* 826)

Saltus, Marie (1883–1960). *Edgar Saltus, the Man.* Chicago: Pascal Covici, 1925.

Santayana, George (1863–1950). *The Last Puritan: A Memoir in the Form of a Novel.* London: Constable, 1935. New York: Charles Scribner's Sons, 1936.

Saunders, [Margaret] Marshall (1861–1947). *Beautiful Joe: An Autobiography.* Philadelphia: Charles H. Banes, 1894.

Sayers, Dorothy L. (1893–1957), ed. *The Omnibus of Crime* <1928> .Garden City, NY: Garden City Publishing Co., 1931. (*LL* 830)

Scott, Walter (1771–1832). *St. Ronan's Well.* Edinburgh: Printed for A. Constable, Edinburgh and Hurst, Robinson, and Co. ; London, 1824.

Scudder, Horace E. (1838–1902). *Boston Town.* Boston: Houghton Mifflin, 1883.

Ships and Shipmasters of Old Providence. Providence, RI, 1919.

Sinclair, May (1863–1946). *Uncanny Stories.* New York: Macmillan, 1923.

Singleton, Esther (1865–1930). *The Furniture of Our Forefathers.* With Critical Descriptions of Plates by Russell Sturgis. Garden City, NY: Doubleday, Page, 1922. (*LL* 875)

Smith, Clark Ashton (1893–1961). "The Abominations of Yondo." *Overland Monthly* 84, No. 4 (April 1926): 100–101, 114, 126.

———. *Ebony and Crystal: Poems in Verse and Prose.* [Auburn, CA: The Auburn Journal, 1922.] (*LL* 881)

———. *Odes and Sonnets.* Preface by George Sterling. San Francisco: Book Club of California, 1918. (*LL* 882)

———. *Sandalwood.* [Auburn, CA: The Auburn Journal, 1925.] (*LL* 883)

———. *The Star-Treader and Other Poems.* San Francisco: A. M. Robertson, 1912. (*LL* 884)

Spencer, R. E. (1896–1956). *The Lady Who Came to Stay.* New York: Book League of America, 1931.

Spofford, Harriett Elizabeth (Prescott) (1835–1921), Louise Imogen Guiney (1861–1920), and Alice Brown (1857–1948). *Three Heroines of New England Romance.* With many little picturings, authentic and fanciful, by Edmund H. Garrett. Boston: Little, Brown, 1895. (*LL* 903)

Staples, William Reed (1798–1868). *Annals of the Town of Providence, from Its First Settlement to the Organization of the City Government, in June, 1832.* Vol. 5 (1843) of Rhode Island Historical Society. *Collections.* Providence, 1827–1941. 34 vols. (*LL* 801)

[State Street Trust Company, Boston.] *Towns of New England and Old England, Ireland and Scotland.* Printed to commemorate the landing of the Pilgrims. [Written by Allan Forbes.] Boston, 1920–21. (*LL* 907)

Sterling, George (1869–1926). "The Shadow Maker." *American Mercury* 6, No. 1 (September 1925): 10–19.

Stevenson, Robert Louis (1850–1894). *Dr. Jekyll and Mr. Hyde and The Merry Men and Other Tales.* <1886; 1887> London: J. M. Dent; New York: E. P. Dutton (Everyman's Library), [1914]–[1932]. (*LL* 922)

———. *Treasure Island.* London: Cassell, 1883. (*LL* 923)

Stiles, Ezra (1727–1795). *The Literary Diary of Ezra Stiles.* New York: Scribner, 1901.

Stormonth, James (1824–1882). *A Dictionary of the English Language.* <1871> The Pronunciation Carefully Revised by the Rev. P. H. Help. New York: Harper & Brothers, 1885. (*LL* 928)

Summers, Montague (1880–1948). *The Vampire: His Kith and Kin.* London: Kegan Paul, Trench, Trübner, 1928.

Symmes, Mrs. William B. (Cassie Mansfield Doty Symmes, 1872–1935). *Old World Footprints.* With a Preface by Frank Belknap Long, Jr. [actually by HPL]. Athol, MA: Published by W. Paul Cook/The Recluse Press, 1928. (*LL* 940)

Synge, J[ohn] M[illington] (1871–1909). *The Tinker's Wedding, Riders to the Sea, and The Shadow of the Glen.* London: George Allen & Unwin, 1904.

Talman, Wilfred Blanch (1904–1986). *Cloisonné and Other Poems.* Providence: The Bear Press, Brown University. 1925. (*LL* 943)

Thackeray, William Makepeace (1811–1863). *The English Humourists of the Eighteenth Century.* <1853> Edited with an Introduction and Explanatory and Critical Notes by William Lyon Phelps. New York: Henry Holt & Co., 1900. (*LL* 953)

Thomson, James (1700–1748). *The Seasons; with The Castle of Indolence.* <1726–30; 1748> New-York: Published by W. B. Gilley, . . . Clayton & Kingsland, Printers, 1819. (*LL* 967)

Thwing, Annie Haven (1851–1940). *The Crooked and Narrow Streets of the Town of Boston 1630–1822.* Boston: Marshall Jones Co., 1920. (*LL* 968)

Trench, Richard Chevenix (1807–1886). *On the Study of Words: Five Lectures.* London: John W. Parker & Son, 1851. (*LL* 979)

Vanderbilt, Gertrude Lefferts (1824–1902). *The Social History of Flatbush, and Manners and Customs of the Dutch Settlers in King County.* New York: D. Appleton, 1881.

Wakefield, H. Russell (1890–1964). *Others Who Returned: Fifteen Disturbing Tales.* New York: D. Appleton & Co., 1929. (*LL* 1003)

Walker, John (1732–1807). *A Rhetorical Grammar; or, Course of Lessons in Elocution* <1785> (1st American ed. Boston: J. T. Buckingham, 1814. (*LL* 1006)

Wallace, Lew (1827–1905). *Ben-Hur: A Tale of the Christ.* New York, Harper & Brothers, 1880.

Walpole, Horace (1717–1797). *Jeffery's Edition of the Castle of Otranto, a Gothic Story.* <1764> London: Printed by W. Blackader . . . for the Publisher [Edward Jeffery], 1800. (*LL* 1007)

Walpole, Hugh (1884–1941). *The Inquisitor.* Garden City, NY: Doubleday, Doran, 1935.

Wandrei, Donald (1908–1987). *Ecstasy and Other Poems.* Athol, MA: Recluse Press, 1928. (*LL* 1010)

Webster, John (1578?–1632?). *The White Devil and the Duchess of Malfy* [*sic*]. Edited by Martin W. Sampson. Boston: D. C. Heath, 1904. (*LL* 1020)

Webster, Noah (1758–1834). *An American Dictionary of the English Language.* Revised and enlarged by Chauncey Goodrich. Springfield, MA: G. & C. Merriam, 1848. (*LL* 1022)

———. *The American Spelling Book.* Boston: Isaiah Thomas & Ebenezer T. Andrews, 1789. [Many subsequent editions.]

———. *Webster's International Dictionary of the English Language.* Springfield, MA: G. & C. Merriam, 1891. (*LL* 1024)

Wells, H[erbert] G[eorge] (1866–1946). *The Outline of History.* <1920> Written with the Advice and Editorial Help of Mr. Ernest Barker, Sir H. H. Johnston, Sir E. Ray Lankester, and Professor Gilbert Murray. Garden City, NY: Garden City Publishing Co., [1920?]–[1931]. (*LL* 1028)

———. *The Time Machine.* London: William Heinemann, 1895.

Wharton, Edith (1862–1937). *The Age of Innocence.* New York: D. Appleton & Company, 1920.

White, Edward Lucas (1866–1934). *Andivius Hedulio: Adventures of a Roman Nobleman in the Days of the Empire.* New York: E. P. Dutton, [1923]. (*LL* 1035)

White, Gilbert (1720–1793). *The Natural History of Selborne.* <1789> New York: Harper & Brothers, 1842. (*LL* 1038)

Whitehead, Henry S. (1882–1932). "The Black Beast." *Adventure* 79, No. 3 (15 July 1931): 136–57.

———. *Pinkie and Camp Cherokee.* New York: G. P. Putnam's Sons, 1931.

Whitman, Sarah Helen Power (1803–1878). *Poems.* Providence: Preston & Rounds, 2nd ed. 1894. (*LL* 1046)

Wilde, Oscar (1854–1900). "The Critic as Artist." *Nineteenth Century* (July & September 1891) (as "The Function and Value of Criticism"). In Wilde's *Intentions.* New York: Dodd, Mead, 1891.

———. "The Decay of Lying." *Nineteenth Century* (January 1889). In Wilde's *Intentions* (q.v.).

———. *Poems.* New York: Modern Library, [19—]. (*LL* 1052)

Williams, Harper (pseud. of Margery Williams Bianco, 1881–1944). *The Thing in the Woods.* New York: Robert M. McBride Co., 1924.

Wilson, Rufus Rockwell (1865–1949). *New York: Old and New; Its Story, Streets, and Landmarks.* Philadelphia: J. B. Lippincott Co., 1902, 1903, or 1909. 2 vols. (*LL* 1058)

Worcester, Joseph E[merson] (1784–1865). *A Comprehensive Pronouncing and Explanatory Dictionary of the English Language.* Boston: Hillard, Gray, Little & Wilkins, 1830.

Young, Charles Augustus (1834–1908). *Lessons in Astronomy Including Uranography.* <1893> Rev. ed. Boston: Ginn & Co., 1903. (*LL* 1076)

Young, Francis Brett (1884–1954). *Cold Harbour.* London: Collins, 1924. New York: Alfred A. Knopf, 1925.

Young, Rida Johnson (1875–1926). *Little Old New York.* New York: Grosset & Dunlap, 1923.

Index

HPL's Christmas poem to, 513; and
Samuel Loveman, 144, 396; residence of, 458, 459, 461; travels with
HPL, 241, 267, 268, 273–76, 278,
286, 287
Kirk, William 252
Kleiner, Rheinhart: as amateur journalist, 33, 37, 85, 90, 91, 231, 323, 377;
as calligrapher, 475, 483, 497, 507,
932–33; employment of, 552, 590;
health of, 142–43; and Kalem Club,
15, 144, 145, 166, 169, 172, 178,
184, 193–94, 239, 260, 299, 308,
316–17, 319–20, 327–28, 333, 347,
366, 387–88, 406, 433, 439, 478,
479, 491–92, 496, 501, 504, 509,
552, 553, 557, 565, 568, 591, 599–
600, 632–44, 654, 655, 656, 658,
660, 855, 962; with HPL in New
York, 56, 59, 63–64, 68, 69, 71, 74,
76, 77, 78–79, 81, 100, 138, 140,
141, 150, 161, 186, 190, 198, 211,
221, 247, 249–50, 265–66, 267, 306,
318, 330, 343, 356, 359, 360, 383,
399, 431, 448–49, 550, 595, 602,
935, 936, 938–39, 941, 966; with
HPL in Providence, 9, 10; HPL's
Christmas poem to, 512; and HPL's
marriage, 125; and James F. Morton,
245; travels with HPL, 369–70, 372,
373, 374, 375
Knopf, Alfred A. (publisher) 221, 223
Koenig, H. C. 963, 965, 966–67, 976,
993, 994
Koopman, Harry Lyman 829
Kosztolányi, Dezsö 751
Koussevitzky, Serge 579
Krom, Asbury 397
Krutch, Joseph Wood 816
Knyphausen, Wilhelm von 187
Kuntz, Eugene B. 315, 336, 512

Ladd Observatory (Brown University)
551
Lady into Fox (Garnett) 759
Lady Who Came to Stay, The (Spencer)
960
Lafayette, Gilbert du Motier, marquis
de 285, 622, 775, 783, 918, 919
Lagerlöf, Selma 545
Lamia (Keats) 342, 378

Landonmère, René de 895
Landor, Walter Savage 196
Laplace, Pierre-Simon, marquis de 544,
560
Larcom, Lucy 569
Larsen, Ray 202
Last Laugh, The (film) 260
Last Puritan, The (Santayana) 1021
Laswell, George D. 99n3, 100, 129,
182, 436, 480, 501, 578
Latrobe, Benjamin 271, 274
Laverty sisters 333, 458, 661, 665, 827
Lawrence, Carroll 54
Lawton, Frank 122, 174, 256
Lawton, Mrs. 954
Lazare, Edward 54, 155, 166, 167, 169,
176, 246, 250, 312
Leacock, Stephen 32, 561
League of American Penwomen 843n4
Lee, Charles 899
Lee, George Washington Custis 284
Lee, Robert E. 279, 284, 446, 773, 775,
791
Lee family (Vermont) 688–89, 696,
697, 699–700
Leeds, Arthur: as author, 257, 263,
309, 312, 333, 431, 490, 968; and
David Van Bush, 160; clothing of,
303, 460–61, 463, 470; and crossword puzzles, 196; employment of,
590, 935; finances of, 330, 398, 434;
gifts to HPL, 560; and Kalem Club,
15, 144, 145, 172, 176, 184, 193,
260, 299, 320, 328, 334, 380, 433,
478, 479, 490, 504, 509, 540, 552,
553, 557, 599–600, 962, 975; and
George Kirk, 431–32, 434; with HPL
in New York, 138, 140, 147, 161,
194, 199, 238, 336, 337, 341, 343,
346, 352, 356, 381, 382, 388, 389,
935, 954; HPL's Christmas poem to,
513; and Everett McNeil, 142, 185;
mental health of, 958; travels with
HPL, 241; and Mr. Yesley, 296–98,
307, 308
Leeman, Tom 724
"Legions of Lemuria" (Long) 504
L'Enfant, Pierre 269, 276
Leonard, William Ellery 66, 91
Leptis Magna 183